Liberty and Justice

A HISTORICAL RECORD OF
AMERICAN CONSTITUTIONAL DEVELOPMENT

Liberty and Justice

Justice

A Historical Record of American

Constitutional Development

EDITED BY JAMES MORTON SMITH

INSTITUTE OF EARLY AMERICAN HISTORY AND CULTURE

AND PAUL L. MURPHY

UNIVERSITY OF MINNESOTA

NEW YORK   ALFRED A. KNOPF 1958

L.C. catalog card number: 58–5061

© *James Morton Smith and Paul L. Murphy, 1958*

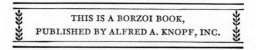

THIS IS A BORZOI BOOK,
PUBLISHED BY ALFRED A. KNOPF, INC.

FIRST EDITION

PREFACE

IN ANY ANALYSIS of the American tradition the theme of constitutional government is a central feature. Although no one would argue today that the history of the United States from colonial times to the present can be wholly understood in terms of its constitutional record, few would deny that a study of the evolution of our constitutional system gets as close to the mainstream of American development as any single historical approach. The mighty torrent of constitutional history is a blending of the troubled waters of political turmoil, the steady current of economic change, the swirling eddys of social tension, and the allegedly placid pools of intellectual ferment. To integrate constitutional evolution with these aspects of America's democratic development, therefore, we have stressed materials of broad historical significance above those of purely legal importance.

A study of the role of the Constitution in American society must deal not only with the shaping and interpretation of that historic document, but also with it as symbol and instrument. Today it is venerated for its age, its success, and its source of authority. Now the oldest written constitution in the world, it has survived the tumultuous twists that have characterized human affairs in America; one hundred and seventy years old in 1957, it remains a vital instrument of government.

There is no doubt that the American doctrine of a written constitution owes much to English and European theorists, but it owes much more to colonial experience. James Madison, the "Father of the Constitution," observed during its formative period that although Americans had "paid a decent regard to the opinions of former times and other nations," they had not allowed "a blind veneration for antiquity, for custom, or for names, to overrule the suggestions of their own good sense, the knowledge of their own situations, and the lessons of their own experience." Although space limitations are partly responsible, it is chiefly the pragmatic nature of American constitutionalism and culture—the concentration on experience rather than logic, on practice rather than theory—which explains our emphasis on practical problems throughout the book.

From the standpoint of the history of ideas, it is probably true that few, if any, of the "self-evident" principles of the American Revolution, and perhaps of the American experience, were wholly new. The basic concept of popular government, which has since evolved into democracy; the principle of equality; the doctrine of limited government; the principle of federalism—all these had long histories as concepts. The peculiar contribution of the Founding Fathers was that they translated theory into practice, actualizing the doctrines by putting them to the acid test of experience in what Carl Becker has called "an experiment in democracy." Starting with the fundamental proposition of popular sovereignty—that government rests on the consent of the governed—they institutionalized this revolutionary concept by perfecting constitutional conventions, both state and federal. By prescribing governmental limits with a written constitution, with built-in checks and balances, and with an additional bill of rights insisted upon by the rank and file, they broke with the monolithic concept of governmental sovereignty and actualized the principle of limited government—"a government of laws and not of men," as John Adams phrased it in the Massachusetts Constitution of 1780. At the same time, they divided the indivisible; by splitting sovereignty, they established a workable federal system.

During the lifetime of the Constitution, the United States has grown from less than 4 million to more than 171 million people; it has been transformed from an agrarian republic into a highly industrialized urban democracy, from a minor nation to the major world power. The documents in this book were chosen to illustrate the integral role of constitutional evolution in these fundamental alterations of the American social order. To present the growth of American constitutionalism in modern historical perspective, we have included much more than Supreme Court decisions, for the "American experience in lawmaking (and lawbreaking)," as Morris R. Cohen has pointed out, "has been extraordinarily rich in novelty and diversity." This collection of source materials features the essential documents, such as the Declaration of Independence and the Federal Constitution, but we have tried to seek out a wide variety of materials which illuminate some of the historic problems encountered in working out a system of ordered liberty. Thus we have chosen statutes, reports, resolutions, petitions, presidential messages, and other official acts, as well as letters, pamphlets, newspaper commentaries, and sermons. To broaden the scope of the book, we have condensed our introductory essays sharply, and edited the documents as economically as possible. The diversified coverage will give the student some idea of the range of constitutional history; it will also allow the instructor to stress whatever aspects he desires.

The chronological and topical organization is designed not only to supply a framework of historical continuity and perspective but also to present persistent problems which may illuminate contemporary issues. Of the twenty-eight chapters, twelve are devoted to the period up to the Civil War. The next eight trace trends through the Twenties. We have included eight final chapters on the last thirty years for three reasons: (1) the most recent readings book in American constitutional history appeared in 1926, (2) the period has witnessed a revolution in constitutional law in two vital areas—government-business relations and civil liberties —and (3) public interest in recent constitutional problems, such as loyalty, segregation, concentrated economic power, and the treaty-making issue, has focused attention on the extent of governmental authority in modern industrial society. Indeed, the relationships of government to the economy and of the individual to the state have become crucial concerns of our time, and they merit close study in the light of earlier constitutional developments.

Although the book is designed primarily for classroom use, we hope that it will appeal to nonacademic groups as well, for we have tried to make it reflect our belief in the Jeffersonian doctrine that the diffusion of knowledge among the people is the only sure foundation "for the preservation of freedom and happiness."

We wish to thank John T. Hawes, head of the College Department of Alfred A. Knopf, Inc., for his encouragement, patience, and friendly counsel, and Ray Ginger, also of the College Department, for his careful, intelligent editorial work. We acknowledge our gratitude to Ruhl J. Bartlett of the Fletcher School of Law and Diplomacy, Foster Rhea Dulles of the Ohio State University, Morton Frisch of the College of William and Mary, and Richard Berner of the University of Idaho for their interest, assistance, and helpful suggestions. We are also in-debted to our mentors—Curtis P. Nettels and Robert E. Cushman of Cornell University and Lawrence A. Harper and Charles Aikin of the University of Cali-fornia—for inspiring our interest and guiding our efforts in the often technical but always intriguing areas of constitutional development. And finally to our wives, who put up with it all, our apologies for mistakenly assuring them that a three-year project could be completed in one.

October 18, 1957   JAMES MORTON SMITH   *and*   PAUL L. MURPHY
                          Williamsburg, Virginia   *Minneapolis, Minnesota*

CONTENTS

x

Contents

Contents

Contents

Liberty and Justice

A HISTORICAL RECORD OF
AMERICAN CONSTITUTIONAL DEVELOPMENT

CHAPTER I

Origins of the
American
Constitutional Tradition

HISTORY is full of beginnings. In probing for the origins of representative government, this is especially true. One school of medieval historians contends that representative government can be traced to Roman law; another argues persuasively that it gradually evolved from administrative procedures and taxation policies of thirteenth-century English government. Some political theorists assign prime importance to John Locke, although they usually agree that his ideas were derivative rather than original. No matter where one begins, the search seems always to lead toward the distant horizon.

In America, the best starting place is the first permanent English colony, the beginning of what later became the United States. In the first charter of Virginia (No. 1), drafted in its final form by Sir Edward Coke, Attorney General, and Sir John Dodderidge, Solicitor General, there was little provision for local self-government, although this written instrument served as the basis for colonial government. In an effort to render the colony attractive to prospective settlers, the Company issued a preliminary order authorizing a representative assembly which met in 1619 (No. 2). Two years later the representative system was confirmed in an ordinance of 1621 (No. 3). In the Mayflower Compact (No. 4), the people themselves, without the aid of an outside agency, created a self-governing community; the document was signed by all the adult males, except eight servants and a dying Pilgrim. The covenanters were not translating abstract theory into practice but were applying customary church practices to meet political necessities. Thus both of the original colonies established the rudiments of representative government early in their development.

It was in Connecticut that the settlers first codified their fundamental law in what is usually described as the first written constitution in America. Carrying the principles of social compact and popular representation one step farther, the Fundamental Orders of Connecticut (No. 5) omitted even a fleeting reference to the King or to Massachusetts, the colony from which Connecticut sprang. In Massachusetts itself, the Puritan leaders of the General Court zealously guarded their own prerogatives, but insisted on persecuting religious nonconformity. In 1635 Roger Williams was found guilty of spreading "new and dangerous opinions against the authority of magistrates" and was banished. His most influential work (No. 6), written after he had had eight years in which to test his theories by practical application in Rhode Island, was a frontal assault on an established church and on the theocratic frame of government. His writings and Rhode Island's practices were milestones on the road to such later democratic principles as separation of church and state, religious liberty, and popular government.

Although Parrington called Locke's *Two Treatises on Civil Government* (No. 7) "the textbook of the American Revolution," recent scholarship has indicated that Locke "was definitely not so important a figure as we have hitherto assumed." It is true, of course, that he drafted in 1669 one of the most impractical of the colonial charters, the "Fundamental Constitutions" for Carolina, but his defense of the Glorious Revolution was essentially a rationalizing of previous political practices into a liberal political philosophy that stressed the concepts of social compact, natural law, inalienable rights, government by consent, and the right of revolution. Locke is also famed for *A Letter Concerning Toleration* (1689), a theoretical exposition on freedom of conscience.

Although *A Vindication of the Government of New England Churches* by John Wise (No. 8) grew out of a theological controversy, it was an important work on political as well as ecclesiastical theory. He grounded his defense of democracy in church government on a comprehensive theory of the democratic origin of civil government, leading Moses Coit Tyler to label him "the first great American democrat." "The end of all good government," Wise proclaimed, "is to cultivate humanity and promote the happiness of all."

Prior to the American Revolution, there were two attempts to form a voluntary American colonial union, and both were motivated in part by a desire for self-defense. The first, the New England Confederation (No. 9), resulted in a union of the colonies of Massachusetts, Connecticut, Plymouth, and New Haven and was active for over twenty years. The Albany Plan of Union (No. 10), devised a century later by Benjamin Franklin, proposed a self-governing confederation for the continental colonies. Although none of the colonies accepted the plan, this attempt at colonial unity was prophetic, for its embryonic federalism stressed the necessity of centralized administration of common problems while leaving local self-government the widest possible control.

The Beginnings of Representative Government

1. The First Permanent English Colony, April 10, 1606

Benjamin Perley Poore, *The Federal and State Constitutions, Colonial Charters, and Other Organic Laws of the United States* (Washington, 1878), II, 1889-93.

1. JAMES, by the Grace of God, King of *England, Scotland, France,* and *Ireland,* Defender of the Faith, &c. WHEREAS our loving and well-disposed Subjects, Sir *Thomas Gates,* and [other] . . . Gentlemen, and divers others of our loving Subjects, have been humble Suitors unto us, that We would vouchsafe unto them our Licence, to make Habitation, Plantation, and to deduce a Colony of sundry of our People into that Part of *America,* commonly called VIRGINIA, and other Parts and Territories in *America,* either appertaining unto us, or which are not now actually possessed by any *Christian* Prince or People. . . .

And to that End, and for the more speedy Accomplishment of their said intended Plantation and Habitation there, are desirous to divide themselves into two several Colonies and Companies; The one consisting of certain Knights, Gentlemen, Merchants, and other Adventurers, of our City of *London* . . . And the other consisting of sundry Knights, Gentlemen, Merchants, and other Adventurers, of our Cities of *Bristol* and *Exeter,* and of our Town of *Plimouth.* . . .

We, greatly commending, and graciously accepting of, their Desires for the Furtherance of so noble a Work, which may, by the Providence of Almighty God, hereafter tend to the Glory of his Divine Majesty, in propagating of *Christian* Religion to such People, as yet live in Darkness and miserable Ignorance of the true Knowledge and Worship of God, and may in time bring the Infidels and Savages, living in those Parts, to human Civility, and to a settled and quiet Government; Do, by these our Letters Patents, graciously accept of, and agree to, their humble and well-intended Desires;

AND do therefore, for Us, our Heirs, and Successors, GRANT and agree, that the said Sir *Thomas Gates* . . . and all such others, as are, or shall be, joined unto them of that Colony, shall be called the *first Colony;* And they shall and may begin their said first Plantation and Habitation, at any Place upon the said Coast of *Virginia* or *America,* where they shall think fit and convenient, between the said four and thirty and one and forty Degrees of the said Latitude. . . .

AND we do likewise . . . GRANT and agree, that the said *Thomas Hanham,* and *Ralegh Gilbert* . . . and all others of the Town of *Plimouth* . . . shall be called the *second Colony;* And that they shall and may begin their said Plantation and Seat of their first Abode and Habitation, at any Place upon the said Coast of *Virginia* and *America,* where they shall think fit and convenient, between eight and thirty Degrees of the said Latitude, and five and forty Degrees of the same Latitude. . . .

AND we do also ordain . . . that each of the said Colonies shall have a Council, which shall govern and order all Matters and Causes, which shall arise, grow, or happen, to or within the same several Colonies, according to such Laws, Ordinances, and Instructions, as shall be, in that behalf, given and signed with Our Hand or

Sign Manual, and pass under the Privy Seal of our Realm of *England;* Each of which Councils shall consist of thirteen Persons, to be ordained, made, and removed, from time to time, according as shall be directed and comprised in the same instructions. . . .

AND that also there shall be a Council established here in *England,* which shall, in like Manner, consist of thirteen Persons, to be, for that Purpose, appointed by Us, . . . which shall be called our *Council of Virginia;* And shall, from time to time, have the superior Managing and Direction, only of and for all Matters, that shall or may concern the Government, as well of the said several Colonies, as of and for any other Part or Place, within the aforesaid Precincts of four and thirty and five and forty Degrees, above mentioned. . . .

AND moreover, we do GRANT . . . that the said several Councils, of and for the said several Colonies, shall and lawfully may, by Virtue hereof, from time to time, without any Interruption of Us . . . , give and take Order, to dig, mine, and search for all Manner of Mines of Gold, Silver, and Copper, as well within any part of their said several Colonies, as for the said main Lands on the Backside of the same Colonies. . . . YIELDING therefore, to Us . . . the fifth Part only of all the same Gold and Silver, and the fifteenth Part of all the same Copper, so to be gotten or had. . . .

Also we do . . . DECLARE . . . that all and every the Persons, being our Subjects, which shall dwell and inhabit within every or any of the said several Colonies and Plantations, and every of their children, which shall happen to be born within any of the Limits and Precincts of the said several Colonies and Plantations, shall HAVE and enjoy all Liberties, Franchises, and Immunities, within any of our other Dominions, to all Intents and Purposes, as if they had been abiding and born, within this our Realm of *England,* or any other of our said Dominions. . . .

And finally, we do . . . GRANT and agree, to and with the said Sir *Thomas Gates* . . . and all others of the said first Colony, that We . . . , upon Petition in that Behalf to be made, shall, . . . GIVE and GRANT unto such Persons, their Heirs, and Assigns, as the Council of that Colony, or the most Part of them, shall, for that Purpose nominate and assign, all the Lands, Tenements, and Hereditaments, which shall be within the Precincts limited for that Colony, as is aforesaid, TO BE HOLDEN of Us, our Heirs, and Successors, as of our Manor at *East-Greenwich* in the County of *Kent,* in free and common Soccage only, and not in Capite. . . .

2. *The Virginia Company Authorizes a Representative Assembly, 1619*

Susan Kingsbury, ed., *The Records of the Virginia Company of London* (Washington, 1906), I, 303.

Itt was ordered . . . by generall Consent that such Captaines or Leaders of Perticulerr Plantacons that shall goe there to inhabite . . . in Virginia, shall have liberty, till a forme of Goverment be here settled for them, Associatinge unto them divers of the gravest and discreetes of their companies, to make Orders, Ordinances, and Constitucons for the better orderinge and dyrectinge of their Servants and buisines, Provided they be not Repugnant to the Lawes of England.

3. *Representative Government is Established in Virginia*, 1621

William Stith, *The History of the First Discovery and Settlement of Virginia* (Williamsburg, 1747), Appendix, No. 4, 32-4.

An Ordinance and Constitution of the Treasurer, Council, and Company in England, for a Council of State and General Assembly.

I.—To all People, to whom these Presents shall come, be seen, or heard, The Treasurer, Council, and Company of Adventurers and Planters for the city of *London* for the first Colony of *Virginia* send Greeting. KNOW YE, that we, the said Treasurer, Council, and Company, taking into our Consideration the present State of the said Colony of Virginia, and intending, by the Divine Assistance, to settle such a Form of Government there, as may be to the greatest Benefit and Comfort of the People, and whereby all Injustice, Grievances, and Oppression may be prevented and kept off as much as possible from the said Colony, have thought fit to make our Entrance, by ordering and establishing such Supreme Councils as may not only be assisting to the Governor for the time being, in the Administration of Justice, and the Executing of other Duties to this Office belonging, but also, by their vigilant Care and Prudence, may provide as well for a Remedy of all Inconveniences, growing from time to time, as also for the advancing of Increase, Strength, Stability, and Prosperity of the said Colony:

II.—WE therefore, the said Treasurer, Council, and Company, by Authority directed to us from his Majesty under the great Seal, upon mature Deliberation, do hereby order and declare, that, from hence forward, there shall be Two SUPREME COUNCILS in *Virginia,* for the better Government of the said Colony aforesaid.

III.—THE one of which Councils, to be called THE COUNCIL OF STATE (and whose Office shall chiefly be assisting, with their Care, Advice, and Circumspection, to the said Governor) shall be chosen, nominated, placed, and displaced, from time to time, by Us, the said Treasurer, Council, and Company, and our Successors: Which Council of State shall consist, for the present, only of these persons, as are here inserted. . . . [Twenty Counsellors are listed.] Which said Counsellors and Council we earnestly pray and desire, and in his Majesty's Name strictly charge and command, that (all Factions, Partialities, and sinister Respect laid aside) they bend their Care and Endeavours to assist the said Governor; first and principally, in the Advancement of the Honour and Service of God, and the Enlargement of his Kingdom amongst the Heathen People; and next, in erecting of the said Colony in due Obedience to his Majesty, and all lawful Authority from his Majesty's Directions; and lastly, in maintaining the said People in Justice and *Christian* Conversation amongst themselves, and in Strength and Ability to withstand their Enemies. And this Council to be always, or for the most Part, residing about or near the Governor.

IV.—THE other Council, more generally to be called by the Governor once Yearly, and no oftener but for very extraordinary and important Occasions, shall consist, for the present, of the said Council of State, and of two Burgesses out of every Town, Hundred, or other particular Plantation, to be respectively chosen by the Inhabitants: Which Council shall be called THE GENERAL ASSEMBLY, wherein (as also in the said Council of State) all Matters shall be decided, determined, and ordered, by the greater Part of the Voices then present; reserving to the Governor always a Negative Voice. And this General Assembly shall have free Power to treat, consult, and conclude, as well of all emergent Occasions concerning the Publick

Weal of the said Colony and every Part thereof, as also to make, ordain, and enact such general Laws and Orders for the Behoof of the said Colony, and the good Government thereof, as shall, from time to time, appear necessary or requisite;

V.—WHEREAS in all other Things, we require the said General Assembly, as also the said Council of State, to imitate and follow the Policy of the Form of Government, Laws, Customs, and Manner of Trial, and other Administration of Justice, used in the Realm of *England,* as near as may be, even as ourselves, by his Majesty's Letters Patent are required.

VI.—PROVIDED, that no Law or Ordinance, made in the said General Assembly, shall be or continue in Force of Validity, unless the same shall be solemnly ratified and confirmed in a General Quarter Court of the said Company here in *England,* and so ratified, be returned to them under our Seal; It being our Intent to afford the like Measure also unto the said Colony, that after the Government of the said Colony shall once have been well framed, and settled accordingly, which is to be done by Us, as by Authority derived from his Majesty, and the same shall have been so by us declared, no Orders of Court afterwards shall bind the said Colony, unless they be ratified in like Manner in the General Assemblies. . . .

4. *The Mayflower Compact, November 11, 1620*

Poore, *Federal and State Constitutions,* I, 931.

IN The Name of God, Amen. We, whose names are underwritten, the Loyal Subjects of our dread Sovereign Lord King *James,* by the Grace of God, of *Great Britain, France,* and *Ireland,* King, *Defender of the Faith,* &c. Having undertaken for the Glory of God, and Advancement of the Christian Faith, and the Honour of our King and Country, a Voyage to plant the first colony in the northern Parts of Virginia; Do by these Presents, solemnly and mutually in the Presence of God and one another, covenant and combine ourselves together into a civil Body Politick, for our better Ordering and Preservation, and Furtherance of the Ends aforesaid: And by Virtue hereof do enact, constitute, and frame, such just and equal Laws, Ordinances, Acts, Constitutions, and Offices, from time to time, as shall be thought most meet and convenient for the general Good of the Colony; unto which we promise all due Submission and Obedience. In WITNESS whereof we have hereunto subscribed our names at *Cape Cod* the eleventh of *November,* in the Reign of our Sovereign Lord King *James* of *England, France,* and *Ireland,* the eighteenth and of *Scotland,* the fifty-fourth. *Anno Domini,* 1620. . . .

Written Guarantees of Liberty

5. The Fundamental Orders of Connecticut, January 14, 1639

Poore, *Federal and State Constitutions*, I, 249-51.

Forasmuch as it hath pleased the All-mighty God by the wise disposition of his divyne pruvidence so to Order and dispose of things that we the Inhabitants and Residents of Windsor, Harteford and Wethersfield are now cohabiting and dwelling in and uppon the River of Conectecotte and the Lands thereunto adioyneing; And well knowing where a people are gathered togather the word of God requires that to mayntayne the peace and union of such a people there should be an orderly and decent Government established according to God, to order and dispose of the affayres of the people at all seasons as occation shall require; doe therefore assotiate and conioyne our selves to be as one Publike State or Commonwelth; and doe, for our selves and our Successors and such as shall be adioyned to us att any tyme hereafter, enter into Combination and Confederation togather, to mayntayne and presearve the liberty and purity of the gospell of our Lord Jesus which we now professe, as also the disciplyne of the Churches, which according to the truth of the said gospell is now practised amongst us; As also in our Civell Affaires to be guided and governed according to such Lawes, Rules, Orders and decrees as shall be made, ordered & decreed, as followeth:—

1. It is Ordered . . . that there shall be yerely two generall Assemblies or Courts, the one the second thursday in Aprill, the other the second thursday in September, following; the first shall be called the Courte of Election, wherein shall be yerely Chosen . . . soe many Magestrats and other publike Officers as shall be found requisitte: Whereof one to be chosen Governour for the yeare ensueing and untill another be chosen, and noe other Magestrate to be chosen for more than one yeare; provided allwayes there be six chosen besids the Governour; which being chosen and sworne according to an Oath recorded for that purpose shall have power to administer iustice according to the Lawes here established, and for want thereof according to the rule of the word of God; which choise shall be made by all that are admitted freemen and have taken the Oath of Fidellity, and doe cohabitte within this Jurisdiction, (having beene admitted Inhabitants by the major part of the Towne wherein they live,) or the major parte of such as shall be then present. . . .

4. It is Ordered . . . that noe person be chosen Governor above once in two yeares, and that the Governor be always a member of some approved congregation, and formerly of the Magestracy within this Jurisdiction; and all the Magestrats Freemen of this Commonwelth: . . .

5. It is Ordered . . . that to the aforesaid Courte of Election the severall Townes shall send their deputyes, and when the Elections are ended they may proceed in any publike searvice as at other Courts. Also the other Generall Courte in September shall be for makeing of lawes, and any other publike occasion, which conserns the good of the Commonwelth. . . .

7. It is Ordered . . . that after there are warrants given out for any of the said Generall Courts, the Constable . . . of ech Towne shall forthwith give notice distinctly to the inhabitants of the same, . . . that at a place and tyme by him or them

lymited and sett, they meet and assemble them selves togather to elect and chuse certen deputyes to be att the Generall Courte then following to agitate the afayres of the commonwelth; which said Deputyes shall be chosen by all that are admitted Inhabitants in the severall Townes and have taken the oath of fidelity; provided that non be chosen a Deputy for any Generall Courte which is not a Freeman of this Commonwelth. . . .

8. It is Ordered . . . that Wyndsor, Hartford and Wethersfield shall have power, ech Towne, to send fower of their freemen as their deputyes to every Generall Courte; and whatsoever other Townes shall be hereafter added to this Jurisdiction, they shall send so many deputyes as the Courte shall judge meete, a reasonable proportion to the number of Freemen that are in the said Townes being to be attended therein; which deputyes shall have the power of the whole Towne to give their voats and alowance to all such lawes and orders as may be for the publike good, and unto which the said Townes are to be bownd.

9. It is ordered . . . that the deputyes thus chosen shall have power and liberty to appoynt a tyme and a place of meeting togather before any Generall Courte to advise and consult of all such things as may concerne the good of the publike, as also to examine their owne Elections. . . .

10. It is Ordered . . . that every Generall Courte . . . shall consist of the Governor, or some one chosen to moderate the Court, and 4 other Magestrats at lest, with the major parte of the deputyes of the severall Townes legally chosen; and in case the Freemen or major parte of them, through neglect or refusall of the Governor and major parte of the magestrats, shall call a Courte, it shall consist of the major parte of Freemen that are present or their deputyes, with a Moderator chosen by them: In which said Generall Courts shall consist the supreme power of the Commonwealth, and they only shall have power to make lawes or repeale them, to graunt levyes, to admitt of Freemen, dispose of lands undisposed of, to severall Townes or persons, and also shall have power to call ether Courte or Magestrate or any other person whatsoever into question for any misdemeanour, and may for just causes displace or deale otherwise according to the nature of the offence; and also may deale in any other matter that concerns the good of this commonwealth, excepte election of Magestrats, which shall be done by the whole boddy of Freemen.

In which Courte the Governour or Moderator shall have power to order the Courte to give liberty of spech, and silence unceasonable and disorderly speakeings, to put all things to voate, and in case the vote be equall to have the casting voice. But non of these Courts shall be adjorned or dissolved without the consent of the major parte of the Court.

11. It is ordered . . . that when any Generall Courte uppon the occasions of the Commonwelth have agreed uppon any summe or sommes of mony to be levyed uppon the severall Townes within this Jurisdiction, that a Committee be chosen to sett out and appoynt what shall be the proportion of every Towne to pay of the said levy, provided the Committees be made up of an equall number out of each Towne.

6. *Roger Williams Pleads for Religious Liberty*

Roger Williams, *The Bloudy Tenent, of Persecution, for cause of Conscience, discussed, in A conference betweene Truth and Peace* (1644) in Samuel L. Caldwell, ed., *Publications of the Narragansett Club* (1st Ser., Providence, 1867), III, 3-4, 247-50.

First, That the blood of so many hundred thousand souls of protestants and papists, spilt in the wars of present and former ages, for their respective consciences, is not required nor accepted by Jesus Christ the Prince of Peace.

Secondly, Pregnant scriptures and arguments are throughout the work proposed against the doctrine of persecution for cause of conscience.

Thirdly, Satisfactory answers are given to scriptures and objections produced by Mr. Calvin, Beza, Mr. Cotton, and the ministers of the New English churches and others former and later, tending to prove the doctrine of persecution for cause of conscience.

Fourthly, The doctrine of persecution for cause of conscience, is proved guilty of all the blood of the souls crying for vengeance under the altar.

Fifthly, All civil states, with their officers of justice, in their respective constitutions and administrations are proved essentially civil, and therefore not judges, governors, or defenders of the spiritual or Christian state and worship.

Sixthly, It is the will and command of God that (since the coming of his Son the Lord Jesus) a permission of the most Paganish, Jewish, Turkish, or anti-christian consciences and worships be granted to all men in all nations and countries: and they are only to be fought against with that sword which is only (in soul matters) able to conquer: to wit, the sword of God's Spirit, the word of God.

Seventhly, The state of the land of Israel, the kings and people thereof in peace and war, is proved figurative and ceremonial, and no pattern nor precedent for any kingdom or civil state in the world to follow.

Eighthly, God requireth not an uniformity of religion to be enacted and enforced in any civil state; which enforced uniformity (sooner or later) is the greatest occasion of civil war, ravishing of conscience, persecution of Christ Jesus in his servants, and of the hypocrisy and destruction of millions of souls.

Ninthly, In holding an enforced uniformity of religion in a civil state, we must necessarily disclaim our desires and hopes of the Jews' conversion to Christ.

Tenthly, An enforced uniformity of religion throughout a nation or civil state, confounds the civil and religious, denies the principles of Christianity and civility, and that Jesus Christ is come in the flesh.

Eleventhly, The permission of other consciences and worships than a state professeth, only can (according to God) procure a firm and lasting peace (good assurance being taken, according to the wisdom of the civil state, for uniformity of civil obedience from all sorts.)

Twelfthly, Lastly, true civility and Christianity may both flourish in a state or kingdom, notwithstanding the permission of divers and contrary consciences, either of Jew or Gentile. . . .

Peace. First, the proper means whereby the civil power may and should attain its end are only political, and principally these five.

First, the erecting and establishing what form of civil government may seem in wisdom most meet, according to general rules of the Word, and state of the people.

Secondly, the making, publishing, and establishing of wholesome civil laws, not only such as concern civil justice, but also the free passage of true religion: for, outward civil peace ariseth and is maintained from them both, from the latter as well as from the former.

Civil peace cannot stand entire where religion is corrupted. . . . And yet such laws, though conversant about religion, may still be counted civil laws, as on the contrary, an oath doth still remain religious, though conversant about civil matters.

Thirdly, election and appointment of civil officers, to see execution of those laws.

Fourthly, civil punishments and rewards of transgressors and observers of these laws.

Fifthly, taking up arms against the enemies of civil peace.

Secondly, the means whereby the church may and should attain her ends are only ecclesiastical, which are chiefly five.

First, setting up that form of church government only, of which Christ hath given them a pattern in his Word.

Secondly, acknowledging and admitting of no lawgiver in the Church, but Christ, and the publishing of his laws.

Thirdly, electing and ordaining of such officers only, as Christ hath appointed in his Word.

Fourthly, to receive into their fellowship them that are approved, and inflicting spiritual censures against them that offend.

Fifthly, prayer and patience in suffering any evil from them that be without who disturb their peace.

So that magistrates, as magistrates, have no power of setting up the form of church government, electing church officers, punishing with church censures, but to see that the church doth her duty herein. And on the other side, the churches as churches, have no power (though as members of the commonweal they may have power) of erecting or altering forms of civil government, electing of civil officers, inflicting civil punishments (no not on persons excommunicate) as by desposing magistrates from their civil authority, or withdrawing the hearts of the people against them, to their laws, no more than to discharge wives, or children, or servants, from due obedience to their husbands, parents, or masters: or by taking up arms against their magistrates, though he persecute them for conscience. For though members of churches who are public officers also of the civil state, may suppress by force the violence of usurpers, as Iehoiada did Athaliah, yet this they do not as members of the church, but as officers of the civil state.

Truth. Here are divers considerable passages which I shall briefly examine, so far as concerns our controversy.

First, whereas they say that the civil power may erect and establish what form of civil government may seem in wisdom most meet, I acknowledge the position to be most true, both in itself, and also considered with the end of it, that a civil government is an ordinance of God, to conserve the civil peace of people, so far as concerns their bodies and goods, as formerly hath been said.

But from this grant I infer (as before hath been touched) that the sovereign, original, and foundation of civil power lies in the people (whom they must needs mean by the civil power distinct from the government set up). And if so, that a people may erect and establish what form of government seems to them most meet for their civil condition. It is evident that such governments as are by them erected and established, have no more power, nor for no longer time, than the civil power or people consenting and agreeing shall betrust them with. This is clear not only in reason, but in the experience of all commonweals where the people are not deprived of their natural freedom by the power of tyrants.

Representation, Democracy, and Colonial Unity

7. John Locke Discusses the Political Theory of Representative Government

John Locke, *Second Treatise of Civil Government* (1690), in Charles L. Sherman, ed., *Treatise of Civil Government and A Letter Concerning Toleration* (New York, 1937), 56, 63-4, 82, 85, 89, 95-6, 153, 163-4. Reprinted by permission of Appleton-Century-Crofts, Inc.

Man being born, as has been proved, with a title to perfect freedom, and an uncontrolled enjoyment of all the rights and privileges of the law of nature equally with any other man or number of men in the world, hath by nature a power not only to preserve his property—that is, his life, liberty, and estate—against the injuries and attempts of other men, but to judge of and punish the breaches of that law in others as he is persuaded the offense deserves, even with death itself, in crimes where the heinousness of the fact in his opinion requires it. But because no political society can be nor subsist without having in itself the power to preserve the property, and, in order thereunto, punish the offenses of all those of that society, there, and there only, is political society, where every one of the members hath quitted this natural power, resigned it up into the hands of the community in all cases that exclude him not from appealing for protection to the law established by it; and thus all private judgment of every particular member being excluded, the community comes to be umpire; and by understanding indifferent rules and men authorized by the community for their execution, decides all the differences that may happen between any members of that society concerning any matter of right, and punishes those offenses which any member hath committed against the society with such penalties as the law has

established; whereby it is easy to discern who are and who are not in political society together. Those who are united into one body, and have a common established law and judicature to appeal to, with authority to decide controversies between them and punish offenders, are in civil society one with another; but those who have no such common appeal—I mean on earth—are still in the state of nature, each being, where there is no other, judge for himself and executioner, which is, as I have before shown it, the perfect state of nature. . . .

Men being, as has been said, by nature all free, equal, and independent, no one can be put out of this estate and subjected to the political power of another without his own consent, which is done by agreeing with other men, to join and unite into a community for the comfortable, safe, and peaceable living, one amongst another, in a secure enjoyment of their properties, and a greater security against any that are not of it. This any number of men may do, because it injures not the freedom of the rest; they are left, as they were, in the liberty of the state of Nature. When any number of men have so consented to make one community or government, they are thereby presently incorporated, and make one body politic, wherein the majority have a right to act and conclude the rest.

For, when any number of men have, by

the consent of every individual, made a community, they have thereby made that community one body, with a power to act as one body, which is only by the will and determination of the majority. For that which acts any community, being only the consent of the individuals of it, and it being one body, must move one way, it is necessary the body should move that way whither the greater force carries it, which is the consent of the majority, or else it is impossible it should act or continue one body, one community, which the consent of every individual that united into it agreed that it should; and so every one is bound by that consent to be concluded by the majority. And therefore we see that in assemblies empowered to act by positive laws where no number is set by that positive law which empowers them, the act of the majority passes for the act of the whole, and of course determines as having, by the law of Nature and reason, the power of the whole. . . .

If man in the state of Nature be so free as has been said, if he be absolute lord of his own person and possessions, equal to the greatest and subject to nobody, why will he part with his freedom, this empire, and subject himself to the dominion and control of any other power? To which it is obvious to answer, that though in the state of Nature he hath such a right, yet the enjoyment of it is very uncertain and constantly exposed to the invasion of others; for all being kings as much as he, every man his equal, and the greater part no strict observers of equity and justice, the enjoyment of the property he has in this state is very unsafe, very insecure. This makes him willing to quit this condition which, however free, is full of fears and continual dangers; and it is not without reason that he seeks out and is willing to join in society with others who are already united, or have a mind to unite for the mutual preservation of their lives, liberties and estates, which I call by the general name—property.

The great and chief end, therefore, of men uniting into commonwealths, and putting themselves under government, is the preservation of their property. . . .

Though the legislative, whether placed in one or more, whether it be always in being or only by intervals, though it be the supreme power in every commonwealth, yet, first, it is not, nor can possibly be, absolutely arbitrary over the lives and fortunes of the people. For it being but the joint power of every member of the society given up to that person or assembly which is legislator, it can be no more than those persons had in a state of Nature before they entered into society, and gave it up to the community. For nobody can transfer to another more power than he has in himself, and nobody has an absolute arbitrary power over himself, or over any other, to destroy his own life, or take away the life or property of another. A man, as has been proved, cannot subject himself to the arbitrary power of another; and having, in the state of Nature, no arbitrary power over the life, liberty, or possession of another, but only so much as the law of Nature gave him for the preservation of himself and the rest of mankind, this is all he doth, or can give up to the commonwealth, and by it to the legislative power, so that the legislative can have no more than this. Their power in the utmost bounds of it is limited to the public good of the society. It is a power that hath no other end but preservation, and therefore can never have a right to destroy, enslave, or designedly to impoverish the subjects; the obligations of the law of Nature cease not in society, but only in many cases are drawn closer, and have by human laws, known penalties annexed to them to enforce their observation. Thus the law of Nature stands as an eternal rule to all men, legislators as well as others. The rules that they make for other men's actions must, as well as their own and other men's actions, be conformable to the law of Nature—i.e., to the will of God, of which that is a declaration, and the fundamental law of Nature being the preservation of mankind, no human sanction can be good or valid against it. . . .

These are the bounds which the trust that is put in them by the society and the law of God and Nature have set to the legislative power of every commonwealth, in all forms of government. First: They are to govern by promulgated established laws, not to be varied in particular cases, but to have one rule for rich and poor, for the favourite at Court, and the country-man at plough. Secondly: These laws also ought to be designed for no other end ultimately but the good of the people. Thirdly: They must not raise taxes on the property of the people without the consent of the people given by themselves or their deputies. And this properly concerns only such governments where the legislative is always in being, or at least where the people have not reserved any part of the legislative to deputies, to be from time to time chosen by themselves. Fourthly: Legislative neither must nor can transfer the power of making laws to anybody else, or place it anywhere but where the people have. . . .

The end of government is the good of mankind. . . .

To conclude. The power that every individual gave the society when he entered into it can never revert to the individuals again, as long as the society lasts, but will always remain in the community; because without this there can be no community—no commonwealth, which is contrary to the original agreement; so also when the society hath placed the legislative in any assembly of men, to continue in them and their successors, with direction and authority for providing such successors, the legislative can never revert to the people whilst that government lasts; because, having provided a legislative with power to continue for ever, they have given up their political power to the legislative, and cannot resume it. But if they have set limits to the duration of their legislative, and made this supreme power in any person or assembly only temporary; or else when, by the miscarriages of those in authority, it is forfeited; upon the forfeiture of their rulers, or at the determination of the time set, it reverts to the society, and the people have a right to act as supreme, and continue the legislative in themselves or place it in a new form, or new hands, as they think good.

8. *John Wise Argues for Democracy,* 1717

John Wise, *A Vindication of the Government of New England Churches* . . . (Boston, 1772), 23-45.

Government . . . is necessary—in that no society of men can subsist without it; and that particular form of government is necessary which best suits the temper and inclination of a people. Nothing can be God's ordinance, but what he has particularly declared to be such; there is no particular form of civil government described in God's word, neither does nature prompt it. . . . Government is not formed by nature, as other births or productions; if it were, it would be the same in all countries; because nature keeps the same method, in the same thing, in all climates. . . .

The prime immunity in man's state, is that he is most properly the subject of the law of nature. He is the favourite animal on earth; in that this part of God's image, *viz.* reason is congenate with his nature, wherein by a law immutable, instampt upon his frame, God has provided a rule for men in all their actions, obliging each one to the performance of that which is right, not only as to justice, but likewise as to all other moral virtues. . . .

The second great immunity of man is an original liberty instampt upon his rational nature. He that intrudes upon this liberty, violates the law of nature. . . .

The native liberty of man's nature implies, a faculty of doing or omitting things according to the direction of his judgment. But in a more special meaning, this liberty does not consist in a loose and ungovernable freedom. . . . As *Plutarch* says, *Those persons only who live in obedience to reason, are worthy to be accounted free: They alone live as they will, who have learnt what they ought to will.* . . .

The third capital immunity belonging to man's nature, is an equality amongst men; which is not to be denied by the law of nature, till man has resigned himself with all his rights for the sake of a civil state; and then his personal liberty and equality is to be cherished, and preserved to the highest degree, as will consist with all just distinctions amongst men of honor, and shall be agreeable with the public good. . . .

The first human subject and original of civil power is the people. For as they have a power every man over himself in a natural state, so upon a combination they can and do bequeath this power unto others; and settle it according as their united discretion shall determine. For that this is very plain that when the subject of sovereign power is quite extinct, that power returns to the people again. And when they are free, they may set up what species of government they please; or if they rather incline to it, they may subside into a state of natural being, if it be plainly for the best. . . .

The forms of a regular state are three only, which forms arise from the proper and particular subject, in which the supreme power resides. As,

A democracy, which is when the sovereign power is lodged in a council consisting of all the members, and where every member has the privilege of a vote. This form of government, appears in the greatest part of the world to have been the most ancient. For that reason seems to show it to be most probable, That when men (being originally in a condition of natural freedom and equality) had thoughts of joining in a civil body, would without question be inclined to administer their common affairs, by their common judgment, and so must necessarily to gratify that inclination establish a democracy. . . .

A democracy is then erected, when a number of free persons, do assemble together, in order to enter into a covenant for uniting themselves in a body: And such a preparative assembly hath some appearance already of a democracy; it is a democracy in *embrio*, properly in this respect, that every man hath the privilege freely to deliver his opinion concerning the common affairs. Yet he who dissents from the vote of the majority, is not in the least obliged by what they determine, till by a second covenant, a popular form be actually established; for not before then can we call it a democratical government, *viz.* Till the right of determining all matters relating to the public safety, is actually placed in a general assembly of the whole people; or by their own compact and mutual agreement, determine themselves the proper subjects for the exercise of sovereign power. . . .

The second species of regular government, is an aristocracy; and this is said then to be constituted when the people, or assembly united by a first covenant, and having thereby cast themselves into the first rudiments of a state; do then by common decree, devolve the sovereign power, on a council consisting of some select members; and these having accepted of the designation, are then properly invested with sovereign command; and then an aristocracy is formed.

The third species of a regular government, is a monarchy, which is settled when the sovereign power is conferred on some one worthy person. It differs from the former, because a monarch who is but one person in natural, as well as in moral account, and so is furnished with an immediate power of exercising sovereign command in all instances of government; but the forenamed must needs have particular time and place assigned; but the power and authority is equal in each. . . .

But to abbreviate; it seems most agreeable with the light of nature, that if there be any of the regular government settled in the church of God it must needs be.

A democracy. This is a form [of] government, which the light of nature does highly value, and often directs to, as most agreeable to the just and natural prerogatives of human beings. This was of great account, in the early times of the world. And not only so, but upon the experience of several thousand years, after the world had been tumbled, and tost from one species of government to another, at a great expense of blood and treasure, many of the wise nations of the world have sheltered themselves under it again; or at least have blendished, and balanced their governments with it.

It is certainly a great truth. That man's original liberty after it is resigned, (yet under due restrictions) ought to be cherished in all wise governments; or otherwise a man in making himself a subject, he alters himself from a freeman, into a slave, which to do is repugnant to the law of nature. Also the natural equality of men amongst men must be duly favored; in that government was never established by God or nature, to give one man a prerogative to insult over another; therefore in a civil, as well as in a natural state of being, a just equality is to be indulged so far, as that every man is bound to honor every man, which is agreeable both with nature and religion. . . .

But to wind up the whole discourse in a few words. . . .

Three particulars; or so many golden maxims, securing the honor of congregational churches.

Particular 1. That the people or fraternity under the gospel, are the first subject of power; or else religion sinks the dignity of human nature into a baser capacity with relation to ecclesiastical, than it is in, in a natural state of being with relation to civil government.

Particular 2. That a democracy in church or state, is a very honorable and regular government according to the dictates of right reason. And therefore,

Particular 3. That these churches of New England, in their ancient constitution of church order; it being a democracy, are manifestly justified and defended by the law and light of nature. . . .

9. *The New England Confederation, May 19, 1643*

Francis Newton Thorpe, *The Federal and States Constitutions, Colonial Charters, and Other Organic Laws* . . . (Washington, 1909), I, 77-81.

The Articles of Confederation between the Plantations under the Government of the Massachusetts, . . . New Plymouth, . . . Connecticut, and . . . New Haven with the Plantations in Combination therewith:

Whereas we all came into these parts of America with one and the same end and aim, namely, to advance the Kingdom of our Lord Jesus Christ and to enjoy the liberties of the Gospel in purity with peace; and whereas in our settling (by a wise providence of God) we are further dis- persed upon the sea coasts and rivers than was at first intended, so that we can not according to our desire with convenience communicate in one government and jurisdiction; and whereas we live encompassed with people of several nations and strange languages which hereafter may prove injurious to us or our posterity. And forasmuch as the natives have formerly committed sundry insolence and outrages upon several Plantations of the English and have of late combined themselves against us: and seeing by reason of those sad distractions in England which they have heard of, and by which they know we are hindered from that humble way of seeking advice, or reaping those comfortable fruits of protection, which at other times we might well expect. . . . Wherefore it is fully agreed and concluded by and between the parties or Jurisdictions above named, and they jointly and severally do by these presents agree and conclude that they all be and henceforth be called by the name of the United Colonies of New England.

2. The said United Colonies for themselves and their posterities do jointly and severally hereby enter into a firm and perpetual league of friendship and amity for offence and defence, mutual advice and succor upon all just occasions both for preserving and propagating the truth and liberties of the Gospel and for their own mutual safety and welfare. . . .

4. It is by these Confederates agreed that the charge of all just wars, whether offensive or defensive, upon what part or member of this Confederation soever they fall, shall both in men, provisions, and all other disbursements be borne by all the parts of this Confederation in different proportions according to their different ability in manner following, namely, . . . that according to the different numbers which from time to time shall be found in each Jurisdiction upon a true and just account, the service of men and all charges of the war be borne by the poll: each Jurisdiction or Plantation being left to their own just course and custom of rating themselves and people according to their different estates with due respects to their qualities and exemptions amongst themselves though the Confederation take no notice of any such privilege: and that according to their different charge of each Jurisdiction and Plantation the whole advantage of the war (if it please God so to bless their endeavors) whether it be in lands, goods, or persons, shall be proportionately divided among the said Confederates.

5. It is further agreed, that if any of these Jurisdictions or any Plantation under or in combination with them, be invaded by any enemy whomsoever, upon notice and request of any three magistrates of that Jurisdiction so invaded, the rest of the Confederates without any further meeting or expostulation shall forthwith send aid to the Confederate in danger but in different proportions; namely, the Massachusetts an hundred men sufficiently armed and provided for such a service and journey, and each of the rest, forty-five so armed and provided, or any less number, if less be required according to this proportion. . . . But in any such case of sending men for present aid, whether before or after such order or alteration, it is agreed that at the meeting of the Commissioners for this Confederation, the cause of such war or invasion be duly considered: and if it appear that the fault lay in the parties so invaded then that Jurisdiction or Plantation make just satisfaction, both to the invaders whom they have injured, and bear all the charges of the war themselves, without requiring any allowance from the rest of the Confederates towards the same. And further that if any Jurisdiction see any danger of invasion approaching, and there be time for a meeting, that in such a case three magistrates of the Jurisdiction may summon a meeting at such convenient place as themselves shall think meet, to consider and provide against the threatened danger. . . .

6. It is also agreed, that for the managing and concluding of all affairs proper, and concerning the whole Confederation two Commissioners shall be chosen by and out of each of these four Jurisdictions . . . being all in Church-fellowship with us, which shall bring full power from their several General Courts respectively to hear, examine, weigh, and determine all affairs of our war, or peace, leagues, aids, charges, and numbers of men for war, division of spoils and whatsoever is gotten by conquest, receiving of

more Confederates for Plantations into combination with any of the Confederates, and all things of like nature, which are the proper concomitants or consequents of such a Confederation for amity, offence, and defence: not intermeddling with the government of any of the Jurisdictions, which by the third article is preserved entirely to themselves. . . . It is further agreed that these eight Commissioners shall meet once every year besides extraordinary meetings (according to the fifth article) to consider, treat, and conclude of all affairs belonging to this Confederation. . . .

8. It is also agreed that the Commissioners for this Confederation hereafter at their meetings, whether ordinary or extraordinary, as they may have commission or opportunity, do endeavor to frame and establish agreements and orders in general cases of a civil nature, wherein all the Plantations are interested, for preserving of peace among themselves, for preventing as much as may be all occasion of war or differences with others, as about the free and speedy passage of justice in every Jurisdiction, to all the Confederates equally as to their own, receiving those that remove from one Plantation without due certificate, how all the Jurisdictions may carry it towards the Indians, that they neither

grow insolent nor be injured without due satisfaction, lest war break in upon the Confederates through such miscarriages. . . .

9. And for that the justest wars may be of dangerous consequence, especially to the smaller Plantations in these United Colonies, it is agreed that neither the Massachusetts, Plymouth, Connecticut, nor New Haven, nor any of the members of them, shall at any time hereafter begin, undertake or engage themselves, or this Confederation, or any part thereof in any war whatsoever . . . without the consent and agreement of the forementioned eight Commissioners, or at least six of them, as in the sixth article is provided: and that no charge be required of any of the Confederates, in case of a defensive war, till the said Commissioners have met, and approved the justice of the war, and have agreed upon the sum of money to be levied. . . .

11. It is further agreed that if any of the Confederates shall hereafter break any of these present articles, or be any other ways injurious to any one of the other Jurisdictions; such breach of agreement or injury shall be duly considered and ordered by the Commissioners for the other Jurisdictions, that both peace and this present Confederation may be entirely preserved without violation. . . .

10. *The Imperial Problem and The Albany Plan of Union, 1754*

Albert Henry Smyth, ed., *The Writings of Benjamin Franklin* (New York, 1905-07), III, 207-26.

It is proposed that humble application be made for an act of Parliament of Great Britain, by virtue of which one general government may be formed in America, including all the said colonies, within and under which government each colony may retain its present constitution, except in the particulars wherein a change may be directed by the said act, as hereafter follows.

[1.] That the said general government be administered by a President-General, to be appointed and supported by the crown; and a Grand Council, to be chosen by the representatives of the people of the several Colonies met in their respective assemblies.

[2.] That within —— months after the passing such act, the House of Representatives that happen to be sitting within that time, or that shall be especially for that purpose convened, may and shall choose members for the Grand Council, in the following proportion, that is to say,

Massachusetts Bay	7
New Hampshire	2
Connecticut	5
Rhode Island	2
New York	4
New Jersey	3
Pennsylvania	6
Maryland	4
Virginia	7
North Carolina	4
South Carolina	4
	—
	48

[3.] —— who shall meet for the first time at the city of Philadelphia, being called by the President-General as soon as conveniently may be after his appointment.

[4.] That there shall be a new election of the members of the Grand Council every three years; and, on the death or resignation of any member, his place should be supplied by a new choice at the next sitting of the Assembly of the Colony he represented.

[5.] That after the first three years, when the proportion of money arising out of each Colony to the general treasury can be known, the number of members to be chosen for each Colony shall, from time to time, in all ensuing elections, be regulated by that proportion, yet so as that the number to be chosen by any one Province be not more than seven, nor less than two.

[6.] That the Grand Council shall meet once in every year, and oftener if occasion require, at such time and place as they shall adjourn to at the last preceding meeting, or as they shall be called to meet at by the President-General on any emergency; he having first obtained in writing the consent of seven of the members to such call, and sent duly and timely notice to the whole.

[7.] That the Grand Council have power to choose their speaker; and shall neither be dissolved, prorogued, nor continued sitting longer than six weeks at one time, without their own consent or the special command of the crown.

[8.] That the members of the Grand Council shall be allowed for their service ten shillings sterling per diem, during their session and journey to and from the place of meeting; twenty miles to be reckoned a day's journey.

[9.] That the assent of the President-General be requisite to all acts of the Grand Council, and that it be his office and duty to cause them to be carried into execution.

[10.] That the President-General, with the advice of the Grand Council, hold or direct all Indian treaties, in which the general interest of the Colonies may be concerned; and make peace or declare war with Indian nations.

[11.] That they make such laws as they judge necessary for regulating all Indian trade.

[12.] That they make all purchases from Indians, for the crown, of lands not now within the bounds of particular Colonies, or that shall not be within their bounds when some of them are reduced to more convenient dimensions.

[13.] That they make new settlements on such purchases, by granting lands in the King's name, reserving a quitrent to the crown for the use of the general treasury.

[14.] That they make laws for regulating and governing such new settlements, till the crown shall think fit to form them into particular governments.

[15.] That they raise and pay soldiers and build forts for the defence of any of the Colonies, and equip vessels of force to guard the coasts and protect the trade on the ocean, lakes, or great rivers; but they shall not impress men in any Colony, without the consent of the Legislature.

[16.] That for these purposes they

have power to make laws, and lay and levy such general duties, imposts, or taxes, as to them shall appear most equal and just (considering the ability and other circumstances of the inhabitants in the several Colonies), and such as may be collected with the least inconvenience to the people; rather discouraging luxury, than loading industry with unnecessary burdens.

[17.] That they may appoint a General Treasurer and Particular Treasurer in each government when necessary; and, from time to time, may order the sums in the treasuries of each government into the general treasury; or draw on them for special payments, as they find most convenient.

[18.] Yet no money to issue but by joint orders of the President-General and Grand Council; except where sums have been appropriated to particular purposes, and the President-General is previously empowered by an act to draw such sums.

[19.] That the general accounts shall be yearly settled and reported to the several Assemblies.

[20.] That a quorum of the Grand Council, empowered to act with the President-General, do consist of twenty-five members; among whom there shall be one or more from a majority of the Colonies.

[21.] That the laws made by them for the purposes aforesaid shall not be repugnant, but, as near as may be, agreeable to the laws of England, and shall be transmitted to the King in Council for approbation, as soon as may be after their passing; and if not disapproved within three years after presentation, to remain in force.

[22.] That, in case of the death of the President-General, the Speaker of the Grand Council for the time being shall succeed, and be vested with the same powers and authorities, to continue till the King's pleasure be known.

[23.] That all military commission officers, whether for land or sea service, to act under this general constitution, shall be nominated by the President-General; but the approbation of the Grand Council is to be obtained, before they receive their commissions. And all civil officers are to be nominated by the Grand Council, and to receive the President-General's approbation before they officiate.

[24.] But, in case of vacancy by death or removal of any officer, civil or military, under this constitution, the Governor of the Province in which such vacancy happens may appoint, till the pleasure of the President-General and Grand Council can be known.

[25.] That the particular military as well as civil establishments in each Colony remain in their present state, the general constitution notwithstanding; and that on sudden emergencies any Colony may defend itself, and lay the accounts of expense thence arising before the President-General and General Council, who may allow and order payment of the same, as far as they judge such accounts just and reasonable.

CHAPTER II

Revolutionary Ideas in Action

THE road to independence was marked by several clearly discernible milestones. By the mid-eighteenth century the colonists were familiar with the workings of representative government, the nature of the social compact, the necessity of limiting government with written constitutions, the right of free political association, and the need for colonial unity. The great end of government, Jonathan Mayhew wrote in 1754, "can be no other than the good of man, the common benefit of society." One of the most outstanding of the dissenting preachers, Mayhew had abandoned the Puritan frame of reference and stressed the right of resistance to tyranny, advocating religious and political freedom, and democratic control in church and state. These concepts are well illustrated in his *Discourse Concerning Unlimited Submission* (No. 11), a classic example of the political maturity of the eighteenth-century colonial mind.

Colonial rejection of passive obedience also was proclaimed in 1761 by James Otis in his speech against writs of assistance (No. 12). "This writ," he argued, "is against the fundamental principles of law. . . . An act against the Constitution is void; an act against natural equity is void; and if an act of Parliament should be made, in the very words of this petition [for a writ], it would be void. The executive Courts must pass such acts into disuse." In effect, Otis inaugurated the basic constitutional debate of the Revolutionary era with his denial of unlimited Parliamentary power over the colonies; indeed, John Adams later wrote that "then and there, the child of Independence was born."

The nature of the constitutional relationship of the colonies to Parliament, however, was a little-explored subject prior to the enactment of the Sugar Act of 1764. One of the measures designed to consolidate and strengthen England's colonial system following the French and Indian War, the measure also proposed to raise a revenue to help defray the costs of maintaining an army in the colonies. This single act of Parliament, Otis later wrote, "set people a thinking, in six months, more than they had done in their whole lives before." The New England lawyer's *Rights of the British Colonies* (No. 13) denounced for the first time "taxation without representation."

The Stamp Act of 1765, a direct internal tax, made the extent of Parliamentary power more than a theoretical problem. The official position of the American colonies was set forth by the Stamp Act Congress, the first intercolonial meeting assembled by local initiative. In the Resolutions of this Congress (No. 14), the colonies opposed any taxation without consent, condemning the Stamp Act as unconstitutional and the Sugar Act as burdensome. Although Parliament denied the unconstitutionality of internal taxes, economic pressure forced the repeal of the Stamp Act. At the same time, however, Parliament took an adamant position, asserting in the Declaratory Act (No. 15) that King and Parliament "have full power and authority to bind the colonies in all cases whatsoever."

The enactment of the Townshend Acts in 1767 inaugurated the second stage of constitutional argument between the colonies and the mother country. Carefully avoiding any direct internal taxation, these measures were nonetheless designed to raise revenue for paying royal appointees, thus undermining the colonial legislature's chief weapon of coercion, the power of the purse. In his *Letters from a Farmer in Pennsylvania* (No. 16), John Dickinson formulated the new colonial position, agreeing that Parliament could levy duties to regulate trade but again denying the constitutionality of levies designed to raise revenue. At the same time, he also focused colonial attention on the imperial suspension of the New York legislature in 1767, an arbitrary action which he branded as "pernicious to American freedom." Once again legislative protests and economic pressures led to the repeal of all the odious duties, except the tax on tea; this was retained as a "peppercorn of acknowledgment" of imperial authority.

The period of constitutional calm which replaced the earlier strife was broken by a spirited exchange between Governor Thomas Hutchinson and the Boston Town-meeting, spurred on by James Warren and Samuel Adams. In a comprehensive discussion of "The Rights of the Colonists" (No. 17), Adams and a Committee of Correspondence suggested a communications network, which was used to revive suspicion of British aims and to unite colonial opposition. Thus, when Parliament played into the hands of Adams and his compatriots with the passage of the Tea Act of 1773, the colonists' response was immediate. In the most decisive action of the pre-revolutionary period, Bostonians held a destructive Tea Party, which brought prompt retaliation by the British. In a series of Coercive Acts, Parliament struck at colonial self-government, asserted unlimited power to regulate commerce, reaffirmed the power of Parliament to tax the colonies for the support of government in America, and subjected the colonial judiciary to royal supervision. Taken together, these measures raised new issues transcending the mere question of taxation, and rendered Dickinson's arguments obsolete. Forced now to choose between submission and self-reliance, the colonists created a new constitutional argument to meet the changed situation.

Although such colonial statesmen as Thomas Jefferson, John and Samuel Adams, Richard Henry Lee, and others reached similar conclusions in 1774, James Wilson's *Considerations* (No. 18), written in 1768 but not published until 1774, offer the most lucid and logical statement of the colonial position which denied Parliamentary power while acknowledging allegiance to the King. Acting on Wilson's concept of the British Empire, the First Continental Congress adopted a declaration of rights (No. 19) which embodied his constitutional theories.

In a semiofficial rebuttal, the learned Samuel Johnson—writing "at the desire of those who were then in power," according to Boswell—declared unequivocally that an Englishman could be taxed without the consent of his representatives and upheld the absolute authority of Parliament without regard to the rights of Englishmen or American colonists (No. 20).

The colonial dialectic of allegiance to the King and disobedience to Parliament was subjected to a tough test by events late in 1775. In August the King branded colonial leaders as traitors in his "Proclamation . . . for Repressing Rebellion and Sedition." When vessels from His Majesty's Navy bombarded and destroyed Falmouth, Maine, and Norfolk, Virginia, patriot leaders credited these actions to a tyrannical king. The final shattering blow to the colonial concept of allegiance to the Crown came in Thomas Paine's *Common Sense* (No. 21), published in January, 1776. In a slashing attack on monarchy, Paine hammered at the one link uniting the colonies with the mother country. Casting off a king, the pamphleteer warned, "may at first seem strange and difficult, but like all other steps which we have already passed over, will in a little time become familiar and agreeable; and until an independence is declared, the Continent will feel itself like a man who continues putting off some unpleasant business from day to day, yet knows it must be done, hates to set about it, wishes it over, and is continually haunted with the thoughts of its necessity." By the spring of 1776, it remained only to formalize this new attitude in an official declaration of independence. Thus far had the colonial constitutional position evolved from protests against taxation.

The Seeds of Dissent

11. *Jonathan Mayhew Discusses Unlimited Submission, January 30, 1750*

John Wingate Thornton, ed., *The Pulpit of the American Revolution* (Boston, 1876), 53-104 *passim*

Although there be a sense, and a very plain and important sense, in which Christ's kingdom is not of this world, his inspired apostles have, nevertheless, laid down some general principles concerning the office of civil rulers, and the duty of subjects, together with the reason and obligation of that duty. . . .

That the end of magistracy is the good of civil society, *as such.*

That civil rulers, *as such,* are the ordinance and ministers of God; it being by his permission and providence that any bear rule, and agreeable to his will that there should be *some persons* vested with authority in society for the well-being of it.

That which is here said concerning civil rulers extends to all of them in common. It relates indifferently to monarchical, republican, and aristocratical government, and to all other forms which truly answer the sole end of government—the happiness of society; and to all the different degrees of authority in any particular state; to inferior officers no less than to the supreme.

That disobedience to civil rulers in the due exercise of their authority is not merely a political sin, but a heinous offence against God and religion. . . . [What is] the *extent* of that subjection to the higher powers which is here enjoined as a duty upon all Christians? Some have thought it warrantable and glorious to disobey the civil powers in certain circumstances, and in cases of very great and general oppression, when humble re-

monstrances fail of having any effect; and, when the public welfare cannot be otherwise provided for and secured, to rise unanimously even against the sovereign himself, in order to redress their grievances; to vindicate their natural and legal rights. . . .

But in opposition to this principle it has often been asserted that the Scripture . . . makes all resistance to princes a crime, in any case whatever. . . . There is, indeed, one passage in the New Testament where it may seem, at first view, that an unlimited submission to civil rulers is enjoined: "Submit yourselves to every ordinance of man for the Lord's sake." . . . But the true solution of this difficulty (if it be one) is this: By "every ordinance of man" is not meant every command of the civil magistrate without exception, but every order of magistrates appointed by man, whether superior or inferior; for so the apostle explains himself in the very next words: "Whether it be to the king as supreme, or to governors, as unto them that are sent," etc. But although the apostle had not subjoined any such explanation, the reason of the thing itself would have obliged us to limit the expression "every ordinance of man" to such human ordinances and commands as are not inconsistent with the ordinances and commands of God, the Supreme Lawgiver, or with any other higher and antecedent obligations. . . .

Thus it appears that the common argument grounded upon this passage in favor of universal and passive obedience really overthrows itself, by proving too much. . . . We may very safely assert these two things in general, without undermining government: One is, that no civil rulers are to be obeyed when they enjoin things that are inconsistent with the commands of God. All such disobedience is lawful and glorious. . . . The only reason of the institution of civil government, and the only rational ground of submission to it, is the common safety and utility. If, therefore, in any case, the common safety and utility would not be promoted by submission to government, but the contrary, there is no ground or motive for obedience and submission, but for the contrary.

Whoever considers the nature of civil government, must indeed be sensible that a great degree of implicit confidence must unavoidably be placed in those that bear rule: this is implied in the very notion of authority's being originally a trust committed by the people to those who are vested with it—as all just and righteous authority is. All besides is mere lawless force, and usurpation; neither God nor nature having given any man a right of dominion over any society independently of that society's approbation and consent to be governed by him. Now, as all men are fallible, it cannot be supposed that the public affairs of any state should be al-ways administered in the best manner possible, even by persons of the greatest wisdom and integrity. Nor is it sufficient to legitimate disobedience to the higher powers that they are not so administered, or that they are in some instances very ill-managed; for, upon this principle, it is scarcely supposable that any government at all could be supported, or subsist. Such a principle manifestly tends to the dissolution of government, and to throw all things into confusion and anarchy. . . . While those who govern do it with any tolerable degree of moderation and justice, and in any good measure act up to their office and character by being public benefactors, the people will generally be easy and peaceable, and be rather inclined to flatter and adore them [than] to insult and resist them. . . .

To conclude: Let us all learn to be free and to be loyal; let us not profess ourselves vassals to the lawless pleasure of any man on earth; but let us remember, at the same time, government is sacred, and not to be trifled with. . . . Let us prize our freedom but not "use our liberty for a cloak of maliciousness." There are men who strike at liberty under the term licentiousness; there are others who aim at popularity under the disguise of patriotism. Be aware of both. Extremes are dangerous. . . .

12. *James Otis Denounces Unlimited Search and Seizure, February 24, 1761*

Charles Francis Adams, ed., *The Works of John Adams* (Boston, 1850-56), II, 523-5.

May it please your honors, I was desired by one of the Court to look into the books, and consider the question now before them concerning writs of assistance. I have accordingly considered it, and now appear, not only in obedience to your order, but likewise in behalf of the inhabitants of this town, who have presented another petition, and out of regard to the liberties of the subject. And I take this opportunity to declare, that whether under a fee or not (for in such a cause as this I despise a fee) I will to my dying day oppose with all the powers and faculties God has given me, all such instruments of slavery on the one hand, and villany on the other, as this writ of assistance is.

It appears to me the worst instrument

of arbitrary power, the most destructive of English liberty and the fundamental principles of law, that ever was found in an English law-book. . . . In the first place, may it please your Honors, I will admit that writs of one kind may be legal; that is, special writs, directed to special officers, and to search certain houses, &c. specially set forth in the writ, may be granted by the Court of Exchequer at home, upon oath made before the Lord Treasurer by the person who asks it, that he suspects such goods to be concealed in those very places he desires to search. The act of 14 Charles II, which Mr. Gridley mentions, proves this. And in this light the writ appears like a warrant from a Justice of the Peace to search for stolen goods. Your Honors will find in the old books concerning the office of a Justice of the Peace, precedents of general warrants to search suspected houses. But in more modern books you will find only special warrants to search such and such houses specially named, in which the complainant has before sworn that he suspects his goods are concealed; and you will find it adjudged that special warrants only are legal. In the same manner I rely on it, that the writ prayed for in this petition, being general, is illegal. It is a power, that places the liberty of every man in the hands of every petty officer. I say I admit that special writs of assistance, to search special places, may be granted to certain persons on oath; but I deny that the writ now prayed for can be granted, for I beg leave to make some observations on the writ itself, before I proceed to other acts of Parliament. In the first place, the writ is universal, being directed "to all and singular Justices, Sheriffs, Constables, and other officers and subjects;" so, that, in short, it is directed to every subject in the King's dominions. Every one with this writ may be a tyrant; if this commission be legal, a tyrant in a legal manner also may control, imprison, or murder any one within the realm. In the next place, it is perpetual; there is no return. A man is accountable

to no person for his doings. Every man may reign secure in his petty tyranny, and spread terror and desolation around him. In the third place, a person with this writ, in the daytime, may enter all houses, shops, &c. at will, and command all to assist him. Fourthly, by this writ not only deputies &c. but even their menial servants, are allowed to lord it over us. Now one of the most essential branches of English liberty is the freedom of one's house. A man's house is his castle; and whilst he is quiet, he is as well guarded as a prince in his castle. This writ, if it should be declared legal, would totally annihilate this privilege. Custom-house officers may enter our houses, when they please; we are commanded to permit their entry. Their menial servants may enter, may break locks, bars, and every thing in their way; and whether they break through malice or revenge, no man, no court, can inquire. Bare suspicion without oath is sufficient. This wanton exercise of his power is not a chimerical suggestion of a heated brain. I will mention some facts. Mr. Pew had one of these writs, and when Mr. Ware succeeded him, he endorsed this writ over to Mr. Ware; so that these writs are negotiable from one officer to another; and so your Honors have no opportunity of judging the persons to whom this vast power is delegated. Another instance is this: Mr. Justice Walley had called this same Mr. Ware before him, by a constable, to answer for a breach of Sabbath-day acts, or that of profane swearing. As soon as he had finished, Mr. Ware asked him if he had done. He replied, Yes/Well then, said Mr. Ware, I will show you a little of my power. I command you to permit me to search your house for uncustomed goods. And went on to search his house from the garret to the cellar; and then served the constable in the same manner. But to show another absurdity in this writ; if it should be established, I insist upon it, every person by the 14 Charles II. has this power as well as custom-house officers. The words are, "It shall be lawful for any person or persons authorized," &c. What a scene does this open! Every man, prompted by revenge, ill humor, or wantonness, to inspect the inside of his neighbor's house, may get a writ of assistance. Others will ask it from self-defence; one arbitrary exertion will provoke another, until society be involved in tumult and in blood.

Again, these writs are not returned. Writs in their nature are temporary things. When the purposes for which they are issued are answered, they exist no more; but these live forever; no one can be called to account. Thus reason and the constitution are both against this writ. Let us see what authority there is for it. Not more than one instance can be found of it in all our law-books; and that was in the zenith of arbitrary power, namely, in the reign of Charles II, when star-chamber powers were pushed to extremity by some ignorant clerk of the exchequer. But had this writ been in any book whatever, it would have been illegal. All precedents are under the control of the principles of law. Lord Talbot says it is better to observe these than any precedents, though in the House of Lords, the last resort of the subject. No Acts of Parliament can establish such a writ; though it should be made in the very words of the petition, it would be void. An act against the constitution is void. (vid. Viner.) But these prove no more than what I before observed, that special writs may be granted *on oath and probable suspicion.* The act of 7 & 8 William III. that the officers of the plantation shall have the same powers, &c., is confined to this sense; that an officer should show probable ground; should take his oath of it; should do this before a magistrate; and that such magistrate, if he thinks proper, should issue a special warrant to a constable to search the places. That of 6 Anne can prove no more.

Parliamentary Taxation and Colonial Self-government

13. *James Otis,* The Rights of the British Colonies, 1764

Charles F. Mullett, ed., *Some Political Writings of James Otis* in *The University of Missouri Studies* (Columbia, Mo., 1929), 53, 69-73, 78-9, 81, 91. Reprinted by permission of Charles F. Mullett.

The *end* of government being the *good* of mankind, points out its great duties: It is above all things to provide for the security, the quiet, and happy enjoyment of life, liberty, and property. There is no one act which a government can have a *right* to make, that does not tend to the advancement of the security, tranquility, and prosperity of the people. . . .

I also lay it down as one of the first principles from whence I intend to deduce the civil rights of the British colonies, that all of them are subject to, and dependent on Great Britain; and that therefore as over subordinate governments, the parliament of Great Britain has an undoubted power and lawful authority to make acts for the general good, that by naming them, shall and ought to be equally binding, as upon the subjects of Great Britain within the realm. This principle, I presume will be readily granted on the other side of the Atlantic. It has been practiced upon for twenty years to my knowledge, in the province of the *Massachusetts Bay;* and I have ever received it, that it has been so from the beginning, in this and the sister provinces, thro' the continent. . . .

Every British subject born on the continent of America, or in any other of the British dominions, is by the law of God and nature, by the common law, and by act of parliament, (exclusive of all charters from the Crown) entitled to all the natural, essential, inherent, and inseparable rights of our fellow subjects in Great Britain. Among those rights are the following, which it is humbly conceived no man or body of men, not excepting the parliament, justly, equitably and consistently with their own rights and the constitution, can take away.

1st. *That the supreme and subordinate powers of the legislation should be free and sacred in the hands where the community have once rightfully placed them.*

2dly. *The supreme national legislative cannot be altered justly 'till the commonwealth is dissolved, nor a subordinate legislative taken away without forfeiture or other good cause.* Nor then can the subjects in the subordinate government be reduced to a state of slavery, and subject to the despotic rule of others. A state has no right to make slaves of the conquered. Even when the subordinate right of legislature is forfeited, and so declared, this cannot affect the natural persons either of those who were invested with it, or the inhabitants, so far as to deprive them of the rights of subjects and of men. The colonists will have an equitable right notwithstanding any such forfeiture of charter, to be represented in Parliament, or to have some new subordinate legislature among themselves. It would be best if they had both. . . .

No representation of the Colonies in parliament alone, would however be equivalent to a subordinate legislative among themselves. . . .

3rdly. *No legislative, supreme or subordinate, has a right to make itself arbitrary.*

It would be a most manifest contradic-

tion, for a free legislative, like that of Great Britain, to make itself arbitrary.

4thly. *The supreme legislative cannot justly assume a power of ruling by extempore arbitrary decrees, but is bound to dispense justice by known settled rules,* and by duly *authorized independent judges.*

5thly. *The supreme power cannot take from any man any part of his property,* without his consent in *person, or by representation.*

6thly. *The legislature cannot transfer the power of making laws to any other hands.*

These are their bounds, which by God and nature are fixed, hitherto have they a right to come, and no further.

1. *To govern by stated laws.*

2. *Those laws should have no other end ultimately, but the good of the people.*

3. *Taxes are not to be laid on the people, but by their consent in person, or by deputation.*

4. *Their whole power is not transferable.*

These are the first principles of law and justice, and the great barriers of a free state, and of the British constitution in particular. I ask, I want no more—Now let it be shown how 'tis reconcilable with principles, or to many other fundamental maxims of the British constitution, as well as the natural and civil rights, which by the laws of their country, all British subjects are entitled to, as their best inheritance and birth-right, that all the northern colonies, who are without one representative in the house of Commons, should be taxed by the British parliament.

That the colonists, black and white, born here, are free born British subjects, and entitled to all the essential civil rights of such, is a truth not only manifest from the provincial charters, from the principles of the common law, and acts of parliament; but from the British constitution, which was reestablished at the revolution, with a professed design to lecture the liberties of all the subjects to all generations. . . .

I can see no reason to doubt, but that the imposition of taxes, whether on trade, or on land, or houses, or ships, on real or personal, fixed or floating property, in the colonies, is absolutely irreconcilable with the rights of the Colonists, as British subjects, and as men. I say men, for in a state of nature, no man can take my property from me, without my consent: If he does, he deprives me of my liberty, and makes me a slave. If such a proceeding is a breach of the law of nature, no law of society can make it just—The very act of taxing, exercised over those who are not represented, appears to me to be depriving them of one of their most essential rights, as freemen; and if continued, seems to be in effect an entire disfranchisement of every civil right. . . .

The power of parliament is uncontrollable, but by themselves, and we must obey. They only can repeal their own acts. There would be an end of all government, if one or a number of subjects or subordinate provinces should take upon them so far to judge of the justice of an act of parliament, as to refuse obedience to it. If there was nothing else to restrain such a step, prudence ought to do it, for forcibly resisting the parliament and the King's laws, is high treason. Therefore let the parliament lay what burthens they please on us, we must, it is our duty to submit and patiently bear them, till they will be pleased to relieve us. And 'tis to be presumed, the wisdom and justice of that august assembly, always will afford us relief by repealing such acts, as through mistake, or other human infirmities, have been suffered to pass, if they can be convinced that their proceedings are not constitutional, or not for the common good. . . .

To say the parliament is absolute and arbitrary, is a contradiction. The parliament cannot make 2 and 2, 5; Omnipotency cannot do it. . . . Parliaments are in all cases to *declare* what is for the good of the whole; but it is not the declaration of Parliament that makes it so:

There must be in every instance, a higher authority, viz. GOD. Should an act of parliament be against any of *his* natural laws, which are *immutably* true, their declaration would be contrary to eternal truth, equity and justice, and consequently void. . . . Upon this great principle, parliaments repeal such acts, as soon as they find they have been mistaken, in having declared them to be for the public good, when in fact they were not so. When such mistake is evident and palpable . . . the judges of the executive courts have declared the act 'of a whole parliament void.' See here the grandeur of the British constitution! See the wisdom of our ancestors! The supreme *legislative*, and the supreme *executive* are a perpetual check and balance to each other. If the supreme executive errs, it is informed by the supreme legislative in parliament: If the supreme legislative errs, it is informed by the supreme executive in the King's courts of law—Here, the King appears, as represented by his judges, in the highest lustre and majesty, as supreme executor of the commonwealth; and he never shines brighter, but on his Throne, at the head of the supreme legislative. This is government! This, is a constitution! to preserve which, either from foreign or domestic foes, has cost oceans of blood and treasure in every age; and the blood and the treasure have upon the whole been well spent. . . .

We all think ourselves happy under Great Britain. We love, esteem, and reverence our mother country, and adore our King. And could the choice of independency be offered the colonies, or subjection to Great Britain upon any terms above absolute slavery, I am convinced they would accept the latter. . . .

The sum of my argument is, That civil government is of God: That the administrators of it were originally the whole people: That they might have devolved it on whom they pleased: That this devolution is fiduciary, for the good of the whole: That by the British constitution, this devolution is on the King, lords, and commons, the supreme, sacred, and uncontrollable legislative power, not only in the realm, but thro' the dominions: That by the abdication, the original compact was broken to pieces: That by the revolution, it was renewed, and more firmly established, and the rights and liberties of the subject in all parts of the dominions, more fully explained and confirmed: That in consequence of this establishment, and the acts of succession and union his Majesty GEORGE III is rightful king and sovereign, and with his parliament, the supreme legislative of Great Britain, France and Ireland, and the dominions thereto belonging: That this constitution is the most free one, and by far the best, now existing on earth: That by this constitution, every man in the dominion is a free man: That no parts of his Majesty's dominions can be taxed without their consent: That every part has a right to be represented in the supreme or some subordinate legislature: That the refusal of this, would seem to be a contradiction in practice to the theory of the constitution: That the colonies are subordinate dominions, and are now in such a state, as to make it best for the good of the whole, that they should not only be continued in the enjoyment of subordinate legislation, but be also represented in some proportion to their number and estates, in the grand legislature of the nation: That this would firmly unite all parts of the British empire, in the greatest peace and prosperity; and render it invulnerable and perpetual.

14. *The Stamp Act Congress and Parliamentary Taxation, October 19, 1765*

Hezekiah Niles, *Principles and Acts of the Revolution in America* (New York, 1876), 163.

The members of this congress, sincerely devoted with the warmest sentiments of affection and duty to his Majesty's person and government; inviolably attached to the present happy establishment of the Protestant succession, and with minds deeply impressed by a sense of the present and impending misfortunes of the British colonies on this continent; having considered as maturely as time will permit, the circumstances of the said colonies, esteem it our indispensable duty to make the following declarations, of our humble opinion, respecting the most essential rights and liberties of the colonists, and of the grievances under which they labour, by reason of several late acts of Parliament.

I. That his Majesty's subjects in these colonies, owe the same allegiance to the Crown of Great Britain that is owing from his subjects born within the realm, and all due subordination to that august body, the Parliament of Great Britain.

II. That his Majesty's liege subjects in these colonies are intitled to all the inherent rights and liberties of his natural born subjects within the kingdom of Great Britain.

III. That it is inseparably essential to the freedom of a people, and the undoubted right of Englishmen, that no taxes be imposed on them, but with their own consent, given personally, or by their representatives.

IV. That the people of these colonies are not, and from their local circumstances cannot be, represented in the House of Commons in Great Britain.

V. That the only representatives of the people of these colonies, are persons chosen therein, by themselves, and that no taxes ever have been, or can be constitutionally imposed on them, but by their respective legislatures.

VI. That all supplies to the Crown, being free gifts of the people, it is unreasonable and inconsistent with the principles and spirit of the British constitution, for the people of Great Britain to grant to his Majesty the property of the colonists.

VII. That trial by jury is the inherent and invaluable right of every British subject in these colonies.

VIII. That the late Act of Parliament, entitled An Act for granting and applying certain Stamp Duties, and other Duties, in the British Colonies and Plantations in America, etc., by imposing taxes on the inhabitants of these colonies; and the said Act, and several other Acts, by extending the jurisdiction of the courts of Admiralty beyond its ancient limits, have a manifest tendency to subvert the rights and liberties of the colonists.

IX. That the duties imposed by several late Acts of Parliament, from the peculiar circumstances of these colonies, will be extremely burthensome and grievous, and from the scarcity of specie, the payment of them absolutely impracticable.

X. That as the profits of the trade of these colonies ultimately center in Great Britain, to pay for the manufactures which they are obliged to take from thence, they eventually contribute very

largely to all supplies granted there to the Crown.

XI. That the restrictions imposed by several late Acts of Parliament, on the trade of these colonies, will render them unable to purchase the manufactures of Great Britain.

XII. That the increase, prosperity and happiness of these colonies depend on the full and free enjoyment of their rights and liberties, and an intercourse with Great Britain mutually affectionate and advantageous.

XIII. That it is the right of the British subjects in these colonies, to petition the King or either House of Parliament.

Lastly, That it is the indispensable duty of these colonies to the best of sovereigns, to the mother country, and to themselves, to endeavour by a loyal and dutiful address to his Majesty, and humble applications to both houses of Parliament, to procure the repeal of the Act for granting and applying certain stamp duties, of all clauses of any other Acts of Parliament, whereby the jurisdiction of the admiralty is extended as aforesaid, and of the other late Acts for the restriction of American commerce.

15. *The Declaratory Act, March 18, 1766*

Danby Pickering, ed., *Statutes at Large from Magna Charta.* . . . (Cambridge, 1762-1807), XXVII, 19-20.

Whereas several of the houses of representatives in his Majesty's colonies and plantations in America, have of late, against law, claimed to themselves, or to the general assemblies of the same, the sole and exclusive right of imposing duties and taxes upon his Majesty's subjects in the said colonies and plantations; and have, in pursuance of such claim, passed certain votes, resolutions, and orders, derogatory to the legislative authority of Parliament, and inconsistent with the dependency of the said colonies and plantations upon the Crown of Great Britain: . . . be it declared . . . , that the said

colonies and plantations in America have been, are, and of right ought to be, subordinate unto, and dependent upon the imperial Crown and Parliament of Great Britain; and that the King's Majesty, by and with the advice and consent of the Lords Spiritual and Temporal, and Commons of Great Britain, in Parliament assembled, had, hath, and of right ought to have, full power and authority to make laws and statutes of sufficient force and validity to bind the colonies and people of America, subjects of the Crown of Great Britain, in all cases whatsoever.

II. And be it further declared . . . ,

that all resolutions, votes, orders, and proceedings, in any of the said colonies or plantations, whereby the power and authority of the Parliament of Great Britain, to make laws and statutes as aforesaid, is denied, or drawn into question, are, and are hereby declared to be, utterly null and void to all intents and purposes whatsoever.

Colonial Constitutional Arguments: The Second Stage

16. John Dickinson Distinguishes Regulatory from Revenue Levies, 1767-68

The Political Writings of John Dickinson, Esquire, Late President of the State of Delaware, and of the Commonwealth of Pennsylvania (Wilmington, 1801), 151-62.

There is another late act of parliament, which appears to me to be unconstitutional, and . . . destructive to the liberty of these colonies . . . that is, the act for granting the duties on paper, glass, &c.

The parliament unquestionably possesses a legal authority to *regulate* the trade of *Great-Britain,* and all her colonies. Such an authority is essential to the relations between a mother country and its colonies; and necessary for the common good of all. He, who considers these provinces as states distinct from the *British empire,* has very slender notions of *justice,* or of their *interests.* We are but parts of a *whole;* and therefore there must exist a power somewhere to preside, and preserve the connection in due order. This power is lodged in the parliament; and we are as much dependent on *Great-Britain* as a perfectly free people can be on another.

I have looked over *every statute* relating to these colonies, from their first settlement to this time, and I find every one of them founded on this principle, till the *stamp-act* administration. *All before,* are calculated to regulate trade, and preserve or promote a mutually beneficial intercourse between the several constituent parts of the empire; and though many of them imposed duties on trade, yet those duties were always imposed *with design* to restrain the commerce of one part, that were injurious to another, and thus to promote the general welfare. The raising a revenue thereby was never intended. . . . Never did the *British* parliament, till the period above mentioned, think of imposing duties in *America, for the purpose of raising a revenue. . . .*

Here we may observe an authority *expressly* claimed and exerted to impose duties on these colonies; not for the regulation of trade; not for the preservation or promotion of a mutually beneficial intercourse between the several constituent parts of the empire, heretofore the *sole objects* of parliamentary institutions; *but for the single purpose of levying money upon us.*

This I call an innovation; and a most dangerous innovation. It may perhaps be objected that *Great-Britain* has a right to lay what duties she pleases upon her exports, and it makes no difference to *us,* whether they are paid here or there.

To this I answer. These colonies require many things for their use, which the laws of *Great-Britain* prohibit them from getting anywhere but from her. Such are paper and glass.

That we may be legally bound to pay any *general* duties on these commodities, relative to the regulation of trade, is granted; but we being *obliged by her laws* to take them from *Great-Britain,* any *special* duties imposed on their exportation *to us only, with intention to raise a revenue from us only,* are as much *taxes* upon us, as those imposed by the *stamp act.* . . .

Some persons perhaps may say, that this act lays us under no necessity to pay the duties imposed, because we may ourselves manufacture the articles on which they are laid; whereas by the *stamp act* no instrument could be good, unless made on *British* paper, and that, too, stamped. . . .

I am told there are but two or three *glass-houses* on this continent, and but very few *paper-mills;* and suppose more should be erected, a long course of years must elapse before they can be brought to per-

fection. This continent is a country of planters, farmers and fishermen; not of manufacturers. The difficulty of establishing particular manufactures in such a country is almost insuperable. . . .

Great-Britain has prohibited the manufacturing of *iron* and *steel* in these colonies, without any objection being made to her *right* of doing it. The *like* right she must have to prohibit any other manufacture among us. Thus she is possessed of an undisputed *precedent* on that point. This authority, she will say, is founded on the original intention of settling these colonies; that is, that she should manufacture for them, and that they should supply her with materials. . . .

Here, then, my dear countrymen, *rouse* yourselves, and behold the ruin hanging over your heads. If you ONCE admit that *Great-Britain* may lay duties upon her exportations to us, *for the purpose of levying money on us only,* she then will have nothing to do, but to lay those duties on the articles which she prohibits us to manufacture—and the tragedy of *American* liberty is finished. . . .

17. *Boston Proclaims the "Natural Rights of the Colonists," November 20, 1772*

Harry Alonzo Cushing, ed., *The Writings of Samuel Adams* (New York, 1904-08), II, 354-9.

It is the greatest absurdity to suppose it in the power of one or any number of men at the entering into society, to renounce their essential natural rights, or the means of preserving those rights when the great end of civil government from the very nature of its institution is for the support, protection and defence of those very rights: the principal of which as is before observed, are life liberty and property. If men through fear, fraud or mistake, should *in terms* renounce and give up any essential natural right, the eternal law of reason and the great end of society, would absolutely vacate such renunciation; the right to freedom being

the gift of God Almighty, it is not in the power of Man to alienate this gift, and voluntarily become a slave. . . .

The Rights of the
Colonists as Subjects

A Common Wealth or state is a body politick or civil society of men, united together to promote their mutual safety and prosperity, by means of their union.

The *absolute Rights* of Englishmen, and all freemen in or out of Civil society, are principally, *personal security personal liberty* and *private property.*

All Persons born in the British American Colonies are by the laws of God and nature, and by the Common law of England, *exclusive of all charters from the Crown,* well Entitled, and by the Acts of the British Parliament are declared to be entitled to all the natural essential, inherent & inseperable Rights Liberties and Privileges of Subjects born in Great Britain, or within the Realm. Among those Rights are the following; which no men or body of men, consistently with their own rights as men and citizens or members of society, can for themselves give up, or take away from others.

First, "The first fundamental positive law of all Commonwealths or States, is the establishing [of] the legislative power; as the first fundamental *natural* law also, which is to govern even the legislative power itself, is the preservation of the Society."

Secondly, The Legislative has no right to absolute arbitrary power over the lives and fortunes of the people: Nor can mortals assume a prerogative, not only too high for men, but for Angels; and therefore reserved for the exercise of the *Deity* alone. . . .

Thirdly, The supreme power cannot Justly take from any man, any part of his property without his consent, in person or by his Representative.—

These are some of the first principles of natural law & Justice, and the great Barriers of all free states, and of the British Constitution in particular. It is utterly irreconcilable to these principles, and to many other fundamental maxims of the common law, common sense and reason, that a British house of commons, should have a right, at pleasure, to give and grant the property of the Colonists. . . . Now what liberty can there be, where property is taken away without consent? . . . Had the Colonists a right to return members to the british parliament, it would only be hurtfull; as from their local situation and circumstances it is impossible they should be ever truly and properly represented there. The inhabitants of this country in all probability in a few years will be more numerous, than those of Great Britain and Ireland together; yet it is absurdly expected by the promoters of the present measures, that these, with their posterity to all generations, should be easy while their property, shall be disposed of by a house of commons at three thousand miles distant from them; and who cannot be supposed to have the least care or concern for their real interest: Who have not only no natural care for their interest, but must be *in effect* bribed against it; as every burden they lay on the colonists is so much saved or gained to themselves. Hitherto many of the Colonists have been free from Quit Rents; but if the breath of a british house of commons can originate an act for taking away all our money, our lands will go next or be subject to rack rents from haughty and relentless landlords who will ride at ease, while we are trodden in the dirt. The Colonists have been branded with the odious names of traitors and rebels, only for complaining of their grievances; How long such treatment will, or ought to be born is submitted.

The Colonies, the Crown, and Parliament

18. *James Wilson*, Considerations on the Nature and Extent of the Legislative Authority of the British Parliament, *August 17, 1774*

James DeWitt Andrews, ed., *The Works of James Wilson* (Chicago, 1896), II, 505-41 *passim.*

No question can be more important to Great Britain, and to the colonies, than this—does the legislative authority of the British parliament extend over them? . . .

Those who allege that the parliament of Great Britain have power to make laws binding the American colonies, reason in the following manner. "That there is and must be in every state a supreme, irresistible, absolute, uncontrolled authority, in which the . . . rights of sovereignty, reside;" "That this supreme power is, by the constitution of Great Britain, vested in the king, lords, and commons:" "That, therefore, the acts of the king, lords, and commons, or, in other words, acts of parliament, have, by the British constitution, a binding force on the American colonies, they composing a part of the British empire."

I admit that the principle, on which this argument is founded, is of great importance: its importance, however, is derived from its tendency to promote the ultimate end of all government. But if the application of it would, in any instance, destroy, instead of promoting, that end, it ought, in that instance, to be rejected: for to admit it, would be to sacrifice the end to the means, which are valuable only so far as they advance it. . . .

Can the Americans, who are descended from British ancestors, and inherit all their rights, be blamed—can they be blamed *by their brethren in Britain*—for claiming

still to enjoy those rights? But can they enjoy them, if they are bound by the acts of a British parliament? Upon what principle does the British parliament found their power? . . . If it resides anywhere . . . it must reside in the house of commons. . . .

But from what source does this mighty, this uncontrolled authority of the house of commons flow? From the collective body of the commons of Great Britain. This authority must, therefore, originally reside in them; for whatever they convey to their representatives, must ultimately be in themselves. And have those, whom we have hitherto been accustomed to consider as our fellow-subjects, an absolute and unlimited power over us? Have they a natural right to make laws, by which we may be deprived of our properties, of our liberties, of our lives? By what title do they claim to be our masters? What act of ours has rendered us subject to those, to whom we were formerly equal? Is British freedom denominated from the *soil*, or from the *people* of Britain? If from the latter, do they lose it by quitting the soil? Do those, who embark, freemen, in Great Britain, disembark, slaves, in America? . . . Is this the return made us for leaving our friends and our country—for braving the danger of the deep—for planting a wilderness, inhabited only by savage men and savage beasts—for extending the dominions of the British crown—for in-

creasing the trade of the British merchants
—for augmenting the rents of the British
landlords—for heightening the wages of
the British artificers? Britons should blush
to make such a claim: Americans would
blush to own it. . . .

What has been already advanced will
suffice to show, that it is repugnant to the
essential maxims of jurisprudence, to the
ultimate end of all governments, to the
genius of the British constitution, and to
the liberty and happiness of the colonies,
that they should be bound by the legislative authority of the parliament of Great
Britain. Such a doctrine is not less repugnant to the voice of her laws. In order to
evince this, I shall appeal to some authorities from the books of the law, which
show expressly, or by a necessary implication, that the colonies are not bound by
the acts of the British parliament; because
they have no share in the British legislature. . . .

From this authority it follows, that it is
by no means a rule, that the authority of
parliament extends to all the subjects of
the crown. The inhabitants of Ireland
were the subjects of the king as of his
crown of England; but it is expressly resolved, in the most solemn manner, that
the inhabitants of Ireland are not bound
by the statutes of England. Allegiance to
the king and obedience to the parliament
are founded on very different principles.
The former is founded on protection; the
latter on representation. . . .

Those who launched into the unknown
deep, in quest of new countries and in-
habitations, still considered themselves as
subjects of the English monarchs, and be-
haved suitably to that character; but it
nowhere appears, that they still considered
themselves as represented in an English
parliament, or that they thought the authority of the English parliament extended
over them. They took possession of the
country in the *king's* name: they treated,
or made war with the Indians by *his* authority: they held the lands under *his*

grants, and paid *him* the rents reserved
upon them: they established governments
under the sanction of *his* prerogative, or
by virtue of *his* charters:—no application
for those purposes was made to the parliament: no ratification of the charters or
letters patent was solicited from that assembly, as is usual in England with regard
to grants and franchises of much less importance. . . .

The colonists ought to be dependent
on the king, because they have hitherto
enjoyed, and still continue to enjoy, his
protection. . . . Every subject, so soon as
he is born, is under the royal protection,
and is entitled to all the advantages arising from it. He therefore owes obedience
to that royal power, from which the protection, which he enjoys, is derived. . . .

Now we have explained the dependence of the Americans. They are the subjects of the king of Great Britain. They
owe him allegiance. They have a right to
the benefits which arise from preserving
that allegiance inviolate. They are liable
to the punishments which await those who
break it. This is a dependence, which they
have always boasted of. . . .

From this dependence, abstracted from
every other source, arises a strict connection between the inhabitants of Great
Britain and those of America. They are
fellow-subjects; they are under allegiance
to the same prince; and this union of
allegiance naturally produces a union of
hearts. It is also productive of a union of
measures through the whole British dominions. To the king is intrusted the direction and management of the great machine of government. He therefore is fittest to adjust the different wheels, and to
regulate their motions in such a manner
as to co-operate in the same general designs. He makes war: he concludes peace:
he forms alliances: he regulates domestic
trade by his prerogative, and directs foreign commerce by his treaties with those
nations, with whom it is carried on. He
names the officers of government; so that

he can check every jarring movement in the administration. He has a negative on the different legislatures throughout his dominions, so that he can prevent any repugnancy in their different laws.

The connection and harmony between Great Britain and us, which it is her interest and ours mutually to cultivate, and on which her prosperity, as well as ours, so materially depends, will be better preserved by the operation of the legal prerogatives of the crown, than by the exertion of an unlimited authority by parliament.

19. *The Continental Congress Declares Colonial Rights,* *October 14, 1774*

Worthington C. Ford, ed., *Journals of the Continental Congress, 1774-1789* (Washington, D. C., 1904-37), I, 63-73.

Whereas, since the close of the last war, the British parliament, claiming a power of right to bind the people of America, by statute in all cases whatsoever, hath, in some acts expressly imposed taxes on them, and in others, under various pretences, but in fact for the purpose of raising a revenue, hath imposed rates and duties payable in these colonies, established a board of commissioners, with unconstitutional powers, and extended the jurisdiction of courts of Admiralty, not only for collecting the said duties, but for the trial of causes merely arising within the body of a county.

And whereas, in consequence of other statutes, judges who before held only estates at will in their offices, have been made dependent on the Crown alone for their salaries, and standing armies kept in times of peace:

And it has lately been resolved in Parliament that . . . colonists may be transported to England, and tried there upon accusations for treasons, and misprisions, or concealments of treasons committed in the colonies; and by a late statute, such trials have been directed in cases therein mentioned.

And whereas, in the last session of Parliament, three statutes were made . . . [the Coercive Acts], and another statute was then made [the Quebec Act] . . . All which statutes are impolitic, unjust, and cruel, as well as unconstitutional, and most dangerous and destructive of American rights.

And whereas, Assemblies have been frequently dissolved, contrary to the rights of the people, when they attempted to deliberate on grievances; and their dutiful, humble, loyal, & reasonable petitions to the crown for redress, have been repeatedly treated with contempt, by His Majesty's ministers of state:

The good people of the several Colonies . . . justly alarmed at these arbitrary proceedings of parliament and administration, have severally elected, constituted, and appointed deputies to meet and sit in general congress, in the city of Philadelphia, in order to obtain such establishment, as that their religion, laws, and liberties, may not be subverted:

Whereupon the deputies so appointed being now assembled, in a full and free representation of these Colonies, taking into their most serious consideration the best means of attaining the ends aforesaid, do in the first place, as Englishmen their ancestors in like cases have usually done, for asserting and vindicating their rights and liberties, declare,

That the inhabitants of the English Colonies in North America, by the immutable laws of nature, the principles of the English constitution, and the several charters or compacts, have the following Rights:

Resolved, N. C. D.

1. That they are entitled to life, liberty, and property, & they have never ceded to any sovereign power whatever, a right to dispose of either without their consent.

2. That our ancestors, who first settled these colonies, were at the time of their emigration from the mother country, entitled to all the rights, liberties, and immunities of free and natural-born subjects within the realm of England.

3. That by such emigration they by no means forfeited, surrendered, or lost any of those rights, but that they were, and their descendants now are entitled to the exercise and enjoyment of all such of them, as their local and other circumstances enable them to exercise and enjoy.

4. That the foundation of English liberty, and of all free government, is a right in the people to participate in their legislative council: and as the English colonists are not represented, and from their local and other circumstances, cannot properly be represented in the British parliament, they are entitled to a free and exclusive power of legislation in their several provincial legislatures, where their right of representation can alone be preserved, in all cases of taxation and internal polity, subject only to the negative of their sovereign, in such manner as has been heretofore used and accustomed. But, from the necessity of the case, and a regard to the mutual interest of both countries, we cheerfully consent to the operation of such acts of the British parliament, as are bona fide restrained to the regulation of our external commerce, for the purpose of securing the commercial advantages of the whole empire to the mother country, and the commercial benefits of its respective members excluding every idea of taxation, internal or external, for raising a revenue on the subjects in America without their consent.

5. That the respective colonies are entitled to the common law of England, and more especially to the great and inestimable privilege of being tried by their peers of the vicinage, according to the course of that law.

6. That they are entitled to the benefit of such of the English statutes, as existed at the time of their colonization; and which they have, by experience, respectively found to be applicable to their several local and other circumstances.

7. That these, his majesty's colonies, are likewise entitled to all the immunities and privileges granted and confirmed to them by royal charters, or secured by their several codes of provincial laws.

8. That they have a right peaceably to assemble, consider of their grievances, and petition the King; and that all prosecutions, prohibitory proclamations, and commitments for the same, are illegal.

9. That the keeping a Standing army in these colonies, in times of peace, without the consent of the legislature of that colony in which such army is kept, is against law.

10. It is indispensably necessary to good government, and rendered essential by the English constitution, that the constituent branches of the legislature be independent of each other; that, therefore, the exercise of legislative power in several colonies, by a council appointed during pleasure, by the crown, is unconstitutional, dangerous, and destructive to the freedom of American legislation. . . .

Resolved, That the following acts of Parliament are infringements and violations of the rights of the colonists; and that the repeal of them is essentially necessary, in order to restore harmony between Great-Britain and the American colonies, viz.:

The several Acts . . . which impose duties for the purpose of raising a revenue in America, extend the powers of the admiralty courts beyond their ancient limits, deprive the American subject of trial by jury, authorize the judges' certificate to indemnify the prosecutor from damages that he might otherwise be liable to, requiring oppressive security from a claimant of ships and goods seized before he shall be allowed to defend his property; and are subversive of American rights.

Also . . . "An act for the better preserving his Majesty's dockyards, magazines, ships, ammunition, and stores," which declares a new offense in America, and deprives the American subject of a constitutional trial by jury of the vicinage, by authorizing the trial of any person charged with the committing any offense described in the said act, out of the realm, to be indicted and tried for the same in any shire or county within the realm.

Also the three acts passed in the last session of parliament, for stopping the port and blocking up the harbour of Boston, for altering the charter & government of the Massachusetts-bay, and that which is entitled "An Act for the better administration of Justice," &c.

Also the act passed the same session for establishing the Roman Catholick Religion in the province of Quebec, abolishing the equitable system of English laws, and erecting a tyranny there, to the great danger, from so great a dissimilarity of Religion, law, and government, of the neighbouring British colonies. . . .

Also the act passed the same session for the better providing suitable quarters for officers and soldiers in his Majesty's service in North-America.

Also, that the keeping a standing army in several of these colonies, in time of peace, without the consent of the legislature of that colony in which the army is kept, is against law.

To these grievous acts and measures Americans cannot submit, but in hopes that their fellow subjects in Great-Britain will, on a revision of them, restore us to that state in which both countries found happiness and prosperity, we have for the present only resolved to pursue the following peaceable measures. . . . 1st. To enter into a non-importation, non-consumption, and non-exportation agreement or association. 2. To prepare an address to the people of Great-Britain, and a memorial to the inhabitants of British America, & 3. To prepare a loyal address to his Majesty, agreeable to resolutions already entered into.

20. *Samuel Johnson*, Taxation No Tyranny, 1775

Arthur Murphy, ed., *The Works of Samuel Johnson* (London, 1824), VIII, 155-92.

In all the parts of human knowledge, whether terminating in science merely speculative, or operating upon life private or civil, are admitted some fundamental principles, or common axioms, which being generally received are little doubted, and being little doubted have been rarely proved. . . .

Of this kind is the position, that *the supreme power of every community has the right of requiring from all its subjects such contributions as are necessary to the publick safety or publick prosperity*, which was considered by all mankind as comprising the primary and essential condition of all political society, till it became disputed by those zealots of anarchy, who have denied to the Parliament of Britain the right of taxing the American colonies. . . .

There are those who . . . tell us that to tax the colonies is usurpation and oppression, an invasion of natural and legal rights, and a violation of those principles which support the constitution of English government.

This question is of great importance. That the Americans are able to bear taxation is indubitable; that their refusal may be over-ruled is highly probable; but power is no sufficient evidence of truth. Let us examine our own claim, and the objections of the recusants, with caution proportioned to the event of the decision, which must convict one part of robbery, or the other of rebellion. . . .

The colonies of England differ no otherwise from those of other nations, than as the English constitution differs from theirs. All government is ultimately and essentially absolute, but subordinate societies may have more immunities, or individuals greater liberty, as the operations of government are differently conducted. An Englishman in the common course of life and action feels no restraint. An English colony has very liberal powers of regulating its own manners and adjusting its own affairs. But an English individual may by the supreme authority be deprived of liberty, and a colony divested of its powers, for reasons of which that authority is the only judge.

In sovereignty there are no gradations. There may be limited royalty, there may be limited consulship; but there can be no limited government. There must in every society be some power or other from which there is no appeal, which admits no restrictions, which pervades the whole mass of the community, regulates and adjusts all subordination, enacts laws or repeals them, erects or annuls judicatures, extends or contracts privileges, exempt itself from question or control, and bounded only by physical necessity. . . .

To him that considers the nature, the original, the progress, and the constitution of the colonies, who remembers that the first discoveries had commissions from the crown, that the first settlers owe to a charter their civil forms and regular magistracy, and that all personal immunities and legal securities by which the condition of the subject has been from time to time improved have been extended to the colonists, it will not be doubted but the Parliament of England has a right to bind them by statutes, and *to bind them in all cases whatsoever,* and has therefore a natural and constitutional power of laying upon them any tax or impost, whether external or internal, upon the product of land, or the manufactures of industry, in the exigencies of war, or in the time of profound peace, for the defence of America, *for the purpose of raising a revenue,* or for any other end beneficial to the empire. . . .

It is, say the American advocates, the natural distinction of a freeman, and the legal privilege of an Englishman, that he is able to call his possessions his own, that he can sit secure in the enjoyment of inheritance or acquisition, that his house is fortified by the law, and that nothing can be taken from him but by his own consent. This consent is given for every man by his representative in parliament. The Americans unrepresented cannot consent to English taxations, as a corporation, and they will not consent as individuals.

Of this argument, it has been observed by more than one, that its force extends equally to all other laws, for a freeman is not to be exposed to punishment or be called to any onerous service but by his own consent. The congress has extracted a position from the fanciful Montesquieu, that *in a free state every man being a free agent ought to be concerned in his own government.* Whatever is true of taxation is true of every other law, that he who is bound by it, without his consent, is not free, for he is not concerned in his own government.

He that denies the English Parliament the right of taxation, denies it likewise the right of making any other laws civil or criminal, yet this power over the colonies was never yet disputed by themselves. They have always admitted statutes for the punishment of offences and for the redress or prevention of inconveniencies, and the reception of any law draws after it, by a chain which cannot be broken, the unwelcome necessity of submitting to taxation. . . .

They have not, by abandoning their part in one legislature, obtained the power of constituting another, exclusive and independent, any more than the multitudes, who are now debarred from voting, have a right to erect a separate Parliament for themselves. . . .

Many populous and opulent towns neither enjoy nor desire particular representatives; they are included in the general scheme of publick administration and cannot suffer but with the rest of the empire. . . .

It must always be remembered that . . .

[Americans] are represented by the same virtual representation as the greater part of Englishmen; and that if by change of place they have less share in the legislature than is proportionate to their opulence, they by their removal gained that opulence, and had originally, and have now, their choice of a vote at home or riches at a distance. . . .

21. *Thomas Paine Talks* Common Sense, *January, 1776*

Moncure Daniel Conway, ed., *The Writings of Thomas Paine* (New York, 1894), 69-101.

THOUGHTS ON THE PRESENT STATE OF AMERICAN AFFAIRS

Volumes have been written on the subject of the struggle between England and America. Men of all ranks have embarked in the controversy, from different motives, and with various designs: but all have been ineffectual, and the period of debate is closed. Arms as the last resource, must decide the contest. . . .

The Sun never shined on a cause of greater worth. 'Tis not the affair of a City, a County, a Province, or a Kingdom, but of a Continent—of at least one eighth part of the habitable Globe. 'Tis not the concern of a day, a year, or an age; posterity are virtually involved in the contest, and will be more or less affected, even to the end of time, by the proceedings now. Now is the seed-time of Continental union, faith, and honour. The least fracture now will be like a name engraved with the point of a pin on the tender rind of a young oak; the wound will enlarge with the tree, and posterity read it in full grown characters. . . .

As much hath been said of the advantages of reconciliation, which, like an agreeable dream, hath passed away and left us as we were, it is but right, that we should examine the contrary side of the argument, and inquire into some of the many material injuries which these Colonies sustain, and always will sustain, by

being connected with and dependant on Great-Britain. . . .

I have heard it asserted by some, that as America hath flourished under her former connexion with Great-Britain, the same connexion is necessary towards her future happiness, and will always have the same effect. . . . I answer roundly, that America would have flourished as much, and probably much more, had no European power had any thing to do with her. The articles of commerce, by which she hath enriched herself, are the necessaries of life, and will always have a market while eating is the custom of Europe. . . .

We have boasted the protection of Great-Britain, without considering, that her motive was *interest* not *attachment;* and that she did not protect us from *our enemies* on *our account*, but from *her enemies* on *her own account*, from those who had no quarrel with us on any *other account*, and who will always be our enemies on the *same account*. Let Britain waive her pretensions to the continent, or the continent throw off the dependance, and we should be at peace with France and Spain, were they at war with Britain. . . .

But Britain is the parent country, say some. Then the more shame upon her conduct. Even brutes do not devour their young, nor savages make war upon their families; wherefore, the assertion, if true, turns to her reproach; but it happens not to be true, or only partly so . . . Europe, and not England, is the parent country of America. This new World hath been the asylum for the persecuted lovers of civil and religious liberty from *every part* of Europe. . . .

I challenge the warmest advocate for reconciliation, to show a single advantage that this continent can reap, by being connected with Great Britain. . . .

Everything that is right or natural pleads for separation. The blood of the slain, the weeping voice of nature cries, *'tis time to part*. Even the distance at which the Almighty hath placed England and America, is a strong and natural proof, that the authority of one over the other, was never the design of Heaven. . . .

As to government matters, 'tis not in the power of Britain to do this continent justice: the business of it will soon be too weighty and intricate to be managed with any tolerable degree of convenience, by a power so distant from us, and so very ignorant of us; for if they cannot conquer us, they cannot govern us. To be always running three or four thousand miles with a tale or a petition, waiting four or five months for an answer, which, when obtained, requires five or six more to explain it in, will in a few years be looked upon as folly and childishness—there was a time when it was proper, and there is a proper time for it to cease.

Small islands not capable of protecting themselves, are the proper objects for kingdoms to take under their care; but there is something absurd, in supposing a continent to be perpetually governed by an island. In no instance hath nature made the satellite larger than its primary planet; and as England and America, with respect to each other, reverses the common order of nature, it is evident that they belong to different systems: England to Europe: America to itself. . . .

America is only a secondary object in the system of British politics—England consults the good of *this* country no fur-

ther than it answers her *own* purpose. Wherefore, her own interest leads her to suppress the growth of *ours* in every case which doth not promote her advantage, or in the least interferes with it. . . .

But the most powerful of all arguments, is, that nothing but independence, i.e. a continental form of government, can keep the peace of the continent and preserve it inviolate from civil wars. I dread the event of a reconciliation with Britain now, as it is more than probable that it will be followed by a revolt somewhere or other, the consequences of which may be far more fatal than all the malice of Britain. . . .

A government of our own is our natural right: and when a man seriously reflects on the precariousness of human affairs, he will become convinced, that it is infinitely wiser and safer, to form a constitution of our own in a cool deliberate manner, while we have it in our power, than to trust such an interesting event to time and chance. . . . Ye that oppose independence now, ye know not what ye do; ye are opening a door to eternal tyranny, by keeping vacant the seat of government. There are thousands and tens of thousands, who would think it glorious to expel from the Continent that barbarous and hellish power, which hath stirred up the Indians and Negroes to destroy us— the cruelty hath a double guilt, it is dealing brutally by us, and treacherously by them. . . .

O! ye that love mankind! Ye that dare oppose, not only the tyranny, but the tyrant, stand forth! Every spot of the old world is overrun with oppression. Freedom hath been hunted round the globe. Asia, and Africa, have long expelled her. Europe regards her like a stranger, and England hath given her warning to depart. O! receive the fugitive, and prepare in time an asylum for mankind. . . . *Wherefore,* instead of gazing at each other, with suspicious or doubtful curiosity, let each of us, hold out to his neighbor the hearty hand of friendship, and unite in drawing a line, which, like an act of oblivion, shall bury in forgetfulness every former dissention. Let the names of whig and tory be extinct; and let none other be heard among us, than those of *a good citizen; an open and resolute friend;* and *a virtuous supporter of the* RIGHTS *of* MANKIND, *and of the* FREE AND INDEPENDENT STATES OF AMERICA.

CHAPTER III

The Declaration, the Articles, and the Constitution

THE King's rejection of the Olive Branch Petition in 1775, coupled with his "Proclamation . . . for Suppressing Rebellion and Sedition," undermined the one remaining link between colonies and mother country. By May, 1776, the ferment of freedom was working in the states as well as in Congress. At almost the same time that the North Carolina (April 12) and Virginia provincial congresses (May 15) instructed their delegates in the Continental Congress to vote for independence, Congress itself advised all the colonies to reject Britain's authority (May 10) and to erect new governments based on common consent (May 15). In conformity with Virginia's instructions, Richard Henry Lee introduced in Congress on June 7 resolutions asserting that the "colonies are, and of right ought to be, free and independent States." On July 2 Congress passed the resolution declaring independence, and on July 4 it adopted the Declaration of Independence (No. 22). "Neither aiming at originality of principles or sentiments," Jefferson later wrote, "nor yet copied from any particular and previous writing, it was intended to be an expression of the American mind." In submitting the document "to a candid world," Congress no longer defended their rights as Englishmen but shifted their argument to the higher plane of the universal rights of man.

But how could the rights of the people be protected from government encroachment? Written bills of rights imposing limitations on political power were the persistent answer. The most influential and eloquent of these statements was the Virginia Declaration of Rights (No. 23), written by George Mason as "the basis and foundation of government." This document, one of America's outstanding contributions to political thought, was the model not only for similar declarations in several state constitutions and the federal Bill of Rights but also for European manifestoes, especially the French Declaration of the Rights of Man and Citizen.

At the same time that R. H. Lee proposed independence, he also suggested that "a plan of confederation be prepared and transmitted to the respective Colonies." On July 12, 1776, a committee reported the first draft, and after considerable delay and a few changes, Congress submitted the Articles of Confederation (No. 24) to the states on November 15, 1777. Until 1781, the Continental Congress functioned as a *de facto* government without a definite constitutional basis. The four-year delay resulted from a bitter controversy involving claims on western land, but with the cession of these lands to the central government the Articles were finally ratified, binding the United States into a "perpetual Union."

The acquisition of these lands made possible the Confederation's outstanding achievement, the enactment of the Northwest Ordinance of 1787 (No. 25), a remarkably workable solution to the imperial problem of governing territorial settlements. Thus, the thorny problem of colonial status, so long troublesome to British administrators, was solved in a unique, pragmatic American manner. Included in the Ordinance were the "articles of compact," a brief bill of rights similar to those incorporated in the state constitutions. This prevailing emphasis upon the libertarian principles of the American Revolution was best epitomized by the Virginia Statute for Religious Freedom (No. 26). This work of Thomas Jefferson sets forth the basic American principle of separation of church and state and elaborates a classic defense of intellectual freedom.

Despite these advances, however, two persistent problems revealed the inadequacies of the Articles: (1) the lack of an effective federal coercive power, and (2) the distribution of powers between the nation and the states. At a convention called for "the sole and express purpose of revising the Articles of Confederation," a distinguished group of delegates, almost all from the conservative wing of the Revolutionary movement, illustrated their political genius by establishing a workable system of republican federalism. Of the plans presented at the Constitutional Convention, two were of basic importance. The large states favored the Randolph plan which proposed a new national government to replace the Articles. The Paterson draft, which won the support of the small states, provided for a revision of the Articles. Although the completed Constitution more closely resembled the former than the latter proposal, one of its crucial concepts—the "supreme law of the land" clause—came from the small-state plan. The willingness of the framers to select features from the various plans, coupled with their ability to reach a series of significant compromises, made possible a new Constitution (No. 27) designed to establish "a more perfect Union."

Radical leaders, nurtured on the Revolutionary concept that government was a necessary evil, feared that strengthening the central government posed potential threats to the people's liberties. Indeed, Elbridge Gerry of Massachusetts and George Mason and Edmund Randolph of Virginia refused to sign the proposed

Constitution on the last day of the Convention. Although Thomas Jefferson was favorably impressed by the general frame of government, he argued forceably "that a bill of rights is what the people are entitled to against every government on earth" (No. 28A). One of the most popular pamphlets of the day was Richard Henry Lee's *Letters from the Federal Farmer*, a moderate plea for amendment rather than rejection. He feared that the Constitution, without a Bill of Rights, would "put Civil Liberty and the happiness of the people at the mercy of Rulers who may possess the great unguarded powers given." Mercy Otis Warren, in a pamphlet long attributed to Elbridge Gerry, went further. Convinced that the proposed Constitution would "lay the foundation of Government of force and fraud" and terminate civil liberties, she opposed its ratification in a blistering attack (No. 28B).

Opposition to the Constitution called forth numerous defenses of it. The most famous of these were *The Federalist Papers*, praised by Jefferson as "the best commentary on the principles of government ever written." Composed by Alexander Hamilton, James Madison, and John Jay, the *Papers* were not intended as a theoretical treatise in political theory but were designed for the specific purpose, as Madison pointed out, of vindicating and recommending "the new Constitution to the State of New York whose ratification of the instrument, was doubtful as well as important." Nevertheless, *The Federalist Papers* were a masterful analysis of the Constitution and the fundamental principles on which the federal government was erected. In the most famous of these papers, *Federalist* No. 10, Madison discusses politics, property, and power in a republic (No. 29).

The American Revolution and the First Constitution of the United States

22. *The Declaration of Independence Justifies Revolution, July 4, 1776*

WHEN in the Course of human events, it becomes necessary for one people to dissolve the political bands which have connected them with another, and to assume among the powers of the earth, the separate and equal station to which the Laws of Nature and of Nature's God entitle them, a decent respect to the opinions of mankind requires that they should declare the causes which impel them to the separation.—We hold these truths to be self-evident, that all men are created equal, that they are endowed by their Creator with certain unalienable Rights, that among these are Life, Liberty and the pursuit of Happiness.—That to secure these rights, Governments are instituted among Men, deriving their just powers from the consent of the governed.—That whenever any Form of Government becomes destructive of these ends, it is the Right of the People to alter or to abolish it, and to institute new Government, laying its foundation on such principles and organizing its powers in such forms, as to them shall seem most likely to effect their Safety and Happiness. Prudence, indeed, will dictate that Governments long established should not be changed for light and transient causes; and accordingly all experience hath shewn, that mankind are more disposed to suffer, while evils are sufferable, than to right themselves by abolishing the forms to which they are accustomed. But when a long train of abuses and usurpations, pursuing invariably the same Object evinces a design to reduce them under absolute Despotism, it is their right, it is their duty, to throw off such Government, and to provide new Guards for their future security.—Such has been the patient sufferance of these Colonies; and such is now the necessity which constrains them to alter their former Systems of Government. The history of the present King of Great Britain is a history of repeated injuries and usurpations, all having in direct object the establishment of an absolute Tyranny over these States. To prove this, let Facts be submitted to a candid world.—He has refused his Assent to Laws, the most wholesome and necessary for the public good.—He has forbidden his Governors to pass Laws of immediate and pressing importance, unless suspended in their operation till his Assent should be obtained; and when so suspended, he has utterly neglected to attend to them.—He has refused to pass other Laws for the accommodation of large districts of people, unless those people would relinquish the right of Representation in the Legislature, a right inestimable to them and formidable to tyrants only.— He has called together legislative bodies at places unusual, uncomfortable, and distant from the depository of their Public Records, for the sole purpose of fatiguing

them into compliance with his measures. —He has dissolved Representative Houses repeatedly, for opposing with manly firmness his invasions on the rights of the people.—He has refused for a long time, after such dissolutions, to cause others to be elected; whereby the Legislative Powers, incapable of Annihilation, have returned to the People at large for their exercise; the State remaining in the mean time exposed to all the dangers of invasion from without, and convulsions within.— He has endeavoured to prevent the population of these States; for that purpose obstructing the Laws for Naturalization of Foreigners; refusing to pass others to encourage their migration hither, and raising the conditions of new Appropriations of Lands.—He has obstructed the Administration of Justice, by refusing his Assent to Laws for establishing Judiciary Powers. —He has made Judges dependent on his will alone, for the tenure of their offices, and the amount and payment of their salaries.—He has erected a multitude of New Offices, and sent hither swarms of Officers to harass our People, and eat out their substance.—He has kept among us, in times of peace, Standing Armies without the Consent of our legislature.—He has affected to render the Military independent of and superior to the Civil Power.—He has combined with others to subject us to a jurisdiction foreign to our constitution, and unacknowledged by our laws; giving his Assent to their acts of pretended legislation:—For quartering large bodies of armed troops among us:—For protecting them, by a mock Trial, from Punishment for any Murders which they should commit on the Inhabitants of these States:—For cutting off our Trade with all parts of the world:—For imposing taxes on us without our Consent:—For depriving us in many cases, of the benefits of Trial by Jury:—For transporting us beyond Seas to be tried for pretended offence:—For abolishing the free System of English Laws in a neighbouring Province, establishing therein an Arbitrary government, and enlarging its Boundaries so as to render it at once an example and fit instrument for introducing the same absolute rule into these Colonies:—For taking away our Charters, abolishing our most valuable Laws, and altering fundamentally the Forms of our Governments: —For suspending our own Legislature, and declaring themselves invested with Power to legislate for us in all cases whatsoever.—He has abdicated Government here, by declaring us out of his Protection and waging War against us.—He has plundered our seas, ravaged our Coasts, burnt our towns, and destroyed the lives of our people.—He is at this time transporting large armies of foreign mercenaries to compleat the works of death, desolation and tyranny, already begun with circumstances of Cruelty & perfidy scarcely paralleled in the most barbarous ages, and totally unworthy the Head of a civilized nation.—He has constrained our fellow Citizens taken Captive on the high Seas to bear Arms against their Country, to become the executioners of their friends and Brethren, or to fall themselves by their Hands.—He has excited domestic insurrections amongst us, and has endeavoured to bring on the inhabitants of our frontiers, the merciless Indian Savages, whose known rule of warfare, is an undistinguished destruction of all ages, sexes and conditions. In every stage of these Oppressions We have Petitioned for Redress in the most humble terms: Our repeated Petitions have been answered only by repeated injury. A Prince, whose character is thus marked by every act which may define a Tyrant, is unfit to be the ruler of a free people. Nor have We been wanting in attentions to our British brethren. We have warned them from time to time of attempts by their legislature to extend an unwarrantable jurisdiction over us. We have reminded them of the circumstances of our emigration and settlement here. We have appealed to their native justice and magnanimity, and we have conjured them by the ties of common kindred to disavow these usurpations, which would inevitably interrupt our connections and correspondence. They too have been deaf to the voice of justice and of consanguinity. We must, therefore, acquiesce in the necessity, which denounces our Separation, and hold them, as we hold the rest of mankind, Enemies in War, in Peace Friends.—

We, therefore, the Representatives of the united States of America, in General Congress, Assembled, appealing to the Supreme Judge of the world for the rectitude of our intentions, do, in the Name, and by Authority of the good People of these Colonies, solemnly publish and declare, That these United Colonies are, and of Right ought to be, Free and Independent States; that they are Absolved from all Allegiance to the British Crown, and that all political connection between them and the State of Great Britain, is and ought to be totally dissolved; and that as Free and Independent States, they have full Power to levy War, conclude Peace, contract Alliances, establish Commerce, and to do all other Acts and Things which Independent States may of right do.—And for the support of this Declaration, with a firm reliance on the protection of divine Providence, we mutually pledge to each other our Lives, our Fortunes and our sacred Honor.

23. George Mason, The Virginia Declaration of Rights, June 12, 1776

Ordinances Passed at General Convention . . . of Virginia, . . . in the City of Williamsburg, on . . . the 6th of May, . . . 1776 (Williamsburg, [1776]), 100-3.

A Declaration of Rights made by the representatives of the good people of Virginia, *assembled in full and free Convention; which rights do pertain to them, and their posterity, as the basis and foundation of government.*

1. That all men are by nature equally free and independent, and have certain inherent rights, of which, when they enter into a state of society, they cannot by any compact deprive or divest their posterity; namely, the enjoyment of life and liberty, with the means of acquiring and possessing property, and pursuing and obtaining happiness and safety.

2. That all power is vested in, and consequently derived from, the people; that magistrates are their trustees and servants, and at all times amenable to them.

3. That government is, or ought to be instituted for the common benefit, protection, and security, of the people, nation, or community; of all the various modes and forms of government that is best, which is capable of producing the greatest degree of happiness and safety, and is most effectually secured against the danger of mal-administration; and that when any government shall be found inadequate or contrary to these purposes, a majority of the community hath an indubitable, un-alienable, and indefeasible right to reform, alter, or abolish it, in such manner as shall be judged most conducive to the publick weal.

4. That no man, or set of men, are entitled to exclusive or separate emoluments or privileges from the community, but in consideration of publick services; which, not being descendible, neither ought the offices of magistrate, legislator, or judge, to be hereditary.

5. That the legislative and executive powers of the state should be separate and distinct from the judiciary; and that the members of the two first may be restrained from oppression, by feeling and participating the burthens of the people, they should, at fixed periods, be reduced to a private station, return into that body from which they were originally taken, and the vacancies be supplied by frequent, certain, and regular elections, in which all, or any part of the former members, to be again eligible, or ineligible, as the laws shall direct.

6. That elections of members to serve as representatives of the people, in assembly, ought to be free; and that all men, having sufficient evidence of permanent common interest with, and attachment to, the community, have the right of suffrage, and can not be taxed or deprived of their property for publick uses without their own consent, or that of their representatives so elected, nor bound by any law to which they have not, in like manner, assented for the publick good.

7. That all power of suspending laws, or the execution of laws, by any authority without consent of the representatives of the people, is injurious to their rights, and ought not to be exercised.

8. That in all capital or criminal prosecutions a man hath a right to demand the cause and nature of his accusation, to be confronted with the accusers and witnesses, to call for evidence in his favour, and to a speedy trial by an impartial jury of his vicinage, without whose unanimous consent he cannot be found guilty, nor can he be compelled to give evidence against himself; that no man be deprived of his liberty, except by the law of the land, or the judgment of his peers.

9. That excessive bail ought not to be required, nor excessive fines imposed, nor cruel and unusual punishments inflicted.

10. That general warrants, whereby an officer or messenger may be commanded to search suspected places without evidence of a fact committed, or to seize any person or persons not named, or whose offence is not particularly described and supported by evidence, are grievous and oppressive, and ought not to be granted.

11. That in controversies respecting property, and in suits between man and man, the ancient trial by jury is preferable to any other, and ought to be held sacred.

12. That the freedom of the press is one of the great bulwarks of liberty, and can never be restrained but by despotick governments.

13. That a well regulated militia, composed of the body of the people, trained to arms, is the proper, natural and safe defence of a free state; that standing armies, in time of peace should be avoided, as dangerous to liberty; and that, in all cases,

the military should be under strict subordination to, and governed by, the civil power.

14. That the people have a right to uniform government; and therefore, that no government separate from, or independent of, the government of *Virginia,* ought to be erected or established within the limits thereof.

15. That no free government, or the blessings of liberty, can be preserved to any people but by a firm adherence to justice, moderation, temperance, frugality, and virtue, and by frequent recurrence to fundamental principles.

16. That religion, or the duty which we owe to our CREATOR, and the manner of discharging it, can be directed only by reason and conviction, not by force or violence; and therefore all men are equally entitled to the free exercise of religion, according to the dictates of conscience; and that it is the mutual duty of all to practise Christian forbearance, love, and charity, towards each other.

24. *The Articles of Confederation and Perpetual Union*

Adopted November 15, 1777; ratified March 1, 1781.

To ALL TO WHOM these Presents shall come, we the undersigned Delegates of the States affixed to our Names send greeting. Whereas the Delegates of the United States of America in Congress assembled did on the fifteenth day of November in the Year of our Lord One Thousand Seven Hundred and Seventy seven, and in the Second Year of the Independence of America agree to certain articles of Confederation and perpetual Union between the States of Newhampshire, Massachusetts-bay, Rhodeisland and Providence Plantations, Connecticut, New York, New Jersey, Pennsylvania, Delaware, Maryland, Virginia, North-Carolina, South-Carolina and Georgia in the Words following, viz. "Articles of Confederation and perpetual Union between the states of Newhampshire, Massachusetts-bay, Rhode-

island and Providence Plantations, Connecticut, New-York, New-Jersey, Pennsylvania, Delaware, Maryland, Virginia, North-Carolina, South-Carolina and Georgia."

Art. I. The Stile of this confederacy shall be "The United States of America."

Art. II. Each state retains its sovereignty, freedom and independence, and every Power, Jurisdiction and right, which is not by this confederation expressly delegated to the United States, in Congress assembled.

Art. III. The said states hereby severally enter into a firm league of friendship with each other, for their common defence, the security of their Liberties, and their mutual and general welfare, binding themselves to assist each other, against all force offered to, or attacks made upon them, or any of them, on account of religion, sovereignty, trade, or any other pretence whatever.

Art. IV. The better to secure and perpetuate mutual friendship and intercourse among the people of the different states in this union, the free inhabitants of each of these states, paupers, vagabonds and fugitives from Justice excepted, shall be entitled to all privileges and immunities of free citizens in the several states; and the people of each state shall have free ingress and regress to and from any other state, and shall enjoy therein all the privileges of trade and commerce, subject to the same duties, impositions and restrictions as the inhabitants thereof respectively, provided that such restriction shall not extend so far as to prevent the removal of property imported into any state, to any other state of which the Owner is an inhabitant; provided also that no imposition, duties or restriction shall be laid by any state, on the property of the united states, or either of them.

If any Person guilty of, or charged with treason, felony, or other high misdemeanor in any state, shall flee from Justice, and be found in any of the united states, he shall upon demand of the Governor or executive power, of the state from which he fled, be delivered up and removed to the state having jurisdiction of his offence.

Full faith and credit shall be given in each of these states to the records, acts and judicial proceedings of the courts and magistrates of every other state.

Art. V. For the more convenient management of the general interests of the united states, delegates shall be annually appointed in such manner as the legislature of each state shall direct, to meet in Congress on the first Monday in November, in every year, with a power reserved to each state, to recall its delegates, or any of them, at any time within the year, and to send others in their stead, for the remainder of the Year.

No state shall be represented in Congress by less than two, nor by more than seven Members; and no person shall be capable of being a delegate for more than three years in any term of six years; nor shall any person, being a delegate, be capable of holding any office under the united states, for which he, or another for his benefit receives any salary, fees or emolument of any kind.

Each state shall maintain its own delegates in a meeting of the states, and while they act as members of the committee of the states.

In determining questions in the united states, in Congress assembled, each state shall have one vote.

Freedom of speech and debate in Congress shall not be impeached or questioned in any Court, or place out of Congress, and the members of congress shall be protected in their persons from arrests and imprisonments, during the time of their going to and from, and attendance on congress, except for treason, felony, or breach of the peace.

Art. VI. No state without the Consent of the united states in congress assembled, shall send any embassy to, or receive any embassy from, or enter into any conference, agreement, or alliance or treaty with any King, prince or state; nor shall any person holding any office of profit or trust under the united states, or any of them, accept of any present, emolument, office or title of any kind whatever from any king, prince or foreign state; nor shall the united states in congress assembled, or any of them, grant any title of nobility.

No two or more states shall enter into any treaty, confederation or alliance whatever between them, without the consent of the united states in congress assembled, specifying accurately the purposes for which the same is to be entered into, and how long it shall continue.

No state shall lay any imposts or duties, which may interfere with any stipulations in treaties, entered into by the united states in congress assembled, with any king, prince or state, in pursuance of any treaties already proposed by congress, to the courts of France and Spain.

No vessels of war shall be kept up in time of peace by any state, except such number only, as shall be deemed necessary by the united states in congress assembled, for the defence of such state, or its trade; nor shall any body of forces be kept up by any state, in time of peace, except such number only, as in the judgment of the united states, in congress assembled, shall be deemed requisite to garrison the forts necessary for the defence of such state; but every state shall always keep up a well regulated and disciplined militia, sufficiently armed and accoutred, and shall provide and constantly have ready for use, in public stores, a due number of field pieces and tents, and a proper quantity of arms, ammunition and camp equipage.

No state shall engage in any war without the consent of the united states in congress assembled, unless such state be actually invaded by enemies, or shall have received certain advice of a resolution being formed by some nation of Indians to invade such state, and the danger is so imminent as not to admit of a delay, till the united states in congress assembled can be consulted: nor shall any state grant commissions to any ships or vessels of war, nor letters of marque or reprisal, except it be after a declaration of war by the united states in congress assembled, and then only against the kingdom or state and the subjects thereof, against which war has been so declared, and under such regulations as shall be established by the united states in congress assembled, unless such state be infested by pirates, in which case vessels of war may be fitted out for that occasion, and kept so long as the danger shall continue, or until the united states in congress assembled shall determine otherwise.

Art. VII. When land-forces are raised by any state for the common defence, all officers of or under the rank of colonel, shall be appointed by the legislature of each state respectively by whom such forces shall be raised, or in such manner as such state shall direct, and all vacancies shall be filled up by the state which first made the appointment.

Art. VIII. All charges of war, and all other expences that shall be incurred for the common defence or general welfare, and allowed by the united states in congress assembled, shall be defrayed out of a common treasury, which shall be supplied by the several states, in proportion to the value of all land within each state, granted to or surveyed for any Person, as such land and the buildings and improvements thereon shall be estimated according to such mode as the united states in congress assembled, shall from time to time direct and appoint. The taxes for paying that proportion shall be laid and levied by the authority and direction of the legislatures of the several states within the time agreed upon by the united states in congress assembled.

Art. IX. The united states in congress assembled, shall have the sole and exclusive right and power of determining on peace and war, except in the cases mentioned in the sixth article—of sending and receiving ambassadors—entering into treaties and alliances, provided that no treaty of commerce shall be made whereby the legislative power of the respective states shall be restrained from imposing such imposts and duties on foreigners, as their own people are subjected to, or from prohibiting the exportation or importation of any species of goods or commodities whatsoever—of establishing rules for deciding in all cases, what captures on land or water shall be legal, and in what manner prizes taken by land or naval forces in the service of the united states shall be divided or appropriated—of granting letters of marque and reprisal in times of peace—appointing courts for the trial of piracies and felonies committed on the high seas and establishing courts for receiving and determining finally appeals in all cases of captures, provided that no member of congress shall be appointed a judge of any of the said courts.

The united states in congress assembled shall also be the last resort on appeal in all disputes and differences now subsisting or that hereafter may arise between two or more states concerning boundary, jurisdiction or any other cause whatever; which authority shall always be exercised in the manner following. Whenever the legislative or executive authority or lawful agent of any state in controversy with another shall present a petition to congress stating the matter in question and praying for a hearing, notice thereof shall be given by order of congress to the legislative or executive authority of the other state in controversy, and a day assigned for the appearance of the parties by their lawful agents, who shall then be directed to appoint by joint consent, commissioners or judges to constitute a court for hearing and determining the matter in question: but if they cannot agree, congress shall name three persons out of each of the united states, and from the list of such persons each party shall alternately strike out one, the petitioners beginning, until the number shall be reduced to thirteen; and from that number not less than seven, nor more than nine names as congress shall direct, shall in the presence of congress be drawn out by lot, and the persons whose names shall be so drawn or any five of them, shall be commissioners or judges, to hear and finally determine the controversy, so always as a major part of the judges who shall hear the cause shall agree in the determination: and if either party shall neglect to attend at the day appointed, without shewing reasons, which congress shall judge sufficient, or being present shall refuse to strike, the congress shall proceed to nominate three persons out of each state, and the secretary of congress shall strike in behalf of such party absent or refusing; and the judgment and sentence of the court to be appointed, in the manner before prescribed, shall be final and conclusive; and if any of the parties shall refuse to submit to the authority of such court, or to appear to defend their claim or cause, the court shall nevertheless proceed to pronounce sentence, or judgment, which shall in like manner be final and decisive, the judgment or sentence and other proceedings being in either case transmitted to congress, and lodged among the acts of congress for the security of the parties concerned: provided that every commissioner, before he sits in judgment, shall take an oath to be administered by one of the judges of the supreme or superior court of the state, where the cause shall be tried, "well and truly to hear and determine the matter in question, according to the best of his judgment, without favour, affection or hope of reward:" provided also that no state shall be deprived of territory for the benefit of the united states.

All controversies concerning the private right of soil claimed under different grants of two or more states, whose jurisdictions as they may respect such lands, and the states which passed such grants are adjusted, the said grants or either of them being at the same time claimed to have originated antecedent to such settlement of jurisdiction, shall on the petition of either party to the congress of the united states, be finally determined as near as may be in the same manner as is before prescribed for deciding disputes respecting territorial jurisdiction between different states.

The united states in congress assembled shall also have the sole and exclusive right and power of regulating the alloy and value of coin struck by their own authority, or by that of the respective states—fixing the standard of weights and measures throughout the united states—regulating the trade and managing all affairs with the Indians, not members of any of the states, provided that the legislative right of any state within its own limits be not infringed or violated—establishing and regulating post-offices from one state to another, throughout all the united states, and exacting such postage on the papers passing thro' the same as may be requisite to defray the expences of the said office—appointing all officers of the land forces, in the service of the united states, excepting regimental officers —appointing all the officers of the naval forces, and commissioning all officers whatever in the service of the united states—making rules for the government and regulation of the said land and naval forces, and directing their operations.

The united states in congress assembled shall have authority to appoint a committee, to sit in the recess of congress, to be denominated "A Committee of the States," and to consist of one delegate from each state; and to appoint such other committees and civil officers as may be necessary for managing the general affairs of the united states under their direction—to appoint one of their number to preside, provided that no person be allowed to serve in the office of president more than one year in any term of three years; to ascertain the necessary sums of Money to be raised for the service of the united states, and to appropriate and apply the same for defraying the public expences—to borrow money, or emit bills on the credit of the united states, transmitting every half year to the respective states an account of the sums of money so borrowed or emitted,—to build and equip a navy—to agree upon the number of land forces, and to make requisitions from each state for its quota, in proportion to the number of white inhabitants in such state; which requisition shall be binding, and thereupon the legislature of each state shall appoint the regimental officers, raise the men and cloath, arm and equip them in a soldier like manner, at the expence of the united states, and the officers and men so cloathed, armed and equipped shall march to the place appointed, and within the time agreed on by the united states in congress assembled: But if the united states in congress assembled shall, on consideration of cir-

cumstances judge proper that any state should not raise men, or should raise a smaller number than its quota, and that any other state should raise a greater number of men than the quota thereof, such extra number shall be raised, officered, cloathed, armed and equipped in the same manner as the quota of such state, unless the legislature of such state shall judge that such extra number cannot be safely spared out of the same, in which case they shall raise officer, cloath, arm and equip as many of such extra number as they judge can be safely spared. And the officers and men so cloathed, armed and equipped, shall march to the place appointed, and within the time agreed on by the united states in congress assembled.

The united states in congress assembled shall never engage in a war, nor grant letters of marque and reprisal in time of peace, nor enter into any treaties or alliances, nor coin money, nor regulate the value thereof, nor ascertain the sums and expences necessary for the defence and welfare of the united states, or any of them, nor emit bills, nor borrow money on the credit of the united states, nor appropriate money, nor agree upon the number of vessels of war, to be built or purchased, or the number of land or sea forces to be raised, nor appoint a commander in chief of the army or navy, unless nine states assent to the same: nor shall a question on any other point, except for adjourning from day to day be determined, unless by the votes of a majority of the united states in congress assembled.

The congress of the united states shall have power to adjourn to any time within the year, and to any place within the united states, so that no period of adjournment be for a longer duration than the space of six Months, and shall publish the Journal of their proceedings monthly, except such parts thereof relating to treaties, alliances or military operations as in their judgment require secrecy; and the yeas and nays of the delegates of each state on any question shall be entered on the Journal, when it is desired by any delegate; and the delegates of a state, or any of them, at his or their request shall be furnished with a transcript of the said Journal, except such parts as are above excepted, to lay before the legislatures of the several states.

Art. X. The committee of the states, or any nine of them, shall be authorised to execute, in the recess of congress, such of the powers of congress as the united states in congress assembled, by the consent of nine states, shall from time to time think expedient to vest them with; provided that no power be delegated to the said committee, for the exercise of which, by the articles of confederation, the voice of nine states in the congress of the united states assembled is requisite.

Art. XI. Canada acceding to this confederation, and joining in the measures of the united states, shall be admitted into, and entitled to all the advantages of this union: but no other colony shall be admitted into the same, unless such admission be agreed to by nine states.

Art. XII. All bills of credit emitted, monies borrowed and debts contracted by, or under the authority of congress, before the assembling of the united states, in pursuance of the present confederation, shall be deemed and considered as a charge against the united states, for payment and satisfaction whereof the said united states, and the public faith are hereby solemnly pledged.

Art. XIII. Every state shall abide by the determinations of the united states in congress assembled, on all questions which by this confederation are submitted to them. And the Articles of this confederation shall be inviolably observed by every state, and the union shall be perpetual; nor shall any alteration at any time hereafter he made in any of them; unless such alteration be agreed to in a congress of the united states, and be afterwards confirmed by the legislatures of every state.

AND WHEREAS it hath pleased the Great Governor of the World to incline the hearts of the legislatures we respectively represent in congress, to approve of, and to authorize us to ratify the said articles of confederation and perpetual union. KNOW YE that we the undersigned delegates, by virtue of the power and authority to us given for that purpose, do by these presents, in the name and in behalf of our respective constituents, fully and entirely ratify and confirm each and every of the said articles of confederation and perpetual union, and all and singular the matters and things therein contained: And we do further solemnly plight and engage the faith of our respective constituents, that they shall abide by the determinations of the united states in congress assembled, on all questions, which by the said confederation are submitted to them. And that the articles thereof shall be inviolably observed by the states we respectively represent, and that the union shall be perpetual. In Witness whereof we have hereunto set our hands in Congress. Done at Philadelphia in the state of Pennsylvania the ninth Day of July in the Year of our Lord one Thousand seven Hundred and Seventy-eight, and in the third year of the independence of America.

Constitutional Problems of the Confederation Period

25. *The Northwest Ordinance Solves the Imperial Problem, July 13, 1787*

W. C. Ford, ed., *Journals of the Continental Congress, 1774-1789,* XXXII, 337-43.

Be it ordained by the United States in Congress Assembled that the said territory for the purposes of temporary government be one district, subject however to be divided into two districts as future circumstances may in the opinion of Congress make it expedient. . . .

Be it ordained by the authority aforesaid, that there shall be appointed, from time to time, by Congress, a governor, whose commission shall continue in force for the term of three years, unless sooner revoked by Congress; he shall reside in the district, and have a freehold estate therein in 1000 acres of land, while in the exercise of his office.

There shall be appointed, from time to time, by Congress, a secretary, whose commission shall continue in force for four years unless sooner revoked; he shall reside in the district, and have a freehold estate therein in 500 acres of land, while in the exercise of his office; it shall be his duty to keep and preserve the acts and laws passed by the legislature, and the public records of the district, and the proceedings of the governor in his Executive department; and transmit authentic copies of such acts and proceedings, every six months, to the Secretary of Congress: There shall also be appointed a court to consist of three judges, any two of whom to form a court, who shall have a common law jurisdiction, and reside in the district, and have each therein a freehold estate in 500 acres of land while in the exercise of their offices; and their commissions shall continue in force during good behavior.

The governor and judges, or a majority of them, shall adopt and publish in the district such laws of the original States, criminal and civil, as may be necessary and best suited to the circumstances of the district, and report them to Congress from time to time: which laws shall be in force in the district until the organization of the General Assembly therein, unless disapproved of by Congress; but, afterwards, the legislature shall have authority to alter them as they shall think fit.

The governor, for the time being, shall be commander-in-chief of the militia, appoint and commission all officers in the same below the rank of general officers; all general officers shall be appointed and commissioned by Congress.

Previous to the organization of the General Assembly, the governor shall appoint such magistrates and other civil officers, in each county or township, as he shall find necessary for the preservation of the peace and good order in the same. After the General Assembly shall be organized, the powers and duties of the magistrates and other civil officers shall be regulated and defined by the said Assembly; but all . . . civil officers not herein otherwise directed shall during the continuance of this temporary government be appointed by the governor.

For the prevention of crimes and injuries the laws to be adopted or made shall have force in all parts of the district; and for the execution of process, criminal and civil, the governor shall make proper divisions thereof, and he shall proceed from time to time as circumstances may require to lay out the parts of the District in which the Indian titles shall have been extinguished into counties and townships subject however to such alterations as may thereafter be made by the legislature.

So soon as there shall be five thousand free male inhabitants of full age in the district, upon giving proof thereof to the governor, they shall receive authority with time and place to elect representatives from their counties or townships to represent them in the general Assembly, provided that for every five hundred free male inhabitants there shall be one representative; and so on progressively with the number of free male inhabitants shall the right of representation encrease until the number of representatives shall amount to twenty five, after which the number and proportion of representatives shall be regulated by the legislature; provided that no person be eligible or qualified to act as a representative unless he shall have been a citizen of one of the United States three years and be a resident in the district or unless he shall have resided in the district three years, and in either case shall likewise hold in his own right in fee simple two hundred acres of land within the same; provided also that a freehold in fifty acres of land in the district having been a citizen of one of the states and being resident in the district, or the like freehold and two years residence in the district shall be necessary to qualify a man as an elector of a representative.

The representatives thus elected shall serve for the term of two years, and in case of the death of a representative or removal from office, the governor shall issue a writ to the county or township for which he was a member, to elect another in his stead to serve for the residue of the term.

The general Assembly or legislature shall consist of the governor, legislative council and a house of representatives. The legislative council shall consist of five members to continue in Office five years

unless sooner removed by Congress, any three of whom to be a quorum and the members of the council shall be nominated and appointed in the following manner, to wit: As soon as representatives shall be elected, the governor shall appoint a time and place for them to meet together; and, when met, they shall nominate ten persons, residents in the district, and each possessed of a freehold in 500 acres of land, and return their names to Congress; five of whom Congress shall appoint and commission to serve as aforesaid; and, whenever a vacancy shall happen in the council, by death or removal from office, the house of representatives shall nominate two persons, qualified as aforesaid, for each vacancy, and return their names to Congress; one of whom Congress shall appoint and commission for the residue of the term. And every five years, four months at least before the expiration of the time of service of the members of council, the said house shall nominate ten persons, qualified as aforesaid, and return their names to Congress; five of whom Congress shall appoint and commission to serve as members of the council five years, unless sooner removed. And the governor, legislative council, and house of representatives, shall have authority to make laws in all cases, for the good government of the district, not repugnant to the principles and articles in this ordinance established and declared. And all bills, having passed by a majority in the house, and by a majority in the council, shall be referred to the governor for his assent; but no bill, or legislative act whatever, shall be of any force without his assent. The governor shall have power to convene, prorogue, and dissolve the General Assembly, when, in his opinion, it shall be expedient.

The governor, judges, legislative council, secretary, and such other officers as Congress shall appoint in the district, shall take an oath or affirmation of fidelity and of office; the governor before the President of Congress, and all other officers before the governor. As soon as a legislature shall be formed in the district, the council and house assembled in one room, shall have authority, by joint ballot, to elect a delegate to Congress, who shall have a seat in Congress, with a right of debating but not of voting during this temporary government.

And, for extending the fundamental principles of civil and religious liberty, which form the basis whereon these republics, their laws and constitutions are erected; to fix and establish those principles as the basis of all laws, constitutions, and governments, which forever hereafter shall be formed in the said territory: to provide also for the establishment of States, and permanent Government therein, and for their admission to a Share in the federal Councils on an equal footing with the original States, at as early periods as may be consistent with the general interest—

It is hereby Ordained and declared by the authority aforesaid, That the following Articles shall be considered as Articles of compact between the Original States and the People and States in the said territory, and forever remain unalterable, unless by common consent, *to wit,.* . . .

Article the Fourth. The said Territory, and the States which may be formed therein, shall forever remain a part of this Confederacy . . . subject to the Articles of Confederation, and to such alterations therein as shall be constitutionally made; and to all the acts and ordinances of the United States in Congress assembled, conformable thereto. . . .

Article the Fifth. There shall be formed in the said territory, not less than three nor more than five States. . . . And, whenever any of the said States shall have 60,000 free inhabitants therein, such State shall be admitted, by its delegates, into the Congress of the United States, on an equal footing with the original States in all respects whatever, and shall be at liberty to form a permanent constitution and State government: *Provided,* the constitution and government, so to be formed, shall be republican, and in conformity to the principles contained in these articles; and, so far as it can be consistent with the general interest of the confederacy, such admission shall be allowed at an earlier period, and when there may be a less number of free inhabitants in the State than 60,000.

Article the Sixth. There shall be neither slavery nor involuntary servitude in the said territory, otherwise than in the punishment of crimes, whereof the party shall have been duly convicted: provided, always, That any person escaping into the same, from whom labor or service is lawfully claimed in any one of the original States, such fugitive may be lawfully reclaimed and conveyed to the person claiming his or her labor or service as aforesaid.

26. *An Act for Establishing Religious Freedom in Virginia, January, 1786*

Hening, ed., *Statutes at Large of Virginia,* XII, 84-6.

I. WHEREAS Almighty God hath created the mind free; that all attempts to influence it by temporal punishments or burthens, or by civil incapacitations, tend only to beget habits of hypocrisy and meanness, and are a departure from the plan of the Holy author of our religion, who being Lord both of body and mind, yet chose not to propagate it by coercions on either, as was in his Almighty power to do; that the impious presumption of legislators and rulers, civil as well as ecclesiastical, who being themselves but fallible and uninspired men, have assumed dominion over the faith of others, setting up their own opinions and modes of thinking as the only true and infallible, and as such endeavouring to impose them on others, hath established and maintained false religions over the greatest part of the world, and through all time; that to compel a man to furnish contributions of money for the propagation of opinions which he disbelieves, is sinful and tyrannical; that even the forcing him to support this or that teacher of his own religious persuasion, is depriving him of the comfortable liberty of giving his contributions to the particular pastor whose morals he would make his pattern, and whose powers he feels most persuasive to righteousness, and is withdrawing from the ministry those temporary rewards, which proceeding from an approbation of their personal conduct, are an additional incitement to earnest and unremitting labours for the instruction of mankind; that our civil rights have no dependence on our religious opinions, any more than our opinions in physics or geometry; that therefore the proscribing any citizen as unworthy the public confidence by laying upon him an incapacity of being called to offices of trust and emolument, unless he profess or renounce this or that religious opinion, is depriving him injuriously of those privileges and advantages to which in common with his fellow-citizens he has a natural right; that it tends only to corrupt the principles of that religion it is meant to encourage, by bribing with a monopoly of worldly honours and emoluments, those who will externally profess and conform to it; that though indeed these are criminal who do not withstand such temptation, yet neither are those innocent who lay the bait in their way; that to suffer the civil magistrate to intrude his powers into the field of opinion, and to restrain the profession or propagation of principles on supposition of their ill tendency, is a dangerous fallacy,

which at once destroys all religious liberty, because he being of course judge of that tendency will make his opinions the rule of judgment, and approve or condemn the sentiments of others only as they shall square with or differ from his own; that it is time enough for the rightful purposes of civil government, for its officers to interfere when principles break out into overt acts against peace and good order; and finally, that truth is great and will prevail if left to herself, that she is the proper and sufficient antagonist to error, and has nothing to fear from the conflict, unless by human interposition disarmed of her natural weapons, free argument and debate, errors ceasing to be dangerous when it is permitted freely to contradict them.

II. *Be it enacted by the General Assembly*, that no man shall be compelled to frequent or support any religious worship, place or ministry whatsoever, nor shall be enforced, restrained, molested, or burthened in his body or goods, nor shall otherwise suffer on account of his religious opinions or belief; but that all men shall be free to profess, and by argument to maintain, their opinion in matters of religion, and that the same shall in no wise diminish, enlarge or affect their civil capacities.

III. And though we well know that this assembly, elected by the people for the ordinary purposes of legislation only, have no power to restrain the acts of succeeding assemblies, constituted with powers equal to our own, and that therefore to declare this act to be irrevocable would be of no effect in law; yet as we are free to declare, and do declare, that the rights hereby asserted are of the natural rights of mankind, and that if any act shall hereafter be passed to repeal the present, or to narrow its operation, such act will be an infringement of natural right.

Forging the Federal Union

27. The Constitution of the United States

Adopted September 17, 1787; ratified June, 1788.

We the People of the United States, in Order to form a more perfect Union, establish Justice, insure domestic Tranquility, provide for the common defence, promote the general Welfare, and secure the Blessings of Liberty to ourselves and our Posterity, do ordain and establish this CONSTITUTION for the United States of America.

ARTICLE I

SECTION 1. All legislative Powers herein granted shall be vested in a Congress of the United States, which shall consist of a Senate and House of Representatives.

SECTION 2. The House of Representatives shall be composed of Members chosen every second Year by the People of the several States, and the Electors in each State shall have the Qualifications requisite for electors of the most numerous Branch of the State Legislature.

No Person shall be a Representative who shall not have attained to the Age of twenty five Years, and been seven Years a Citizen of the United States, and who shall not, when elected, be an Inhabitant of that State in which he shall be chosen.

Representatives and direct Taxes shall be apportioned among the several States which may be included within this Union, according to their respective numbers which shall be determined by adding to the whole Number of free Persons, including those bound to Service for a Term of Years, and excluding Indians not taxed, three fifths of all other Persons. The actual Enumeration shall be made within three Years after the first Meeting of the Congress of the United States, and within every subsequent Term of ten Years, in such Manner as they shall by Law direct. The number of Representatives shall not exceed one for every thirty Thousand, but each State shall have at Least one Representative; and until such enumeration shall be made, the State of New Hampshire shall be entitled to chuse three, Massachusetts eight, Rhode-Island and Providence Plantations one, Connecticut five, New-York six, New Jersey four, Pennsylvania eight, Delaware one, Maryland six, Virginia ten, North Carolina five, South Carolina five, and Georgia three.

When vacancies happen in the Representation from any State, the Executive Authority thereof shall issue Writs of Election to fill such Vacancies.

The House of Representatives shall chuse their Speaker and other Officers; and shall have the sole Power of Impeachment.

SECTION 3. The Senate of the United States shall be composed of two Senators from each State, chosen by the Legislature thereof, for six Years; and each Senator shall have one Vote.

Immediately after they shall be assembled in Consequence of the first Election, they shall be divided as equally as may be into three Classes. The Seats of the Senators of the first Class shall be vacated at the Expiration of the second Year, of the second Class at the Expiration of the fourth Year, and of the third Class at the Expiration of the sixth Year, so that one third may be chosen every second Year; and if Vacancies happen by Resignation, or otherwise, during the Recess of the Legislature of any State, the Executive thereof may make temporary Appointments until the next Meeting of the Legislature, which shall then fill such Vacancies.

No Person shall be a Senator who shall not have attained to the Age of thirty Years, and been nine Years a Citizen of the United States, and who shall not, when elected, be an Inhabitant of that State for which he shall be chosen.

The Vice President of the United States shall be President of the Senate, but shall have no Vote, unless they be equally divided.

The Senate shall chuse their other Officers, and also a President pro tempore, in the Absence of the Vice President, or when he shall exercise the Office of President of the United States.

The Senate shall have the sole Power to try all Impeachments. When sitting for that Purpose, they shall be on Oath or Affirmation. When the President of the United States is tried, the Chief Justice shall preside: And no Person shall be convicted without the Concurrence of two thirds of the Members present.

Judgment in Cases of Impeachment shall not extend further than to removal from Office, and disqualification to hold and enjoy any Office of honor, Trust, or Profit under the United States: but the Party convicted shall nevertheless be liable and subject to Indictment, Trial, Judgment, and Punishment, according to Law.

SECTION 4. The Times, Places, and Manner of holding Elections for Senators and Representatives shall be prescribed in each State by the Legislature thereof; but the Congress may at any time by Law make or alter such Regulations, except as to the Places of chusing Senators.

The Congress shall assemble at least once in every Year, and such Meeting shall be on the first Monday in December, unless they shall by Law appoint a different Day.

SECTION 5. Each House shall be the Judge of the Elections, Returns, and Qualifications of its own Members, and a Majority of each shall constitute a Quorum to do Business; but a smaller Number may adjourn from day to day, and may be authorized to compel the Attendance of absent Members, in such Manner, and under such Penalties as each House may provide.

Each House may determine the Rules of its Proceedings, punish its Members for disorderly Behaviour, and, with the Concurrence of two thirds, expel a member.

Each House shall keep a Journal of its Proceedings, and from time to time publish the same, excepting such Parts as may in their Judgment require Secrecy; and the Yeas and Nays of the Members of either House on any question shall, at the Desire of one fifth of those Present, be entered on the Journal.

Neither House, during the Session of Congress, shall, without the Consent of the other, adjourn for more than three days, nor to any other Place than that in which the two Houses shall be sitting.

SECTION 6. The Senators and Representatives shall receive a Compensation for their Services, to be ascertained by Law, and paid out of the Treasury of the United States. They shall in all Cases, except Treason, Felony, and Breach of the Peace, be privileged from Arrest during their Attendance of the Session of their respective Houses, and in going to and returning from the same; and for any Speech or Debate in either House, they shall not be questioned in any other Place.

No Senator or Representative shall, during the Time for which he was elected, be appointed to any civil Office under the Authority of the United States, which shall have been created, or the Emoluments whereof shall have been encreased during such time; and no Person holding any Office under the United States, shall be a Member of either House during his Continuance in Office.

SECTION 7. All Bills for raising Revenue shall originate in the House of Representatives; but the Senate may propose or concur with Amendments as on other Bills.

Every Bill which shall have passed the House of Representatives and the Senate, shall, before it become a Law, be presented to the President of the United States; If he approve he shall sign it, but if not he shall return it, with his Objections, to that House in which it shall have originated, who shall enter the Objections at large on their Journal, and proceed to reconsider it. If after such Reconsideration two thirds of that House shall agree to pass the Bill, it shall be sent, together with the Objections, to the other House, by which it shall likewise be reconsidered, and if approved by two thirds of that House, it shall become a Law. But in all such Cases the Votes of both Houses shall be determined by Yeas and Nays, and the Names of the Persons voting for and against the Bill shall be entered on the Journal of each House respectively. If any Bill shall not be returned by the President within ten Days (Sundays excepted) after it shall have been presented to him, the Same shall be a law, in like Manner as if he had signed it, unless the Congress by their Adjournment prevent its Return, in which Case it shall not be a Law.

Every Order, Resolution, or Vote to which the Concurrence of the Senate and House of Representatives may be necessary (except on a question of Adjournment) shall be presented to the President of the United States; and before the Same shall take Effect, shall be approved by him, or being disapproved by him, shall be repassed by two thirds of the Senate and House of Representatives, according to the Rules and Limitations prescribed in the Case of a Bill.

SECTION 8. The Congress shall have Power To lay and collect Taxes, Duties, Imposts, and Excises, to pay the Debts and provide for the common Defence and general Welfare of the United States; but all Duties, Imposts, and Excises shall be uniform throughout the United States;

To borrow Money on the Credit of the United States;

To regulate Commerce with foreign Nations, and among the several States, and with the Indian Tribes;

To establish an uniform Rule of Naturalization, and uniform Laws on the subject of Bankruptcies throughout the United States;

To coin Money, regulate the Value thereof, and of foreign Coin, and fix the Standard of Weights and Measures;

To provide for the Punishment of counterfeiting the Securities and current Coin of the United States;

To establish Post Offices and post Roads;

To promote the Progress of Science and useful Arts, by securing for limited Times to Authors and Inventors the exclusive Right to their respective Writings and Discoveries;

To constitute Tribunals inferior to the supreme Court;

To define and punish Piracies and Felonies committed on the high Seas, and Offences against the Law of Nations;

To declare War, grant Letters of Marque and Reprisal, and make Rules concerning Captures on Land and Water;

To raise and support Armies, but no Appropriation of Money to that Use shall be for a longer Term than two Years;

To provide and maintain a Navy;

To make Rules for the Government and Regulation of the land and naval Forces;

To provide for calling forth the Militia to execute the Laws of the Union, suppress Insurrections and repel Invasions;

To provide for organizing, arming, and disciplining, the Militia, and for governing such Part of them as may be employed in the Service of the United States, reserving to the States respectively, the Appointment of the Officers, and the Authority of training the Militia according to the discipline prescribed by Congress;

To exercise exclusive Legislation in all

Cases whatsoever, over such District (not exceeding ten Miles square) as may, by Cession of particular States, and the Acceptance of Congress, become the Seat of the Government of the United States, and to exercise like Authority over all Places purchased by the Consent of the Legislature of the State in which the same shall be, for the Erection of Forts, Magazines, Arsenals, dock-Yards, and other needful Buildings;—And

To make all Laws which shall be necessary and proper for carrying into Execution the foregoing Powers, and all other Powers vested by this Constitution in the Government of the United States, or in any Department or Officer thereof.

SECTION 9. The Migration or Importation of such Persons as any of the States now existing shall think proper to admit, shall not be prohibited by the Congress prior to the Year one thousand eight hundred and eight, but a Tax or duty may be imposed on such Importation, not exceeding ten dollars for each Person.

The Privilege of the Writ of Habeas Corpus shall not be suspended, unless when in Cases of Rebellion or Invasion the public Safety may require it.

No Bill of Attainder or ex post facto Law shall be passed.

No Capitation, or other direct, Tax shall be laid, unless in Proportion to the Census or Enumeration herein before directed to be taken.

No Tax or Duty shall be laid on Articles exported from any State.

No Preference shall be given by any Regulation of Commerce or Revenue to the Ports of one State over those of another: nor shall Vessels bound to, or from, one State, be obliged to enter, clear, or pay Duties in another.

No Money shall be drawn from the Treasury, but in Consequence of Appropriations made by Law; and a regular Statement and Account of the Receipts and Expenditures of all public Money shall be published from time to time.

No Title of Nobility shall be granted by the United States: And no Person holding any Office of Profit or Trust under them, shall, without the Consent of the Congress, accept of any present, Emolument, Office, or Title, of any kind whatever, from any King, Prince, or foreign State.

SECTION 10. No State shall enter into any Treaty, Alliance, or Confederation; grant Letters of Marque and Reprisal; coin Money; emit Bills of Credit; make any Thing but gold and silver Coin a Tender in Payment of Debts; pass any Bill of Attainder, ex post facto Law, or Law impairing the Obligation of Contracts, or grant any Title of Nobility.

No State shall, without the Consent of the Congress, lay any Imposts or Duties on Imports or Exports, except what may be absolutely necessary for executing its inspection Laws: and the net Produce of all Duties and Imposts, laid by any State on Imports or Exports, shall be for the Use of the Treasury of the United States; and all such Laws shall be subject to the Revision and Controul of the Congress.

No State shall, without the Consent of Congress, lay any Duty of Tonnage, keep Troops, or Ships of War in time of Peace, enter into any Agreement or Compact with another State, or with a foreign Power, or engage in War, unless actually invaded, or in such imminent Danger as will not admit of delay.

ARTICLE II

SECTION 1. The executive Power shall be vested in a President of the United States of America. He shall hold his Office during the Term of four Years, and, together with the Vice President, chosen for the same Term, be elected, as follows

Each State shall appoint, in such Manner as the Legislature thereof may direct, a Number of Electors, equal to the whole Number of Senators and Representatives to which the State may be entitled in the Congress: but no Senator or Representative, or Person holding an Office of

Trust or Profit under the United States, shall be appointed an Elector.

The Electors shall meet in their respective States, and vote by Ballot for two Persons, of whom one at least shall not be an Inhabitant of the same State with themselves. And they shall make a List of all the Persons voted for, and of the Number of Votes for each; which List they shall sign and certify, and transmit sealed to the Seat of the Government of the United States, directed to the President of the Senate. The President of the Senate shall, in the Presence of the Senate and House of Representatives, open all the Certificates, and the Votes shall then be counted. The Person having the greatest Number of Votes shall be the President, if such Number be a Majority of the whole Number of Electors appointed; and if there be more than one who have such Majority, and have an equal Number of Votes, then the House of Representatives shall immediately chuse by Ballot one of them for President; and if no Person have a Majority, then from the five highest on the List the said House shall in like Manner chuse the President. But in chusing the President, the Votes shall be taken by States, the Representation from each State having one Vote; A quorum for this Purpose shall consist of a Member or Members from two thirds of the States, and a Majority of all the States shall be necessary to a Choice. In every Case, after the Choice of the President, the Person having the greatest Number of Votes of the Electors shall be the Vice President. But if there should remain two or more who have equal Votes, the Senate shall chuse from them by Ballot the Vice President.

The Congress may determine the Time of chusing the Electors, and the Day on which they shall give their Votes; which Day shall be the same throughout the United States.

No Person except a natural born Citizen, or a Citizen of the United States, at the time of the Adoption of this Constitution, shall be eligible to the Office of President; neither shall any Person be eligible to that Office who shall not have attained to the Age of thirty five Years, and been fourteen Years a Resident within the United States.

In Case of the Removal of the President from Office, or of his Death, Resignation, or Inability to discharge the Powers and Duties of the said Office, the Same shall devolve on the Vice President, and the Congress may by Law provide for the Case of Removal, Death, Resignation, or Inability, both of the President and Vice President, declaring what Officer shall then act as President, and such Officer shall act accordingly, until the Disability be removed, or a President shall be elected.

The President shall, at stated Times, receive for his Services, a Compensation, which shall neither be encreased nor diminished during the Period for which he shall have been elected, and he shall not receive within that Period any other Emolument from the United States, or any of them.

Before he enter on the Execution of his Office, he shall take the following Oath or Affirmation:—

"I do solemnly swear (or affirm) that I will faithfully execute the Office of President of the United States, and will to the best of my Ability, preserve, protect, and defend the Constitution of the United States."

SECTION 2. The President shall be Commander in Chief of the Army and Navy of the United States, and of the Militia of the several States, when called into the actual Service of the United States; he may require the Opinion, in writing, of the principal Officer in each of the executive Departments, upon any Subject relating to the Duties of their respective Offices, and he shall have Power to grant Reprieves and Pardons for Offences against the United States, except in Cases of Impeachment.

He shall have Power, by and with the Advice and Consent of the Senate, to make Treaties, provided two thirds of the

Senators present concur; and he shall nominate, and by and with the Advice and Consent of the Senate, shall appoint Ambassadors, other public Ministers and Consuls, Judges of the supreme Court, and all other Officers of the United States, whose Appointments are not herein otherwise provided for, and which shall be established by Law: but the Congress may by Law vest the Appointment of such inferior Officers, as they think proper, in the President alone, in the Courts of Law, or in the Heads of Departments.

The President shall have Power to fill up all Vacancies that may happen during the Recess of the Senate, by granting Commissions which shall expire at the End of their next Session.

SECTION 3. He shall from time to time give to the Congress Information of the State of the Union, and recommend to their Consideration such Measures as he shall judge necessary and expedient; he may, on extraordinary Occasions, convene both Houses, or either of them, and in Case of Disagreement between them, with Respect to the Time of Adjournment, he may adjourn them to such Time as he shall think proper; he shall receive Ambassadors and other public Ministers; he shall take Care that the Laws be faithfully executed, and shall Commission all the Officers of the United States.

SECTION 4. The President, Vice President, and all civil Officers of the United States shall be removed from office on Impeachment for, and conviction of, Treason, Bribery, or other high Crimes and Misdemeanours.

ARTICLE III

SECTION 1. The judicial Power of the United States, shall be vested in one supreme Court, and in such inferior Courts as the Congress may from time to time ordain and establish. The Judges, both of the supreme and inferior Courts, shall hold their Offices during good Behavior, and shall, at stated Times, receive for their Services, a Compensation, which shall not be diminished during their Continuance in Office.

SECTION 2. The judicial Power shall extend to all Cases, in Law and Equity, arising under this Constitution, the Laws of the United States, and Treaties made, or which shall be made, under their Authority;—to all Cases affecting Ambassadors, other public Ministers and Consuls;—to all Cases of admiralty and maritime Jurisdiction;—to Controversies to which the United States shall be a Party;—to Controversies between two or more States;—between a State and Citizens of another State;—between Citizens of different States,—between Citizens of the same State claiming lands under Grants of different States,—and between a State, or the Citizens thereof, and foreign States, Citizens or Subjects.

In all Cases affecting Ambassadors, other public Ministers and Consuls, and those in which a State shall be Party, the supreme Court shall have original Jurisdiction. In all the other Cases before mentioned, the supreme Court shall have appellate Jurisdiction, both as to Law and Fact, with such Exceptions, and under such Regulations as the Congress shall make.

The trial of all Crimes, except in Cases of Impeachment, shall be by Jury; and such Trial shall be held in the State where the said Crimes shall have been committed; but when not committed within any State, the Trial shall be at such Place or Places as the Congress may by Law have directed.

SECTION 3. Treason against the United States, shall consist only in levying War against them, or in adhering to their Enemies, giving them Aid and Comfort. No Person shall be convicted of Treason unless on the Testimony of two Witnesses to the same overt Act, or on Confession in open Court.

The Congress shall have Power to declare the Punishment of Treason, but no attainder of Treason shall work Corruption of Blood, or Forfeiture except during the Life of the Person attainted.

ARTICLE IV

SECTION 1. Full Faith and Credit shall be given in each State to the public Acts, Records, and judicial Proceeding of every other State. And the Congress may by general Laws prescribe the Manner in which such Acts, Records and Proceedings shall be proved, and the Effect thereof.

SECTION 2. The Citizens of each State shall be entitled to all Privileges and immunities of Citizens in the several States.

A Person charged in any State with Treason, Felony, or other Crime, who shall flee from Justice, and be found in another State, shall on Demand of the executive Authority of the State from which he fled, be delivered up, to be removed to the State having Jurisdiction of the Crime.

No Person held to Service or Labour in one State, under the Laws thereof, escaping into another, shall, in Consequence of any Law or Regulation therein, be discharged from such Service or Labour, but shall be delivered up on claim of the Party to whom such Service or Labour may be due.

SECTION 3. New States may be admitted by the Congress into this Union; but no new State shall be formed or erected within the Jurisdiction of any other State; nor any State be formed by the Junction of two or more States, or Parts of States, without the consent of the Legislatures of the States concerned as well as of the Congress.

The Congress shall have Power to dispose of and make all needful Rules and Regulations respecting the Territory or other Property belonging to the United States; and nothing in this Constitution shall be so construed as to Prejudice any Claims of the United States, or of any particular State.

SECTION 4. The United States shall guarantee to every State in this Union a Republican Form of Government, and shall protect each of them against Invasion; and on Application of the Legislature, or of the Executive (when the Legislature cannot be convened) against domestic Violence.

ARTICLE V

The Congress, whenever two thirds of both Houses shall deem it necessary, shall propose Amendments to this Constitution, or, on the Application of the Legislatures of two thirds of the several States, shall call a Convention for proposing Amendments, which, in either Case, shall be valid to all Intents and Purposes, as Part of this Constitution, when ratified by the Legislatures of three fourths of the several States, or by Conventions in three fourths thereof, as the one or the other Mode of ratification may be proposed by the Congress; Provided that no Amendment which may be made prior to the Year One thousand eight hundred and eight shall in any Manner affect the first and fourth Clauses in the Ninth Section of the first Article; and that no State, without its Consent, shall be deprived of its equal Suffrage in the Senate.

ARTICLE VI

All Debts contracted and Engagements entered into, before the Adoption of this Constitution, shall be as valid against the United States under this Constitution, as under the Confederation.

This Constitution, and the Laws of the United States which shall be made in Pursuance thereof; and all Treaties made, or which shall be made, under the Authority of the United States, shall be the supreme Law of the Land; and the Judges in every State shall be bound thereby, any Thing in the Constitution or Laws of any State to the Contrary notwithstanding.

The Senators and Representatives before mentioned, and the Members of the several State Legislatures, and all executive and judicial Officers, both of the United

States and of the several States, shall be bound by Oath or Affirmation, to support this Constitution; but no religious Test shall ever be required as a Qualification to any Office or public Trust under the United States.

ARTICLE VII

The Ratification of the Conventions of nine States, shall be sufficient for the Establishment of this Constitution between the States so ratifying the Same.

28. *The Argument Against the Constitution*

A. THOMAS JEFFERSON ON THE ABSENCE OF A BILL OF RIGHTS

Thomas Jefferson to James Madison, December 20, 1787, Julian P. Boyd and others, eds., *The Papers of Thomas Jefferson* (Princeton, 1950-), XII, 439-40. Reprinted by permission of Princeton University Press.

I like much the general idea of framing a government which should go on of itself peaceably, without needing continual recurrence to the state legislatures. I like the organization of the government into Legislative, Judiciary and Executive. I like the power given the Legislature to levy taxes; and for that reason solely approve of the greater house being chosen by the people directly. For tho' I think a house chosen by them will be very illy qualified to legislate for the Union, for foreign nations &c. yet this evil does not weigh against the good of preserving inviolate the fundamental principle that the people are not to be taxed but by representatives chosen immediately by themselves. I am captivated by the compromise of the opposite claims of the great and little states, of the latter to equal, and the former to proportional influence. I am much pleased too with the substitution of the method of voting by persons, instead of that of voting by states: and I like the negative given to the Executive with a third of either house, though I should have liked it better had the Judiciary been associated for that purpose, or invested with a similar and separate power. There are other good things of less moment. I will now add what I do not like. First the omission of a bill of rights providing clearly and without the aid of

sophisms for freedom of religion, freedom of the press, protection against standing armies, restriction against monopolies, the eternal and unremitting force of the habeas corpus laws, and trials by jury in all matters of fact triable by the laws of the land and not by the law of Nations. To say, as Mr. [James] Wilson does that a bill of rights was not necessary because all is reserved in the case of the general government which is not given, while in the particular ones all is given which is not reserved might do for the Audience to whom it was addressed, but is surely gratis dictum, opposed by strong inferences from the body of the instrument, as well as from the omission of the clause of our present confederation which had declared that in express terms. It was a hard conclusion to say because there has been no uniformity among the states as to the cases triable by jury, because some have been so incautious as to abandon this mode of trial, therefore the more prudent states shall be reduced to the same level of calamity. It would have been much more just and wise to have concluded the other way that as most of the states had judiciously preserved this palladium, those who had wandered should be brought back to it, and to have established general right instead of general wrong. Let me add that a bill of rights is what the people are entitled to against every government on earth, general or particular, and what no just government should refuse, or rest on inference. . . . After all, it is my principle that the will of the Majority should always prevail. If they approve the proposed Convention in all it's parts, I shall concur in it chearfully, in hopes that they will amend it whenever they shall find it work wrong. . . . Above all things I hope the education of the common people will be attended to; convinced that on their good sense we may rely with the most security for the preservation of a due degree of liberty. . . .

B. [MERCY OTIS WARREN], "OBSERVATIONS ON THE NEW CONSTITUTION, AND ON THE FEDERAL AND STATE CONVENTIONS," 1788

Lawrence W. Towner, ed., *Old South Leaflets*, No. 226 (Boston, 1955), 5-13, 20-1.

It is with inexpressible anxiety, that many of the best friends of the Union of the States—to the peaceable and equal participation of the rights of nature, and to the glory and dignity of this country, behold the insiduous arts, and the strenuous efforts of the partisans of arbitrary power, by their vague definitions of the best established truths, endeavoring to envelope the mind in darkness the concomitant of slavery, and to lock the strong chains of domestic despotism on a country, which by the most glorious and successful struggles is but newly emancipated from the spectre of foreign dominion. . . .

There are few who do not unite in the general wish for the restoration of public faith, the revival of commerce, arts, agriculture, and industry, under a lenient, peaceable and energetick government: But the most sagacious advocates for the party have not by fair discussion, and rational argumentation, evinced the necessity of adopting this many headed monster; of such motley mixture, that its enemies cannot trace a feature of Democratick or Republican extract; nor have its friends the courage to denominate [it] a Monarchy, an Aristocracy, or an Oligarchy, and the favoured bantling must have passed through the short period of its existence without a name, had not Mr. *Wilson*, in the fertility of his genius, suggested the happy epithet of a *Federal Republic.* But I leave the field of general censure on the secrecy of its birth, the rapidity of its growth, and the fatal consequences of suffering it to live to the age of maturity, and will particularize some of the most weighty objections to its passing through this continent in a gigantic size. —It will be allowed by every one that the fundamental principle of a free government, is the equal representation of a free people. . . . And when society has . . . deputed a certain number of their equals to take care of their personal rights, and the interest of the whole community, it must be considered that responsibility is the great security of integrity and honour; and that annual election is the basis of responsibility.—Man is not immediately corrupted, but power without limitation, or amenability, may endanger the brightest virtue—whereas a frequent return to the bar of their Constituents is the strongest check against the corruptions to which men are liable, either from the intrigues of others of more subtle genius, or the propensities of their own hearts. . . .

2. There is no security in the profered system, either for the rights of conscience or the liberty of the Press: Despotism usually while it is gaining ground, will suffer men to think, say, or write what they please; but when once estab-

lished, if it is thought necessary to subserve the purposes, of arbitrary power, the
most unjust restrictions may take place in
the first instance, and an *imprimator* on
the Press in the next, may silence the
complaints, and forbid the most decent
remonstrances of an injured and oppressed people.

3. There are no well defined limits of
the Judiciary Powers, they seem to be left
as a boundless ocean, that has broken
over the chart of the Supreme Lawgiver,
"thus far shalt thou go and no further,"
and as they cannot be comprehended by
the clearest capacity, or the most sagacious mind, it would be an Herculean
labour to attempt to describe the dangers
with which they are replete.

4. The Executive and the Legislative
are so dangerously blended as to give just
cause of alarm, and every thing relative
thereto, is couched in such ambiguous
terms—in such vague and indefinite expression, as is a sufficient ground without any objection, for the reprobation of
a system, that the authors dare not hazard
to a clear investigation.

5. The abolition of trial by jury in
civil causes.—This mode of trial the
learned Judge Blackstone observes, "has
been coeval with the first rudiments of
civil government, that property, liberty
and life, depend on maintaining in its
legal force the constitutional trial by
jury. . . ."

6. Though it has been said by Mr.
[James] *Wilson* and many others, that a
Standing-Army is necessary for the dignity and safety of America, yet freedom
revolts at the idea, when the Divan, or
the Despot, may draw out his dragoons to
suppress the murmurs of a few, who may
yet cherish those sublime principles which
call forth the exertions, and lead to
the best improvement of the human
mind. . . .

7. Notwithstanding the delusory promise to guarantee a Republican form of
government to every State in the Union
—If the most discerning eye could dis-

cover any meaning at all in the engagement, there are no resources left for the
support of internal government, or the
liquidation of the debts of the State.
Every source of revenue is in the monopoly of Congress, and if the several
legislatures in their enfeebled state,
should against their own feelings be necessitated to attempt a dry tax for the
payment of their debts, and the support
of internal police, even this may be required for the purposes of the general
government.

8. As the new Congress are empowered to determine their own salaries, the
requisitions for this purpose may not be
very moderate, and the drain for public
moneys will probably rise past all calcu-
lation. . . .

9. There is no provision for a rotation, nor anything to prevent the perpetuity of office in the same hands for life;
which by a little well timed bribery, will
probably be done, to the exclusion of
men of the best abilities from their share
in the offices of government.—By this
neglect we lose the advantages of that
check to the overbearing insolence of office, which by rendering him ineligible at
certain periods, keeps the mind of man
in equilibrio, and teaches him the feelings of the governed, and better qualifies
him to govern in his turn.

10. The inhabitants of the United
States, are liable to be draged from the
vicinity of their own country, or state, to
answer the litigious or unjust suit of an
adversary, on the most distant borders of
the Continent: in short the appelate jurisdiction of the Supreme Federal Court,
includes an unwarrantable stretch of
power over the liberty, life, and property
of the subject, through the wide Continent of America. . . .

12. If the sovereignty of America is
designed to be elective, the circumscrib-
ing the votes to only ten electors in this
State, and the same proportion in all the
others, is nearly tantamount to the exclusion of the voice of the people in the

choice of their first magistrate. It is vesting the choice solely in an aristocratic junto, who may easily combine in each State to place at the head of the Union the most convenient instrument for despotic sway.

13. A Senate chosen for six years will, in most instances, be an appointment for life, as the influence of such a body over the minds of the people will be coequal to the extensive powers with which they are vested, and they will not only forget, but be forgotten by their constituents— a branch of the Supreme Legislature thus set beyond all responsibility is totally repugnant to every principle of a free government.

14. There is no provision by a bill of rights to guard against the dangerous encroachments of power in too many instances to be named: but I cannot pass over in silence the insecurity in which we are left with regard to warrants unsupported by evidence—the daring experiment of granting *writs of assistance* in a former arbitrary administration is not yet forgotten in . . . Massachusetts. . . . The rights of individuals ought to be the primary object of all government, and cannot be too securely guarded by the most explicit declarations in their favor. . . .

15. The difficulty, if not impracticability, of exercising the equal and equitable powers of government by a single legislature over an extent of territory that reaches from the Mississippi to the Western lakes, and from them to the Atlantic Ocean, is an insuperable objection to the adoption of the new system. . . .

17. The first appearance of the article which declares the ratification of nine states sufficient for the establishment of the new system, wears the face of dissension, is a subversion of the union of Confederated States, and tends to the introduction of anarchy and civil convulsions, and may be a means of involving the whole country in blood. . . .

But it is needless to enumerate other instances, in which the proposed constitution appears contradictory to the first principles which ought to govern mankind; and it is equally so to enquire into the motives that induced to so bold a step as the annihilation of the independence and sovereignty of the thirteen distinct states. . . .

But it is a republican principle that the majority should rule; and if a spirit of moderation should be cultivated on both sides, till the voice of the people at large could be fairly heard it should be held sacred.—And if, on such a scrutiny, the proposed constitution should appear repugnant to their character and wishes . . . . who would then have the effrontery to say, it ought not to be thrown out with indignation. . . . But if after all, on a dispassionate and fair discussion, the people generally give their voice for a voluntary dereliction of their privileges, let every individual who chooses the active scenes of life, strive to support the peace and unanimity of his country, though every other blessing may expire. . . .

29. The Federalist Papers *Defend the Constitution*

A. MADISON DISCUSSES POLITICS, PROPERTY, AND POWER IN A REPUBLIC, 1787

Henry Cabot Lodge, ed., *The Federalist* No. 10
(New York, 1902), 51-60.

Among the numerous advantages promised by a well-constructed Union, none deserves to be more accurately developed than its tendency to break and control the violence of faction. The friend of popular governments never finds himself so much alarmed for their character and fate, as when he contemplates their propensity to this dangerous vice. . . . Complaints are everywhere heard from our most considerate and virtuous citizens, equally the friends of public and private faith, and of public and personal liberty, that our governments are too unstable, that the public good is disregarded in the conflicts of rival parties, and that measures are too often decided, not according to the rules of justice and the rights of the minor party, but by the superior force of an interested and overbearing majority. However anxiously we may wish that these complaints had no foundation, the evidence of known facts will not permit us to deny that they are in some degree true. It will be found, indeed, on a candid review of our situation, that some of the distresses under which we labor have been erroneously charged on the operation of our governments; but it will be found, at the same time, that other causes will not alone account for many of our heaviest misfortunes; and, particularly, for that prevailing and increasing distrust of public engagements, and alarm for private rights, which are echoed from one end of the continent to the other. These must be chiefly, if not wholly, effects of the unsteadiness and injustice with which a factious spirit has tainted our public administrations.

By a faction, I understand a number of citizens, whether amounting to a majority or minority of the whole, who are united and actuated by some common impulse of passion, or of interest, adverse to the rights of other citizens, or to the permanent and aggregate interests of the community.

There are two methods of curing the mischiefs of faction: the one, by removing its causes; the other, by controlling its effects.

There are again two methods of removing the causes of faction: the one by destroying the liberty which is essential to its existence; the other, by giving to every citizen the same opinions, the same passions, and the same interests.

It could never be more truly said than of the first remedy, that it was worse than the disease. Liberty is to faction what air is to fire, an aliment without which it instantly expires. But it could not be less folly to abolish liberty, which is essential to political life, because it nourishes faction, than it would be to wish the annihilation of air, which is essential to animal life, because it imparts to fire its destructive agency.

The second expedient is as impracticable as the first would be unwise. As long as the reason of man continues fallible, and he is at liberty to exercise it, different opinions will be formed. As long as the connection subsists between his reason and his self-love, his opinions and his passions will have a reciprocal influence on each other; and the former will be objects to which the latter will attach themselves. The diversity in the faculties of men, from which the rights of property originate, is not less an insuperable obstacle to a uniformity of interests. The protection of these faculties is the first object of government. From the protection of different and unequal faculties of acquiring property, the possession of different degrees and kinds of property immediately results; and from the influence of these on the sentiments and views of the respective proprietors, ensues a division of the society into different interests and parties.

The latent causes of faction are thus sown in the nature of man; and we see them everywhere brought into different degrees of activity, according to the different circumstances of civil society. A zeal for different opinions concerning religion, concerning government, and many other points, as well of speculation as of practice; an attachment to different leaders ambitiously contending for pre-eminence and power; or to persons of other descriptions whose fortunes have been interesting to the human passions, have, in turn, divided mankind into parties, inflamed them with mutual animosity, and rendered them much more disposed to vex and oppress each other than to co-operate for their common good. . . . The most common and durable source of factions has been the various and unequal distribution of property. Those who hold and those who are without property have ever formed distinct interests in society. Those who are creditors, and those who are debtors, fall under a like discrimination. A landed interest, a manufacturing interest, a mercantile interest, a moneyed interest, with many lesser interests, grow up of necessity in civilized nations, and divide them into different classes, actuated by different sentiments and views. The regulation of these various and interfering interests forms the principal task of modern legislation, and involves the spirit of party and faction in the necessary and ordinary operations of the government.

No man is allowed to be a judge in his own cause, because his interest would certainly bias his judgment, and, not improbably, corrupt his integrity. With equal, nay with greater reason, a body of men are unfit to be both judges and parties at the same time; yet what are many of the most important acts of legislation, but so many judicial determinations, not indeed concerning the rights of single persons, but concerning the rights of large bodies of citizens? And what are the different classes of legislators but advocates and parties to the causes which they determine? Is a law proposed concerning private debts? It is a question to which the creditors are parties on one side and the debtors on the other. Justice ought to hold the balance between them. Yet the parties are, and must be, themselves the judges; and the most numerous party, or, in other words, the most powerful faction must be expected to prevail. Shall domestic manufacturers be encouraged, and in what degree, by restrictions on foreign manufactures? are questions which would be differently decided by the landed and the manufacturing classes, and probably by neither with a sole regard to justice and the public good. The apportionment of taxes on the various descriptions of property is an act which seems to require the most exact impartiality; yet there is, perhaps, no legislative act in which greater opportunity and temptation are given to a predominant party to trample on the rules of justice. . . .

It is in vain to say that enlightened statesmen will be able to adjust these clashing interests, and render them all subservient to the public good. Enlightened statesmen will not always be at the helm. Nor, in many cases, can such an adjustment be made at all without taking into view indirect and remote considerations, which will rarely prevail over the immediate interest which one party may find in disregarding the rights of another or the good of the whole.

The inference to which we are brought is, that the causes of faction cannot be removed, and that relief is only to be sought in the means of controlling its *effects.*

If a faction consists of less than a majority, relief is supplied by the republican principle, which enables the majority to defeat its sinister views by regular vote. It may clog the administration, it may convulse the society; but it will be unable to execute and mask its violence under the forms of the Constitution. When a majority is included in a faction, the form of popular government, on the other hand, enables it to sacrifice to its ruling passion or interest both the public good and the rights of other citizens. To secure the public good and private rights against the danger of such a faction, and at the same time to preserve the spirit and the form of popular government, is then the great object to which our inquiries are directed. . . .

By what means is this object attainable? Evidently by one of two only. Either the existence of the same passion or interest in a majority at the same time must be prevented, or the majority, having such coexisent passion or interest, must be rendered, by their number and local situation, unable to concert and carry into effect schemes of oppression. If the impulse and the opportunity be suffered to coincide, we well know that neither moral nor religious motives can be relied on as an adequate control. . . .

From this view of the subject it may be concluded that a pure democracy, by which I mean a society consisting of a small number of citizens, who assemble and administer the government in person, can admit of no cure for the mischiefs of faction. A common passion or interest will, in almost every case, be felt by a majority of the whole; a communication and concert result from the form of government itself; and there is nothing to check the inducements to sacrifice the weaker party or an obnoxious individual. Hence it is that such democracies have ever been spectacles of turbulence

and contention; have ever been found incompatible with personal security or the rights of property; and have in general been as short in their lives as they have been violent in their deaths. Theoretic politicians, who have patronized this species of government, have erroneously supposed that by reducing mankind to a perfect equality in their political rights, they would, at the same time, be perfectly equalized and assimilated in their possessions, their opinions, and their passions.

A republic, by which I mean a government in which the scheme of representation takes place, opens a different prospect, and promises the cure for which we are seeking. Let us examine the points in which it varies from pure democracy, and we shall comprehend both the nature of the cure and the efficacy which it must derive from the Union.

The two great points of difference between a democracy and a republic are: first, the delegation of the government, in the latter, to a small number of citizens elected by the rest; secondly, the greater number of citizens, and greater sphere of country, over which the latter may be extended.

The effect of the first difference is, on the one hand, to refine and enlarge the public views, by passing them through the medium of a chosen body of citizens, whose wisdom may best discern the true interest of their country, and whose patriotism and love of justice will be least likely to sacrifice it to temporary or partial considerations. Under such a regulation, it may well happen that the public voice, pronounced by the representatives of the people, will be more consonant to the public good than if pronounced by the people themselves, convened for the purpose. On the other hand, the effect may be inverted. Men of factious tempers, of local prejudices, or of sinister designs, may, by intrigue, by corruption, or by other means, first obtain the suffrages, and then betray the interests, of the people. The question resulting is, whether small or extensive republics are more favorable to the election of proper guardians of the public weal; and it is clearly decided in favor of the latter by two obvious considerations:

In the first place, it is to be remarked that, however small the republic may be, the representatives must be raised to a certain number, in order to guard against the cabals of a few; and that, however large it may be, they must be limited to a certain number, in order to guard against the confusion of a multitude. Hence, the number of representatives in the two cases not being in proportion to that of the two constituents, and being proportionally greater in the small republic, it follows that, if the proportion of fit characters be not less in the large than in the small republic, the former will present a greater option, and consequently a greater probability of a fit choice.

In the next place, as each representative will be chosen by a greater number of citizens in the large than in the small republic, it will be more difficult for unworthy candidates to practise with success the vicious arts by which elections are too often carried; and the suffrages of the people being more free, will be more likely to center in men who possess the most attractive merit and the most diffusive and established characters.

It must be confessed that in this, as in most other cases, there is a mean, on both sides of which inconveniences will be found to lie. By enlarging too much the number of electors, you render the representative too little acquainted with all their local circumstances and lesser interests; as by reducing it too much, you render him unduly attached to these, and too little fit to comprehend and pursue great and national objects. The federal Constitution forms a happy combination in this respect; the great and aggregate interests being referred to the national, the local and particular to the State legislatures.

The other point of difference is, the greater number of citizens and extent of territory which may be brought within the compass of republican than of democratic government; and it is this circumstance principally which renders factious combinations less to be dreaded in the former than in the latter. The smaller the society, the fewer probably will be the distinct parties and interests composing it; the fewer the distinct parties and interests, the more frequently will a majority be found of the same party; and the smaller the number of individuals composing a majority, and the smaller the compass within which they are placed, the more easily will they concert and execute their plans of oppression. Extend the sphere, and you take in a greater variety of parties and interests; you make it less probable that a majority of the whole will have a common motive to invade the rights of other citizens; or if such a common motive exists, it will be more difficult for all who feel it to discover their own strength, and to act in unison with each other. Besides other impediments, it may be remarked that, where there is a consciousness of unjust or dishonorable purposes, communication is always checked by distrust in proportion to the number whose concurrence is necessary.

Hence, it clearly appears, that the same advantage which a republic has over a democracy, in controlling the effects of faction, is enjoyed by a large over a small republic,—is enjoyed by the Union over the States composing it. Does the advantage consist in the substitution of representatives whose enlightened views and virtuous sentiments render them superior to local prejudices and to schemes of injustice? It will not be denied that the representation of the Union will be most likely to possess these requisite endowments. Does it consist in the greater security afforded by a greater variety of parties, against the event of any one party being able to outnumber and oppress the rest? In an equal degree does the increased variety of parties comprised within the Union, increase this security. Does it, in fine, consist in the greater obstacles opposed to the concert and accomplishment of the secret wishes of an unjust and interested majority? Here, again, the extent of the Union gives it the most palpable advantage.

The influence of factious leaders may kindle a flame within their particular States, but will be unable to spread a general conflagration through the other States. A religious sect may degenerate into a political faction in a part of the Confederacy; but the variety of sects dispersed over the entire face of it must secure the national councils against any danger from that source. A rage for paper money, for an abolition of debts, for an equal division of property, or for any other improper or wicked project, will be less apt to pervade the whole body of the Union than a particular member of it; in the same proportion as such a malady is more likely to taint a particular county or district, than an entire State.

In the extent and proper structure of the Union, therefore, we behold a republican remedy for the diseases most incident to republican government. . . .

CHAPTER IV

The Founding Fathers Translate Principles into Practice

ALTHOUGH the Federalists were successful in their ratification campaign for the Constitution, John Marshall was probably correct when he wrote later that "in some of the adopting states, a majority of the people were in opposition. In all of them," he observed, "the numerous amendments which were proposed, demonstrate the reluctance with which the new government was accepted; and that a dread of dismemberment, not an approbation of the particular system under consideration, had induced an acquiescence in it." But as Jefferson observed at the time, there had been "just opposition enough to produce probably further guarantees of liberty without touching the energy of the government;" this, he observed, "will bring over the bulk of the opposition to the side of the new government."

As a matter of fact, seven ratification conventions proposed amendments to almost every article in the new Constitution, and North Carolina and Rhode Island failed to join the Union until Congress had met and initiated the amending process. The great majority of the 124 alterations officially suggested by the state conventions dealt with guarantees of individual rights. James Madison, "the Father of the Constitution," presented to the first session of Congress the popular demand for amendments and recommended propositions that "expressly declare the great rights of mankind secured under this constitution" (No. 30). Of the seventeen rights voted by the House, twelve were endorsed by the Senate (No. 31) and ten were adopted as the federal Bill of Rights in order to extend "the ground of public confidence in the government" (No. 32).

Although most of these amendments impose general limitations on the government, the First Amendment specifically restricts the federal Congress. The scope of the others was unclear until *Barron v. Baltimore* (No. 33) forced the Supreme Court in 1833 to decide whether these guarantees of civil liberty ought to be interpreted as restraints on the state governments as well as the federal government. Chief Justice Marshall ruled that "these amendments contain no expression indicating an intention to apply them to the state governments." Thus, prior to the adoption of the Fourteenth Amendment, denials by the state of such rights as free speech or fair trial could be contested only in state courts.

During the first decade after the Constitution was adopted, the Eleventh Amendment was ratified. In *Chisholm v. Georgia* (No. 34), one of the historic pre-Marshall decisions, the Supreme Court upheld the right of a citizen of one state to sue another state. This decision was viewed by states' rights advocates as an alarming assertion of national power. Although no state went as far as Georgia's legislature, which threatened to punish with death "without benefit of clergy" any official attempting to carry out the Court's decree, Massachusetts, New York, and other states led the fight in Congress to abrogate the decision. The Eleventh Amendment (No. 35) was the result.

Every step taken by the new government during its formative years was important, setting precedents of force equal to that of the Constitution. The Founding Fathers had to solve problems as diverse as congressional organization and the question of presidential titles; the proper relationship between the three branches of government, and the issue of strict or broad construction of the Constitution's provisions; the Vice President's role as presiding officer of the Senate, and the establishment of a federal judicial system. The chief defect of the Articles, Hamilton had written in *The Federalist* No. 22, was "the want of a judicial power," and President Washington asserted in 1789 that "the first arrangement of the judicial department . . . [was] essential to the happiness of our country and the stability of its political system." In the Judiciary Act of 1789 (No. 36), Congress created a federal judicial system emphasizing the principle of national supremacy, determining federal court procedure, and defining federal-state jurisdiction.

Although the word *cabinet* does not appear in the Constitution, the President was authorized to "require the opinion in writing of the principle officer in each of the executive departments upon any subject relating to the duties of their respective offices." This provision, however, was not helpful on questions of general policy, and Washington, cognizant of this shortcoming, turned to other agencies. In the field of foreign policy, the Constitution grants the President power, "by and with the advice and consent of the Senate, to make treaties, provided two-thirds of the senators present concur." Only once did Washington attempt to use this power, but the experiment was unsatisfactory, ending the Senate's role as an effective advisory body to the President. Washington then turned to the Supreme Court, but Chief Justice John Jay established a binding precedent by refusing to give advisory opinions (No. 37).

Another defect of the Articles which the Constitution remedied was the absence of a federal coercive power. The first important challenge to federal authority came as a result of the whiskey tax levied in 1791, a part of the Federalist financial program. Although the right to levy excises is mentioned specifically in the Constitution, the tax was unpopular in the back country. Anticipating opposition, Congress enacted a bill authorizing the use of the militia to execute the laws of the Union and to suppress insurrections. When resistance to the excise act broke out, President Washington invoked the new militia statute. Although the military force vindicated federal authority, the use of repressive measures created popular fear of centralized power.

Other aspects of the Hamiltonian system aroused considerable constitutional debate, particularly the establishment of the Bank of the United States. Attacked in Congress as class legislation, an instrument of consolidation, and a violation of constitutional limitations, the measure was sufficiently controversial for Washington to request written opinions from his Cabinet. The interpretations of Jefferson and Hamilton turned on the scope of the "necessary and proper" clause, Jefferson (No. 38A) denying the necessity and therefore the constitutionality of the Bank, and Hamilton (No. 38B) upholding both. It should be noted that Jefferson's mention of the Twelfth Amendment actually refers to the Tenth Amendment; this was due to the pending ratification of the twelve proposed amendments, ten of which were adopted in December, 1791.

Domestic policy was not the only area of constitutional concern during the 1790's. The declaraton of war by France on England and Spain in 1793 raised grave problems in international affairs. America's position was complicated by a Revolutionary War treaty with France. Was a policy of neutrality consistent with this treaty? If so, should the policy be announced by the President or Congress? Again the members of the Cabinet disagreed on details, but President Washington's proclamation of neutrality (in which the word *neutrality* does not appear) resolved the immediate issue. At the same time, however, it raised the whole question of Presidential prerogative in the conduct of foreign policy. Jay's Treaty in 1795 precipitated a year-long controversy over this issue. Since the treaty required an appropriation to implement one of its provisions and since the Constitution assigns the right to originate appropriations to the House, the treaty also raised the question of the role of the House of Representatives in treaty making. Washington's defense of presidential authority is set forth cogently in his message to the House (No. 39A). The Blount Resolutions are a formal reply to the President's position (No. 39B).

In only one early case did the Supreme Court become involved in the controversy over the treaty-making power. In *Ware v. Hylton* (No. 40), a case involving a Virginia wartime statute and the treaty ending the Revolution, the Court established an important precedent that state laws are subordinate to treaties made by the United States.

An interesting constitutional sidelight of the period was the role of Congress in "unmaking" a treaty. Antagonized by America's treaty with Great Britain, France adopted a hostile attitude toward the United States, which eventuated in an undeclared war in 1798. With the approval of President John Adams, Congress passed legislation that ended the Revolutionary treaty of alliance with France. In 1800 France agreed to this unilateral abrogation in a new treaty that cancelled American spoliation claims against France.

Although Washington's role as President is often overshadowed by the Hamiltonian-Jeffersonian conflict, his leadership had a profound influence on constitutional and political evolution. Many of the constitutional problems listed in this chapter were settled by his action, and his signature validated all Federalist legislation; indeed, he was the outstanding political leader of the new government. Another aspect of Washington's leadership which is too often overlooked is his role in the rise of political parties, an extraconstitutional development that the Founding Fathers had failed to foresee. Despite the fame of Washington's Farewell Address for its advice on foreign policy, his warning against political partisanship is seldom noted. Paradoxically, although Washington's remarks were thinly disguised warnings against the factionalism of the Republicans, it was the Federalist party that carried partisanship to extremes in the Alien and Sedition Laws of 1798 (No. 41 A, B). Viewing these acts not only as a frontal assault on the Bill of Rights but also as a dangerous extension of governmental centralization, the Republicans replied with the Kentucky (No. 42) and Virginia Resolutions, classic arguments on behalf of individual liberties and states' rights. Stressing the Half War with France, the Federalists defended their repressive measures as national defense legislation (No. 43), justifying the Alien Law as a protective measure against factious foreigners and denying that the Sedition Act violated the First Amendment. In the election of 1800, Jeffersonian principles were vindicated at the polls and subsequently President Jefferson pardoned victims of the Sedition Law still in jail.

The election of 1800, like that of 1796, revealed the necessity for constitutional recognition of political parties. In 1796, although Jefferson—the Republican presidential candidate—lost to Adams—a Federalist—he, nevertheless, was chosen Vice-President. The electoral machinery again failed to work smoothly in 1800, resulting in a tie between Jefferson and Burr. Both incidents indicated the emergence of disciplined politicial parties, and the adoption of the Twelfth Amendment (No. 44) successfully integrated the two-party system into election procedures.

Federal Guarantees of Fundamental Rights

30. Madison Voices the People's Demands, June 8, 1789

Annals of Congress, 1st Cong., 1st Sess., 449-57 passim.

It cannot be a secret to the gentlemen in this House, that, notwithstanding the ratification of this system of Government by eleven of the thirteen United States, in some cases unanimously, in others by large majorities;

yet still there is a great number of our constituents who are dissatisfied with it; among whom are many respectable for their talents and patriotism, and respectable for the jealousy they have for their liberty, which, though mistaken in its object, is laudable in its motive. There is a great body of the people falling under this description, who at present feel much inclined to join their support to the cause of Federalism, if they were satisfied on this one point. We ought not to disregard their inclination, but, on principles of amity and moderation, conform to their wishes, and expressly declare the great rights of mankind secured under this constitution. The acquiescence which our fellow-citizens show under the Government, calls upon us for a like return of moderation. But perhaps there is a stronger motive than this for our going into a consideration of the subject. It is to provide those securities for liberty which are required by a part of the community; I allude in a particular manner to those two States that have not thought fit to throw themselves into the bosom of the Confederacy. It is a desirable thing, on our part as well as theirs, that a reunion should take place as soon as possible. I have no doubt, if we proceed to take those steps which would be prudent and requisite at this juncture, that in a short time we should see that disposition prevailing in those States which have not come in, that we have seen prevailing in those States which have embraced the constitution.

But I will candidly acknowledge, that, over and above all these considerations, I do conceive that the constitution may be amended; that is to say, if all power is subject to abuse, that then it is possible the abuse of the powers of the General Government may be guarded against in a more secure manner than is now done, while no one advantage arising from the exercise of that power shall be damaged or endangered by it. We have in

this way something to gain, and, if we proceed with caution, nothing to lose. And in this case it is necessary to proceed with caution; for while we feel all these inducements to go into a revisal of the constitution, we must feel for the constitution itself, and make that revisal a moderate one. I should be unwilling to see a door opened for a reconsideration of the whole structure of the Government—for a reconsideration of the principles and the substance of the powers given; because I doubt, if such a door were opened, we should be very likely to stop at that point which would be safe to the Government itself. But I do wish to see a door opened to consider, so far as to incorporate those provisions for the security of rights, against which I believe no serious objection has been made by any class of our constituents: such as would be likely to meet with the concurrence of two-thirds of both Houses, and the approbation of three-fourths of the State Legislatures. I will not propose a single alteration which I do not wish to see take place, as intrinsically proper in itself, or proper because it is wished for by a respectable number of my fellow-citizens; and therefore I shall not propose a single alteration but is likely to meet the concurrence required by the constitution. There have been objections of various kinds made against the constitution. Some were levelled against its structure because the President was without a council; because the Senate, which is a legislative body, had judicial powers in trials on impeachments; and because the powers of that body were compounded in other respects, in a manner that did not correspond with a particular theory; because it grants more power than is supposed to be necessary for every good purpose, and controls the ordinary powers of the State Governments. I know some respectable characters who opposed this Government on these grounds; but I believe that the great mass of the people who opposed it, disliked it because it did not contain effectual provisions against encroachments on particular rights, and those safeguards which they have been long accustomed to have interposed between them and the magistrate who exercises the sovereign power; nor ought we to consider them safe, while a great number of our fellow-citizens think these securities necessary. . . .

It has been said, that it is unnecessary to load the constitution with this provision, because it was not found effectual in the constitution of the particular States. It is true, there are a few particular States in which some of the most valuable articles have not, at one time or other, been violated; but it does not follow but they may have, to a certain degree, a salutary effect against the abuse of power. If they are incorporated into the constitution, independent tribunals of justice will consider themselves in a peculiar manner the guardians of those rights; they will be an impenetrable bulwark against every assumption of power in the legislative or executive; they will be naturally led to resist every encroachment upon rights expressly stipulated for in the constitution by the declaration of rights. Besides this security, there is a great probability that such a declaration in the federal system would be enforced; because the State Legislatures will jealously and closely watch the operations of this Government, and be able to resist with more effect every assumption of power, than any other power on earth can do; and the greatest opponents to a Federal Government admit the State Legislatures to be sure guardians of the people's liberty. I conclude, from this view of the subject, that it will be proper in itself, and highly politic, for the tranquillity of the public mind, and the stability of the Government, that we should offer something, in the form I have proposed, to be incorporated in the system of Government as a declaration of the rights of the people.

31. Resolution for Adding a Bill of Rights, September 25, 1789

Jonathan Elliot, ed., Debates in the Several State Conventions, on the Adoption of the Federal Constitution . . . (Washington, 1863), I, 338.

The conventions of a number of the states having, at the time of their adopting the Constitution, expressed a desire, in order to prevent misconstruction or abuse of its powers, that further declaratory and restrictive clauses should be added; and as extending the ground of public confidence in the government will best insure the beneficent ends of its institution;—

Resolved by the Senate and House of Representatives of the United States of America, in Congress assembled, two thirds of both houses concurring, that the following articles be proposed by the legislatures of the several states, as amendments to the Constitution of the United States, all or any of which articles, when ratified by three fourths of the said legislatures, to be valid, to all intents and purposes, as part of the said Constitution. . . . [Of the twelve proposed, ten were adopted.]

32. *The First Ten Amendments,* 1791

ARTICLE I

Congress shall make no law respecting an establishment of religion, or prohibiting the free exercise thereof; or abridging the freedom of speech or of the press; or the right of the people peaceably to assemble, and to petition the government for a redress of grievances.

ARTICLE II

A well-regulated militia being necessary to the security of a free State, the right of the people to keep and bear arms shall not be infringed.

ARTICLE III

No soldier shall, in time of peace, be quartered in any house without the consent of the owner, nor in time of war, but in a manner to be prescribed by law.

ARTICLE IV

The right of the people to be secure in their persons, houses, papers, and effects, against unreasonable searches and seizures, shall not be violated, and no warrants shall issue but upon probable cause, supported by oath or affirmation, and particularly describing the place to be searched, and the person or things to be seized.

ARTICLE V

No person shall be held to answer for a capital or otherwise infamous crime, unless on a presentment or indictment of a grand jury, except in cases arising in the land or naval forces, or in the militia, when in actual service in time of war or public danger; nor shall any person be subject for the same offense to be twice put in jeopardy of life or limb; nor shall be compelled in any criminal case to be a witness against himself, nor be deprived of life, liberty, or property, without due process of law; nor shall private property be taken for public use without just compensation.

ARTICLE VI

In all criminal prosecutions the accused shall enjoy the right to a speedy and public trial, by an impartial jury of the State and district wherein the crime shall have been committed, which district shall have been previously ascertained by law, and to be informed of the nature and cause of the accusation; to be confronted with the witnesses against him; to have compulsory process for obtaining witnesses in his favor, and to have the assistance of counsel for his defense.

ARTICLE VII

In suits at common law, where the value in controversy shall exceed twenty dollars, the right of trial by jury shall be preserved, and no fact tried by a jury shall be otherwise re-examined in any court of the United States, than according to the rules of the common law.

ARTICLE VIII

Excessive bail shall not be required, nor excessive fines imposed, nor cruel and unusual punishments inflicted.

ARTICLE IX

The enumeration in the Constitution of certain rights shall not be construed to deny or disparage others retained by the people.

ARTICLE X

The powers not delegated to the United States by the Constitution, nor prohibited by it to the States, are reserved to the States respectively or to the people.

33. Does the Bill of Rights Restrain the States?

Barron v. Baltimore, 7 Peters 243 (1833).

MARSHALL, C.J.: The judgment brought up by this writ of error having been rendered by the Court of a State, this tribunal can exercise no jurisdiction over it, unless it be shown to come within the provisions of the twenty-fifth section of the Judicial Act [of 1789]. The plaintiff in error contends that it comes within that clause in the fifth amendment to the constitution, which inhibits the taking of private property for public use, without just compensation. He insists that this amendment, being in favor of the liberty of the citizen, ought to be so construed as to restrain the legislative power of a state, as well as that of the United States. If this proposition be untrue, the court can take no jurisdiction of the cause.

The question thus presented is, we think, of great importance, but not of much difficulty.

The constitution was ordained and established by the people of the United States for themselves, for their own government, and not for the government of the individual States. Each State established a constitution for itself, and, in that constitution, provided such limitations and restrictions on the powers of its particular government as its judgment dictated. The people of the United States framed such a government for the United States as they supposed best adapted to their situation, and best calculated to promote their interests. The powers they conferred on this government were to be exercised by itself; and the limitations on power, if expressed in general terms, are naturally, and, we think, necessarily applicable to the government created by the instrument. They are limitations of power granted in the instrument itself; not of distinct governments, framed by different persons and for different purposes.

If these propositions be correct, the fifth amendment must be understood as restraining the power of the general government, not as applicable to the States. In their several constitutions they have imposed such restrictions on their respective governments as their own wisdom suggested; such as they deemed most proper for themselves. It is a subject on which they judge exclusively, and with which others interfere no farther than they are supposed to have a common interest.

The counsel for the plaintiff in error insists that the constitution was intended to secure the people of the several States against the undue exercise of power by their respective state governments; as well as against that which might be attempted by their general government. In support of this argument he relies on the inhibitions contained in the tenth section of the first article.

We think that section affords a strong if not a conclusive argument in support of the opinion already indicated by the court.

The preceding section contains restrictions which are obviously intended for the exclusive purpose of restraining the exercise of power by the departments of the general government. Some of them use language applicable only to Congress; others are expressed in general terms. The third clause, for example, declares that "no bill of attainder or *ex post facto* law shall be passed." No language can be more general; yet the demonstration is complete that it applies solely to the government of the United States. In addition to the general arguments furnished by the instrument itself, some of which have been already suggested, the succeeding section, the avowed purpose of which is to restrain state legislation, contains in terms the very prohibition. It declares that "no State shall pass any bill of attainder or *ex post facto* law." This provision, then, of the ninth section, however comprehensive its language, contains no restriction on state legislation.

The ninth section having enumerated, in the nature of a bill of rights, the limitations intended to be imposed on the powers of the general government, the tenth proceeds to enumerate those which were to operate on the state legislatures. These restrictions are brought together in the same section, and are by express words applied to the States. "No State shall enter into any treaty," etc. Perceiving that in a constitution framed by the people of the United States for the government of all, no limitation of the action of government on the people would apply to the state government, unless expressed in terms; the restrictions contained in the tenth section are in direct words so applied to the States.

It is worthy of remark, too, that these inhibitions generally restrain state legislation on subjects intrusted to the general government, or in which the people of all the States feel an interest. . . .

It would be tedious to recapitulate the several limitations on the powers of the States which are contained in this section. They will be found, generally, to restrain state legislation on subjects intrusted to the government of the Union, in which the citizens of all the States are interested. In these alone were the whole people concerned. The question of their application to States is not left to construction. It is averred in positive words.

If the original constitution, in the ninth and tenth sections of the first article, draws this plain and marked line of discrimination between the limitations it imposes on the powers of the general government, and on those of the States; if in every inhibition intended to act on state power, words are employed which directly express that intent; some strong reason must be assigned for departing from this safe and judicious course in framing the amendments, before that departure can be assumed.

We search in vain for that reason. . . .

We are of opinion that the provision in the fifth amendment to the constitution, declaring that private property shall not be taken for public use without just compensation, is intended solely as a limitation on the exercise of power by the government of the United States, and is not applicable to the legislation of the States. . . . This court, therefore, has no jurisdiction of the cause; and it is dismissed.

34. *Can a Citizen Sue a State in the Federal Courts?*

Chisholm v. Georgia, 2 Dallas 419 (1793).

JAY, C.J.: The question we are now to decide has been accurately stated namely, is a State suable by individual citizens of another State?

It is said that Georgia refuses to appear and answer to the plaintiff in this action, because she is a sovereign State, and therefore not liable to such actions. In order to ascertain the merits of this objection, let us inquire:—1st. In what sense Georgia is a sovereign State. 2nd. Whether suability is incompatible with such sovereignty. 3rd. Whether the Constitution, to which Georgia is a party, authorizes such an action against her.

1st. . . . the sovereignty of the nation is in the people of the nation, and the residuary sovereignty of each State in the people of each State. . . .

2nd. The second object of inquiry now presents itself, namely, whether suability is compatible with State sovereignty. . . .

If there be any such incompatibility as is pretended, whence does it arise? In what does it consist? There is at least one strong undeniable fact against this in-compatibility, and that is this: Any one State in the Union may sue all the people of another State. It is plain then that a State may be sued, and hence it plainly follows that suability and State sover-eignty are not incompatible. . . . But why should it be more incompatible that all the people of a State should be sued by one citizen, than by one hundred thousand, I cannot perceive, the process in both cases being alike, and the conse-quences of a judgment alike. Nor can I observe any greater inconveniences in the one case than in the other, except what may arise from the feelings of those who may regard a lesser number in an inferior light. But if any reliance be made on this inferiority, as an objection, at least one-half of its force is done away by this fact, namely, that it is conceded that a State may appear in this court as plaintiff against a single citizen as de-fendant; and the truth is that the State of Georgia is at this moment prosecuting an action in this court against two citizens of South Carolina. . . .

3rd. Let us now proceed to inquire whether Georgia has not, by being a party to the national compact, consented to be suable by individual citizens of an-other State. . . .

The question now before us renders it necessary to pay particular attention to that part of the second section which ex-tends the judicial power "to controver-sies between a State and citizens of an-other State." It is contended that this ought to be construed to reach none of these controversies, excepting those in which a State may be plaintiff. The ordi-nary rules for construction will easily de-cide whether those words are to be un-derstood in that limited sense.

This extension of power is remedial, because it is to settle controversies. It is, therefore, to be construed liberally. It is

politic, wise, and good, that not only the controversies in which a State is plaintiff, but also those in which a State is de-fendant, should be settled; both cases, therefore, are within the reason of the remedy; and ought to be so adjudged, un-less the obvious, plain, and literal sense of the words forbid it. If we attend to the words, we find them to be express, positive, free from ambiguity, and with-out room for such implied expressions: "The judicial power of the United States shall extend to controversies between a State and citizens of another State." If the constitution really meant to extend these powers only to those controversies in which a State might be plaintiff, to the exclusion of those in which citizens had demands against a State, it is inconceiva-ble that it should have attempted to con-vey that meaning in words not only so incompetent, but also repugnant to it; if it meant to exclude a certain class of these controversies, why were they not expressly excepted; on the contrary, not even an intimation of such intention ap-pears in any part of the constitution. It cannot be pretended that where citizens urge and insist upon demands against a State, which the State refuses to admit and comply with, that there is no con-troversy between them. If it is a contro-versy between them, then it clearly falls not only within the spirit, but the very words of the constitution. What is it to the cause of justice, and how can it affect the definition of the word controversy, whether the demands which cause the dis-pute are made by a State against citizens of another State, or by the latter against the former? When power is thus ex-tended to a controversy, it necessarily, as to all judicial purposes, is also extended to those between whom it subsists. . . .

For the reasons before given, I am clearly of opinion that a State is sua-ble by citizens of another State. . . .

35. *The Eleventh Amendment Limits Federal Judicial Power*

Proposed March 5, 1794; adopted January 8, 1798.

ARTICLE XI

The judicial power of the United States shall not be construed to extend to any suit in law or equity, commenced or prosecuted against one of the United States by citizens of another State, or by citizens or subjects of any foreign State.

The Organization of the New Government

36. *Judiciary Act of 1789, September 24, 1789*

U. S. Stat. at L., I, 73-93.

SEC. 1. *Be it enacted* . . . That the supreme court of the United States shall consist of a chief justice and five associate justices, any four of whom shall be a quorum, and shall hold annually at the seat of government two sessions, the one commencing the first Monday of February, and the other the first Monday of August. That the associate justices shall have precedence according to the date of their commissions, or when the commissions of two or more of them bear date on the same day, according to their respective ages.

SEC. 2. That the United States shall be, and they hereby are divided into thirteen districts. . . .

SEC. 3. That there be a court called a District Court, in each of the afore mentioned districts, to consist of one judge, who shall reside in the district for which he is appointed, and shall be called a District Judge, and shall hold annually four sessions. . . .

SEC. 4. That the beforementioned districts, except those of Maine and Kentucky, shall be divided into three circuits, and be called the eastern, the middle, and the southern circuit. . . . That there shall be held annually in each district of said circuits, two courts which shall be called Circuit Courts, and shall consist of any two justices of the Supreme Court and the district judge of such districts, any two of whom shall constitute a quorum: *Provided,* That no district judge shall give a vote in any case of appeal or error from his own decision; but may assign the reasons of such his decision. . . .

SEC. 9. That the district courts shall have, exclusively of the courts of the several States, cognizance of all crimes and offences that shall be cognizable under the authority of the United States, committed within their respective districts, or upon the high seas; where no other punishment than whipping, not exceeding thirty stripes, a fine not exceeding one hundred dollars, or a term of imprisonment not exceeding six months, is to be inflicted; and shall also have exclusive original cognizance of all civil cases of admiralty and maritime jurisdiction, including all seizures under laws of impost, navigation or trade of the United States. . . . And shall also have cognizance, concurrent with the courts of the several States, or the circuit courts, as the case may be, of all causes where an alien sues for a tort only in violation of the law of nations or a treaty of the United States. And shall also have cognizance, concurrent as last mentioned, of all suits at common law where the United States sue, and the matter in dispute amounts, exclusive of costs, to the sum or value of one hundred dollars. And shall also have jurisdiction exclusively of the courts of the several States, of all suits against consuls or vice-consuls, except for offences above the description aforesaid. And the trial of issues in fact, in the district courts, in all cases except civil causes of admiralty and maritime jurisdiction, shall be by jury. . . .

SEC. 11. That the circuit courts shall have original cognizance, concurrent with the courts of the several States, of all suits of a civil nature at common law or in equity, where the matter in dispute exceeds, exclusive of costs, the sum or value of five hundred dollars, and the United States are plaintiffs or petitioners; or an alien is a party, or the suit is between a citizen of the State where the suit is brought and a citizen of another State. And shall have exclusive cognizance of all crimes and offences cognizable under the authority of the United States, except where this act otherwise provides, or the laws of the United States shall otherwise direct, and concurrent jurisdiction with the district courts of the crimes and offences cognizable therein. . . . And the circuit courts shall also have appellate jurisdiction from the district courts under the regulations and restrictions hereinafter provided. . . .

SEC. 13. That the Supreme Court shall have exclusive jurisdiction of all controversies of a civil nature, where a state is a party, except between a state and its citizens; and except also between a state and citizens of other states, or aliens, in which latter case it shall have original but not exclusive jurisdiction. And shall have

exclusively all such jurisdiction of suits or proceedings against ambassadors or other public ministers, or their domestics, or domestic servants, as a court of law can have or exercise consistently with the law of nations; and original, but not exclusive jurisdiction of all suits brought by ambassadors or other public ministers, or in which a consul or vice-consul shall be a party. And the trial of issues in fact in the Supreme Court in all actions at law against citizens of the United States shall be by jury. The Supreme Court shall also have appellate jurisdiction from the circuit courts and courts of the several states in the cases hereinafter specially provided for; and shall have power to issue writs of prohibition to the district courts, when proceeding as courts of admiralty and maritime jurisdiction, and writs of *mandamus,* in cases warranted by the principle and usages of law, to any courts appointed, or persons holding office under the authority of the United States. . . .

SEC. 25. That a final judgment or decree in any suit, in the highest court of law or equity of a State in which a decision in the suit could be had, where is drawn in question the validity of a treaty or statute of, or an authority exercised under, the United States, and the decision is against their validity; or where is drawn in question the validity of a statute of, or an authority exercised under, any State, on the ground of their being repugnant to the constitution, treaties, or laws of the United States, and the decision is in favour of such their validity, or where is drawn in question the construction of any clause of the constitution, or of a treaty, or statute of, or commission held under, the United States, and the decision is against the title, right, privilege, or exemption, specially set up or claimed by either party, under such clause of the said Constitution, treaty, statute, or commission, may be re-examined, and reversed or affirmed in the Supreme Court of the United States upon a writ of error, the citation being signed by the chief justice, or judge or chancellor of the court rendering or passing the judgment or decree complained of, or by a justice of the Supreme Court of the United States, in the same manner and under the same regulations, and the writ shall have the same effect as if the judgment or decree complained of had been rendered or passed in a circuit court, and the proceedings upon the reversal shall also be the same, except that the Supreme Court, instead of remanding the cause for a final decision as before provided, may, at their discretion, if the cause shall have been once remanded before, proceed to a final decision of the same, and award execution. But no other error shall be assigned or regarded as a ground of reversal in any such case as aforesaid, than such as appears on the face of the record, and immediately respects the before-mentioned questions of validity or construction of the said constitution, treaties, statutes, commissions, or authorities in dispute. . . .

SEC. 35. . . . And there shall also be appointed a meet person learned in the law to act as attorney-general for the United States, who shall be sworn or affirmed to a faithful execution of his office; whose duty it shall be to prosecute and conduct all suits in the Supreme Court in which the United States shall be concerned, and to give his advice and opinion upon questions of law when required by the President of the United States, or when requested by the heads of any of the departments, touching any matters that may concern their departments, and shall receive such compensation for his services as shall by law be provided.

37. *The Supreme Court Refuses to Render Advisory Opinions*

Chief Justice John Jay to President Washington, August 8, 1793, Henry P. Johnston, ed., *The Correspondence and Public Papers of John Jay* (New York, 1891), III, 488-9.

We have considered the previous question stated in a letter written by your direction to us by the Secretary of State on the 18th of last month, [regarding] the lines of separation drawn by the Constitution between the three departments of the government. These being in certain respects checks upon each other, and our being judges of a court in the last resort, are considerations which afford strong arguments against the propriety of our extra-judicially deciding the questions alluded to, especially as the power given by the Constitution to the President, of calling on the heads of departments for opinions, seems to have been *purposely* as well as expressly united to the *executive* departments.

We exceedingly regret every event that may cause embarrassment to your administration, but we derive consolation from the reflection that your judgment will discern what is right, and that your usual prudence, decision, and firmness will surmount every obstacle to the preservation of the rights, peace, and dignity of the United States. . . .

38. *The Bank of the United States: Broad versus Strict Construction*

A. THOMAS JEFFERSON TO GEORGE WASHINGTON, FEBRUARY 15, 1791

Andrew A. Lipscomb and Albert Ellery Bergh, eds., *The Writings of Thomas Jefferson* (Washington, 1903), III, 146-53.

I consider the foundation of the Constitution as laid on this ground—that "all powers not delegated to the United States, by the Constitution, nor prohibited by it to the states, are reserved to the states, or to the people" [XIIth amendment]. To take a single step beyond the boundaries thus specially drawn around the powers of Congress, is to take possession of a boundless field of power, no longer susceptible of any definition.

The incorporation of a bank, and the powers assumed by this bill, have not, in my opinion, been delegated to the United States by the Constitution.

I. They are not among the powers specially enumerated: for these are:

1st. A power to lay taxes for the purpose of paying the debts of the United States. But no debt is paid by this bill, nor any tax laid. Were it a bill to raise money, its organization in the Senate would condemn it by the Constitution.

2d. "To borrow money." But this bill neither borrows money nor insures the borrowing of it. The proprietors of the bank will be just as free as any other money-holders to lend, or not to lend, their money to the public. The operation proposed in the bill, first to lend them two millions, and then borrow them back again, cannot change the nature of the latter act, which will still be a payment, and not a loan, call it by what name you please.

3d. To "regulate commerce with foreign nations, and among the states, and with the Indian tribes." To erect a bank, and to regulate commerce, are very different acts. He who erects a bank creates a subject of commerce in its bills; so does he who makes a bushel of wheat, or digs a dollar out of the mines; yet neither of these persons regulates commerce thereby. To make a thing which may be bought and sold, is not to prescribe regulations for buying and selling. Besides, if this were an exercise of the power of regulating commerce, it would be void, as extending as much to the internal commerce of every state, as it is external. For the power given to Congress by the Constitution does not extend to the internal regulation of the commerce of a state . . . which remains exclusively with its own legislature; but to its external commerce only, that is to say, its commerce with another state, or with foreign nations, or with the Indian tribes. Accordingly, the bill does not propose the measure as a regulation of trade, but as "productive of considerable advantage to trade." Still less are these powers covered by any other of the special enumerations.

II. Nor are they within either of the general phrases, which are the two following:—

1. To lay taxes to provide for the general welfare of the United States, that is to say, "to lay taxes for *the purpose* of providing for the general welfare." For the laying of taxes is the *power,* and the general welfare the *purpose* for which the power is to be exercised. Congress are not to lay taxes *ad libitum for any purpose they please:* but only to *pay the*

debts, or provide for the welfare, of the Union. In like manner, they are not *to do anything they please* to provide for the general welfare, but only to *lay taxes* for that purpose. To consider the latter phrase, not as describing the purpose of the first, but as giving a distinct and independent power to do any act they please, which might be for the good of the Union, would render all the preceding and subsequent enumerations of power completely useless.

It would reduce the whole instrument to a single phrase, that of instituting a Congress with power to do whatever would be for the good of the United States; and, as they would be the sole judges of the good or evil, it would be also a power to do whatever evil they please.

It is an established rule of construction, where a phrase will bear either of two meanings, to give it that which will allow some meaning to the other parts of the instrument, and not that which will render all the others useless. Certainly no such universal power was meant to be given them. It was intended to lace them up straitly within the enumerated powers, and those without which, as means, these powers could not be carried into effect. It is known that the very power now proposed *as a means,* was rejected *as an end* by the Convention which formed the Constitution. A proposition was made to them, to authorize Congress to open canals, and an amendatory one to empower them to incorporate. But the whole was rejected; and one of the reasons of objection urged in debate was, that they then would have a power to erect a bank, which would render great cities, where there were prejudices and jealousies on that subject, adverse to the reception of the Constitution.

2. The second general phrase is, "to make all laws *necessary* and proper for carrying into execution the enumerated powers." But they can all be carried into

execution without a bank. A bank, therefore, is not *necessary,* and consequently not authorized by this phrase.

It has been much urged that a bank will give great facility or convenience in the collection of taxes. Suppose this were true: yet the Constitution allows only the means which are *"necessary,"* not those which are merely "convenient," for effecting the enumerated powers. If such a latitude of construction be allowed to this phrase as to give any non-enumerated power, it will go to every one; for there is not one which ingenuity may not torture into a *convenience* in some instance *or other,* to *some one* of so long a list of enumerated powers. It would swallow up all the delegated powers, and reduce the whole to one phrase, as before observed. Therefore it was that the Constitution restrained them to the *necessary* means; that is to say, to those means without which the grant of the power would be nugatory. . . .

Perhaps bank bills may be a more *convenient* vehicle than treasury orders. But a little *difference* in the degree of *convenience* cannot constitute the necessity which the Constitution makes the ground for assuming any non-enumerated power. . . .

Can it be thought that the Constitution intended that, for a shade or two of *convenience,* more or less, Congress should be authorized to break down the most ancient and fundamental laws of the several states; such as those against Mortmain, the laws of Alienage, the rules of descent, the acts of distribution, the laws of escheat and forfeiture, and the laws of monopoly. Nothing but a necessity invincible by other means, can justify such a prostitution of laws, which constitute the pillars of our whole system of jurisprudence. Will Congress be too strait-laced to carry the Constitution into honest effect, unless they may pass over the foundation laws of the state governments, for the slightest convenience to theirs?

The negative of the President is the

shield provided by the Constitution to protect, against the invasions of the legislature, 1. The rights of the Executive; 2. Of the Judiciary; 3. Of the States and State legislatures. The present is the case of a right remaining exclusively with the States, and is, consequently, one of those intended by the Constitution to be placed under his protection.

It must be added, however, that, unless the President's mind, on a view of everything which is urged for and against this bill, is tolerably clear that it is unauthorized by the Constitution, if the pro and the con hang so evenly as to balance his judgment, a just respect for the wisdom of the legislature would naturally decide the balance in favor of their opinion. It is chiefly for cases where they are clearly misled by error, ambition, or interest, that the Constitution has placed a check in the negative of the President.

B. ALEXANDER HAMILTON TO GEORGE WASHINGTON, FEBRUARY 23, 1791

John C. Hamilton, ed., *The Works of Alexander Hamilton* (New York, 1851), IV, 105-33.

In entering upon the argument it ought to be premised that the objections of the Secretary of State and the Attorney-General are founded on a general denial of the authority of the United States to erect corporations. The latter, indeed, expressly admits, that if there be anything in the bill which is not warranted by the Constitution, it is the clause of incorporation.

Now it appears to the Secretary of the Treasury that this *general principle* is *inherent* in the very *definition* of government, and *essential* to every step of the progress to be made by that of the United States, namely: That every power vested in a government is in its nature *sovereign,* and includes, by *force* of the *term* a right to employ all the *means* requisite and fairly applicable to the attainment of the ends of such power, and which are not precluded by restrictions and exceptions specified in the Constitution, or not immoral, or not contrary to the *essential ends* of political society. . . .

If it would be necessary to bring proof to a proposition so clear, as that which affirms that the powers of the federal government, as to *its objects,* were sovereign, there is a clause of the Constitution which would be decisive. It is

that which declares that the Constitution, and the laws of the United States made in pursuance of it . . . shall be the *supreme law of the land.* The power which can create a *supreme law of the land* in *any case,* is doubtless *sovereign* as to such case.

This general and indisputable principle puts at once an end to the *abstract* question, whether the United States have power to erect a *corporation;* that is to say, to give a *legal* or *artificial capacity* to one or more persons, distinct from the *natural.* For it is unquestionably incident to *sovereign power* to erect corporations, and consequently to *that* of the United States, in *relation* to the *objects* intrusted to the management of the government. The difference is this: where the authority of the government is general, it can create corporations in *all cases;* where it is confined to certain branches of legislation, it can create corporations *only* in those cases. . . .

It is not denied that there are *implied* as well as *express powers,* and that the *former* are as effectually delegated as the *latter.* . . .

It is conceded that *implied powers* are to be considered as delegated equally with *express ones.* Then it follows, that as a power of erecting a corporation may as well be *implied* as any other thing, it may as well be employed as an *instrument* or *mean* of carrying into execution any of the specified powers, as any other *instrument* or *mean* whatever. The only question must be, in this, as in every other case, whether the mean to be employed, or in this instance, the corporation to be erected, has a natural relation to any of the acknowledged objects or lawful ends of the government. Thus a corporation may not be erected by Congress for superintending the police of the city of Philadelphia, because they are not authorized to *regulate* the *police* of that city. But one may be erected in relation to the collection of taxes, or to the trade with foreign countries, or to the trade between the States, or with the Indian tribes; because it is the province of the federal government to *regulate* those objects and because it is incident to a general *sovereign* or *legislative* power to *regulate* a thing, to employ all the means which relate to its regulation to the best and greatest advantage. . . .

Through this mode of reasoning respecting the right of employing all the means requisite to the execution of the specified powers of the government, it is objected, that none but necessary and proper means are to be employed; and the Secretary of State maintains, that no means are to be considered as *necessary* but those without which the grant of the power would be *nugatory*. . . .

It is essential to the being of the national government, that so erroneous a conception of the meaning of the word *necessary* should be exploded.

It is certain, that neither the grammatical nor popular sense of the term requires that construction. According to both, *necessary* often means no more than *needful, requisite, incidental, useful,* or *conducive to.* . . . And it is the true one in which it is to be understood as used in the Constitution. The whole turn of the clause containing it indicates, that it was the intent of the Convention, by that clause, to give a liberal latitude to the exercise of the specified powers. The expressions have peculiar comprehensiveness. They are, "to make all *laws* necessary and proper for *carrying into execution* the *foregoing powers*, and *all other powers* vested by the Constitution in the *government* of the United States, or in any *department* or *officer* thereof."

To understand the word as the Secretary of State does, would be to depart from its obvious and popular sense, and to give it a restrictive operation, an idea never before entertained. It would be to give it the same force as if the word *absolutely* or *indispensably* had been prefixed to it. . . .

The *degree* in which a measure is necessary, can never be a *test* of the legal right to adopt it; that must be a matter of opinion, and can only be a *test* of expediency. The *relation* between the *measure* and the *end;* between the *nature* of the *mean* employed towards the execution of a power, and the object of that power, must be the criterion of constitutionality, not the more or less of *necessity* or *utility.* . . .

This restrictive interpretation of the word *necessary* is also contrary to this sound maxim of construction; namely, that the powers contained in a constitution of government, especially those which concern the general administration of the affairs of a country, its finances, trade, defence &c., ought to be construed liberally in advancement of the public good. . . .

But the doctrine which is contended for is not chargeable with the consequences imputed to it. It does not affirm that the national government is sovereign in all respects, but that it is sovereign to a certain extent; that is, to the extent of the objects of its specified powers.

It leaves, therefore, a criterion of

what is constitutional and of what is not so. This criterion is the *end,* to which the measure relates as a *mean.* If the *end* be clearly comprehended within any of the specified powers, and if the measure have an obvious relation to that *end,* and is not forbidden by any particular provision of the Constitution, it may safely be deemed to come within the compass of the national authority. There is also this further criterion, which may materially assist the decision; Does the proposed measure abridge a pre-existing right of any State or of any individual? If it does not, there is a strong presumption in favor of its constitutionality, and slighter relations to any declared object of the Constitution may be permitted to turn the scale. . . .

It is presumed to have been satisfactorily shown in the course of the preceding observations:

1. That the power of the government, *as* to the objects intrusted to its management, is, in its nature, sovereign.

2. That the right of erecting corporations is one inherent in, and inseparable from, the idea of sovereign power.

3. That the position, that the government of the United States can exercise no power but such as is delegated to it by its Constitution, does not militate against this principle.

4. That the word *necessary,* in the general clause, can have no *restrictive* operation derogating from the force of this principle; indeed, that the degree in which a measure is or is not *necessary,* cannot be a *test* of *constitutional right,* but of *expediency only.*

5. That the power to erect corporations is not to be considered as an *independent* or *substantive* power, but as an *incidental* and *auxiliary* one, and was therefore more properly left to implication than expressly granted.

6. That the principle in question does not extend the power of the government beyond the prescribed limits, because it only affirms a power to *incorporate* for purposes *within the sphere* of the *specified powers.*

And lastly, that the right to exercise such a power in certain cases is unequivocally granted in the most *positive* and *comprehensive* terms. . . .

A hope is entertained that it has, by this time, been made to appear, to the satisfaction of the President, that a bank has a natural relation to the power of collecting taxes—to that of regulating trade—to that of providing for the common defence—and that, as the bill under consideration contemplates the government in the light of a joint proprietor of the stock of the bank, it brings the case within the provision of the clause of the Constitution which immediately respects the property of the United States. . . .

Forging a Foreign Policy

39. *The Original Controversy over the Treaty-Making Power*

A. PRESIDENT WASHINGTON TO THE HOUSE OF REPRESENTATIVES, MARCH 30, 1796

Annals of Congress, 4th Cong., 1st Sess., 760-2.

Gentlemen of the House of Representatives:

With the utmost attention I have considered your resolution of the 24th instant, requesting me to lay before your House a copy of the instructions to the Minister of the United States, who negotiated the Treaty with the King of Great Britain, together with the correspondence and other documents relative to that Treaty, excepting such of the said papers as any existing negotiation may render improper to be disclosed.

In deliberating upon this subject, it was impossible for me to lose sight of the principle which some have avowed in its discussion, or to avoid extending my views to the consequences which must flow from the admission of that principle.

I trust that no part of my conduct has ever indicated a disposition to withhold any information which the Constitution has enjoined upon the President, as a duty, to give, or which could be required of him by either House of Congress as a right; and, with truth, I affirm, that it has been, as it will continue to be, while I have the honor to preside in the Government, my constant endeavor to harmonize with the other branches thereof, so far as the trust delegated to me by the people of the United States, and my sense of the obligation it imposes, to "preserve, pro-tect, and defend the Constitution," will permit.

The nature of foreign negotiations requires caution; and their success must often depend on secrecy; and even, when brought to a conclusion, a full disclosure of all the measures, demands, or eventual concessions which may have been proposed or contemplated would be extremely impolitic; for this might have a pernicious influence on future negotiation; or produce immediate inconveniences, perhaps danger and mischief, in relation to other Powers. The necessity of such caution and secrecy was one cogent reason for vesting the power of making Treaties in the President with the advice and consent of the Senate; the principle on which the body was formed confining it to a small number of members. To admit, then, a right in the House of Representatives to demand, and to have, as a matter of course, all the papers respecting a negotiation with a foreign Power, would be to establish a dangerous precedent.

It does not occur that the inspection of the papers asked for can be relative to any purpose under the cognizance of the House of Representatives, except that of an impeachment; which the resolution has not expressed. I repeat, that I have no disposition to withhold any information which the duty of my station will permit, or the public good shall require, to be disclosed; and, in

96   LIBERTY AND JUSTICE

fact, all the papers affecting the negotiation with Great Britain were laid before the Senate, when the Treaty itself
was communicated for their consideration and advice.

The course which the debate has
taken on the resolution of the House,
leads to some observations on the mode
of making Treaties under the Constitution of the United States.

Having been a member of the General Convention, and knowing the
principles on which the Constitution
was formed, I have ever entertained but
one opinion on this subject, and from
the first establishment of the Government
to this moment, my conduct has exemplified that opinion, that the power of
making Treaties is exclusively vested in
the President, by and with the advice
and consent of the Senate, provided
two-thirds of the Senators present concur; and that every Treaty so made, and
promulgated, thenceforward becomes the
law of the land. It is thus that the
Treaty-making power has been understood by foreign nations, and in all the
Treaties made with them, *we* have declared, and *they* have believed, that
when ratified by the President, with the
advice and consent of the Senate, they
became obligatory. In this construction
of the Constitution every House of Representatives has heretofore acquiesced,
and until the present time not a doubt
or suspicion has appeared to my knowledge that this construction was not the
true one. Nay, they have more than acquiesced; for until now, without con-
troverting the obligation of such Treaties, they have made all the requisite
provisions for carrying them into effect.

There is also reason to believe that

this construction agrees with the opinions entertained by the State Conventions, when they were deliberating on
the Constitution, especially by those
who objected to it, because there was
not required in Commercial Treaties the
consent of two-thirds of the whole
number of the members of the Senate,
instead of two-thirds of the Senators
present, and because, in Treaties respecting territorial and certain other
rights and claims, the concurrence of
three-fourths of the whole number of
the members of both Houses respectively was not made necessary. . . .

If other proofs than these, and the
plain letter of the Constitution itself,
be necessary to ascertain the point under consideration, they may be found in
the Journals of the General Convention,
which I have deposited in the office
of the Department of State. In those
Journals it will appear, that a proposition was made, "that no Treaty should
be binding on the United States which
was not ratified by a law," and that the
proposition was explicitly rejected.

As, therefore, it is perfectly clear to
my understanding, that the assent of the
House of Representatives is not necessary to the validity of a Treaty; as the
Treaty with Great Britain exhibits in itself all the objects requiring Legislative
provision, and on these the papers
called for can throw no light; and as it
is essential to the due administration of
the Government, that the boundaries
fixed by the Constitution between the
different departments should be preserved—a just regard to the Constitution and to the duty of my office, under all the circumstances of this case,
forbid a compliance with your request.

B. THE BLOUNT RESOLUTIONS, APRIL 6, 1796

Annals of Congress, 4th Cong., 1st Sess., 771-2.

Resolved, That, it being declared by the second section of the second article of the Constitution, "that the President shall have power, by and with the advice of the Senate, to make Treaties, provided two-thirds of the Senate present concur," the House of Representatives do not claim any agency in making Treaties; but, that when a Treaty stipulates regulations on any of the subjects submitted by the Constitution to the power of Congress, it must depend for its execution, as to such stipulations, on a law or laws to be passed by Congress. And it is the constitutional right and duty of the House of Representatives, in all such cases, to deliberate on the expediency or inexpediency of carrying such Treaty into effect, and to determine and act thereon, as, in their judgment, may be most conducive to the public good.

Resolved, That it is not necessary to the propriety of any application from this House to the Executive, for information desired by them, and which may relate to any constitutional functions of the House, that the purpose for which such information may be wanted, or to which the same may be applied, should be stated in the application.

[Although the Blount Resolutions were carried by a vote of 57 to 35, the House later voted to carry the treaty into effect by a vote of 51 to 48.]

40. *Are Treaties Paramount over State Law?*

Ware v. Hylton, 3 Dallas 199 (1796).

CUSHING, J.: My state[ment] of this case will, agreeably to my view of it, be short. I shall not question the right of a State to confiscate debts. Here is an act of the assembly of Virginia, passed in 1777, respecting debts; which contemplating to prevent the enemy deriving strength by the receipt of them during the war, provides, that if any British debtor will pay his debt into the loan-office, obtain a certificate and receipt as directed, he shall be discharged from so much of the debt. But an intent is expressed in the act not to confiscate, unless Great Britain should set the example. This act, it is said, works a discharge and a bar to the payer. If such payment is to be considered as a discharge, or a bar, so long as the act had force, the question occurs—was there a power, by the treaty, supposing it contained proper words, entirely to remove this law, and this bar, out of the creditor's way? . . . This power seems not to have been contended against by the defendant's counsel; and, indeed, it cannot be denied; the treaty having been sanctioned, in all its parts, by the constitution of the United States, as the supreme law of the land.

Then arises the great question, upon the import of the fourth article of the treaty: And to me, the plain and obvious meaning of it goes to nullify . . . all laws, or the impediments of any law, as far as they might have been designed to impair or impede the creditor's right or remedy against his original debtor. "Creditors on either side shall meet with no lawful impediment to the recovery of the full value in sterling money, of all *bona fide* debts heretofore contracted." . . .

A State may make what rules it

pleases; and those rules must necessarily have place within itself. But here is a treaty, the supreme law, which overrules all State laws upon the subject, to all intents and purposes; and that makes the difference. Diverse objections are made to this construction: that it is an odious one, and as such ought to be avoided. . . .

But it can hardly be considered as an odious thing to enforce the payment of an honest debt, according to the true intent and meaning of the parties contracting, especially if, as in this case, the State having received the money, is bound in justice and honor to indemnify the debtor, for what it in fact received. In whatever other lights this act of assembly may be reviewed, I consider it in one, as containing a strong implied engagement on the part of the State, to indemnify every one who should pay money under it, pursuant to the invitation it held out. . . .

Again, the treaty regarded the existing state of things, by removing the laws then existing, which intended to defeat the creditor of his usual remedy at law. . . .

The provision, that "creditors shall meet with no lawful impediment," &c., is as absolute, unconditional, and peremptory, as words can well express, and made not to depend on the will and pleasure, or the optional conduct of any body of men whatever.

To effect the object intended, there is no want of proper and strong language; there is no want of power, the treaty being sanctioned as the supreme law, by the constitution of the United States, which nobody pretends to deny to be paramount and controlling to all state laws, and even state constitutions, wheresoever they interfere or disagree.

The treaty, then, as to the point in question, is of equal force with the constitution itself; and certainly with any law whatsoever. And the words, "shall meet with no lawful impediment," &c., are as strong as the wit of man could devise, to avoid all effects of sequestration, confiscation, or any other obstacle thrown in the way, by any law particularly pointed against the recovery of such debts. . . .

Constitutional Reflections of Political Partisanship

41. The Federalists Attack the Bill of Rights, 1798

A. AN ACT CONCERNING ALIENS

U. S. Stat. at L., 570-2.

SEC. 1. *Be it enacted* . . . , That it shall be lawful for the President of the United States at any time during the continuance of this act, to *order* all such *aliens* as he shall judge dangerous to the peace and safety of the United States, or shall have reasonable grounds to suspect are concerned in any treasonable or secret machinations against the government thereof, to depart out of the territory of the United States, within such time as shall be expressed in such order, which order shall be served on such alien by delivering him a copy thereof, or leaving the same at his usual abode, and returned to the office of the Secretary of State, by the marshal or other person to whom the same shall be directed. And in case any alien, so ordered to depart, shall be found at large within the United States after the time limited in such order for his departure, and not having obtained a *license* from the President to reside therein, or having obtained such *license* shall not have conformed thereto, every such alien shall, on conviction thereof, be imprisoned for a term not exceeding three years, and shall never after be admitted to become a citizen of the United States. *Provided always, and be it further enacted,* that if any alien so ordered to depart shall prove to the satisfaction of the President, by evidence to be taken before such person or persons as the President shall direct, who are for that purpose hereby authorized to administer oaths, that no injury or danger to the United States will arise from suffering such alien to reside therein, the President may grant a *license* to such alien to remain within the United States for such time as he shall judge proper, and at such place as he may designate. And the President may also require of such alien to enter into a bond to the United States, in such penal sum as he may direct, with one or more sufficient sureties to the satisfaction of the person authorized by the President to take the same, conditioned for the good behavior of such alien during his residence in the United States, and not violating his license, which license the President may revoke, whenever he shall think proper.

Sec. 2. *And be it further enacted,* That it shall be lawful for the President of the United States, whenever he may deem it necessary for the public safety, to order to be removed out of the territory thereof, any alien who may or shall be in prison in pursuance of this act; and to cause to be arrested and sent out of the United States such of those aliens as shall have been ordered to depart therefrom and shall not have obtained a license as aforesaid, in all cases where, in the opinion of the President, the public safety requires a speedy removal. And if any alien so removed or sent out of the United States by the President shall voluntarily return thereto, unless by permission of the President of the United States, such alien on conviction thereof, shall be imprisoned so long as, in the opinion of the President, the public safety may require. . . .

Sec. 4. *And be it further enacted,* That the circuit and district courts of the United States, shall respectively have cognizance of all crimes and offences against this act. . . .

Sec. 6. *And be it further enacted,* That this act shall continue and be in force for and during the term of two years from the passing thereof.

B. THE SEDITION ACT

U. S. Stat. at L., 596-7.

Sec. 1. *Be it enacted* . . . , That if any persons shall unlawfully combine or conspire together, with intent to oppose any measure or measures of the government of the United States, which are or shall be directed by proper authority, or to impede the operation of any law of the United States, or to intimidate or prevent any person holding a place or office in or under the government of the United States, from undertaking, performing or executing his trust or duty; and if any person or persons, with intent as aforesaid, shall counsel, advise or attempt to procure any insurrection, riot, unlawful assembly, or combination, whether such conspiracy, threatening, counsel, advice, or attempt shall have the proposed effect or not, he or they shall be deemed guilty of a high misdemeanor, and on conviction, before any court of the United States having jurisdiction thereof, shall be punished by a fine not exceeding five thousand dollars, and by imprisonment during a term not less than six months nor exceeding five years; and further, at the discretion of the court may be holden to find sureties for his good behaviour in such sum, and for such time, as the said court may direct.

SEC. 2. . . . That if any person shall write, print, utter, or publish, or shall cause or procure to be written, printed, uttered or published, or shall knowingly and willingly assist or aid in writing, printing, uttering or publishing any false, scandalous and malicious writing or writings against the government of the United States, or either house of the Congress of the United States, or the President of the United States, with intent to defame the said government, or either house of the said Congress, or the said President, or to bring them, or either of them, into contempt or disrepute; or to excite against them, or either or any of them, the hatred of the good people of the United States, or to stir up sedition within the United States, or to excite any unlawful combinations therein, for opposing or resisting any law of the United States, or any act of the President of the United States, done in pursuance of any such law, or of the powers in him vested by the constitution of the United States, or to resist, oppose, or defeat any such law or act, or to aid, encourage or abet any hostile designs of any foreign nation against the United States, their people or government, then such person, being thereof convicted before any court of the United States having jurisdiction thereof, shall be punished by a fine not exceeding two thousand dollars, and by imprisonment not exceeding two years.

SEC. 3. . . . That if any person shall be prosecuted under this act, for the writing or publishing any libel aforesaid, it shall be lawful for the defendant, upon the trial of the cause, to give in evidence in his defence, the truth of the matter contained in the publication charged as a libel. And the jury who shall try the cause, shall have a right to determine the law and the fact, under the direction of the court, as in other cases.

SEC. 4. . . . That this act shall continue to be in force until March 3, 1801, and no longer: *Provided,* that the expiration of the act shall not prevent or defeat a prosecution and punishment of any offence against the law, during the time it shall be in force.

42. *The Kentucky Resolutions, November 16, 1798*

Facsimile reproduction in Paul Leicester Ford, ed., *The Writings of Thomas Jefferson* (New York, 1896), VII, 288-9.

I. *Resolved,* that the several states composing the United States of America, are not united on the principle of unlimited submission to their General Government; but that by compact under the style and title of a Constitution for the United States and of amendments thereto, they constituted a General Government for special purposes, delegated to that Government certain definite powers, reserving each state to itself, the residuary mass of right to their own self-Government; and that whensoever the General Government assumes undelegated powers, its acts are unauthoritative, void, and of no force: That to this compact each state acceded as a state, and is an integral party, its co-states forming, as to itself, the other party; That the government created by this compact was not made the exclusive or final *judge* of the extent of the powers delegated to itself; since that would have made its discretion, and not the constitution, the measure of its powers; but that as in all other cases of compact among parties having no common Judge, each party has an equal right to judge for itself, as well of infractions as of the mode and measure of redress.

II. *Resolved,* that the Constitution of the United States having delegated to Congress a power to punish treason, counterfeiting the securities and current coin of the United States, piracies and felonies committed on the High Seas, and offenses against the laws of nations, and no other crimes whatever, and it being true as a general principle, and one of the amendments to the Constitution having also declared "that the powers not delegated to the United States by the Constitution, nor prohibited by it to the States, are reserved to the States respectively, or to the people," therefore also . . . [the Sedition Act]; as also the act passed by them on the 27th day of June, 1798, entitled "An act to punish frauds committed on the Bank of the United States" (and all other their acts which assume to create, define, or punish crimes other than those enumerated in the constitution), are altogether void and of no force, and that the power to create, define, and punish such other crimes is reserved, and of right appertains solely and exclusively to the respective states, each within its own Territory.

III. *Resolved,* that it is true as a general principle, and is also expressly declared by one of the amendments to the Constitution that "the powers not delegated to the United States by the Constitution, nor prohibited by it to the States, are reserved to the States respectively or to the people;" and that no power over the freedom of religion, freedom of speech, or freedom of the press being delegated to the United States by the Constitution, nor prohibited by it to the states, all lawful powers respecting the same did of right remain, and were reserved to the States, or to the people: That thus was manifested their determination to retain to themselves the right of judging how far the licentiousness of speech and of the press may be abridged without lessening their useful freedom,

and how far those abuses which cannot be separated from their use should be tolerated rather than the use be destroyed; and thus also they guarded against all abridgment by the United States of the freedom of religious opinions and exercises, and retained to themselves the right of protecting the same, as this state, by a Law passed on the general demand of its Citizens, had already protected them from all human restraint or interference: And that in addition to this general principle and express declaration, another and more special provision has been made by one of the amendments to the Constitution which expressly declares, that "Congress shall make no law respecting an establishment of religion, or prohibiting the free exercise thereof, or abridging the freedom of speech, or of the press," thereby guarding in the same sentence, and under the same words, the freedom of religion, of speech, and of the press, insomuch, that whatever violates either, throws down the sanctuary which covers the others, and that libels, falsehoods, defamation equally with heresy and false religion, are withheld from the cognizance of federal tribunals. That therefore . . . [the Sedition Act], which does abridge the freedom of the press, is not law, but is altogether void and of no effect.

IV. *Resolved,* that alien friends are under the jurisdiction and protection of the laws of the State wherein they are; that no power over them has been delegated to the United States, nor prohibited to the individual States distinct from their power over citizens; and it being true as a general principle, and one of the amendments to the Constitution having also declared that "the powers not delegated to the United States by the Constitution, nor prohibited by it to the States, are reserved to the States respectively, or to the people," the . . . [Alien Act of June 25, 1798], which assumes power over alien friends not delegated by the Constitution, is not law, but is altogether void and of no force.

V. *Resolved,* that in addition to the general principle as well as the express declaration, that powers not delegated are reserved, another and more special provision inserted in the Constitution from abundant caution has declared, "that the *migration* or importation of such persons as any of the States now existing shall think proper to admit, shall not be prohibited by the Congress prior to the year 1808." That this Commonwealth does admit the migration of alien friends described as the subject of the said act concerning aliens; that a provision against prohibiting their migration is a provision against all acts equivalent thereto, or it would be nugatory; that to remove them when migrated is equivalent to a prohibition of their migration, and is therefore contrary to the said provision of the Constitution, and void.

VI. *Resolved,* that the imprisonment of a person under the protection of the Laws of this Commonwealth on his failure to obey the simple *order* of the President to depart out of the United States, as is undertaken by the said act entitled "An act concerning Aliens," is contrary to the Constitution, one amendment to which has provided, that "no person shall be deprived of liberty without due process of law," and that another having provided "that in all criminal prosecutions, the accused shall enjoy the right to a public trial by an impartial jury, to be informed of the nature and cause of the accusation, to be confronted with the witnesses against him, to have compulsory process for obtaining witnesses in his favour, and to have the assistance of counsel for his defense," the same act undertaking to authorize the President to remove a person out of the United States who is under the protection of the Law, on his own suspicion, without accusation, without jury, without public trial, without confrontation of the witnesses against him, without having witnesses in his favour, without defense, without counsel, is contrary to these provisions also of the Constitution, is

therefore not law, but utterly void and of no force.

That transferring the power of judging any person who is under the protection of the laws, from the Courts to the President of the United States, as is undertaken by the same act concerning Aliens, is against the article of the Constitution which provides, that "the judicial power of the United States shall be vested in courts, the judges of which shall hold their offices during good behavior," and that the said act is void for that reason also; and it is further to be noted, that this transfer of Judiciary power is to that magistrate of the General Government who already possesses all the Executive, and a qualified negative in all the Legislative powers.

VII. *Resolved,* that the construction applied by the General Government (as is evinced by sundry of their proceedings) to those parts of the Constitution of the United States which delegate to Congress a power to lay and collect taxes, duties, imposts, and excises; to pay the debts, and provide for the common defense, and general welfare of the United States, and to make all laws which shall be necessary and proper for carrying into execution the powers vested by the Constitution in the Government of the United States, or any department thereof, goes to the destruction of all the limits prescribed to their power by the Constitution: That words meant by that instrument to be subsidiary only to the execution of the limited powers ought not to be so construed as themselves to give unlimited powers, nor a part so to be taken as to destroy the whole residue of the instrument: That the proceedings of the General Government under colour of these articles will be a fit and necessary subject for revisal and correction at a time of greater tranquillity, while those specified in the preceding resolutions call for immediate redress.

VIII. *Resolved,* that the preceding Resolutions be transmitted to the Senators and Representatives in Congress from this Commonwealth, who are hereby enjoined to present the same to their respective Houses, and to use their best endeavors to procure, at the next session of Congress, a repeal of the aforesaid unconstitutional and obnoxious acts.

IX. *Resolved,* lastly, that the Governor of this Commonwealth be, and is hereby authorized and requested to communicate the preceding Resolutions to the Legislatures of the several States, to assure them that this Commonwealth considers Union for specified National purposes, and particularly for those specified in their late Federal Compact, to be friendly to the peace, happiness, and prosperity of all the States: that faithful to that compact according to the plain intent and meaning in which it was understood and acceded to by the several parties, it is sincerely anxious for its preservation: that it does also believe, that to take from the States all the powers of self-government, and transfer them to a general and consolidated Government, without regard to the special delegations and reservations solemnly agreed to in that compact, is not for the peace, happiness, or prosperity of these States: And that, therefore, this Commonwealth is determined, as it doubts not its Co-states are, tamely to submit to undelegated and consequently unlimited powers in no man or body of men on earth: that if the acts before specified should stand, these conclusions would flow from them; that the General Government may place any act they think proper on the list of crimes and punish it themselves, whether enumerated or not enumerated by the Constitution as cognizable by them: that they may transfer its cognizance to the President or any other person, who may himself be the accuser, counsel, judge, and jury, whose *suspicions* may be the evidence, his order the sentence, his officer the executioner, and his breast the sole record of the transaction: that a very numerous and valuable description of the inhabitants of these States being by this precedent reduced as outlaws to the absolute dominion of one

man, and the barrier of the Constitution thus swept away from us all, no rampart now remains against the passions and the powers of a majority of Congress, to protect from a like exportation or other more grievous punishment the minority of the same body, the Legislatures, Judges, Governors, and Counsellors of the states, nor their other peaceable inhabitants who may venture to reclaim the constitutional rights and liberties of the state and people, or who for other causes, good or bad, may be obnoxious to the views or marked by the suspicions of the President, or be thought dangerous to his or their elections or other interests, public or personal: that the friendless alien has indeed been selected as the safest subject of a first experiment, but the citizen will soon follow, or rather has already followed: for, already has a Sedition Act marked him as its prey: that these and successive acts of the same character, unless arrested on the threshold, may tend to drive these states into revolution and blood, and will furnish new calumnies against Republican Governments, and new pretexts for those who wish it to be believed, that man cannot be governed but by a rod of iron: that it would be a dangerous delusion were a confidence in the men of our choice to silence our fears for the safety of our rights: that confidence is everywhere the parent of despotism: free government is founded in jealousy and not in confidence; it is jealousy and not confidence which prescribes limited Constitutions to bind down those whom we are obliged to trust with power: that our Constitution has accordingly fixed the limits to which and no further our confidence may go; and let the honest advocate of confidence read the Alien and Sedition Acts, and say if the Constitution has not been wise in fixing limits to the government it created, and whether we should be wise in destroying those limits. Let him say what the government is if it be not a tyranny, which the men of our choice have conferred on the President, and the President of our choice has assented to and accepted over the friendly strangers, to whom the mild spirit of our Country and its laws had pledged hospitality and protection: that the men of our choice have more respected the bare suspicions of the President than the solid rights of innocence, the claims of justification, the sacred force of truth, and the forms and substance of law and justice. In questions of power then let no more be heard of confidence in man, but bind him down from mischief by the claims of the Constitution. That this Commonwealth does therefore call on its Co-states for an expression of their sentiments on the acts concerning Aliens, and for the punishment of certain crimes herein before specified, plainly declaring whether these acts are or are not authorized by the Federal Compact. And it doubts not that their sense will be so announced as to prove their attachment unaltered to limited Government, whether general or particular, and that the rights and liberties of their Co-states will be exposed to no dangers by remaining embarked on a common bottom with their

own: That they will concur with this Commonwealth in considering the said acts so palpably against the Constitution as to amount to an undisguised declaration, that the Compact is not meant to be the measure of the powers of the General Government, but that it will proceed in the exercise over these states of all powers whatsoever: That they will view this as seizing the rights of the states and consolidating them in the hands of the General Government with a power assumed to bind the states (not merely in cases made Federal) but in all cases whatsoever, by laws made, not with their consent, but by others against their consent: That this would be to surrender the form of government we have chosen, and to live under one deriving its powers from its own will, and not from our authority; and that the Co-states, recurring to their natural right in cases not made federal, will concur in declaring these acts void and of no force, and will each unite with this Commonwealth in requesting their repeal at the next session of Congress.

43. *The Federalist Defense of the Alien and Sedition Laws*

Report of a House Committee, February 25, 1799,
Annals of Congress, 5th Cong., 3d Sess., 2985-93.

The . . . sedition act, contains provisions of a twofold nature; first, against seditious acts, and, second, against libellous and seditious writings. The first have never been complained of, nor has any objection been made to its validity. The objection applies solely to the second; and on the ground, in the first place, that Congress have no power by the Constitution to pass any act for punishing libels, no such power being expressly given, and all powers not given to Congress, being reserved to the States respectively, or the people thereof.

To this objection it is answered, that a law to punish false, scandalous, and malicious writings against the Government,

with intent to stir up sedition, is a law necessary for carrying into effect the power vested by the Constitution in the Government of the United States, and in the departments and officers thereof, and, consequently, such a law as Congress may pass; because the direct tendency of such writings is to obstruct the acts of the Government by exciting opposition to them, to endanger its existence by rendering it odious and contemptible in the eyes of the people, and to produce seditious combinations against the laws, the power to punish which has never been questioned; because it would be manifestly absurd to suppose that a Government might punish sedition, and yet be void of power to prevent it by punishing those acts which plainly and necessarily lead to it; and, because, under the general power to make all laws proper and necessary for carrying into effect the powers vested by the Constitution in the Government of the United States, Congress has passed many laws for which no express provision can be found in the Constitution, and the constitutionality of which has never been questioned. . . .

The act in question is said to be an "abridgment of the liberty of the press," and therefore unconstitutional.

To this it is answered, in the first place, that the liberty of the press consists not in a license for every man to publish what he pleases without being liable to punishment, if he should abuse this license to the injury of others, but in a permission to publish, without previous restraint, whatever he may think proper, being answerable to the public and individuals, for any abuse of this permission to their prejudice. . . .

It is answered, in the second place, that the liberty of the press did never extend, according to the laws of any State, or of the United States, or of England, from whence our laws are derived, to the publication of false, scandalous, and malicious writings against the Government, written or published with intent to do mischief, such publications being unlawful, and punishable in every State; from whence it follows, undeniably, that a law to punish seditious and malicious publications is not an abridgment of the liberty of the press, for it would be a manifest absurdity to say, that a man's liberty was abridged by punishing him for doing that which he never had a liberty to do.

It is answered, thirdly, that the act in question cannot be unconstitutional, because it makes nothing penal that was not penal before, and gives no new powers to the court, but is merely declaratory of the common law, and useful for rendering that law more generally known, and more easily understood. This cannot be denied,

if it be admitted, as it must be, that false, scandalous, and malicious libels against the Government of the country, published with intent to do mischief, are punishable by the common law; for, by the 2d section of the 3d article of the Constitution, the judicial power of the United States is expressly extended to all offences arising under the Constitution. By the Constitution, the Government of the United States is established, for many important objects, as the Government of the country; and libels against that Government, therefore, are offences arising against the Constitution, and, consequently, are punishable at common law by the courts of the United States. The act, indeed, is so far from having extended the law and the power of the court, that it has abridged both, and has enlarged instead of abridging the liberty of the press; for, at common law, libels against the Government might be punished with fine and imprisonment at the discretion of the court, whereas the act limits the fine to two thousand dollars, and the imprisonment to two years; and it also allows the party accused to give the truth in evidence for his justification, which, by the common law, was expressly forbidden.

And, lastly, it is answered, that had the Constitution intended to prohibit Congress from legislating at all on the subject of the press, which is the construction whereon the objections to this law are founded, it would have used the same expressions as in that part of the clause which relates to religion and religious tests. . . . It is evident they may legislate respecting the press, may pass laws for its regulation, and to punish those who pervert it into an engine of mischief, provided those laws do not abridge its liberty. . . .

Although the committee believe, that each of the measures adopted by Congress during the last session, is susceptible of an analytical justification, on the principles of the Constitution, and national policy, yet they prefer to rest their vindication on the true ground of considering them as parts of a general system of defence, adapted to a crisis of extraordinary difficulty and danger.

It cannot be denied, that the power to declare war, to raise and support armies, to provide and maintain a navy, to suppress insurrection, and repel invasions, and also the power to defray the necessary expense by loans or taxes, are vested in Congress. . . . In the internal history of France, and in the conduct of her forces and partisans in the countries which have fallen under her power, the public councils of our country were required to discern the dangers which threatened the United States, and to guard not only against the usual consequences of war, but also against the effects of an unprecedented combination to establish new principles of social action, on the subversion

of religion, morality, law, and government. . . .

The alien and sedition acts, so called, form a part, and, in the opinion of the committee, an essential part in these precautionary and protective measures, adopted for our security. . . .

The principles of the sedition law, so called, are among the most ancient principles of our Governments. They have been engrafted into statutes, or practised upon as maxims of the common law, according as occasion required. They were often and justly applied in the Revolutionary war. Is it not strange, that now they should first be denounced as oppressive, when they have long been recognised in the jurisprudence of these States!

The necessity that dictated these acts, in the opinion of the committee, still exists. . . .

44. *The Twelfth Amendment Recognizes Political Parties*

Proposed December 12, 1803; adopted September 25, 1804.

The Electors shall meet in their respective states, and vote by ballot for President and Vice-President, one of whom, at least, shall not be an inhabitant of the same state with themselves; they shall name in their ballots the person voted for as President, and in distinct ballots the person voted for as Vice-President, and they shall make distinct lists of all persons voted for as President, and of all persons voted for as Vice-President, and of the number of votes for each, which lists they shall sign and certify, and transmit sealed to the seat of the government of the United States, directed to the President of the Senate;—The President of the Senate shall, in presence of the Senate and House of Representatives, open all the certificates and the votes shall then be counted;—The person having the greatest number of votes for President, shall be the President, if such number be a majority of the whole number of Electors appointed; and if no

person have such majority, then from the persons having the highest numbers not exceeding three on the list of those voted for as President, the House of Representatives shall choose immediately, by ballot, the President. But in choosing the President, the votes shall be taken by states, the representation from each state having one vote; a quorum for this purpose shall consist of a member or members from two-thirds of the states, and a majority of all the states shall be necessary to a choice. And if the House of Representatives shall not choose a President whenever the right of choice shall devolve upon them, before the fourth day of March next following, then the Vice-President shall act as President, as in the case of the death or other constitutional disability of the President. The person having the greatest number of votes as Vice-President, shall be the Vice-President, if such number be a majority of the whole number of Electors appointed, and if no person have a majority, then from the two highest numbers on the list, the Senate shall choose the Vice-President; a quorum for the purpose shall consist of two-thirds of the whole number of Sena- tors, and a majority of the whole number shall be necessary to a choice. But no person constitutionally ineligible to the office of President shall be eligible to that of Vice-President of the United States.

CHAPTER V

Jeffersonian Republicanism and Federal Judicial Power

SHORTLY after his inauguration, Jefferson wrote that "the revolution of 1800 was as real a revolution in the principles of our government as that of 1776 was in its form." In his first inaugural address (No. 45), the new President reverted to the democratic principles of the Declaration of Independence, proclaiming his faith in the republican experiment in popular government and stressing the primary means of maintaining it through free inquiry and expression.

Indeed, Jefferson and the Republicans, still smarting from rigorous enforcement of the Sedition Law, questioned the Federalist interpretation of the scope of judicial authority. The historic case of *Marbury v. Madison* (No. 46), a blend of high politics and constitutional technicalities, grew out of the Republican refusal to validate the commission of a Federalist "midnight appointee." Although Chief Justice John Marshall wished to uphold the Federalist appointments, he refused to issue a writ of mandamus, ruling unconstitutional the section of the Judiciary Act of 1789 granting the Supreme Court this power. This was the first time that the Court overruled a law of Congress and asserted the fundamental principle of judicial review.

Another precedent of tremendous importance to national growth was also established in 1803. Because the Constitution had made no provision for the acquisition of territory, the question of purchasing Louisiana and incorporating foreign territory into the Union forced a reconsideration of the Republican party's strict construction principles. Although Jefferson originally favored an amendment authorizing acquisition, he reluctantly discarded his constitutional scruples, lamenting that "the executive . . . have done an act beyond the Constitution." The Treaty of Purchase not only extended the national domain to more than twice its original size but also expanded national power. In an interesting reversal, the Federalists deplored this expansion (Roger Griswold, No. 47A). The question of incorporating foreign territory as a part of the United States was not ruled upon by the Supreme Court until the significant decisions in the Insular Cases following the Spanish-American War (see Chapter XVI), but in the Canter case (No. 47B) Chief Justice Marshall and a unanimous Court upheld the power of the federal government to acquire and govern territory.

Napoleon, fortified with fifteen million dollars from the sale of Louisiana, resumed warfare with Great Britain in 1803. As a neutral nation, the United States became involved in international maritime controversies. Heavy shipping losses and England's persistent impressment of American seamen threatened to force the United States into war. To avoid this extremity, Jefferson resorted to economic coercion, arguing that by withholding American supplies the European powers would be forced to respect American commercial rights. Congress complied by enacting the Embargo Act. Although the Supreme Court did not rule on the Act, the federal district court of Massachusetts, presided over by Judge John Davis, a long-time Federalist, upheld in broad terms the validity of the statute as a legitimate exercise of the commerce power (*U.S. v. Brigantine William*, 1808), and Chief Justice Marshall later cited the "universally acknowledged power of the government to impose embargoes" (Gibbons v. Ogden, 1827). Most Federalists, however, and particularly those in maritime New England, denied this power and resorted to the Republican-inspired technique of legislative remonstrance. When the Connecticut Assembly, in a statement similar to the Kentucky and Virginia resolutions, denounced the Embargo as "grievous to the good people of this state, dangerous to their common liberties, incompatible with the Constitution of the United States, and encroaching upon the immunities of this state," the *Richmond Enquirer* summarized the situation in a terse headline: "Things turned Topsy Turvey—Federalists turned Anti-Federalist—the Friends of Order turned Jacobin."

Economic coercion did not prevent the War of 1812, nor did war lessen Federalist opposition to the government's policy. All the New England states, for instance, refused to authorize the integration of state militia into the federal army. The climax of opposition came in the Hartford Convention in 1814, when the five New England states met in secret session and drafted demands even more adamant than those against the Embargo (No. 48A). The only aspect of this controversy which eventually reached the Supreme Court was the question of the President's discretionary power to call forth the state militia. In *Martin v. Mott* (No. 48B), Justice Joseph Story of Massachusetts ruled that the President is the sole judge of the existence of an emergency and that his decision is binding upon all persons, including state authorities.

The Jeffersonian Philosophy

45. Jefferson's First Inaugural Address, March 4, 1801

James D. Richardson, ed., *Messages and Papers of the Presidents* (Washington, 1896), I, 322-4.

During the contest of opinion through which we have passed the animation of discussions and of exertions has sometimes worn an aspect which might impose on strangers unused to think freely and to speak and to write what they think; but this being now decided by the voice of the nation, announced according to the rules of the Constitution, all will, of course, arrange themselves under the will of the law, and unite in common efforts for the common good. All, too, will bear in mind this sacred principle, that though the will of the majority is in all cases to prevail, that will to be rightful must be reasonable; that the minority possess their equal rights, which equal law must protect, and to violate would be oppression. Let us, then, fellow-citizens, unite with one heart and one mind. Let us restore to social intercourse that harmony and affection without which liberty and even life itself are but dreary things. And let us reflect that, having banished from our land that religious intolerance under which mankind so long bled and suffered, we have yet gained little if we countenance a political intolerance as despotic, as wicked, and capable of as bitter and bloody persecutions. During the throes and convulsions of the ancient world, during the agonizing spasms of infuriated man, seeking through blood and slaughter his long-lost liberty, it was not wonderful that the agitation of the billows should reach even this distant and peaceful shore; that this should be more felt and feared by some and less by others, and should divide opinions as to measures of safety. But every difference of opinion is not a difference of principle. We have called by different names brethren of the same principle. We are all Republicans, we are all Federalists. If there be any among us who would wish to dissolve this Union or to change its republican form, let them stand undisturbed as monuments of the safety with which error of opinion may be tolerated where reason is left free to combat it. I know, indeed, that some honest men fear that a republican government can not be strong, that this Government is not strong enough; but would the honest patriot, in the full tide of successful experiment, abandon a government which has so far kept us free and firm on the theoretic and visionary fear that this Government, the world's best hope, may by possibility want energy to preserve itself? I trust not. I believe this, on the contrary, the strongest Government on earth. I believe it the only one where every man, at the call of the law, would fly to the standard of the law, and would meet invasions of the public order as his own personal concern. Sometimes it is said that man can not be trusted with the government of himself. Can he, then, be trusted with the government of others? Or have we found angels in the forms of kings to govern him? Let history answer this question. . . .

Let us, then, with courage and confidence pursue our own Federal and Republican principles, our attachment to union and representative government. . . .

About to enter, fellow-citizens, on the exercise of duties which comprehend everything dear and valuable to you, it is proper you should understand what I deem the essential principles of our Government, and consequently those which ought to shape its Administration. I will compress them within the narrowest compass they will bear, stating the general principle, but not all its limitations. Equal and exact justice to all men, of whatever state or persuasion, religious or political; peace, commerce, and honest friendship with all nations, entangling alliances with none; the support of the State governments in all their rights, as the most competent administrations for our domestic concerns and the surest bulwarks against antirepublican tendencies; the preservation of the General Government in its whole constitutional vigor, as the sheet anchor of our peace at home and safety abroad; a jealous care of the right of election by the people—a mild and safe corrective of abuses which are lopped by the sword of revolution where peaceable remedies are unprovided; absolute acquiescence in the decisions of the majority, the vital principle of republics, from which is no appeal but to force, the vital principle and immediate parent of despotism; a well-disciplined militia, our best reliance in peace and for the first moments of war, till regulars may relieve them; the supremacy of the civil over the military authority; economy in the public expense, that labor may be lightly burthened; the honest payment of our debts and sacred preservation of the public faith; encouragement of agriculture, and of commerce as its handmaid; the diffusion of information and arraignment of all abuses at the bar of the public reason; freedom of religion; freedom of the press, and freedom of person under the protection of the habeas corpus, and trial by juries impartially selected. These principles form the bright constellation which has gone before us and guided our steps through an age of revolution and reformation. The wisdom of our sages and blood of our heroes have been devoted to their attainment. They should be the creed of our political faith, the text of civic instruction, the touchstone by which to try the services of those we trust; and should we wander from them in moments of error or of alarm, let us hasten to retrace our steps and to regain the road which alone leads to peace, liberty, and safety. . . .

The Supreme Court and Judicial Review

46. "The very essence of judicial duty"

Marbury v. Madison, 1 Cranch 137 (1803).

MARSHALL, C.J.: . . . The peculiar delicacy of this case, the novelty of some of its circumstances, and the real difficulty attending the points which occur in it, require a complete exposition of the principles on which the opinion to be given by the court is founded. . . .

In the order in which the court has viewed this subject, the following questions have been considered and decided.

1st. Has the applicant a right to the commission he demands?

2dly. If he has a right and that right has been violated, do the laws of his country afford him a remedy?

3dly. If they do afford him a remedy, is it a *mandamus* issuing from this court? . . .

The first object of enquiry is,

Has the applicant a right to the commission he demands? . . .

Where an officer is removable at the will of the executive, the circumstance which completes his appointment is of no concern, because the act is at any time revocable; and the commission may be arrested, if still in the office. But when the officer is not removable at the will of the executive, the appointment is not revocable, and cannot be annulled. It has conferred legal rights which cannot be resumed. . . . The right to the office is then in the person appointed, and he has the absolute, unconditional power of accepting or rejecting it. . . .

Mr. Marbury, . . . since his commission was signed by the President, and sealed by the secretary of state, was appointed; and as the law creating the office, gave the officer a right to hold for five years, independent of the executive, the appointment was not revocable; but vested in the officer legal rights, which are protected by the laws of his country.

To withhold his commission, therefore, is an act deemed by the court not warranted by law, but violative of a vested legal right.

2. This brings us to the second enquiry: which is,

If he has a right, and that right has been violated, do the laws of his country afford him a remedy? . . .

The conclusion . . . is, that where the heads of departments are the political or confidential agents of the executive, merely to execute the will of the President, or rather to act in cases in which the executive possesses a constitutional or legal discretion, nothing can be more perfectly clear than that their acts are only politically examinable. But where a specific duty is assigned by law, and individual rights depend upon the performance of that duty, it seems equally clear that the individual who considers himself injured, has a right to resort to the laws of his country for a remedy. . . .

It is, then, the opinion of the Court,

1st. That by signing the commission of Mr. Marbury, the president of the United States appointed him a justice of peace for the county of Washington in the district of Columbia; and that the seal of the United States, affixed thereto by the secretary of state, is conclusive testimony of the verity of the signature, and of the completion of the appointment; and that the appointment conferred on him a legal right to the office for the space of five years.

2dly. That, having this legal title to the office, he has a consequent right to the commission; a refusal to deliver which, is a plain violation of that right, for which the laws of his country afford him a remedy.

It remains to be enquired whether,

3dly. He is entitled to the remedy for which he applies. This depends on,

1st. The nature of the writ applied for, and,

2dly. The power of this court. . . .

This . . . is a plain case for a mandamus, either to deliver the commission, or a copy of it from the record; and it only remains to be enquired,

Whether it can issue from this court.

The act to establish the judicial courts of the United States authorizes the supreme court "to issue writs of mandamus, in cases warranted by the principles and usages of law, to any courts appointed, or persons holding office, under the authority of the United States."

The secretary of state, being a person holding an office under the authority of the United States is precisely within the letter of the description; and if this court is not authorized to issue a writ of mandamus to such an officer, it must be because the law is unconstitutional, and therefore absolutely incapable of conferring the authority and assigning the duties which its words purport to confer and assign.

The constitution vests the whole judicial power of the United States in one supreme court, and such inferior courts as congress shall, from time to time, ordain and establish. This power is expressly extended to all cases arising under the laws of the United States; and consequently, in some form, may be exercised over the present case; because the right claimed is given by a law of the United States.

In the distribution of this power it is declared, that "the supreme court shall have original jurisdiction in all cases affecting ambassadors, other public ministers and consuls, and those in which a state shall be a party. In all other cases, the supreme court shall have appellate jurisdiction." . . .

When an instrument organizing fundamentally a judicial system, divides it into one supreme, and so many inferior courts as the legislature may ordain and establish; then enumerates its powers, and proceeds so far to distribute them, as to define the jurisdiction of the supreme court by declaring the cases in which it shall take original jurisdiction, and that in others it shall take appellate jurisdiction; the plain import of the words seems to be, that in one class of cases the jurisdiction is original and not appellate; in the other it is appellate, and not original. If any other construction would render the clause inoperative, that is an additional reason for rejecting such other construction, and for adhering to their obvious meaning.

To enable this court, then, to issue a mandamus, it must be shown to be an exercise of appellate jurisdiction, or to be necessary to enable them to exercise appellate jurisdiction. . . .

It is the essential criterion of appellate jurisdiction, that it revises and corrects the proceedings in a cause already instituted, and does not create that cause. Although, therefore, a mandamus may be directed to courts, yet to issue such a writ to an officer for the delivery of a paper, is in effect the same as to sustain an original action for that paper, and therefore, seems not to belong to appellate, but to original jurisdiction. Neither is it necessary in such

a case as this, to enable the court to exercise its appellate jurisdiction.

The authority, therefore, given to the supreme court, by the act establishing the judicial courts of the United States, to issue writs of *mandamus* to public officers, appears not to be warranted by the constitution; and it becomes necessary to inquire whether a jurisdiction so conferred can be exercised.

The question, whether an act, repugnant to the constitution, can become the law of the land, is a question deeply interesting to the United States; but, happily, not of an intricacy proportioned to its interest. It seems only necessary to recognize certain principles, supposed to have been long and well established, to decide it.

That the people have an original right to establish for their future government, such principles as, in their opinion, shall most conduce to their own happiness, is the basis in which the whole American fabric has been erected. The exercise of this original right is a very great exertion; nor can it, nor ought it to be frequently repeated. The principles, therefore, so established, are deemed fundamental. And as the authority from which they proceed is supreme, and can seldom act, they are designed to be permanent.

This original and supreme will organizes the government, and assigns, to different departments, their respective powers. It may either stop here, or establish certain limits not to be transcended by those departments.

The government of the United States is of the latter description. The powers of the legislature are defined and limited; and that those limits may not be mistaken, or forgotten, the constitution is written. To what purpose are powers limited, and to what purpose is that limitation committed to writing, if these limits may, at any time, be passed by those intended to be restrained? The distinction between a government with limited and unlimited powers is abolished, if those limits do not confine the persons on whom they are imposed, and if acts prohibited and acts allowed are of equal obligation. It is a proposition too plain to be contested, that the constitution controls any legislative act repugnant to it; or, that the legislature may alter the constitution by an ordinary act.

Between these alternatives there is no middle ground. The constitution is either a superior, paramount law, unchangeable by ordinary means, or it is on a level with ordinary legislative acts, and like other acts, is alterable when the legislature shall please to alter it.

If the former part of the alternative be true, then a legislative act contrary to the constitution, is not law; if the latter part be true, then written constitutions are absurd attempts, on the part of the people, to limit a power in its own nature illimitable.

Certainly all those who have framed written constitutions contemplate them as forming the fundamental and paramount law of the nation, and consequently the theory of every such government must be that an act of the legislature, repugnant to the constitution, is void.

This theory is essentially attached to a written constitution, and is consequently to be considered, by this court, as one of the fundamental principles of our society. It is not therefore to be lost sight of in the further consideration of this subject.

If an act of the legislature, repugnant to the constitution, is void, does it, notwithstanding its invalidity, bind the courts, and oblige them to give it effect? Or, in other words, though it be not law, does it constitute a rule as operative as if it was a law? This would be to overthrow in fact what was established in theory; and would seem, at first view, an absurdity too gross to be insisted on. It shall, however, receive a more attentive consideration.

It is emphatically the province and duty of the judicial department to say what the law is. Those who apply the rule to particular cases, must of necessity expound and interpret that rule. If two laws conflict with each other, the courts must decide on the operation of each.

So if a law be in opposition to the constitution; if both the law and the constitution apply to a particular case, so that the court must either decide that case conformably to the law, disregarding the constitution; or conformably to the constitution disregarding the law, the court must determine which of these conflicting rules governs the case. This is of the very essence of judicial duty.

If, then, the courts are to regard the constitution, and the constitution is superior to any ordinary act of the legislature, the constitution, and not such ordinary act, must govern the case to which they both apply.

Those, then, who controvert the principle that the constitution is to be considered, in court, as a paramount law, are reduced to the necessity of maintaining that courts must close their eyes on the constitution, and see only the law.

This doctrine would subvert the very foundation of all written constitutions. It would declare that an act which, according to the principles and theory of our government, is entirely void, is yet, in practice, completely obligatory. It would declare, that if the legislature shall do what is expressly forbidden, such act, notwithstanding the express prohibition, is in reality effectual. It would be giving to the legislature a practical and real omnipotence, with the same breath which professes to restrict their powers within narrow limits. It is prescribing limits, and declaring that those limits may be passed at pleasure. . . .

It is also not entirely unworthy of observation, that in declaring what shall be the *supreme* law of the land, the *constitution* itself is first mentioned; and not the laws of the United States generally, but those only which shall be made in *pursuance* of the constitution, have that rank.

Thus, the particular phraseology of the constitution of the United States confirms and strengthens the principle, supposed to be essential to all written constitutions, that a law repugnant to the constitution is void; and that *courts,* as well as other departments, are bound by that instrument.

The rule must be discharged.

The Power to Acquire Territory

47. The Purchase of Louisiana from France

A. CONGRESSMAN ROGER GRISWOLD OPPOSES THE ACQUISITION, 1803

Annals of Congress, 8th Cong., 1st Sess., 459-65.

I have been one of those who have long believed that the power of making treaties belongs exclusively to the President, with the consent of the Senate, and that a treaty, when constitutionally made and ratified, becomes a law, and must be executed accordingly. But it is essential to the existence of a treaty that it should be consistent with the Constitution, in every respect—both as it regards the subject-matter, and the form of ratification. If a treaty is repugnant to the Constitution, either in the matter of which it treats or in the form of ratification, it cannot be considered, within the meaning of the Constitution, a treaty. It is not within the words of the Constitution, "made under the authority of the United States,"—it is a dead letter, and void. If it shall then be found, that the instrument under consideration, contains stipulations which the Constitution does not warrant, it will result, that it cannot be respected as a treaty; that Congress, so far from being bound to carry it into execution, are obliged, by their duty and their oaths, to support the Constitution, and to refuse their assent to laws which go to infringe this great charter of our Government. . . .

I will again call the attention of the Committee to those parts of the instrument which have been noticed by other gentlemen, and which have equally excited in my mind doubts of its constitutionality. The third article of the treaty is thus expressed.

"The inhabitants of the ceded territory shall be incorporated in the union of the United States, and admitted as soon as possible, according to the principles of the Federal Constitution, to the enjoyment of all the rights, advantages and immunities of citizens of the United States; and in the mean time they shall be maintained and protected in the free enjoyment of their liberty, property, and the religion which they profess." . . .

It is, perhaps, somewhat difficult to ascertain the precise effect which it was intended to give the words which have been used in this stipulation. It is, however, clear, that it was intended to incorporate the inhabitants of the ceded territory into the Union, by the treaty itself, or to pledge the faith of the nation that such an incorporation should take place within a reasonable time. It is proper, therefore to consider the question with a reference to both constructions.

It is, in my opinion, scarcely possible

for any gentleman on this floor to advance an opinion that the President and Senate may add to the members of the Union by treaty whenever they please, or, in the words of this treaty, may "incorporate in the union of the United States" a foreign nation who, from interest or ambition, may wish to become a member of our Government. Such a power would be directly repugnant to the original compact between the States, and a violation of the principles on which that compact was formed. It has been already well observed that the union of the States was formed on the principle of a copartnership, and it would be absurd to suppose that the agents of the parties who have been appointed to execute the business of the compact, in behalf of the principals, could admit a new partner, without the consent of the parties themselves. And yet, if the first construction is assumed, such must be the case under this Constitution, and the President and Senate may admit at will any foreign nation into this copartnership without the consent of the States.

The Government of this country is formed by a union of States, and the people have declared, that the Constitution was established "to form a more perfect union of the United States." The United States here mentioned cannot be mistaken. They were the States then in existence, and such other new States as should be formed, within the then limits of the Union, conformably to the provisions of the Constitution. Every measure, therefore, which tends to infringe the perfect union of the States herein described, is a violation of the first sentiment expressed in the Constitution. The incorporation of a foreign nation into the Union, so far from tending to preserve the Union, is a direct inroad upon it; it destroys the perfect union contemplated between the original parties by interposing an alien and a stranger to share the powers of Government with them.

The Government of the United States was not formed for the purpose of distributing its principles and advantages to foreign nations. It was formed with the sole view of securing those blessings to ourselves and our posterity. It follows from these principles that no power can reside in any public functionary to contract any engagement, or to pursue any measure which shall change the Union of the States. . . . The President, with the advice of the Senate, has undoubtedly the right to form treaties, but in exercising these powers, he cannot barter away the Constitution, or the rights of particular States. It is easy to conceive that it must have been considered very important, by the original parties to the Constitution, that the limits of the United States should not be extended. The Government having been formed by a union of States, it is supposable that the fear of an undue or preponderating influence, in certain parts of this Union, must have great weight in the minds of those who might apprehend that such an influence might ultimately injure the interests of the States to which they belonged; and although they might consent to become parties to the Union, as it was then formed, it is highly probable they would never have consented to such a connexion, if a new world was to be thrown into the scale, to weigh down the influence which they might otherwise possess in the national councils.

From this view of the subject, I have been persuaded that the framers of the Constitution never intended that a power should reside in the President and Senate to form a treaty by which a foreign nation and people shall be incorporated into the Union, and that this treaty, so far as it stipulates for such an incorporation, is void . . .

Without detaining the Committee longer upon this subject, I will only observe that it is my wish that every doubt touching the constitutionality of the treaty may be removed. I do not personally feel any peculiar hostility to it. The importance of the navigation of the Mississippi, and a place of deposit at the mouth of it, has long convinced me of the necessity of adopting measures to place those objects beyond all future hazard. At the same time, I must be permitted to say, that I have not viewed the advantages from possessing the country on the west, as some gentlemen appear to have considered them. This subject was much considered during the last session of Congress, but it will not be found either in the report of the secret committee, which has recently been published, or in any document or debate, that any individual entertained the least wish to obtain the province of Louisiana; our views were then confined to New Orleans and the Floridas, and, in my judgment, it would have been happy for this country, if they were still confined within those limits. The vast and unmanageable extent which the accession of Louisiana will give to the United States; the consequent dispersion of our population, and the destruction of that balance which it is so important to maintain between the Eastern and the Western States, threatens, at no very distant day, the subversion of our Union. For these reasons, and many others which I will not detain the Committee to detail, I have doubted the policy of the treaty itself, when taken altogether; but the only points on which I feel myself at liberty to decide, are those which have been before explained, respecting the constitutionality of the treaty, and, until the doubts on these points are cleared up, I shall be compelled to vote against the resolution for carrying the treaty into execution.

B. THE UNITED STATES "POSSESSES THE POWER OF ACQUIRING TERRITORY, EITHER BY CONQUEST OR BY TREATY"

American Insurance Co. v. Canter, 1 Peters 511 (1828).

MARSHALL, C.J.: . . . The course which the argument has taken, will require, that, in deciding this question, the court should take into view the relation in which Florida stands to the United States.

The constitution confers absolutely on the government of the Union, the powers of making war, and of making treaties; consequently, that government possesses the power of acquiring territory, either by conquest or by treaty.

The usage of the world is, if a nation be not entirely subdued, to consider the holding of conquered territory as a mere military occupation, until its fate shall be determined at the treaty of peace. If it be ceded by the treaty, the acquisition is confirmed, and the ceded territory becomes a part of the nation to which it is annexed; either on the terms stipulated in the treaty of cession, or on such as its new master shall impose. On such transfer of territory, it has never been held that the relations of the inhabitants with each other undergo any change. Their relations with their former sovereign are dissolved, and new relations are created between them and the government which has acquired their territory. The same act which transfers their country, transfers the allegiance of those who remain in it; and the law, which may be denominated political, is necessarily changed, although that which regulates the intercourse and general conduct of individuals, remains in force until altered by the newly created power of the state.

On the 2d of February, 1819, Spain ceded Florida to the United States. The 6th article of the treaty of cession, contains the following provision: "The inhabitants of the territories which his Catholic Majesty cedes to the United States by this treaty, shall be incorporated in the Union of the United States, as soon as may be consistent with the principles of the federal Constitution; and admitted to the enjoyment of the privileges, rights, and immunities of the citizens of the United States."

This treaty is the law of the land, and admits the inhabitants of Florida to the enjoyment of the privileges, rights, and immunities of the citizens of the United States. It is unnecessary to inquire whether this is not their condition, independent of stipulation. They do not, however, participate in political power; they do not share in the government till Florida shall become a State. In the meantime, Florida continues to be a territory of the United States, governed by virtue of that clause in the constitution which empowers Congress "to make all needful rules and regulations, respecting the territory, or other property belonging to the United States."

Perhaps the power of governing a territory belonging to the United States, which has not, by becoming a State, acquired the means of self-government, may result necessarily from the facts that it is not within the jurisdiction of any particular State, and is within the power and jurisdiction of the United States. The right to govern, may be the inevitable consequence of the right to acquire territory. Whichever may be the source whence the power is derived, the possession of it is unquestioned. In execution of it, Congress, in 1822, passed "an act for the establishment of a territorial government in Florida," and on the 3d of March, 1823, passed another act to amend the act of 1822. Under this act, the territorial legislature enacted the law now under consideration. . . .

The Embargo and Northern Championship of States' Rights

48. Neutrality and the War of 1812

A. NULLIFICATION IN NEW ENGLAND, 1815

Resolutions of the Hartford Convention, Theodore Dwight, *History of the Hartford Convention, with a Review of the Policy . . . which led to the War of 1812* (New York, 1833), 368-78.

Nothing more can be attempted in this report than a general allusion to the principal outlines of the policy which has produced this vicissitude. Among these may be enumerated—

First.—A deliberate and extensive system for effecting a combination among certain states, by exciting local jealousies and ambition, so as to secure to popular leaders in one section of the Union, the controul of public affairs in perpetual succession. To which primary object most other characteristics of the system may be reconciled.

Secondly.—The political intolerance displayed and avowed in excluding from office men of unexceptionable merit, for want of adherence to the executive creed.

Thirdly.—The infraction of the judiciary authority and rights, by depriving judges of their offices in violation of the constitution.

Fourthly.—The abolition of existing taxes, requisite to prepare the country for those changes to which nations are always exposed, with a view to the acquisition of popular favour.

Fifthly.—The influence of patronage in the distribution of offices, which in these states has been almost invariably made among men the least entitled to such distinction, and who have sold themselves as ready instruments for distracting public opinion, and encouraging administration to hold in contempt the wishes and remonstrances of a people thus apparently divided.

Sixthly.—The admission of new states into the Union formed at pleasure in the western region, has destroyed the balance of power which existed among the original States, and deeply affected their interest.

Seventhly.—The easy admission of naturalized foreigners, to places of trust, honour or profit, operating as an inducement to the malcontent subjects of the old world to come to these States, in quest of executive patronage, and to repay it by an abject devotion to executive measures.

Eighthly.—Hostility to Great Britain, and partiality to the late government of France, adopted as coincident with popular prejudice, and subservient to the main object, party power. Connected with these must be ranked erroneous and distorted estimates of the power and resources of those nations, of the probable results of their controversies, and of our political relations to them respectively.

Lastly and principally.—A visionary and superficial theory in regard to commerce, accompanied by a real hatred but a feigned regard to its interests, and a ruinous perseverance in efforts to render it an instrument of coercion and war.

But it is not conceivable that the obliquity of any administration could, in so short a period, have so nearly consummated the work of national ruin, unless favoured by defects in the constitution.

To enumerate all the improvements of which that instrument is susceptible, and to propose such amendments as might render it in all respects perfect, would be a task which this convention has not thought proper to assume. They have confined their attention to such as experience has demonstrated to be essential, and even among these, some are considered entitled to a more serious attention than others. They are suggested without any intentional disrespect to other states, and are meant to be such as all shall find an interest in promoting. Their object is to strengthen, and if possible to perpetuate, the union of the states, by removing the grounds of existing jealousies, and providing for a fair and equal representation, and a limitation of powers, which have been misused. . . .

THEREFORE RESOLVED,

That it be and hereby is recommended to the legislatures of the several states represented in this Convention, to adopt all such measures as may be necessary effectually to protect the citizens of said states from the operation and effects of all acts which have been or may be passed by the Congress of the United States, which shall contain provisions, subjecting the militia or other citizens to forcible drafts, conscriptions, or impressments, not authorised by the constitution of the United States.

Resolved, That it be and hereby is recommended to the said Legislatures, to authorize an immediate and earnest application to be made to the government of the United States, requesting their consent to some arrangement, whereby the said states may, separately or in concert, be empowered to assume upon themselves the defence of their territory against the enemy; and a reasonable portion of the taxes, collected within said States, may be paid into the respective treasuries thereof, and appropriated to the payment of the balance due said states, and to the future defence of the same. The amount so paid into the said treasuries to be credited, and the disbursements made as aforesaid to be charged to the United States.

Resolved, That it be, and hereby is, recommended to the legislatures of the aforesaid states, to pass laws (where it has not already been done) authorizing the governors or commanders-in-chief of their militia to make detachments from the same, or to form voluntary corps, as shall be most convenient and conformable to their constitutions, and to cause the same to be well armed, equipped, and disciplined, and held in readiness for service; and upon the request of the governor of either of the other states to employ the whole of such detachment or corps, as well as the regular forces of the state, or such part thereof as may be required and can be spared consistently with the safety of the state, in assisting the state, making such request to repel any invasion thereof which shall be made or attempted by the public enemy.

Resolved, That the following amendments of the constitution of the United States be recommended to the states represented as aforesaid, to be proposed by them for adoption by the state legislatures, and in such cases as may be deemed expedient by a convention chosen by the people of each state.

And it is further recommended, that the said states shall persevere in their efforts to obtain such amendments, until the same shall be effected.

First. Representatives and direct taxes shall be apportioned among the several states which may be included within this Union, according to their respective numbers of free persons, including those bound to serve for a term of years, and excluding Indians not taxed, and all other persons.

Second. No new state shall be admitted into the Union by Congress, in virtue of the power granted by the constitution, without the concurrence of two thirds of both houses.

Third. Congress shall not have power to lay any embargo on the ships or vessels of the citizens of the United States, in the ports or harbours thereof, for more than sixty days.

Fourth. Congress shall not have power, without the concurrence of two thirds of both houses, to interdict the commercial intercourse between the United States and any foreign nation, or the dependencies thereof.

Fifth. Congress shall not make or declare war, or authorize acts of hostility against any foreign nation, without the concurrence of two thirds of both houses, except such acts of hostility be in defence of the territories of the United States when actually invaded.

Sixth. No person who shall hereafter be naturalized, shall be eligible as a member of the senate or house of representatives of the United States, nor capable of holding any civil office under the authority of the United States.

Seventh. The same person shall not be elected president of the United States a second time; nor shall the president be elected from the same state two terms in succession.

Resolved, That if the application of these states to the government of the United States, recommended in a foregoing resolution, should be unsuccessful and peace should not be concluded, and the defence of these states should be neglected, as it has since the commencement of the war, it will, in the opinion of this convention, be expedient for the legislatures of the several states to appoint delegates to another convention, to meet at Boston . . . with such powers and instructions as the exigency of a crisis so momentous may require.

B. THE PRESIDENT HAS THE POWER TO CALL FORTH THE MILITIA IN TIMES OF EMERGENCY

Martin v. Mott, 12 Wheaton 19 (1827).

STORY, J.: This is a writ of error to the judgment of the Court for the Trial of Impeachments and the Correction of Errors of the State of New York, being the highest court of that state, and is brought here in virtue of the 25th section of the Judiciary Act of 1789, ch. 20. . . .

The avowry, in substance, asserts a justification of . . . a fine and forfeiture imposed upon the original plaintiff by a court-martial, for a failure to enter the service of the United States as a militiaman, when thereto required by the President of the United States in pursuance of the act of the 28th of February, 1795. . . .

The constitution declares that Congress shall have power "to provide for calling forth the militia, to execute the laws of the Union, suppress insurrections, and repel invasions": and also "to provide for organizing, arming and disciplining the militia, and for governing such part of them as may be employed in the service of the United States." In pursuance of this authority, the act of 1795 has provided "that whenever the United States shall be invaded, or be in imminent danger of invasion from any foreign nation or Indian tribe, it shall be lawful for the President of the United States to call for such number of the militia of the State or States most convenient to the place of danger, or scene of action, as he may judge necessary to repel such invasion, and to issue his order for that purpose, to such officer or officers of the militia as he shall think proper." . . . It has not been denied here, that the act of 1795 is within the constitutional authority of Congress, or that Congress may not lawfully provide for cases of imminent danger of invasion, as well as for cases where an invasion has actually taken place. In our opinion there

is no ground for a doubt on this point, even if it had been relied on, for the power to provide for repelling invasions includes the power to provide against the attempt and danger of invasion, as the necessary and proper means to effectuate the object. One of the best means to repel invasion is to provide the requisite force for action before the invader himself has reached the soil.

The power thus confided by Congress to the President, is, doubtless, of a very high and delicate nature. A free people are naturally jealous of the exercise of military power; and the power to call the militia into actual service is certainly felt to be one of no ordinary magnitude. But it is not a power which can be executed without a correspondent responsibility. It is, in its terms, a limited power, confined to cases of actual invasion, or of imminent danger of invasion. If it be a limited power, the question arises, by whom is the exigency to be judged of and decided? Is the President the sole and exclusive judge whether the exigency has arisen, or is it to be considered as an open question, upon which every officer to whom the orders of the President are addressed, may decide for himself, and equally open to be contested by every militia-man who shall refuse to obey the orders of the President? We are all of the opinion that the authority to decide whether the exigency has arisen belongs exclusively to the President, and that his decision is conclusive upon all other persons. We think that this construction necessarily results from the nature of the power itself, and from the manifest object contemplated by the act of Congress. The power itself is to be exercised upon sudden emergencies, upon great occasions of state, and under circumstances which may be vital to the ex-

istence of the Union. A prompt and un-
hesitating obedience to orders is indispensable to the complete attainment of
the object. The service is a military service, and the command of a military nature;
and in such cases, every delay, and every
obstacle to an efficient and immediate
compliance, necessarily tends to jeopard
the public interests. While subordinate
officers or soldiers are pausing to consider
whether they ought to obey, or are scrupulously weighing the evidence of the
facts upon which the commander-in-chief
exercises the right to demand their services, the hostile enterprise may be accomplished without the means of resistance.
If "the power of regulating the militia,
and of commanding its services in times
of insurrection and invasion, are (as it has
been emphatically said they are) natural
incidents to the duties of superintending
the common defense, and of watching
over the internal peace of the confederacy," these powers must be so construed as
to the modes of their exercise as not to
defeat the great end in view. If a superior
officer has a right to contest the orders of
the President upon his own doubts as to
the exigency having arisen, it must be
equally the right of every inferior officer
and soldier; and any act done by any person in furtherance of such orders would
subject him to responsibility in a civil
suit, in which his defense must finally rest
upon his ability to establish the facts by
competent proofs. Such a course would be
subversive of all discipline, and expose the
best-disposed officers to the chances of
ruinous litigation. Besides, in many instances, the evidence upon which the President might decide that there is imminent
danger of invasion, might be of a nature
not constituting strict technical proof, or
the disclosure of the evidence might reveal important secrets of state, which the
public interest, and even safety, might imperiously demand to be kept in conceal-
ment. . . .

CHAPTER VI

The Nationalism of the Marshall Court

For a third of a century the Supreme Court was dominated by that durable Federalist, John Marshall, and his persevering nationalism. Although Governor John Jay of New York, a former Chief Justice, had rejected reappointment because the Court lacked "energy, weight, and dignity," Marshall realized the Court's potential as a co-ordinate branch of government. Long an advocate of strong central government, Marshall had played a prominent role in Virginia's ratification of the Constitution, and as Chief Justice he became the leading spokesman of national supremacy. In the delicate area of federal-state relations, he consistently championed federal authority.

In addition to *Marbury v. Madison* (Chapter V), Marshall's most important opinion during his early years on the Court was in *Fletcher v. Peck* (No. 49). Having upheld the right of the Court to review federal legislation in the first of these decisions, he established in the second the precedent of setting aside state legislation conflicting with the Constitution. In 1795 the legislature of Georgia sold 35 million acres of Western lands at the bargain price of 1½ cents an acre to a syndicate of real-estate speculators, headed by United States Senator James Gunn of Georgia. A completely corrupt transaction, the deal had been facilitated by the open bribery of a majority of the state legislature at the going rate of $1,000 a man. Interested in a quick profit, the speculators sold the land to Northern investors for approximately 14 cents an acre. An indignant Georgia electorate in

1796 replaced the corrupt legislature with new representatives who rescinded the original sale. Purchasers anxious to validate their title to the Yazoo lands, finding themselves prevented by the Eleventh Amendment from suing the State of Georgia, eventually turned to the federal courts. *Fletcher v. Peck* stands as a landmark in constitutional law for two reasons: (1) the economic importance of Marshall's interpretation of the contract clause (see Chapter VII, No. 56) and, (2) the political importance of the assertion by the federal judiciary of the right to invalidate state laws.

In subsequent decisions Marshall continued to stress national supremacy. In the famous case of *Martin v. Hunter's Lessee* (No. 50), again involving land titles, the important issue was the constitutional right of the Supreme Court to review the rulings of "the highest court of a sovereign state." In a defiant decision, Judge Spencer Roane of Virginia had denied the appellate jurisdiction of the Supreme Court and declared section 25 of the Judiciary Act of 1789 unconstitutional. Because of his personal economic interest in the land titles in the case, Marshall disqualified himself, but Justice Joseph Story defined the Court's right to review state cases dealing with the interpretation of the federal Constitution, national treaties, and federal laws.

The two Virginia antagonists, Marshall and Roane, did not tangle over this question until *Cohens v. Virginia* (No. 51). The offense, involving the sale of District of Columbia lottery tickets in violation of a Virginia statute, was trival and on the immediate issue Marshall ruled in favor of the state. At the same time, however, the case gave him a forum for expressing his broad views on the nature of the federal Union and the extent of the power of the federal judiciary.

It is altogether appropriate that the opinion regarded as Marshall's greatest state paper not only stressed national supremacy by proclaiming the doctrine of implied powers but also struck down a state statute impinging upon an agency chartered by the federal government. After the establishment of the Second Bank of the United States in 1816, Maryland imposed a heavy tax on its notes. McCulloch, a federal cashier, issued notes without paying the tax, and Maryland sued. In *McCulloch v. Maryland* (No. 52), the Court sustained the validity of the Congressional act chartering the Bank, and overruled the Maryland tax.

Like most of his nationalistic pronouncements, this decision by Marshall aroused a storm of protest. Some strict constructionists, tacitly accepting Marshall's theory of judicial review, argued against the broad doctrine of implied powers, contending that it was the Court's duty to strike down the federal law establishing the Bank. Jefferson's persistent fear of consolidation led him to characterize the Court as "constantly working under ground to undermine the foundations of our confederated fabric." On the issue of constitutional interpretation, he argued that the Court was not the exclusive arbiter, but rather one of three coordinate branches of the government. Although Jefferson formulated no systematic statement of his position, several of his letters (No. 53) indicate his alarm over the dangers of judicial power unresponsive to the popular will. The most prolific Jeffersonian advocate of decentralized government was John Taylor of Caroline. Between 1814 and 1823 he wrote four detailed treatises attacking consolidated government and opposing federal encroachments on state prerogatives. In all of these he analyzed the role of the Supreme Court in the American constitutional system, devoting five chapters to the McCulloch case in his *Construction Construed and Constitutions Vindicated* (1820). In his final book, *New Views of the Constitution* (No. 54), may be found the most complete statement of his constitutional logic.

One of the few instances of the Supreme Court limiting its jurisdiction during the Marshall era was the case of the *United States v. Hudson and Goodwin* (No. 55). Significantly enough, it was one of Jefferson's appointees, Associate Justice William Johnson, who ruled that federal common law jurisdiction was not within the implied powers of the federal courts. This rejection of inherent power in the government, according to Charles Warren, was a sound limitation on the "indefinite powers of Federal Courts."

The Supreme Court Reviews State Legislation and Judicial Decisions

49. *The Federal Judiciary Voids a State Law for the First Time*

Fletcher v. Peck, 6 Cranch 87 (1810).

MARSHALL, C. J.: . . . That the legislature of Georgia, unless restrained by its own constitution, possesses the power of disposing of the unappropriated lands within its own limits, in such manner as its own judgment shall dictate, is a proposition not to be controverted. The only question, then, presented by this demurrer, for the consideration of the court, is this, did the then constitution of the State of Georgia prohibit the legislature to dispose of the lands, which were the subject of this contract, in the manner stipulated by the contract? . . .

In the constitution of Georgia, adopted in the year 1789, the court can perceive no restriction on the legislative power, which inhibits the passage of the act of 1795. The court cannot say that, in passing that act, the legislature has tran-

scended its powers, and violated the constitution. In overruling the demurrer, therefore, to the first plea, the circuit court committed no error. . . .

That corruption should find its way into the governments of our infant republics, and contaminate the very source of legislation, or that impure motives should contribute to the passage of a law, or the formation of a legislative contract, are circumstances most deeply to be deplored. How far a court of justice would, in any case, be competent, on proceedings instituted by the State itself, to vacate a contract thus formed, and to annul rights acquired, under that contract, by third persons having no notice of the improper means by which it was obtained, is a question which the court would approach with much circumspection. . . .

In this case the legislature may have had ample proof that the original grant was obtained by practices which can never be too much reprobated, and which would have justified its abrogation so far as respected those to whom crime was imputable. But the grant, when issued, conveyed an estate in fee-simple to the grantees, clothed with all the solemnities which law can bestow. This estate was transferable; and those who purchased parts of it were not stained by that guilt which infected the original transaction. . . .

Is the power of the legislature competent to the annihilation of such title, and to a resumption of the property thus held? The principle asserted is, that one legislature is competent to repeal any act which a former legislature was competent to pass; and that one legislature cannot abridge the powers of a succeeding legislature. The correctness of this principle, so far as respects general legislation, can never be controverted. But if an act be done under a law, a succeeding legislature cannot undo it. The past cannot be recalled by the most absolute power. Conveyances have been made, those conveyances have vested legal estates, and, if those estates may be seized by the sovereign authority, still, that they originally vested is a fact, and cannot cease to be a fact. When, then, a law is in its nature a contract, when absolute rights have vested under that contract, a repeal of the law cannot divest those rights; and the act of annulling them, if legitimate, is rendered so by a power applicable to the case of every individual in the community.

It may well be doubted whether the nature of society and of the government does not prescribe some limits to the legislative power; and if any be prescribed, where are they to be found, if the property of an individual, fairly and honestly acquired, may be seized without compensation? To the legislature all legislative power is granted; but the question whether the act of transferring the property of an individual to the public be in the nature of legislative power, is well worthy of serious reflection. . . .

The validity of this rescinding act, then, might well be doubted, were Georgia a single sovereign power. But Georgia cannot be viewed as a single, unconnected, sovereign power, on whose legislature no other restrictions are imposed than may be found in its own constitution. She is a part of a large empire; she is a member of the American Union; and that union has a constitution, the supremacy of which all acknowledge, and which imposes limits to the legislatures of the several States, which none claim a right to pass. The constitution of the United States declares that no state shall pass any bill of attainder, *ex post facto* law, or law impairing the obligation of contracts.

Does the case now under consideration come within this prohibitory section of the constitution? . . .

The contract between Georgia and the purchasers was executed by the grant. A contract executed, as well as one which is executory, contains obligations binding on the parties. A grant, in its own nature, amounts to an extinguishment of the right of the grantor, and implies a contract not to reassert that right. A party is, therefore, always estopped by his own grant. . . .

Whatever respect might have been felt for the state sovereignties, it is not to be disguised that the framers of the constitution viewed, with some apprehension, the violent acts which might grow out of the feelings of the moment; and that the people of the United States, in adopting that instrument, have manifested a determination to shield themselves and their property from the effects of those sudden and strong passions to which men are exposed. The restrictions on the legislative power of the states are obviously founded in this sentiment; and the constitution of the United States contains what may be deemed a bill of rights for the people of each state. . . .

It is, then, the unanimous opinion of the court, that, in this case, the estate having passed into the hands of a purchaser for a valuable consideration, without notice, the state of Georgia was restrained, either by general principles which are common to our free institutions, or by the particular provisions of the constitution of the United States, from passing a law whereby the estate of the plaintiff in the premises so purchased could be constitutionally and legally impaired and rendered null and void. . . .

50. *The Federal Judiciary and State Judicial Decisions*

Martin v. Hunter's Lessee, 1 Wheaton 304 (1816).

STORY, J.: . . . The third article of the constitution is that which must principally attract our attention. . . .

This leads us to the consideration of the great question as to the nature and extent of the appellate jurisdiction of the United States. We have already seen that appellate jurisdiction is given by the constitution to the supreme court in all cases where it has not original jurisdiction, subject, however, to such exceptions and regulations as congress may prescribe. It is, therefore, capable of embracing every case enumerated in the constitution, which is not exclusively to be decided by way of original jurisdiction. But the exercise of appellate jurisdiction is far from being limited by the terms of the constitution to the supreme court. There can be no doubt that congress may create a succession of inferior tribunals, in each of which it may vest appellate as well as original jurisdiction. The judicial power is delegated by the constitution in the most general terms, and may, therefore, be exercised by Congress under every variety of form, of appellate or original jurisdiction. And as there is nothing in the constitution which restrains or limits this power, it must, therefore, in all other cases, subsist in the utmost latitude of which, in its own nature, it is susceptible.

As, then, by the terms of the constitution, the appellate jurisdiction is not limited as to the supreme court, and as to this court it may be exercised in all other cases than those of which it has original cognizance, what is there to restrain its exercise over state tribunals in the enumerated cases? The appellate power is not limited by the terms of the third article to any particular courts. The words are, "the judicial power (which includes appellate power) shall extend *to all cases*," &c., and "in all other cases before mentioned the supreme court shall have appellate jurisdiction." It is the *case*, then, and not *the court*, that gives the jurisdiction. If the judicial power extends to the case, it will be in vain to search in the letter of the constitution for any qualifications as to the tribunal where it depends. It is incumbent, then, upon those who assert such a qualification to show its existence by necessary implication. If the text be clear and distinct, no restriction upon its plain and obvious import ought to be admitted, unless the inference be irresistible.

If the constitution meant to limit the appellate jurisdiction to cases pending in the courts of the United States, it would necessarily follow that the jurisdiction of these courts would, in all the cases enumerated in the constitution, be exclusive of state tribunals. How otherwise could the jurisdiction extend to all cases arising under the constitution, laws, and treaties of the United States, or to all cases of admiralty and maritime jurisdiction? If some of these cases might be entertained by state tribunals, and no appellate jurisdiction as to them should exist, then the appellate power would not extend to all, but to some, cases. If state tribunals might exercise concurrent jurisdiction over all or some of the other classes of cases in the constitution without control, then the appellate jurisdiction of the United States, might, as to such cases, have no real existence, contrary to the manifest intent of the constitution. Under such circumstances, to give effect to the judicial power, it must be construed to be exclusive; and this not only when the *casus fœderis* should arise directly, but when it should arise, incidentally, in cases pending in state courts. This construction would abridge the jurisdiction of such court far more than has been ever contemplated in any act of congress.

On the other hand, if, as has been contended, a discretion be vested in congress to establish, or not to establish, inferior courts at their own pleasure, and congress should not establish such courts, the appellate jurisdiction of the supreme court would have nothing to act upon, unless it could act upon cases pending in the state courts. Under such circumstances, it must be held that the appellate power would extend to state courts; for the constitution is peremptory that it shall extend to certain enumerated cases, which cases could exist in no other courts. Any other construction, upon this supposition, would involve this strange contradiction, that a discretionary power vested in congress, and which they might rightfully omit to exercise, would defeat the absolute injunctions of the constitution in relation to the whole appellate power.

But it is plain that the framers of the constitution did contemplate that cases within the judicial cognizance of the United States not only might but would arise in the state courts, in the exercise of their ordinary jurisdiction. With this view the sixth article declares, that "this constitution, and the laws of the United States which shall be made in pursuance thereof, and all treaties made, or which shall be made, under the authority of the United States, shall be the supreme law of the land, and the judges in every State shall be bound thereby, anything in the constitution, or laws of any State to the contrary notwithstanding." It is obvious that this obligation is imperative upon the state judges in their official, and not merely in their private, capacities. From the very nature of their judicial duties they would be called upon to pronounce the law applicable to the case in judgment. They were not to decide merely according to the laws or constitution of the State, but according to the constitution, laws, and treaties of the United States, "the supreme law of the land." . . .

It must, therefore, be conceded that the constitution not only contemplated, but meant to provide for cases within the scope of the judicial power of the United States, which might yet depend before state tribunals. It was foreseen that in the exercise of their ordinary jurisdiction, state courts would incidentally take cognizance of cases arising under the constitution, the laws, and treaties of the United States. Yet to all these cases the judicial power, by the very terms of the constitution, is to extend. It cannot extend by original jurisdiction if that was already rightfully and exclusively attached in the state courts, which (as has been already shown) may occur; it must therefore extend by appellate jurisdiction, or not at all. It would seem to follow that the appellate power of the United States must, in such cases, extend to state tribunals; and if in such cases, there is no reason why it should not equally attach upon all others within the purview of the constitution. . . .

On the whole, the court are of opinion, that the appellate power of the United States does extend to cases pending in the state courts; and that the 25th section of the Judiciary Act, which authorizes the exercise of this jurisdiction in the specified cases, by a writ of error, is supported by the letter and spirit of the constitution. We find no clause in that instrument which limits this power; and we dare not interpose a limitation where the people have not been disposed to create one. . . .

It is the opinion of the whole court, that the judgment of the court of appeals of Virginia, rendered on the mandate in this cause, be reversed. . . .

51. "A constitution is framed for ages to come."

Cohens v. Virginia, 6 Wheaton 264 (1821).

MARSHALL, C. J.: . . . The American States, as well as the American people, have believed a close and firm Union to be essential to their liberty and to their happiness. They have been taught by experience, that this Union cannot exist without a government for the whole; and they have been taught by the same experience that this government would be a mere shadow, that must disappoint all their hopes, unless invested with large portions of that sovereignty which belongs to independent States. Under the influence of this opinion, and thus instructed by experience, the American people, in the conventions of their respective States, adopted the present constitution.

If it could be doubted whether, from its nature, it were not supreme in all cases where it is empowered to act, that doubt would be removed by the declaration that "this constitution, and the laws of the United States which shall be made in pursuance thereof, and all treaties made, or which shall be made, under the authority of the United States, shall be the supreme law of the land; and the judges in every State shall be bound thereby, anything in the constitution or laws of any State to the contrary notwithstanding."

This is the authoritative language of the American people; and, if gentlemen please, of the American States. It marks with lines too strong to be mistaken, the characteristic distinction between the government of the Union and those of the States. The general government, though limited as to its objects, is supreme with respect to those objects. This principle is a part of the constitution; and if there be any who deny its necessity, none can deny its authority.

To this supreme government ample powers are confided; and if it were possible to doubt the great purposes for which they were so confided, the people of the United States have declared that they are given "in order to form a more perfect union, establish justice, insure domestic tranquility, provide for the common defense, promote the general welfare, and secure the blessings of liberty to themselves and their posterity."

With the ample powers confided to this supreme government, for these interesting purposes, are connected many express and important limitations on the sovereignty of the States, which are made for the same purposes. The powers of the Union on the great subjects of war, peace, and commerce, and on many others, are in themselves limitations of the sovereignty of the States; but in addition to these, the sovereignty of the States is surrendered in many instances where the surrender can only operate to the benefit of the people, and where, perhaps, no other power is conferred on Congress than a conservative power to maintain the principles established in the constitution. The maintenance of these principles in their purity is certainly among the great duties of the government. One of the instruments by which this duty may be peaceably performed is the judicial department. It is authorized to decide all cases, of every description, arising under the constitution or laws of the United States. From this general grant of jurisdiction, no exception is made of those cases in which a State may be a party. When we consider the situation of the government of the Union and of a State, in relation to each other; the nature of our constitution, the subordination of the state governments to the constitution; the great purpose for which jurisdiction over all cases arising under the constitution and laws of the United States, is confided to the judicial department, are we at liberty to insert in this general grant, an exception of those cases in which a State may be a party? Will the spirit of the constitution justify this attempt to control its words? We think it will not. We think a case arising under the constitution or laws of the United States, is cognizable in the courts of the Union, whoever may be the parties to that case. . . .

The second objection to the jurisdiction of the court is, that its appellate power cannot be exercised, in any case, over the judgment of a state court. . . .

That the United States form, for many, and for most important purposes, a single nation, has not yet been denied. In war, we are one people. In making peace, we are one people. In all commercial regulations, we are one and the same people. In many other respects, the American people are one; and the government which is alone capable of controlling and managing their interests, in all these respects, is the government of the Union. It is their government, and in that character they have no other. America has chosen to be, in many respects, and to many purposes, a nation; and for all these purposes her government is complete; to all these objects, it is competent. The people have declared, that in the exercise of all powers given for these objects, it is supreme. It

can, then, in effecting these objects, legitimately control all individuals or governments within the American territory. The constitution and laws of a State, so far as they are repugnant to the constitution and laws of the United States, are absolutely void. These States are constituent parts of the United States. They are members of one great empire—for some purposes sovereign, for some purposes subordinate.

In a government so constituted, is it unreasonable that the judicial power should be competent to give efficacy to the constitutional laws of the legislature? That department can decide on the validity of the constitution or law of a State, if it be repugnant to the constitution or to a law of the United States. Is it unreasonable that it should also be empowered to decide on the judgment of a state tribunal enforcing such unconstitutional law? Is it so very unreasonable as to furnish a justification for controlling the words of the constitution?

We think it is not. We think that in a government acknowledgedly supreme, with respect to objects of vital interest to the nation, there is nothing inconsistent with sound reason, nothing incompatible with the nature of government, in making all its departments supreme, so far as respects those objects, and so far as is necessary to their attainment. The exercise of the appellate power over those judgments of the state tribunals which may contravene the constitution or laws of the United States, is, we believe, essential to the attainment of those objects. . . .

Liberal Construction and National Supremacy

52. *The Doctrine of Implied Powers*

McCulloch v. Maryland, 4 Wheaton 316 (1819).

MARSHALL, C.J.: . . . The first question made in the cause is, has congress power to incorporate a bank? . . .

This government is acknowledged by all to be one of enumerated powers. The principle, that it can exercise only the powers granted to it, would seem too apparent to have required to be enforced by all those arguments which its enlightened friends, while it was depending before the people, found it necessary to urge. That principle is now universally admitted. But the question respecting the extent of the powers actually granted, is perpetually arising, and will probably continue to arise, so long as our system shall exist.

In discussing these questions, the conflicting powers of the general and State governments must be brought into view, and the supremacy of their respective laws, when they are in opposition, must be settled.

If any one proposition could command the universal assent of mankind, we might expect it would be this—that the government of the Union, though limited in its powers, is supreme within its sphere of action. This would seem to result necessarily from its nature. It is the government of all; its powers are delegated by all; it represents all, and acts for all. Though any one State may be willing to control its operations, no State is willing to allow others to control them. The nation, on those subjects on which it can act, must necessarily bind its component parts. But this question is not left to mere reason: the people have, in express terms, decided it, by saying, "this constitution, and the laws of the United States, which shall be made in pursuance thereof," "shall be the supreme law of the land," and by requiring that the members of the State legislatures, and the officers of the executive and judicial departments of the States, shall take the oath of fidelity to it.

The government of the United States, then, though limited in its powers, is supreme; and its laws, when made in pursuance of the constitution, form the supreme law of the land, "anything in the constitution or laws of any State to the contrary notwithstanding." . . .

Although, among the enumerated powers of government, we do not find the word "bank" or "incorporation," we find the great powers to lay and collect taxes; to borrow money; to regulate commerce; to declare and conduct a war; and to raise and support armies and navies. The sword and the purse, all the external relations, and no inconsiderable portion of the industry of the nation, are entrusted to its government. It can never be pretended that these vast powers draw after them others of inferior importance, merely because they are inferior. Such an idea can never be advanced. But it may, with great reason, be contended, that a government, intrusted with such ample powers, on the due execution of which the happiness and prosperity of the nation so vitally depends, must also be intrusted with ample means for their execution. The power being given, it is the interest of the nation to facilitate its execution. It can never be their interest, and cannot be presumed to have been their intention, to clog and embarrass its execution by withholding the most appropriate means. Throughout this vast republic, from the St. Croix to the Gulf of Mexico, from the Atlantic to the Pacific, revenue is to be collected and expended, armies are to be marched and supported. The exigencies of the nation may require that the treasure raised in the North should be transported to the South, that raised in the East conveyed to the West, or that this order should be reversed. Is that construction of the constitution to be preferred which would render these operations difficult, hazardous, and expensive? Can we adopt that construction (unless the words imperiously require it) which would impute to the framers of that instrument, when granting these powers for the public good, the intention of impeding their exercise by withholding a choice of means? If, indeed, such be the mandate of the constitution, we have only to obey; but that instrument does not profess to enumerate the means by which the powers it confers may be executed; nor does it prohibit the creation of a corporation, if the existence of such a being be essential to the beneficial exercise of those powers. It is, then, the subject of fair inquiry, how far such means may be employed. . . .

But the constitution of the United States has not left the right of congress to employ the necessary means, for the execution of the powers conferred on the government, to general reasoning. To its enumeration of powers is added that of making "all laws which shall be necessary and proper, for carrying into execution the foregoing powers, and all other powers vested by this constitution in the government of the United States, or in any department thereof." . . .

The argument on which most reliance is placed is drawn from the peculiar language of this clause. Congress is not empowered by it to make all laws, which may have relation to the powers conferred on the government, but such only as may be "necessary and proper" for carrying them into execution. The word "necessary" is considered as controlling the whole sentence, and as limiting the right to pass laws for the execution of the granted powers, to such as are indispensable, and without which the power would be nugatory. That it excludes the choice of means, and leaves to congress, in each case, that only which is most direct and simple.

Is it true, that this is the sense in which the word "necessary" is always used? Does it always import an absolute physical necessity, so strong that one thing, to which another may be termed necessary, cannot exist without that other? We think it does not. If reference be had to its use, in the common affairs of the world, or in approved authors, we find that it frequently imports no more than that one thing is convenient, or useful, or essential to another. To employ the means necessary to an end, is generally understood as employing any means calculated to produce the end, and not as being confined to those single means, without which the end would be entirely unattainable. . . . This word, then, like others, is used in various senses; and, in its construction, the subject, the context, the intention of the person using them, are all to be taken into view.

Let this be done in the case under consideration. The subject is the execution of those great powers on which the welfare of a nation essentially depends. It must have been the intention of those who gave these powers, to insure, as far as human prudence could insure, their beneficial execution. This could not be done by confiding the choice of means to such narrow limits as not to leave it in the power of congress to adopt any which might be appropriate, and which were conducive to the end. This provision is made in a constitution intended to endure for ages to come, and, consequently, to be adapted to the various *crises* of human affairs. To have prescribed the means by which government should, in all future time, execute its powers, would have been to change, entirely, the character of the instrument, and give it the properties of a legal code. It would have been an unwise attempt to provide, by immutable rules, for exigencies which, if foreseen at all, must have been seen dimly, and which can be best provided for as they occur. To have declared that the best means shall not be used, but those alone without which the power given would be nugatory, would have been to deprive the legislature of the capacity to avail itself of experience, to exercise its reason, and to accommodate its legislation to circumstances. . . .

The result of the most careful and attentive consideration bestowed upon this clause is, that if it does not enlarge, it cannot be construed to restrain the powers of Congress, or to impair the right of the legislature to exercise its best judgment in the selection of measures to carry into execution the constitutional powers of the government. If no other motive for its insertion can be suggested, a sufficient one is found in the desire to remove all doubts respecting the right to legislate on that vast mass of incidental powers which must be involved in the constitution, if that instrument be not a splendid bauble.

We admit, as all must admit, that the powers of the government are limited, and that its limits are not to be transcended. But we think the sound construction of the constitution must allow to the national legislature that discretion, with respect to the means by which the powers it confers are to be carried into execution, which will enable that body to perform the high duties assigned to it, in the manner most beneficial to the people. Let the end be legitimate, let it be within the scope of the constitution, and all means which are appropriate, which are plainly adapted to that end, which are not prohibited, but consist with the letter and spirit of the constitution, are constitutional. . . .

After the most deliberate consideration, it is the unanimous and decided opinion of this court, that the act to incorporate the Bank of the United States is a law made in pursuance of the constitution, and is a part of the supreme law of the land. . . .

It being the opinion of the Court, that the act incorporating the bank is constitutional; and that the power of establishing a branch in the State of Maryland might be properly exercised by the bank itself, we proceed to inquire—

2. Whether the State of Maryland may, without violating the constitution, tax that branch?

That the power of taxation is one of vital importance; that it is retained by the States; that it is not abridged by the grant of a similar power to the government of the Union; that it is to be concurrently exercised by the two governments: are truths which have never been denied. But, such is the paramount character of the constitution, that its capacity to withdraw any subject from the action of even this power, is admitted. The States are expressly forbidden to lay any duties on imports or exports. . . . If the obligation of this prohibition must be conceded . . . , the same paramount character . . . certainly may restrain a state from such other exercise of this power, as is in its nature incompatible with, and repugnant to, the constitutional laws of the Union. A law, absolutely repugnant to another, as entirely repeals the other as if express terms of repeal were used.

On this ground the counsel for the bank place its claim to be exempted from the power of a State to tax its operations. . . .

That the power to tax involves the power to destroy; that the power to destroy may defeat and render useless the power to create; that there is a plain repugnance, in conferring on one government a power to control the constitutional measures of another, which other, with respect to those very measures, is declared to be supreme over that which exerts the control, are propositions not to be denied. But all inconsistencies are to be reconciled by the magic of the word Confidence. Taxation, it is said, does not necessarily and unavoidably destroy. To carry it to the excess of destruction would be an abuse, to presume which, would banish that confidence which is essential to all government.

But is this a case of confidence? Would the people of any one State trust those of another with a power to control the most insignificant operations of their State government? We know they would not. Why, then, should we suppose that the people of any one State should be willing to trust those of another with a power to control the operations of a government to which they have confided their most important and most valuable interests? In the legislature of the Union alone, are all represented. The legislature of the Union alone, therefore, can be trusted by the people with the power of controlling measures which concern all, in the confidence that it will not be abused. This, then, is not a case of confidence, and we must consider it as it really is.

If we apply the principle for which the State of Maryland contends, to the constitution generally, we shall find it capable of changing totally the character of that instrument. We shall find it capable of arresting all the measures of the government, and of prostrating it at the foot of the states. The American people have declared their constitution, and the laws made in pursuance thereof, to be supreme; but this principle would transfer the supremacy, in fact, to the States.

If the States may tax one instrument, employed by the government in the execution of its powers, they may tax any and every other instrument. They may tax the mail; they may tax the mint; they may tax patent rights; they may tax the papers of the custom-house; they may tax judicial process; they may tax all the means employed by the government, to an excess which would defeat all the ends of government. This was not intended by the American people. They did not design to make their government dependent on the States. . . .

This is not all. If the controlling power of the States be established; if their supremacy as to taxation be acknowledged; what is to restrain their exercising this control in any shape they may please to give it? Their sovereignty is not confined to taxation. That is not the only mode in which it might be displayed. The question is, in truth, a question of supremacy; and if the right of the States to tax the means employed by the general government be conceded, the declaration that the constitution, and the laws made in pursuance thereof, shall be the supreme law of the land, is empty and unmeaning declamation. . . .

The court has bestowed on this subject its most deliberate consideration. The result is a conviction that the States have no power, by taxation or otherwise, to retard, impede, burden, or in any manner control, the operations of the constitutional laws enacted by congress to carry into execution the powers vested in the general government. This is, we think, the unavoidable consequence of that supremacy which the constitution has declared.

We are unanimously of opinion, that the law passed by the legislature of Maryland, imposing a tax on the Bank of the United States, is unconstitutional and void. . . .

Nationalism and States' Rights

53. *Jefferson: The judiciary is a "subtle corps of sappers and miners."*

A. JEFFERSON TO W. H. TORRANCE, JUNE 11, 1815

Ford, ed., *Writings of Thomas Jefferson*, IX, 517-19

The . . . question, whether the judges are invested with exclusive authority to decide on the constitutionality of a law, has been heretofore a subject of consideration with me in the exercise of official duties. Certainly there is not a word in the constitution which has given that power to them more than to the executive or legislative branches. Questions of property, of character and of crime being ascribed to the judges, through a definite course of legal proceeding, laws involving such questions belong, of course, to them; and as they decide on them ultimately and without appeal, they of course decide *for themselves*. The constitutional validity of the law or laws again prescribing executive action, and to be administered by that branch ultimately and without appeal, the executive must decide *for themselves* also, whether, under the constitution, they are valid or not. So also as to laws governing the proceedings of the legislature, that body must judge *for itself* the constitutionality of the law, and equally without appeal or control from its co-ordinate branches. And, in general, that branch which is to act ultimately, and without appeal, on any law, is the rightful expositor of the validity of the law, uncontrolled by the opinions of the other co-ordinate authorities. It may be said that contradictory decisions may arise in such case, and pro-

duce inconvenience. This is possible, and is a necessary failing in all human proceedings. Yet the prudence of the public functionaries, and authority of public opinion, will generally produce accommodation. . . . This is what I believe myself to be sound. But there is another opinion entertained by some men of such judgment and information as to lessen my confidence in my own. That is, that the legislature alone is the exclusive expounder of the sense of the constitution, in every part of it whatever. And they allege in its support, that this branch has authority to impeach and punish a member of either of the others acting contrary to its declaration of the sense of the constitution. It may indeed be answered, that an act may still be valid although the party is punished for it, right or wrong. However, this opinion which ascribes exclusive exposition to the legislature, merits respect for its safety, there being in the body of the nation a control over them, which, if expressed by rejection on the subsequent exercise of their elective franchise, enlists public opinion against their exposition, and encourages a judge or executive on a future occasion to adhere to their former opinion. Between these two doctrines, every one has a right to choose, and I know of no third meriting any respect. . . .

B. JEFFERSON TO JUDGE SPENCER ROANE, SEPTEMBER 6, 1819

Ford, *Writings of Thomas Jefferson*, X, 140-3.

I had read in the Enquirer, and with great approbation, the pieces signed Hampden, and have read them again with redoubled approbation, in the copies you have been so kind as to send me. I subscribe to every tittle of them. They contain the true principles of the revolution of 1800, for that was as real a revolution in the principles of our government as that of 1776 was in its form; not effected indeed by the sword, as that, but by the rational and peaceable instrument of reform, the suffrage of the people. The nation declared its will by dismissing functionaries of one principle, and electing those of another, in the two branches, executive and legislative, submitted to their election. Over the judiciary department, the constitution had deprived them of their control. That, therefore, has continued the reprobated system, and although new matter has been occasionally incorporated into the old, yet the leaven of the old mass seems to assimilate to itself the new, and after twenty years' confirmation of the federal system by the voice of the nation, declared through the medium of elections, we find the judiciary on every occasion, still driving us into consolidation.

In denying the right they usurp of exclusively explaining the constitution, I go further than you do, if I understand rightly your quotation from the *Federalist*, of an opinion that "the judiciary is the last resort in relation *to the other departments* of the government, but not in relation to the rights of the parties to the compact under which the judiciary is derived." If this opinion be sound, then indeed is our constitution a complete *felo de se*. For intending to establish three departments, coordinate and independent, that they might check and balance one another, it has given, according to this opinion, to one of them alone, the right to prescribe rules for the government of the others, and to that one too, which is unelected by, and independent of the nation. . . . The constitution, on this hypothesis, is a mere thing of wax in the hands of the judiciary, which they may twist and shape into any form they please. . . . My construction of the constitution is very different from that you quote. It is that each department is truly independent of the others, and has an equal right to decide for itself what is the meaning of the constitution in the cases submitted to its action; and especially, where it is to act ultimately and without appeal. . . .

54. The Constitution did not create "a concentrated supremacy in the federal government."

John Taylor, *New Views of the Constitution of the United States* (Washington, 1823), 18-19, 36-7, 143, 163-5, 238-9, 241, 244-6.

It can never be conceived that the principle of a negative over state laws . . . had silently crept into the constitution. This was quite consistent with the national form of government proposed, but quite inconsistent with the federal form adopted. . . .

Revived by construction, it assumes a far more formidable and consolidating aspect than as it was originally offered, because the usurped negative over state laws, by a majority of a court or of Congress, would not have its malignity to the states alleviated by the checks to which the project itself resorted. Without these checks, even the advocates for a national form of government thought such a negative intolerable. The project contemplated a mixed legislative, executive, and judicial supremacy over state laws, so that one department of this sovereignty, like that of the English, might check the other, in construing "the articles of the union," and did not venture even to propose, that a government should be established, in which a single court was to be invested with a supreme power over these articles, or the constitution. The idea seems to be a political monster never seen in fable or in fact. . . .

Sovereignty is the highest degree of political power, and the establishment of a form of government, the highest proof which can be given of its existence. The states could not have reserved any rights by the articles of their union, if they had not been sovereign, because they could have no rights unless they flowed from that source. In the creation of the federal government, the states exercised the highest act of sovereignty, and they may, if they please, repeat the proof of their sovereignty, by its annihilation. But the union possesses no innate sovereignty, like the states; it was not self-constituted; it is conventional, and of course subordinate to the sovereignties by which it was formed. . . . I have no idea of a sovereignty constituted upon better ground than that of each state, nor of one which can be pretended to on worse, than that claimed for the federal government, or some portion of it. . . . The sovereignties which imposed the limitations upon the federal government, far from supposing that they perished by the exercise of a part of their faculties, were vindicated, by reserving powers in which their deputy, the federal government, could not participate; and the usual right of sovereigns to alter or revoke its commissions. . . .

The federal legislative and judicial powers are both plainly intended to be limited by the constitution, and any mode by which this limitation can be evaded, must destroy our federal system, or be destroyed by it. If Congress can give a judicial supremacy to a federal court, the federal legislative power must be itself supreme, and may extend its boundary to the executive also. . . .

There are some principles necessary for the existence of the political system of the United States. One of these is, the supremacy, both of the state and federal constitutions, over the repositories of power created by their articles. Another, that this is a limited supremacy in both cases, subject in one, to the supremacy of the people in each state, and in the other, to the supremacy of three-fourths of the states. And a third, that no power created by these constitutions, can violate their articles, or evade the supremacies to which the constitutions are themselves subject. From these principles it results, that neither laws nor judgments are valid, which do not conform to constitutions; and that a mutual control of political departments, is the only mode of enforcing this doctrine, necessary to sustain both the supremacy of constitutions, and of those who make them. The federal judges do not take an oath to obey the state constitutions, because, as they derive no jurisdiction from them, there is no privity between the rights and powers which they establish, and these judges. If the federal courts could abridge these rights and powers, it would defeat the principle of the supremacy of the people of each state, over their constitutions. This would vitally destroy the federal compact, supposed to exist between republicks, because the states would not be republicks, if their constitutions were made subordinate to the will or the power of the court, instead of being only subordinate to the will or power of the people. . . . As state constitutions are subject to the supremacy of the people of each state, and the federal constitution to three-fourths of the states, neither are subject to laws or judgments state or federal, or to a consolidated American nation. A supremacy in a federal court to construe the articles of the declaration of independence, and of the federal and state constitutions, united with a power to enforce its constructions, would as effectually destroy the supremacy of the people, and of three-fourths of the states, as the same species of supreme power in state legislatures would destroy the supremacy of state constitutions, and of the people of each state.

If the constitution of a state should be so altered, as to bestow on the legislature a supreme power of construing its articles, and excluding the judiciary from the right or the duty of disobeying unconstitutional laws; or if the constitution of the United States should invest the federal judiciary with the same supreme power as to the construction of the federal constitution; the principles, necessary for the existence of our political system, would be abolished, and both the federal and state governments would substantially be reinstated, according to the English policy, by which the government itself can modify its own powers. . . .

The objection, that the state governments may obstruct federal supremacy,

unless they are subordinate to some federal supremacy, is only equivalent to the objection that the federal government may obstruct state measures, unless it is subordinate to a state supremacy. . . . Reason, compact, and a common interest, and not a supreme power, are the only resources for settling such collisions, compatible with a division of power. . . .

Society, well constructed, must be compounded of restraint and freedom, and this was carefully attended to in framing our union. . . . Freedom without restraint, or restraint without freedom, is either anarchy or despotism. . . . A concentrated power destroys the counterpoise between freedom and restraint, and never fails to become the executioner of human happiness. The constitution, with consummate wisdom, has effected this counterpoise, and also provided against foreign and state collisions, without sacrificing state prosperity. It did not design to embitter the best fruits of government, by tacitly creating a concentrated supremacy. . . .

Limitations of Judicial Authority

55. Is there a federal common law jurisdiction?

U. S. v. Hudson and Goodwin, 7 Cranch 32 (1812).

JOHNSON, J.: The only question which this case presents is, whether the circuit courts of the United States can exercise a common law jurisdiction in criminal cases. We state it thus broadly because a decision on a case of libel will apply to every case in which jurisdiction is not vested in those courts by statute.

Although this question is brought up now for the first time to be decided by

this court, we consider it as having been long since settled in public opinion. In no other case for many years has this jurisdiction been asserted; and the general acquiescence of legal men shews the prevalence of opinion in favor of the negative of the proposition.

The course of reasoning which leads to this conclusion is simple, obvious, and admits of but little illustration. The powers of the general government are made up of concessions from the several States—whatever is not expressly given to the former, the latter expressly reserve. The judicial power of the United States is a constituent part of those concessions—that power is to be exercised by courts organized for the purpose, and brought into existence by an effort of the legislative power of the Union. Of all the courts which the United States may, under their general powers, constitute, one only, the supreme court, possesses jurisdiction derived immediately from the constitution, and of which the legislative power cannot deprive it. All other courts created by the general government possess no jurisdiction but what is given them by the power that creates them, and can be vested with none but what the power ceded to the general government will authorize them to confer.

It is not necessary to inquire whether the general government, in any and what extent, possesses the power of conferring on its courts a jurisdiction in cases similar to the present; it is enough that such jurisdiction has not been conferred by any legislative act, if it does not result to those courts as a consequence of their creation.

And such is the opinion of the majority of this court. For, the power which congress possess to create Courts of inferior jurisdiction, necessarily implies the power to limit the jurisdiction of those courts to particular objects; and when a court is created, and its operations confined to certain specific objects, with what propriety can it assume to itself a jurisdiction—much more extended—in its nature very indefinite—applicable to a great variety of subjects—varying in every State in the Union—and with regard to which there exists no definite criterion of distribution between the district and circuit courts of the same district?

The only ground on which it has ever been contended that this jurisdiction could be maintained is, that, upon the formation of any political body, an implied power to preserve its own existence and promote the end and object of its creation, necessarily results to it. But without examining how far this consideration is applicable to the peculiar character of our constitution, it may be remarked that it is a principle by no means peculiar to the common law. It is coeval, probably, with the first formation of a limited government; belongs to a system of universal law, and may as well support the assumption of many other powers as those more peculiarly acknowledged by the common law of England.

But if admitted as applicable to the state of things in this country, the consequence would not result from it which is here contended for. If it may communicate certain implied powers to the general government, it would not follow that the courts of that government are vested with jurisdiction over any particular act done by an individual in supposed violation of the peace and dignity of the sovereign power. The legislative authority of the Union must first make an act a crime, affix a punishment to it, and declare the court that shall have jurisdiction of the offence.

Certain implied powers must necessarily result to our courts of justice from the nature of their institution. But jurisdiction of crimes against the State is not among those powers. To fine for contempt—imprison for contumacy—inforce the observance of order, etc., are powers which cannot be dispensed with in a court, because they are necessary to the exercise of all others; and so far our courts no doubt possess powers not immediately derived from statute; but all exercise of criminal jurisdiction in common law cases we are of opinion is not within their implied powers.

CHAPTER VII

The Marshall Court,
Constitutional Machinery,
and Economic Policy

THE Constitution was framed by men familiar with the economic as well as the political shortcomings of the Confederation era. They were therefore careful to incorporate safeguards of individual enterprise including centralized control over currency, prohibitions on state legal-tender laws, protection against impairment of the obligation of contracts, provision for bankruptcy laws, and the guarantee of inventive rights through patent and copyright monopolies for limited periods. In the decades before the Civil War, adjudication in the courts was the chief instrument of government influence on the expanding American economy. The first case interpreting the impairment of contract clause was *Fletcher v. Peck* (No. 56), the political aspects of which were discussed in Chapter VI. There the Court held that the corrupt Yazoo land grant constituted a contract and could not be canceled by subsequent state legislation. By ruling that the contract clause made no distinction between private and public contracts, Marshall began the process of extending the protection of the clause far beyond the intention of the Framers. Although he was quite sure that the land grant was a contract, he did not know exactly why the rescinding act was invalid. Indeed, the concluding paragraph of his opinion cites no specific constitutional clause, asserting rather that "the State of Georgia was restrained, either by general principles, which are common to our free institutions, or by the particular provisions of the constitution of the United States."

Within two years in *New Jersey v. Wilson* (1812) Marshall explicitly extended the contract clause to sanctify and perpetuate a state exemption from taxation, sacrificing a vital state financial power in order to protect the vested rights of property. The climax of the process of expanding the contract clause came in the famous Dartmouth College case (No. 57). Ruling that a corporate charter is a contract, the Marshall Court in effect placed charters of private corporations, economic as well as educational, outside of control by the state that chartered them. This construction of the contract clause protected the corporate form of industry from state regulation during its early years of growth, serving as business's principle legal weapon against legislative interference until it was superseded by the due process clause of the Fourteenth Amendment.

In addition to the contract clause, Marshall also gave an expansive interpretation to the commerce clause. One of the most far-reaching decisions of the aging Chief Justice was *Gibbons v. Ogden* (No. 58). This popular ruling, which struck a blow at a transportation monopoly, was the first interstate commerce controversy since the Potomac meetings that resulted in a call for the Constitutional Convention in 1787. The case involved state powers under the commerce clause, but Marshall chose to give a sweeping definition of federal control, indicating that it encompassed "every species of commercial intercourse." Although he did not state flatly that congressional power was exclusive, neither did he define the extent of state power in the absence of federal legislation. The practical effect, like that of the Dartmouth College case, was to free economic enterprise, in this instance, transportation, from state restraints.

In *Brown v. Maryland* (No. 59) Marshall partially defined the line between state and federal control of commerce, formulating the technical but important "original package" doctrine. In his thirty-four years on the Court, Marshall ruled on only one other commerce case, *Willson v. Blackbird Creek Marsh Company* (1829). The Chief Justice upheld a state regulation affecting interstate commerce, ruling that in the absence of federal action the local regulation was valid. It is clear, however, that state power was sustained by sufferance of the Court, which alone was to serve as arbiter of the federal system.

Marshall's decisions on the commerce cases were consistent with his opinions in other areas of constitutional law. All his rulings asserted and defended broad construction, and they upheld the power of the national government within the areas delegated to it. In his decisive delineations of limitations on the states, he emphatically upheld the right of the Court to review both state legislation and state judicial decisions that threatened to infringe on constitutional grants. Moreover, he stretched constitutional restrictions on the states to protect property from legislative interference. In no less than thirteen cases did he set aside state laws as contrary to constitutional principles, but only in *Worcester v. Georgia* was his decision openly flouted.

Andrew Jackson also disagreed with Marshall's ruling in the McCulloch case, but the President battled the Bank of the United States in the political rather than in the judicial arena. In his veto of a congressional enactment extending the life of the Bank (No. 60), Jackson not only denied its constitutionality but also took "a stand against all new grants of monopolies and exclusive privileges, against any prostitution of our government to the advancement of the few at the expense of the many." This attack on corporate capitalism—"a concentration of power," Jackson said, "in the hands of a few men irresponsible to the people"—was greeted by the *Washington Globe* as a second Declaration of Independence which freed the country from the grasp of a moneyed monopoly.

After Jackson's re-election in 1832, he attempted to implement the provision of the Bank charter which authorized the removal of the public funds at the discretion of the Secretary of the Treasury. Interpreting this clause as vesting discretion in them, rather than in the President, two Secretaries refused to order the removal. Jackson finally appointed a bitter anti-Bank Democrat, Roger B. Taney, shortly to become Marshall's successor as Chief Justice of the Supreme Court. In a noteworthy statement drafted by Taney, the President read to his Cabinet a paper (No. 61) giving his reasons for the removal and defining the responsibilities of a cabinet official in the American constitutional framework. When President Jackson refused to comply with a Senate request for a copy of this paper, that body, controlled by the Whigs, passed resolutions censuring the administration's Bank policy. Jackson's message of protest to the Senate (No. 62) was a classic formulation of the scope of presidential authority, stressing the idea of the President as the direct and immediate representative of the American people and of the nation as a whole; in short, it is a concise definition of Jacksonian Democracy.

The Contract Clause and Early Corporations

56. "A compact between two or more parties."

Fletcher v. Peck, 6 Cranch 87 (1810).

MARSHALL, C. J.: . . . When . . . a law is in its nature a contract, when absolute rights have vested under that contract, a repeal of the law cannot divest those rights; and the act of annulling them, if legitimate, is rendered so by a power applicable to the case of every individual in the community. . . .

We immediately ask ourselves what is a contract? Is a grant a contract? A contract is a compact between two or more parties, and is either executory or executed. An executory contract is one in which a party binds himself to do, or not to do, a particular thing; such was the

law under which the conveyance was made by the governor. A contract executed is one in which the object of contract is performed; and this, says Blackstone, differs in nothing from a grant. . . .

Since, then, in fact, a grant is a contract executed, the obligation of which still continues, and since the constitution uses the general term contract, without distinguishing between those which are executory and those which are executed, it must be construed to comprehend the latter as well as the former. . . .

If, under a fair construction of the constitution, grants are comprehended under the term "contracts," is a grant from the State excluded from the operation of the provision? Is the clause to be considered as inhibiting the State from impairing the obligation of contracts between two individuals, but as excluding from that inhibition contracts made with itself? The words themselves contain no such distinction. They are general, and are applicable to contracts of every description. If contracts made with the State are to be exempted from their operation, the exception must arise from the character of the contracting party, not from the words which are employed. . . .

57. *Constitutional Protection of Corporation Charters*

Dartmouth College v. Woodward, 4 Wheaton 518 (1819).

MARSHALL, C. J.: . . . On the judges of this Court . . . is imposed the high and solemn duty of protecting, from even legislative violation, those contracts which the Constitution of our country has placed beyond legislative control; and, however irksome the task may be, this is a duty from which we dare not shrink. . . .

It can require no argument to prove, that the circumstances of this case constitute a contract. An application is made to the crown for a charter to incorporate a religious and literary institution. In the application it is stated that large contributions have been made for the object, which will be conferred on the corporation as soon as it shall be created. The charter is granted, and on its faith the property is conveyed. Surely, in this transaction, every ingredient of a complete and legitimate contract is to be found.

The points for consideration are, 1. Is this contract protected by the constitution of the United States? 2. Is it impaired by the acts under which the defendant holds? . . .

If the act of incorporation be a grant of political power, if it create a civil institution to be employed in the administration of the government, or if the funds of the college be public property, or if the State of New Hampshire, as a government, be alone interested in its transactions, the subject is one in which the legislature of the State may act according to its own judgment, unrestrained by any limitation of its power imposed by the constitution of the United States. . . .

Whence . . . can be derived the idea, that Dartmouth College has become a public institution, and its trustees public officers. . . . Not from the source whence its funds were drawn; for its foundation is purely private and eleemosynary. Not from the application of those funds; for money may be given for education and the persons receiving it do not, by being employed in the education of youth, become members of the civil government. Is it from the act of incorporation? Let this subject be considered.

A corporation is an artificial being, invisible, intangible, and existing only in contemplation of law. Being the mere creature of law, it possesses only those properties which the charter of its creation confers upon it, either expressly or as incidental to its very existence. These are such as are supposed best calculated to effect the object for which it was created. Among the most important are immortality, and, if the expression may be allowed, individuality; properties, by which a perpetual succession of many persons are considered as the same, and may act as a single individual. They enable a corporation to manage its own affairs, and to hold property without the perplexing intricacies, the hazardous and endless necessity of perpetual conveyances, for the purpose of transmitting it from hand to hand. It is chiefly for the purpose of clothing bodies of men, in succession, with these qualities and capacities that corporations were invented, and are in use. By these means, a perpetual succession of individuals are capable of acting for the promotion of the particular object, like one immortal being. . . .

According to the theory of the British constitution, their parliament is omnipotent. To annul corporate rights might give a shock to public opinion, which that government has chosen to avoid; but its power is not questioned. Had parliament, immediately after the emanation of this charter, and the execution of those conveyances which followed it, annulled the instrument, so that the living donors would have witnessed the disappointment of their hopes, the perfidy of the transaction would have been universally acknowledged. . . . What has since occurred to strip it of its inviolability? Circumstances have not changed it. In reason, in justice, and in law, it is now what it was in 1769. . . .

Almost all eleemosynary corporations, those which are created for the promotion of religion, of charity, or of education, are of the same character. The law of this case is the law of all. . . .

The opinion of the court, after mature deliberation, is, that this is a contract, the obligation of which cannot be impaired without violating the constitution of the United States. This opinion appears to us to be equally supported by reason and by the former decisions of this court.

2. We next proceed to the inquiry, whether its obligation has been impaired by those acts of the legislature of New Hampshire to which the special verdict refers. . . .

The obligations, then, which were created by the charter to Dartmouth College were the same in the new that they had been in the old government. The power of the government was also the same. A repeal of this charter at any time prior to the adoption of the present constitution of the United States would have been an extraordinary and unprecedented act of power, but one which could have been contested only by the restrictions upon the legislature to be found in the constitution of the State. But the constitution of the United States has imposed this additional limitation, that the legislature of a state shall pass no act "impairing the obligation of contracts." . . .

The will of the State is substituted for the will of the donors in every essential operation of the college. This is not an immaterial change. . . . This system is totally changed. The charter of 1769 exists no longer. It is reorganized; and reorganized in such a manner as to convert a literary institution, moulded according to the will of its founders and placed under the control of private literary men, into a machine entirely subservient to the will of government. This may be for the advantage of this college in particular, and may be for the advantage of literature in general; but it is not according to the will of the donors, and is subversive of that contract on the faith of which their property was given. . . .

The Commerce Clause Under the Marshall Court

58. *Commerce Includes Every Species of Commercial Intercourse*

Gibbons v. Ogden, 9 Wheaton 1 (1824).

MARSHALL, C. J.: The appellant contends that this decree is erroneous, because the laws which purport to give the exclusive privilege it sustains are repugnant to the constitution and laws of the United States. They are said to be repugnant— 1st. To that clause in the constitution which authorizes congress to regulate commerce. 2d. To that which authorizes congress to promote the progress of science and useful arts. . . .

The words [used in the Constitution] are: "Congress shall have power to regulate commerce with foreign nations, and among the several States, and with the Indian tribes." The subject to be regulated is commerce; and our constitution being, as was aptly said at the bar, one of enumeration, and not of definition, to ascertain the extent of the power, it becomes necessary to settle the meaning of the word. The counsel for the appellee would limit it to traffic, to buying and selling, or the interchange of commodities, and do not admit that it comprehends navigation. This would restrict a general term, applicable to many objects, to one of its significations. Commerce, undoubtedly, is traffic, but it is something more; it is intercourse. It describes the commercial intercourse between nations, and parts of nations, in all its branches, and is regulated by prescribing rules for carrying on that intercourse. The mind can scarcely conceive a system for regulating commerce between nations which shall exclude all laws concerning navigation, which shall be silent on the admission of the vessels of the one nation into the ports of the

other, and be confined to prescribing rules for the conduct of individuals, in the actual employment of buying and selling, or of barter.

If commerce does not include navigation, the government of the Union has no direct power over that subject, and can make no law prescribing what shall constitute American vessels, or requiring that they shall be navigated by American seamen. Yet this power has been exercised from the commencement of the government, has been exercised with the consent of all, and has been understood by all to be a commercial regulation. All America understands, and has uniformly understood, the word "commerce" to comprehend navigation. It was so understood, and must have been so understood, when the constitution was framed. The power over commerce, including navigation, was one of the primary objects for which the people of America adopted their government, and must have been contemplated in forming it. The convention must have used the word in that sense, because all have understood it in that sense; and the attempt to restrict it comes too late. . . .

The word used in the constitution, then, comprehends, and has been always understood to comprehend, navigation within its meaning; and a power to regulate navigation is as expressly granted as if that term had been added to the word "commerce."

To what commerce does this power extend? The constitution informs us, to commerce "with foreign nations, and among the several States, and with the Indian tribes." It has, we believe, been universally admitted that these words comprehend every species of commercial intercourse between the United States and foreign nations. No sort of trade can be carried on between this country and any other to which this power does not extend. It has been truly said that commerce, as the word is used in the constitution, is a unit, every part of which is indicated by the term. If this be the admitted meaning of the word, in its application to foreign nations, it must carry the same meaning throughout the sentence, and remain a unit, unless there be some plain intelligible cause which alters it.

The subject to which the power is next applied is to commerce "among the several States." The word "among" means intermingled with. A thing which is among others is intermingled with them. Commerce among the States cannot stop at the external boundary line of each State, but may be introduced into the interior.

It is not intended to say that these words comprehend that commerce which is completely internal, which is carried on between man and man in a State, or between different parts of the same State, and which does not extend to or affect other States. Such a power would be inconvenient and is certainly unnecessary.

Comprehensive as the word "among" is, it may very properly be restricted to that commerce which concerns more States than one. The phrase is not one which would probably have been selected to indicate the completely interior traffic of a State, because it is not an apt phrase for that purpose; and the enumeration of the particular classes of commerce to which the power was to be extended would not have been made had the intention been to extend the power to every description. The enumeration presupposes something not enumerated; and that something, if we regard the language or the subject of the sentence, must be the exclusively internal commerce of a State. The genius and character of the whole government

seem to be, that its action is to be applied to all the external concerns of the nation, and to those internal concerns which affect the States generally; but not to those which are completely within a particular State, which do not affect other States, and with which it is not necessary to interfere for the purpose of executing some of the general powers of the government. The completely internal commerce of a State, then, may be considered as reserved for the State itself.

But, in regulating commerce with foreign nations, the power of congress does not stop at the jurisdictional lines of the several States. It would be a very useless power, if it could not pass those lines. The commerce of the United States with foreign nations is that of the whole United States. Every district has a right to participate in it. The deep streams which penetrate our country in every direction pass through the interior of almost every State in the Union, and furnish the means of exercising this right. If congress has the power to regulate it, that power must be exercised whenever the subject exists. If it exists within the States, if a foreign voyage may commence or terminate at a port within a State, then the power of congress may be exercised within a State.

This principle is, if possible, still more clear, when applied to commerce "among the several States." They either join each other, in which case they are separated by a mathematical line, or they are remote from each other, in which case other States lie between them. What is commerce "among" them; and how is it to be conducted? Can a trading expedition between two adjoining States commence and terminate outside of each? And if the trading intercourse be between two States remote from each other, must it not commence in one, terminate in the other, and probably pass through a third? Commerce among the States must, of necessity, be commerce with the States. In the regulation of trade with the Indian tribes, the action of the law, especially when the constitution was made, was chiefly within a State. The power of Congress, then, whatever it may be, must be exercised within the territorial jurisdiction of the several States. The sense of the nation on this subject is unequivocally manifested by the provisions made in the laws for transporting goods, by land, between Baltimore and Providence, between New York and Philadelphia, and between Philadelphia and Baltimore.

We are now arrived at the inquiry—What is this power?

It is the power to regulate; that is, to prescribe the rule by which commerce is to be governed. This power, like all others vested in congress, is complete in itself, may be exercised to its utmost extent, and acknowledges no limitations other than are prescribed in the constitution. These are expressed in plain terms, and do not affect the questions which arise in this case, or which have been discussed at the bar. If, as has always been understood, the sovereignty of congress, though limited to specified objects, is plenary as to those objects, the power over commerce with foreign nations, and among the several States, is vested in congress as absolutely as it would be in a single government, having in its constitution the same restrictions on the exercise of the power as are found in the constitution of the United States. . . . The power of congress, then, comprehends navigation, within the limits of every State in the Union, so far as that navigation may be, in any manner, connected with "commerce with foreign nations, or among the several States, or with the Indian tribes." It may, of consequence, pass the jurisdiction line of New York, and act upon the very waters to which the prohibition now under consideration applies.

But it has been urged with great earnestness that, although the power of congress to regulate commerce with foreign nations, and among the several States, be coextensive with the subject itself, and have no other limits than are prescribed in the constitution, yet the States may sev-

erally exercise the same power, within their respective jurisdictions. . . .

Since, however, in exercising the power of regulating their own purely internal affairs, whether of trading or police, the States may sometimes enact laws, the validity of which depends on their interfering with, and being contrary to, an act of congress passed in pursuance of the constitution, the court will enter upon the inquiry, whether the laws of New York, as expounded by the highest tribunal of that State, have, in their application to this case, come into collision with an act of congress, and deprived a citizen of a right to which that act entitles him. Should this collision exist, it will be immaterial whether those laws were passed in virtue of a concurrent power "to regulate commerce with foreign nations and among the several States," or in virtue of a power to regulate their domestic trade and police. In one case and the other the acts of New York must yield to the law of congress; and the decision sustaining the privilege they confer against a right given by a law of the Union, must be erroneous.

This opinion has been frequently expressed in this court, and is founded as well on the nature of the government as on the words of the constitution. In argument, however, it has been contended that, if a law passed by a State, in the exercise of its acknowledged sovereignty, comes into conflict with a law passed by congress in pursuance of the constitution, they affect the subject, and each other, like equal opposing powers.

But the framers of the constitution foresaw this state of things, and provided for it by declaring the supremacy not only of itself, but of the laws made in pursuance of it. The nullity of any act, inconsistent with the constitution, is produced by the declaration, that the constitution is supreme law. . . . In every such case the act of congress, or the treaty, is supreme; and the law of the State, though enacted in the exercise of powers not controverted, must yield to it. . . .

This Court is, therefore, of opinion, that the decree of the Court of New York . . . is erroneous, and ought to be reversed, and the same is hereby reversed and annulled and . . . the bill of . . . Aaron Ogden . . . is hereby dismissed. . . .

59. The "Original Package" Rule

Brown v. Maryland, 12 Wheaton 419 (1827).

MARSHALL, C. J.: . . . The cause depends entirely on the question, whether the legislature of a State can constitutionally require the importer of foreign articles to take out a license from the State, before he shall be permitted to sell a bale or package so imported. . . .

The plaintiffs in error . . . insist that the act under consideration is repugnant to two provisions in the constitution . . .

1. To that which declares that "no State shall, without the consent of Congress, lay any imposts, or duties on imports or exports, except what may be absolutely necessary for executing its inspection laws."

2. To that which declares that Congress shall have power "to regulate commerce with foreign nations, and among the several States, and with the Indian tribes.". . .

The constitutional prohibition on the States to lay a duty on imports, a prohibition which a vast majority of them must feel an interest in preserving, may certainly come in conflict with their acknowledged power to tax persons and property within their territory. The power, and the restriction on it, though quite distinguishable when they do not approach each other, may yet, like the intervening colours between white and black, approach so nearly as to perplex the understanding, as colours perplex the vision in marking the distinction between them. Yet the distinction exists, and must be marked as the cases arise. Till they do arise, it might be premature to state any rule as being universal in its application. It is sufficient for the present to say, generally, that when the importer has so acted upon the thing imported, that it has become incorporated and mixed up with the mass of property in the country, it has, perhaps, lost its distinctive character as an import, and has become subject to the taxing power of the state; but while remaining the property of the importer, in his warehouse, in the original form or package in which it was imported, a tax upon it is too plainly a duty on imports to escape the prohibition in the constitution. . . .

Commerce is intercourse: one of its most ordinary ingredients is traffic. It is inconceivable, that the power to authorize this traffic, when given in the most comprehensive terms, with the intent that its efficacy should be complete, should cease at the point when its continuance is indispensable to its value. To what purpose should the power to allow importation be given, unaccompanied with the power to authorize a sale of the thing imported? Sale is the object of importation, and is an essential ingredient of that intercourse, of which importation constitutes a part. It is as essential an ingredient, as indispensable to the existence of the entire thing, then, as importation itself. It must be considered as a component part of the power to regulate commerce. Congress has a right, not only to authorize importation, but to authorize the importer to sell. . . .

The conclusion that the right to sell is connected with the law permitting importation, as an inseparable incident, is inevitable. . . .

Any penalty inflicted on the importer for selling the article in his character of importer, must be in opposition to the act of congress which authorizes importation. Any charge on the introduction and incorporation of the articles into and with the mass of property in the country, must be hostile to the power given to congress to regulate commerce, since an essential part of that regulation, and principal object of it, is to prescribe the regular means for accomplishing that introduction and incorporation. . . .

It has been contended that this construction of the power to regulate commerce . . . would abridge the acknowledged power of a State to tax its own citizens, or their property within its territory.

We admit this power to be sacred; but cannot admit that it may be used so as to obstruct the free course of a power given to congress. We cannot admit that it may be used so as to obstruct or defeat the power to regulate commerce. . . . It results, necessarily, from this principle, that the taxing power of the States must have some limits. It cannot reach and restrain the action of the national government within its proper sphere. It cannot reach the administration of justice in the courts

of the Union, or the collection of the taxes of the United States, or restrain the operation of any law which congress may constitutionally pass. It cannot interfere with any regulation of commerce. If the States may tax all persons and property found on their territory, what shall restrain them from taxing goods in their transit through the State from one port to another, for the purpose of re-exportation? The laws of trade authorize this operation, and general convenience requires it. Or what should restrain a State from taxing any article passing through it from one State to another, for the purpose of traffic? or from taxing the transportation of articles passing from the State itself to another State, for commercial purposes? These cases are all within the sovereign power of taxation, but would obviously derange the measures of congress to regulate commerce, and affect materially the purpose for which that power was given. . . .

The Jacksonian Attack on Monopoly Banking

60. *Jackson's Bank Veto Message, July 10, 1832*

Richardson, ed., *Messages and Papers of the Presidents*, II, 576-91 *passim*.

The bill "to modify and continue" the act entitled "An act to incorporate the subscribers to the Bank of the United States" was presented to me on the 4th July instant. Having . . . come to the conclusion that it ought not to become law, I herewith return it to the Senate, in which it originated, with my objections. . . .

The present corporate body . . . enjoys an exclusive privilege of banking under the authority of the General Government, a monopoly of its favor and support, and, as

a necessary consequence, almost a monopoly of the foreign and domestic exchange. The powers, privileges, and favors bestowed upon it in the original charter, by increasing the value of the stock far above its par value, operated as a gratuity of many millions to the stockholders. . . .

The act before me proposes another gratuity to the holders of the same stock. . . . On all hands it is conceded that its passage will increase at least 20 or 30 per cent more the market price of the stock, subject to the payment of the annuity of $200,000 per year secured by the act, thus adding in a moment one-fourth to its par value. It is not our own citizens only who are to receive the bounty of our Government. More than eight millions of the stock of this bank are held by foreigners. By this act the American Republic proposes virtually to make them a present of some millions of dollars. For these gratuities to foreigners and to some of our own opulent citizens the act secures no equivalent whatever. . . . Every monopoly and all exclusive privileges are granted at the expense of the public which ought to receive a fair equivalent. . . . But the act does not permit competition in the purchase of this monopoly. It seems to be predicated on the erroneous idea that the present stockholders have a prescriptive right not only to the favor but to the bounty of government. . . .

It is maintained by the advocates of the bank that its constitutionality in all its features ought to be considered as settled by precedent and by the decision of the Supreme Court. To this conclusion I cannot assent. Mere precedent is a dangerous source of authority, and should not be regarded as deciding questions of constitutional power except where the acquiescence of the people and the States can be considered as well settled. So far from this being the case on this subject, an argument against the bank might be based on precedent. One Congress, in 1791, decided in favor of a bank; another, in 1811, decided against it. One Congress, in 1815, decided against a bank; another, in 1816, decided in its favor. Prior to the present Congress, therefore, the precedents drawn from that source were equal. If we resort to the States, the expressions of legislative, judicial, and executive opinions against the bank have been probably to those in its favor as 4 to 1. . . .

If the opinion of the Supreme Court covered the whole ground of this act, it ought not to control the co-ordinate authorities of this Government. The Congress, the Executive, and the Court must each for itself be guided by its own opinion of the Constitution. Each public officer who takes an oath to support the Constitution swears that he will support it as he understands it, and not as it is understood by others. It is as much the duty of the House of Representatives, of the Senate, and of the President to decide upon the constitutionality of any bill or resolution which may be presented to them for passage or approval as it is of the supreme judges when it may be brought before them for judicial decision. The opinion of the judges has no more authority over Congress than the opinion of Congress has over the judges, and on that point the President is independent of both. The authority of the Supreme Court must not, therefore, be permitted to control the Congress or the Executive when acting in their legislative capacities, but to have only such influence as the force of their reasoning may deserve.

But in the case relied upon the Supreme Court have not decided that all the features of this corporation are compatible with the Constitution. It is true that the court have said that the law incorporating the bank is a constitutional exercise of power by Congress; but taking into view the whole opinion of the court and the reasoning by which they have come to that conclusion, I understand them to have decided that inasmuch as a bank is an appropriate means for carrying into effect the enumerated powers of the General Government, therefore the law incorporating it is in accordance with that provision of the Constitution which declares that Congress shall have power "to make all laws which shall be necessary and proper for carrying those powers into execution." Having satisfied themselves that the word "necessary" in the Constitution means "needful," "requisite," "essential," "conducive to," and that "a bank" is a convenient, a useful, and essential instrument in the prosecution of the Government's "fiscal operations," they conclude that to "use one must be within the discretion of Congress" and that "the act to incorporate the Bank of the United States is a law made in pursuance of the Constitution"; "but," say they, *where the law is not prohibited and is really calculated to effect any of the objects intrusted to the Government, to undertake here to inquire into the degree of its necessity would be to pass the line which circumscribes the judicial department and to tread on legislative ground."*

The principle here affirmed is that the "degree of its necessity," involving all the details of a banking institution, is a question exclusively for legislative consideration. A bank is constitutional, but it is the province of the Legislature to determine whether this or that particular power, privilege, or exemption is "necessary and proper" to enable the bank to discharge its duties to the Government, and from their decision there is no appeal to the courts of justice. Under the decision of the Supreme Court, therefore, it is the exclusive province of Congress and the President to decide whether the particular features of this act are *necessary* and *proper* in order to enable the bank to perform conveniently and efficiently the public duties assigned to it as a fiscal agent, and therefore constitutional, or *unnecessary* and *improper,* and therefore unconstitutional. . . .

If our power over means is so absolute that the Supreme Court will not call in question the constitutionality of an act of Congress the subject of which "is not prohibited, and is really calculated to effect any of the objects intrusted to the Government," although, as in the case before me, it takes away powers expressly granted to Congress and rights scrupulously reserved to the States, it becomes us to proceed in our legislation with the utmost caution. Though not directly, our own powers and the rights of the States may be indirectly legislated away in the use of means to execute substantive powers. We may not enact that Congress shall not have the power of exclusive legislation over the District of Columbia, but we may pledge the faith of the United States that as a means of executing other powers it shall not be exercised for twenty years or forever. We may not pass an act prohibiting the States to tax the banking business carried on within their limits, but we may, as a means of executing our powers over other objects, place that business in the hands of our agents and then declare it exempt from State taxation in their hands. Thus may our own powers and the rights of the States, which we cannot directly curtail or invade, be frittered away and extinguished in the use of means employed by us to execute other powers. That a bank of the United States, competent to all the duties which may be required by the Government, might be so organized as not to infringe on our own delegated powers or the reserved rights of the States I do not entertain a doubt. . . .

The bank is professedly established as an agent of the executive branch of the Government, and its constitutionality is maintained on that ground. Neither upon the propriety of present action nor upon the provisions of this act was the Executive consulted. It has had no opportunity to say that it neither needs nor wants an agent clothed with such powers and favored by such exemptions. There is nothing in its legitimate functions which makes it necessary or proper. Whatever interest or influence, whether public or private, has given birth to this act, it cannot be found either in the wishes or necessities of the executive department, by which present action is deemed premature, and the powers conferred upon its agent not only unnecessary, but dangerous to the Government and country.

It is to be regretted that the rich and powerful too often bend the acts of government to their selfish purposes. Distinctions in society will always exist under every just government. Equality of talents, of education, or of wealth cannot be produced by human institutions. In the full enjoyment of the gifts of Heaven and the fruits of superior industry, economy, and virtue, every man is equally entitled to protection by law; but when the laws undertake to add to these natural and just advantages artificial distinctions, to grant titles, gratuities, and exclusive privileges to make the rich richer, and the potent more powerful, the humble members of society —the farmers, mechanics, and laborers— who have neither the time nor the means of securing like favor to themselves, have a right to complain of the injustice of their government. There are no necessary evils in government. Its evils exist only in its abuses. If it would confine itself to equal protection, and, as Heaven does its rains, shower its favors alike on the high and the low, the rich and the poor, it would be an unqualified blessing. In the act before me there seems to be a wide and unnecessary departure from these just principles. . . .

Experience should teach us wisdom. Most of the difficulties our Government now encounters and most of the dangers which impend over our Union have sprung from an abandonment of the legitimate objects of Government by our national legislation, and the adoption of such principles as are embodied in this act. Many of our rich men have not been content with equal protection and equal benefits, but have besought us to make them richer by act of Congress. By attempting to gratify their desires we have in the results of our legislation arrayed section against section, interest against interest, and man against man, in a fearful commotion which threatens to shake the foundations of our Union. It is time to pause in our career to review our principles, and if possible revive that devoted patriotism and spirit of compromise which distinguished the sages of the Revolution and the fathers of our Union. If we cannot at once, in justice to interests vested under improvident legislation, make our government what it ought to be, we can at least take a stand against all new grants of monopolies and exclusive privileges, against any prostitution of our government to the advancement of the few at the expense of the many, and in favor of compromise and gradual reform in our code of laws and system of political economy.

61. Andrew Jackson's Paper to the Cabinet on the Bank Deposit Withdrawal, September 18, 1833

Richardson, ed., *Messages and Papers of the Presidents*, III, 18-19.

It is the desire of the President that the control of the banks and the currency shall, as far as possible, be entirely separated from the political power of the country as well as wrested from an institution which has already attempted to subject the Government to its will. In his opinion the action of the General Government on this subject ought not to extend beyond the grant in the Constitution, which only authorizes Congress "to coin money and regulate the value thereof;" all else belongs to the States and the people, and must be regulated by public opinion and the interests of trade. . . .

The President must be permitted to remark that he looks upon the pending question as of higher consideration than the mere transfer of a sum of money from one bank to another. Its decision may affect the character of our government for ages to come. Should the bank be suffered longer to use the public moneys, in the accomplishment of its purposes, with the proofs of its faithlessness and corruption before our eyes, the patriotic among our citizens will despair of success in struggling against its power; and we shall be responsible for entailing it upon our country forever. Viewing it as a question of transcendant importance, both in the principles and consequences it involves, the President could not, in justice to the responsibility which he owes to the country, refrain from pressing upon the Secretary of the Treasury, his view of the considerations which impel to immediate action. Upon him has been devolved by the Constitution and the suffrages of the American people, the duty of superintending the operation of the Executive Departments of the government, and seeing that the laws are faithfully executed. In the performance of this high trust, it is his undoubted right to express to those whom the laws and his own choice have made his associates in the administration of the Government, his opinion of their duties under circumstances as they arise. It is this right which he now exercises. Far be it from him to expect or require, that any member of the Cabinet should, at his request, order, or dictation, do any act which he believes unlawful, or in his conscience condemns. From them and from his fellow citizens in general, he desires only that aid and support, which their reason approves and their conscience sanctions.

In the remarks he has made on this all-important question, he trusts the Secretary of the Treasury will see only the frank and respectful declarations of the opinions which the President has formed on a measure of great national interest deeply affecting the character and usefulness of his Administration, and not a spirit of dictation, which the President would be as careful to avoid as ready to resist. Happy will he be, if the facts now disclosed produce uniformity of opinion and unity of action among the members of the Administration.

The President again repeats that he begs his Cabinet to consider the proposed measure as his own, in the support of which he shall require no one of them to make a sacrifice of opinion or principle. Its responsibility has been assumed, after the most mature deliberation and reflection, as necessary to preserve the morals of the people, the freedom of the press, and the purity of the elective franchise, without which all will unite in saying that the blood and treasure expended by our forefathers in the establishment of our happy system of government will have been vain and fruitless. Under these convictions, he feels that a measure so important to the American people cannot be commenced too soon; and he therefore names the first day of October next as a period proper for the change of the deposits, or sooner, provided the necessary arrangements with the State banks can be made.

62. *Jackson Protests the Senate's Censure, April 15, 1834*

Richardson, ed., *Messages and Papers of the Presidents*, III, 72-3, 90-2.

The resolution of the Senate is wholly unauthorized by the Constitution, and in derogation of its entire spirit. It assumes that a single branch of the legislative department may for the purposes of a public censure, and without any view to legislation or impeachment, take up, consider, and decide upon the official acts of the Executive. But in no part of the Constitution is the President subjected to any such responsibility; and in no part of that instrument is any such power conferred on either branch of the Legislature. . . .

The resolution above quoted charges, in substance, that in certain proceedings relating to the public revenue the President has usurped authority and power not conferred upon him by the constitution and laws, and that in doing so he violated both. Any such act constitutes a high crime—one of the highest, indeed, which the President can commit—a crime which justly exposes him to impeachment by the House of Representatives, and upon due conviction, to removal from office, and to the complete and immutable disfranchisement prescribed by the Constitution. . . .

The honest differences of opinion which occasionally exist between the Senate and the President, in regard to matters in which both are obliged to participate, are sufficiently embarrassing. But if the course recently adopted by the Senate shall hereafter be frequently pursued, it is not only obvious that the harmony of the relations between the President and the Senate will be destroyed, but that other and graver effects will ultimately ensue. If the censures of the Senate be submitted to by the President, the confidence of the people in his ability and virtue, and the character and usefulness of his Administration will soon be at an end, and the real power of the Government will fall into the hands of a body holding their offices for long terms, not elected by the people, and not to them directly responsible. If, on the other hand, the illegal censures of the Senate should be resisted by the President, collisions and angry controversies might ensue, discreditable in their progress, and in the end compelling the people to adopt the conclusion, either that their Chief Magistrate was unworthy of their respect, or that the senate was chargeable with calumny and injustice. Either of these results would impair public confidence in the perfection of the system, and lead to serious alterations of its frame work, or to the practical abandonment of some of its provisions.

The influence of such proceedings on the other departments of the Government, and more especially on the States, could not fail to be extensively pernicious. When the judges in the last resort of official misconduct themselves overleap the bounds of their authority, as prescribed by the Constitution, what general disregard of its provisions might not their example be expected to produce? And who does not perceive that such con-

tempt of the Federal Constitution by one of its most important departments would hold out the strongest temptation to resistance on the part of the State sovereignties whenever they shall suppose their just rights to have been invaded? Thus all the independent departments of the Government, and the States which compose our confederated Union, instead of attending to their appropriate duties, and leaving those who may offend to be reclaimed or punished in the manner pointed out in the Constitution, would fall to mutual crimination and recrimination and give to the people confusion and anarchy instead of order and law; until at length some form of aristocratic power would be established on the ruins of the Constitution or the States be broken into separate communities.

Far be it from me to charge or to insinuate that the present Senate of the United States intend, in the most distant way to encourage such a result. It is not of their motives or designs, but only of the tendency of their acts, that it is my duty to speak. It is, if possible, to make Senators themselves sensible of the danger which lurks under the precedent set in their resolution, and at any rate to perform my duty as the responsible head of one of the coequal departments of the Government, that I have been compelled to point out the consequences to which the discussion and passage of the resolution may lead if the tendency of the measure be not checked in its inception. It is due to the high trust with which I have been charged, to those who may be called to succeed me in it, to the representatives of the people whose constitutional prerogative has been unlawfully assumed, to the people and to the States, and to the Constitution they have established that I should not permit its provisions to be broken down by such an attack on the executive department without at least some effort "to preserve, protect, and defend" them. With this view, and for the reasons which have been stated, I do hereby *solemnly protest* against the afore-mentioned proceedings of the Senate as unauthorized by the Constitution, contrary to its spirit and to several of its express provisions, subversive of that distribution of the powers of government which it has ordained and established, destructive of the checks and safeguards by which those powers were intended on the one hand to be controlled and on the other to be protected, and calculated by their immediate and collateral effects, by their character and tendency, to concentrate in the hands of a body not directly amenable to the people a degree of influence and power dangerous to their liberties and fatal to the Constitution of their choice. . . .

CHAPTER VIII

Jacksonian Democracy and the
Sectional Challenge

THE doctrine that "all men are created equal" was the central theme of Jacksonian democracy. In an era of dynamic economic and social change, the rational liberalism of the Jeffersonians was expanded in an effort to maintain the Revolutionary goals of individual freedom and equality of opportunity. Jackson's denunciation of monopoly in his Bank Veto (Chapter VII) was essentially a manifestation in the economic realm of this trend. The most conspicuous reflection of the equalitarian character of American democracy was in the fields of political and constitutional practice. The admittance of the masses of the people to political participation, the elimination of property qualifications for public office, the substitution of a representative convention for "King Caucus," rotation in office, and the perfection of national party organization were some of the key developments in an era of democratic reform.

No one better captured the spirit of the age than the youthful French aristocrat, Alexis de Tocqueville. In his perceptive analysis, *Democracy in America*, he gives a comprehensive description of the rise of the common man. Especially significant were his observations on the sovereignty of the people (No. 63), and on judicial power in the United States and its influence on political society (No. 64).

Manhood suffrage could be achieved only by constitutional change, and this fact explains the rash of state constitutional conventions held in the 1820's and 1830's. Aristocracy was strongly attacked in all these conventions and a wider franchise was demanded. But strong opposition developed among conservative constitutionalists, who generally agreed with John Randolph's dictum that it was impossible "to divorce property from power." One of the chief spokesman of the old order was Justice Joseph Story of the United States Supreme Court, who presented his arguments in the Massachusetts convention (No. 65). Once the liberals had triumphed, however, the conservatives were forced to relinquish their theory that universal suffrage was inconsistent with liberty and, operating on the principle "if you can't beat them, join them," went on to become equally vociferous advocates of the new political order.

Despite this surface unity on political principles, the practical problem of adjusting federal-state relations apparently defied solution. Even President Jackson, whose chief constitutional problem—aside from the Bank issue—was sectional conflict, oscillated between states' rights and nationalism. Although Jackson's first annual message to Congress is noteworthy for his confidence in the average man's capacity for political participation, important also is the President's statement of one of "the most deeply rooted convictions of my mind," a defense of "the legitimate sphere of State sovereignty." This position appealed to strict constructionists and states' rights advocates as did Jackson's early opposition to federal appropriations for state and local transportation projects, and his acquiescence in Georgia's open defiance of the Constitution, a federal treaty, and Marshall's powerful decision (*Worcester v. Georgia* [1832]). Marshall had voided a Georgia law and declared that the national government had exclusive jurisdiction in the territory of the Cherokee Nation. Although Jackson's oft-quoted response—"John Marshall has made his decision, now let him enforce it!"—is generally conceded to be apocryphal, he did observe at the time that, "The decision of the Supreme Court has fell still born, and they find it cannot coerce Georgia to yield."

In the same year, however, Jackson's nationalism was reflected in the way he handled South Carolina's attempt to nullify a federal tariff law. The increasing complexity of the American economy following the War of 1812 almost inevitably bred sectional conflict. The nationalism of 1816 was the product of general sectional agreement on the necessity of a national bank and a protective tariff. This unanimity was shortlived. The Panic of 1819, the progressive soil exhaustion of the southeastern seaboard, the threat of Western expansion to the political dominance of the older states, and the Northern manufacturers' demands for increased protection from foreign competition created sectional controversies that concentrated attention on the government's role in economic life and revived constitutional debates in the South reminiscent of New England's states' rights position at the Hartford Convention.

South Carolina and its illustrious spokesman, John C. Calhoun, afford the classic case study of the shift from ardent nationalism to strident localism. Although the land-sapping system of cotton culture and the disastrous competition of the newly opened fields of the Old Southwest were the fundamental causes of South Carolina's distress, she blamed her descent from prosperity to poverty on federal measures. Attacking the tariff as a discriminatory and unconstitutional burden on the South for the benefit of the prosperous North, Vice President Calhoun, formerly a strong nationalist, secretly drafted the *South Carolina Exposi-*

tion. Although it traced its parentage to the Kentucky and Virginia Resolutions of 1798, its announcement of the doctrine of nullification by a *single* state was completely different from the Jeffersonian-Madisonian remedy of repeal of objectionable legislation by majority action.

The most devastating criticism of the South Carolina doctrine was the reply of Senator Daniel Webster of Massachusetts (No. 66) to a reformulation of the theory of nullification by Calhoun's fellow Carolinian, Senator Robert Y. Hayne. Although the original issue in this Congressional debate involved the sale of Western lands, the discussion quickly turned to the broad field of federal-state relations. Because the North and South were voicing antipathetic theories of constitutional interpretation, attention focused on the West and its leading spokesman, Jackson. Hoping to win the President's support, Calhoun and the nullifiers attempted to ally the West and the South at a Jefferson Day dinner. Hayne's prepared address was followed by twenty-four formal toasts, most of them stressing state sovereignty and nullification as orthodox Democratic tenets. Jackson's reply repudiated the Southern bid—"Our Federal Union—it must be preserved." Accepting the challenge, Calhoun responded: "The Union—next to our liberty, most dear. May we all remember that it can only be preserved by respecting the rights of the states and distributing equally the benefits and burdens of the Union."

President and Vice President were now pitted against each other, and neither backed down. After the enactment of a new tariff in 1832, South Carolina actualized Calhoun's theory by declaring the tariff "null, void, and no law, nor binding upon this State" (No. 67). In an effort to elicit public sympathy for their stand, a special state convention pleaded their economic plight under the tariff as a justification for invoking nullification, which they defended as a constitutional means of redress for acts deemed injurious to the state (No. 68). Jackson's response was predictable. Privately vowing if blood were shed, to hang the first nullifier he could put his hands on to the first tree he could find, he publicly cautioned that "disunion by armed force is *treason*," and bluntly denounced nullification as "contradicted expressly by the letter of the Constitution" (No. 69). A month later the President asked for crisis powers, and Congress passed the Force Bill authorizing the use of military power if necessary. Congress also made tariff concessions to the hard pressed South Carolinians, however, and did not resort to this drastic measure of compulsion. The nullification convention then reassembled, repealed the Nullification Ordinance and, in a gratuitous act of defiance, nullified the Force Bill. Both sides claimed victory, but it should be pointed out that no state endorsed the South Carolina position, and the Force Act, despite South Carolina's meaningless challenge, remained on the federal law books as a tacit assertion of the invalidity of nullification as a constitutional remedy.

In his farewell address in March, 1837, the retiring chief executive summarized the hectic years of the early Republic. "Our Constitution is no longer a doubtful experiment . . . It is no longer a question whether this great country can remain happily united and flourish under our present form of government. Experience . . . has shown the wisdom and foresight of those who formed it, and has proved that in the union of these States there is a sure foundation for the brightest hopes of freedom and for the happiness of the people."

Broadening the Base of Popular Government

63. *"The people reign in the American political world"*

Alexis de Tocqueville, 1835, in Phillips Bradley, ed., *Democracy in America by Alexis de Tocqueville* (New York, 1954), 55-60.

In America the aristocratic element has always been feeble from its birth; and if at the present day it is not actually destroyed, it is at any rate so completely disabled that we can scarcely assign to it any degree of influence on the course of affairs.

The democratic principle, on the contrary, has gained so much strength by time, by events, and by legislation, as to have become not only predominant, but all-powerful. No family or corporate authority can be perceived; very often one cannot even discover in it any very lasting individual influence.

America, then, exhibits in her social state an extraordinary phenomenon. Men are there seen on a greater equality in point of fortune and intellect, or, in other words, more equal in their strength, than in any other country of the world, or in any age of which history has preserved the remembrance.

The political consequences of such a social condition as this are easily deducible.

It is impossible to believe that equality will not eventually find its way into the political world, as it does everywhere else. To conceive of men remaining forever unequal upon a single point, yet equal on all others, is impossible; they must come in the end to be equal upon all.

Now, I know of only two methods of establishing equality in the political world; rights must be given to every citizen, or none at all to anyone. For nations which are arrived at the same stage of social existence as the Anglo-Americans, it is, therefore, very difficult to discover a

medium between the sovereignty of all and the absolute power of one man: and it would be vain to deny that the social condition which I have been describing is equally liable to each of these consequences.

There is, in fact, a manly and lawful passion for equality that excites men to wish all to be powerful and honored. This passion tends to elevate the humble to the rank of the great; but there exists also in the human heart a depraved taste for equality, which impels the weak to attempt to lower the powerful to their own level and reduces men to prefer equality in slavery to inequality with freedom. Not that those nations whose social condition is democratic naturally despise liberty; on the contrary, they have an instinctive love of it. But liberty is not the chief and constant object of their desires; equality is their idol: they make rapid and sudden efforts to obtain liberty and, if they miss their aim, resign themselves to their disappointment; but nothing can satisfy them without equality, and they would rather perish than lose it.

On the other hand, in a state where the citizens are all practically equal, it becomes difficult for them to preserve their independence against the aggressions of power. No one among them being strong enough to engage in the struggle alone with advantage, nothing but a general combination can protect their liberty. Now, such a union is not always to be found.

From the same social position, then, nations may derive one or the other of two great political results; these results are extremely different from each other, but they both proceed from the same cause.

The Anglo-Americans are the first nation who, having been exposed to this formidable alternative, have been happy enough to escape the dominion of absolute power. They have been allowed by their circumstances, their origin, their intelligence, and especially by their morals to establish and maintain the sovereignty of the people.

THE PRINCIPLE OF THE SOVEREIGNTY OF THE PEOPLE OF AMERICA

Whenever the political laws of the United States are to be discussed, it is with the doctrine of the sovereignty of the people that we must begin.

The principle of the sovereignty of the people, which is always to be found, more or less, at the bottom of almost all human institutions, generally remains there concealed from view. It is obeyed without being recognized, or if for a moment it be brought to light, it is hastily cast back into the gloom of the sanctuary.

"The will of the nation" is one of those expressions that have been most largely abused by the wily and the despotic of every age. Some have seen the expression of it in the purchased suffrages of a few of the satellites of power; others, in the votes of a timid or an interested minority; and some have even discovered it in the silence of a people, on the supposition that the fact of submission established the right to command. . . .

When a nation begins to modify the elective qualifications, it may easily be foreseen that, sooner or later, that qualification will be entirely abolished. There is no more invariable rule in the history of society: the further electoral rights are extended, the greater is the need of extending them; for after each concession the strength of the democracy increases, and its demands increase with its strength. The ambition of those who are below the appointed rate is irritated in exact proportion to the great number of those who are above it. The exception at last becomes the rule, concession follows concession, and no stop can be made short of universal suffrage.

At the present day the principle of the sovereignty of the people has acquired in the United States, all the practical development that the imagination can conceive. It is unencumbered by those fictions that are thrown over it in other countries, and it appears in every possible form, according to the exigency of the occasion. Sometimes the laws are made by the people in a body, as at Athens; and sometimes its representatives, chosen by universal suffrage, transact business in its name and under its immediate supervision.

In some countries a power exists which, though it is in a degree foreign to the social body, directs it, and forces it to pursue a certain track. In others the ruling force is divided, being partly within and partly without the ranks of the people. But nothing of the kind is to be seen in the United States; there society governs itself for itself. All power centers in its bosom, and scarcely an individual is to be met with who would venture to conceive or, still less, to express the idea of seeking it elsewhere. The nation participates in the making of its laws by the choice of its legislators, and in the execution of them by the choice of the agents of the executive government; it may almost be said to govern itself, so feeble and so restricted is the share left to the administration, so little do the authorities forget their popular origin and the power from which they emanate. The people reign in the American political world as the Deity does in the universe. They are the cause and the aim of all things; everything comes from them, and everything is absorbed in them.

64. *The Judiciary as a Barrier Against Legislative Tyranny*

Alexis de Tocqueville, 1835, in Philips Bradley, ed., *Democracy in America by Alexis de Tocqueville* (New York, 1954), 106-7.

Whenever a law that the judge holds to be unconstitutional is invoked in a tribunal of the United States, he may refuse to admit it as a rule; this power is the only one peculiar to the American magistrate, but it gives rise to immense political influence. In truth, few laws can escape the searching analysis of the judicial power for any length of time, for there are few that are not prejudicial to some private interest or other, and none that may not be brought before a court of justice by the choice of parties or by the necessity of the case. But as soon as a judge has refused to apply any given law in a case, that law immediately loses a portion of its moral force. Those to whom it is prejudicial learn that means exist of evading its authority, and similar suits are multiplied until it becomes powerless. The alternative, then, is that the people must alter the Constitution or the legislature must repeal the law. The political power which the Americans have entrusted to their courts of justice is therefore immense, but the evils of this power are considerably diminished by the impossibility of attacking the laws except through the courts of justice. If the judge had been empowered to contest the law on the ground of theoretical generalities, if he were able to take the initiative and to censure the legislator, he would play a prominent political part; and as the champion or the antagonist of a party, he would have brought the hostile passions of the nation into the conflict. But when a judge contests a law in an obscure debate on some particular case, the importance of his attack is concealed from public notice; his decision bears upon the interests of an individual, and the law is slighted only incidentally. Moreover, although it is censured, it is not abolished;

its moral force may be diminished, but its authority is not taken away; and its final destruction can be accomplished only by the reiterated attacks of judicial functionaries. It will be seen, also, that by leaving it to private interest to censure the law, and by intimately uniting the trial of the law with the trial of an individual, legislation is protected from wanton assaults and from the daily aggressions of party spirit. The errors of the legislator are exposed only to meet a real want; and it is always a positive and appreciable fact that must serve as the basis of a prosecution.

I am inclined to believe this practice of the American courts to be at once most favorable to liberty and to public order. If the judge could attack the legislator only openly and directly, he would sometimes be afraid to oppose him; and at other times party spirit might encourage him to brave it at every turn. The laws would consequently be attacked when the power from which they emanate was weak, and obeyed when it was strong; that is to say, when it would be useful to respect them, they would often be contested; and when it would be easy to convert them into an instrument of oppression, they would be respected. But the American judge is brought into the political arena independently of his own will. He judges the law only because he is obliged to judge a case. The political question that he is called upon to resolve is connected with the interest of the parties, and he cannot refuse to decide it without a denial of justice. He performs his functions as a citizen by fulfilling the precise duties which belong to his profession as a magistrate. It is true that, upon this system, the judicial censorship of the courts of justice over the legislature cannot extend to all laws indiscriminately, inasmuch as some of them can never give rise to that exact species of contest which is termed a lawsuit; and even when such a contest is possible, it may happen that no one cares to bring it before a court of justice. The Americans have often felt this inconvenience; but they have left the remedy incomplete, lest they should give it an efficacy that might in some cases prove dangerous. Within these limits the power vested in the American courts of justice of pronouncing a statute to be unconstitutional forms one of the most powerful barriers that have ever been devised against the tyranny of political assemblies.

65. *Joseph Story speaks for "the property-holding part of the community"*

Journal of Debates and Proceedings in the Convention of Delegates Chosen to Revise the Constitution of Massachusetts [1820] (rev. ed., Boston, 1853), 283-8.

The proposition of my friend from Roxbury is to make population the basis for apportioning the senate. . . . Those who contend on the other hand, for the basis of valuation, propose nothing new, but stand upon the letter and spirit of the present constitution. . . .

The qualifications are to remain as before, and the rich and the poor, and the high and the low are to meet at the polls upon the same level of equality. . . . I agree that the poor man is not to be deprived of his rights any more than the rich man, nor have I as yet heard of any proposition to that effect; and if it should come, I should feel myself bound to resist it. The poor man ought to be protected in his rights, not merely of life and liberty, but of his scanty and hard earnings. I do not deny that the poor man may possess as much patriotism as the rich; but it is unjust to suppose that he necessarily possesses more. Patriotism and poverty do not necessarily march hand in hand; nor is wealth that monster which some imaginations have depicted, with a heart of adamant and a sceptre of iron, surrounded with scorpions stinging every one within its reach, and planting its feet of oppression upon the needy and the dependent. Such a representation is not just with reference to our country. There is no class of very rich men in this happy land, whose wealth is fenced in by hereditary titles, by entails, and by permanent elevation to the highest offices. Here there is a gradation of property from the highest to the lowest, and all feel an equal interest in its preservation. If, upon the principle of valuation, the rich man in a district, which pays a high tax, votes for a larger number of senators, the poor man in the same district enjoys the same distinction. There is not then a conflict, but a harmony of interests between them; nor under the present constitution has any discontent or grievance been seriously felt from this source.

When I look around and consider the blessings which property bestows, I cannot persuade myself that gentlemen are serious in their views, that it does not deserve our utmost protection. I do not here speak of your opulent and munificent citizens, whose wealth has spread itself into a thousand channels of charity and public benevolence. . . . I speak not of these, not because they are not worthy of all praise; but because I would dwell rather on those general blessings, which prosperity diffuses through the whole mass of the community. . . . I consider property as the source of all the comforts and advantages we enjoy, and every man, from him who possesses but a single dollar up to him who possesses the greatest fortune, is equally interested in its security and its preservation. Government indeed stands on a combination of interests and circumstances. It must always be a question of the highest moment, how the property-holding part of the community may be sustained against the inroads of poverty and vice. Poverty leads to temptation, and temptation often leads to vice, and vice to military despotism. The rights of man are never heard in a despot's palace. The very rich man, whose estate consists in personal property, may escape from such evils by flying for refuge to some foreign land. But the hardy yeoman, the owner of a few acres of the soil, and supported by it, cannot leave his home without becoming a wanderer on the face of the earth. In the preservation of property and virtue, he has, therefore, the deepest and most permanent interest.

Gentlemen have argued as if personal rights only were the proper objects of government. But what, I would ask, is life worth, if a man cannot eat in security the bread earned by his own industry? . . . I will say no more about the rich and the poor. There is no parallel to be run between them, founded on permanent constitutional distinctions. The rich help the poor, and the poor in turn administer to the rich. In our country, the highest man is not *above* the people; the humblest is not *below* the people. If the rich may be said to have additional protection, they have not additional power. Nor does wealth here form a permanent distinction of families. Those who are wealthy today pass to the tomb, and their children divide their estates. Property thus is divided quite as fast as it accumulates. No family can, without its own exertions, stand erect for a long time under our statute of descents and distributions, the only true and legitimate agrarian law. . . . It is a mistaken theory, that government is founded for one object only. It is organized for the protection of life, liberty and property, and all the comforts of society—to enable us to indulge in our domestic affections, and quietly to enjoy our homes and our firesides. . . .

It has been also suggested, that great property, of itself, gives great influence, and that it is unnecessary that the constitution should secure to it more. I have already stated what I conceive to be the true answer; that a representation in the senate founded on valuation, is not a representation of property in the abstract. . . . The basis of valuation was undoubtedly adopted by the framers of our constitution, with reference to a just system of checks, and balances, and the principles of rational liberty. Representation and taxation was the doctrine of those days—a doctrine for which our fathers fought and bled, in the battles of the revolution. Upon the basis of valuation, property is not directly represented; but property in the aggregate, combined with personal rights—where the greatest burthen of taxation falls, there the largest representation is apportioned; but still the choice depends upon the will of the majority of voters, and not upon that of the wealthier class within the district. There is a peculiar beauty in our system of taxation and equalizing the public burthens. . . . But even if it were true that the representation in the senate were founded on property, I would respectfully ask gentlemen, if its natural influence would be weakened or destroyed by assuming the basis of population. I presume not. It would still be left to exert that influence over friends and dependents in the same manner that it now does; so that the change would not in the slightest degree aid the asserted object, I mean the suppression of the supposed predominating authority of wealth.

Gentlemen have argued, as though it was universally conceded as a political axiom, that population is in all cases and under all circumstances the safest and best basis of representation. I beg leave to doubt the proposition. . . . What should be the basis on which representation should be founded, is not an abstract theoretical question, but depends upon the habits, manners, character and institutions of the people, who are to be represented. It is a question of political policy, which every nation must decide for itself, with reference to its own wants and circumstances. . . .

Nullification and Nationalism: The South Carolina Episode

66. "Liberty and Union, now and forever, one and inseparable!"

Daniel Webster's Reply to Robert Hayne, January 26, 1830, in J. W. McIntyre, ed., *The Writings and Speeches of Daniel Webster* (Boston, 1903), VI, 51, 53-5, 67-8, 73.

I understand the honorable gentleman from South Carolina to maintain, that it is a right of the State legislatures to interfere, whenever, in their judgment, this government transcends its constitutional limits, and to arrest the operation of its laws. . . .

What he contends for is, that it is constitutional to interrupt the administration of the Constitution itself, in the hands of those who are chosen and sworn to administer it, by the direct interference, in form of law, of the States, in virtue of their sovereign capacity. The inherent right in the people to reform their government I do not deny; and they have another right, and that is, to resist unconstitutional laws, without overturning the government. It is no doctrine of mine, that unconstitutional laws bind the people. The great question is, Whose prerogative is it to decide on the constitutionality or unconstitutionality of the laws? On that, the main debate hinges. The proposition, that, in case of a supposed violation of the Constitution by Congress, the States have a constitutional right to interfere, and annul the law of Congress, is the proposition of the gentleman. I do not admit it. If the gentleman had intended no more than to assert the right of revolution for justifiable cause, he would have said only what all agree to. But I cannot conceive that there can be a middle course, between submission to the laws, when regularly pronounced constitutional, on the one hand, and open resistance, which is revolution or rebellion, on the other. I say, the right of a State to annul a law of Congress, cannot be maintained but on the ground of the unalienable right of man to resist oppression; that is to say, upon the ground of revolution. I admit that there is an ultimate violent remedy, above the Constitution and in defiance of the Constitution, which may be resorted to when a revolution is to be justified. But I do not admit, that, under the Constitution and in conformity with it, there is any mode in which a State government, as a member of the Union, can interfere and stop the progress of the general government, by force of her own laws, under any circumstances whatever.

This leads us to inquire into the origin of this government and the source of its power. Whose agent is it? Is it the creature of the State legislatures, or the creature of the people? If the government of the United States be the agent of the State governments, then they may control it, provided they can agree in the manner of controlling it; if it be the agent of the people, then the people alone can control it, restrain it, modify, or reform it. It is observable enough, that the doctrine for which the honorable gentleman contends leads him to the necessity of maintaining, not only that this general government is the creature of the States, but that it is the creature of each of the States severally, so that each may assert the power for itself of determining whether it acts within the limits of its authority. It is the servant of four-and-twenty masters, of different wills and different purposes, and yet bound to obey all. This absurdity (for it seems no less) arises from a misconception as to the origin of this government and its true character. It is, Sir, the people's Constitution, the people's government, made for the people, made by the people, and answerable to the people. The people of the United States have declared that this Constitution shall be the supreme law. We must either admit the proposition, or dispute their authority. The States are, unquestionably, sovereign, so far as their sovereignty is not affected by this supreme law. But the State legislatures, as political bodies, however sovereign, are yet not sovereign over the people. So far as the people have given power to the general government, so far the grant is unquestionably good, and the government holds of the people, and not of the State governments. We are all agents of the same supreme power, the people. The general government and the State governments derive their authority from the same source. Neither can, in relation to the other, be called primary, though one is definite and restricted, and the other general and residuary. The national government possesses those powers which it can be shown the people have conferred on it, and no more.

All the rest belongs to the State governments, or to the people themselves. So far as the people have restrained State sovereignty, by the expression of their will, in the Constitution of the United States, so far, it must be admitted, State sovereignty is effectually controlled. I do not contend that it is, or ought to be, controlled farther. The sentiment to which I have referred propounds that State sovereignty is only to be controlled by its own "feeling of justice"; that is to say, it is not to be controlled at all, for one who is to follow his own feelings is under no legal control. Now, however men may think this ought to be, the fact is, that the people of the United States have chosen to impose control on State sovereignties. There are those, doubtless, who wish they had been left without restraint; but the Constitution has ordered the matter differently. To make war, for instance, is an exercise of sovereignty; but the Constitution declares that no State shall make war. To coin money is another exercise of sovereign power; but no State is at liberty to coin money. Again, the Constitution says that no sovereign State shall be so sovereign as to make a treaty. These prohibitions, it must be confessed are a control on the State sovereignty of South Carolina, as well as of the other States, which does not arise "from her own feelings of honorable justice." The opinion referred to, therefore, is in defiance of the plainest provisions of the Constitution. . . .

But, Sir, the people have wisely provided, in the Constitution itself, a proper, suitable mode and tribunal for settling questions of constitutional law. There are in the Constitution grants of powers to Congress, and restrictions on these powers. There are, also, prohibitions on the States. Some authority must, therefore, necessarily exist, having the ultimate jurisdiction to fix and ascertain the interpretation of these grants, restrictions, and prohibitions. The Constitution has itself pointed out, ordained, and established that authority. How has it accomplished this great and essential end? By declaring, Sir, that *"the Constitution, and the laws of the United States made in pursuance thereof, shall be the supreme law of the land, any thing in the constitution or laws of any State to the contrary notwithstanding."*

This, Sir, was the first great step. By this the supremacy of the Constitution and laws of the United States is declared. The people so will it. No State law is to be valid which comes in conflict with the Constitution, or any law of the United States passed in pursuance of it. But who shall decide this question of interference? To whom lies the last appeal? This, Sir, the Constitution itself decides also, by declaring *"that the judicial power shall extend to all cases arising under the constitution and laws of the United States."* These two provisions, Sir, cover the whole ground. They are, in truth, the key-stone of the arch! With these, it is a Constitution; without them, it is a confederation. In pursuance of these clear and express provisions, Congress established, at its very first session, in the judicial act, a mode for carrying them into full effect, and for bringing all questions of constitutional power to the final decision of the Supreme Court. It then, Sir, became a Government. . . .

If any thing be found in the national Constitution, either by original provision or subsequent interpretation, which ought not to be in it, the people know how to get rid of it. If any construction, unacceptable to them, be established, so as to become practically a part of the Constitution, they will amend it, at their own sovereign pleasure. But while the people choose to maintain it as it is, while they are satisfied with it, and refuse to change it, who has given, or who can give, to the State legislatures a right to alter it, either by interference, construction, or otherwise? Gentlemen do not seem to recollect that the people have any power to do any thing for themselves. They imagine there is no safety for them, any longer than they are under close guardianship of the State legislatures. Sir, the people have not trusted their safety, in regard to the general Constitution, to these hands. They have required other security, and taken other bonds. They have chosen to trust themselves, first, to the plain words of the instrument, and to such construction as the government themselves, in doubtful cases, should put on their own powers, under their oaths of office, and subject to their responsibility to them; just as the people of a State trust their own State governments with a similar power. Secondly, they have reposed their trust in the efficacy of frequent elections, and in their own power to remove their own servants and agents whenever they see cause. Thirdly, they have reposed trust in the judicial power, which, in order that it might be trustworthy, they have made as respectable, as disinterested, and as independent as was practicable. Fourthly, they have seen fit to rely, in case of necessity, on high expediency, on their known and admitted power to alter or amend the Constitution, peaceably and quietly, whenever experience shall point out defects or imperfections. And, finally, the people of the United States have at no time, in no way, directly or indirectly, authorized any State legislature to construe or interpret *their* high instrument of government; much less, to interfere, by their own power, to arrest its course and operation. . . .

67. *South Carolina Ordinance of Nullification, November 24, 1832*

Thomas Cooper, ed., *Statutes at Large of South Carolina* (Columbia, S.C., 1836), I, 329-31.

Whereas the Congress of the United States, by various acts, purporting to be acts laying duties and imposts on foreign imports, but in reality intended for the protection of domestic manufactures, and the giving of bounties to classes and individuals engaged in particular employments, at the expense and to the injury and oppression of other classes and individuals, and by wholly exempting from taxation certain foreign commodities, such as are not produced or manufactured in the United States, to afford a pretext for imposing higher and excessive duties on articles similar to those intended to be protected, hath exceeded its just powers under the Constitution, which confers on it no authority to afford such protection, and hath violated the true meaning and intent of the Constitution, which provides for equality in imposing the burthens of taxation upon the several States and portions of the confederacy: And whereas the said Congress, exceeding its just power to impose taxes and collect revenue for the purpose of effecting and accomplishing the specific objects and purposes which the Constitution of the United States authorizes it to effect and accomplish, hath raised and collected unnecessary revenue for objects unauthorized by the Constitution:

We, therefore, the people of the State of South Carolina in Convention assembled, do declare and ordain, . . . that the several acts and parts of acts of . . . Congress . . . purporting to be laws for the imposing of duties and imposts on the importation of foreign commodities, . . . and, more especially, . . . [the 1828 and 1832 tariffs] . . . are unauthorized by the Constitution of the United States, and violate the true meaning and intent

thereof, and are null, void, and no law, nor binding upon this State, its officers or citizens; and all promises, contracts, and obligations, made or entered into, or to be made or entered into, with purpose to secure the duties imposed by the said acts, and all judicial proceedings which shall be hereafter had in affirmance thereof, are and shall be held utterly null and void.

And it is further ordained, that it shall not be lawful for any of the constituted authorities, whether of this State or of the United States, to enforce the payment of duties imposed by the said acts within the limits of this State; but it shall be the duty of the Legislature to adopt such measures and pass such acts as may be necessary to give full effect to this ordinance, and to prevent the enforcement and arrest the operation of the said acts and parts of acts of the Congress of the United States within the limits of this State, from and after the 1st day of February next, and the duty of all other constituted authorities, and of all persons residing or being within the limits of this State, and they are hereby required and enjoined, to obey and give effect to this ordinance, and such acts and measures of the Legislature as may be passed or adopted in obedience thereto. . . .

And we, the people of South Carolina, to the end that it may be fully understood by the Government of the United States, and the people of the co-States, that we are determined to maintain this, our ordinance and declaration, at every hazard, do further declare that we will not submit to the application of force, on the part of the Federal Government, to reduce this State to obedience; but that we will consider the passage, by Congress, of any act authorizing the employment of a military or naval force against the State of South Carolina, her constituted authorities or citizens; or any act abolishing or closing the ports of this State, or any of them, or otherwise obstructing the free ingress and egress of vessels to and from the said ports, or any other act on the part of the Federal Government, to coerce the State, shut up her ports, destroy or harrass her commerce, or to enforce the acts hereby declared to be null and void, otherwise than through the civil tribunals of the country, as inconsistent with the longer continuance of South Carolina in the Union: and that the people of this State will thenceforth hold themselves absolved from all further obligation to maintain or preserve their political connexion with the people of the other States, and will forthwith proceed to organize a separate Government, and do all other acts and things which sovereign and independent States may of right do.

68. South Carolina Defends Its Views on Federal-State Relations, November 24, 1832

Address to the People of the United States, Cooper, ed., Stat. at L. of S. C., I, 346-9.

We hold . . . that on their separation from the Crown of Great Britain, the several colonies became free and independent States, each enjoying the separate and independent right of self government; and that no authority can be exercised over them or within their limits, but by their consent, respectively given as States. It is equally true, that the Constitution of the United States is a compact formed between the several States, acting as sovereign communities; that the government created by it is a joint agency of the States, appointed to execute the powers enumerated and granted by that instrument; that all its acts not intentionally authorized are of themselves essentially null and void, and that the States have the right, in the same sovereign capacity in which they adopted the Federal Constitution, to pronounce, in the last resort, authoritative judgment on the usurpations of the Federal Government, and to adopt such measures as they may deem necessary and expedient to arrest the operation of the unconstitutional acts of that Government, within their respective limits. Such we deem to be inherent rights of the States; rights, in the very nature of things, absolutely inseparable from sovereignty. Nor is the duty of a State, to arrest an unconstitutional and oppressive act of the Federal Government less imperative, than the right is incontestible. Each State, by ratifying the Federal Constitution, and becoming a member of the confederacy, contracted an obligation to "protect and defend" that instrument, as well by resisting the usurpations of the Federal Government, as by sustaining that government in the exercise of the powers actually conferred upon it. . . .

It is true, that in ratifying the Federal Constitution, the States placed a large and important portion of the rights of their citizens under the joint protection of all the States, with a view to their more effectual security; but it is not less true that they reserved a portion still larger and not less important under their own immediate guardianship, and in relation to which their original obligation to protect their citizens, from whatever quarter assailed, remains unchanged and undiminished.

But clear and undoubted as we regard the right, and sacred as we regard the duty of the States to interpose their sovereign power for the purpose of protecting their citizens from the unconstitutional and oppressive acts of the Federal Government, yet we are as clearly of the opinion, that nothing short of that high moral and political necessity, which results from acts of usurpation, subversive of the rights and liberties of the people, should induce a member of this confederacy to resort to this interposition. Such, however, is the melancholy and painful necessity under which we have declared the acts of Congress imposing protecting duties, null and void within the limits of South Carolina. The spirit and the principles which animated your ancestors and ours in the councils and in the fields of their common glory, forbid us to submit any longer to a system of Legislation now become the established policy of the Federal Government, by which we are reduced to a condition of colonial vassalage, in all its aspects more oppressive and intolerable than that from which our common ancestors relieved themselves by the war of the revolution. There is no right which enters more essentially into a just conception of liberty, than that of the free and unrestricted use of the productions of our industry wherever they can be most advantageously exchanged, whether in foreign or domestic markets. South Carolina produces, almost exclusively, agricultural staples, which derive their principal value from the demand for them in foreign countries. Under these circumstances, her natural markets are abroad; and restrictive

duties imposed upon her intercourse with those markets, diminish the exchangeable value of her productions very nearly to the full extent of those duties.

Under a system of free trade, the aggregate crop of South Carolina could be exchanged for a larger quantity of manufactures, by at least one third, than it can be now exchanged for under the protecting system. It is no less evident, that the value of that crop is diminished by the protecting system very nearly, if not precisely, to the extent that the aggregate quantity of manufactures which can be obtained for it, is diminished. . . .

Almost the entire crop of South Carolina, amounting annually to more than six millions of dollars, is ultimately exchanged either for foreign manufactures, subject to protecting duties, or for similar domestic manufactures. The *natural* value of the crop would be all the manufactures which we could obtain for it, under a system of unrestricted commerce. The *artificial* value, produced by the unjust and unconstitutional Legislation of Congress, is only such part of those manufactures as will remain after paying a duty of fifty per cent to the Government, or, to speak with more precision, to the Northern manufacturers. . . .

69. *Jackson asserts that nullification is "incompatible with the existence of the Union"*

Proclamation to the People of South Carolina, December 10, 1832, Richardson, ed., *Messages and Papers of the Presidents*, II, 641-52.

The ordinance is founded, not on the indefeasible right of resisting acts which are plainly unconstitutional and too oppressive to be endured, but on the strange position that any one State may not only declare an act of Congress void, but prohibit its execution; that they may do this consistently with the Constitution; that the true construction of that instrument permits a State to retain its place in the

Union and yet be bound by no other of its laws than those it may choose to consider as constitutional. It is true, they add, that to justify this abrogation of a law it must be palpably contrary to the Constitution; but it is evident that to give the right of resisting laws of that description, coupled with the uncontrolled right to decide what laws deserve that character, is to give the power of resisting all laws; for as by the theory there is no appeal, the reasons alleged by the State, good or bad, must prevail. If it should be said that public opinion is a sufficient check against the abuse of this power, it may be asked why it is not deemed a sufficient guard against the passage of an unconstitutional act by Congress? There is, however, a restraint in this last case which makes the assumed power of a State more indefensible, and which does not exist in the other. There are two appeals from an unconstitutional act passed by Congress—one to the judiciary, the other to the people and the States. There is no appeal from the State decision in theory, and the practical illustration shows that the courts are closed against an application to review it, both judges and jurors being sworn to decide in its favor. But reasoning on this subject is superfluous when our social compact, in express terms, declares that the laws of the United States, its Constitution, and treaties made under it are the supreme law of the land, and, for greater caution, adds "that the judges in every State shall be bound thereby, anything in the constitution or laws of any State to the contrary notwithstanding." And it may be asserted without fear of refutation that no federative government could exist without a similar provision. . . .

If this doctrine had been established at an earlier day, the Union would have been dissolved in its infancy. The excise law in Pennsylvania, the embargo and nonintercourse law in the Eastern States, the carriage tax in Virginia, were all deemed unconstitutional, and were more unequal in their operation than any of the laws now complained of; but, fortunately, none of those States discovered that they had the right now claimed by South Carolina. The war into which we were forced to support the dignity of the nation and the rights of our citizens might have ended in defeat and disgrace, instead of victory and honor, if the States who supposed it a ruinous and unconstitutional measure had thought they possessed the right of nullifying the

act by which it was declared and denying supplies for its prosecution. Hardly and unequally as those measures bore upon several members of the Union, to the legislatures of none did this efficient and peaceable remedy, as it is called, suggest itself. The discovery of this important feature in our Constitution was reserved to the present day. To the statesmen of South Carolina belongs the invention, and upon the citizens of that State will unfortunately fall the evils of reducing it to practice.

If the doctrine of a State veto upon the laws of the Union carries with it internal evidence of its impracticable absurdity, our constitutional history will also afford abundant proof that it would have been repudiated with indignation had it been proposed to form a feature in our Government. . . .

I consider, then, the power to annul a law of the United States, assumed by one State, *incompatible with the existence of the Union, contradicted expressly by the letter of the Constitution, unauthorized by its spirit, inconsistent with every principle on which it was founded, and destructive of the great object for which it was formed.*

After this general view of the leading principle, we must examine the particular application of it which is made in the ordinance.

The preamble rests its justification on these grounds: It assumes as a fact that the obnoxious laws, although they purport to be laws for raising revenue, were in reality intended for the protection of manufactures, which purpose it asserts to be unconstitutional; that the operation of these laws is unequal; that the amount raised by them is greater than is required by the wants of the Government; and, finally, that the proceeds are to be applied to objects unauthorized by the Constitution. These are the only causes alleged to justify an open opposition to the laws of the country and a threat of seceding from the Union if any attempt should be made to enforce them. The first virtually acknowledges that the law in question was passed under a power expressly given by the Constitution to lay and collect imposts; but its constitutionality is drawn in question from the *motives* of those who passed it. However apparent this purpose may be in the present case, nothing can be more dangerous than to admit the position that an unconstitutional purpose entertained by the members who assent to a law enacted under a constitutional power shall make that law void. For how is that purpose to be ascertained? Who is to make the scrutiny? How often may bad purposes be falsely imputed, in how many cases are they concealed by false professions, in how many is no declaration of motive made? Admit this doctrine, and you give to the States an uncontrolled right to decide, and every law may be annulled under this pretext. If, therefore, the absurd and dangerous doctrine should be admitted that a State may annul an unconstitutional law, or one that it deems such, it will not apply to the present case.

The next objection is that the laws in question operate unequally. This objection may be made with truth to every law that has been or can be passed. The wisdom of man never yet contrived a system of taxation that would operate with perfect equality. If the unequal operation of a law makes it unconstitutional, and if all laws of that description may be abrogated by any State for that cause, then, indeed, is the Federal Constitution unworthy of the slightest effort for its preservation. . . .

The Constitution declares that the judicial powers of the United States extend to cases arising under the laws of the United States, and that such laws, the Constitution, and treaties shall be paramount to the State constitutions and laws. The judiciary act prescribes the mode by which the case may be brought before a court of the United States by appeal when a State tribunal shall decide against this provision of the Constitution. The ordinance declares there shall be no appeal—makes the State law paramount to the Constitution and laws of the United States, forces judges and jurors to swear that they will disregard their provisions, and even makes it penal in a suitor to attempt relief by appeal. It further declares that it shall not be lawful for the authorities of the United States or of that State to enforce the payment of duties imposed by the revenue laws within its limits.

Here is a law of the United States, not even pretended to be unconstitutional, repealed by the authority of a small majority of the voters of a single State. Here is a provision of the Constitution which is solemnly abrogated by the same authority.

On such expositions and reasonings the ordinance grounds not only an assertion of the right to annul the laws of which it complains, but to enforce it by a threat of seceding from the Union if any attempt is made to execute them.

This right to secede is deduced from the nature of the Constitution, which, they say, is a compact between sovereign States who have preserved their whole sovereignty and therefore are subject to no superior; that because they made the compact they can break it when in their opinion it has been departed from by the other States. Fallacious as this course of reasoning is, it enlists State pride and finds advocates in the honest prejudices of those who have not studied the nature of our Government sufficiently to see the radical error on which it rests. . . .

The Constitution of the United States, then, forms a *government*, not a league; and whether it be formed by compact between the States or in any other manner, its character is the same. It is a Government in which all the people are represented, which operates directly on the people individually, not upon the States; they retained all the power they did not grant. But each State, having expressly parted with so many powers as to constitute, jointly with the other States, a single nation, can not, from that period, possess any right to secede, because such secession does not break a league, but destroys the unity of a nation; and any injury to that unity is not only a breach which would result from the contravention of a compact, but it is an offense against the whole Union. To say that any State may at pleasure secede from the Union is to say that the United States are not a nation, because it would be a solecism to contend that any part of a nation might dissolve its connection with the other parts, to their injury or ruin, without committing any offense. Secession, like any other revolutionary act, may be morally justified by the extremity of oppression; but to call it a constitutional right is confounding the meaning of terms, and can only be done through gross error or to deceive those who are willing to assert a right, but would pause before they made a revolution or incur the penalties consequent on a failure. . . .

The laws of the United States must be executed. I have no discretionary power on the subject; my duty is emphatically pronounced in the Constitution. Those who told you that you might peaceably prevent their execution deceived you; they could not have been deceived themselves. They know that a forcible opposition could alone prevent the execution of the laws, and they know that such opposition must be repelled. Their object is disunion. But be not deceived by names. Disunion by armed force is *treason*. Are you really ready to incur its guilt? If you are, on the heads of the instigators of the act be the dreadful consequences; on their heads be the dishonor, but on yours may fall the punishment. . . .

Fellow-citizens of the United States. . . . I rely with equal confidence on your undivided support in my determination to execute the laws, to preserve the Union by all constitutional means, to arrest, if possible, by moderate and firm measures the necessity of a recourse to force; and if it be the will of Heaven that the recurrence of its primeval curse on man for the shedding of a brother's blood should fall upon our land, that it be not called down by any offensive act on the part of the United States.

CHAPTER IX

The Taney Court and the
Expansion of Business Enterprise

I F THE Supreme Court was dominated during the first third of the nine-teenth century by John Marshall, it was likewise under the influence of another strong personality during the period from Jackson to Lincoln. Roger B. Taney of Maryland, a former Federalist but now a confirmed Jacksonian, and a democratized Supreme Court—Jackson appointed six Associate Justices in addition to Chief Justice Taney—greatly modified, and in a few instances repudiated, the Federalist constitutional law of Marshall. Indeed, Taney's draft of Jackson's Bank Veto (Chapter VII) was a basic statement of his belief that special privilege is as undemocratic in economics as in politics.

In the first decision he wrote as Chief Justice, Taney formalized this faith in free, competitive enterprise by severely modifying Marshall's dictum on the sanctity of contract. In the Charles River Bridge case (No. 70), he formulated the doctrine of the social responsibilities of private property, observing that "While the rights of private property are sacredly guarded, we must not forget that the community also have rights, and that the happiness and well-being of every citizen depends on their faithful preservation." The technical issue involved was the claim by a Massachusetts bridge company that its charter of incorporation gave it exclusive, monopolistic business rights by implication. In rejecting this contention, the new Chief Justice ruled that no corporate charter could confer implied powers beyond the specific terms of the grant. Attacked by Justice Story and other conservatives as an open assault on the rights of property, the decision has long been regarded as favorable to the progress of economic enterprise because it freed new businesses from the fear of monopolistic claims of older corporations with ambiguously phrased charters.

Another indication of the changing temper of the Court under Taney was the opinion in *Briscoe v. Bank of Kentucky* (No. 71). In 1830 the Marshall Court had upset a Missouri statute authorizing the issuance of state loan certificates as an unconstitutional emission of bills of credit by the state (*Craig v. Missouri*). In the Briscoe case, the Taney Court, in an opinion by a Craig dissenter, upheld a Kentucky law establishing a state-owned bank that issued paper currency. Justice McLean ruled that these notes were not bills of credit, for the state had not pledged their redemption, but had substituted a public corporation capable of suing and being sued. Not only was the case a realistic recognition of the demise of the Bank of the United States; it was a further assertion of state regulatory power in the economic sphere.

One of the most important of Taney's decisions in relation to the growth of American business enterprise was *Bank of Augusta v. Earle* (No. 72), a landmark in constitutional law as well as constitutional history. The case involved an appeal from the federal circuit court in Alabama which had denied to a banking corporation chartered in Georgia the right of transacting business in Alabama. This decision, declared Justice Story, "frightened half the lawyers and all the corporations of the country out of their proprieties." Steering skillfully between the lower court's assertion of state sovereignty and the corporation's claim to all the legal rights guaranteed to citizens by the Constitution, Taney, although he recognized the right of a corporation to do business outside the home state, made it clear that the other state could regulate or exclude "foreign" corporations. Five years later, in *Louisville, Cincinnati, and Charleston R.R. Co. v. Letson* (1844), the Taney Court extended the legal fiction of citizenship to corporations, thus insuring them the protection of federal judicial review from state assaults. This decision expanded the scope of federal judicial power by asserting that for purposes of a suit in the federal courts a corporation was presumed to be a citizen of the state in which it was chartered. In addition, it stimulated the development of corporate enterprise.

Commercial regulation offers another contrast between the Marshall and Taney Courts. In a series of cases between 1837 and 1851, the Taney Court attempted to delineate the permissible area of state jurisdiction over interstate commerce in the absence of explicit congressional enactments. Whereas the Marshall Court inclined strongly toward exclusive federal control, the Taney Court, although sharply divided in earlier cases, reached a workable compromise on the negative implication of the commerce clause in the Cooley case (No. 73). Applying the new doctrine of "selective exclusiveness," Justice Curtis sustained a state act regulating harbor pilots in Philadelphia. At the same time, Curtis asserted that the commerce clause, when implemented by congressional legislation, excludes state interference. When Congress is silent, however, states may act unless the specific subject requires "uniform national control." This deceptively simple formula has forced upon the Court the increasingly difficult task of determining whether a single uniform rule is necessary, or whether the subject is sufficiently local to make state regulation permissible.

Throughout the nineteenth century and well into the twentieth, one sphere of economic activity existed in which the federal government did not contest the states' police power. The legal rights of workers to organize labor unions were governed by the common law of the various states, which generally regarded workingmen's organizations as "conspiracies." Early judicial decisions uniformly agreed that combinations of laborers organized to raise wages or to regulate terms of employment were illegal. Long after the leveling philosophy of Jacksonian democracy had challenged the inequalities of the emerging industrial system, a New York court penalized strikers for attempting to secure higher wages (*People v. Fisher*, No. 74ᴀ). Not until 1842 did a state uphold the right of workers to unite for their own protection. In *Commonwealth v. Hunt* (No. 74ᴮ), Chief Justice Lemuel Shaw reversed a lower Massachusetts court, not only ruling that unions are legal associations, but also exempting them from responsibility for illegal acts committed by individual members, and recognizing the legality of a strike for the closed shop. The development of the legal position of unions in an increasingly industrialized society is directly traceable to this decision.

70. *The Court, Corporations, and the Social Responsibility of Private Property*

Charles River Bridge v. Warren Bridge, 11 Peters 420 (1837).

TANEY, C. J.: . . . Borrowing, as we have done, our system of jurisprudence from the English law. . . . it would present a singular spectacle, if, while the courts in England are restraining, within the strictest limits, the spirit of monopoly, and exclusive privileges in nature of monopolies, and confining corporations to the privileges plainly given to them in their charter; the courts of this country should be found enlarging these privileges by implication; and construing a statute more unfavorably to the public, and to the rights of the community, than would be done in a like case in an English court of justice.

But we are not now left to determine for the first time the rules by which public grants are to be construed in this country. The subject has already been considered in this court, and the rules of construction above stated fully established. In the case of the *United States v. Arre-*

dondo . . . the leading cases upon this subject are collected together by the learned judge who delivered the opinion of the court, and the principle recognized that, in grants by the public nothing passes by implication. . . .

The case now before the court, is, in principle, precisely the same. It is a charter from a state; the act of incorporation is silent in relation to the contested power. The argument in favor of the proprietors of the Charles River bridge, is . . . that the power claimed by the state, if it exists, may be so used as to destroy the value of the franchise they have granted to the corporation. . . . The fact that the power has been already exercised, so as to destroy the value of the franchise, cannot in any degree affect the principle. The existence of the power does not, and cannot, depend upon the circumstance of its having been exercised or not. . . .

The object and end of all government

is to promote the happiness and prosperity of the community by which it is established; and it can never be assumed, that the government intended to diminish its power of accomplishing the end for which it was created. And in a country like ours, free, active and enterprising, continually advancing in numbers and wealth, new channels of communication are daily found necessary, both for travel and trade, and are essential to the comfort, convenience and prosperity of the people. . . .

No one will question that the interests of the great body of the people of the state, would, in this instance, be affected by the surrender of this great line of travel to a single corporation, with the right to exact toll, and exclude competition, for seventy years. While the rights of private property are sacredly guarded, we must not forget that the community also have rights, and that the happiness and well-being of every citizen depends on their faithful preservation.

Adopting the rule of construction above stated as the settled one, we proceed to apply it to the charter of 1785 to the proprietors of the Charles River bridge. This act of incorporation is in the usual form, and the privileges such as are commonly given to corporations of that kind. It confers on them the ordinary faculties of a corporation, for the purpose of building the bridge; and establishes certain rates of toll, which the company are authorized to take. This is the whole grant. There is no exclusive privilege given to them over the waters of Charles river, above or below their bridge; no right to erect another bridge themselves, nor to prevent other persons from erecting one, no engagement from the State, that another shall not be erected; and no undertaking not to sanction competition, nor to make improvements that may diminish the amount of its income. Upon all these subjects the charter is silent; and nothing is said in it about a line of travel, so much insisted on in the argument, in which they are to have exclusive

privileges. No words are used from which an intention to grant any of these rights can be inferred. If the plaintiff is entitled to them, it must be implied, simply from the nature of the grant, and cannot be inferred from the words by which the grant is made. . . .

The inquiry then is, does the charter contain such a contract on the part of the State? Is there any such stipulation to be found in that instrument? It must be admitted on all hands, that there is none— no words that even relate to another bridge, or to the diminution of their tolls, or to the line of travel. If a contract on that subject can be gathered from the charter, it must be by implication, and cannot be found in the words used. Can such an agreement be implied? The rule of construction before stated is an answer to the question. In charters of this description, no rights are taken from the public, or given to the corporation, beyond those which the words of the charter, by their natural and proper construction, purport to convey. There are no words which import such a contract as the plaintiffs in error contend for, and none can be implied. . . . The whole community are interested in this inquiry, and they have a right to require that the power of promoting their comfort and convenience, and of advancing the public prosperity, by providing safe, convenient, and cheap ways for the transportation of produce and the purposes of travel, shall not be construed to have been surrendered or diminished by the State, unless it shall appear by plain words that it was intended to be done. . . .

And what would be the fruits of this doctrine of implied contracts on the part of the States, and of property in a line of travel by a corporation, if it should now be sanctioned by this court? To what results would it lead us? If it is to be found in the charter to this bridge, the same process of reasoning must discover it, in the various acts which have been passed, within the last forty years, for turnpike companies. . . . If this court should establish the principles now contended for, what is to become of the numerous railroads established on the same line of travel with turnpike companies, and which have rendered the franchises of the turnpike corporations of no value? Let it once be understood that such charters carry with them these implied contracts, and give this unknown and undefined property in a line of travelling, and you will soon find the old turnpike corporations awakening from their sleep and calling upon this court to put down the improvements which have taken their place. The millions of property which have been invested in railroads and canals upon lines of travel which had been before occupied by turnpike corporations will be put in jeopardy. We shall be thrown back to the improvements of the last century, and obliged to stand still until the claims of the old turnpike corporations shall be satisfied, and they shall consent to permit these States to avail themselves of the lights of modern science, and to partake of the benefit of those improvements which are now adding to the wealth and prosperity, and the convenience and comfort, of every other part of the civilized world. . . .

71. *State Regulation of Currency and Banking*

Briscoe v. Bank of Kentucky, 11 Peters 257 (1837).

McLean, J.: . . . The question is presented whether the notes issued by the bank are bills of credit, emitted by the State, in violation of the constitution of the United States. . . . The definition . . . which does include all classes of bills of credit emitted by the colonies or States, is, a paper issued by the sovereign power, containing a pledge of its faith, and designed to circulate as money. Having arrived at this point the next inquiry is, whether the notes of the Bank of the Commonwealth were bills of credit within the meaning of the constitution. . . .

The notes issued by the bank were in the usual form of bank-notes, in which the Bank of the Commonwealth promised to pay to the bearer on demand, the sum specified on the face of the note. . . . On the part of the plaintiffs in error, it is contended, that the provision in the constitution, that "no State shall coin money," "emit bills of credit," or "make any thing but gold and silver coin a tender in payment of debts," are three distinct powers which are inhibited to the States. . . . [and] that the Bank of the Common- wealth, in emitting the bills in question, acted as the agent of the State; and that, consequently, the bills were issued by the State.

If this argument be correct, and the position that a State cannot do indirectly what it is prohibited from doing directly, be a sound one, then it must follow, as a necessary consequence, that all banks incorporated by a State are unconstitutional. . . . This doctrine is startling, as it strikes a fatal blow against the state banks, which have a capital of near $400,000,000, and which supply almost the entire circulating medium of the country. But let us for a moment consider it dispassionately. . . .

A State cannot emit bills of credit. . . . But a State may grant acts of incorporation for the attainment of those objects which are essential to the interests of society. This power is incident to sovereignty, and there is no limitation in the federal constitution, on its exercise by the States, in respect to the incorporation of banks. . . . If, then, the powers not delegated to the federal government, nor denied to the States, are retained by the States, or the people, and by a fair construction of the term bills of credit, as used in the constitution, they do not include ordinary bank-notes, does it not follow that the power to incorporate banks to issue these notes may be exercised by a State? . . .

But the question arises, what is a bill of credit within the meaning of the constitution? On the answer of this must depend the constitutionality or unconstitutionality of the act in question. . . . To constitute a bill of credit within the constitution, it must be issued by a State, on the faith of the State, and be designed to circulate as money. It must be a paper which circulates on the credit of the State; and is so received and used in the ordinary business of life. The individual or committee who issue the bill must have the power to bind the State; they must act as agents, and, of course, do not incur any personal responsibility, nor impart, as individuals, any credit to the paper. These are the leading characteristics of a bill of credit which a State cannot emit. Were the notes of the Bank of the Commonwealth bills of credit issued by the State? . . . Upon their face they do not purport to be . . . but by the president and directors of the bank. They promise to pay to bearer on demand the sums stated. Were they issued on the faith of the State? The notes contain no pledge of the faith of the State in any form. They purport to have been issued on the credit of the funds of the bank, and must have been so received in the community. But these funds, it is said, belonged to the State; and the promise to pay on the face of the notes were made by the president and directors as agents of the State. They do not assume to act as agents, and there is no law which authorizes them to bind the State. As in, perhaps, all bank charters, they had the power to issue a certain amount of notes; but they determined the time and circumstances which should regulate these issues.

When a State emits bills of credit the amount to be issued is fixed by law, as also the fund out of which they are to be paid, if any fund be pledged for their redemption; and they are issued on the credit of the State, which, in some form, appears upon the face of the notes, or by the signature of the person who issues them. As to the funds of the Bank of the Commonwealth, they were, in part only derived from the State. The capital, it is true, was to be paid by the State; but in making loans the bank was required to take good securities, and these constituted a fund to which the holders of the notes could look for payment, and which could be made legally responsible. In this respect the notes of this bank were essentially different from any class of bills of credit, which are believed to have been issued. . . .

But there is another quality which distinguished these notes from bills of credit. Every holder of them could not only look to the funds of the bank for payment, but he had in his power the means of enforcing it. The bank could be sued; and the records of this court show that while its paper was depreciated, a suit was prosecuted to judgment against it by a depositer, and who obtained from the bank, it is admitted, the full amount of his judgment in specie. . . .

If these positions be correct, is there not an end to this controversy? If the Bank of the Commonwealth is not the State, nor the agent of the State; if it possesses no more power than is given to it in the act of incorporation, and precisely the same as if the stock were owned by private individuals, how can it be contended that the notes of the bank can be called bills of credit, in contradistinction from the notes of the banks? . . .

We are of the opinion that the act incorporating the Bank of the Commonwealth was a constitutional exercise of power by the State of Kentucky; and, consequently, that the notes issued by the bank are not bills of credit, within the meaning of the federal constitution. . . .

72. *Regulation of Corporations Chartered in Another State*

Bank of Augusta v. Earle, 13 Peters 519 (1839).

TANEY, C. J.: . . . A multitude of corporations for various purposes have been chartered by the several States; a large portion of certain branches of business has been transacted by incorporated companies, or through their agency; and contracts to a very great amount have undoubtedly been made by different corporations out of the jurisdiction of the particular State by which they were created. In deciding the case before us, we in effect determine whether these numerous contracts are valid or not. And if, as has been argued at the bar, a corporation, from its nature and character, is incapable of making such contracts, or if they are inconsistent with the rights and sovereignty of the States in which they are made, they cannot be enforced in the courts of justice. . . .

But it has been urged in the argument that, notwithstanding the powers thus conferred by the terms of the charter, a corporation, from the very nature of its being, can have no authority to contract out of the limits of the State; that the laws of a State can have no extra-territorial operation; and that, as a corporation is the mere creature of a law of the State, it can have no existence beyond the limits in which that law operates; and that it must necessarily be incapable of making a contract in another place.

It is very true that a corporation can have no legal existence out of the boundaries of the sovereignty by which it is created. It exists only in contemplation of law, and by force of the law; and where that law ceases to operate and is no longer obligatory, the corporation can have no existence. It must dwell in the place of its creation, and cannot migrate to another sovereignty. But although it must live and have its being in that State only, yet it does not by any means follow that its existence there will not be recognized in other places; and its residence in one State creates no insuperable objection to its power of contracting in another. It is indeed a mere artificial being, invisible and intangible; yet it is a person, for certain purposes in contemplation of law, and has been recognized as such by the decisions of this court. . . . Now, natural persons, through the intervention of agents, are continually making contracts in countries in which they do not reside, and where they are not personally present when the contract is made; and nobody has ever doubted the validity of these agreements. And what greater objection can there be to the capacity of an artificial person, by its agents, to make a contract within the scope of its limited powers, in a sovereignty in which it does not reside; provided such contracts are permitted to be made by them by the laws of the place?

The corporation must no doubt show that the law of its creation gave it authority to make such contracts, through such agents. Yet, as in the case of a natural person, it is not necessary that it should actually exist in the sovereignty in which the contract is made. It is sufficient that its existence as an artifical person, in the State of its creation, is acknowledged and recognized by the law of the nation where the dealing takes place; and that it is permitted by the laws of that place to exercise there the powers with which it is endowed.

Every power, however, of the description of which we are speaking, which a corporation exercises in another State, depends for its validity upon the laws of the sovereignty in which it is exercised; and a corporation can make no valid contract without their sanction, express or implied. And this brings us to the question which has been so elaborately discussed; whether, by the comity of nations and between these States, the corporations of one State are permitted to make contracts in another. . . .

It cannot be necessary to pursue the argument further. We think it is well settled that by the law of comity among nations, a corporation created by one sovereignty is permitted to make contracts in another, and to sue in its courts; and that the same law of comity prevails among the several sovereignties of this Union. The public and well known and long continued usages of trade; the general acqui-

escence of the States; the particular legislation of some of them as well as the legislation of Congress; all concur in proving the truth of this proposition.

But we have already said that this comity is presumed from the silent acquiescence of the State. Whenever a State sufficiently indicates that contracts which derive their validity from its comity are repugnant to its policy, or are considered as injurious to its interest, the presumption in favor of its adoption can no longer be made. . . .

73. *Federalism, the Commerce Clause, and the Judiciary*

Cooley v. Board of Wardens of the Port of Philadelphia, 12 Howard 299 (1852).

CURTIS, J.: . . . The power to regulate navigation is the power to prescribe rules in conformity with which navigation must be carried on. It extends to the persons who conduct it, as well as to the instruments used. Accordingly, the first congress assembled under the constitution passed laws, requiring the masters of ships and vessels of the United States to be citizens of the United States, and established many rules for the government and regulation of officers and seamen. . . . These have been from time to time added to and changed, and we are not aware that their validity has been questioned.

Now, a pilot, so far as respects the navigation of the vessel in that part of the voyage which is his pilotage-ground, is the temporary master charged with the safety of the vessel and cargo, and of the lives of those on board, and intrusted with the command of the crew. He is not only one of the persons engaged in navigation, but he occupies a most important and responsible place among those thus engaged. And if congress has power to regulate the seamen who assist the pilot in the management of the vessel, a power never denied, we can perceive no valid

reason why the pilot should be beyond the reach of the same power. . . .

Nor should it be lost sight of, that this subject of the regulation of pilots and pilotage has an intimate connection with, and an important relation to, the general subject of commerce with foreign nations and among the several States, over which it was one main object of the constitution to create a national control. . . .

And a majority of the Court are of opinion, that a regulation of pilots is a regulation of commerce, within the grant to congress of the commercial power, contained in the third clause of the eighth section of the first article of the constitution.

It becomes necessary, therefore, to consider whether this law of Pennsylvania, being a regulation of commerce, is valid.

The act of Congress of the 7th of August, 1789, section 4, is as follows:

"That all pilots in the bays, inlets, rivers, harbors, and ports of the United States shall continue to be regulated in conformity with the existing laws of the states, respectively, wherein such pilots may be, or with such laws as the states may respectively hereafter enact for the purpose, until further legislative provision shall be made by Congress.". . .

We are brought directly and unavoidably to the consideration of the question, whether the grant of the commercial power to congress did, *per se* deprive the States of all power to regulate pilots. This question has never been decided by this court, nor, in our judgment, has any case depending upon all the considerations which must govern this one, come before this court. The grant of commercial power to congress does not contain any terms which expressly exclude the States from exercising an authority over its subject-matter. If they are excluded, it must be because the nature of the power thus granted to congress requires that a similar authority should not exist in the States. If it were conceded on the one side that the nature of this power, like that to legislate for the District of Columbia, is absolutely and totally repugnant to the existence of similar power in the States, probably no one would deny that the grant of the power to congress, as effectually and perfectly excludes the States from all future legislation on the subject, as if express words had been used to exclude them. And on the other hand, if it were admitted that the existence of this power in congress, like the power of taxation, is compatible with the existence of a similar power in the States, then it would be in conformity with the contemporary exposition of the constitution (Federalist, No. 32), and with the judicial construction given from time to time by this court, after the most deliberate consideration, to hold that the mere grant of such a power to congress, did not imply a prohibition on the states to exercise the same power; that it is not the mere existence of such a power, but its exercise by congress, which may be incompatible with the exercise of the same power by the States, and that the States may legislate in the absence of congressional regulations. . . .

The diversities of opinion, therefore, which have existed on this subject have arisen from the different views taken of the nature of this power. But when the nature of a power like this is spoken of, when it is said that the nature of the power requires that it should be exercised exclusively by congress, it must be intended to refer to the subjects of that power, and to say they are of such a nature as to require exclusive legislation by congress. Now, the power to regulate commerce embraces a vast field, containing not only many, but exceedingly various subjects, quite unlike in their nature; some imperatively demanding a single uniform rule, operating equally on the commerce of the United States in every port; and some, like the subject now in question, as imperatively demanding that diversity, which alone can meet the local necessities of navigation.

Either absolutely to affirm, or deny that the nature of this power requires exclusive legislation by congress, is to lose sight of the nature of the subjects of this power, and to assert concerning all of them, what is really applicable but to a part. Whatever subjects of this power are in their nature national, or admit only of one uniform system, or plan of regulation, may justly be said to be of such a nature as to require exclusive legislation by congress. That this cannot be affirmed of laws for the regulation of pilots and pilotage, is plain. The act of 1789 contains a clear and authoritative declaration by the first congress, that the nature of this subject is such that until congress should find it necessary to exert its power, it should be left to the legislation of the States; that it is local and not national; that it is likely to be the best provided for, not by one system, or plan of regulation, but by as many as the legislative discretion of the several States should deem applicable to the local peculiarities of the ports within their limits. . . .

It is the opinion of a majority of the court that the mere grant to congress of the power to regulate commerce, did not deprive the States of power to regulate pilots, and that although congress has legislated on this subject, its legislation manifests an intention, with a single exception, not to regulate this subject, but to leave its regulation to the several States. To these precise questions, which are all we are called on to decide, this opinion must be understood to be confined. It does not extend to the question [of] what other subjects, under the commercial power, are within the exclusive control of congress, or may be regulated by the States in the absence of all congressional legislation; nor to the general question, how far any regulation of a subject by congress may be deemed to operate as an exclusion of all legislation by the States upon the same subject. We decide the precise questions before us, upon what we deem sound principles, applicable to this particular subject in the state in which the legislation of congress has left it. We go no further. . . .

74. *State Courts, Labor Organizations, and the Conspiracy Doctrine*

A. PEOPLE *V*. FISHER, NEW YORK (1835)

N. Y. Reports, 14 Wend. 9.

SAVAGE, C. J.: The legislature have given us their definition of conspiracies, and abrogated the common law on the subject. We must, therefore, see whether this case comes within the statute. The legislature have said, ". . . 6. To commit any act injurious to the public health, to public morals, or to trade or commerce; or for the perversion or obstruction of justice of the due administration of the laws —they shall be deemed guilty of a misdemeanor" . . . and in section 9 it is declared that "no conspiracies, other than such as are enumerated in the last section, are punishable criminally." If the conspiracy charged in the indictment is an offence under this statute, it must be embraced under the sixth subdivision, and is an act injurious to trade or commerce. . . .

The question therefore is: is a conspiracy to raise the wages of journeymen shoemakers, an act injurious to trade or commerce? . . .

Whatever disputes may exist among political economists upon the point, I think there can be no doubt in a legal sense, but what the wages of labor compose a material portion of the value of manufactured articles. The products of mechanical labor compose a large proportion of the materials with which trade is carried on. By trade, I now understand traffic or mutual dealings between members of the same community, or internal trade. Coarse boots and shoes are made in many parts of our country; not for particular persons who are to wear them, but as an article of trade and commerce. Probably such is the case in Geneva, where this offence was committed. If journeymen bootmakers, by extravagant demands for wages, so enhance the price of boots made in Geneva, for instance, that boots made elsewhere, in Auburn for example, can be sold cheaper, is not such an act injurious to trade? It is surely so to the trade of Geneva in that particular article, and that I apprehend is all that is necessary to bring the offence within the statute. It is important to the best interests of society that the price of labor be left to regulate itself, or rather, be limited by the demand for it. Combinations and confederacies to enhance or reduce the prices of labor, or of any articles of trade or commerce, are injurious. They may be oppressive by compelling the public to give more for an article of necessity or of convenience than it is worth; or, on the other hand, of compelling the labor of the mechanic for less than its value. Without any officious and improper interference on the subject, the price of labor or the wages of mechanics will be regulated by the demand for the manufactured article, and the value of that which is paid for it; but the right does not exist either to enhance the price of the article or the wages of the mechanic, by any forced and artificial means. The man who owns an article of trade or commerce is not obliged to sell it for any particular price. Nor is the mechanic obliged by law to labor for any particular price. He may say that he will not make coarse boots for less than one dollar per pair, but he has no right to say that no other mechanic shall make them for less. The cloth merchant may say that he will not sell his goods for less than so much per yard, but has no right to say that any other merchant shall not sell for a less price. If one individual does not possess such a right over the conduct of another, no number of individuals can possess such a right. All combinations, therefore, to effect such an object are in-

jurious, not only to the individual particularly oppressed, but to the public at large.

It is true, that no great danger is to be apprehended on account of the impracticability of . . . universal combinations. But if universally or even generally entered into, they would be prejudicial to trade and to the public; they are wrong in each particular case. The truth is, that industry requires no such means to support it. Competition is the life of trade. If the defendants cannot make coarse boots for less than one dollar per pair, let them refuse to do so; but let them not directly or indirectly undertake to say that others shall not do the work for a less price. It may be that Pennock, from greater industry or greater skill, made more profit by making boots at 75 cents per pair than the defendants at a dollar. He had a right to work for what he pleased. His employer had a right to employ him for such price as they could agree upon. The interference of the defendants was unlawful; its tendency is not only to individual oppression, but to public inconvenience and embarrassment.

I am of the opinion that the offence is indictable, and that the judgment of the general sessions of Ontario county should be reversed, and that a *venire de novo* should issue.

Judgment accordingly.

B. COMMONWEALTH *V.* HUNT, MASSACHUSETTS (1842)

Mass. Reports, 4 Metcalf 45.

SHAW, C. J.: . . . We have no doubt, that by the operation of the constitution of this Commonwealth, the general rules of the common law, making conspiracy an indictable offence, are in force here, and that this is included in the description of laws which had, before the adoption of the constitution, been used and approved in the Province, Colony, or State of Massa-

chusetts Bay, and usually practised in the courts of law. . . . Still it is proper in this connexion to remark, that although the common law in regard to conspiracy in this Commonwealth is in force, yet it will not necessarily follow that every indictment at common law for this offence is a precedent for a similar indictment in this State. The general rule of the common law is, that it is a criminal and indictable offence, for two or more to confederate and combine together, by concerted means, to do that which is unlawful or criminal, to the injury of the public, or portions or classes of the community, or even to the rights of an individual. This rule of law may be equally in force as a rule of the common law, in England and in this Commonwealth; and yet it must depend upon the local laws of each country to determine, whether the purpose to be accomplished by the combination, or the concerted means of accomplishing it, be unlawful or criminal in the respective countries. All those laws of the parent country, whether rules of the common law, or early English statutes, which were made for the purpose of regulating the wages of laborers, the settlement of paupers, and making it penal for anyone to use a trade or handicraft to which he had not served a full apprenticeship—not being adapted to the circumstances of our colonial condition—were not adopted, used or approved, and therefore do not come within the description of the laws adopted and confirmed by the provision of the constitution already cited. . . .

Stripped then of these introductory recitals and alleged injurious consequences, and of the qualifying epithets attached to the facts, the averment is this; that the defendants and others formed themselves into a society, and agreed not to work for any person who should employ any journeyman or other person, not a member of such society, after notice given him to discharge such workman. The manifest intent of the association is, to induce all those engaged in the same occupation to become members of it. Such a purpose is not unlawful. It would give them a power which might be exerted for useful and honorable purposes, or for dangerous and pernicious ones. If the latter were the real and actual object, and susceptible of proof, it should have been specially charged. Such an association might be used to afford each other assistance in

times of poverty, sickness and distress; or to raise their intellectual, moral and social condition; or to make improvement in their art; or for other proper purposes. Or the association might be designed for purposes of oppression and injustice. . . .

Nor can we perceive that the objects of this association, whatever they may have been, were to be attained by criminal means. The means which they proposed to employ, as averred in this count, and which, as we are now to presume, were established by the proof, were, that they would not work for a person, who, after due notice, should employ a journeyman not a member of their society. Supposing the object of the association to be laudable and lawful, or at least not unlawful, are these means criminal? The case supposes that these persons are not bound by contract, but free to work for whom they please, or not to work, if they so prefer. In this state of things, we cannot perceive, that it is criminal for men to agree together to exercise their own acknowledged rights, in such a manner as best to subserve their own interests. One way to test this is, to consider the effect of such an agreement, where the object of the association is acknowledged on all hands to be a laudable one. Suppose a class of workmen, impressed with the manifold evils of intemperance, should agree with each other not to work in a shop in which ardent spirit was furnished, or not to work in a shop with any one who used it, or not to work for an employer, who should, after notice, employ a journeyman who habitually used it. The consequences might be the same. A workman, who should still persist in the use of ardent spirit, would find it more difficult to get employment; a master employing such an one might, at times, experience inconvenience in his work, in losing the services of a skilful but intemperate workman. Still it seems to us, that as the object would be lawful, and the means not unlawful, such an agreement could not be pronounced a criminal conspiracy. . . .

We think, therefore, that associations may be entered into, the object of which is to adopt measures that may have a tendency to impoverish another, that is, to diminish his gains and profits, and yet so far from being criminal or unlawful, the object may be highly meritorious and public spirited. The legality of such an association will therefore depend upon the means to be used for its accomplishment. . . .

CHAPTER X

Slavery and Sectionalism

ONE of the ironies of American constitutional development was the almost simultaneous appearance in the colonies of the institutions of representative government and slavery. By the time of the Declaration of Independence, the inconsistency of freedom and servitude was so evident that Jefferson's original draft contained a severe indictment of George III for perpetuating slavery in America by suppressing every legislative action by the colonies "to prohibit or to restrain this execrable commerce"—the slave trade (No. 75).

During the Revolution, a majority of the states provided for outright or gradual abolition of slavery. Although questions pertaining to slavery, the slave trade, and counting slaves for apportionment and direct taxation required sectional compromises, the Constitutional Convention apparently accepted the premise that the Union could "endure permanently half slave and half free." There was general agreement that the foreign slave trade should be halted, although prior to 1808 Congressional action was prohibited. In 1806 President Jefferson reminded Congress of its authority, and the result was the Act of 1807 banning the slave trade (No. 76).

As cotton culture expanded in the South, the temptation to violate the importation ban increased. In an effort to police the source of supply more effectively, the United States and Great Britain ratified the Webster-Ashburton Treaty in 1842, establishing a joint patrol of African waters. As a result of the growing humanitarian protests of the 1840's, both the foreign and the domestic slave trades were severely condemned, and Congress, in the famed Compromise of 1850, made a minor concession by abolishing the slave trade in the nation's capital.

One of the most delicate constitutional problems connected with slavery was the interstate rendition of runaway slaves. In 1793 Congress passed the original fugitive slave act, imposing dual responsibility on the federal government and the states. The rise of antislavery sentiment in the North, however, led several states to enact "personal liberty laws" which virtually nullified the federal statute's provisions. The constitutionality of this Northern challenge to federal authority was reviewed in *Prigg v. Pennsylvania* (No. 77) with ambiguous results. Although Justice Story struck down the Pennsylvania liberty law and upheld the exclusive character of federal authority, he also ruled that no state official had to assist in implementing the fugitive slave law. As a result, an even greater number of state liberty laws were passed forbidding local authorities to enforce the federal act. In the Compromise of 1850, Congress passed a new fugitive slave act that forbade any interference with enforcement. Open defiance of this statute by Wisconsin (No. 78) raised the ominous issue of nullification in the North at the very moment that states'-righters were discussing secession in the South.

The chief constitutional and political manifestation of the growing slavery controversy was the extent of congressional control over the future of that peculiar institution. One of the early acts of Congress under the Constitution was a renewal of the Northwest Ordinance of 1787, including its antislavery provisions. The acquisition of the Louisiana Territory posed the problem anew, but Congress quietly disregarded it and failed to extend the Northwest Territory stipulations. When Missouri applied for admission to the Union, the issue could no longer be ignored. Indeed, the issue of slavery in the territories was almost a by-product of the question of Congress's right to impose conditions on incoming states. Could Congress constitutionally restrict slavery in new states, or interfere with Negro servitude in any manner? The North's resounding affirmative answer was the Tallmadge Amendment, prohibiting further importation of slaves into Missouri and freeing slave children at age 25. An adamant South, however, deadlocked Congress and it was not until Maine petitioned for admittance as a free state that a compromise became possible. When the North backed down on its effort to impose conditions on new states and agreed to Missouri's proslavery constitution, Congress reasserted its power to control slavery in the territories; in all the remaining portions of the Louisiana Purchase north of 36° 30′ slavery was to be forever prohibited.

After the Missouri Compromise, the slavery controversy as a sectional issue was eclipsed by such economic problems as the tariff issue, banking and currency, land policy, and internal improvements. Calhoun admitted as early as 1830, however, that "the real cause of the present unhappy state of things" was "the peculiar domestic institution of the Southern States." At the time of the nullification conflict over the tariff, Jackson also predicted that the next great sectional crisis would be "the Negro, or slavery question." Jackson's fear was well grounded, for a growing abolition movement was stimulated by the appearance on New Year's Day, 1831, of William Lloyd Garrison's *Liberator*. Garrison was instrumental in organizing the New England Anti-Slavery Society in 1832 and the American Anti-

Slavery Convention in 1833. Although the defiant *Declaration of Sentiments* of the latter society (No. 79) denounced as "utterly null and void" in the sight of God all laws that recognized slavery, the abolitionists agreed that the Constitution gave Congress no right to interfere with the peculiar institution in any slave State. But they also maintained that slavery should be removed "by moral and political action, as prescribed in the Constitution of the United States."

The Southern reaction to these aggressive views was to demand censorship of the mails (South Carolina Resolutions, No. 80). Jackson, himself a slaveowner, sympathized with this suggestion, and recommended a federal censorship law to Congress in 1835 (No. 81). Although Congress refused to take this action, the House restricted the right of petition by adopting the "Gag Rule" in 1836 to prevent discussion of abolitionist pleas (No. 82A). Over the vehement constitutional protests of ex-President John Quincy Adams, the House flatly rejected all abolitionist petitions in 1840, but the growth of antislavery sentiment made it possible four years later for the Adams view to prevail (No. 82B).

Although the proslavery advocates insisted that chattel servitude was positively protected by the federal Constitution, they also maintained that it was a purely domestic institution. The dichotomy in their thinking is well illustrated by Calhoun's position on federal censorship. Fearful of the nationalistic implications of federal postal control, the South Carolinian rejected this method of protecting slavery and turned to the state sovereignty arguments of the nullification period. In a series of six Senate resolutions in 1837, he converted his constitutional theory of state sovereignty into a defense of slavery (No. 83). Thus the "Marx of the Master Class" forged a double-barreled constitutional weapon that served as a Southern defense against both nationalism and abolitionism.

The Mexican War opened new avenues of agitation to the antislavery advocates. For the first time since the Missouri Compromise, the whole question of slavery extension in the territories was revived in Congress as a central political and constitutional issue. Immediately responsible for this was David Wilmot, who introduced a proviso "that, as an express and fundamental condition to the acquisition of any territory from the Republic of Mexico by the United States . . . neither slavery nor involuntary servitude shall ever exist in any part of said territory." Though not enacted, the Wilmot proviso set off a series of historic debates about slavery in the newly acquired territories. Between 1847 and 1850 four major solutions to the vexing problem were presented. The Southern argument followed closely Calhoun's resolutions of 1837 and many Northerners subscribed to Wilmot's views. Some moderates agreed with President Polk's suggestion that the Missouri Compromise line should be extended to the West Coast. In a letter to Governor A. O. P. Nicholson of Tennessee, Senator Lewis Cass of Michigan offered the new doctrine of "squatter sovereignty," which was popular because of its compromise character and favored by many politicians because it would transfer the issue from Congress to the people in the territories (No. 84).

With the admission of California as a free state and the application of the "popular sovereignty" formula to the rest of the Mexican Territory, slavery extension seemed a dead issue, but territorial politics and railroad rivalries combined to frustrate the hopes of the compromisers. In his desire to obtain a northern transcontinental railroad route, Senator Douglas of Illinois, chairman of the committee on territories, proposed to transplant "popular sovereignty" to the remaining unorganized Louisiana Purchase Territory. The Kansas-Nebraska Act (No. 85), therefore, repealed the Missouri Compromise and opened the final stage of the slavery controversy.

Southerners generally favored the Kansas-Nebraska Act because it opened to slavery a vast territory closed since 1820. But in 1857 they rejoiced when the Taney Court handed down the Dred Scott decision (No. 86), which they hoped would fix for all time the constitutional status of slavery in the territories. Instead, the Supreme Court decision, the first exercise of judicial invalidation of a congressional measure since *Marbury v. Madison*, was opposed by an overwhelming majority in the North. Neither the first nor the best-known adversary was a former Whig Congressman from Illinois, Abraham Lincoln. But his views (No. 87) appealed to the new Republican party in his home state, which chose him as its senatorial candidate against Stephen A. Douglas. In a series of famous debates, Lincoln hammered at the inconsistency of the Dred Scott opinion and Douglas's formula of popular sovereignty. Douglas's Freeport Doctrine (No. 88) contended that the people in a territory could exclude slavery, notwithstanding the Supreme Court ruling. Although this clever solution to his dilemma won for Douglas reelection to the Senate, Lincoln, in a prophetic comment a year later, got in the final word: "There was something about that answer," he confided, "that has probably been a trouble to . . . Judge [Douglas] ever since" (No. 89).

The Slave Trade and Fugitive Slaves

THE SLAVE TRADE: "THIS EXECRABLE COMMERCE"

75. *What the Declaration of Independence Did Not Say About Slavery*

Boyd, ed., *Papers of Thomas Jefferson*, I, 426.

He [the King of Great Britain] has waged cruel war against human nature itself, violating its most sacred rights of life & liberty in the persons of a distant people who never offended him, captivating & carrying them into slavery in another hemisphere, or to incur miserable death in their transportation thither. This piratical warfare, the opprobrium of *infidel* powers, is the warfare of the *Christian* King of Great Britain. Determined to keep open a market where MEN should be bought & sold, he has prostituted his negative for suppressing every legislative attempt to prohibit or to restrain this execrable commerce: and that this assemblage of horrors might want no fact of distinguished die, he is now exciting those very people to rise in arms among us, and to purchase that liberty of which *he* has deprived them by murdering the people upon whom *he* also obtruded them; thus paying off former crimes committed against the *liberties* of one people, with crimes which he urges them to commit against the *lives* of another.

76. *Congress Prohibits the Slave Trade, 1807*

U. S. Stat. at L., II, 426-8.

Be it enacted . . . That from and after the first day of January, one thousand eight hundred and eight, it shall not be lawful to import or bring into the United States or the territories thereof from any foreign kingdom, place, or country, any negro, mulatto, or person of colour, as a slave, or to be held to service or labour.

SEC. 2. That no citizen of the United States, or any other person, shall, from and after the first day of January, in the year of our Lord one thousand eight hundred and eight, for himself, or themselves, or any other person whatsoever, either as master, factor, or owner, build, fit, equip, load or to otherwise prepare any ship or vessel, in any port or place within the jurisdiction of the United States, nor shall cause any ship or vessel to sail from any port or place within the same, for the purpose of procuring any negro, mulatto, or person of colour, from any foreign kingdom, place, or country, to be transported to any port or place whatsoever within the jurisdiction of the United States, to be held, sold, or disposed of as slaves, or to be held to service or labour: and if any ship or vessel shall be so fitted out for the purpose aforesaid, or shall be caused to sail so as aforesaid, every such ship or vessel, her tackle, apparel, and furniture, shall be forfeited to the United States, and shall be liable to be seized, prosecuted, and condemned in any of the circuit courts or district courts, for the district where the said ship or vessel may be found or seized. . . .

SEC. 4. If any citizen or citizens of the United States, or any person resident within the jurisdiction of the same, shall, from and after the first day of January, one thousand eight hundred and eight, take on board, receive or transport from any of the coasts or kingdoms of Africa, or from any other foreign kingdom, place, or country, any negro, mulatto, or person of colour in any ship or vessel, for the purpose of selling them in any port or place within the jurisdiction of the United States as slaves, or to be held to service or labour, or shall be in any ways aiding or abetting therein, such citizen or citizens, or person, shall severally forfeit and pay five thousand dollars, one moiety thereof to the use of any person or persons who shall sue for and prosecute the same to effect. . . .

SEC. 6. That if any person or persons whatsoever, shall, from and after the first day of January, one thousand eight hundred and eight, purchase or sell any negro, mulatto, or person of colour, for a slave, or to be held to service or labour, who shall have been imported, or brought from any foreign kingdom, place, or country, or from the dominions of any foreign state, immediately adjoining to the United States, after the last day of December, one thousand eight hundred and seven, knowing at the time of such purchase or sale, such negro, mulatto, or person of colour, was so brought within the jurisdiction of the United States, as aforesaid, such purchaser and seller shall severally forfeit and pay for every negro, mulatto, or person of colour, so purchased or sold as aforesaid, eight hundred dollars. . . .

SEC. 7. That if any ship or vessel shall be found, from and after the first day of January, one thousand eight hundred and eight, in any river, port, bay, or harbor, or on the high seas, within the jurisdictional limits of the United States, or hovering on the coast thereof, having on board any negro, mulatto, or person of colour, for the purpose of selling them as slaves, or with intent to land the same, in any port or place within the jurisdiction of the United States, contrary to the prohibition of the act, every such ship or vessel, together with her tackle, apparel, and furniture, and the goods or effects which shall be found on board the same, shall be forfeited to the use of the United States, and may be seized, prosecuted, and condemned, in any court of the United States, having jurisdiction thereof. And it shall be lawful for the President of the United States, and he is hereby authorized, should he deem it expedient, to cause any of the armed vessels of the United States to be manned and employed to cruise on any part of the coast of the United States, or territories thereof, where he may judge attempts will be made to violate the provisions of this act, and to instruct and direct the commanders of armed vessels of the United States, to seize, take, and bring into any port of the United States all such ships or vessels, and moreover to seize, take, or bring into any port of the United States all ships or vessels of the United States, wheresoever found on the high seas, contravening the provisions of this act, to be proceeded against according to law. . . .

FUGITIVE SLAVES AND INTERSTATE RENDITION

77. *Congressional Power over the Rendition of Fugitive Slaves*

Prigg v. Pennsylvania, 16 Peters 539 (1842).

STORY, J.: . . . The facts are briefly these: the plaintiff in error was indicted in . . . York County for having, . . . taken and carried away from that county to the State of Maryland, a certain negro woman, named Margaret Morgan, with a design and intention of selling and disposing of, and keeping her as a slave or servant for life, contrary to a statute of Pennsylvania, passed on the 26th of March 1826. That statute in the first section, . . . provides, that if any person or persons shall from and after the passing of the act, by force and violence take and carry away . . . and shall by fraud and false pretense seduce . . . any negro or mulatto from any part of that Commonwealth, . . . [he] shall on conviction thereof, be deemed guilty of a felony. . . .

The counsel for the plaintiff have contended that the statute of Pennsylvania is unconstitutional. . . . Few questions which have ever come before this court involve more delicate and important considerations; and few upon which the public at large may be presumed to feel a more profound and pervading interest. . . .

There are two clauses in the constitution upon the subject of fugitives which stand in juxtaposition with each other, and have been thought mutually to illustrate each other. They are both contained in the second section of the fourth article. . . .

The last clause is that, the true interpretation whereof is directly in judgment before us. Historically, it is well known that the object of this clause was to secure to the citizens of the slaveholding States the complete right and title of ownership in their slaves, as property, in every State in the Union into which they might escape from the State where they were held in servitude. . . .

We have not the slightest hesitation in holding that, under and in virtue of the constitution, the owner of a slave is clothed with entire authority, in every State in the Union, to seize and recapture his slave, whenever he can do it without any breach of the peace or any illegal violence. . . .

This leads us to the consideration of the other part of the clause which implies at once a guarantee and duty. It says: "But he (the slave) shall be delivered up on claim of the party to whom such service or labor may be due." . . .

A claim is to be made. What is a claim? It is, in a just juridical sense, a demand of some matter as of right made by one person upon another, to do or to forbear to do some act or thing as a matter of duty. . . . The slave is to be delivered up on the claim. By whom to be delivered up? In what mode to be delivered up? How, if a refusal takes place, is the right of delivery to be enforced? Upon what proofs? What shall be the evidence of a rightful recaption or delivery? When and under what circumstances shall the possession of the owner, after it is obtained, be conclusive of his right, so as to preclude any further inquiry or examination into it by local tribunals or otherwise, while the slave, in possession of the owner, is in transitu to the State from which he fled?

These . . . questions . . . require the aid of legislation to protect the right, to enforce the delivery, and to secure the subsequent possession of the slave. . . .

Congress has taken this very view of the power and duty of the national government. . . . The result of their deliberations, was the passage of the [Fugitive Slave] act of the 12th of February, 1793. . . .

We hold the act to be clearly constitutional in all its leading provisions, and, indeed, with the exception of that part which confers authority upon State magistrates, to be free from reasonable doubt and difficulty. . . . As to the authority so conferred upon state magistrates, while a difference of opinion has existed, and may

exist still on the point, in different States, whether state magistrates are bound to act under it, none is entertained by this court, that state magistrates may, if they choose, exercise that authority, unless prohibited by state legislation.

The remaining question is, whether the power of legislation upon this subject is exclusive in the national government, or concurrent in the States, until it is exercised by congress. In our opinion it is exclusive; and we shall now proceed briefly to state our reasons for that opinion. . . . In the first place it is material to state . . . that the right to seize and retake fugitive slaves and the duty to deliver them up, in whatever State of the Union they may be found, and of course the corresponding power of Congress to use the appropriate means to enforce the right and duty, derive their whole validity and obligation exclusively from the Constitution of the United States. . . . Under the constitution, it is recognized as an absolute, positive right and duty, pervading the whole Union with an equal and supreme force, uncontrolled and uncontrollable by state sovereignty or state legislation. It is, therefore, in a just sense, a new and positive right, independent of comity, confined to no territorial limits, and bounded by no state institutions or policy. The natural inference deducible from this consideration certainly is, in the absence of any positive delegation of power to the state legislatures, that it belongs to the legislative department of the national government, to which it owes its origin and establishment. . . .

In the next place, the nature of the provision and the objects to be attained by it require that it should be controlled by one and the same will, and act uniformly by the same system of regulations throughout the Union. If, then, the States have a right, in the absence of legislation by congress, to act upon the subject, each State is at liberty to prescribe just such regulations as suit its own policy, local convenience, and local feelings. . . .

It is scarcely conceivable that the slave-holding States would have been satisfied with leaving to the legislation of the non-slaveholding States a power of regulation, in the absence of that of congress, which would or might practically amount to a power to destroy the rights of the owner. If the argument, therefore, of a concurrent power in the States to act upon the subject-matter in the absence of legislation by congress be well founded; then, if congress had never acted at all, or if the act of congress should be repealed without providing a substitute, there would be a resulting authority in each of the States to regulate the whole subject at its pleasure, and to dole out its own remedial justice, or withhold it at its pleasure and according to its own views of policy and expediency. Surely such a state of things never could have been intended, under such a solemn guarantee of right and duty. On the other hand, construe the right of legislation as exclusive in congress, and every evil and every danger vanishes. The right and the duty are then co-extensive and uniform in remedy and operation throughout the whole Union. The owner has the same security, and the same remedial justice, and the same ex-emption from state regulation and control through however many States he may pass with his fugitive slave in his posses-sion. . . .

These are some of the reasons but by no means all upon which we hold the power of legislation on this subject to be exclu-sive in Congress. To guard, however, against any possible misconstruction of our views, it is proper to state that we are by no means to be understood, in any manner whatsoever to doubt or to inter-fere with the police power belonging to the States, in virtue of their general sover-eignty. That police power extends over all subjects within the territorial limits of the States, and has never been conceded to the United States. . . . But such regu-lations can never be permitted to inter-fere with or to obstruct the just rights of the owner to reclaim his slave, derived from the constitution of the United States, or with the remedies prescribed by congress to aid and enforce the same.

Upon these grounds we are of opinion that the act of Pennsylvania upon which this indictment is founded, is unconstitu-tional and void. . . .

Judgment . . . reversed . . .

78. *Wisconsin Attempts to Nullify the Fugitive Slave Act*

Ableman v. Booth, 21 Howard 506 (1859).

TANEY, C. J.: . . . In the case before the Supreme Court of Wisconsin, a right was claimed under the Constitution and laws of the United States, and the decision was against the right claimed; and it re-fuses obedience to the writ of error, and regards its own judgment as final. It has not only reversed and annulled the judg-ment of the District Court of the United States, but it has reversed and annulled the provisions of the Constitution itself, and the act of Congress of 1789, and made the superior and appellate tribunal the in-ferior and subordinate one.

We do not question the authority of State court, or judge, who is authorized by the laws of the State to issue the writ of *habeas corpus*, to issue it in any case where the party is imprisoned within its territorial limits, provided it does not ap-pear, when the application is made, that the person imprisoned is in custody under the authority of the United States. The court or judge has a right to inquire, in this mode of proceeding, for what cause and by what authority the prisoner is con-fined within the territorial limits of the State sovereignty. And it is the duty of the marshal, or other person having the custody of the prisoner, to make known to the judge or court, by a proper return, the authority by which he holds him in custody. This right to inquire by process of *habeas corpus*, and the duty of the officer to make a return, grows, necessarily, out of the complex character of our Government, and the existence of two distinct and separate sovereignties within the same territorial space, each of them restricted in its powers, and each within its sphere of action, prescribed by the Constitution of the United States, independent of the other. But, after the return is made, and the State judge or court judicially apprized that the party is in custody under the authority of the United States, they can proceed no further. They then know that the prisoner is within the dominion and jurisdiction of another Government, and that neither the writ of *habeas corpus,* nor any other process issued under State authority, can pass over the line of division between the two sovereignties. He is then within the dominion and exclusive jurisdiction of the United States. If he has committed an offence against their laws, their tribunals alone can punish him. If he is wrongfully imprisoned, their judicial tribunals can release him and afford him redress. And although, as we have said, it is the duty of the marshal, or other person holding him, to make known, by a proper return, the

authority under which he detains him, it is at the same time imperatively his duty to obey the process of the United States, to hold the prisoner in custody under it, and to refuse obedience to the mandate or process of any other Government. And consequently it is his duty not to take the prisoner, nor suffer him to be taken, before a State judge or court upon a *habeas corpus* issued under State authority. No State judge or court, after they are judicially informed that the party is imprisoned under the authority of the United States, has any right to interfere with him, or to require him to be brought before them. And if the authority of a State, in the form of judicial process or otherwise, should attempt to control the marshal or other authorized officer or agent of the United States in any respect, in the custody of his prisoner, it would be his duty to resist it, and to call to his aid any force that might be necessary to maintain the authority of law against illegal interference. No judicial process, whatever form it may assume, can have any lawful authority outside of the limits of the jurisdiction of the court or judge by whom it is issued; and an attempt to enforce it beyond these boundaries is nothing less than lawless violence. . . .

Judgment reversed.

Congressional Control Over Slavery

THE ABOLITIONIST ATTACK

79. *The American Anti-Slavery Society's "Declaration of Sentiments," December 6, 1833*

Wendell Phillips Garrison and Francis Jackson Garrison, *William Lloyd Garrison, 1805-1879: The Story of His Life Told by His Children* (New York, 1885), I, 408-12.

We have met together for the achievement of an enterprise without which that of our fathers is incomplete; and which, for its magnitude, solemnity, and probable results upon the destiny of the world, as far transcends theirs as moral truth does physical force. . . .

Their grievances, great as they were, were trifling in comparison with the wrongs and sufferings of those for whom we plead. Our fathers were never slaves— never bought and sold like cattle—never shut out from the light of knowledge and religion—never subjected to the lash of brutal taskmasters.

But those for whose emancipation we are striving—constituting at the present time at least one-sixth part of our country-men—are recognized by law, and treated by their fellow-beings, as marketable commodities, as goods and chattels, as brute beasts; are plundered daily of the fruits of their toil without redress; really enjoy no constitutional nor legal protection from licentious and murderous outrages upon their persons; and are ruthlessly torn asunder—the tender babe from the arms of its frantic mother—the heart-broken wife from her weeping husband— at the caprice or pleasure of irresponsible tyrants. For the crime of having a dark complexion, they suffer the pangs of hunger, the infliction of stripes, the ignominy of brutal servitude. They are kept in heathenish darkness by laws expressly enacted to make their instruction a criminal offence.

These are the prominent circumstances in the condition of more than two millions of our people, the proof of which may be found in thousands of indisputable facts, and in the laws of the slaveholding States.

Hence we maintain—that, in view of the civil and religious privileges of this nation, the guilt of its oppression is unequalled by any other on the face of the earth; and, therefore, that it is bound to repent instantly, to undo the heavy burdens, and to let the oppressed go free. . . .

It is piracy to buy or steal a native African, and subject him to servitude. Surely, the sin is as great to enslave an American as an African.

Therefore we believe and affirm—that there is no difference, in principle, between the African slave trade and American slavery:

That every American citizen who detains a human being in involuntary bondage as his property, is, according to Scripture, (Ex. xxi 16), a man-stealer:

That the slaves ought instantly to be set free, and brought under the protection of law:

That if they had lived from the time of Pharaoh down to the present period, and had been entailed through successive generations, their right to be free could never have been alienated, but their claims would have constantly risen in solemnity:

That all those laws which are now in force, admitting the right of slavery, are therefore, before God, utterly null and void; being an audacious usurpation of the Divine prerogative, a daring infringement on the law of nature, a base overthrow of the very foundations of the social compact, a complete extinction of all the relations, endearments and obligations of mankind, and a presumptuous transgression of all the holy commandments; and that therefore they ought instantly to be abrogated.

We further believe and affirm—that all persons of color, who possess the qualifications which are demanded of others, ought to be admitted forthwith to the enjoyment of the same privileges, and the exercise of the same prerogatives, as others; and that the paths of preferment, of wealth and of intelligence, should be opened as widely to them as to persons of a white complexion.

We maintain that no compensation should be given to the planters emancipating their slaves:

Because it would be a surrender of the great fundamental principle, that man cannot hold property in man; . . .

We regard as delusive, cruel and dangerous, any scheme of expatriation which pretends to aid, either directly or indirectly, in the emancipation of the slaves, or to be a substitute for the immediate and total abolition of slavery.

We fully and unanimously recognize the sovereignty of each State, to legislate exclusively on the subject of the slavery which is tolerated within its limits; we concede that Congress, under the present national compact, has no right to interfere with any of the slave States, in relation to this momentous subject:

But we maintain that Congress has a right, and is solemnly bound, to suppress the domestic slave trade between the several States, and to abolish slavery in those portions of our territory which the Constitution has placed under its exclusive jurisdiction.

We also maintain that there are, at the present time, the highest obligations resting upon the people of the free States to remove slavery by moral and political action, as prescribed in the Constitution of the United States. They are now living under a pledge of their tremendous physical force, to fasten the galling fetters of tyranny upon the limbs of millions in the Southern States; they are liable to be called at any moment to suppress a general insurrection of the slaves; they authorize the slave owner to vote for three-fifths of his slaves as property, and thus enable him to perpetuate his oppression; they support a standing army at the South for its protection; and they seize the slave who has escaped into their territories, and send him back to be tortured by an enraged master or a brutal driver. This relation to slavery is criminal, and full of danger: IT MUST BE BROKEN UP.

These are our views and principles— these our designs and measures. With entire confidence in the overruling justice of God, we plant ourselves upon the Declaration of our Independence and the truths of Divine Revelation, as upon the Everlasting Rock. . . .

THE SOUTH ATTEMPTS TO SUPPRESS ABOLITIONIST AGITATION

80. *South Carolina Resolutions on Abolitionist Propaganda, December 16, 1835*

Acts and Resolutions of South Carolina, 1835, 26-7.

1. *Resolved,* That the formation of the abolition societies, and the acts and doings of certain fanatics, calling themselves abolitionists, in the non-slaveholding states of this confederacy, are in direct violation of the obligations of the compact of the union, dissocial, and incendiary in the extreme.

2. *Resolved,* That no state having a just regard for her own peace and security can acquiesce in a state of things by which such conspiracies are engendered within the limits of a friendly state, united to her by the bonds of a common league of political association, without either surrendering or compromising her most essential rights.

3. *Resolved,* That the Legislature of South Carolina, having every confidence in the justice and friendship of the non-slaveholding states, announces to her co-states her confident expectation, and she earnestly requests that the governments of these states will promptly and effectually suppress all those associations within their respective limits, purporting to be abolition societies, and that they will make it highly penal to print, publish, and distribute newspapers, pamphlets, tracts and pictorial representations calculated and having an obvious tendency to excite the slaves of the southern states to insurrection and revolt.

4. *Resolved,* That, regarding the domestic slavery of the southern states as a subject exclusively within the control of each of the said states, we shall consider every interference, by any other state or the general government, as a direct and unlawful interference, to be resisted at once, and under every possible circumstance.

5. *Resolved,* In order that a salutary negative may be put on the mischievous and unfounded assumption of some of the abolitionists—the non-slaveholding states are requested to disclaim by legislative declaration, all right, either on the part of themselves or the government of the United States, to interfere in any manner with domestic slavery, either in the states, or in the territories where it exists.

6. *Resolved,* That we should consider the abolition of slavery in the District of Columbia, as a violation of the rights of the citizens of that District, derived from the implied conditions on which that territory was ceded to the general government, and as an usurpation to be at once resisted as nothing more than the commencement of a scheme of much more extensive and flagrant injustice.

7. *Resolved,* That the Legislature of South Carolina, regards with decided approbation, the measures of security adopted by the Post Office Department of the United States, in relation to the transmission of incendiary tracts. But if this highly essential and protective policy, be counteracted by congress, and the United States mail becomes a vehicle for the transmission of the mischievous documents, with which it was recently freighted, we, in this contingency, expect that the Chief Magistrate of our state, will forthwith call the legislature together, that timely measures may be taken to prevent its traversing our territory. . . .

81. *Andrew Jackson Recommends a Federal Censorship Law, December, 1835*

Richardson, *Messages and Papers of the Presidents,* III, 175-6.

In connection with these provisions in relation to the Post-Office Department, I must also invite your attention to the painful excitement produced in the South by attempts to circulate through the mails inflammatory appeals addressed to the passions of the slaves, in prints and in various sorts of publications, calculated to stimulate them to insurrection and to produce all the horrors of a servile war. There is doubtless no respectable portion of our countrymen who can be so far misled as to feel any other sentiment than that of indignant regret at conduct so destructive of the harmony and peace of the country, and so repugnant to the principles of our national compact and to the dictates of humanity and religion. Our happiness and prosperity essentially depend upon peace within our borders, and peace depends upon the maintenance in good faith of those compromises of the Constitution upon which the Union is founded. It is fortunate for the country that the good sense, the generous feeling, and the deep-rooted attachment of the people of the nonslaveholding States to the Union and to their fellow-citizens of the same blood in the South have given so strong and impressive a tone to the sentiments entertained against the proceedings of the misguided persons who have engaged in these unconstitutional and wicked attempts, and especially against the emissaries from foreign parts who

have dared to interfere in this matter, as to authorize the hope that those attempts will no longer be persisted in. But if these expressions of the public will shall not be sufficient to effect so desirable a result, not a doubt can be entertained that the non-slaveholding States, so far from countenancing the slightest interference with the constitutional rights of the South, will be prompt to exercise their authority in suppressing so far as in them lies whatever is calculated to produce this evil.

In leaving the care of other branches of this interesting subject to the State authorities, to whom they properly belong, it is nevertheless proper for Congress to take such measures as will prevent the Post-Office Department, which was designed to foster an amicable intercourse and correspondence between all the members of the Confederacy, from being used as an instrument of an opposite character. The General Government, to which the great trust is confided of preserving inviolate the relations created among the States by the Constitution, is especially bound to avoid in its own action anything that may disturb them. I would therefore call the special attention of Congress to the subject, and respectfully suggest the propriety of passing such a law as will prohibit, under severe penalties, the circulation in the Southern States, through the mail, of incendiary publications intended to instigate the slaves to insurrection.

82. *The Gag Rule in Congress*

A. ADOPTION OF THE RULE BY THE HOUSE, MAY, 1836

Congressional Globe, 24th Cong., 1st Sess., 469, 499, 505.

Resolved, That Congress possess no constitutional authority to interfere in any way with the institution of slavery in any of the States of this Confederacy.

Resolved, That Congress ought not to interfere in any way with slavery in the District of Columbia.

And whereas it is extremely important and desirable that the agitation of this subject should be finally arrested, for the purpose of restoring tranquillity to the public mind, your committee respectfully recommend the adoption of the following additional resolution, viz:

Resolved, That all petitions, memorials, resolutions, propositions, or papers, relating in any way, or to any extent, whatever, to the subject of slavery, or the abolition of slavery, shall, without being either printed or referred, be laid upon the table, and that no further action whatever shall be had thereon.

B. JOHN QUINCY ADAMS ON THE REPEAL OF THE GAG RULE, 1844

Charles Francis Adams, ed., *Memoirs of John Quincy Adams, Comprising Portions of His Diary from 1795 to 1848* (Philadelphia, 1877), XII, 115-16.

December 3, 1844. At the meeting of the House this day, . . . R. M. Saunders moved the appointment of the standing committees; which was agreed to. In pursuance of the notice I had given yesterday, I moved the following resolution: "Resolved, That the twenty-fifth standing rule for conducting business in this House, in the following words, 'No petition, memorial, resolution, or other paper praying the abolition of slavery in the District of Columbia or any State or Territory, or the slave-trade between the States or Territories in which it now exists, shall be received by this House, or entertained in any way whatever,' be, and the same is hereby, rescinded." I called for the yeas and nays. Jacob Thompson, of Mississippi, moved to lay the resolution on the table. I called for the yeas and nays on that motion. As the Clerk was about to begin the call, the President's message was announced and received. A member called for the reading of the message. I said I hoped the question upon my resolution would be taken. The Clerk called the roll, and the motion to lay on the table was rejected—eighty-one to one hundred and four. The question was then put on the resolution; and it was carried—one hundred and eight to eighty. Blessed, forever blessed, be the name of God!

83. *Calhoun Unites the Proslavery and State Sovereignty Arguments, December 27, 1837*

Congressional Globe, 25th Cong., 2d Sess., 55.

Resolved, That in the adoption of the Federal Constitution, the States adopting the same acted, severally, as free, independent, and sovereign States; and that each, for itself, by its own voluntary assent, entered the Union with the view to its increased security against all dangers, domestic as well as foreign, and the more perfect and secure enjoyment of its advantages, natural, political, and social.

Resolved, That in delegating a portion of their powers to be exercised by the Federal Government, the States retained, severally, the exclusive and sole right over their own domestic institutions and police, and are alone responsible for them, and that any intermeddling of any one or more States, or a combination of their citizens, with the domestic institutions and police of the others, on any ground, or under any pretext whatever, political, moral, religious, with the view to their alteration, or subversion, is an assumption of superiority not warranted by the Constitution; insulting to the States interfered with, tending to endanger their domestic peace and tranquility, subversive of the objects for which the Constitution was formed, and, by necessary consequence, tending to weaken and destroy the Union itself.

Resolved, That this Government was instituted and adopted by the several States of this Union as a common agent, in order to carry into effect the powers which they had delegated by the Constitution for their mutual security and prosperity; and that, in fulfilment of this high and sacred trust, this Government is bound so to exercise its powers as to give, as far as may be practicable, increased stability and security to the domestic institutions of the States that compose the Union; and that it is the solemn duty of the Government to resist all attempts by one portion of the Union to use it as an instrument to attack the domestic institutions of another, or to weaken or destroy such institutions, instead of strengthening and upholding them, as it is in duty bound to do.

Resolved, That domestic slavery, as it exists in the Southern and Western States of this Union, composes an important part of their domestic institutions, inherited from their ancestors, and existing at the adoption of the Constitution, by which it is recognised as constituting an essential element in the distribution of its powers among the States; and that no change of opinion, or feeling, on the part of the other States of the Union in relation to it can justify them or their citizens in open and systematic attacks thereon, with the view to its overthrow; and that all such attacks are in manifest violation of the mutual and solemn pledge to protect and defend each other, given by the States, respectively, on entering into the Constitutional compact, which formed the Union, and as such is a manifest breach of faith, and a violation of the most solemn obligations, moral and religious.

Resolved, That the intermeddling of any State or States, or their citizens, to abolish slavery in this District, or any of the Territories, on the ground, or under the pretext, that it is immoral or sinful; or the passage of any act or measure of Congress, with that view, would be a direct and dangerous attack on the institutions of all the slaveholding States.

Resolved, That the union of these States rest on an equality of rights and advantages among its members; and that whatever destroys that equality, tends to destroy the Union itself; and that it is the solemn duty of all, and more especially of this body, which represents the States in their corporate capacity, to resist all attempts to discriminate between the States in extending the benefits of the Government to the several portions of the Union; and that to refuse to extend to the Southern and Western States any advantage which would tend to strengthen, or render them more secure, or increase their limits or population by the annexation of new territory or States, on the assumption or under the pretext that the institution of slavery, as it exists among them, is immoral or sinful, or otherwise obnoxious, would be contrary to that equality of rights and advantages which the Constitution was intended to secure alike to all the members of the Union, and would, in effect, disfranchise the slaveholding States, withholding from them the advantages, while it subjected them to the burthens, of the Government.

THE MEXICAN WAR AND SLAVERY IN THE TERRITORIES

84. *Lewis Cass, Letter to Governor Nicholson on "Squatter Sovereignty," December 24, 1847*

Niles' Register, LXXIII (1847-48), 293-4.

The theory of our Government presupposes that its various members have reserved to themselves the regulation of all subjects relating to what may be termed their internal police. They are sovereign within their boundaries, except in those cases where they have surrendered to the General Government a portion of their rights, in order to give effect to the objects of the Union, whether these concern foreign nations or the several States themselves. Local institutions, if I may so speak, whether they have reference to slavery or to any other relations, domestic or public, are left to local authority, either original or derivative. Congress has no right to say there shall be slavery in New York, or that there shall be no slavery in Georgia; nor is there any other human power, but the people of those States, respectively, which can change the relation existing therein; and they can say, if they will, "We will have slavery in the former, and we will abolish it in the latter."

In various respects, the Territories differ from the States. Some of their rights are inchoate, and they do not possess the peculiar attributes of sovereignty. Their relation to the General Government is very imperfectly defined by the Constitution; and it will be found, upon examination, that in that instrument the only grant of power concerning them is conveyed in the phrase, "Congress shall have the power to dispose of and make all needful rules and regulations respecting the territory and other property belonging to the United States." Certainly this phraseology is very loose, if it designed to include in the grant the whole power of legislation over persons, as well as things. The expression, the "territory and other property," fairly construed, related to the public lands, as such; to arsenals, dockyards, forts, ships, and all the various kinds of property which the United States may and must possess.

But surely the simple authority to *dispose of and regulate* these does not extend to the unlimited power of legislation; to the passage of all *laws,* in the most general acceptation of the word, which, by the by, is carefully excluded from the sentence. And, indeed, if this were so, it would render unnecessary another provision of the Constitution, which grants to Congress the power to legislate, with the consent of the States, respectively, over all places purchased for the "erection of forts, magazines, arsenals, dockyards," etc. These being the *"property"* of the United States, if the power to make "needful rules and regulations concerning" them includes the general power of legislation, then the grant of authority to regulate "the territory and other property of the United States" is unlimited, wherever subjects are found for its operation, and its exercise needed no auxiliary provision. If, on the other hand, it does not include such power of legislation over the "other property" of the United States, then it does not include it over their *"territory;"* for the same terms which grant the one grant the other. *"Territory"* is here classed with property, and treated as such; and the object was evidently to enable the General Government, as a property-holder—which, from necessity, it must be—to manage, preserve and *"dispose of"* such property as it might possess, and which authority is essential almost to its being. But the lives and persons of our citizens, with the vast variety of objects connected with them, cannot be controlled by an authority which is merely called into existence for the purpose of making *rules and regulations for the disposition and management of property.*

Such, it appears to me, would be the construction put upon this provision of the Constitution, were this question now first presented for consideration, and not controlled by imperious circumstances. The original ordinance of the Congress of the Confederation, passed in 1787, and which was the only act upon this subject in force at the adoption of the Constitution, provided a complete frame of government for the country north of the Ohio, while in a territorial condition, and for its eventual admission in separate States into the Union. And the persua-

sion that this ordinance contained within itself all the necessary means of execution, probably prevented any direct reference to the subject in the Constitution, further than vesting in Congress the right to admit the States formed under it into the Union. However, circumstances arose, which required legislation, as well over the territory north of the Ohio, as over other territory, both within and without the original Union, ceded to the General Government, and, at various times, a more enlarged power has been exercised over the Territories—meaning thereby the different Territorial Governments—than is conveyed by the limited grant referred to. How far an existing necessity may have operated in producing this legislation, and thus extending, by rather a violent implication powers not directly given, I know not. But certain it is that the principle of interference should not be carried beyond the necessary implication, which produces it. It should be limited to the creation of proper governments for new countries, acquired or settled, and to the necessary provisions for their eventual admission into the Union; leaving, in the meantime, to the people inhabiting them, to regulate their internal concerns in their own way. They are just as capable of doing so as the people of the States; and they can do so, at any rate as soon as their political independence is recognized by admission into the Union. During this temporary condition, it is hardly expedient to call into exercise a doubtful and invidious authority which questions the intelligence of a respectable portion of our citizens, and whose limitation, whatever it may be, will be rapidly approaching its termination—an authority which would give to Congress despotic power, uncontrolled by the Constitution, over most important sections of our common country. . . .

The Disruption of the Compromise

85. The Kansas-Nebraska Act, May 30, 1854

U. S. Stat. at L., X, 277-90.

Be it enacted . . . , That all that part of the territory of the United States included within the following limits, except such portions thereof as are hereinafter expressly exempted from the operations of this act . . . be, and the same is hereby, created into a temporary government by the name of the Territory of Nebraska; and when admitted as a State or States, the said Territory, or any portion of the same, shall be received into the Union with or without slavery, as their constitution may prescribe at the time of their admission: . . .

SEC. 14. *And be it further enacted, . . .* That the Constitution, and all Laws of the United States which are not locally inapplicable, shall have the same force and effect within the said Territory of Nebraska as elsewhere within the United States, except the eighth section of the act preparatory to the admission of Missouri into the Union, approved March sixth, eighteen hundred and twenty, which, being inconsistent with the principle of nonintervention by Congress with slavery in the States and Territories, as recognized by the legislation of eighteen hundred and fifty, commonly called the Compromise Measures, is hereby declared inoperative and void; it being the true intent and meaning of this act not to legislate slavery into any Territory or State, nor to exclude it therefrom, but to leave the people thereof perfectly free to form and regulate their domestic institutions in their own way, subject only to the Constitution of the United States: *Provided,* That nothing herein contained shall be construed to revive or put in force any law or regulation which may have existed prior to the act of sixth March, eighteen hundred and twenty, either protecting, establishing, prohibiting, or abolishing slavery. . . .

SEC. 19. *And be it further enacted,* That all that part of the Territory of the United States included within the following limits, except such portions thereof as are hereinafter expressly exempted from the operations of this act, . . . be, and the same is hereby, created into a temporary government by the name of the Territory of Kansas; and when admitted as a State or States, the said Territory, or any portion of the same, shall be received into the Union with or without slavery, as their constitution may prescribe at the time of their admission. . . .

86. The Court Adopts the Calhoun Argument

Dred Scott v. Sandford, 19 Howard 393 (1857).

TANEY, C. J.: . . . There are two leading questions presented by the record:

1. Had the Circuit Court of the United States jurisdiction to hear and determine the case between these parties? And

2. If it had jurisdiction, is the judgment it has given erroneous or not? . . .

The question is simply this: Can a negro, whose ancestors were imported into this country, and sold as slaves, become a member of the political community formed and brought into existence by the Constitution of the United States, and as such become entitled to all the rights, privileges and immunities, guarantied by that instrument to the citizen? One of which rights is the privilege of suing in a court of the United States in the cases specified in the Constitution. . . .

It is true, every person, and every class and description of persons, who were at the time of the adoption of the Constitution recognized as citizens in the several States, became also citizens of this new political body; but none other; it was formed by them, and for them and their posterity, but for no one else. And the personal rights and privileges guarantied to citizens of this new sovereignty were intended to embrace those only who were then members of the several State communities, or who should afterwards, by birthright or otherwise, become members, according to the provisions of the Constitution and the principles on which it was founded. . . .

It becomes necessary, therefore, to determine who were citizens of the several States when the Constitution was adopted. And in order to do this, we must recur to the Governments and institutions of the thirteen colonies, when they separated from Great Britain and formed new sovereignties, and took their places in the family of independent nations. . . .

In the opinion of the court, the legislation and histories of the times, and the language used in the Declaration of Independence, show, that neither the class of persons who had been imported as slaves, nor their descendants, whether they had become free or not, were then acknowledged as a part of the people, nor intended to be included in the general words used in that memorable instrument. . . .

They had for more than a century before been regarded as beings of an in-ferior order, and altogether unfit to associate with the white race, either in social or political relations; and so far inferior, that they had no rights which the white man was bound to respect; and that the negro might justly and lawfully be reduced to slavery for his benefit. . . .

The legislation of the States therefore shows, in a manner not to be mistaken, the inferior and subject condition of that race at the time the Constitution was adopted, and long afterwards, throughout the thirteen States by which that instrument was framed; and it is hardly consistent with the respect due to these States, to suppose that they regarded at that time, as fellow-citizens and members of the sovereignty, a class of beings whom they had thus stigmatized; whom, as we are bound, out of respect to the State sovereignties, to assume they had deemed it just and necessary thus to stigmatize, and upon whom they had impressed such deep and enduring marks of inferiority and degradation; or, that when they met in convention to form the Constitution, they looked upon them as a portion of their constituents, or designed to include them in the provisions so carefully inserted for the security and protection of the liberties and rights of their citizens. It cannot be supposed that they intended to secure to them rights, and privileges, and rank, in the new political body throughout the Union, which every one of them denied within the limits of its own dominion. More especially, it cannot be believed that the large slave-holding States regarded them as included in the word citizens, or would have consented to a constitution which might compel them to receive them in that character from another State. . . .

To all this mass of proof we have still to add, that Congress has repeatedly legislated upon the same construction of the Constitution that we have given. . . .

The conduct of the Executive Department of the Government has been in perfect harmony upon this subject with this course of legislation. . . .

And upon a full and careful consideration of the subject, the court is of opinion, that, upon the facts stated in the plea in abatement, Dred Scott was not a citizen of Missouri within the meaning of the Constitution of the United States, and not entitled as such to sue in its courts; and, consequently, that the Circuit Court had no jurisdiction of the case, and that the judgment on the plea in abatement is erroneous. . . .

We proceed, therefore, to inquire whether the facts relied on by the plaintiff entitled him to his freedom. . . .

In considering this part of the controversy, two questions arise: 1. Was he, together with his family, free in Missouri by reason of the stay in the territory of the United States hereinbefore mentioned? And 2. If they were not, is Scott himself free by reason of his removal to Rock Island, in the State of Illinois, as stated in the above admissions?

We proceed to examine the first question.

The Act of Congress, upon which the plaintiff relies, declares that slavery and involuntary servitude, except as a punishment for crime, shall be forever prohibited . . . north of thirty-six degrees thirty minutes north latitude, and not included within the limits of Missouri. And the difficulty which meets us at the threshold of this part of the inquiry is, whether Congress was authorized to pass this law under any of the powers granted to it by the Constitution; for if the authority is not given by that instrument, it is the duty of this court to declare it void and inoperative, and incapable of conferring freedom upon any one who is held as a slave under the laws of any one of the States.

The counsel for the plaintiff has laid much stress upon that article in the Constitution which confers on Congress the power "to dispose of and make all needful rules and regulations respecting the territory or other property belonging to the United States;" but, in the judgment of the court, that provision has no bearing on the present controversy, and the power there given, whatever it may be, is confined, and was intended to be confined, to the territory which at that time belonged to, or was claimed by, the United States, and was within their boundaries as settled by the treaty with Great Britain, and can have no influence upon a territory afterwards acquired from a foreign Government. It was a special provision for a known and particular territory, and to meet a present emergency, and nothing more. . . .

At the time when the territory in question was obtained by cession from France, it contained no population fit to be associated together and admitted as a State; and it therefore was absolutely necessary to hold possession of it, as a Territory belonging to the United States, until it was settled and inhabited by a civilized community capable of self-government, and in a condition to be admitted on equal terms with the other States as a member of the Union. But, as we have before said, it was acquired by the General Government, as the representative and trustee of the people of the United States, and it must therefore be held in that character for their common and equal benefit; for it was the people of the several States, acting through their agent and representative, the Federal Government, who in fact acquired the Territory in question, and the Government holds it for their common use until it shall be associated with the other States as a member of the Union.

But until that time arrives, it is undoubtedly necessary that some Government should be established, in order to organize society, and to protect the inhabitants in their persons and property; and as the people of the United States could act in this matter only through the Government which represented them, and through which they spoke and acted when the Territory was obtained, it was not only within the scope of its powers, but it was its duty to pass such laws and establish such a Government as would enable those by whose authority they acted to reap the advantages anticipated from its acquisition, and to gather there a population which would enable it to assume the position to which it was destined among the States of the Union. . . .

But the power of Congress over the person or property of a citizen can never be a mere discretionary power under our Constitution and form of Government. The powers of the Government and the rights and privileges of the citizen are regulated and plainly defined by the Constitution itself. . . .

Thus the rights of property are united with the rights of person, and placed on the same ground by the fifth amendment to the Constitution, which provides that no person shall be deprived of life, liberty, and property, without due process of law. And an act of Congress which deprives a citizen of the United States of his liberty or property, merely because he came himself or brought his property into a particular Territory of the United States, and who had committed no offense against the laws, could hardly be dignified with the name of due process of law. . . .

Now . . . the right of property in a slave is distinctly and expressly affirmed in the Constitution. The right to traffic in it, like an ordinary article of merchandise and property, was guaranteed to the citizens of the United States, in every State that might desire it, for twenty years. And the Government in express terms is pledged to protect it in all future time, if the slave escapes from his owner. This is done in plain words—too plain to be misunderstood. And no word can be found in the Constitution which gives Congress a greater power over slave property, or which entitles property of that kind to less protection than property of any other description. The only power conferred is the power coupled with the duty of guarding and protecting the owner in his rights.

Upon these considerations, it is the opinion of the court that the act of Congress which prohibited a citizen from holding or owning property of this kind in the territory of the United States north of the line therein mentioned, is not warranted by the Constitution, and is therefore void; and that neither Dred Scott himself, nor any of his family, were made free by being carried into this territory; even if they had been carried there by the owner, with the intention of becoming a permanent resident. . . .

But there is another point in the case which depends upon State power and State law. And it is contended, on the part of the plaintiff, that he is made free by being taken to Rock Island, in the State of Illinois, independently of his residence in the territory of the United States; and being so made free, he was not again reduced to a state of slavery by being brought back to Missouri.

Our notice of this part of the case will be very brief; for the principle on which it depends was decided in this court, upon much consideration, in the case of *Strader et al. v. Graham.* . . . In that case, the slaves had been taken from Kentucky to Ohio, with the consent of the owner, and afterwards brought back to Kentucky. And this court held that their status or condition, as free or slave, depended upon the laws of Kentucky, when they were brought back into that State, and not of Ohio; and that this court had no jurisdiction to revise the judgment of a State court upon its own laws. . . .

So in this case. As Scott was a slave when taken into the State of Illinois by his owner, and was there held as such, and brought back in that character, his *status,* as free or slave, depended on the laws of Missouri, and not of Illinois. . . .

Upon the whole, therefore, it is the judgment of this court, that it appears by the record before us, that the plaintiff in error is not a citizen of Missouri, in the sense in which that word is used in the Constitution; and that the Circuit Court of the United States, for that reason, had no jurisdiction in the case, and could give no judgment in it. Its judgment for the defendant must, consequently, be reversed, and a mandate issued, directing the suit to be dismissed for want of jurisdiction.

87. *Lincoln Denounces the Dred Scott Decision,* 1858

John G. Nicolay and John Hay, eds., *Complete Works of Abraham Lincoln* (New York, 1894), XI, 110-11.

What constitutes the bulwark of our own liberty and independence? It is not our frowning battlements, our bristling sea coasts, our army and our navy. These are not our reliance against tyranny. All of those may be turned against us without making us weaker for the struggle. Our reliance is in the love of liberty which God has planted in us. Our defence is in the spirit which prized liberty as the heritage of all men, in all lands everywhere. Destroy this spirit and you have planted the seeds of despotism at your own doors. Familiarize yourself with the chains of bondage and you prepare your own limbs to wear them. Accustomed to trample on the rights of others, you have lost the genius of your own independence and become the fit subjects of the first cunning tyrant who rises among you. And let me tell you, that all these things are prepared for you by the teachings of history, if the elections shall promise that the next Dred Scott decision and all future decisions will be quietly acquiesced in by the people.

88. *Stephen A. Douglas, Freeport Doctrine,* 1858

Edwin Erle Sparks, ed., *The Lincoln-Douglas Debates of 1858* (Vol. III, *Collections of the Illinois State Historical Library,* Springfield, 1908), 160-2.

In reference to Kansas, it is my opinion that as she has population enough to constitute a slave State, she has people enough for a free State. I will not make Kansas an exceptional case to the other States of the Union. I hold it to be a sound rule, of universal application, to require a Territory to contain the requisite population for a member of Congress before it is admitted as a State into the Union. I made that proposition in the Senate in 1856, and I renewed it during the last session, in a bill providing that no Territory of the United States should form a constitution and apply for admission until it had the requisite population. On another occasion I proposed that neither Kansas nor any other Territory should be admitted until it had the requisite population. Congress did not adopt any of my propositions containing this general rule, but did made an exception of Kansas. I will stand by that exception. Either Kansas must come in as a free State, with whatever population she may have, or the rule must be applied to all the other Territories alike. I therefore answer at once, that, it having been decided that Kansas has people enough for a slave State, I hold that she has enough for a free State. . . .

The next question propounded to me by Mr. Lincoln is: Can the people of a Territory in any lawful way, against the wishes of any citizen of the United States, exclude slavery from their limits prior to the formation of a State constitution? I answer emphatically, as Mr. Lincoln has heard me answer a hundred times from every stump in Illinois, that in my opinion the people of a Territory can, by lawful means, exclude slavery from their limits prior to the formation of a State constitution. Mr. Lincoln knew that I had answered that question over and over again. He heard me argue the Nebraska Bill on that principle all over the State in 1854, in 1855, and in 1856, and he has no excuse for pretending to be in doubt as to my position on that question. It matters not what way the Supreme Court may hereafter decide as to the abstract question whether slavery may or may not go into a Territory under the Constitution, the people have the lawful means to introduce it or exclude it as they please, for the reason that slavery cannot exist a day or an hour anywhere, unless it is supported by local police regulations. Those police regulations can only be established by the local legislature, and if the people are opposed to slavery they will elect representatives to that body who will by unfriendly legislation effectually prevent the introduction of it into their midst. If, on the contrary, they are for it, their legislation will favor its extension. Hence, no matter what the decision of the Supreme Court may be on that abstract question, still the right of the people to make a slave Territory or a free Territory is perfect and complete under the Nebraska Bill. I hope Mr. Lincoln deems my answer satisfactory on that point. . . .

89. *Lincoln Comments on the Freeport Doctrine, September, 1859*

Political Debates between Abraham Lincoln and Stephen A. Douglas (Cleveland, Ohio, 1894), 294-6.

I wish to say something now in regard to the Dred Scott decision, as dealt with by Judge Douglas. In that "memorable debate" between Judge Douglas and myself, last year, the Judge thought fit to commence a process of catechising me, and at Freeport I answered his questions, and propounded some to him. Among others propounded to him was one that I have here now. The substance, as I remember it, is, "Can the people of a United States Territory, under the Dred Scott decision, in any lawful way, against the wish of any citizen of the United States, exclude slavery from its limits, prior to the formation of a State Constitution?" He answered that they could lawfully exclude slavery from the United States Territories, notwithstanding the Dred Scott decision. There was something about that answer that has probably been a trouble to the Judge ever since.

The Dred Scott decision expressly gives every citizen of the United States a right to carry his slaves into the United States Territories. And now there was some inconsistency in saying that the decision was right, and saying, too, that the people of the Territory could lawfully drive slavery out again. When all the trash, the words, the collateral matter, was cleared away from it—all the chaff was fanned out of it, it was a bare absurdity—*no less than that a thing may be lawfully driven away from where it has a lawful right to be.* Clear it of all the verbiage, and that is the naked truth of his proposition—that a thing may be lawfully driven from the place where it has a lawful right to stay. . . .

But I undertake to give the opinion, at least, that if the Territories attempt by any direct legislation to drive the man with his slave out of the Territory, or to decide that his slave is free because of his being taken in there, or to tax him to such an extent that he cannot keep him there, the Supreme Court will unhesitatingly decide all such legislation unconstitutional, as long as that Supreme Court is constructed as the Dred Scott Supreme Court is. The first two things they have already decided, except that there is a little quibble among lawyers between the words *"dicta"* and "decision." They have already decided a negro cannot be made free by Territorial legislation. . . .

What is that Dred Scott decision? Judge Douglas labors to show that it is one thing, while I think it is altogether different. It is a long opinion, but it is all embodied in this short statement: "The Constitution of the United States forbids Congress to deprive a man of his property, without due process of law; the right of property in slaves is distinctly and expressly affirmed in that Constitution; therefore if Congress shall undertake to say that a man's slave is no longer his slave, when he crosses a certain line into a Territory, that is depriving him of his property without due process of law, and is unconstitutional." There is the

whole Dred Scott decision. They add that if Congress cannot do so itself, Congress cannot confer any power to do so, and hence any effort by the Territorial Legislature to do either of these things is absolutely decided against. It is a foregone conclusion by that court.

Now, as to this indirect mode by "unfriendly legislation," all lawyers here will readily understand that such a proposition cannot be tolerated for a moment, because a legislature cannot indirectly do that which it cannot accomplish directly. Then I say any legislation to control this property, as property, for its benefit as property, would be hailed by this Dred Scott Supreme Court, and fully sustained; but any legislation driving slave property out, or destroying it as property, directly or indirectly, will most assuredly, by that court, be held unconstitutional. . . .

CHAPTER XI

Crisis, Coercion, and Civil War

THE new Republican party was originally a political organization dedicated to but a single proposition—Congressional prohibition of slavery in the territories. By 1860 it had evolved into a party representing a variety of Northern economic interests without sacrificing its original goal. Its carefully contrived platform of 1860, designed to appeal to advocates of tariffs, free land, and federal aid to transportation and internal improvements, nevertheless devoted two-thirds of its provisions to the constitutional status of slavery, the slave trade, and the nature of the Union. Because the triumph of the Republicans and their platform (No. 90) led to secession, this document deserves priority in any discussion of "the irrepressible conflict."

With the election of Lincoln, South Carolina immediately set in motion the secession machinery perfected by Calhoun. Thus when President Buchanan sent his last annual message to Congress, the Union was in danger of disruption. Following a formal opinion of Attorney-General Jeremiah S. Black, Buchanan, in futile despair, agreed that although secession was illegal the federal government lacked the power to preserve the Union by force (No. 91). Less than two weeks later, South Carolina's secession convention decided unanimously "that the union now subsisting between South Carolina and other States under the name of the United States is hereby dissolved" (No. 92). On Christmas Eve, the convention justified its action in a declaration defending slavery, secession, state sovereignty, and the compact theory of government (No. 93).

When Chief Justice Taney, whom Lincoln had criticized for his Dred

Scott decision, administered the oath of office to the incoming President, seven states of the Deep South had united into the Confederate States of America. Unlike Buchanan, Lincoln, in his inaugural address, rejected the Supreme Court's protection of slavery in the territories, and announced the physical and constitutional impossibility of secession. In a conciliatory but firm affirmation of national authority, he denied any intenton to make war on the South, but pledged the enforcement of federal laws and the protection of federal property. In short, there need be no violence "unless it be forced upon the national authority" (No. 94).

One week later, however, adamant Southern representatives replaced their Provisional Government, adopted in February, with a permanent constitution that contained clauses expressly guaranteeing protection of slavery and the admission of additional slave states. Since the most striking thing about the Confederate Constitution was its almost verbatim restatement of the Constitution of the United States, No. 95 contains only those sections differing from the federal charter. Brief notations indicate how the first twelve federal amendments were incorporated in the new governmental framework.

The war started on April 12, 1861, with the bombardment of Fort Sumter. Accordingly, Lincoln declared that "insurrection" existed and, in the absence of Congress, issued the call to arms (No. 96). Insisting that it was not state governments who had rebelled but combinations of individuals "too powerful to be suppressed" by ordinary legal processes, Lincoln avoided a formal acknowledgment of a state of war, but in proclaiming a blockade of the Confederacy (No. 97) he accorded *de facto* recognition to a state of belligerency.

Since Congress was not in session when hostilities broke out, the new administration of necessity formulated policies that concentrated power in the hands of the Chief Executive. When Congress met in special session on Independence Day, 1861, Lincoln requested approval of the steps taken, and asked for additional powers. His message is noteworthy, too, for its emphasis on the importance of the conflict not only as a means of preserving the Union but "for maintaining in the world that form and substance of government whose leading object is to elevate the condition of men—to lift artificial weights from all shoulders; to clear the path of laudable pursuit for all; to afford all an unfettered start, and a fair chance in the race of life" (No. 98).

Responding to Lincoln's plea, Congress approved and legalized retrospectively "all the acts, proclamations, and orders of the President . . . respecting the Army and Navy . . . or relating to the militia or volunteers from the States." On July 22 the House and Senate declared that their sole object in carrying on the conflict was to maintain the Constitution and to preserve the Union. Finally, Congress authorized the President to proclaim a state of insurrection. Lincoln did so on August 16, 1861 (No. 99). The most famous statement of the purposes for which the war was fought came halfway through the cataclysmic struggle in Lincoln's expressed hope at Gettysburg "that government of the people, by the people, and for the people, shall not perish from the earth."

Disunion and Secession

90. "We hold in abhorrence all schemes for Disunion"

Republican Party Platform, 1860, Edward Stanwood, *A History of Presidential Elections* (Boston, 1892), 228-31.

That the maintenance of the principles promulgated in the Declaration of Independence and embodied in the Federal Constitution, "That all men are created equal; that they are endowed by their Creator with certain inalienable rights; that among these are life, liberty and the pursuit of happiness; that, to secure these rights, governments are instituted among men, deriving their just powers from the consent of the governed," is essential to the preservation of our Republican institutions; and that the Federal Constitution, the Rights of the States, and the Union of the States, must and shall be preserved.

3. That to the Union of the States this nation owes its unprecedented increase in population, its surprising development of material resources, its rapid augmentation of wealth, its happiness at home and its honor abroad; and we hold in abhorrence all schemes for Disunion, come from whatever source they may; And we congratulate the country that no Republican member of Congress has uttered or countenanced the threats of Disunion so often made by Democratic members, without rebuke and with applause from their political associates; and we denounce those threats of Disunion, in case of a popular overthrow of their ascendency, as denying the vital principles of a free government, and as an avowal of contemplated treason, which it is the imperative duty of an indignant People sternly to rebuke and forever silence.

4. That the maintenance inviolate of the rights of the States, and especially the right of each State to order and control its own domestic institutions according to its own judgment exclusively, is essential to that balance of powers on which the perfection and endurance of our political fabric depends; and we denounce the lawless invasion by armed force of the soil of any State or Territory, no matter under what pretext, as among the gravest of crimes.

5. That the present Democratic Administration has far exceeded our worst apprehensions, in its measureless subserviency to the exactions of a sectional interest, as especially evinced in its desperate exertions to force the infamous Lecompton constitution upon the protesting people of Kansas; in construing the personal relation between master and servant to involve an unqualified property in persons; in its attempted enforcement, everywhere, on land and sea, through the intervention of Congress and of the Federal Courts of the extreme pretensions of a purely local interest; and in its general and unvarying abuse of the power intrusted to it by a confiding people. . . .

7. That the new dogma that the Constitution, of its own force, carries Slavery into any or all of the Territories of the United States, is a dangerous political heresy, at variance with the explicit provisions of that instrument itself, with contemporaneous exposition, and with legislative and judicial precedent; is revolutionary in its tendency, and subversive of the peace and harmony of the country.

8. That the normal condition of all the territory of the United States is that of

freedom; That as our Republican fathers, when they had abolished slavery in all our national territory, ordained that "no person should be deprived of life, liberty, or property, without due process of law," it becomes our duty, by legislation, whenever such legislation is necessary, to maintain this provision of the Constitution against all attempts to violate it; and we deny the authority of Congress, of a territorial legislature, or of any individuals, to give legal existence to Slavery in any Territory of the United States. . . .

12. That, while providing revenue for the support of the General Government by duties upon imports, sound policy requires such an adjustment of these imposts as to encourage the development of the industrial interests of the whole country; and we commend that policy of national exchanges which secures to the working men liberal wages, to agriculture remunerating prices, to mechanics and manufacturers an adequate reward for their skill, labor and enterprise, and to the nation commercial prosperity and independence.

13. That we protest against any sale or alienation to others of the Public Lands held by actual settlers, and against any view of the Homestead policy which regards the settlers as paupers or supplicants for public bounty; and we demand the passage by Congress of the complete and satisfactory Homestead measure which has already passed the house.

14. That the Republican Party is opposed to any change in our Naturalization Laws or any State legislation by which the rights of our citizenship hitherto accorded to immigrants from foreign lands shall be abridged or impaired; and in favor of giving a full and efficient protection to the rights of all classes of citizens, whether native or naturalized, both at home and abroad.

15. That appropriations by Congress for River and Harbor improvements of a National character, required for the accommodation and security of an existing commerce, are authorized by the Constitution, and justified by the obligations of Government to protect the lives and property of its citizens.

16. That a Railroad to the Pacific Ocean is imperatively demanded by the interests of the whole country; that the Federal Government ought to render immediate and efficient aid in its construction; and that, as preliminary thereto, a daily Overland Mail should be promptly established. . . .

91. *The Constitutional Dilemma of President Buchanan*

Message to Congress, December 3, 1860, Richardson, ed., *Messages and Papers of the Presidents*, V, 630-6.

The long-continued and intemperate interference of the Northern people with the question of slavery in the Southern States has at length produced its natural effects. The different sections of the Union are now arrayed against each other, and the time has arrived, so much dreaded by the Father of his Country, when hostile geographical parties have been formed. . . .

All for which the slave States have ever contended, is to be let alone and permitted to manage their domestic institutions in their own way. As sovereign States, they, and they alone, are responsible before God and the world for the slavery existing among them. For this the people of the North are not more responsible and have no more right to interfere than with similar institutions in Russia or in Brazil. . . .

It has been claimed within the last few years that any State, whenever this shall be its sovereign will and pleasure, may secede from the Union in accordance with the Constitution and without any violation of the constitutional rights of the other members of the Confederacy; that as each became parties to the Union by the vote of its own people assembled in convention, so any one of them may retire from the Union in a similar manner by the vote of such a convention.

In order to justify secession as a constitutional remedy, it must be on the principle that the Federal Government is a mere voluntary association of States, to be dissolved at pleasure by any one of the contracting parties. If this be so, the Confederacy is a rope of sand, to be penetrated and dissolved by the first adverse wave of public opinion in any of the States. . . .

Such a principle is wholly inconsistent with the history as well as the character of the Federal Government. . . .

It was intended to be perpetual, and not to be annulled at the pleasure of any one of the contracting parties. . . .

It may be asked, then, Are the people of the States without redress against the tyranny and oppression of the Federal Government? By no means. The right of resistance on the part of the governed against the oppression of their governments can not be denied. It exists independently of all constitutions, and has been exercised at all periods of the world's history. Under it old governments have been destroyed and new ones have taken their place. It is embodied in strong and express language in our own Declaration of Independence. But the distinction must ever be observed that this is revolution against an established government, and not a voluntary secession from it by virtue of an inherent constitutional right. In short, let us look the danger fairly in the face. Secession is neither more nor less than revolution. It may or it may not be a justifiable revolution, but still it is revolution.

What, in the meantime, is the responsibility and true position of the Executive? He is bound by solemn oath, before God and the country, "to take care that the laws be faithfully executed," and from this obligation he can not be absolved by any human power. But what if the performance of this duty, in whole or in part, has been rendered impracticable by events over which he could have exercised no control? Such at the present moment is the case throughout the State of South Carolina so far as the laws of the United States to secure the administration of justice by means of the Federal judiciary are concerned. All the Federal officers within its limits through whose agency alone these laws can be carried into execution have already resigned. We no longer have a district judge, a district attorney, or a marshal in South Carolina. In fact, the whole machinery of the Federal Government necessary for the distribution of remedial justice among the people has been demolished, and it would be difficult, if not impossible, to replace it.

The only acts of Congress on the statute book bearing upon this subject are those of February 28, 1795, and March 3, 1807. These authorize the President, after he shall have ascertained that the marshal, with his *posse comitatus*, is unable to execute civil or criminal process in any particular case, to call forth the militia and employ the Army and Navy to aid him in performing this service, having first by proclamation commanded the insurgents "to disperse and retire peaceably to their respective abodes within a limited time." This duty can not by possibility be performed in a State where no judicial authority exists to issue process, and where there is no marshal to execute it, and where, even if there were such an officer, the entire population would constitute one solid combination to resist him.

The bare enumeration of these provisions proves how inadquate they are without further legislation to overcome a united opposition in a single State, not to speak of other States who may place themselves in a similar attitude. Congress alone has power to decide whether the present laws can or can not be amended so as to carry out more effectually the objects of the Constitution. . . .

Apart from the execution of the laws, so far as this may be practicable, the Executive has no authority to decide what shall be the relations between the Federal Government and South Carolina. . . . It is therefore my duty to submit to Congress the whole question in all its bearings. . . .

The question fairly stated is, Has the Constitution delegated to Congress the power to coerce a State into submission which is attempting to withdraw or has actually withdrawn from the Confederacy? If answered in the affirmative, it must be on the principle that the power has been conferred upon Congress to declare and to make war against a State. After much serious reflection I have arrived at the conclusion that no such power has been delegated to Congress or to any other department of the Federal Government. . . .

Without descending to particulars, it may be safely asserted that the power to make war against a State is at variance with the whole spirit and intent of the Constitution. . . .

The fact is that our Union rests upon public opinion, and can never be cemented by the blood of its citizens shed in civil war. If it can not live in the affections of the people, it must one day perish. Congress possesses many means of preserving it by conciliation, but the sword was not placed in their hand to preserve it by force. . . .

92. *South Carolina Ordinance of Secession, December 20, 1860*

Frank Moore, ed., *The Rebellion Record*, I, Doc. 2, 2.

We, the people of the State of South Carolina, in Convention assembled, do declare and ordain, and it is hereby declared and ordained, that the ordinance adopted by us in Convention, on the 23d day of May, in the year of our Lord 1788, whereby the Constitution of the United States of America was ratified, and also all Acts and parts of Acts of the General Assembly of this State ratifying the amendments of the said Constitution, are hereby repealed, and that the union now subsisting between South Carolina and other States under the name of the United States of America is hereby dissolved.

93. *South Carolina Declaration of the Causes of Secession, December 24, 1860*

Moore, ed., *The Rebellion Record*, I, Doc. 3, 3-4.

The State of South Carolina having resumed her separate and equal place among nations, deems it due to herself, to the remaining United States of America, and to the nations of the world, that she should declare the immediate causes which have led to this act. . . .

We hold that the Government . . . is subject to the two great principles asserted in the Declaration of Independence; and we hold further, that the mode of its formation subjects it to a third fundamental principle, namely, the law of compact. We maintain that in every compact between two or more parties, the obligation is mutual; that the failure of one of the contracting parties to perform a material part of the agreement, entirely releases the obligation of the other; and that, where no arbiter is provided, each party is remitted to his own judgment to determine the fact of failure, with all its consequences.

In the present case, that fact is established with certainty. We assert that fourteen of the States have deliberately refused for years past to fulfil their constitutional obligations, and we refer to their own statutes for the proof.

The Constitution of the United States, in its fourth Article, provides as follows: "No person held to service or labor in one State under the laws thereof, escaping into another, shall, in consequence of any law or regulation therein, be discharged from such service or labor, but shall be delivered up, on claim of the party to whom such service or labor may be due."

This stipulation was so material to the compact that without it that compact would not have been made. . . .

The constitutional compact has been deliberately broken and disregarded by the non-slaveholding States; and the consequence follows that South Carolina is released from her obligation. . . .

We affirm that these ends for which this Government was instituted have been defeated, and the Government itself has been destructive of them by the action of the non-slaveholding States. Those States have assumed the right of deciding upon the propriety of our domestic institutions; and have denied the rights of property established in fifteen of the States and recognized by the Constitution; they have denounced as sinful the institution of Slavery; they have permitted the open establishment among them of societies, whose avowed object is to disturb the peace of and eloin the property of the citizens of other States. They have encouraged and assisted thousands of our slaves to leave their homes; and those who remain, have been incited by emissaries, books, and pictures, to servile insurrection.

For twenty-five years this agitation has been steadily increasing, until it has now secured to its aid the power of the common Government. Observing the *forms* of the Constitution, a sectional party has found within that article establishing the Executive Department, the means of subverting the Constitution itself. A geographical line has been drawn across the Union, and all the States north of that line have united in the election of a man to the high office of President of the United States whose opinions and purposes are hostile to Slavery. He is to be intrusted with the administration of the common Government, because he has declared that "Government cannot endure permanently half slave, half free," and that the public mind must rest in the belief that Slavery is in the course of ultimate extinction.

This sectional combination for the subversion of the Constitution has been aided, in some of the States, by elevating to citizenship persons who, by the supreme law of the land, are incapable of becoming citizens; and their votes have been used to inaugurate a new policy, hostile to the South, and destructive of its peace and safety.

On the 4th of March next this party will take possession of the Government. It has announced that the South shall be excluded from the common territory, that the Judicial tribunal shall be made sectional, and that a war must be waged against Slavery until it shall cease throughout the United States.

The guarantees of the Constitution will then no longer exist; the equal rights of the States will be lost. The Slaveholding States will no longer have the power of self-government, or self-protection, and the Federal Government will have become their enemy.

Sectional interest and animosity will deepen the irritation; and all hope of remedy is rendered vain, by the fact that the public opinion at the North has invested a great political error with the sanctions of a more erroneous religious belief.

We, therefore, the people of South Carolina, by our delegates in Convention assembled, appealing to the Supreme Judge of the world for the rectitude of our intentions, have solemnly declared that the Union heretofore existing between this State and the other States of North America is dissolved, and that the State of South Carolina has resumed her position among the nations of the world, as a separate and independent state, with full power to levy war, conclude peace, contract alliances, establish commerce, and to do all other acts and things which independent States may of right do.

94. Lincoln: "the Union is much older than the Constitution," March 4, 1861

First Inaugural Address, Richarson, ed., *Messages and Papers of the Presidents*, VI, 7-8.

Apprehension seems to exist among the people of the Southern States that by the accession of a Republican administration their property and their peace and personal security are to be endangered. There has never been any reasonable cause for such apprehension. . . . [On the contrary, as I have stated] "I have no purpose, directly or indirectly, to interfere with the institution of slavery in the States where it exists. I believe I have no lawful right to do so, and I have no inclination to do so." . . .

I add . . . that all the protection which, consistently with the Constitution and the laws, can be given, will be cheerfully given to all the States when lawfully demanded, for whatever cause—as cheerfully to one section as to another. . . .

[However] a disruption of the Federal Union, heretofore only menaced, is now formidably attempted.

I hold that in contemplation of universal law and of the Constitution the Union of these States is perpetual. Perpetuity is implied, if not expressed, in the fundamental law of all national governments. It is safe to assert that no government proper ever had a provision in its organic law for its own termination. Continue to execute all the express provisions of our National Constitution, and the Union will endure forever, it being impossible to destroy it except by some action not provided for in the instrument itself.

Again: If the United States be not a government proper, but an association of States in the nature of contract merely, can it, as a contract, be peaceably unmade by less than all the parties who made it? One party to a contract may violate it—break it, so to speak—but does it not require all to lawfully rescind it?

Descending from these general principles, we find the proposition that in legal contemplation the Union is perpetual confirmed by the history of the Union itself. The Union is much older than the Constitution. It was formed, in fact, by the Articles of Association in 1774. It was matured and continued by the Declaration of Independence in 1776. It was further matured, and the faith of all the then thirteen States expressly plighted and engaged that it should be perpetual, by the Articles of Confederation in 1778. And finally, in 1787, one of the declared objects for ordaining and establishing the Constitution was *"to form a more perfect Union."*

But if destruction of the Union by one or by a part only of the States be lawfully possible, the Union is *less* perfect than before the Constitution, having lost the vital element of perpetuity.

It follows from these views that no State upon its own mere motion can lawfully get out of the Union, that *resolves* and *ordinances* to that effect are legally void, and that acts of violence within any State or States against the authority of the United States are insurrectionary or revolutionary, according to circumstances.

I therefore consider that in view of the Constitution and the laws the Union is unbroken, and to the extent of my ability I shall take care, as the Constitution itself expressly enjoins upon me, that the laws of the Union be faithfully executed in all the States. Doing this I deem to be only a simple duty on my part, and I shall perform it so far as practicable unless my rightful masters, the American people, shall withhold the requisite means or in some authoritative manner direct the contrary. I trust this will not be regarded as a menace, but only as the declared purpose of the Union that it *will* constitutionally defend and maintain itself.

In doing this there needs to be no bloodshed or violence, and there shall be none unless it be forced upon the national authority. The power confided to me will be used to hold, occupy, and possess the property and places belonging to the Government and to collect the duties and imposts; but beyond what may be necessary for these objects, there will be no invasion, no using of force against or among the people anywhere. Where hostility to the United States in any interior locality shall be so great and universal as to prevent competent resident citizens from holding the Federal offices, there will be no attempt to force obnoxious strangers among the people for that object. While the strict legal right may exist in the Government to enforce the exercise of these offices, the attempt to do so would be so irritating and so nearly impracticable withal that I deem it better to forego for the time the uses of such offices.

The mails, unless repelled, will continue to be furnished in all parts of the Union. So far as possible the people everywhere shall have that sense of perfect security which is most favorable to calm thought and reflection. The course here indicated will be followed unless current events and experience shall show a modification or change to be proper, and in every case and exigency my best discretion will be exercised, according to circumstances actually existing and with a view and a hope of a peaceful solution of the national troubles and the restoration of fraternal sympathies and affections. . . .

95. *The Confederate Constitution, March 11, 1861*

James D. Richardson, ed., *A Compilation of the Messages and Papers of the Confederacy . . . 1861-1865* (Nashville, 1906), I, 37-53.

We, the people of the Confederate States, each State acting in its sovereign and independent character, in order to form a permanent federal government, establish justice, insure domestic tranquillity, and secure the blessings of liberty to ourselves and our posterity—invoking the favor and guidance of Almighty God—do ordain and establish this Constitution for the Confederate States of America.

ARTICLE I

SECTION 2. (5) The House of Representatives shall choose their Speaker and other officers; and shall have the sole power of impeachment; except that any judicial or other federal officer resident and acting solely within the limits of any State, may be impeached by a vote of two-thirds of both branches of the Legislature thereof. . . .

SECTION 7. (2) . . . The President may approve any appropriation and disapprove any other appropriation in the same bill. In such case he shall, in signing the bill, designate the appropriations disapproved; and shall return a copy of such appropriations, with his objections, to the House in which the bill shall have originated; and the same proceedings shall then be had as in case of other bills disapproved by the President. . . .

SECTION 8. The Congress shall have power—

(1) To lay and collect taxes, duties, imposts, and excises, for revenue necessary to pay the debts, provide for the common defence, and carry on the Government of the Confederate States; but no bounties shall be granted from the treasury; nor shall any duties or taxes on importations from foreign nations be laid to promote or foster any branch of industry; and all duties, imposts, and excises shall be uniform throughout the Confederate States. . . .

(3) To regulate commerce with foreign nations, and among the several States, and with the Indian tribes; but neither this, nor any other clause contained in the Constitution shall be construed to delegate the power to Congress to appropriate money for any internal improvement intended to facilitate commerce; except for the purpose of furnishing lights, beacons, and buoys, and other aids to navigation upon the coasts, and the improvement of harbors, and the removing of obstructions in river navigation, in all which cases, such duties shall be laid on the navigation facilitated thereby, as may be necessary to pay the costs and expenses thereof.

(4) To establish uniform laws of naturalization, and uniform laws on the subject of bankruptcies throughout the Confederate States, but no law of Congress shall discharge any debt contracted before the passage of the same. . . .

(7) To establish post-offices and post-routes; but the expenses of the Post-office Department, after the first day of March, in the year of our Lord eighteen hundred and sixty-three, shall be paid out of its own revenues. . . .

SECTION 9. (1) The importation of negroes of the African race, from any foreign country, other than the slaveholding States or Territories of the United States of America, is hereby forbidden; and Congress is required to pass such laws as shall effectually prevent the same.

(2) Congress shall also have power to prohibit the introduction of slaves from any State not a member of, or Territory not belonging to, this Confederacy. . . .

(4) No bill of attainder, or *ex post facto* law, or law denying or impairing the right of property in negro slaves shall be passed. . . .

(6) No tax or duty shall be laid on articles exported from any State, except by a vote of two-thirds of both Houses.

(7) No preference shall be given by any regulation of commerce or revenue to the ports of one State over those of another. . . .

(9) Congress shall appropriate no money from the treasury except by a vote of two-thirds of both Houses, taken by yeas and nays, unless it be asked and estimated for by some one of the heads of departments, and submitted to Congress by the President; or for the purpose of paying its own expenses and contingencies; or for the payment of claims against the Confederate States, the justice of which shall have been judicially declared by a tribunal for the investigation of claims against the Government, which it is hereby made the duty of Congress to establish.

(10) All bills appropriating money shall specify in federal currency the exact amount of each appropriation and the purposes for which it is made; and Congress shall grant no extra compensation to any public contractor, officer, agent, or servant, after such contract shall have been made or such service rendered. . . .

[Paragraphs 12 through 19 incorporate the first 8 amendments to the U.S. Constitution.]

(20) Every law, or resolution having the force of law, shall relate to but one subject, and that shall be expressed in the title.

SECTION 10. (3) No State shall, without the consent of Congress, lay any duty on tonnage, except on sea-going vessels, for the improvement of its rivers and harbors navigated by the said vessels; but such duties shall not conflict with any treaties of the Confederate States with foreign nations; and any surplus of revenue, thus derived, shall, after making such improvement, be paid into the common treasury; nor shall any State keep troops or ships of war in time of peace, enter into any agreement or compact with another State, or with a foreign power, or engage in war, unless actually invaded, or in such imminent danger as will not admit of delay. But when any river divides or flows through two or more States, they may enter into compacts with each other to improve the navigation thereof.

ARTICLE II

SECTION 1. (1) The Executive power shall be vested in a President of the Confederate States of America. He and the Vice-President shall hold their offices for the term of six years; but the President shall not be reeligible. . . .

[Paragraph 3 incorporates the twelfth amendment.]

(7) No person except a natural born citizen of the Confederate States, or a citizen thereof, at the time of the adoption of this Constitution, or a citizen thereof born in the United States prior to the 20th December, 1860, shall be eligible to the office of President. . . .

SECTION 2. (3) The principal officer in each of the Executive Departments, and all persons connected with the diplomatic service, may be removed from office at the pleasure of the President. All other civil officers of the Executive Department may be removed at any time by the President, or other appointing power, when their services are unnecessary, or for dishonesty,

incapacity, inefficiency, misconduct, or neglect of duty; and when so removed, the removal shall be reported to the Senate, together with the reasons therefor.

(4) The President shall have power to fill all vacancies that may happen during the recess of the Senate, by granting commissions which shall expire at the end of the next session; but no person rejected by the Senate shall be reappointed to the same office during their ensuing recess. . . .

ARTICLE III

[SECTION 2, paragraph 1 incorporates the eleventh amendment.]

ARTICLE IV

SECTION 2. (1) The citizens of each State shall be entitled to all the privileges and immunities of citizens of the several States, and shall have the right of transit and sojourn in any State of this Confederacy, with their slaves and other property; and the right of property in said slaves shall not be thereby impaired. . . .

(3) No slave or other person held to service or labor in any State or Territory of the Confederate States, under the laws thereof, escaping or unlawfully carried into another, shall, in consequence of any law or regulation therein, be discharged from such service or labor; but shall be delivered up on claim of the party to whom such slave belongs, or to whom such service or labor may be due.

SECTION 3. (1) Other States may be admitted into this Confederacy by a vote of two-thirds of the whole House of Representatives, and two-thirds of the Senate, the Senate voting by States. . . .

(2) The Congress shall have power to dispose of and make all needful rules and regulations concerning the property of the Confederate States, including the lands thereof.

(3) The Confederate States may acquire new territory; and Congress shall have power to legislate and provide gov-

ernments for the inhabitants of all territory belonging to the Confederate States, lying without the limits of the several States, and may permit them, at such times, and in such manner as it may by law provide, to form States to be admitted into the Confederacy. In all such territory, the institution of negro slavery, as it now exists in the Confederate States, shall be recognized and protected by Congress and by the territorial government; and the inhabitants of the several Confederate States and Territories shall have the right to take to such territory any slaves lawfully held by them in any of the States or Territories of the Confederate States. . . .

ARTICLE V

SECTION 1. (1) Upon the demand of any three States, legally assembled in their several Conventions, the Congress shall summon a Convention of all the States, to take into consideration such amendments to the Constitution as the said States shall concur in suggesting at the time when the said demand is made; and should any of the proposed amendments to the Constitution be agreed on by the said Convention—voting by States—and the same be ratified by the Legislatures of two-thirds of the several States, or by conventions in two-thirds thereof—as the one or the other mode of ratification may be proposed by the general convention—they shall thenceforward form a part of this Constitution. But no State shall, without its consent, be deprived of its equal representation in the Senate.

ARTICLE VI

(1) The Government established by this Constitution is the successor of the Provisional Government of the Confederate States of America, and all the laws passed by the latter shall continue in force until the same shall be repealed or modified; and all the officers appointed by the same shall remain in office until their successors are appointed and qualified, or the offices abolished. . . .

[Paragraph 5 incorporates the ninth amendment.]

(6) The powers not delegated to the Confederate States by the Constitution, nor prohibited by it to the States, are reserved to the States, respectively, or to the people thereof.

ARTICLE VII

(2) When five States shall have ratified this Constitution in the manner before specified, the Congress, under the provisional Constitution, shall prescribe the time for holding the election of President and Vice-President, and for the meeting of the electoral college, and for counting the votes and inaugurating the President. They shall also prescribe the time for holding the first election of members of Congress under this Constitution, and the time for assembling the same. Until the assembling of such Congress, the Congress under the provisional Constitution shall continue to exercise the legislative powers granted them; not extending beyond the time limited by the Constitution of the Provisional Government.

Lincoln Accepts the Southern Challenge

96. *The President Mobilizes the State Militia, April 15, 1861*

Richardson, ed., *Messages and Papers of the Presidents,* VI, 13.

Whereas the laws of the United States have been for some time past and now are opposed and the execution thereof obstructed in the States of South Carolina, Georgia, Alabama, Florida, Mississippi, Louisiana, and Texas by combinations too powerful to be suppressed by the ordinary course of judicial proceedings or by the powers vested in the marshals by law:

Now, therefore, I, Abraham Lincoln, President of the United States, in virtue of the power in me vested by the Constitution and the laws, have thought fit to call forth, and hereby do call forth, the militia of the several States of the Union to the aggregate number of 75,000, in order to suppress said combinations and to cause the laws to be duly executed. . . .

97. *Lincoln Proclaims a Blockade of the Confederacy, April 19, 1861*

Richardson, ed., *Messages and Papers of the Presidents,* VI, 14.

Whereas an insurrection against the Government of the United States has broken out in the States of South Carolina, Georgia, Alabama, Florida, Mississippi, Louisiana, and Texas, and the laws of the United States for the collection of the revenue can not be effectually executed therein conformably to that provision of the Constitution which requires duties to be uniform throughout the United States; and

Whereas a combination of persons engaged in such insurrection have threatened to grant pretended letters of marque to authorize the bearers thereof to commit assaults on the lives, vessels, and property of good citizens of the country lawfully engaged in commerce on the high seas and in waters of the United States; and

Whereas an Executive proclamation has been already issued requiring the persons engaged in these disorderly proceedings to desist therefrom, calling out a militia force for the purpose of repressing the same, and convening Congress in extraordinary session to deliberate and determine thereon:

Now, therefore, I, Abraham Lincoln, President of the United States, with a view to the same purposes before mentioned and to the protection of the public peace and the lives and property of quiet and orderly citizens pursuing their lawful occupations, until Congress shall have assembled and deliberated on the said unlawful proceedings or until the same shall have ceased, have further deemed it advisable to set on foot a blockade of the ports within the States aforesaid, in pursuance of the laws of the United States and of the law of nations in such case provided. . . .

And I hereby proclaim and declare that if any person, under the pretended authority of the said States or under any other pretense, shall molest a vessel of the United States or the persons or cargo on board of her, such person will be held amenable to the laws of the United States for the prevention and punishment of piracy. . . .

98. *"There can be no successful appeal . . . to bullets"*

Abraham Lincoln, July 4, 1861, Richardson, ed., *Messages and Papers of the Presidents*, VI, 23-30.

This issue embraces more than the fate of these United States. It presents to the whole family of man the question whether a constitutional republic, or democracy—a government of the people by the same people—can or can not maintain its territorial integrity against its own domestic foes. It presents the question whether discontented individuals, too few in number to control administration according to organic laws in any case, can always, upon the pretenses made in this case, or on any other pretenses, or arbitrarily without any pretense, break up their government, and thus practically put an end to free government upon the earth. It forces us to ask: Is there in all republics this inherent and fatal weakness? Must a Government of necessity be too *strong* for the liberties of its own people, or too *weak* to maintain its own existence?

So viewing the issue, no choice was left but to call out the war power of the government, and so to resist force employed for its destruction by force for its preservation. . . .

It might seem, at first thought, to be of little difference whether the present movement at the South be called "secession" or "rebellion." The movers, however, well understand the difference. At the beginning they knew they could never raise their treason to any respectable magnitude by any name which implies violation of law. They knew their people possessed as much of moral sense, as much of devotion to law and order, and as much pride in and reverence for the history and government of their common country as any other civilized and patriotic people.

They knew they could make no advancement directly in the teeth of these strong and noble sentiments. Accordingly, they commenced by an insidious debauching of the public mind. They invented an ingenious sophism which, if conceded, was followed by perfectly logical steps, through all the incidents, to the complete destruction of the Union. The sophism itself is that any State of the Union may consistently with the national Constitution, and therefore lawfully and peacefully, withdraw from the Union without the consent of the Union or of any other State. . . .

Having never been States either in substance or in name, *outside* of the Union, whence this magical omnipotence of "State rights," asserting a claim of power to lawfully destroy the Union itself? Much is said about the "sovereignty" of the States, but the word even is not in the national Constitution, nor, as is believed, in any of the State constitutions. What is "sovereignty" in the political sense of the term? Would it be far wrong to define it as "a political community without a political superior"? Tested by this, no one of our States, except Texas, ever was a sovereignty. . . . The States have their status in the Union, and they have no other legal status. If they break from this, they can only do so against law and by revolution. . . .

What is now combated is the position that secession is *consistent* with the Constitution—is *lawful* and *peaceful*. It is not contended that there is any express law for it, and nothing should ever be implied as law which leads to unjust or absurd consequences. . . .

The seceders insist that our Constitution admits of secession. They have assumed to make a national constitution of their own, in which of necessity they have either *discarded* or *retained* the right of secession as they insist it exists in ours. If they have discarded it, they thereby admit that on principle it ought not to be in ours. If they have retained it, by their own construction of ours, they show that to be consistent they must secede from one another whenever they shall find it the easiest way of settling their debts, or effecting any other selfish or unjust object. The principle itself is one of disintegration and upon which no government can possibly endure. . . .

It may well be questioned whether there is to-day a majority of the legally qualified voters of any State, except, perhaps, South Carolina, in favor of disunion. There is much reason to believe that the Union men are the majority in many, if not in every other one, of the so-called seceded States. . . .

This is essentially a people's contest. On the side of the Union it is a struggle for maintaining in the world that form and substance of government whose leading object is to elevate the condition of men; to lift artificial weights from all shoulders; to clear the paths of laudable pursuit for all; to afford all an unfettered start and a fair chance in the race of life. Yielding to partial and temporary departures, from necessity, this is the leading object of the Government for whose existence we contend. . . .

Our popular government has often been called an experiment. Two points in it our people have already settled—the successful *establishing* and the successful *administering* of it. One still remains—its successful *maintenance* against a formidable internal attempt to overthrow it. It is now for them to demonstrate to the world that those who can fairly carry an election can also suppress a rebellion; that ballots are the rightful and peaceful successors of bullets; and that when ballots have fairly and constitutionally decided, there can be no successful appeal back to bullets; that there can be no successful appeal, except to ballots themselves, at succeeding elections. Such will be a great lesson of peace: teaching men that what they cannot take by an election, neither can they take it by war; teaching all the folly of being the beginners of a war. . . .

99. *Lincoln Proclaims a State of Insurrection, August 16, 1861*

Richardson, ed., *Messages and Papers of the Presidents*, VI, 37-8.

Whereas on the 15th day of April, 1861, the President of the United States, in view of an insurrection against the laws, Constitution, and Government of the United States . . . did call forth the militia to suppress said insurrection and to cause the laws of the Union to be duly executed, and the insurgents have failed to disperse by the time directed by the President; and . . .

Whereas the insurgents in all the said States claim to act under the authority thereof, and such claim is not disclaimed or repudiated by the persons exercising the functions of government in such State or States or in the part or parts thereof in which such combinations exist, nor has such insurrection been suppressed by said States:

Now, therefore, I, Abraham Lincoln, President of the United States, in pursuance of an act of Congress approved July 13, 1861, do hereby declare that the inhabitants of the said States of Georgia, South Carolina, Virginia, North Carolina, Tennessee, Alabama, Louisiana, Texas, Arkansas, Mississippi, and Florida (except the inhabitants of that part of the State of

Virginia lying west of the Alleghany Mountains and of such other parts of that State and the other States hereinbefore named as may maintain a loyal adhesion to the Union and the Constitution or may be from time to time occupied and controlled by forces of the United States engaged in the dispersion of said insurgents) are in a state of insurrection against the United States, and that all commercial intercourse between the same and the inhabitants thereof, with the exceptions aforesaid, and the citizens of other States and other parts of the United States is unlawful, and will remain unlawful until such insurrection shall cease or has been suppressed. . . .

CHAPTER XII

The Civil War and the Constitution

THE legal status of the civil conflict was a complicated constitutional, political, and diplomatic issue. What was the nature of this armed struggle—was it simply a domestic insurrection, a rebellion of dissidents, or a war between nation and nation? The official position of Lincoln, later supported by Congress and the Supreme Court, was that the Union is perpetual; secessionists, therefore, were engaged in an insurrection against their lawful government. The blockade of Confederate ports seriously challenged this theory, for international law viewed the right of blockade as an incident of war between belligerent nations. The seizure of neutral vessels raised the whole question of the legality of the blockade, and the Supreme Court in the Prize Cases (No. 100) performed a brilliant feat of judicial juggling, upholding the "insurrection theory" but at the same time interpreting insurrection as war, despite the absence of a congressional declaration. In other words, the Union retained the insurrection doctrine as a constitutional theory, using it when necessary, but also resorted to a belligerency theory when it was advantageous, as in justifying the blockade.

The problem of dealing with treason and confiscation was also characterized by this dualism. If the policy of the government were based on the insurrection doctrine, the Confederates could be treated as traitors but their property rights were protected by constitutional guarantees. If the belligerency theory were followed, the Confederates were enemies, not traitors, and their property was subject to the rules of international law. Congress utilized a strange mixture of constitutional and international law, treating Confederates as enemies for purposes of confiscation and as traitorous insurrectionists for purposes of punishment (No. 101). Although the law of treason was modified to permit fine and imprisonment as a substitute for the death penalty, few persons were convicted of treason for giving aid to the rebellion, and in no case was the death penalty applied.

In the absence of congressional delegations of power, the responsibilities for meeting the secession crisis fell on the President. To justify the series of extraordinary measures which he took prior to the convening of Congress in 1861, Lincoln evolved a constitutional interpretation which completely revolutionized the Executive's function as Commander-in-Chief. His "war power" theory resulted from the union of the clause making it the duty of the President "to take care that the laws be faithfully executed" and the "Commander-in-Chief" clause, which states that "the President shall be the Commander-in-Chief of the Army and Navy of the United States, and of the Militia of the several States, when called into the actual service of the United States." Relying on this plenary doctrine, Lincoln proclaimed a blockade, suspended the writ of habeas corpus, instituted a militia draft, and issued the Emancipation Proclamation.

Perhaps the President's most controversial action in the early days of the crisis was the suspension of the fundamental guarantee that "the privilege of the writ of habeas corpus shall not be suspended, unless when in cases of rebellion or invasion the public safety may require it." Although this provision does not specify which branch of the government possesses the power of suspension, Lincoln ordered the withholding of the privilege between Washington and Philadelphia only two weeks after Sumter (No. 102). The chief argument against Lincoln's action was Chief Justice Taney's opinion in *Ex parte* Merryman (No. 103). Denying the violation of any law, President Lincoln justified his action in his special message to Congress (No. 104). Although Lincoln left to Congress the question of legislating on this vital issue, it was not until March, 1863, that Congress responded. In practice, however, the 1863 law made no noticeable difference in enforcement procedures, and widespread criticism continued.

The suspension of the habeas corpus privilege did not necessarily institute martial law. In September, 1862, President Lincoln definitely assumed the power to proclaim martial law generally. The ambivalent position of the judiciary toward military trial of civilians is best illustrated by the contrast between the handling of the Vallandigham case in 1864 and the postwar Milligan decision. In the former case, the Supreme Court refused to review the proceedings of a military commission, but in *Ex parte* Milligan (No. 105), decided after hostilities had ended, the Court reversed a military tribunal in a classic opinion that has long been considered one of the basic defenses of American civil liberty.

The eradication of slavery by presidential authority involved one of the boldest uses of the Chief Executive's "war power" theory. The conversion of the Republican party from one opposing slavery extension to one demanding universal emancipation was a slow process, and its leader only gradually accepted, with severe constitutional misgivings, the necessity of abolition. Lincoln's single-minded war aim to preserve the Union outraged Northerners who demanded immediate emancipation, but even editor Horace Greeley's blistering "Prayer of Twenty Millions" did not shake the President's determination to subordinate the issue of slavery to that of unity (No. 106). When Lincoln finally requested congressional action against slavery on December 1, 1862, his constitutional scruples dictated the resort to constitutional amendments guaranteeing compensation to the former owners (No. 107). Lincoln's conservatism and caution, however, had already been undermined by both domestic and foreign antislavery sentiment; indeed, he informed his Cabinet on July 22, 1862, of his intention to proclaim "emancipation of all slaves within States remaining in insurrection on the first of January, 1863." After a preliminary proclamation of September 22, 1862, the President accordingly issued on New Year's day, 1863, the famed Emancipation Proclamation (No. 108), which, paradoxically enough, did not free a single slave immediately. Thus, as Lincoln later said, "the moment came when I felt that slavery must die that the nation might live."

In Lincoln's home state, his opponents held a mass meeting in the House of Representatives and denounced the Proclamation as "a total subversion of the Federal Union" (No. 109). In defending his policies, Lincoln frankly confessed that his actions had been shaped by the course of events and asserted that "measures otherwise unconstitutional might become lawful by becoming indispensable to the preservation of the Constitution through the preservation of the nation." Constitutional justification of emancipation was provided by the Thirteenth Amendment (No. 110), which was operative nine months after the war ended.

Eight years after Appomattox the Supreme Court ruled on the vital question of whether one of the states of the Union could constitutionally secede. Recognizing that this issue had been permanently settled by the clash of arms, the Court sustained Lincoln's reasoning and established the still enduring concept of the constitutional nature of the postwar Union (*Texas v. White* [No. 111]). This decision confined itself largely to a discussion of the nature of the Union itself rather than the nature of the powers possessed by the central government. This latter question came before the Court in the Legal Tender Cases, which involved the power of the federal government to issue paper currency in wartime. In *Hepburn v. Griswold* (1870) the Court rejected Congress's attempt to make greenbacks legal tender for debts contracted before the passage of the act in 1862. To the minority, the act was a wartime "necessity, in the most stringent sense in which that word can be used." In the second Legal Tender Case (1871) two new justices joined the minority and reversed the Hepburn ruling. Upholding the constitutionality of the act in cases involving contracts negotiated both before and after its enactment, the new majority validated the Legal Tender Acts in the broadest possible manner as a justifiable exercise of the national government's powers in time of emergency, not necessarily limited to war. In a concurring opinion, Justice Bradley elaborated on this theme: "I do not say that it is a war power, or that it is only to be called into exercise in time of war; for other public exigencies may arise in the history of a nation which may make it expedient and imperative to exercise it." The new justice also announced a doctrine in reference to other aspects of the expansion of governmental powers that was to prove important in later constitutional development. In a strongly nationalistic opinion, he declared that "the United States is . . . a national government, and the only government in this country that has the character of nationality." Its jurisdiction extended over all general subjects of legislation affecting the interests of the whole people and requiring uniformity of regulation. "Such being the character of the general government," he concluded, "it seems to be a self-evident proposition that it is invested with all those inherent and implied powers which, at the time of adopting the Constitution, were generally considered to belong to every government as such, and as being essential to the exercise of its functions."

Consistent with this expansive view of federal power, the Court ruled in *Julliard v. Greenman* (1884) that Congress had the power to make treasury notes legal tender at any time, emergency or not. The authority relied upon included not only the power to coin and borrow money but also related congressional powers designed to achieve the great objects for which a "national government, with sovereign powers," was framed.

Nature of the War

100. "*A civil war, with belligerent parties in hostile array*"

The Prize Cases, 2 Black 635 (1863).

GRIER, J.: . . . Let us inquire whether, at the time this blockade was instituted, a state of war existed which would justify a resort to these means of subduing the hostile force. . . .

Insurrection against a government may or may not culminate in an organized rebellion, but a civil war always begins by insurrection against the lawful authority of the Government. A civil war is never solemnly declared; it becomes such by its accidents—the number, power, and organization of the persons who originate and carry it on. When the party in rebellion occupy and hold in a hostile manner a certain portion of territory; have declared their independence; have cast off their allegiance; have organized armies; have commenced hostilities against their former sovereign, the world acknowledges

them as belligerents, and the contest a *war*. *They* claim to be in arms to establish their liberty and independence, in order to become a sovereign State, while the sovereign party treats them as insurgents and rebels who owe allegiance, and who should be punished with death for their treason.

The laws of war, as established among nations, have their foundation in reason, and all tend to mitigate the cruelties and misery produced by the scourge of war. Hence the parties to a civil war usually concede to each other belligerent rights. They exchange prisoners, and adopt the other courtesies and rules common to public or national wars. . . .

This greatest of civil wars was not gradually developed by popular commotion, tumultuous assemblies, or local unorganized insurrections. However long may have been its previous conception, it nevertheless sprung forth suddenly from the parent brain, a Minerva in the full panoply of *war*. The President was bound to meet it in the shape it presented itself, without waiting for Congress to baptize it with a name; and no name given to it by him or them could change the fact.

It is not the less a civil war, with belligerent parties in hostile array, because it may be called an "insurrection" by one side, and the insurgents be considered as rebels or traitors. It is not necessary that the independence of the revolted province or State be acknowledged in order to constitute it a party belligerent in a war according to the law of nations. Foreign nations acknowledge it as war by a declaration of neutrality. The condition of neutrality cannot exist unless there be two belligerent parties. . . .

The law of nations is also called the law of nature; it is founded on the common consent as well as the common sense of the world. It contains no such anomalous doctrine as that which this Court are now for the first time desired to pronounce, to wit: That insurgents who have risen in rebellion against their sovereign, expelled her courts, established a revolutionary government, organized armies, and commenced hostilities, are not *enemies* because they are *traitors;* and a war levied on the government by traitors, in order to dismember and destroy it, is not a *war* because it is an "insurrection."

Whether the President, in fulfilling his duties as Commander-in-chief in suppressing an insurrection, has met with such armed hostile resistance, and a civil war of such alarming proportions, as will compel him to accord to them the character of belligerents, is a question to be decided *by him,* and this Court must be governed by the decisions and acts of the political department of the Government to which this power was intrusted. "He must determine what degree of force the crisis demands." The proclamation of blockade is itself official and conclusive evidence to the Court that a state of war existed which demanded and authorized a recourse to such a measure, under the circumstances peculiar to the case. . . .

On this first question therefore we are of the opinion that the President had a right, *jure belli*, to institute a blockade of ports in possession of the States in rebellion, which neutrals are bound to regard.

Congress, Confiscation, and Treason

101. *The Second Confiscation Act, July 17, 1862*

U. S. Stat. at L., XII, 589-92.

Be it enacted by the Senate and House of Representatives . . . that every person who shall hereafter commit the crime of treason against the United States, and shall be adjudged guilty thereof, shall suffer death, and all his slaves, if any, shall be declared and made free; or, at the discretion of the court, he shall be imprisoned for not less than five years and fined not less than ten thousand dollars, and all his slaves, if any, shall be declared and made free; said fine shall be levied and collected on any or all of the property, real and personal, excluding slaves, of which the said person so convicted was the owner at the time of committing the said crime, any sale or conveyance to the contrary notwithstanding.

SEC. 2. *And be it further enacted,* That, if any person shall hereafter incite, set on foot, assist, or engage in any rebellion or insurrection against the authority of the United States, or the laws thereof, or shall give aid or comfort thereto, or shall engage in, or give aid and comfort to, any such existing rebellion or insurrection, and be convicted thereof, such person shall be punished by imprisonment for a period not exceeding ten years, or by a fine not exceeding ten thousand dollars, and by the liberation of all his slaves, if any he have; or by both of said punishments, at the discretion of the Court. . . .

SEC. 5. *And be it further enacted* . . . That, to insure the speedy termination of the present rebellion, it shall be the duty of the President of the United States to cause the seizure of all the estate and property, money, stocks, credits, and effects of the persons hereinafter named in this section, and to apply and use the same and the proceeds thereof for the support of the army of the United States, that is to say:

First. Of any person hereafter acting as an officer of the army or navy of the rebels in arms against the government of the United States.

Secondly. Of any person hereafter acting as President, Vice-President, member of Congress, judge of any court, cabinet officer, foreign minister, commissioner or consul of the so-called confederate states of America.

Thirdly. Of any person acting as a governor of a state, member of a so-called convention or legislature, or judge of any court of any of the so-called confederate states of America.

Fourthly. Of any person who, having held an office of honor, trust, or profit in the United States, shall hereafter hold an office in the so-called confederate states of America. . . .

Sixthly. Of any person who, owning property in any loyal State or Territory of the United States or the District of Columbia, shall hereafter assist and give aid and comfort to such rebellion; and all sales, tranfers, or conveyances of any such property shall be null and void; and it shall be a sufficient bar to any suit brought by such person for the possession or the use of such property, or any of it, to allege and prove that he is one of the persons described in this section. . . .

SEC. 9. *And be it further enacted,* That all slaves of persons who shall hereafter be engaged in rebellion against the government of the United States, or who shall in any way give aid or comfort thereto, escaping from such persons and taking refuge within the lines of the army; and all slaves captured from such persons or deserted by them and coming under the control of the government of the United States; and all slaves of such persons found . . . [or] being within any place occupied by rebel forces and afterwards occupied by the forces of the United States, shall be deemed captives of war, and shall be forever free of their servitude and not again held as slaves.

SEC. 10. *And be it further enacted,* That no slave escaping into any State, Territory, or the District of Columbia, from any other State, shall be delivered up, or in any way impeded or hindered of his liberty, except for crime, or some offence against the laws, unless the person claiming said fugitive shall first make oath that the person to whom the labor or service of such fugitive is alleged to be due is his lawful owner, and has not borne arms against the United States in the present rebellion, nor in any way given aid and comfort thereto. . . .

SEC. 11. *And be it further enacted,* That the President of the United States is authorized to employ as many persons of African descent as he may deem necessary and proper for the suppression of this rebellion, and for this purpose he may or- ganize and use them in such manner as he may judge best for the public welfare. . . .

SEC. 13. *And be it further enacted,* That the President is hereby authorized, at any time hereafter, by proclamation, to extend to persons who may have partici- pated in the existing rebellion in any State or part thereof, pardon and amnesty, with such exceptions and at such time and on such condition as he may deem expedi- ent for the public welfare. . . .

The President as Commander in Chief

102. *Lincoln Suspends Habeas Corpus, April 27, 1861*

Richardson, ed., *Messages and Papers of the Presidents*, VI, 18.

THE COMMANDING GENERAL OF THE ARMY OF THE UNITED STATES:

You are engaged in suppressing an in- surrection against the laws of the United States. If at any point on or in the vicinity of any military line which is now or which shall be used between the city of Philadelphia and the city of Washington you find resistance which renders it neces- sary to suspend the writ of *habeas corpus* for the public safety, you personally, or through the officer in command at the point where resistance occurs, are author- ized to suspend that writ.

103. Ex Parte *Merryman, 1861*

Federal Case No. 9487, *The Federal Cases, Comprising Cases Argued and Determined in the Circuit and District Courts of the United States* (St. Paul, 1895), XVII, 144-53.

TANEY, C.J.: . . . A military officer re- siding in Pennsylvania issues an order to arrest a citizen of Maryland, upon vague and indefinite charges, without any proof, so far as appears. Under this order his house is entered in the night; he is seized as a prisoner, and conveyed to Fort Mc- Henry, and there kept in close confine- ment. And when a *habeas corpus* is served on the commanding officer, requiring him to produce the prisoner before a justice of the Supreme Court, in order that he may examine into the legality of the imprison- ment, the answer of the officer is that he is authorized by the President to suspend the writ of *habeas corpus* at his discretion, and, in the exercise of that discretion, sus- pends it in this case, and on that ground refuses obedience to the writ.

As the case comes before me, therefore, I understand that the President not only claims the right to suspend the writ of *habeas corpus* himself, at his discretion, but to delegate that discretionary power to a military officer, and to leave it to him to determine whether he will or will not obey judicial process that may be served upon him.

No official notice has been given to the Courts of Justice, or to the public, by proclamation or otherwise, that the President claimed this power and had exercised it in the matter stated in the return. And I certainly listened to it with some surprise, for I had supposed it to be one of those points of constitutional law upon which there was no difference of opinion, and that it was admitted on all hands that the privilege of the writ could not be suspended except by act of Congress. . . . The great importance which the framers of the Constitution attached to the privilege of the writ of *habeas corpus* to protect the liberty of the citizen, is proved by the fact that its suspension, except in cases of invasion and rebellion, is first in the list of prohibited power; and even in these cases the power is denied and its exercise prohibited unless the public safety shall require it. It is true that in the cases mentioned Congress is of necessity to judge whether the public safety does or does not require it; and its judgment is conclusive. But the introduction of these words is a standing admonition to the legislative body of the danger of suspending it and of the extreme caution they should exercise before they give the Government of the United States such power over the liberty of a citizen.

It is the second Article of the Constitution that provides for the organization of the Executive Department, and enumerates the powers conferred on it, and prescribes its duties. And if the high power over the liberty of the citizens now claimed was intended to be conferred on the President, it would undoubtedly be found in plain words in this article. But there is not a word in it that can furnish the slightest ground to justify the exercise of the power. . . .

And the only power, therefore, which the President possesses, where the "life, liberty and property" of a private citizen is concerned, is the power and duties prescribed in the third section of the Second Article which requires, "that he shall take care that the laws be faithfully executed." He is not authorized to execute them himself, or through agents or officers, civil or military, appointed by himself, but he is to take care that they be faithfully carried into execution as they are expounded and adjudged by the co-ordinate branch of the government, to which that duty is assigned by the Constitution. It is thus made his duty to come in aid of the judicial authority, if it shall be resisted by force too strong to be overcome without the assistance of the Executive arm. But in exercising this power, he acts in subordination to judicial authority, assisting it to execute its process and enforce its judgements.

With such provisions in the Constitution, expressed in language too clear to be misunderstood by anyone, I can see no ground whatever for supposing that the President in any emergency or in any state of things can authorize the suspension of the privilege of the writ of *habeas corpus,* or arrest a citizen except in aid of the judicial power. He certainly does not faithfully execute the laws if he takes upon himself legislative power by suspending the writ of *habeas corpus*—and the judicial power, also, by arresting and imprisoning a person without due process of law. Nor can any argument be drawn from the nature of sovereignty, or the necessities of government for self-defence, in times of tumult and danger. The Government of the United States is one of delegated and limited powers. It derives its existence and authority altogether from the Constitution, and neither of its branches—executive, legislative, or judicial—can exercise any of the powers of government beyond those specified and granted. . . . The documents before me show that the military authority in this case has gone far beyond the mere suspension of the privilege of the writ of *habeas corpus.* It has, by force of arms, thrust aside the judicial authorities and officers to whom the Constitution has confided the power and duty of interpreting and administering the laws, and substituted a military government in its place, to be administered and executed by military officers. . . .

The Constitution provides, as I have before said, that "no person shall be deprived of life, liberty, or property without due process of law." It declares that "the right of the people to be secure in their persons, houses, papers, and effects against unreasonable searches and seizures shall not be violated, and no warrant shall issue but upon probable cause, supported by oath or affirmation, and particularly describing the place to be searched and the persons or things to be seized." It provides that the party accused shall be entitled to a speedy trial in a court of justice.

And these great and fundamental laws, which Congress itself could not suspend, have been disregarded and suspended, like the writ of *habeas corpus,* by a military order, supported by force of arms. Such is the case now before me; and I can only say that if the authority which the Constitution has confided to the judiciary department and judicial officers may thus upon any pretext or under any circumstances be usurped by the military power

at its discretion, the people of the United States are no longer living under a Government of laws, but every citizen holds life, liberty, and property at the will and pleasure of the army officer in whose military district he may happen to be found.

In such a case my duty was too plain to be mistaken. I have exercised all the power which the Constitution and laws confer on me, but that power has been resisted by a force too strong for me to overcome. It is possible that the officer who had incurred this grave responsibility may have misunderstood his instructions, and exceeded the authority intended to be given him. I shall therefore order all the proceedings in this case, with my opinion, to be filed and recorded in the Circuit Court of the United States for the District of Maryland, and direct the clerk to transmit a copy . . . to the President of the United States. It will then remain for that high officer, in fulfillment of his constitutional obligation to "take care that the laws be faithfully executed" to determine what measure he will take to cause the civil process of the United States to be respected and enforced.

104. *Lincoln Defends the Suspension of Habeas Corpus, July 4, 1861*

Richardson, ed., *Messages and Papers of the Presidents,* VI, 24-5.

Soon after the first call for militia it was considered a duty to authorize the Commanding General in proper cases, according to his discretion, to suspend the privilege of the writ of *habeas corpus,* or, in other words, to arrest and detain without resort to the ordinary processes and forms of law such individuals as he might deem dangerous to the public safety. This authority has purposely been exercised but very sparingly. Nevertheless, the legality and propriety of what has been done under it are questioned, and the attention of the country has been called to the proposition that one who is sworn to "take

care that the laws be faithfully executed" should not himself violate them. Of course some consideration was given to the questions of power and propriety before this matter was acted upon. The whole of the laws which were required to be faithfully executed were being resisted and failing of execution in nearly one-third of the States. Must they be allowed to finally fail of execution, even had it been perfectly clear that by the use of the means necessary to their execution some single law, made in such extreme tenderness of the citizen's liberty that practically it relieves more of the guilty than of the innocent, should to a very limited extent be violated? To state the question more directly, Are all the laws *but one* to go unexecuted, and the Government itself go to pieces lest that one be violated? Even in such a case, would not the official oath be broken if the Government should be overthrown when it was believed that disregarding the single law would tend to preserve it? But it was not believed that this question was presented. It was not believed that any law was violated. The provision of the Constitution that "the privilege of the writ of *habeas corpus* shall not be suspended unless when, in cases of rebellion or invasion, the public safety may require it" is equivalent to a provision—is a provision—that such privilege may be suspended when, in cases of rebellion or invasion, the public safety *does* require it. It was decided that we have a case of rebellion and that the public

safety does require the qualified suspension of the privilege of the writ which was authorized to be made. Now it is insisted that Congress, and not the Executive, is vested with this power; but the Constitution itself is silent as to which or who is to exercise the power; and as the provision was plainly made for a dangerous emergency, it can not be believed the framers of the instrument intended that in every case the danger should run its course until Congress could be called together, the very assembling of which might be prevented, as was intended in this case, by the rebellion.

No more extended argument is now offered, as an opinion at some length will probably be presented by the Attorney-General. Whether there shall be any legislation upon the subject, and, if any, what, is submitted entirely to the better judgment of Congress.

105. *"The Constitution . . . is a law for rulers and people, equally in war and in peace."*

Ex Parte Milligan, 4 Wallace 2 (1866).

DAVIS, J.: . . . The controlling question in the case is this: Upon the *facts* stated in Milligan's petition, and the exhibits filed, had the military commission mentioned in its *jurisdiction,* legally, to try and sentence him? Milligan, not a resident of one of the rebellious states, or a prisoner of war, but a citizen of Indiana for twenty years past, and never in the military or naval service, is, while at his home, arrested by the military power of the United States, imprisoned, and, on certain criminal charges preferred against him, tried, convicted, and sentenced to be hanged by a military commission, organized under the direction of the military commander of the military district of Indiana. Had this tribunal the *legal* power and authority to try and punish this man? . . .

The Constitution of the United States

is a law for rulers and people, equally in war and in peace, and covers with the shield of its protection all classes of men, at all times, and under all circumstances. No doctrine, involving more pernicious consequences, was ever invented by the wit of man than that any of its provisions can be suspended during any of the great exigencies of government. Such a doctrine leads directly to anarchy or despotism, but the theory of necessity on which it is based is false; for the government, within the Constitution, has all the powers granted to it which are necessary to preserve its existence; as has been happily proved by the result of the great effort to throw off its just authority.

Have any of the rights guaranteed by the Constitution been violated in the case of Milligan? and if so, what are they? Every trial involves the exercise of judicial power; and from what source did the military commission that tried him derive their authority? Certainly no part of the judicial power of the country was conferred on them; because the Constitution expressly vests it "in one Supreme Court and such inferior courts as the Congress may from time to time ordain and establish," and it is not pretended that the commission was a court ordained and established by Congress. They cannot justify on the mandate of the President, because he is controlled by law, and has his appropriate sphere of duty, which is to execute, not to make, the laws; and there is "no unwritten criminal code to which resort can be had as a source of jurisdiction."

But it is said that the jurisdiction is complete under the "laws and usages of war."

It can serve no useful purpose to inquire what those laws and usages are, whence they originated, where found, and on whom they operate; they can never be applied to citizens in states which have upheld the authority of the government, and where the courts are open and their process unobstructed. This Court has judicial knowledge that in Indiana the federal authority was always unopposed, and its courts always open to hear criminal accusations and redress grievances; and no usage of war would sanction a military trial there for any offense whatever of a citizen in civil life, in nowise connected with the military service. Congress could grant no such power; and to the honor of our national legislature be it said, it has never been provoked by the state of the country even to attempt its exercise. One of the plainest constitutional provisions was, therefore, infringed when Milligan was tried by a court not ordained and established by Congress, and not composed of judges appointed during good behavior.

Why was he not delivered to the circuit court of Indiana to be proceeded against according to law? . . . If it was danger-

ous, in the distracted condition of affairs, to leave Milligan unrestrained of his liberty, because he "conspired against the government, afforded aid and comfort to rebels, and incited the people to insurrection," the *law* said, arrest him, confine him closely, render him powerless to do further mischief; and then present his case to the grand jury of the district, with proofs of his guilt, and, if indicted, try him according to the course of the common law. If this had been done, the Constitution would have been vindicated, the law of 1863 enforced, and the securities for personal liberty preserved and defended.

Another guarantee of freedom was broken when Milligan was denied a trial by jury. . . .

It is claimed that martial law covers with its broad mantle the proceedings of this military commission. The proposition is this: that in a time of war the commander of an armed force (if, in his opinion, the exigencies of the country demand it, and of which he is to judge) has the power, within the lines of his military district, to suspend all civil rights and their remedies, and subject citizens as well as soldiers to the rule of *his will*; and in the exercise of his lawful authority cannot be restrained, except by his superior officer or the President of the United States. . . .

The statement of this proposition shows its importance; for, if true, republican government is a failure, and there is an end of liberty regulated by law. Martial law, established on such a basis, destroys every guarantee of the Constitution, and effectually renders the "military independent of, and superior to, the civil power,"— the attempt to do which by the king of Great Britain was deemed by our fathers such an offense, that they assigned it to the world as one of the causes which impelled them to declare their independence. Civil liberty and this kind of martial law cannot endure together; the antagonism is irreconcilable; and, in the conflict, one or the other must perish. . . .

The necessities of the service, during

the late rebellion, required that the loyal states should be placed within the limits of certain military districts and commanders appointed in them; and, it is urged, that this, in a military sense, constituted them the theatre of military operations; and, as in this case, Indiana had been and was again threatened with invasion by the enemy, the occasion was furnished to establish martial law. The conclusion does not follow from the premises. If armies were collected in Indiana, they were to be employed in another locality, where the laws were obstructed and the national authority disputed. On *her* soil there was no hostile foot; if once invaded, that invasion was at an end, and with it all pretext for martial law. Martial law cannot arise from a *threatened* invasion. The necessity

must be actual and present; the invasion real, such as effectually closes the courts and deposes the civil administration. . . .

Martial rule can never exist where the courts are open, and in the proper and unobstructed exercise of their jurisdiction. It is also confined to the locality of actual war. Because, during the late rebellion it could have been enforced in Virginia, where the national authority was overturned and the courts driven out, it does not follow that it should obtain in Indiana, where that authority was never disputed, and justice was always administered. And so in the case of a foreign invasion, martial rule may become a necessity in one state, when, in another, it would be "mere lawless violence." . . .

Emancipation

106. *Lincoln Subordinates Slavery to the Union*

Lincoln to Horace Greeley, August 22, 1862, in Roy P. Basler, Marion Dolores Pratt, and Lloyd A. Dunlap, eds., *The Collected Works of Abraham Lincoln* (New Brunswick, 1953), V, 388-9. Reprinted by permission of Rutgers University Press.

I have just read yours of the 19th, addressed to myself through the New-York Tribune. If there be in it any statements, or assumptions of fact, which I may know to be erroneous, I do not, now and here, controvert them. If there be in it any inferences which I may believe to be falsely drawn, I do not now and here, argue against them. If there be perceptable in it an impatient and dictatorial tone, I waive it in deference to an old friend, whose heart I have always supposed to be right.

As to the policy I "seem to be pursuing" as you say, I have not meant to leave any one in doubt.

I would save the Union. I would save it the shortest way under the Constitution. The sooner the national authority can be restored, the nearer the Union will be "the Union as it was." If there be those who would not save the Union, unless they could at the same time *save* slavery, I do not agree with them. If there be those who would not save the Union unless they could at the same time *destroy* slavery, I do not agree with them. My paramount object in this struggle *is* to save the Union, and is *not* either to save or destroy slavery. If I could save the Union without freeing *any* slave I would do it;

and if I could save it by freeing *all* the slaves I would do it; and if I could do it by freeing some and leaving others alone I would also do that. What I do about slavery, and the colored race, I do because I believe it helps to save the Union; and what I forbear, I forbear because I do *not* believe it would help to save the Union. I shall do *less* whenever I shall believe what I am doing hurts the cause, and I shall do *more* whenever I shall believe doing more will help the cause. I shall try to correct errors when shown to be errors; and I shall adopt new views so fast as they shall appear to be true views.

I have here stated my purpose according to my view of *official* duty; and I intend no modification of my oft-expressed *personal* wish that all men every where could be free.

107. *Lincoln Recommends Compensated Emancipation, December 1, 1862*

Richardson, ed., *Messages and Papers of the Presidents*, VI, 136-7, 139, 142.

I recommend the adoption of the following resolution and articles amendatory to the Constitution of the United States: . . .

ART.—. Every State wherein slavery now exists which shall abolish the same therein at any time or times before the 1st day of January, A.D. 1900, shall receive compensation from the United States as follows, to wit:

The President of the United States shall deliver to every such State bonds of the United States bearing interest at the rate of—per cent per annum to an amount equal to the aggregate sum of—— for each slave shown to have been therein by the Eighth Census of the United States, said bonds to be delivered to such State by instalments or in one parcel at the completion of the abolishment, accordingly as the same shall have been gradual or at one time within such State; and interest shall begin to run upon any such bond only from the proper time of its delivery as aforesaid. Any State having received bonds as aforesaid and afterwards reintroducing or tolerating slavery therein shall refund to the United States the bonds so received, or the value thereof, and all interest paid thereon.

ART.—. All slaves who shall have enjoyed actual freedom by the chances of the war at any time before the end of the rebellion shall be forever free; but all owners of such who shall not have been disloyal shall be compensated for them at the same rates as is provided for States adopting abolishment of slavery, but in such way that no slave shall be twice accounted for.

ART.—. Congress may appropriate money and otherwise provide for colonizing free colored persons with their own consent at any place or places without the United States.

I beg indulgence to discuss these proposed articles at some length. Without slavery the rebellion could never have existed; without slavery it could not continue. . . .

The emancipation will be unsatisfactory to the advocates of perpetual slavery, but the length of time should greatly mitigate their dissatisfaction. The time spares both races from the evils of sudden derangement—in fact, from the necessity of any derangement—while most of those whose habitual course of thought will be disturbed by the measure will have passed away before its consummation. They will never see it. Another class will hail the prospect of emancipation, but will deprecate the length of time. They will feel that it gives too little to the now living slaves. But it really gives them much. It saves them from the vagrant destitution which must largely attend immediate emancipation in localities where their numbers are very great, and it gives the inspiring assurance that their posterity shall be free forever. The plan leaves to each State choosing to act under it to abolish slavery now or at the end of the century, or at any intermediate time, or by degrees extending over the whole or any part of the period, and it obliges no two States to proceed alike. It also provides for compensation, and generally the mode of making it. This, it would seem, must further mitigate the dissatisfaction of those who favor perpetual slavery, and especially of those who are to receive the compensation. . . .

In *giving* freedom to the *slave* we *assure* freedom to the *free*—honorable alike in what we give and what we preserve. We shall nobly save or meanly lose the last, best hope of earth. Other means may succeed; this could not fail. The way is plain, peaceful, generous, just—a way which if followed the world will forever applaud and God must forever bless.

108. *The Emancipation Proclamation, January 1, 1863*

U. S. Stat. at L., XII, 1268-9.

Whereas on the twenty-second day of September, A.D. eighteen hundred and sixty two, a proclamation was issued by the President of the United States, containing, among other things, the following, to wit:

"That on the first day of January, A.D. 1863, all persons held as slaves within any State or designated part of a State the people whereof shall then be in rebellion against the United States shall be then, thenceforward, and forever free; and the executive government of the United States, including the military and naval authority thereof, will recognize and maintain the freedom of such persons and will do no act or acts to repress such persons, or any of them, in any efforts they may make for their actual freedom.

"That the executive will on the first day of January aforesaid, by proclamation, designate the States and parts of States, if any, in which the people thereof, respectively, shall then be in rebellion against the United States;" . . .

Now, therefore, I, Abraham Lincoln, President of the United States, by virtue of the power in me vested as Commander-in-Chief of the Army and Navy of the United States in time of actual armed rebellion against the authority and government of the United States, and as a fit and necessary war measure for suppressing said rebellion, do . . . order and declare that all persons held as slaves within said designated States and parts of States are, and henceforward shall be, free; and that the Executive Government of the United States, including the military and naval authorities thereof, will recognize and maintain the freedom of said persons.

And I hereby enjoin upon the people so declared to be free to abstain from all violence, unless in necessary self-defense; and I recommend to them that, in all cases when allowed, they labor faithfully for reasonable wages.

And I further declare and make known that such persons of suitable condition will be received into the armed service of the United States to garrison forts, positions, stations, and other places, and to man vessels of all sorts in said service.

And upon this act, sincerely believed to be an act of justice, warranted by the Constitution upon military necessity, I invoke the considerate judgment of mankind and the gracious favor of Almighty God.

109. *Lincoln's Opponents Deplore Emancipation, January 5, 1863*

Illinois State Register (Springfield), January 6, 1863.

Resolved: That the emancipation proclamation of the president of the United States is as unwarrantable in military as in civil law; a gigantic usurpation, at once converting the war, professedly commenced by the administration for the vindication of the authority of the constitution, into the crusade for the sudden, unconditional and violent liberation of three millions of negro slaves; a result which would not only be a total subversion of the Federal Union but a revolution in the social organization of the southern states, the immediate and remote, the present and far-reaching consequences of which to both races cannot be contemplated without the most dismal foreboding of horror and dismay. The proclamation invites servile insurrection as an element in this emancipation crusade—a means of warfare, the inhumanity and diabolism of which are without example in civilized warfare, and which we denounce, and which the civilized world will denounce, as an ineffaceable disgrace to the American name.

110. *The Thirteenth Amendment Grants Constitutional Recognition of Emancipation*

Proposed February 1, 1865; adopted December 18, 1865.

SECTION 1. Neither slavery nor involuntary servitude, except as a punishment for crime whereof the party shall have been duly convicted, shall exist within the United States or any place subject to their jurisdiction.

SECTION 2. Congress shall have power to enforce this article by appropriate legislation.

The Constitutional Nature and Powers of the New Union

111. *"An indestructible Union, composed of indestructible States"*

Texas v. White, 7 Wallace 700 (1869).

CHASE, C.J.: . . . The first inquiries to which our attention was directed by counsel . . . [is whether] the State of Texas . . . having severed her relations with a majority of the States of the Union, and having by her ordinance of secession attempted to throw off her allegiance to the Constitution and government of the United States, has so far changed her status as to be disabled from prosecuting suits in the National courts. . . .

Texas . . . took part, with the other Confederate States, in the war of the rebellion, which these events made inevitable. During the whole of that war there was no governor, or judge, or any other State officer in Texas, who recognized the National authority. Nor was any officer of the United States permitted to exercise any authority whatever under the National government within the limits of the State, except under the immediate protection of the National military forces.

Did Texas, in consequence of these acts, cease to be a State? Or, if not, did the State cease to be a member of the Union?

It is needless to discuss at length the question whether the right of a State to withdraw from the Union for any cause, regarded by itself as sufficient, is consistent with the Constitution of the United States.

The Union of the States was never a purely artificial and arbitrary relation. It began among the Colonies, and grew out of common origin, mutual sympathies, kindred principles, similar interests, and geographical relations. It was confirmed and strengthened by the necessities of war, and received definite form, and character, and sanction from the Articles of Confederation. By these the Union was solemnly declared to be "perpetual." And when these Articles were found to be inadequate to the exigencies of the country, the Constitution was ordained "to form a more perfect Union." It is difficult to convey the idea of indissoluble unity more clearly than by these words. What can be indissoluble if a perpetual Union made more perfect, is not?

But the perpetuity and indissolubility of the Union by no means implies the loss of distinct and individual existence, or of the right of self-government by the States. Under the Articles of Confederation each State retained its sovereignty, freedom, and independence, and every power, jurisdiction, and right not expressly delegated to the United States. Under the Constitution, though the powers of the States were much restricted, still, all powers not delegated to the United States, nor prohibited to the States, are reserved to the States, respectively, or to the people. And we have already had occasion to remark at this term, that "the people of each State compose a State, having its own government, and endowed with all the functions essential to separate and independent existence," and that "without the States in union, there could be no such political body as the United States." Not only, therefore, can there be no loss of separate and independent autonomy to the States, through their union under the Constitution, but it may be not unreasonably said that the preservation of the States, and the maintenance of their governments, are as much within the design and care of the Constitution as the preservation of the Union and the maintenance of the National government. The Constitution, in all its provisions, looks to an indestructible Union, composed of indestructible States. . . .

When, therefore, Texas became one of the United States, she entered into an indissoluble relation. All the obligations of perpetual union, and all the guaranties of republican government in the Union, attached at once to the State. The act which consummated her admission into the Union was something more than a compact; it was the incorporation of a new member into the political body. And it was final. The union between Texas and the other States was as complete, as perpetual, and as indissoluble as the union between the original States. There was no place for reconsideration or revocation except through revolution, or through consent of the States.

Considered therefore as transactions under the Constitution, the ordinance of secession, adopted by the convention and ratified by a majority of the citizens of Texas, and all the acts of her legislature intended to give effect to that ordinance, were absolutely void. They were utterly without operation in law. The obligations of the State, as a member of the Union, and of every citizen of the State, remained perfect and unimpaired. It certainly follows that the State did not cease to be a State, nor her citizens to be citizens of the Union. If this were otherwise, the State must have become foreign, and her citizens foreigners. The war must have become a war for conquest and subjugation.

Our conclusion therefore is, that Texas continued to be a State, and a State of the Union, notwithstanding the transactions to which we have referred. And this conclusion, in our judgment, is not in conflict with any act or declaration of any department of the national government, but entirely in accordance with the whole series of such acts and declarations since the first outbreak of the rebellion.

But in order to the exercise, by a State, of the right to sue in this court, there needs to be a State government, compe-

tent to represent the State in its relations with the National government, so far at least as the institution and prosecution of a suit is concerned.

And it is by no means a logical conclusion, from the premises which we have endeavored to establish, that the governmental relations of Texas to the Union remained unaltered. . . . No one has been bold enough to contend that, while Texas was controlled by a government hostile to the United States, and in affiliation with a hostile confederation, waging war upon the United States, senators chosen by her legislature, or representatives elected by her citizens, were entitled to seats in Congress; or that any suit, instituted in her name, could be entertained in this court. All admit that, during this condition of civil war, the rights of the State as a member, and of her people as citizens of the Union, were suspended. The government and the citizens of the State, refusing to recognize their constitutional obligations, assumed the character of enemies, and incurred the consequences of rebellion. . . .

CHAPTER XIII

Reconstruction

LIKE the issues of the Civil War, those of Reconstruction were extremely complex, involving social and economic tensions, political and psychological pressures. Similarly, postwar politicians dealt with these problems as they had in the prewar period, translating sectional antagonisms into constitutional controversies. The basic constitutional problem was to determine whether the seceded states were ever out of the Union. The South, by resorting to secession, had clearly indicated its belief in the voluntary nature of a loosely organized confederacy of sovereign states. The Northern wartime position denied the legality of secession, maintaining that the nation was an indestructible union of indestructible states. Projecting these Northern premises into the postwar period, the logical conclusion was that the Southern states were never out of the Union and thus continued to possess all the normal rights and privileges of statehood.

With the end of hostilities, constitutional expediency led to a hasty exchange of sectional wartime logic. Southern secessionists grasped the Northern view, denying that the Union had been dissolved despite their four-year struggle to secure that end. The North, triumphant in its efforts to preserve the American nation, virtually accepted secessionist principles in its desire to prove that the Southern states had forfeited their rights by leaving the federal Union. Only Lincoln was consistent in his constitutional views. Having argued from the beginning that secession was impossible, he avoided the theoretical and vindictive aspects of this thorny problem and, maintaining his Inaugural position that the Union was perpetual, advocated a direct restoration of the seceded states. In a proclamation of December 8, 1863, he formulated the Presidential plan of reconstruction. This magnanimous policy of "malice toward none, with charity for all" he reiterated in his second Inaugural Address (No. 112). Greatly concerned with reconciliation and reconstruction, Lincoln, in what proved to be his last public speech, rejected constitutional theorizing on the status of the Southern states as "a merely pernicious abstraction"; the pragmatic problem was "to again get them into their proper practical relation" (No. 113).

Presidential plans met congressional opposition from the outset. Radical Republicans, whether subscribing to the "conquered province" or "state suicide" theories, argued that rebellion converted the Confederate states into unorganized territory subject to congressional authority. The Wade-Davis Bill of 1864 actualized this concept, but Lincoln's pocket veto temporarily defeated the congressional attempt to wrest the reconstruction process from the President. Not to be denied the last word, defiant men issued the Wade-Davis Manifesto (No. 114), asserting "that the authority of Congress is paramount," and warning Lincoln to "confine himself to his executive duties . . . and leave political reorganization to Congress."

The assassination of Lincoln raised the hopes of Radicals that Andrew Johnson would endorse congressional control of reconstruction. When a congressional committee called on the new President, Senator Wade expressed their faith in him, declaring, "By the gods, there will be no trouble now in running the government." Harmony did not materialize, however, for Johnson adopted substantially the Lincolnian program. Moreover, subsequent actions of the Presidentially reconstructed states played into the hands of the Radicals. The North was especially aroused by the election of prominent ex-Confederates to high governmental offices and the adoption of "Black Codes" (No. 115), which represented the Southern solution to "the Negro problem." The congressional solution was embodied in the Freedman's Bureau Bill which Johnson vetoed in February, 1866.

Open war between the President and Congress ensued. Initial victory was Johnson's, for the Radicals failed to override his veto of the Freedmen's Bill. But Congress regained the initiative in March by passing the Civil Rights Act, a detailed measure designed to protect the freedman from legislative discrimination such as the Black Codes. Vetoed by President Johnson as an unwarrantable stride "toward centralization and the concentration of all legislative powers in the national government" (No. 116), it was quickly re-enacted, signaling the triumph of Congress. This *fait accompli* was formalized two months later in the report of a joint congressional committee on Reconstruction (No. 117). Asserting the supremacy of Congress over the President in outlining a reconstruction program, the report denied the right of representation to the Presidentially reconstructed Confederate states. The committee, fearful of the constitutionality of the Civil Rights Act, also rephrased that measure as the Fourteenth Amendment (No. 118A). One of the most important amendments ever added to the Constitution, it was remarkably inclusive in dealing with the various aspects of the Southern question. Ironically, Congress, while insisting that the Southern states were out of the Union, nevertheless required that they ratify this amendment. Since the citizenship clause of the Amendment was later interpreted by the Supreme Court as a protection of corporate wealth, the intentions of the framers, as revealed in the speech of Representative Thaddeus Stevens (No. 118B), are of more than historical significance.

With the overwhelming victory of the Radicals in the election of 1866, Congress's assertion of complete authority over Reconstruction challenged the principle of the separation of powers. Outraged by Johnson's consistent vetoes, Congress attempted to reduce the President to a figurehead, curbing his power to appoint new Supreme Court Justices, restricting, in the Command of the Army Act, his authority as commander in chief, and subordinating to Senate control his power to remove executive appointees. Johnson's veto of the Tenure of Office Act (No. 119) typified his cogent constitutional objections. After Congress overrode his veto, Johnson decided to test the constitutionality of the measure and dismissed Secretary of War Stanton, who had earlier assisted in drafting the veto message. Alleging violation of the Tenure of Office Act, the House impeached President Johnson for "high crimes and misdemeanors." Chief Justice Salmon P. Chase, a Lincoln appointee, presided over the Senate trial, but despite his insistence on fair legal procedure, the Radicals battered down legal obstacles. The Radical position on the nature of impeachable offenses is set forth by Senator Henry Wilson (No. 120A), later Vice-President under General Grant. Several Republicans resisted party pressure for conviction, and joined with Senator Grimes in his opposition to the "doctrine of the omnipotence of Congress" (No. 120B). By the narrow margin of one vote the President escaped conviction. Senator Lyman Trumbull, who bolted the Radicals, defended Johnson's position and observed that if the Chief Executive were removed for insufficient cause "no future President will be safe who happens to differ with a majority of the House and two thirds of the Senate on any measure deemed by them important, particularly if of a political character."

The congressional majority also attempted to subject the Supreme Court to its will. The Milligan decision of 1866 (Chapter XII) stood as a tacit challenge to the Radical program of military reconstruction instituted in 1867, and in the same year judicial invalidation of discriminatory legislation against ex-Confederates (The Test Oath Cases, No. 121) set off a bitter attack by the Radicals. Aware of its precarious position, the Court avoided the basic issue of the constitutionality of the Military Reconstruction Acts, refusing to enjoin President Johnson's enforcement on the ground that political processes were not subject to judicial restraint (*Mississippi v. Johnson*, No. 122). This temporarily mollified the Radicals, but when the Court agreed in February, 1868, to consider *Ex parte* McCardle, a case challenging by implication the legality of the Congressional program, the Radicals promptly deprived it of jurisdiction. In the only other important decision involving Reconstruction, the Court in *Texas v. White* (Chapter XII), although accepting Lincoln's position on the indestructibility of the Union, acquiesced in Congress's authority to reconstruct the states.

The Presidential Plan

112. Lincoln, Second Inaugural Address, March 4, 1865

Richardson, ed., *Messages and Papers of the Presidents*, VI, 276-7.

At this second appearing to take the oath of the presidential office there is less occasion for an extended address than there was at the first. Then a statement somewhat in detail of a course to be pursued seemed fitting and proper. Now, at the expiration of four years, during which public declarations have been constantly called forth on every point and phase of the great contest which still absorbs the attention and engrosses the energies of the nation, little that is new could be presented. The progress of our arms, upon which all else chiefly depends, is as well known to the public as to myself, and it is, I trust, reasonably satisfactory and encouraging to all. With high hope for the future, no prediction in regard to it is ventured.

On the occasion corresponding to this four years ago all thoughts were anxiously directed to an impending civil war. All dreaded it, all sought to avert it. While the inaugural address was being delivered from this place, devoted altogether to *saving* the Union without war, insurgent agents were in the city seeking to *destroy* it without war—seeking to dissolve the Union and divide effects by negotiation. Both parties deprecated war, but one of them would *make* war rather than let the nation survive, and the other would *accept* war rather than let it perish, and the war came.

One-eighth of the whole population was colored slaves, not distributed generally over the Union, but localized in the southern part of it. These slaves constituted a peculiar and powerful interest. All knew that this interest was somehow the cause of the war. To strengthen, perpetuate, and extend this interest was the object for which the insurgents would rend the Union even by war, while the Government claimed no right to do more than to restrict the territorial enlargement of it. Neither party expected for the war the magnitude or the duration which it has already attained. Neither anticipated that the *cause* of the conflict might cease with or even before the conflict itself should cease. Each looked for an easier triumph, and a result less fundamental and astounding. Both read the same Bible and pray to the same God, and each invokes His aid against the other. It may seem strange that any men should dare to ask a just God's assistance in wringing their bread from the sweat of other men's faces, but let us judge not, that we be not judged. The prayers of both could not be answered. That of neither has been answered fully. The Almighty has His own purposes. "Woe unto the world because of offenses; for it must needs be that offenses come, but woe to that man by whom the offense cometh." If we shall suppose that American slavery is one of those offenses which, in the providence of God, must needs come, but which, having continued through His appointed time, He now wills to remove, and that He gives to both North and South this terrible war as the woe due to those by whom the offense came, shall we discern therein any departure from those divine attributes which the believers in a living God always ascribe to Him? Fondly do we hope, fervently do we pray, that this mighty scourge of war may speedily pass away. Yet, if God wills that it continue until all the wealth piled by the bondsman's two hundred and fifty years of unrequited toil shall be sunk, and until every drop of blood drawn with the lash shall be paid by another drawn with the sword, as was said three thousand years ago, so still it must be said, "The judgments of the Lord are true and righteous altogether."

With malice toward none, with charity for all, with firmness in the right as God gives us to see the right, let us strive on to finish the work we are in, to bind up the nation's wounds, to care for him who shall have borne the battle and for his widow and his orphan, to do all which may achieve and cherish a just and lasting peace among ourselves and with all nations.

113. *Lincoln, Speech on Reconciliation and Reconstruction, April 11, 1865*

John G. Nicolay and John Hay, eds., *Complete Works of Abraham Lincoln* (New York, 1894), II, 672.

We all agree that the seceded States, so called, are out of their proper practical relation with the Union, and that the sole object of the Government, civil and military, in regard to those States is to again get them into that proper practical relation. I believe that it is not only possible, but in fact easier, to do this without deciding or even considering whether these States have ever been out of the Union, than with it. Finding themselves safely at home, it would be utterly immaterial whether they had ever been abroad. Let us all join in doing the acts necessary to restore the proper practical relations between these States and the Union, and each forever after innocently indulge his own opinion whether in doing the acts he brought the States from without into the Union, or only gave them proper assistance, they never having been out of it. . . .

Congressional Opposition to Presidential Reconstruction

114. *The Wade-Davis Manifesto, August 5, 1864*

Edward McPherson, ed., *The Political History of the United States During the Great Rebellion* (4th ed., Washington, 1882), 332.

The President, by preventing this bill from becoming a law, holds the electoral votes of the rebel States at the dictation of his personal ambition. If those votes turn the balance in his favor, is it to be supposed that his competitor, defeated by such means, will acquiesce? If the rebel majority assert their supremacy in those States, and send votes which elect an enemy of the Government, will we not repel his claims? And is not that civil war for the Presidency inaugurated by the votes of rebel States?

Seriously impressed with these dangers,

Congress, *"the proper constituted authority,"* formally declared that there are no State governments in the rebel States, and provided for their erection at a proper time; and both the Senate and the House of Representatives rejected the Senators and Representatives chosen under the authority of what the President calls the free constitution and government of Arkansas. The President's proclamation *"holds for naught"* this judgment, and discards the authority of the Supreme Court, and strides headlong toward the anarchy his proclamation of the 8th of December inaugurated. If electors for President be allowed to be chosen in either of those States, a sinister light will be cast on the motives which induced the President to "hold for naught" the will of Congress rather than his government in Louisiana and Arkansas. That judgment of Congress which the President defies was the exercise of an authority exclusively vested in Congress by the Constitution to determine what is the established government in a State, and in its own nature and by the highest judicial authority binding on all other departments of the Government. . . .

A more studied outrage on the legislative authority of the people has never been perpetrated. Congress passed a bill; the President refused to approve it, and then by proclamation puts as much of it in force as he sees fit, and proposes to execute those parts by officers unknown to the laws of the United States and not subject to the confirmation of the Senate! The bill directed the appointment of Provisional Governors by and with the advice and consent of the Senate. The President, after defeating the law, proposes to appoint without law, and without the advice and consent of the Senate, *Military* Governors for the rebel States! He has already exercised this dictatorial usurpation in Louisiana, and he defeated the bill to prevent its limitation. . . .

The President has greatly presumed on the forbearance which the supporters of his Administration have so long practiced, in view of the arduous conflict in which we are engaged, and the reckless ferocity of our political opponents. But he must understand that our support is of a cause and not of a man; that the authority of Congress is paramount and must be respected; that the whole body of the Union men of Congress will not submit to be impeached by him of rash and unconstitutional legislation; and if he wishes our support, he must confine himself to his executive duties—to obey and execute, not make the laws—to suppress by arms armed rebellion, and leave political reorganization to Congress. If the supporters of the Government fail to insist on this, they become responsible for the usurpations which they fail to rebuke, and are justly liable to the indignation of the people whose rights and security, committed to their keeping, they sacrifice. Let them consider the remedy for these usurpations, and, having found it, fearlessly execute it.

115. *The Presidentially Reconstructed States Enact "Black Codes"*

Acts of the Session of 1865-1866 of the General Assembly of Alabama (Montgomery, 1866), 119-21.

SECTION 1. . . . That the commissioners' court of any county in this State may purchase, rent, or provide such lands, buildings and other property as may be necessary for a poor-house, or house of correction for any such county, and may appoint suitable officers for the management thereof, and make all necessary by-laws, rules and regulations for the government of the inmates thereof, and cause the same to be enforced; but in no case shall the punishment inflicted exceed hard labor, either in or out of said house; the use of chain-gangs, putting in stocks, if necessary, to prevent escapes; such reasonable correction as a parent may inflict upon a stubborn, refractory child; and solitary confinement for not longer than one week, on bread and water; and may cause to be hired out such as are vagrants, to work in chain-gangs or otherwise, for the length of time for which they are sentenced; and the proceeds of such hiring must be paid into the county treasury, for the benefits of the helpless in said poorhouse, or house of correction.

Sec. 2. . . . That the following persons are vagrants in addition to those already declared to be vagrants by law, or that may hereafter be so declared by law; a stubborn or refractory servant; a laborer or servant who loiters away his time, or refuses to comply with any contract for a term of service, without just cause; and such person may be sent to the house of correction in the county in which such offense is committed; and for want of such house of correction, the common jail of the county may be used for that purpose.

Sec. 3. . . . That when a vagrant is found, any justice of the peace of the county must, upon complaint made upon oath, or on his own knowledge, issue his warrant to the sheriff or any constable of the county, to bring such person before him; and if, upon examination and hearing of testimony, it appears to the justice, that such person is a vagrant, he shall assess a fine of fifty dollars and costs against such vagrant; and in default of payment, he must commit such vagrant to the house of correction; or if no such house, to the common jail of the county, for a term not exceeding six months, and until such fine, costs and charges are paid, or such party is otherwise discharged by law; *Provided*, That when committed to jail under this section, the commissioners'

court may cause him to be hired out in like manner as in section one of this act.

Sec. 4. . . . That when any person shall be convicted of vagrancy, as provided for in this act, the justice of the peace, before whom such conviction is had, may, at his discretion, either commit such person to jail, to the house of correction, or hire such person to any person who will hire the same, for a period not longer than six months, for cash, giving three days' notice of the time and place of hiring; and the proceeds of such hiring, after paying all costs and charges, shall be paid into the county treasury for the benefit of the helpless in the poor-house.

Sec. 5. . . . That all fines received by any justice of the peace under the provisions of this act, shall be paid into the county treasury for the purposes as set forth in section one of this act.

Sec. 6. . . . That it shall be the duty of the justice of the peace to settle with the county treasurer at least once a month, for all fines received by him under this act, and for a wilful default so to do, he shall be guilty of a misdemeanor; and upon conviction in any court having jurisdiction, shall be fined in double the amount so received or collected by him, and all costs of suit.

Sec. 7. . . . That the court of county commissioners of each county shall have full and complete control of the public works and public highways therein, and shall make all contracts in relation thereto; and shall have power to appoint a superintendent of said public works and highways, under such rules and regulations as said court shall determine; and any justice of the peace trying any cause under this act, on conviction, shall have power to sentence such vagrant to work on said public works and highways, under the supervision of such superintendent, for not more than forty days.

116. *President Johnson's Veto of the Civil Rights Act, March 27, 1866*

Richardson, ed., *Messages and Papers of the Presidents,* VI, 405-13.

I regret that the bill, which has passed both Houses of Congress . . . contains provisions which I can not approve consistently with my sense of duty to the whole people and my obligations to the Constitution. . . .

By the first section of the bill all persons born in the United States and not subject to any foreign power . . . are declared to be citizens of the United States. . . . It does not purport to give these classes of persons any status as citizens of States, except that which may result from their status as citizens of the United States. The power to confer the right of State citizenship is just as exclusively with the several States as the power to confer the right of Federal citizenship is with Congress.

The right of Federal citizenship thus to be conferred on the several excepted races before mentioned is now for the first time proposed to be given by law. If, as is claimed by many, all persons who are native born already are, by virtue of the Constitution, citizens of the United States, the passage of the pending bill can not be necessary to make them such. If, on the other hand, such persons are not citizens, as may be assumed from the proposed legislation to make them such, the grave question presents itself whether, when eleven of the thirty-six States are unrepresented in Congress at the present time, it is sound policy to make our entire colored population and all other excepted classes citizens of the United States. Four millions of them have just emerged from slavery into freedom. . . . It may also be asked whether it is necessary that they should be declared citizens in order that they may be secured in the enjoyment of the civil rights proposed to be conferred by the bill. Those rights are, by Federal as well as State laws, secured to all domiciled aliens and foreigners, even before the completion of the process of naturalization; and it may safely be assumed that the same enactments are sufficient to give like protection and benefits to those for whom this bill provides special legislation. Besides, the policy of the Government from its origin to the present time seems to have been that persons who are strangers to and unfamiliar with our institutions and our laws should pass through a certain probation, at the end of which, before attaining the coveted prize, they must give evidence of their fitness to receive and to exercise the rights of citizens as contemplated by the Constitution of the United States. The bill in effect proposes a discrimination against large numbers of intelligent, worthy, and patriotic foreigners, and in favor of the negro, to whom, after long years of bondage, the avenues to freedom and intelligence have just now been suddenly opened. . . .

The first section of the bill also contains an enumeration of the rights to be enjoyed by these classes so made citizens "in every State and Territory in the United States." These rights are "to make and enforce contracts; to sue, be parties, and give evidence; to inherit, purchase, lease, sell, hold, and convey real and personal property," and to have "full and equal benefit of all laws and proceedings for the security of person and property as is enjoyed by white citizens." So, too, they are made subject to the same punishment, pains, and penalties in common with white citizens, and to none other. Thus a perfect equality of the white and colored races is attempted to be fixed by Federal law in every State of the Union over the vast field of State jurisdiction covered by these enumerated rights. In no one of these can any State ever exercise any power of discrimination between the different races. . . .

The object of the second section of the bill is to afford discriminating protection to colored persons in the full enjoyment of all the rights secured to them by the preceding section. . . .

This provision of the bill seems to be unnecessary, as adequate judicial remedies could be adopted to secure the desired end without invading the immunities of legislators, always important to be preserved in the interest of public liberty; without assailing the independence of the judiciary, always essential to the preservation of individual rights; and without impairing the efficiency of ministerial officers, always necessary for the maintenance of public peace and order. The remedy proposed by this section seems to be in this respect not only anomalous, but unconstitutional; for the Constitution guarantees nothing with certainty if it does not insure to the several States the right of making and executing laws in regard to all matters arising within their jurisdiction, subject only to the restriction that in cases of conflict with the Constitution and constitutional laws of the United

States the latter should be held to be the supreme law of the land. . . .

In all our history, in all our experience as a people living under Federal and State law, no such system as that contemplated by the details of this bill has ever before been proposed or adopted. They establish for the security of the colored race safeguards which go infinitely beyond any that the General Government has ever provided for the white race. In fact, the distinction of race and color is by the bill made to operate in favor of the colored and against the white race. They interfere with the municipal legislation of the States, with the relations existing exclusively between a State and its citizens, or between inhabitants of the same State—an absorption and assumption of power by the General Government which, if acquiesced in, must sap and destroy our federative system of limited powers and break down the barriers which preserve the rights of the States. It is another step, or rather stride, toward centralization and the concentration of all legislative powers in the National Government. The tendency of the bill must be to resuscitate the spirit of rebellion and to arrest the progress of those influences which are more closely drawing around the States the bonds of union and peace. . . .

117. *Congress Presents a Plan of Radical Reconstruction, June 18, 1866*

Report of the Joint Committee on Reconstruction, 39th Cong., 1st Sess. (1866), xiii-xxi *passim.*

Your committee came to the consideration of the subject referred to them with the most anxious desire to ascertain what was the condition of the people of the States recently in insurrection, and what, if anything, was necessary to be done before restoring them to the full enjoyment of all their original privileges. It was undeniable that the war into which they had plunged the country had materially changed their relations to the people of

the loyal States. Slavery had been abolished by constitutional amendment. A large proportion of the population had become, instead of mere chattels, free men and citizens. Through all the past struggle these had remained true and loyal, and had, in large numbers, fought on the side of the Union. It was impossible to abandon them, without securing them their rights as free men and citizens. The whole civilized world would have cried out against such base ingratitude, and the bare idea is offensive to all right-thinking men. Hence it became important to inquire what could be done to secure their rights, civil and political. It was evident to your committee that adequate security could only be found in appropriate constitutional provisions. By an original provision of the Constitution, representation is based on the whole number of free persons in each State, and three-fifths of all other persons. When all became free, representation for all necessarily follows. As a consequence the inevitable effect of the rebellion would be to increase the political power of the insurrectionary States, whenever they should be allowed to resume their positions as States of the Union. As representation is by the Constitution based upon population, your committee did not think it advisable to recommend a change of that basis. The increase of representation necessarily resulting from the abolition of slavery was considered the most important element in the questions arising out of the changed condition of affairs, and the necessity for some fundamental action in this regard seemed imperative. It appeared to your committee that the rights of these persons by whom the basis of representation had been thus increased should be recognized by the general government. While slaves they were not considered as having any rights, civil or political. It did not seem just or proper that all the political advantages derived from their becoming free should be confined to their former masters, who had fought against the Union, and withheld from themselves, who had always been loyal. Slavery, by building up a ruling and dominant class, had produced a spirit of oligarchy adverse to republican institutions, which finally inaugurated civil war. The tendency of continuing the domination of such a class, by leaving it in the exclusive possession of political power, would be to encourage the same spirit, and lead to a similar result. Doubts were entertained whether Congress had power, even under the amended Constitution, to prescribe the qualifications of voters in a State, or could act directly on the subject. It was doubtful, in the opinion of your committee, whether the States would consent to surrender a power they had always exercised, and to which they were attached. As the best if not the only method of surmounting the difficulty, and as eminently just and proper in itself, your committee came to the conclusion that political power should be possessed in all the States exactly in proportion as the right of suffrage should be granted, without distinction of color or race. This it was thought would leave the whole question with the people of each State, holding out to all the advantage of increased political power as an inducement to allow all to participate in its exercise. Such a provision would be in its nature gentle and persuasive, and would lead, it was hoped, at no distant day, to an equal participation of all, without distinction, in all the rights and privileges of citizenship, thus affording a full and adequate protection to all classes of citizens, since all would have, through the ballot-box, the power of self-protection. . . .

The conclusion of your committee therefore is, that the so-called Confederate States are not, at present, entitled to representation in the Congress of the United States; that, before allowing such representation, adequate security for future peace and safety should be required; that this can only be found in such changes of the organic law as shall determine the civil rights and privileges of all citizens in all parts of the republic, shall place representation on an equitable basis, shall fix a stigma upon treason, and protect the loyal people against future claims for the expenses incurred in support of rebellion and for manumitted slaves, together with an express grant of power in Congress to enforce those provisions. To this end they offer a joint resolution for amending the Constitution of the United States, and the two several bills designed to carry the same into effect, before referred to. . . .

118. *Congress Restricts State Infringements of Civil Rights*

A. THE FOURTEENTH AMENDMENT

Proposed June 16, 1866; adopted July 28, 1868.

SECTION 1. All persons born or naturalized in the United States, and subject to the jurisdiction thereof, are citizens of the United States and of the State wherein they reside. No State shall make or enforce any law which shall abridge the privileges or immunities of citizens of the United States; nor shall any State deprive any person of life, liberty, or property, without due process of law; nor deny to any person within its jurisdiction the equal protection of the laws.

SECTION 2. Representatives shall be apportioned among the several States according to their respective numbers, counting the whole number of persons in each State, excluding Indians not taxed. But when the right to vote at any election for the choice of electors for President and Vice-President of the United States, Representatives in Congress, the executive and judicial officers of a State, or the members of the legislature thereof, is denied to any of the male inhabitants of such State, being twenty-one years of age, and citizens of the United States, or in any way abridged, except for participation in rebellion, or other crime, the basis of representation therein shall be reduced in the proportion which the number of such male citizens shall bear to the whole number of male citizens twenty-one years of age in such State.

SECTION 3. No person shall be a Senator or Representative in Congress, or elector of President and Vice-President, or hold any office, civil or military, under the United States or under any State, who, having previously taken an oath as a member of Congress, or as an officer of the United States, or as a member of any State legislature, or as an executive or judicial officer of any State, to support the Constitution of the United States, shall have engaged in insurrection or rebellion against the same, or given aid or comfort to the enemies thereof. But Congress may, by a vote of two-thirds of each house, remove such disability.

SECTION 4. The validity of the public debt of the United States, authorized by law, including debts incurred for payment of pensions and bounties for services in suppressing insurrection or rebellion, shall not be questioned. But neither the United States nor any State shall assume or pay any debt or obligation incurred in aid of insurrection or rebellion against the United States, or any claim for the loss or emancipation of any slave; but all such debts, obligations, and claims shall be held illegal and void.

SECTION 5. The Congress shall have power to enforce, by appropriate legislation, the provisions of this article.

B. THE FOURTEENTH AMENDMENT: "THE FINAL TRIUMPH OF THE RIGHTS OF MAN"

Thaddeus Stevens, May 8, 1866, *Congressional Globe*, 39th Cong., 1st Sess., XXXVI, Pt. 3, 2459-60.

This proposition is not all that the committee desired. It falls far short of my wishes, but it fulfills my hopes. I believe it is all that can be obtained in the present state of public opinion. . . .

I can hardly believe that any person can

be found who will not admit that every one of these propositions [in the first section] is just. They are all asserted, in some form or other, in our DECLARATION or organic law. But the Constitution limits only the action of Congress, and is not a limitation on the States. This amendment supplies that defect, and allows Congress to correct the unjust legislation of the States, so far that the law which operates upon one man shall operate *equally* upon all. Whatever law punishes a white man for a crime shall punish the black man precisely in the same way and to the same degree. Whatever law protects the white man shall afford "equal" protection to the black man. Whatever means of redress is afforded to one shall be afforded to all. Whatever law allows the white man to testify in court shall allow the man of color to do the same. These are great advantages over their present codes. Now different degrees of punishment are inflicted, not on account of the magnitude of the crime, but according to the color of the skin. Now color disqualifies a man from testifying in courts, or being tried in the same way as white men. I need not enumerate these partial and oppressive laws. Unless the Constitution should restrain them, those States will all, I fear, keep up this discrimination, and crush to death the hated freedmen. . . .

The second section I consider the most important in the article. It fixes the basis of representation in Congress. If any State shall exclude any of her adult male citizens from the elective franchise, or abridge that right, she shall forfeit her right to representation in the same proportion. The effect of this provision will be either to compel the States to grant universal suffrage or so to shear them of their power as to keep them forever in a hopeless minority in the national Government, both legislative and executive. If

they do not enfranchise the freedmen, it would give to the rebel States but thirty-seven Representatives. Thus shorn of their power, they would soon become restive. Southern pride would not long brook a hopeless minority. True, it will take two, three, possibly five years before they conquer their prejudices sufficiently to allow their late slaves to become their equals at the polls. That short delay would not be injurious. In the mean time the freedmen would become more enlightened, and more fit to discharge the high duties of their new condition. In that time, too, the loyal Congress could mature their laws and so amend the Constitution as to secure the rights of every human being, and render disunion impossible. . . .

The third section may encounter more difference of opinion here. Among the people I believe it will be the most popular of all the provisions; it prohibits rebels from voting for members of Congress and electors of President until 1870. My only objection to it is that it is too lenient. . . . I would be glad to see it extended to 1876, and to include all State and municipal as well as national elections. In my judgment we do not sufficiently protect the loyal men of the rebel States from the vindictive persecutions of their victorious rebel neighbors. Still I will move no amendment, nor vote for any, lest the whole fabric should tumble to pieces.

I need say nothing of the fourth section, for none dare object to it who is not himself a rebel. To the friend of justice, the friend of the Union, of the perpetuity of liberty, and the final triumph of the rights of man and their extension to every human being, let me say, sacrifice as we have done your peculiar views, and instead of vainly insisting upon the instantaneous operation of all that is right accept what is possible, and "all these things shall be added unto you."

Constitutional Challenges to Congressional Reconstruction

119. *President Johnson Vetoes the Tenure of Office Act, March 2, 1867*

Richardson, ed., *Messages and Papers of the Presidents*, VI, 492-7.

I have carefully examined the bill "to regulate the tenure of certain civil offices." . . . In effect the bill provides that the President shall not remove from their places any of the civil officers whose terms of service are not limited by law without the advice and consent of the Senate of the United States. The bill in this respect conflicts, in my judgment, with the Constitution of the United States. The question, as Congress is well aware, is by no means a new one. That the power of removal is constitutionally vested in the President of the United States is a principle which has been not more distinctly declared by judicial authority and judicial commentators than it has been uniformly practiced upon by the legislative and executive departments of the Government. . . .

The question has often been raised in subsequent times of high excitement, and the practice of the Government has, nevertheless, conformed in all cases to the decision thus early made.

The question was revived during the Administration of President Jackson, who made . . . a very large number of removals, which were made an occasion of close and rigorous scrutiny and remonstrance. The subject was long and earnestly debated in the Senate, and the early construction of the Constitution was, nevertheless, freely accepted as binding and conclusive upon Congress.

The question came before the Supreme Court in January, 1839, *ex parte* Hennen. It was declared . . . that the power of removal from office was a subject much disputed, and upon which a great diversity of opinion was entertained in the early history of the Government. This related, however, to the power of the President to remove officers appointed with the concurrence of the Senate, and the great question was whether the removal was to be by the President alone or with the concurrence of the Senate, both constituting the appointing power. No one denied the power of the President and Senate jointly to remove where the tenure of the office was not fixed by the Constitution, which was a full recognition of the principle that the power of removal was incident to the power of appointment; but it was very early adopted as a practical construction of the Constitution that this power was vested in the President alone. . . .

Thus has the important question presented by this bill been settled, in the language of the late Daniel Webster . . . by construction, settled by precedent, settled by the practice of the Government, and settled by statute. . . .

120. *The Impeachment of President Johnson*

A. THE RADICAL INDICTMENT

Speech by Senator Henry Wilson, 1868, *Proceedings in the Trial of Andrew Johnson, President of the United States, before the United States Senate . . .* (Washington, 1868), 952-3.

High misdemeanors may or may not be violations of the laws. High misdemeanors may, in my judgment, be misbehavior in office detrimental to the interests of the nation, dangerous to the rights of the people, or dishonoring to the government. I entertain the conviction that the framers of the Constitution intended to impose the high duty upon the House of Representatives to arraign the Chief Magistrate for such misbehavior in office as injured, dishonored, or endangered the nation, and to impose upon the Senate the duty of trying, convicting, and removing the Chief Magistrate proved guilty of such misbehavior. Believing this to be the intention of the framers of the Constitution and its true meaning; believing that the power should be exercised whenever the security of the country and the liberties of the people imperatively demand it; and believing by the evidence adduced to prove the charges of violating the Constitution and the tenure-of-office act, and by the confessed and justified acts of the President, that he is guilty of high misdemeanors, I unhesitatingly vote for his conviction and removal from his high office.

The President is charged by the House of Representatives with violating the Constitution and the tenure-of-office act in removing Mr. Stanton from the office of Secretary of War, and in appointing Adjutant General Thomas Secretary of War *ad interim*. The removal of Mr. Stanton and the appointment of Adjutant General Thomas, and the violation of the tenure-of-office act, if Mr. Stanton be within that act, stand confessed and justified in the answer of the President to the charges of the House of Representatives. The answer of the President, without any other evidence, is to my mind conclusive evidence of his guilt. Upon his answer, confessions, assumptions, and justifications I have no hesitation in recording my vote of "guilty." The assumptions of power put forth by the President in his defense cannot but startle and alarm all men who would maintain the just powers of all branches of the Government. Had the President inadvertently violated the Constitution and the laws; had he pleaded in justification misconstruction of the Constitution and the laws, I might have hesitated to vote for his conviction. But he claims the right to remove civil officers and appoint others *ad interim* during the session of the Senate. If that claim of power is admitted by a vote of acquittal, the President can remove during the session of the Senate tens of thousands of civil officers with their millions of compensation, and appoint his own creatures to fill their places without the advice and consent of the Senate, and thus nullify that provision of the Constitution that empowers the Senate to give its advice and consent to appointments.

Not content with this assumption of power, the President claims the right to pronounce a law of Congress unconstitutional, to refuse to execute it, although he is sworn to do so, and to openly violate it with a view of testing its constitutionality in the courts, although no means may exist for months or years to come, to test the constitutionality of the law so violated in the judicial tribunals of the country.

The President claims and has exercised the right to declare Congress an unconstitutional body, incapable of enacting laws or of proposing amendments to the Constitution; to hold the laws in abeyance; to refuse to execute them, and to defiantly violate them in order to test their constitutionality. These are the positions assumed by Andrew Johnson. These assumptions, if admitted, radically change the character of our Government. If they are sustained by a verdict of acquittal, the President ceases to be the servant of the law, and becomes the master of the people; and a law-non-executing power, a law-defying power, a law-breaking power is created within the Government. Instead of an Executive bound to the faithful execution of the laws of Congress, the nation has an Executive bound only to execute the laws according to his own caprices, whims, and sovereign pleasure. Never can I assent, by a vote of acquittal, to executive assumptions so unconstitutional, so subversive of the Government, so revolutionary in their scope and tendency. These assumptions will introduce into our constitutional system, into our government of nicely adjusted parts, derangement, disorganization, and anarchy. . . .

B. "I AM NO CONVERT TO ANY DOCTRINE OF THE OMNIPOTENCE OF CONGRESS."

Senator James W. Grimes, *Trial of Andrew Johnson*, 871-6.

It is clear to my mind that the *proviso* does not include, and was not intended to include, Mr. Stanton's case. It is not possible to apply to his case the language of the proviso unless we suppose it to have been intended to legislate him out of office; a conclusion, I consider, wholly inadmissible. He was appointed by President Lincoln during his first term of office. He cannot hereafter go out of office at the end of the term of the President by whom he was appointed. That term was ended before the law was passed. The proviso, therefore, cannot have been intended to make a rule for his case; and it is shown that it was not intended. This was plainly declared in debate by the conference committee, both in the Senate and in the House of Representatives, when the proviso was introduced and its effect explained. The meaning and effect of the *proviso* were then explained and understood to be that the only tenure of the Secretaries provided for by this law was a tenure to end with the term of service of the President by whom they were appointed, and as this new tenure could not include Mr. Stanton's case, it was here explicitly declared that it did not include it. . . .

I come now to the question of intent. Admitting that the President had no power under the law to issue the order to remove Mr. Stanton and appoint General Thomas Secretary for the Department of War *ad interim*, did he issue those orders with a manifest *intent* to violate the laws and "the Constitution of the United States," as charged in the articles, or did he issue them, as he says he did, with a view to have the constitutionality of the tenure-of-office act judicially decided?

It is apparent to my mind that the President thoroughly believed the tenure-of-office act to be unconstitutional and void. He was so advised by every member of his cabinet when the bill was presented to him for his approval in February, 1867 . . . including the Attorney General, whose duty it is made by law to give legal advice to him, including the Secretary for the Department of War, also an eminent lawyer and an Attorney General of the United States under a former administration. . . . The question [is] whether Mr. Stanton's case is included in the provisions of that act. If it was not, as I think it clearly was not, then the question of intent is not in issue, for he did no unlawful act. If it was included, then I ask whether, in view of those facts, the President's *guilty intent* to do an unlawful act "shines with such a clear and certain light" as to justify, to require us to pronounce him guilty of a high constitutional crime or misdemeanor? . . .

It is not denied, I think, that the constitutional validity of this law could not be tested before the courts unless a case was made and presented to them. No such case could be made unless the President made a removal. That act of his would necessarily be the basis on which the case would rest. He is sworn to " preserve, protect, and defend the Constitution of the United States." He must *defend* it against all encroachments, from whatever quarter. A question arose between the legislative and executive departments as to their relative powers in the matter of removals and appointments to office. That question was, Does the Constitution confer on the President the power which the tenure-of-office act seeks to take away? It was a question manifestly of construction and interpretation. The Constitution has provided a common arbiter in such cases of controversy—the Supreme Court of the United States. Before that tribunal can take jurisdiction a removal must be made. The President attempted to give the court jurisdiction in that way. For doing so he is impeached, and for the reason, as the Managers say, that—

He has no authority under the Constitution, or by any law, to enter into any schemes or plans for the purpose of testing the validity of the laws of the country, either judicially or otherwise.

If this be true, then if the two Houses of Congress should pass by a two-thirds vote over the President's veto an act depriving the President of the right to exercise the pardoning power, and he should exercise that power nevertheless, or if he should exercise it only in a single case for the purpose of testing the constitutionality of the law, he would be guilty of a high crime and misdemeanor and impeachable accordingly. The Managers' theory establishes at once the complete supremacy of Congress over the other branches of government. I can give my assent to no such doctrine.

This was a *punitive* statute. It was directed against the President alone. It interfered with the prerogatives of his department as recognized from the foundation of the Government. It wrested from him powers which, according to the legislative and judicial construction of 80 years, had been bestowed upon him by the Constitution itself. In my opinion it was not only proper, but it was his duty to cause the disputed question to be determined in the manner and by the tribunal established for such purposes. This Government can only be preserved and the liberty of the people maintained by preserving intact the co-ordinate branches of it—legislative, executive, judicial—alike. I am no convert to any doctrine of the omnipotence of Congress. . . .

121. *The Test Oath Cases: Bills of Attainder and Ex Post Facto Laws*

Ex parte Garland, 4 Wallace 333 (1867).

FIELD, J.: . . . The petitioner . . . now produces his pardon, and asks permission to continue to practise as an at-torney and counsellor of the court without taking the oath required by the act of January 24, 1865, and the rule of the court, which he is unable to take, by reason of the offices he held under the Confederate government. He rests his application principally upon two grounds:

1st. That the act of January 24th, 1865, so far as it affects his status in the court, is unconstitutional and void; and,

2d. That, if the act be constitutional, he is released from compliance with its provisions by the pardon of the President. . . .

The statute is directed against parties who have offended in any of the particulars embraced by these clauses. And its object is to exclude them from the profession of the law, or at least from its practice in the courts of the United States. As the oath prescribed cannot be taken by these parties, the act, as against them, operates as a legislative decree of perpetual exclusion. And exclusion from any of the professions or any of the ordinary avocations of life for past conduct can be regarded in no other light than as punishment for such conduct. The exaction of the oath is the mode provided for ascertaining the parties upon whom the act is intended to operate, and instead of lessening, increases its objectionable character. All enactments of this kind partake of the nature of bills of pains and penalties, and are subject to the constitutional inhibition against the passage of bills of attainder, under which general designation they are included.

In the exclusion which the statute adjudges it imposes a punishment for some of the acts specified which were not punishable at the time they were committed; and for other of the acts it adds a new punishment to that before prescribed, and it is thus brought within the further inhibition of the Constitution against the passage of an *ex post facto* law. . . .

The legislature may undoubtedly prescribe qualifications for the office, to which he must conform, as it may, where it has exclusive jurisdiction, prescribe qualifications for the pursuit of any of the ordinary avocations of life. The question, in this case, is not as to the power of Congress to prescribe qualifications, but whether that power has been exercised as a means for the infliction of punishment, against the prohibition of the Constitution. That this result cannot be effected indirectly by a State under the form of creating qualifications we have held in the case of *Cummings v. The State of Missouri,* and the reasoning by which that conclusion was reached applies equally to similar action on the part of Congress.

This view is strengthened by a consideration of the effect of the pardon produced by the petitioner, and the nature of the pardoning power of the President.

The Constitution provides that the President "shall have power to grant reprieves and pardons for offenses against the United States, except in cases of impeachment."

The power thus conferred is unlimited, with the exception stated. It extends to every offense known to the law, and may be exercised at any time after its commission, either before legal proceedings are taken, or during their pendency, or after conviction and judgment. This power of the President is not subject to legislative control. Congress can neither limit the effect of his pardon, nor exclude from its exercise any class of offenders. The benign prerogative of mercy reposed in him cannot be fettered by any legislative restrictions.

Such being the case, the inquiry arises as to the effect and operation of a pardon, and on this point all the authorities concur. A pardon reaches both the punishment prescribed for the offense and the guilt of the offender; and when the pardon is full, it releases the punishment and blots out of existence the guilt, so that in the eye of the law the offender is as innocent as if he had never committed the offense. If granted before conviction, it prevents any of the penalties and disabilities consequent upon conviction from attaching; if granted after conviction, it removes the penalties and disabilities, and restores him to all his civil rights; it makes him, as it were, a new man, and gives him a new credit and capacity. . . .

The pardon produced by the petitioner is a full pardon "for all offences by him committed, arising from participation, direct or implied, in the Rebellion," and is subject to certain conditions which have been complied with. The effect of this pardon is to relieve the petitioner from all penalties and disabilities attached to the offence of treason, committed by his participation in the Rebellion. So far as that offence is concerned, he is thus placed beyond the reach of punishment of any kind. But to exclude him, by reason of that offence, from continuing in the enjoyment of a previously acquired right, is to en-

force a punishment for that offence notwithstanding the pardon. If such exclusion can be effected by the exaction of an expurgatory oath covering the offence, the pardon may be avoided, and that accomplished indirectly which cannot be reached by direct legislation. It is not within the constitutional power of Congress to inflict punishment beyond the reach of executive clemency. From the petitioner, therefore, the oath required by the act of January 24th, 1865, could not be exacted, even if that act were not subject to any other objection than the one thus stated.

It follows, from the views expressed, that the prayer of the petitioner must be granted.

122. *The Court Sidesteps the Reconstruction Issue*

Mississippi v. Johnson, 4 Wallace 475 (1867).

CHASE, C.J.: A motion was made, some days since, in behalf of the State of Mississippi, for leave to file a bill in the name of the State, praying this court perpetually to enjoin and restrain Andrew Johnson, President of the United States, and E. O. C. Ord, general commanding in the District of Mississippi and Arkansas, from executing, or in any manner carrying out, certain acts of Congress therein named.

The acts referred to are those of March 2d and March 23d, 1867, commonly known as the Reconstruction Acts. . . .

The single point which requires consideration is this: Can the President be restrained by injunction from carrying into effect an act of Congress alleged to be unconstitutional? . . .

By the first of these acts he is required to assign generals to command in the several military districts, and to detail sufficient military force to enable such officers to discharge their duties under the law. By the supplementary act, other duties are imposed on the several commanding generals, and these duties must necessarily be performed under the supervision of the

President as commander-in-chief. The duty thus imposed on the President is in no just sense ministerial. It is purely executive and political.

An attempt on the part of the judicial department of the government to enforce the performance of such duties by the President might be justly characterized, in the language of Chief Justice Marshall, as "an absurd and excessive extravagance."

It is true that in the instance before us the interposition of the court is not sought to enforce action by the Executive under constitutional legislation, but to restrain such action under legislation alleged to be unconstitutional. But we are unable to perceive that this circumstance takes the case out of the general principles which forbid judicial interference with the exercise of Executive discretion.

It was admitted in the argument that the application now made to us is without a precedent; and this is of much weight against it. . . .

The fact that no such application was ever before made in any case indicates the general judgment of the profession that no such application should be entertained.

It will hardly be contended that Congress [*sic*] can interpose, in any case, to restrain the enactment of an unconstitutional law; and yet how can the right to judicial interposition to prevent such an enactment, when the purpose is evident and the execution of that purpose certain, be distinguished, in principle, from the right to such interposition against the execution of such a law by the President?

The Congress is the legislative department of the government; the President is the executive department. Neither can be restrained in its action by the judicial department; though the acts of both, when performed, are, in proper cases, subject to its cognizance.

The impropriety of such interference will be clearly seen upon consideration of its possible consequences.

Suppose the bill filed and the injunction prayed for allowed. If the President refuse obedience, it is needless to observe that the court is without power to enforce its process. If, on the other hand, the President complies with the order of the court and refuses to execute the acts of Congress, is it not clear that a collision may occur between the executive and legislative departments of the government? May not the House of Representatives impeach the President for such refusal? And in that case could this court interfere, in behalf of the President, thus endangered by compliance with its mandate, and restrain by injunction the Senate of the United States from sitting as a court of impeachment? Would the strange spectacle be offered to the public world of an attempt by this court to arrest proceedings in that court?

These questions answer themselves. . . .

It has been suggested that the bill contains a prayer that, if the relief sought cannot be had against Andrew Johnson, as President, it may be granted against Andrew Johnson as a citizen of Tennessee. But it is plain that relief as against the execution of an act of Congress by Andrew Johnson, is relief against its execution by the President. A bill praying an injunction against the execution of an act of Congress by the incumbent of the presidential office cannot be received, whether it describes him as President or as a citizen of a State.

The motion for leave to file the bill is therefore denied.

CHAPTER XIV

Aftermath of Reconstruction

THE Reconstruction Amendments—the Thirteenth, Fourteenth, and Fifteenth—involved the first formal changes in the text of the Constitution for over sixty years, comprising the only alterations made between 1804 and 1913. They necessitated far-reaching readjustments not only in constitutional doctrine but also in social organization, government-business relations, political representation, and definition of suffrage requirements.

The Slaughterhouse Cases (No. 123) were the first judicial pronouncements on the Fourteenth Amendment. These cases had nothing to do with the rights of freedmen but arose over the protest of the Butchers' Benevolent Association of New Orleans against a Louisiana act granting a monopoly of the slaughterhouse business to a favored firm. The ousted butchers challenged the law as a violation of the privileges and immunities clause of the new Amendment. By a majority of 5 to 4, the Court upheld the state enactment. The majority distinguished between state and national citizenship, placing the great bulk of civil rights under the protection of the state governments. Only the rights and privileges of federal citizenship are protected by the Fourteenth Amendment and these the Court defined narrowly. Giving the due process and equal protection clauses of the Amendment only cursory attention, the majority did not consider them limitations on the economic regulatory powers of the state, holding that the equal protection guarantee applied solely to state laws that discriminated against Negroes. By this restrictive interpretation, the majority failed to carry out the nationalistic revolution in the American constitutional system which the Radical framers of the

Amendment intended, and permanently devitalized the privileges and immunities clause as a federal protection against state encroachments. The due process and equal protection clauses, however, have since emerged as vital concepts; indeed, they have been responsible for more adjudication than any other constitutional provision.

In the Slaughterhouse Cases Justice Miller stated that the pervading purpose of the equal protection clause was to remedy the evil caused by state laws that "discriminated with gross injustice and hardship" against "the newly emancipated negroes"; it was "clearly a provision for that race and that emergency." Congress, which had drafted the Fourteenth Amendment to validate the Civil Rights Act of 1866, now enacted a Second Civil Rights Act (No. 124) in their attempt to guarantee civil and legal equality to Negroes. Unlike the earlier measure, which protected the voting rights and legal status of Negroes from state discrimination, this final all-out effort of the Radicals to establish civil equality was frustrated by the Court in the Civil Rights Cases (No. 125). These cases grew out of discriminations by individuals who refused equal accommodations to Negroes in public inns, conveyances, and theatres. In emasculating the Radical legislation, the Court held that "it would be running the slavery argument into the ground to make it apply to every act of discrimination which a person may see fit to make as to the guests he will entertain, or as to the people he will take into his coach or cab or car." Moreover, Justice Bradley stated, "individual invasion of individual rights is not the subject-matter of the amendment," which was prohibitory solely upon the states; wrongful acts of individuals, unsupported by state authority ". . . could not impair the civil rights protected by the Constitution against state aggression." The Court's ruling that these were social rather than civil rights, Harlan argued in his dissent, was "entirely too narrow and artificial," and sacrificed the spirit of the Civil War amendments "by a subtle and ingenious verbal criticism." He viewed the rights as "legal" rather than "social," contending that the majority decision would sanctify the continuation of discrimination with the full acquiescence of the state. "We shall enter upon an era of constitutional law," the former Kentucky Unionist predicted, "when the rights of freedom and American citizenship cannot receive from the nation that efficient protection which heretofore was unhesitatingly accorded to slavery and the rights of the master."

This prediction proved true. In the settlement of the Disputed Election of 1876, Northern Republicans agreed to jettison Radical policies in the South in return for Southern support of Hayes over Tilden. The effect of this compromise was to return control of race relations to the states, which then evolved less crude devices than the Black Codes to prevent Negro equality. The most generally accepted fomula was the "separate but equal" doctrine which gave the states an acceptable legal principle for compulsory segregation of the races. In *Plessy v. Ferguson*, thirteen years after the Court had sanctioned discrimination by individuals, it approved separation of the races by state action. Justice Henry B. Brown agreed that the object of the Fourteenth Amendment "was undoubtedly to enforce the absolute equality of the two races before the law, but in the nature of things it could not have been intended to abolish distinctions based on color, or to enforce social, as distinguished from political equality, or a commingling of the two races upon terms unsatisfactory to either (No. 126)." Although Brown denied that "enforced separation of the two races stamps the colored race with a badge of inferiority," Justice Harlan, in the only dissent, countered with the argument that "the arbitrary separation of citizens, on the basis of race, while they are on a public highway, is a badge of servitude wholly inconsistent with the Constitution" (No. 127). Insisting that the Constitution is "color-blind," he denounced the "thin disguise of 'equal' accommodations" for passengers in railroad coaches—a disguise which "will not mislead anyone, nor atone for the wrong this day done." Three years later, the Court inferred that the "equality" of separate educational accommodations in the states need not be exactly "equal"; indeed, the case of *Cumming v. County Board of Education* (1899) ruled that a Georgia county did not deny equal protection to colored children by failing to provide them with a high school, although it maintained a high school for white students.

Just as the Fourteenth Amendment prompted the freedman to strive for political equality, so it sparked an unexpected movement by women to gain long-denied legal and political equality. In *Minor v. Happersett* (No. 128), however, the Court denied the argument of women that the right to vote was a privilege or immunity of citizenship guaranteed against state infringement by the Fourteenth Amendment.

Another undefined term in that all-important amendment presented the court with difficulties. In the clause prohibiting state deprivation of "life, liberty, or property without due process of law," did the word "liberty" include the guarantees of the federal Bill of Rights? Prior to the adoption of the Fourteenth Amendment, the Court had ruled that the first ten amendments were not limitations upon the states (*Barron v. Baltimore*, Chapter IV). Without specifically saying so, the Slaughterhouse Cases ruled that the Fourteenth Amendment did not alter the Barron doctrine. In *Hurtado v. California* (No. 129), the Court held that the due process clause of the Fourteenth Amendment did not require a grand jury indictment in a state court, even though the Bill of Rights requires one in federal courts. In subsequent cases, the Court ruled that the amendment did not incorporate other liberties of the Bill of Rights as procedural guarantees which the states cannot violate. Thus, just as the Court cut down the meaning of equal protection and privileges and immunities, so did it vitiate the due process clause as a protection of civil liberties against state encroachment.

There was one important exception to this early erosion of the guarantees in the Fourteenth Amendment. Whereas the Supreme Court was unwilling to probe behind state assertions to determine whether separate facilities for Negroes were really "equal," in another instance of racial discrimination (*Yick Wo v. Hopkins,* 1886), it went behind a San Francisco ordinance to examine its actual administration. The local regulation required every laundryman to obtain a permit, unless his business was conducted in a brick or stone building. In administering this measure, city supervisors consistently discriminated against Chinese laundrymen, and thus, the Court ruled, violated the equal protection clause of the Fourteenth Amendment.

A Chinese also figured in another fundamental interpretation of the Fourteenth Amendment. Although the original Constitution recognized citizenship of the United States, it was not until the addition of the Fourteenth Amendment that this citizenship was specifically defined in terms of birth in the United States and subjection to its jurisdiction. As Representative Thaddeus Stevens cogently pointed out (Chapter XIII), this provision was designed to confer citizenship on the freedman, but as time went by the applicability of its provisions to other races raised problems. In the 1880's and 1890's, Congress complicated the issue by barring Chinese and other Asiatics from naturalization. Were native-born children of these disqualified aliens entitled to citizenship? In the Wong Kim Ark Case (No. 130), the definitive ruling on citizenship, the Court ruled that they were.

The last of the Civil War Amendments was the Fifteenth (No. 131). Military Reconstruction of the South was based on the Radical concept that the freedmen should vote, assuming, of course that they would vote Republican. When Southern whites organized the Ku Klux Klan and other secret societies to destroy Radical political power and re-establish white supremacy, the Republicans retaliated with the Fifteenth Amendment and a series of anti-Klan Enforcement Acts designed to protect the electoral and civil rights of the Negro. As in its interpretation of the Fourteenth Amendment, the Supreme Court also narrowly construed the Fifteenth Amendment. In *U.S. v. Reese* (No. 132A), two election inspectors in a Kentucky election were indicted for violating the Enforcement Act by refusing to receive the vote of a Negro. The Court noted that the Amendment did not give anyone a positive right to vote; it simply stated that persons could not be denied the right because of race, color, or previous condition of servitude. The "appropriate legislation" that the Amendment authorized Congress to pass was limited to these specific discriminations. Therefore, the sections of the Enforcement Act which attempted to prevent other kinds of discrimination exceeded Congress's authority and were unconstitutional.

In the same year, the Court dismissed the charge against Louisianans who had, by fraud, violence, and murder, denied Negroes the right to vote, holding that the allegations did not show that the denial had been based on race or color. "We may suspect," the Court concluded laconically, "that race was the cause of the hostility; but it is not so averred" (*U.S. v. Cruikshank*, 1876). Despite the severe judicial limitations on the guarantees of the Fifteenth Amendment, some provisions of the Enforcement Acts were upheld. In *Ex parte* Yarbrough (No. 132B), Justice Miller sustained the conviction of Georgia Klansmen who used physical violence to deprive a Negro of his right to vote for a member of Congress. The Court stated that the right to vote for federal officers is a right of United States citizenship "and Congress has the power to enforce that right."

Civil Rights Under the Fourteenth Amendment

RADICAL RECONSTRUCTION RECONSTRUED

123. The Supreme Court Interprets the Fourteenth Amendment Narrowly

The Slaughterhouse Cases, 16 Wallace 36 (1873).

MILLER, J.: . . . No one can fail to be impressed with the one pervading purpose found in . . . [the Thirteenth, Fourteenth, and Fifteenth Amendments], lying at the foundation of each, and without which none of them would have been even suggested; we mean the freedom of the slave race, the security and firm establishment of that freedom, and the protection of the newly-made freeman and citizen from the oppressions of those who had formerly exercised unlimited dominion over him. It is true that only the Fifteenth Amendment, in terms, mentions the negro by speaking of his color and his slavery. But it is just as true that each of the other articles was addressed to the grievances of that race, and designed to remedy them as the Fifteenth. . . .

In any fair and just construction of any section or phrase of these amendments, it is necessary to look to the purpose which we have said was the pervading spirit of them all, the evil which they were designed to remedy, and the process of continued addition to the Constitution, until that purpose was supposed to be accomplished, as far as constitutional law can accomplish it.

The first section of the fourteenth article, to which our attention is more specially invited, opens with a definition of citizenship—not only citizenship of the United States, but citizenship of the States. No such definition was previously found in the Constitution, nor had any attempt been made to define it by act of Congress. . . . It had been said by eminent judges that no man was a citizen of the United States, except as he was a citizen of one of the States composing the Union. Those, therefore, who had been born and resided always in the District of Columbia or in the Territories, though within the United States, were not citizens. Whether this proposition was sound or not had never been judicially decided. But it had been held by this court, in the celebrated Dred Scott Case, only a few years before the outbreak of the civil war, that a man of African descent, whether a slave or not, could not be a citizen of a State or of the United States. This decision, while it met the condemnation of some of the ablest statesmen and constitutional lawyers of the country, had never been overruled; and if it was to be accepted as a constitutional limitation of the right of citizenship, then all the negro race who had recently been made freemen, were still, not only not citizens, but were incapable of becoming so by anything short of an amendment to the Constitution.

To remove this difficulty primarily, and to establish a clear and comprehensive definition of citizenship . . . , the first clause of the first section was framed. . . .

It is quite clear, then, that there is a citizenship of the United States, and a citizenship of a State, which are distinct from each other, and which depend upon different characteristics or circumstances in the individual.

We think this distinction and its explicit recognition in this amendment of great weight in this argument, because the next paragraph of this same section, which is the one mainly relied on by the plaintiffs in error, speaks only of privileges and immunities of citizens of the United States, and does not speak of those of citizens of the several States. . . .

It is a little remarkable, if this clause was intended as a protection to the citizen of a State against the legislative power of his own State, that the word citizen of the State should be left out when it is so carefully used, and used in contradistinction to citizens of the United States, in the very sentence which precedes it. It is too clear for argument that the change in phraseology was adopted understandingly and with a purpose.

Of the privileges and immunities of the citizen of the United States, and of the privileges and immunities of the citizen of the State, . . . only the former . . . are placed by this clause under the protection of the federal Constitution. . . .

If, then, there is a difference between the privileges and immunities belonging to a citizen of the United States as such, and those belonging to the citizen of the State as such, the latter must rest for their security and protection where they have heretofore rested; for they are not embraced by this paragraph of the amendment.

The first occurrence of the words "privileges and immunities" in our constitutional history, is to be found in the fourth of the Articles of the old Confederation. . . .

In the Constitution of the United States, which superseded the Articles of Confederation, the corresponding provision is found in section two of the fourth article, in the following words: "The citizens of each State shall be entitled to all the privileges and immunities of citizens of the several States." . . .

The constitutional provision . . . did not create those rights, which it called privileges and immunities of citizens of the States. It threw around them in that clause no security for the citizens of the State in which they were claimed or exercised. Nor did it profess to control the power of the state governments over the rights of its own citizens.

Its sole purpose was to declare to the several States, that whatever those rights, as you grant or establish them to your own citizens, or as you limit or qualify, or impose restrictions on their exercise, the same, neither more nor less, shall be the measure of the rights of citizens of other States within your jurisdiction. . . . But with the exception of . . . a few . . . restrictions, the entire domain of the privileges and immunities of citizens of the States, as above defined, lay within the constitutional and legislative power of the States. . . . [Was it the purpose of the Fourteenth Amendment, by the simple declaration that no State should make or enforce any law which shall abridge the privileges and immunities of citizens of the United States, to transfer the security and protection of all the civil rights which we have mentioned, from the States to the federal government?] And where it is declared that Congress shall have the power to enforce that article, was it intended to bring within the power of Congress the entire domain of civil rights heretofore belonging exclusively to the States?

All this and more must follow, if the proposition of the plaintiffs in error be sound. For not only are these rights subject to the control of Congress whenever in its discretion any of them are supposed to be abridged by state legislation, but that body may also pass laws in advance, limiting and restricting the exercise of legislative power by the States, in their most ordinary and usual functions, as in its judgment it may think proper on all such subjects. And still further, such a construction followed by the reversal of the judgments of the Supreme Court of

Louisiana in these cases, would constitute this court a perpetual censor upon all
legislation of the States, on the civil rights
of their own citizens, with authority to
nullify such as it did not approve as consistent with those rights, as they existed
at the time of the adoption of this amendment. The argument, we admit, is not
always the most conclusive which is drawn
from the consequences urged against the
adoption of a particular construction of an
instrument. But when, as in the case before us, these consequences are so serious, so far-reaching and pervading, so
great a departure from the structure and
spirit of our institutions; when the effect
is to fetter and degrade the state governments by subjecting them to the control
of Congress, in the exercise of powers
heretofore universally conceded to them
of the most ordinary and fundamental
character; when in fact it radically
changes the whole theory of the relations
of the state and federal governments to
each other and of both these governments
to the people; the argument has a force
that is irresistible, in the absence of
language which expresses such a purpose
too clearly to admit of doubt.

We are convinced that no such results
were intended by the Congress which
proposed these amendments, nor by the
legislatures of the States which ratified
them. . . . ⎡We are of opinion that the
rights claimed by these plaintiffs in error,
if they have any existence, are not privileges and immunities of citizens of the
United States within the meaning of the
clause of the Fourteenth Amendment under consideration. . . . ⎤

The argument has not been much
pressed in these cases that the defendant's
charter deprives the plaintiffs of their
property without due process of law, or
that it denies to them the equal protection of the law. The first of these paragraphs has been in the Constitution since
the adoption of the Fifth Amendment, as
a restraint upon the federal power. It is
also to be found in some form of expression in the constitutions of nearly all the
States, as a restraint upon the power of the
States. This law, then, has practically been
the same as it now is during the existence
of the government, except so far as the
present amendment may place the restraining power over the States in this
matter in the hands of the federal government. . . .

In the light of the history of these
amendments, and the pervading purpose
of them, which we have already discussed,
it is not difficult to give a meaning to this
[equal protection] clause. The existence
of laws in the States where the newly
emancipated negroes resided, which discriminated with gross injustice and hardship against them as a class, was the evil
to be remedied by this clause, and by it
such laws are forbidden.

If, however, the States did not conform
their laws to its requirements, then by the
fifth section of the article of amendment
Congress was authorized to enforce it by
suitable legislation. We doubt very much
whether any action of a State not directed
by way of discrimination against the negroes as a class, or on account of their
race, will ever be held to come within the
purview of this provision. It is so clearly
a provision for that race and that emergency, that a strong case would be necessary for its application to any other. But
as it is a State that is to be dealt with, and
not alone the validity of its laws, we may
safely leave that matter until Congress
shall have exercised its power, or some
case of state oppression, by denial of equal
justice in its courts, shall have claimed a
decision at our hands. We find no such
case in the one before us. . . .

124. *The Second Civil Rights Act, March 1, 1875*

U. S. Stat. at L., XVIII, Part 3, 335-7.

Whereas it is essential to just government we recognize the equality of all men before the law, and hold that it is the duty of government in its dealings with the people to mete out equal and exact justice to all, of whatever nativity, race, color, or persuasion, religious or political; and it being the appropriate object of legislation to enact great fundamental principles into law: Therefore,

Be it enacted . . . That all persons within the jurisdiction of the United States shall be entitled to the full and equal enjoyment of the accommodations, advantages, facilities, and privileges of inns, public conveyances on land or water, theaters, and other places of public amusement; subject only to the conditions and limitations established by law, and applicable alike to citizens of every race and color, regardless of any previous condition of servitude.

SEC. 2. That any person who shall violate the foregoing section by denying to any citizen, except for reasons by law applicable to citizens of every race and color, and regardless of any previous condition of servitude, the full enjoyment of any of the accommodations, advantages, facilities, or privileges in said section enumerated, or by aiding or inciting such denial, shall, for every such offense, forfeit and pay the sum of five hundred dollars to the person aggrieved thereby, . . . and shall also, for every such offense, be deemed guilty of a misdemeanor, and, upon conviction thereof, shall be fined not less than five hundred nor more than one thousand dollars, or shall be imprisoned not less than thirty days nor more than one year. . . .

SEC. 3. That the district and circuit courts of the United States shall have, exclusively of the courts of the several States, cognizance of all crimes and offenses against, and violations of, the provisions of this act. . . .

SEC. 4. That no citizen possessing all other qualifications which are or may be prescribed by law shall be disqualified for service as grand or petit juror in any court of the United States, or of any State, on account of race, color, or previous condition of servitude; and any officer or other person charged with any duty in the selection or summoning of jurors who shall exclude or fail to summon any citizen for the cause aforesaid shall, on conviction thereof, be deemed guilty of a misdemeanor, and be fined not more than five thousand dollars.

SEC. 5. That all cases arising under the provisions of this act . . . shall be reviewable by the Supreme Court of the United States, without regard to the sum in controversy. . . .

125. *Discrimination by Private Individuals*

The Civil Rights Cases, 109 U.S. 3 (1883).

BRADLEY, J.: . . . It is obvious that the primary and important question in all the cases is the constitutionality of the [Second Civil Rights] law: for if the law is unconstitutional none of the prosecutions can stand.

The sections of the law referred to . . .

[are paragraphs 2 and 3 of the preceding selection].

The essence of the law is, not to declare broadly that all persons shall be entitled to the full and equal enjoyment of the accommodations, advantages, facilities, and privileges of inns, public conveyances, and theatres; but that such enjoyment shall not be subject to any conditions applicable only to citizens of a particular race or color, or who had been in a previous condition of servitude. . . . The second section makes it a penal offense in any person to deny to any citizen of any race or color, regardless of previous servitude, any of the accommodations or privileges mentioned in the first section.

Has Congress constitutional power to make such a law? Of course, no one will contend that the power to pass it was contained in the Constitution before the adoption of the last three amendments. The power is sought, first, in the Fourteenth Amendment. . . .

It is state action of a particular character that is prohibited [by the Fourteenth Amendment]. Individual invasion of individual rights is not the subject-matter of the amendment. It has a deeper and broader scope. It nullifies and makes void all state legislation, and state action of every kind, which impairs the privileges and immunities of citizens of the United States, or which injures them in life, liberty, or property without due process of law, or which denies to any of them the equal protection of the laws. It not only does this, but, in order that the national will, thus declared, may not be a mere brutum fulmen, the last section of the amendment invests Congress with power to enforce it by appropriate legislation. To enforce what? To enforce the prohibition. To adopt appropriate legislation for correcting the effects of such prohibited state law and state acts, and thus to render them effectually null, void, and innocuous. This is the legislative power conferred upon Congress, and this is the whole of it. It does not invest Congress with power to legislate upon subjects which are within the domain of state legislation; but to provide modes of relief against state legislation, or state action, of the kind referred to. It does not authorize Congress to create a code of municipal

law for the regulation of private rights; but to provide modes of redress against the operation of state laws, and the action of state officers, executive or judicial, when these are subversive of the fundamental rights specified in the amendment. Positive rights and privileges are undoubtedly secured by the Fourteenth Amendment; but they are secured by way of prohibition against state laws and state proceedings affecting those rights and privileges, and by power given to Congress to legislate for the purpose of carrying such prohibition into effect; and such legislation must necessarily be predicated upon such supposed state laws or state proceedings, and be directed to the correction of their operation and effect. . . .

In this connection it is proper to state that civil rights, such as are guaranteed by the Constitution against state aggression, cannot be impaired by the wrongful acts of individuals, unsupported by state authority in the shape of laws, customs, or judicial or executive proceedings. The wrongful act of an individual, unsupported by any such authority, is simply a private wrong, or a crime of that individual; an invasion of the rights of the injured party, it is true, whether they affect his person, his property, or his reputation; but if not sanctioned in some way by the state, or not done under state authority, his rights remain in full force, and may presumably be vindicated by resort to the laws of the state for redress. . . .

If the principles of interpretation which we have laid down are correct, . . . it is clear that the law in question cannot be sustained by any grant of legislative power made to Congress by the Fourteenth Amendment. That amendment prohibits the states from denying to any person the equal protection of the laws, and declares that Congress shall have power to enforce, by appropriate legislation, the provisions of the amendment. The law in question, without any reference to adverse state legislation on the subject, declares that all persons shall be entitled to equal accommodations and privileges of inns, public conveyances, and places of public amusement, and imposes a penalty upon any individual who shall deny to any citizen such equal accommodations and privileges. This is not corrective legislation; it is primary and direct; it takes immediate and absolute possession of the subject of the right of admission to inns, public conveyances, and places of amusement. It supersedes and displaces state legislation on the same subject, or only allows it permissive force. It ignores such legislation, and assumes that the matter is one that belongs to the domain of national regulation. Whether it would not have been a more effective protection of the rights of citizens to have clothed Congress with plenary power over the whole subject, is not now the question. What we have to decide is, whether such plenary power has been conferred upon Congress by the Fourteenth Amendment, and, in our judgment, it has not. . . .

But the power of Congress to adopt direct and primary, as distinguished from corrective legislation, on the subject in hand, is sought in the second place, from the Thirteenth Amendment, which abolishes slavery. . . .

It is true that slavery cannot exist without law any more than property in lands and goods can exist without law, and therefore the Thirteenth Amendment may be regarded as nullifying all state laws which establish or uphold slavery. But it has a reflex character also, establishing and decreeing universal civil and political freedom throughout the United States; and it is assumed that the power in Congress to enforce the articles by appropriate legislation, clothes Congress with power to pass all laws necessary and proper for abolishing all badges and incidents of slavery in the United States; and upon this assumption it is claimed that this is sufficient authority for declaring by law that all persons shall have equal accommodations and privileges in all inns, public conveyances, and places of public amuse-

ment; the argument being that the denial of such equal accommodations and privileges is in itself a subjection to a species of servitude within the meaning of the amendment. Conceding the major proposition to be true, that Congress has a right to enact all necessary and proper laws for the obliteration and prevention of slavery with all its badges and incidents, is the minor proposition also true, that the denial to any person of admission to the accommodations and privileges of an inn, a public conveyance, or a theatre, does subject that person to any form of servitude, or tend to fasten upon him any badge of slavery? If it does not, then power to pass the law is not found in the Thirteenth Amendment. . . .

But is there any similarity between such servitudes and a denial by the owner of an inn, a public conveyance, or a theatre, of its accommodations and privileges to an individual, even though the denial be founded on the race or color of that individual? Where does any slavery or servitude, or badge of either, arise from such an act of denial? Whether it might not be a denial of a right which, if sanctioned by the state law, would be obnoxious to the prohibitions of the Fourteenth Amendment, is another question. But what has it to do with the question of slavery? . . .

The long existence of African slavery in this country gave us very distinct notions of what it was, and what were its necessary incidents. Compulsory service of the slave for the benefit of the master, restraint of his movements except by the master's will, disability to hold property, to make contracts, to have a standing in court, to be a witness against a white person, and such like burdens and incapacities were the inseparable incidents of the institution. . . . Can the act of a mere individual, the owner of the inn, the public conveyance, or place of amusement, refusing the accommodation, be justly regarded as imposing any badge of slavery or servitude upon the applicant, or only as inflicting an ordinary civil injury, properly cognizable by the laws of the State, and presumably subject to redress by those laws until the contrary appears?

After giving to these questions all the consideration which their importance demands, we are forced to the conclusion that such an act of refusal has nothing to do with slavery or involuntary servitude, and that if it is violative of any right of the party, his redress is to be sought under the laws of the State; or, if those laws are adverse to his rights and do not protect him, his remedy will be found in the corrective legislation which Congress has adopted, or may adopt, for counteracting the effect of state laws, or state action,

prohibited by the Fourteenth Amendment. It would be running the slavery argument into the ground to make it apply to every act of discrimination which a person may see fit to make as to the guests he will entertain, or as to the people he will take into his coach or cab or car, or admit to his concert or theatre, or deal with in other matters of intercourse or business. . . .

On the whole we are of the opinion that no countenance of authority for the passage of the law in question can be found in either the Thirteenth or Fourteenth Amendment of the Constitution. . . .

THE ORIGINS OF THE "SEPARATE BUT EQUAL" DOCTRINE

126. *The Court Upholds Jim Crow Laws*

Plessy v. Ferguson, 163 U.S. 537 (1896).

BROWN, J.: . . . This case turns upon the Constitutionality of an act of . . . Louisiana, passed in 1890, providing for separate railway carriages for the white and colored races. . . .

The constitutionality of this act is attacked upon the ground that it conflicts both with the Thirteenth Amendment of the Constitution, abolishing slavery, and the Fourteenth Amendment, which prohibits certain restrictive legislation on the part of the States.

1. That it does not conflict with the Thirteenth Amendment, which abolished slavery and involuntary servitude, except as a punishment for crime, is too clear for argument. Slavery implies involuntary servitude—a state of bondage; the ownership of mankind as a chattel, or at least the control of the labor and services of one man for the benefit of another, and the absence of a legal right to the disposal of his own person, property, and services. . . .

A statute which implies merely a legal distinction between the white and col-

ored races—a distinction which is founded in the color of the two races, and which must always exist so long as white men are distinguished from the other race by color—has no tendency to destroy the legal equality of the two races, or re-establish a state of involuntary servitude. Indeed, we do not understand that the Thirteenth Amendment is strenuously relied upon by the plaintiff in error in this connection. . . .

2. . . . The object of the amendment was undoubtedly to enforce the absolute equality of the two races before the law, but in the nature of things it could not have been intended to abolish distinctions based upon color, or to enforce social, as distinguished from political, equality, or a commingling of the two races upon terms unsatisfactory to either. Laws permitting, and even requiring, their separation in places where they are liable to be brought into contact do not necessarily imply the inferiority of either race to the other, and have been generally, if not universally, recognized as within the competency of

the state legislatures in the exercise of their police power. The most common instance of this is connected with the establishment of separate schools for white and colored children, which has been held to be a valid exercise of the legislative power even by courts of States where the political rights of the colored race have been longest and most earnestly enforced. . . .

So far, then, as a conflict with the Fourteenth Amendment is concerned, the case reduces itself to the question whether the statute of Louisiana is a reasonable regulation, and with respect to this there must necessarily be a large discretion on the part of the legislature. In determining the question of reasonableness it is at liberty to act with reference to the established usages, customs, and traditions of the people, and with a view to the promotion of their comfort, and the preservation of the public peace and good order. Gauged by this standard, we cannot say that a law which authorizes or even requires the separation of the two races in public conveyances is unreasonable or more obnoxious to the Fourteen Amendment than the acts of Congress requiring separate schools for colored children in the District of Columbia, the constitutionality of which does not seem to have been questioned, or the corresponding acts of state legislatures.

We consider the underlying fallacy of the plaintiff's argument to consist in the assumption that the enforced separation of the two races stamps the colored race with a badge of inferiority. If this be so, it is not by reason of anything found in the act, but solely because the colored race chooses to put that construction upon it. The argument necessarily assumes that if, as has been more than once the case, and is not unlikely to be so again, the colored race should become the dominant power in the state legislature, and should enact a law in precisely similar terms, it would thereby relegate the white race to an inferior position. We imagine that the white race, at least, would not acquiesce in this assumption. The argument also assumes that social prejudices may be overcome by legislation and that equal rights cannot be secured to the Negro except by an enforced commingling of the two races. We cannot accept this proposition. If the two races are to meet upon terms of social equality, it must be the result of natural affinities, a mutual appreciation of each other's merits, and a voluntary consent of individuals. . . . Legislation is powerless to eradicate racial instincts or to abolish distinctions based upon physical differences, and the attempt to do so can only result in accentuating the difficulties of the present situation. If the civil and political rights of both races be equal, one cannot be inferior to the other civilly or politically. If one race be inferior to the other socially, the Constitution of the United States cannot put them upon the same plane.

127. *Justice Harlan: "Our Constitution is color-blind."*

Plessy v. Ferguson, 163 U.S. 537 (1896).

HARLAN, J., dissenting: . . . In respect of civil rights, common to all citizens, the Constitution of the United States does not, I think, permit any public authority to know the race of those entitled to be protected in the enjoyment of such rights. Every true man has pride of race, and under appropriate circumstances when the rights of others, his equals before the law, are not to be affected, it is his privilege to express such pride and to take such action based upon it as to him seems proper. But I deny that any legislative body or judicial tribunal may have regard to the race of citizens when the civil rights of those citizens are involved. Indeed, such legislation, as that here in question, is inconsistent not only with that equality of rights which pertains to citizenship, National and State, but with the personal liberty enjoyed by everyone within the United States. . . .

It is one thing for railroad carriers to furnish, or to be required by law to furnish, equal accommodations for all whom they are under a legal duty to carry. It is quite another thing for government to forbid citizens of the white and black races from traveling in the same public conveyance, and to punish officers of railroad companies for permitting persons of the two races to occupy the same passenger coach. If a State can prescribe, as a rule of civil conduct, that whites and blacks shall not travel as passengers in the same railroad coach, why may it not so regulate the use of the streets of its cities and towns as to compel white citizens to keep on one side of a street and black citizens to keep on the other? Why may it not, upon like grounds, punish whites and blacks who ride together in streetcars or in open vehicles on a public road or street? Why may it not require sheriffs to assign whites to one side of a courtroom and blacks to the other? And why may it not also prohibit the commingling of the two races in the galleries of legislative halls or in public assemblages convened for the consideration of the political questions of the day? Further, if this statute of Louisiana is consistent with the personal liberty of citizens, why may not the State require the separation in railroad coaches of native and naturalized citizens of the United States, or of Protestants and Roman Catholics?

The answer given at the argument to these questions was that regulations of the kind they suggest would be unreasonable and could not, therefore, stand before the law. Is it meant that the determination of questions of legislative power depends upon the inquiry whether the statute whose validity is questioned is, in the judgment of the courts, a reasonable one, taking all the circumstances into consideration? A statute may be unreasonable merely because a sound public policy forbade its enactment. But I do not understand that the courts have anything to do with the policy or expediency of legislation. . . .

The white race deems itself to be the dominant race in this country. And so it is, in prestige, in achievements, in education, in wealth, and in power. So, I doubt not, it will continue to be for all time, if it remains true to its great heritage and holds fast to the principles of constitutional liberty. But in view of the Constitution, in the eye of the law, there is in this country no superior, dominant, ruling class of citizens. There is no caste here. Our Constitution is color-blind and neither knows nor tolerates classes among citizens. In respect of civil rights, all citizens are equal before the law. The humblest is the peer of the most powerful. The law regards man as man and takes no account of his surroundings or of his color when his civil rights as guaranteed by the supreme law of the land are involved. It is, therefore, to be regretted that this high tribunal, the final expositor of the fundamental law of the land, has reached the conclusion that it is competent for a State to regulate the enjoyment by citizens of their civil rights solely upon the basis of race. . . .

The sure guarantee of the peace and security of each race is the clear, distinct, unconditional recognition by our governments, National and State, of every right that inheres in civil freedom, and of the equality before the law of all the citizens of the United States without regard to race. State enactments, regulating the enjoyment of civil rights, upon the basis of race, and cunningly devised to defeat legitimate results of the war, under the pretense of recognizing equality of rights, can have no other result than to render permanent peace impossible, and to keep alive a conflict of races, the continuance of which must do harm to all concerned. . . .

The arbitrary separation of citizens, on

the basis of race, while they are on a public highway, is a badge of servitude wholly inconsistent with the civil freedom and the equality before the law established by the Constitution. It cannot be justified upon any legal grounds.

If evils will result from the commingling of the two races upon public highways established for the benefit of all, they will be infinitely less than those that will surely come from state legislation regulating the enjoyment of civil rights upon the basis of race. We boast of the freedom enjoyed by our people above all other peoples. But it is difficult to reconcile that boast with a state of the law which, practically, puts the brand of servitude and degradation upon a large class of our fellow-citizens, our equals before the law. The thin disguise of "equal" accommodations for passengers in railroad coaches will not mislead anyone, nor atone for the wrong this day done. . . .

I am of opinion that the statute of Louisiana is inconsistent with the personal liberty of citizens, white and black, in that State, and hostile to both the spirit and letter of the Constitution of the United States. If laws of like character should be enacted in the several States of the Union, the effect would be in the highest degree mischievous. . . . Such a system is inconsistent with the guarantee given by the Constitution to each state of a republican form of government, and may be stricken down by congressional action, or by the courts in the discharge of their solemn duty to maintain the supreme law of the land, anything in the constitution or laws of any state to the contrary notwithstanding.

PRIVILEGES AND IMMUNITIES OF FEDERAL CITIZENSHIP

128. *Suffrage Is Not One of the Privileges and Immunities of Citizenship*

Minor v. Happersett, 21 Wallace 162 (1875).

WAITE, C.J.: . . . The argument is, that as a woman, born or naturalized in the United States and subject to the jurisdiction thereof, is a citizen of the United States and of the State in which she resides, she has the right of suffrage as one of the privileges and immunities of her citizenship, which the State cannot by its laws or constitution abridge.

There is no doubt that women may be citizens. . . . Sex has never been made one of the elements of citizenship in the United States. In this respect men have never had an advantage over women. The same laws precisely apply to both. The Fourteenth Amendment did not affect the citizenship of women any more than it did of men. In this particular, therefore, the rights of Mrs. Minor do not depend upon the amendment. She has always been a citizen from her birth, and entitled to all the privileges and immunities of citizenship. . . .

If the right of suffrage is one of the necessary privileges of a citizen of the United States, then the constitution and laws of Missouri confining it to men are in violation of the Constitution of the United States, as amended, and consequently void. The direct question is, therefore, presented whether all citizens are necessarily voters.

The Constitution does not define the privileges and immunities of citizens. For that definition we must look elsewhere. In this case we need not determine what they are, but only whether suffrage is necessarily one of them.

It certainly is nowhere made so in express terms. The United States has no voters in the States of its own creation. The elective officers of the United States are all elected directly or indirectly by state voters. . . .

The amendment did not add to the privileges and immunities of a citizen. It simply furnished an additional guaranty for the protection of such as he already had. No new voters were necessarily made by it. Indirectly it may have had that effect, because it may have increased the number of citizens entitled to suffrage under the constitution and laws of the States, but it operates for this purpose, if at all, through the States and the state laws, and not directly upon the citizen.

It is clear therefore, we think, that the Constitution has not added the right of suffrage to the privileges and immunities of citizenship as they existed at the time it was adopted. This makes it proper to inquire whether suffrage was coextensive with the citizenship of the States at the time of its adoption. If it was, then it may with force be argued that suffrage was one of the rights which belonged to citizenship, and in the enjoyment of which every citizen must be protected. But if it was not, the contrary may with propriety be assumed.

When the Federal Constitution was adopted, all the States, with the exception of Rhode Island and Connecticut, had constitutions of their own. . . . Upon an examination of these constitutions we find that in no State were all citizens permitted to vote. . . .

In this condition of the law in respect to suffrage in the several States it cannot for a moment be doubted that if it had been intended to make all citizens of the United States voters, the framers of the Constitution would not have left it to implication. . . . In all, save perhaps New Jersey, this right was only bestowed upon men and not upon all of them. . . . Women were excluded from suffrage in nearly all the States by the express provision of their constitutions and laws. . . .

No new State has ever been admitted to the Union which has conferred the right of suffrage upon women, and this has never been considered a valid objection to her admission. On the contrary, . . . the right of suffrage was withdrawn from women as early as 1807 in the State of New Jersey, without any attempt to obtain the interference of the United States to prevent it. . . .

Besides this, citizenship has not in all cases been made a condition precedent to the enjoyment of the right of suffrage. Thus, in Missouri, persons of foreign birth, who have declared their intention to become citizens of the United States, may under certain conditions vote. The same provision is to be found in the constitutions of Alabama, Arkansas, Florida, Georgia, Indiana, Kansas, Minnesota, and Texas.

Certainly if the courts can consider any question settled, this is one. For nearly ninety years the people have acted upon the idea that the Constitution, when it conferred citizenship, did not necessarily confer the right of suffrage. If uniform practice long continued can settle the construction of so important an instrument as the Constitution of the United States confessedly is, most certainly it has been done here. Our province is to decide what the law is, not to declare what it should be. . . . No argument as to woman's need of suffrage can be considered. We can only act upon her rights as they exist. It is not for us to look at the hardship of withholding. Our duty is at an end if we find it is within the power of a State to withhold.

Being unanimously of the opinion that the Constitution of the United States does not confer the right of suffrage upon any one, and that the constitutions and laws of the several States which commit that important trust to men alone are not necessarily void, we affirm the judgment.

PROCEDURAL RIGHTS IN THE STATES UNDER THE FOURTEENTH AMENDMENT

129. *Grand Jury Indictment Is Not Necessary to Justice in the States*

Hurtado v. California, 110 U.S. 516 (1884).

MATTHEWS, J.: . . . The proposition of law we are asked to affirm is that an indictment or presentment by a grand jury, as known to the common law of England, is essential to that "due process of law," when applied to prosecutions for felonies, which is secured and guaranteed by this provision of the Constitution of the United States, and which accordingly it is forbidden to the States respectively to dispense with in the administration of criminal law. . . .

It is maintained on behalf of the plaintiff in error that the phrase "due process of law" is equivalent to "law of the land," as found in the 29th chapter of Magna Charta; that by immemorial usage it has acquired a fixed, definite, and technical meaning; that it refers to and includes, not only the general principles of public liberty and private right, which lie at the foundation of all free government, but the very institutions which, venerable by time and custom, have been tried by experience and found fit and necessary for the preservation of those principles, and which, having been the birthright and inheritance of every English subject, crossed the Atlantic with the colonists and were transplanted and established in the fundamental laws of the State; that, having been originally introduced into the Constitution of the United States as a limitation upon the powers of the government, brought into being by that instrument, it has now been added as an additional security to the individual against oppression by the States themselves; that one of these institutions is that of the grand jury, an indictment or presentment by which against the accused in cases of alleged felonies is an essential part of due process of law, in order that he may not be harassed or destroyed by prosecutions founded only upon private malice or popular fury. . . .

A critical examination and comparison of the text and context will show that it . . . was not intended to assert that an indictment or presentment of a grand jury was essential to the idea of due process of law in the prosecution and punishment of crimes, but was only mentioned as an example and illustration of due process of law as it actually existed in cases in which it was customarily used. . . .

The Constitution of the United States was ordained . . . by descendants of Englishmen, who inherited the traditions of English law and history; but it was made for an undefined and expanding future, and for a people gathered and to be gathered from many nations and of many tongues. And while we take just pride in the principles and institutions of the common law, we are not to forget that in lands where other systems of jurisprudence prevail, the ideas and processes of civil justice are also not unknown. Due process of law, in spite of the absolutism of continental governments, is not alien to that code which survived the Roman Empire as the foundation of modern civilization in Europe. . . . There is nothing in Magna Charta, rightly construed as a broad charter of public right and law, which ought to exclude the best ideas of all systems and of every age; and as it was the characteristic principle of the common law to draw its inspiration from every fountain of justice, we are not to assume that the sources of its supply have been exhausted. On the contrary, we should expect that the new and various experiences of our own situation and system will mould and shape it into new and not less useful forms. . . .

In this country written constitutions were deemed essential to protect the rights and liberties of the people against the encroachments of power delegated to their governments, and the provisions of Magna Charta were incorporated into Bills of Rights. They were limitations upon all the powers of government, legislative as well as executive and judicial.

It necessarily happened, therefore, that as these broad and general maxims of liberty and justice held in our system a different place and performed a different function from their position and office in English constitutional history and law, they would receive and justify a corresponding and more comprehensive interpretation. Applied in England only as guards against executive usurpation and tyranny, here they have become bulwarks also against arbitrary legislation; but, in that application, as it would be incongruous to measure and restrict them by the ancient customary English law, they must be held to guarantee not particular forms of procedure, but the very substance of individual rights to life, liberty, and property. . . .

We are to construe this phrase in the Fourteenth Amendment by the *usus loquendi* of the Constitution itself. The same words are contained in the Fifth Amendment. That article makes specific and express provision for perpetuating the institution of the grand jury, so far as relates to prosecutions for the more aggravated crimes under the laws of the United States. It declares that:

"No person shall be held to answer for a capital or otherwise infamous crime, unless on a presentment or indictment of a grand jury, except in cases arising in the land or naval forces, or in the militia when in actual service in time of war or public danger; nor shall any person be subject for the same offence to be twice put in jeopardy of life or limb; nor shall he be compelled in any criminal case to be witness against himself." [It then immediately adds]: "Nor be deprived of life, liberty, or property, without due process of law."

According to a recognized canon of interpretation, especially applicable to formal and solemn instruments of constitutional law, we are forbidden to assume, without clear reason to the contrary, that any part of this most important amendment is superfluous. The natural and obvious inference is, that in the sense of the Constitution "due process of law" was not meant or intended to include, *ex vi termini*, the institution and procedure of a grand jury in any case. The conclusion is equally irresistible, that when the same phrase was employed in the Fourteenth Amendment to restrain the action of the States, it was used in the same sense and with no greater extent; and that if in the adoption of that amendment it had been part of its purpose to perpetuate the institution of the grand jury in all the States, it would have embodied, as did the Fifth Amendment, express declarations to that effect. Due process of law in the latter refers to that law of the land which derives its authority from the legislative powers conferred upon Congress by the Constitution of the United States, exercised within the limits therein prescribed, and interpreted according to the principles of the common law. In the Fourteenth Amendment, by parity of reason, it refers to that law of the land in each State, which derives its authority from the inherent and reserved powers of the State, exerted within the limits of those fundamental principles of liberty and justice which lie at the base of all our civil and political institutions, and the greatest security for which resides in the right of the people to make their own laws, and alter them at their pleasure.

Definition of American Citizenship

130. Birth constitutes "a sufficient and complete right to citizenship."

U.S. v. Wong Kim Ark, 169 U.S. 649 (1898).

GRAY, J.: . . . The Constitution of the United States, as originally adopted, uses the words "citizen of the United States," and "natural-born citizen of the United States." By the original Constitution, every Representative in Congress is required to have been "seven years a citizen of the United States," and every Senator to have been "nine years a citizen of the United States"; and "no person except a natural-born citizen, or a citizen of the United States at the time of the adoption of this Constitution, shall be eligible to the office of President." The Fourteenth Article of Amendment, besides declaring that "all persons born or naturalized in the United States, and subject to the jurisdiction thereof, are citizens of the United States and of the State wherein they reside," also declares that "no State shall make or enforce any law which shall abridge the privileges or immunities of citizens of the United States; nor shall any State deprive any person of life, liberty, or property, without due process of law; nor deny to any person within its jurisdiction the equal protection of the laws." And the Fifteenth Article of Amendment declares that "the right of citizens of the United States to vote shall not be denied or abridged by the United States, or by any State, on account of race, color, or previous condition of servitude."

The Constitution nowhere defines the meaning of these words, either by way of inclusion or of exclusion, except in so far as this is done by the affirmative declaration that "all persons born or naturalized in the United States, and subject to the jurisdiction thereof, are citizens of the United States." In this, as in other respects, it must be interpreted in the light of the common law, the principles and history of which were familiarly known to the framers of the Constitution. . . .

The fundamental principle of the common law with regard to English nationality was birth within the allegiance—also called "ligealty," "obedience," "faith," or "power," of the King. The principle embraced all persons born within the King's allegiance, and subject to his protection. Such allegiance and protection were mutual . . . and were not restricted to natural-born subjects and naturalized subjects, or to those who had taken an oath of allegiance; but were predicable of aliens in amity, so long as they were within the kingdom. Children, born in England, of such aliens, were therefore natural-born subjects. But the children, born within the realm, of foreign ambassadors, or the children of alien enemies, born during and within their hostile occupation of part of the King's dominions, were not natural-born subjects, because not born within the allegiance, the obedience, or the power, or, as would be said at this day, within the jurisdiction, of the King. . . .

The real object of the Fourteenth Amendment of the Constitution, in qualifying the words "all persons born in the United States," by the addition, "and subject to the jurisdiction thereof," would appear to have been to exclude, by the fewest and fittest words (besides children of members of the Indian tribes, standing in a peculiar relation to the national government, unknown to the common law), the two classes of cases—children born of alien enemies in hostile occupation, and children of diplomatic representatives of a foreign state—both of which, as has already been shown, by the law of England and by our own law, from the time of the first settlement of the English colonies in America, had been recognized exceptions to the fundamental rule of citizenship by birth within the country. . . .

The foregoing considerations and authorities irresistibly lead us to these conclusions: The Fourteenth Amendment affirms the ancient and fundamental rule of citizenship by birth within the territory, in the allegiance and under the protection of the country, including all children here born of resident aliens, with the exceptions or qualifications (as old as the rule itself) of children of foreign sovereigns or their ministers, or born on foreign public ships, or of enemies within and during a hostile occupation of part of our territory, and with the single additional exception

of children of members of the Indian tribes owing direct allegiance to their several tribes. The Amendment, in clear words and in manifest intent, includes the children born within the territory of the United States of all other persons, of whatever race or color, domiciled within the United States. Every citizen or subject of another country, while domiciled here, is within the allegiance and the protection, and consequently subject to the jurisdiction, of the United States. . . .

It is true that Chinese persons born in China cannot be naturalized, like other aliens, by proceedings under the naturalization laws. But this is for want of any statute or treaty authorizing or permitting such naturalization, as will appear by tracing the history of the statutes, treaties, and decisions upon that subject—always bearing in mind that statutes enacted by Congress, as well as treaties made by the President and Senate, must yield to the paramount and supreme law of the Constitution. . . .

The Fifteenth Amendment and the Right to Vote

131. The Fifteenth Amendment

Proposed February 27, 1869; adopted March 30, 1870.

SECTION 1. The right of citizens of the United States to vote shall not be denied or abridged by the United States or by any State on account of race, color, or previous condition of servitude.

SECTION 2. The Congress shall have power to enforce this article by appropriate legislation.

132. *The Ku Klux Klan and the Fifteenth Amendment*

A. "THE FIFTEENTH AMENDMENT DOES NOT CONFER THE RIGHT OF SUFFRAGE UPON ANYONE."

U.S. v. Reese, 92 U.S. 214 (1876).

WAITE, C.J.: . . . The Fifteenth Amendment does not confer the right of suffrage upon anyone. It prevents the States or the United States, however, from giving preference, in this particular, to one citizen of the United States over another on account of race, etc. Before its adoption, this could be done. . . . Now it cannot. If citizens of one race having certain qualifications are permitted to vote, those of another having the same qualifications must be. . . . It follows that the Amendment has invested the citizen of the United States with a new constitutional right which is within the protecting power of Congress. That right is exemp-

tion from discrimination in the exercise of the elective franchise on account of race, color, or previous condition of servitude. . . .

The power of Congress to legislate at all upon the subject of voting at State elections rests upon this Amendment. It cannot be contended that the Amendment confers authority to impose penalties for every wrongful refusal to receive the vote of a qualified elector at State elections. It is only when the wrongful refusal at such an election is on account of race, etc., that Congress can interfere and provide for its punishment. . . .

B. THE KU KLUX KLAN CASE

Ex parte Yarbrough, 110 U.S. 651 (1884).

MILLER, J.: . . . Stripped of its technical verbiage, the offence charged in this indictment is that the defendants conspired to intimidate Berry Saunders, a citizen of African descent, in the exercise of his right to vote for a member of the Congress of the United States, and in the execution of that conspiracy they beat, bruised, wounded and otherwise maltreated him; and in the second count, that they did this on account of his race, color, and previous condition of servitude, by going in disguise and assaulting him on the public highway and on his own premises. . . .

That a government whose essential character is republican, whose executive head and legislative body are both elective, whose most numerous and powerful branch of the legislature is elected by

the people directly, has no power by appropriate laws to secure this election from the influence of violence, of corruption, and of fraud, is a proposition so startling as to arrest attention and demand the gravest consideration.

If this government is anything more than a mere aggregation of delegated agents of other States and governments, each of which is superior to the general government, it must have the power to protect the elections on which its existence depends from violence and corruption.

If it has not this power, it is left helpless before the two great natural and historical enemies of all republics, open violence and insidious corruption.

The proposition that it has no such power is supported by the old argument, often heard, often repeated, and in this court never assented to, that when a question of the power of Congress arises the advocate of the power must be able to place his finger on words which expressly grant it. The brief of the counsel before us, though directed to the authority of that body to pass criminal laws, uses the same language. Because there is no *express* power to provide for preventing violence exercised on the voter as a means of controlling his vote, no such law can be enacted. It destroys at one blow, in construing the Constitution of the United States, the doctrine universally applied to all instruments of writing, that what is implied is as much a part of the instrument as what is expressed. This principle, in its application to the Constitution of the United States, more than to almost any other writing, is a necessity, by reason of the inherent inability to put into words all derivative powers,—a difficulty which the instrument itself recognizes by conferring on Congress the authority to pass all laws necessary and proper to carry into execution the powers expressly granted, and all other powers vested in the government or any branch of it by the Constitution. . . .

The States, in prescribing the qualifications of voters for the most numerous branch of their own legislatures, do not do this with reference to the election for members of Congress. Nor can they prescribe the qualification for voters for those *eo nomine*. They define who are to vote for the popular branch of their own legislature, and the Constitution of the United States says the same persons shall vote for members of Congress in that state. It adopts the qualification thus furnished as

the qualification of its own electors for members of Congress.

It is not true, therefore, that electors for members of Congress owe their right to vote to the state law, in any sense which makes the exercise of the right to depend exclusively on the law of the State. . . .

In a republican government, like ours, where political power is reposed in representatives of the entire body of the people, chosen at short intervals by popular elections, the temptations to control these elections by violence and by corruption is a constant source of danger.

Such has been the history of all republics, and, though ours has been comparatively free from both these evils in the past, no lover of his country can shut his eyes to the fear of future danger from both sources.

If the recurrence of such acts as these prisoners stand convicted of are too common in one quarter of the country, and give omen of danger from lawless violence, the free use of money in elections, arising from the vast growth of recent wealth in other quarters, presents equal cause for anxiety.

If the government of the United States has within its constitutional domain no authority to provide against these evils, if the very sources of power may be poisoned by corruption or controlled by violence and outrage, without legal restraint, then, indeed, is the country in danger, and its best powers, its highest purposes, the hopes which it inspires, and the love which enshrines it, are at the mercy of the combinations of those who respect no right but brute force on the one hand, and unprincipled corruptionists on the other.

CHAPTER XV

The Waite-Fuller Court
and the Industrial Revolution

THE Civil War Amendments did not erect bulwarks of civil liberties protecting individual rights as their sponsors envisioned. Instead, they
were gradually developed into formidable legal protections of corporate-
property rights against state regulation. A classic protest against such governmental
interference is set forth in the Jacobs case (No. 133). A New York court struck
down a state law forbidding the manufacture of cigars in tenement houses because
it could not "perceive how the cigarmaker is to be improved in his health or
morals by forcing him from his home and its hallowed associations and beneficent
influences to ply his trade elsewhere." Although Governor Theodore Roosevelt
condemned the ruling because it showed that judges "knew nothing whatever
of the needs, or the life and labor, of three-fourths of their fellow citizens . . . ,"
the Jacobs view dominated the bench more and more in the late 19th century.
Some protested. A future Supreme Court Justice, for example, foresaw the evils
of unregulated *laissez faire* and proclaimed the judicial necessity "of weighing
considerations of social advantage" (No. 134).

The key to the rapid industrialization of the postwar period was the development of nationwide transportation facilities. Built with the aid of state and federal
legislation and subsidies, the railroads too often ignored the interests of the public.
In 1871 Charles Francis Adams, Lincoln's wartime ambassador to England and
later a railroad executive, noted that interests controlling the railroads "have
declared war, negotiated peace, reduced courts, legislatures, and sovereign states to

an unqualified obedience to their will, disturbed trade, agitated the currency, imposed taxes, and boldly setting both law and public opinion at defiance, have freely exercised many other attributes of sovereignty." In the absence of federal legislation, the states were the only governmental agencies to enact regulatory measures. The Granger cases, which tested these statutes, are of historic importance in American constitutional law. Chief Justice Waite upheld state regulation of railroad and storage facilities as a legitimate exercise of the state's police power to protect the public welfare. In the Munn decision (No. 135), involving warehouse storage charges, he ruled that "when private property is affected with a public interest it ceases to be *juris privati* only." Waite agreed that state regulation might be abused, but suggested that "for protection against abuses by legislatures the people must resort to the polls, not the courts." On the same day the Court applied the same rule to railroad rates, observing that the railroads involved were "employed in state as well as interstate commerce, and until Congress acts, the State must be permitted to adopt such rules and regulations as may be necessary for the promotion of the general welfare of the people within its own jurisdiction, even though in so doing those without may be indirectly affected." (*Peik v. Chicago and Northwestern Railway Co.,* 1877).

Ten years later, however, in the Wabash Case the Court reversed its position (No. 136), invalidating an Illinois statute that prohibited "long-and-short haul" rate discriminations on the ground that state regulation violated Congress's exclusive power over interstate commerce. Since the states had been the only regulators of railroads until this time, the decision temporarily killed all regulation of rail transportation, making it imperative that Congress act. Simultaneously, a congressional committee concluded that "the paramount evil chargeable against transportation systems is unjust discrimination between persons, places, commodities, or particular descriptions of traffic." Viewing the Wabash decision as an invitation to act, Congress passed the Interstate Commerce Act, establishing the first permanent regulatory agency in American history. Designed to regulate railroad abuses, the Interstate Commerce Commission was authorized to investigate complaints against the railroads, but enforcement of its rulings was vested in the Courts.

Although the Act specified that all rail charges should be "reasonable and just," these terms were not defined nor was the Commission specifically empowered to fix "just" rates. Moreover, the burden of proof for alleged violations was placed on the Commission; the railroads were not bound by "cease and desist" orders until they were approved by the judiciary. Indeed, Senator Nelson W. Aldrich candidly admitted that the act was "a delusion and a sham . . . an empty menace to great interests, made to answer the clamor of the ignorant and unreasoning."

Whether one agrees with Senator Aldrich's statement or not, judicial review by a court composed largely of ex-corporation lawyers quickly rendered the Commission ineffective as a regulatory body. Between 1887 and 1905 the Supreme Court heard sixteen cases involving the Interstate Commerce Act; in fifteen it ruled in favor of the railroads. The most important of these decisions was the Maximum Freight Rate Case (No. 137), in which the railroads challenged the Commission's authority to fix rates. Although the I. C. C. had never assumed that it had the power to promulgate rate schedules prior to a complaint, for ten years it had followed up its "cease and desist" orders with alternative rates that were "reasonable." Now the Court ruled that the Commission had never possessed this vital power. The final blow came in the same year in the Alabama Midland Railway Case (1897) when the Court nullified for practical purposes the long- and short-haul clause. "By virtue of judicial decisions," the I. C. C. confessed in its annual report of 1897, "we have ceased to be a body for the regulation of interstate carriers . . . The people should no longer look to this commission for a protection which it is powerless to extend." Thus, as Attorney General Richard S. Olney had predicted five years earlier, the act to regulate railroads was transformed judicially into "a sort of barrier between the railroad corporations and the people" (No. 138).

The concentration of economic power, well exemplified by the organization of transcontinental transportation in large railroad systems, grew steadily in the post-Civil War industrial boom. Like the railroads, other gigantic corporations threatened to monopolize the economic life of the nation, and by the 1880's public opinion began to demand effective regulation of the trusts. In his annual message in 1888, President Cleveland warned that "corporations which should be carefully restrained creatures of the law and servants of the people, are fast becoming the people's masters." In that same year, both major parties inserted antimonopoly planks in their national platforms. This widespread opposition led to the Sherman Anti-Trust Act in 1890. Hailed as a victory over "unlawful restraints and monopolies," the measure carefully avoided defining the terms trust, monopoly, conspiracy, combination, or restraint. Moreover, no enforcement machinery was prescribed, apart from instituting suits in federal courts. Commenting on these ambiguities, Mr. Dooley, the shrewd observer created by the humorist Finley Peter Dunne, prophesied that "what looks like a stone-wall to a layman is a triumphal arch to a corporation lawyer." In the first interpretation by the Supreme Court (No. 139), the law was rendered ineffective by narrow construction of its terms. The Knight case held that control of 98 per cent of the nation's sugar refining capacity did not restrain trade and commerce since "commerce succeeds to manufacture, and is not a part of it." In a lone dissent, Justice Harlan protested that under the guise of economic freedom, individual liberty was being subordinated to industrial combinations "so all-pervading that they threaten the integrity of our institutions." But there were no protests from Attorney-General Olney, who virtually admitted sabotaging the antitrust law in his complacent acceptance of business triumph: "You will have observed that the government has been defeated . . . on the trust question. I always supposed it would be, and have taken the responsibility of not prosecuting under a law I believed to be no good."

If Olney was reluctant to use the Sherman Act against business, the Justice Department was not so hesitant in utilizing it against labor unions. In breaking the Pullman strike of 1894, the federal government used two almost equally effective instruments—troops, and an injunction based partially on the Anti-Trust Act. The injunction against the American Railway Union was upheld in a contempt case at the circuit court level (No. 140). This interpretation was challenged by the

Union's president, Eugene V. Debs, who sued out a writ of habeas corpus in the Supreme Court. Although Olney had specifically directed that the Sherman Act should be "strictly enforced against all violators," his argument in *In re Debs* skirted that issue and urged broader grounds to justify governmental interference. For the most part, the Supreme Court followed Olney's reasoning (No. 141).

The year 1895 saw a third major defense of the gospel of wealth by the Supreme Court. Economically, the Income Tax decision (No. 142) was consistent with the Court's construction of a legal bulwark protecting vested rights and corporate property. As recently as 1881 the Court had unanimously upheld the Civil War income tax, ruling that it did not violate the direct tax clauses of the Constitution since these clauses applied only to taxes on land and on persons (*Springer v. U.S.*). When the Wilson-Gorman Tariff Act of 1894 enacted a 2 per cent tax on incomes over $4,000, however, the Court, grown conservative in the years since 1881, struck down the tax provisions as unconstitutional levies and an assault upon capital. The Sixteenth Amendment (Chapter XVIII) was added to the Constitution as a direct, but long deferred, result of this case.

When the Supreme Court was erecting a constitutional defense against national regulation of property, it evolved an interpretation of the due process clause of the Fourteenth Amendment which eventually made it possible to strike down state supervision. In the Slaughterhouse Cases (Chapter XIV), the first interpretation of due process, Justice Miller refused to convert the clause from a guarantee of just procedure to a device for reviewing the substance of state laws. "Such a ruling," he said, "would constitute this Court a perpetual censor upon all legislation of the states." Four years later in *Munn v. Illinois*, the Court again waved aside substantive due process in favor of the police powers of the states. Denouncing this judicial hands-off position in a vigorous dissent, Justice Field asserted that procedural due process did not afford sufficient protection for property rights. The majority's decision, he concluded, was "subversive of the right of private property, heretofore believed to be protected by constitutional guarantees against legislative interference."

Between 1877 and 1890 seven participants in the Slaughterhouse and Munn cases died or resigned from the Supreme Court. During this period Field and his new colleagues brought about a judicial revolution in the interpretation of due process. As early as 1882, Roscoe Conkling, a member of the congressional committee that drafted the Fourteenth Amendment, supplied the Court with a convenient if not altogether reliable argument, asserting that the committee had used the word "person" instead of "citizen" in the due process clause to protect corporations as well as individuals (*San Mateo County v. Southern Pacific Railroad Co.*). Four years later the Court endorsed this position in *Santa Clara County v. Southern Pacific Railroad Company* (No. 143). In the Minnesota Commission Case (1889) the Court completed the judicial about-face, transforming itself, in Justice Miller's words, into a "perpetual censor" of state legislation, and establishing itself as the final arbiter of the reasonableness of railroad rates. The development of substantive due process culminated in *Smyth v. Ames* (No. 144). In voiding a Nebraska intrastate rate law, the Court decided that "reasonable" rates must yield a "fair return" on a "fair evaluation" of the property regulated. The very vagueness of this terminology buttressed the Court's new censorial role, increasing both the scope and the economic importance of judicial review in an industrialized society.

Presages of Future Change

133. *"Governmental interferences disturb the normal adjustments of the social fabric."*

In re Jacobs, 98 New York 98 (1885).

EARL, J.: . . . Generally it is for the legislature to determine what laws and regulations are needed to protect the public health and secure the public comfort and safety, and while its measures are calculated, intended, convenient and appropriate to accomplish these ends, the exercise of its discretion is not subject to review by the courts. But they must have some relation to these ends. Under the mere guise of police regulations, personal rights and private property cannot arbitrarily be invaded, and the determination of the legislature is not final or conclusive. If it passes an act ostensibly for the public health, and thereby destroys or takes away the property of a citizen, or interferes with his personal liberty, then it is for the courts to scrutinize the act and see whether it really relates to and is convenient and appropriate to promote the public health. It matters not that the legislature may in the title to the act, or in its body, declare that it is intended for the improvement of the public health. . . . What possible relation to the health of the occupants of a large tenement-house could cigarmaking in one of its remote rooms have? If the legislature had in mind the protection of the occupants of the tenement-houses, why was the act confined in its operation to the two cities only? It is plain that this is not a health law, and that it has no relation whatever to the

public health. . . . Such legislation may invade one class of rights to-day and another to-morrow, and if it can be sanctioned under the Constitution, while far removed in time we will not be far away in practical statesmanship from those ages when governmental prefects supervised the building of houses, the rearing of cattle, the sowing of seed and the reaping of grain, and governmental ordinances regulated the movements and labor of artisans, the rate of wages, the price of food, the diet and clothing of the people, and a large range of other affairs long since in all civilized lands regarded as outside of governmental functions. Such governmental interferences disturb the normal adjustments of the social fabric, and usually derange the delicate and complicated machinery of industry and cause a score of ills while attempting the removal of one.

When a health law is challenged in the courts as unconstitutional on the ground that it arbitrarily interferes with personal liberty and private property without due process of law, the courts must be able to see that it has at least in fact some relation to the public health, that the public health is the end actually aimed at, and that it is appropriate and adapted to that end. This we have not been able to see in this law, and we must, therefore, pronounce it unconstitutional and void. . . .

134. Oliver Wendell Holmes, "The Path of the Law," 1897

Harvard Law Review, 10 (1897), 457-78.

The training of lawyers is a training in logic. The processes of analogy, discrimination, and deduction are those in which they are most at home. The language of judicial decision is mainly the language of logic. And the logical method and form flatter that longing for certainty and for repose which is in every human mind. But certainty generally is illusion, and repose is not the destiny of man. Behind the logical form lies a judgment as to the relative worth and importance of competing legislative grounds, often an inarticulate and unconscious judgment, it is true, and yet the very root and nerve of the whole proceeding. You can give any conclusion a logical form. . . . We do not realize how large a part of our law is open to reconsideration upon a slight change in the habit of the public mind. No concrete proposition is self evident, no matter how ready we may be to accept it, not even Mr. Herbert Spencer's "Every man has a right to do what he wills, provided he interferes not with a like right on the part of his neighbors." . . .

I think that the judges themselves have failed adequately to recognize their duty of weighing considerations of social advantage. The duty is inevitable, and the result of the often proclaimed judicial aversion to deal with such considerations is simply to leave the very ground and foundation of judgments inarticulate, and often unconscious, as I have said. When socialism first began to be talked about, the comfortable classes of the community were a good deal frightened. I suspect that this fear has influenced judicial action both here and in England. . . . I think that something similar has led people who no longer hope to control the legislatures to look to the courts as expounders of the Constitutions, and that in some courts new principles have been discovered outside the bodies of those instruments, which may be generalized into acceptance of the economic doctrines which prevailed about fifty years ago, and a wholesale prohibition of what a tribunal of lawyers does not think about right. I cannot but believe that if the training of lawyers led them habitually to consider more definitely and explicitly the social advantage on which the rule they lay down must be justified, they sometimes would hesitate where now they are confident, and see that really they were taking sides upon debatable and often burning questions.

Government Regulation of Economic Enterprise

THE RAILROADS AND THE REVOLT OF THE GRANGERS

135. Private Property and Public Regulation

Munn v. Illinois, 94 U.S. 113 (1877).

WAITE, C.J.: . . . The Constitution contains no definition of the word "deprive," as used in the Fourteenth Amendment. To determine its signification, therefore, it is necessary to ascertain the effect which usage has given it, when employed in the same or a like connection.

While this provision of the amendment is new in the Constitution of the United States, as a limitation upon the powers of the States, it is old as a principle of civilized government. It is found in Magna Charta, and, in substance if not in form, in nearly or quite all the constitutions that have been from time to time adopted by the several States of the Union. By the Fifth Amendment, it was introduced into the Constitution of the United States as a limitation upon the powers of the national government, and by the Fourteenth, as a guarantee against any encroachment upon an acknowledged right of citizenship by the legislatures of the States. . . .

When one becomes a member of society, he necessarily parts with some rights or privileges which, as an individual not affected by his relations to others, he might retain. "A body politic," as aptly defined in the preamble of the constitution of Massachusetts, "is a social compact by which the whole people covenants with each citizen, and each citizen with the whole people, that all shall be governed by certain laws for the common good." This does not confer power upon the whole people to control rights which are purely and exclusively private. . . ; but it does authorize the establishment of laws requiring each citizen to so conduct himself, and so use his own property, as not unnecessarily to injure another. . . . From this source come the police powers, which, as was said by Mr. Chief Justice Taney in the *License Cases* . . . "are nothing more or less than the powers of government inherent in every sovereignty, . . . that is to say, . . . the power to govern men and things." Under these powers the government regulates the conduct of its citizens one towards another, and the manner in which each shall use his own property, when such regulation becomes necessary for the public good. . . .

From this it is apparent that, down to the time of the adoption of the Fourteenth Amendment, it was not supposed that statutes regulating the use, or even the price of the use, of private property necessarily deprived an owner of his property without due process of law. Under some circumstances they may, but not under all. The amendment does not change the law in this particular: it simply prevents the States from doing that which will operate as such a deprivation.

This brings us to inquire as to the principles upon which this power of regulation rests, in order that we may determine what is within and what without its operative effect. Looking, then, to the common law, from whence came the right which the Constitution protects, we find that when private property is "affected with a public interest, it ceases to be *juris privati* only." This was said by Lord Chief Justice Hale more than two hundred years ago, in his treatise *De Portibus Maris*, 1 Harg. Law Tracts, 78, and has been accepted without objection as an essential element in the law of property ever since. Property does become clothed with a public interest when used in a manner to make it of public consequence, and affect the community at large. When, therefore, one devotes his property to a use in which the public has an interest, he, in effect, grants to the public an interest in that use, and must submit to be controlled by the public for the common good, to the extent of the interest he has thus created. He may withdraw his grant by discontinuing the use; but, so long as he maintains the use, he must submit to the control. . . .

Common carriers exercise a sort of public office, and have duties to perform in which the public is interested. . . . Their business is, therefore, "affected with a public interest," within the meaning of the doctrine which Lord Hale has so forcibly stated.

But we need not go further. Enough has already been said to show that, when private property is devoted to a public use, it is subject to public regulation. It remains only to ascertain whether the warehouses of these plaintiffs in error, and the business which is carried on there, come within the operation of this principle. . . .

It must . . . be conceded that it is a business in which the whole public has a direct and positive interest. It presents, therefore, a case for the application of a long-known and well-established principle in social science, and this statute simply extends the law so as to meet this new development of commercial progress. There is no attempt to compel these owners to grant the public an interest in their property, but to decline their obligations, if they use it in this particular manner. . . .

It is insisted, however, that the owner of property is entitled to a reasonable compensation for its use, even though it be clothed with a public interest, and that what is reasonable is a judicial and not a legislative question.

As has already been shown, the practice has been otherwise. In countries where the common law prevails, it has been customary from time immemorial for the legislature to declare what shall be a reasonable compensation under such circumstances, or perhaps more properly speaking, to fix a maximum beyond which any charge made would be unreasonable. Undoubtedly in mere private contracts, relating to matters in which the public has no interest, what is reasonable must be ascertained judicially. But this is because the legislature has no control over such a contract. So, too, in matters which do not affect the public interest, and as to which legislative control may be exercised . . . the courts must determine what is reasonable. The controlling fact is the power to regulate at all. If that exists, the right to establish the maximum charge, as one of the means of regulation, is implied. . . .

136. *Regulation of interstate commerce "should be done by the Congress."*

Wabash, St. Louis and Pacific Railway Company v. Illinois, 118 U.S. 557 (1886).

MILLER, J.: . . . The obvious injustice of such a rule as this, which railroad companies are by heavy penalties compelled to conform to, in regard to commerce among the States, when applied to transportation which includes Illinois in a long line of carriage through several States, shows the value of the constitutional provision which confides the power of regulating interstate commerce to the Congress of the United States, whose enlarged view of the interests of all the States, and of the railroads concerned, better fits it to establish just and equitable rules.

Of the justice or propriety of the principle which lies at the foundation of the Illinois statute it is not the province of this court to speak. As restricted to a transportation which begins and ends within the limits of the State it may be

very just and equitable, and it certainly is the province of the state legislature to determine that question. But when it is attempted to apply to transportation through an entire series of States a principle of this kind, and each one of the States shall attempt to establish its own rates of transportation, its own methods to prevent discrimination in rates, or to permit it, the deleterious influence upon the freedom of commerce among the States, and upon the transit of goods through those States, cannot be overestimated. That this species of regulation is one which must be, if established at all, of a general and national character, and cannot be safely and wisely remitted to local rules and local regulations, we think is clear from what has already been said. And if it be a regulation of commerce, as we think we have demonstrated it is, and as the Illinois court concedes it to be, it must be of that national character; and the regulation can only appropriately exist by general rules and principles, which demand that it should be done by the Congress of the United States under the commerce clause of the Constitution.

137. *The Maximum Freight Rate Case: Judicial Emasculation of the I. C. C.*

I. C. C. v. Cincinnati, New Orleans, and Texas Pacific Railway Company, 167 U.S. 479 (1897).

BREWER, J.: . . . Before the passage of the act it was generally believed that there were great abuses in railroad management and railroad transportation, and the grave question which Congress had to consider was how those abuses should be corrected and what control should be taken of the business of such corporations. The present inquiry is limited to the question as to what it determined should be done with reference to the matter of rates. There were three obvious and dissimilar courses open for consideration. Congress might itself prescribe the rates; or it might commit to some subordinate tribunal this duty; or it might leave with the companies the right to fix rates, subject to regulations and restrictions, as well as to that rule which is as old as the existence of common carriers, to wit, that rates must be reasonable. There is nothing in the act fixing rates. Congress did not attempt to exercise that power, and, if we examine the legislative and public history of the day, it is apparent that there was no serious thought of doing so.

The question debated is whether it vested in the Commission the power and the duty to fix rates; and the fact that this is a debatable question, and has been most strenuously and earnestly debated, is very persuasive that it did not. The grant of such a power is never to be implied. The power itself is so vast and comprehensive, so largely affecting the rights of carrier and shipper, as well as indirectly all commercial transactions, the language by which the power is given

had been so often used and was so familiar to the legislative mind and is capable of such definite and exact statement, that no just rule of construction would tolerate a grant of such power by mere implication. . . .

It will be perceived that in this case the Interstate Commerce Commission assumed the right to prescribe rates which should control in the future, and this application to the court was for a mandamus to compel the companies to comply with their decision; that is, to abide by their legislative determination as to the maximum rates to be observed in the future. Now, nowhere in the Interstate Commerce Act do we find words giving to the Commission power to "increase or reduce any of the rates"; "to establish rates of charges"; "to make and fix reasonable and just rates of freight and passenger tariffs"; "to make a schedule of reasonable maximum rates of charges"; "to fix tables of maximum charges"; to compel the carrier "to adopt such rate, charge or classification as said commissioners shall declare to be equitable and reasonable." The power, therefore, is not expressly given. . . .

We have, therefore, these considerations presented: First. The power to prescribe a tariff or rates for carriage by a common carrier is a legislative and not an administrative or judicial function, and, having respect to the large amount of property invested in railroads, the various companies engaged therein, the thousands of miles of road, and the millions of tons of freight carried, the varying and diverse conditions attaching to such carriage, is a power of supreme delicacy and importance. Second. That Congress has transferred such a power to any administrative body is not to be presumed or implied from any doubtful and uncertain language. The words and phrases efficacious to make such a delegation of power are well understood, and have been frequently used, and, if Congress had intended to grant such a power to the Interstate Commerce Commission it cannot be doubted that it would have used language open to no misconstruction, but clear and direct. Third. Incorporating into a statute the common law obligation resting upon the carrier to make all its charges reasonable and just, and directing the Commission to execute and enforce the provisions of the act, does not by implication carry to the Commission, or invest it with the power to exercise, the legislative function of prescribing rates which shall control in the future. Fourth. Beyond the inference which irresistibly follows from the omission to grant in express terms to the commission this power of fixing rates is the clear language of section 6, recognizing the right of the carrier to establish rates, to increase or reduce them, and prescribing the conditions upon which such increase or reduction may be made, and requiring, as the only conditions of its action, first, publication; and, second, the filing of the tariff with the Commission. The grant to the Commission of the power to prescribe the form of the schedules, and to direct the place and manner of publication of joint rates, thus specifying the scope and limit of its functions in this respect, strengthens the conclusion that the power to prescribe rates or fix any tariff for the future is not among the powers granted to the Commission. . . .

Our conclusion, then, is that Congress has not conferred upon the Commission the legislative power of prescribing rates either maximum or minimum or absolute. As it did not give the express power to the Commission, it did not intend to secure the same result indirectly by empowering that tribunal to determine what in reference to the past was reasonable and just, whether as maximum, minimum or absolute, and then enable it to obtain from the courts a peremptory order that in the future the railroad companies should follow the rates thus determined to have been in the past reasonable and just. . . .

138. The I. C. C. Act is "protection against hasty . . . legislation hostile to railroad interests."

Richard S. Olney to Charles C. Perkins, December 28, 1892, Letterbook, IV, 353-4, Olney Papers (Library of Congress).

My impression would be that, looking at the matter from a railroad point of view exclusively, it would not be a wise thing to undertake to abolish the [Interstate Commerce] Commission. The attempt would not be likely to succeed—if it did not succeed and were made on the ground of the inefficiency and uselessness of the Commission, the result would very probably be giving it the powers it now lacks. The Commission, as its functions have now been limited by the Courts, is, or can be made of great use to the railroads. It satisfies the popular clamor for a government supervision of railroads, at the same time that the supervision is almost entirely nominal. Further, the older such a commission gets to be, the more inclined it will be found to be to take the business and railroad view of things. It thus becomes a sort of barrier between the railroad corporations and the people and a sort of protection against hasty and crude legislation hostile to railroad interests. The Commission costs something, of course. But so long as its powers are advisory merely, for the reasons just stated, it strikes me it is well worth the money. The part of wisdom is not to destroy the Commission, but to utilize it. . . .

MONITORING THE MENACE OF MONOPOLY

139. *"Commerce succeeds to manufacture, and is not a part of it."*

U.S. v. E. C. Knight, 156 U.S. 1 (1895).

FULLER, C.J.: . . . The fundamental question is, whether conceding that the existence of a monopoly in manufacture is established by the evidence, that monopoly can be directly suppressed under the act of Congress in the mode attempted by this bill. . . .

Doubtless the power to control the manufacture of a given thing involves in a certain sense the control of its disposition, but this is a secondary and not the primary sense; and although the exercise of that power may result in bringing the operation of commerce into play, it does not control it, and affects it only incidentally and indirectly. Commerce succeeds to manufacture, and is not a part of it. The power to regulate commerce is the power to prescribe the rule by which commerce shall be governed, and is a power independent of the power to suppress monopoly. But it may operate in repression of monopoly whenever it comes within the rules by which commerce is governed or whenever the transaction is itself a monopoly of commerce.

It is vital that the independence of the commercial power and of the police power, and the delimitation between them, however sometimes perplexing, should always be recognized and observed, for while the one furnishes the strongest bond of union, the other is essential to the autonomy of the States as required by our dual form of government; and acknowledged evils, however grave and urgent they may appear to be, had better be borne, than the risk be run, in the effort to suppress them, of more serious consequences by resort to expedients of even doubtful constitutionality.

It will be perceived how far-reaching the proposition is that the power of dealing with a monopoly directly may be exercised by the general government whenever interstate or international commerce may be ultimately affected. The regulation of commerce applies to the subjects of commerce, and not to matters of internal police. Contracts to buy, sell, or exchange goods to be transported among the several States, the transportation and its instrumentalities, and articles bought, sold, or exchanged for the purposes of such transit among the States, or put in the way of transit, may be regulated, but this is because they form part of interstate trade or commerce. The fact that an article is manufactured for export to another State does not of itself make it an article of interstate commerce, and the intent of the manufacturer does not determine the time when the article or product passes from the control of the State and belongs to commerce. . . .

Contracts, combinations, or conspiracies to control domestic enterprise in manufacture, agriculture, mining production in all its forms, or to raise or lower prices or wages, might unquestionably tend to restrain external as well as domestic trade, but the restraint would be an indirect result, however inevitable and whatever its extent, and such result would not necessarily determine the object of the contract, combination, or conspiracy.

Again, all the authorities agree that in order to vitiate a contract or combination it is not essential that its result should be a complete monopoly; it is sufficient if it really tends to that end and to deprive the public of the advantages which flow from free competition. Slight reflection will show that if the national power extends to all contracts and combinations in manufacture, agriculture, mining, and other productive industries, whose ultimate result may affect external commerce, comparatively little of business operations and affairs would be left for state control.

It was in the light of well-settled principles that the act of July 2, 1890 was framed. Congress did not attempt thereby to assert the power to deal with monopoly directly as such; or to limit and restrict the rights of corporations created by the States or the citizens of the States in the acquisition, control, or disposition of property; or to regulate or prescribe the price or prices at which such property or the products thereof should be sold; or to make criminal the acts of persons in the acquisition and control of property which the States of their residence or creation sanctioned or permitted. Aside from the provisions applicable where Congress might exercise municipal power, what the law struck at was combinations, contracts, and conspiracies to monopolize trade and commerce among the several States or with foreign nations; but the contracts and acts of the defendants related exclusively to the acquisition of the Philadelphia refineries and the business of sugar refining in Pennsylvania, and bore no direct relation to commerce between the States or with foreign nations. The object was manifestly private gain in the manufacture of the commodity, but not through the control of interstate or foreign commerce. It is true that the bill alleged that the products of these refineries were sold and distributed among the several States, and that all the companies were engaged in trade or commerce with the several States and with foreign nations; but this was no more than to say that trade and commerce served manufacture to fulfil its function. . . . There was nothing in the proofs to indicate any intention to put a restraint upon trade or commerce, and the fact, as we have seen, that trade or commerce might be indirectly affected was not enough to entitle complainants to a decree. . . .

140. *Circuit Judge Woods Brings Labor Unions Under the Sherman Act*

U.S. v. Debs et al, 64 Fed. 724 (1894).

WOODS, Circuit Judge: . . . The position of the defendants in respect to this statute, as stated in one of the briefs, is that it "is directed at capital," "at dangers very generally supposed to result from vast aggregations of capital," that "the evil aimed at is one of a contractual character, and not of force and violence." . . . It is said we may gather from the debates in congress, as from any other source, "the history of the evil which the legislation was intended to remedy." Doubt- less this is often true; and in this instance it is perhaps apparent that the original measure, as proposed in the senate, "was directed wholly against trusts, and not at organizations of labor in any form." But it also appears that before the bill left the senate its title had been changed, and material additions made to the text; and it is worthy of note that a proviso to the effect that the act should not be construed to apply "to any arrangements, agreements or combinations made between laborers with a view of lessening hours of labor or of increasing their wages, nor to any arrangements, agreements or combinations among persons engaged in agriculture made with the view of enhancing the price of agricultural . . . products" was not adopted. Such an amendment, doubtless, was not necessary in order to exclude agreements and arrangements of the kind mentioned; but the offering of the proposition shows that the possible application of the statute to cases not in the nature of trusts or monopolies, and in which workmen or farmers should be concerned, was not overlooked. But it is more significant that, upon the introduction of the bill into the house, the chairman of the judiciary committee . . . made the following statement: "Now just what contracts, what combinations in the form of trusts, or what conspiracies will be in restraint of trade or commerce, mentioned in the bill, will not be known until the courts have construed and interpreted this provision."

It is therefore the privilege and duty of the court, uncontrolled by considerations drawn from other sources, to find the meaning of the statute in the terms of its provisions, interpreted by the settled rules of construction. That the original design to suppress trusts and monopolies created by contract or combination in the form of trust, which of course would be of a "contractual character" was adhered to, is clear; but it is equally clear that a further and more comprehensive purpose came to be entertained, and was embodied in the final form of the enactment. Combinations are condemned, not only when they take the form of trusts, but in whatever form found, if they be in restraint of trade. That is the effect of the words "or otherwise." . . . Any proposed restraint of trade, though it be in itself innocent, if it is to be accomplished by conspiracy, is unlawful. . . .

I have not failed, I think, to appreciate the just force of the argument to the contrary, of my opinion,—it has sometimes entangled me in doubt,—but my conclusion is clear, that under the act of 1890, the court had jurisdiction of the case presented in the application, and that the injunction granted was not without authority of law, nor for any reason invalid. . . .

141. *The Court exercises "the strong arm of the national government."*

In re Debs, 158 U.S. 564 (1895).

BREWER, J.: . . . As, under the Constitution, power over interstate commerce and the transportation of the mails is vested in the national government, and Congress by virtue of such grant has assumed actual and direct control, it follows that the national government may prevent any unlawful and forcible interference therewith. . . .

The entire strength of the nation may be used to enforce in any part of the land the full and free exercise of all national powers and the security of all rights entrusted by the Constitution to its care. The strong arm of the national government may be put forth to brush away all obstructions to the freedom of interstate commerce or the transportation of the mails. If the emergency arises, the army of the Nation, and all its militia, are at the service of the Nation to compel obedience to its laws. . . .

But . . . is there no other alternative than the use of force on the part of the executive authorities whenever obstructions arise to the freedom of interstate commerce or the transportation of the mails? Is the army the only instrument by which rights of the public can be enforced and the peace of the nation preserved? Grant that any public nuisance may be forcibly abated either at the instance of the authorities, or by any individual suffering private damage therefrom, the existence of this right of forcible abatement is not inconsistent with nor does it destroy the right of appeal in an orderly way to the court for a judicial determination, and an exercise of their powers by writ of injunction and otherwise to accomplish the same result. . . .

The national government, given by the Constitution power to regulate interstate commerce, has by express statute assumed jurisdiction over such commerce when carried upon railroads. It is charged, therefore, with the duty of keeping those highways of interstate commerce free from obstruction, for it has always been recognized as one of the powers and duties of a government to remove obstructions from the highway under its control. . . .

Summing up our conclusions, we hold that the government of the United States is one having jurisdiction over every foot of soil within its territory, and acting directly upon each citizen; that while it is a government of enumerated powers, it has within the limits of those powers all the attributes of sovereignty; that to it is committed power over interstate commerce and the transmission of the mail; that the powers thus conferred upon the national government are not dormant, but have been assumed and put into practical exercise by the legislation of Congress; that in the exercise of those powers it is competent for the nation to remove all obstructions upon highways, natural or artificial, to the passage of interstate commerce or the carrying of the mail; that while it may be competent for the government (through the executive branch and in the use of the entire executive power of the nation) to forcibly remove all such obstructions, it is equally within its competency to appeal to the civil courts for an inquiry and determination as to the existence and character of any alleged obstructions, and if such are found

to exist, or theaten to occur, to invoke the powers of these courts to remove or restrain such obstruction; that the jurisdiction of courts to interfere in such matters by injunction is one recognized from ancient times and by indubitable authority; that such jurisdiction is not ousted by the fact that the obstructions are accompanied by or consist of acts in themselves violations of the criminal law; that the proceeding by injunction is of a civil character, and may be enforced by proceedings in contempt; that such proceedings are not in execution of the criminal laws of the land; that the penalty for a violation of injunction is no substitute for and no defense to a prosecution for any criminal offenses committed in the course of such violation; that the complaint filed in this case clearly showed an existing obstruction of artificial highways for the passage of interstate commerce and the transmission of the mail—an obstruction not only temporarily existing, but threatening to continue; that under such complaint the circuit court had power to issue its process of injunction; that it having been issued and served on these defendants, the circuit court had authority to inquire whether its orders had been disobeyed, and when it found that they had been, then to proceed under section 725, Revised Statutes, which grants power "to punish by fine or imprisonment, . . . disobedience, . . . by any party . . . or other person, to any lawful writ, process, order, rule, decree or command," and enter the order of punishment complained of; and, finally, that, the circuit court, having full jurisdiction in the premises, its finding of the fact of disobedience is not open to review on *habeas corpus* in this or any other court. . . .

We enter into no examination of the [Sherman] act of July 2, 1890 . . . upon which the Circuit Court relied mainly to sustain its jurisdiction. It must not be understood from this that we dissent from the conclusions of that court in reference to the scope of the act, but simply that we prefer to rest our judgment on the broader ground which has been discussed in this opinion, believing it of importance that the principles underlying it should be fully stated and affirmed.

The petition for a writ of *habeas corpus* is denied.

THE INCOME TAX AND THE GOSPEL OF WEALTH

142. *The Court Rules that Income Taxes Are an Assault on Capital*

Pollock v. Farmers' Loan and Trust Company 158 U.S. 601 (1895).

FULLER, C.J.: . . . Our previous decision was confined to the consideration of the validity of the tax on the income from real estate, and on the income from municipal bonds. . . .

We are now permitted to broaden the field of inquiry, and to determine to which of the two great classes a tax upon a person's entire income, whether derived from rents or products, or otherwise, of real estate, or from bonds, stocks, or other forms of personal property, belongs; and we are unable to conclude that the enforced subtraction from the yield of all the owner's real or personal property, in the manner prescribed, is so different from a tax on the property itself, that it is not a direct, but an indirect, tax in the meaning of the Constitution. . . .

We know of no reason for holding otherwise than that the words "direct taxes" on the one hand, and "duties, imposts and excises," on the other, were used in the Constitution in their natural and obvious sense. Nor, in arriving at what those terms embrace, do we perceive any ground for enlarging them beyond, or narrowing them within, their natural and obvious import at the time the Constitution was framed and ratified. . . .

The Constitution prohibits any direct tax, unless in proportion to numbers as ascertained by the census, and, in the light of the circumstances to which we have referred, is it not an evasion of that prohibition to hold that a general unapportioned tax, imposed upon all property owners as a body for or in respect of their property, is not direct, in the meaning of the Constitution, because confined to the income therefrom?

Whatever the speculative views of political economists or revenue reformers may be, can it be properly held that the Constitution, taken in its plain and obvious sense, and with due regard to the circumstances attending the formation of the government, authorizes a general unapportioned tax on the products of the farm and the rents of real estate, although imposed merely because of ownership, and with no possible means of escape from payment, as belonging to a totally different class from that which includes the property from whence the income proceeds?

There can be but one answer, unless the constitutional restriction is to be treated as utterly illusory and futile, and the object of its framers defeated. We find it impossible to hold that a fundamental requisition deemed so important as to be enforced by two provisions, one affirmative and one negative, can be refined away by forced distinctions between that which gives value to property and the property itself.

Nor can we perceive any ground why the same reasoning does not apply to capital in personalty held for the purpose of income, or ordinarily yielding income, and to the income therefrom. . . .

Personal property of some kind is of general distribution, and so are incomes, though the taxable range thereof might be narrowed through large exemptions. . . .

Nor are we impressed with the contention that, because in the four instances in which the power of direct taxation has been exercised, Congress did not see fit, for reasons of expediency, to levy a tax on personalty, this amounts to such a practical construction of the Constitution that the power did not exist, that we must regard ourselves bound by it. We should regret to be compelled to hold the powers of the general government thus restricted, and certainly we cannot accede to the idea that the Constitution has become weakened by a particular course of inaction under it. . . .

We have unanimously held in this case that, so far as this law operates on the receipts from municipal bonds, it cannot be sustained, because it is a tax on the power of the States and on their instrumentalities to borrow money, and consequently repugnant to the Constitution. But, if, as contended, the interest, when received, has become merely money in the recipient's pocket, and taxable, as such, without reference to the source from which it came, the question is immaterial whether it could have been originally taxed at all or not. This was admitted by the Attorney General, with characteristic candor; and it follows that if the revenue derived from municipal bonds cannot be taxed, because the source cannot be, the same rule applies to revenue from any other source not subject to the tax, and the lack of power to levy any but an apportioned tax on real and personal property equally exists as to the revenue therefrom.

Admitting that this act taxes the income of property, irrespective of its source, still we cannot doubt that such a tax is necessarily a direct tax in the meaning of the Constitution. . . .

The power to tax real and personal property and the income from both, there being an apportionment, is conceded; that such a tax is a direct tax in the meaning of the Constitution has not been, and, in our judgment, cannot be successfully denied; and yet we are thus invited to hesitate in the enforcement of the mandate of the Constitution, which prohibits Congress from laying a direct tax on the revenue from property of the citizen without regard to state lines, and in such manner that the States cannot intervene by payment in regulation of their own resources, lest a government of delegated powers should be found to be, not less powerful, but less absolute, than the imagination of the advocate had supposed.

We are not here concerned with the question whether an income tax be or be not desirable, nor whether such a tax would enable the government to diminish taxes on consumption and duties on imports, and to enter upon what may be believed to be a reform of its fiscal and commercial system. Questions of that character belong to the controversies of political parties, and cannot be settled by judicial decision. In these cases our province is to determine whether this income tax on the revenue from property does or does not belong to the class of direct taxes. If it does, it is, being unapportioned, in violation of the Constitution, and we must so declare. . . .

Our conclusions may, therefore, be summed up as follows:

First. We adhere to the opinion already announced, that, taxes on real estate being indisputably direct taxes, taxes on the rents or income of real estate are equally direct taxes.

Second. We are of opinion that taxes on personal property, or on the income of personal property, are likewise direct taxes.

Third. The tax imposed by sections twenty-seven to thirty-seven, inclusive, of the act of 1894, so far as it falls on the income of real estate and of personal property, being a direct tax within the meaning of the Constitution, and, therefore, unconstitutional and void because not apportioned according to representation, all those sections, constituting one entire scheme of taxation, are necessarily invalid.

Judicial Development of Due Process as a Limitation on Public Control

THE FOURTEENTH AMENDMENT AND STATE REGULATORY POWER

143. *The Corporation as a Person*

Santa Clara County v. Southern Pacific Railroad Company, 118 U.S. 394 (1886).

One of the points made and discussed at length in the brief of counsel for defendants in error was that "Corporations are persons within the meaning of the Fourteenth Amendment to the Constitution of the United States." Before argument

Mr. Chief Justice Waite said: The Court does not wish to hear argument on the question whether the provision in the Fourteenth Amendment to the Constitution, which forbids a State to deny to any person within its jurisdiction the equal protection of the laws, applies to these corporations. We are all of the opinion that it does.

DUE PROCESS AND RAILROAD RATE MAKING

144. *To be reasonable, rates must yield a "fair return."*

Smyth v. Ames, 169 U.S. 466 (1898).

HARLAN, J.: . . . By the Fourteenth Amendment, it is provided that no State shall deprive any person of property without due process of law nor deny to any person within its jurisdiction the equal protection of the laws. That corporations are persons within the meaning of this Amendment is now settled. . . . What amounts to deprivation of property without due process of law or what is a denial of the equal protection of the laws is often difficult to determine, especially where the question relates to the property of a *quasi* public corporation and the extent to which it may be subjected to public control. But this court, speaking by Chief Justice Waite, has said that, while a State has power to fix the charges for railroad companies for the transportation of persons and property within its own jurisdiction, unless restrained by valid contract, or unless what is done amounts to a regulation of foreign or interstate commerce, such power is not without limit; and that, "under pretense of regulating fares, and freights, the state cannot require a railroad corporation to carry persons or property without reward; neither can it do that which in law amounts to a taking of private property for public use without just compensation, or without due process of law." . . .

The plaintiffs contended that a railroad company is entitled to exact such charges for transportation as will enable it, at all times, not only to pay operating expenses, but also to meet the interest regularly accruing upon all its outstanding obligations, and justify a dividend upon all its stock; and that to prohibit it from maintaining rates or charges for transportation adequate to *all* those ends will deprive it of its property without due process of law, and deny to it the equal protection of the laws. This contention . . . should not be passed without examination.

In our opinion, the broad proposition advanced by counsel involves some misconception of the relations between the public and a railroad corporation. It is unsound in that it practically excludes from consideration the fair value of the property used, omits altogether any consideration of the right of the public to be exempt from unreasonable exactions, and makes the interests of the corporation maintaining a public highway the sole test in determining whether the rates established by or for it are such as may be rightfully prescribed as between it and the public. . . .

We hold, however, that the basis of all calculations as to the reasonableness of rates to be charged by a corporation maintaining a highway under legislative sanction must be the fair value of the property being used by it for the convenience of the public. And, in order to ascertain that value, the original cost of construction, the amount expended in permanent improvements, the amount and market value of its bonds and stocks, the present as compared with the original cost of construction, the probable earning capacity of the property, under particular rates prescribed by statute, and the sum required to meet operating expenses, are all matters for consideration, and are to be given such weight as may be just and right in each case. We do not say that there may not be other matters to be regarded in estimating the value of the property. What the company is entitled to ask is a fair return upon the value of that which it employs for the public convenience. On the other hand, what the public is entitled to demand is that no more be exacted from it for the use of a public highway than the services rendered by it are **reasonably worth**. . . .

CHAPTER XVI

Imperialism and the Constitution

OLLOWING the Civil War the powers of the federal government expanded not only in the field of domestic economic regulation but also in the field of foreign policy. The spirit of resurgent nationalism, reflected as early as 1867 in the purchase of Alaska, was also expressed by the Supreme Court in decisions implying the existence of inherent sovereign powers in foreign affairs. In *Chae Chan Ping v. U.S.* (1889), the Court asserted that the United States is "one nation, invested with powers which belong to independent nations." Four years later in Fong Yue Ting (1893), the Court, in another Chinese exclusion case, asserted that "the United States are a sovereign and independent nation, and are vested by the Constitution with the entire control of international relations."

The issues in these cases were simple compared with the political and constitutional complexities posed by the acquisition of a colonial empire as a result of "the splendid little war with Spain." The status of continental territories had been defined by the Northwest Ordinance even before the adoption of the Constitution, and the Constitution authorized Congress "to dispose of and make all needful Rules and Regulations respecting the Territory or other Property belonging to the United States." Alaska, the first non-contiguous territory, presented few new problems, and none at all of governing alien peoples. In 1898, however, the United States, by the annexation of the Hawaiian Islands and the conquest of

Puerto Rico and the Philippines, began exercising sovereign authority over millions of alien subjects. Theoretically, the Treaty of Paris solved the problem simply, by providing that "the civil rights and political status of the native inhabitants hereby ceded to the United States shall be determined by Congress." But this provision did not delineate the nature and extent of congressional power; did it mean that Congress could exercise plenary power without extending the liberties guaranteed by the Constitution, or did it mean that Congress was subject to constitutional limitations in dealing with the newly acquired possessions? Two basic problems arose immediately: (1) does annexed territory become an integral part of the United States, and (2) do the constitutional guarantees also apply to the inhabitants of the territories?

In the Insular Cases, the Court wrestled inconclusively with these problems. *DeLima v. Bidwell* (1901) involved an American importer of Puerto Rican sugar who protested against the payment of tariff duties. The Court ruled that Puerto Rico was no longer a foreign nation but a territory of the United States and ordered the refunding of the duties. By this time, however, Congress had passed the Foraker Act, establishing a civil government for Puerto Rico and levying duties equal to 15 per cent of the regular tariff. Since the Constitution requires tariff uniformity, this clearly indicated that Congress did not consider the island a part of the United States. In *Downes v. Bidwell* (No. 145), the Court upheld Congress, ruling that although Puerto Rico was not a foreign nation, neither was it exactly a part of the United States in a domestic sense. Justice Brown, in the majority opinion, held that Puerto Rico "is a territory appurtenant and belonging to the United States, but not a part of the United States." In Justice White's concurring opinion, the majority evolved the new constitutional doctrine of "incorporation" to justify its negative answer to the popular question of the day: "Does the Constitution follow the flag?" Approving the expansion of American territory and the contraction of the Constitution, White ruled that constitutional provisions did not apply in non-contiguous territory until it was incorporated into the United States by Congress. Mr. Dooley, in one of his shrewd comments lampooning the Court, concluded that "no matter whether the constitution follows the flag or not, th' Supreme Court follows th' illiction returns."

The second problem, involving civil and political rights, came before the Court in a series of cases decided between 1903 and 1922. Drawing a legalistic distinction between fundamental liberties and purely procedural rights, the Court concluded that Congress could not deny the fundamental liberties in any territory, incorporated or unincorporated, nor could it deny procedural rights in incorporated territories. But in unincorporated territories, Congress could extend procedural guarantees at its discretion. The chief difficulty with this delineation, however, was the Court's failure to specify what constituted incorporation. Chief Justice Fuller had deplored the lack of constitutional clarity when Justice White first presented the theory of "incorporation." In his dissent in *Downes*, Fuller had denied that once "an organized and settled province of another sovereignty is acquired by the United States, Congress has the power to keep it, like a disembodied shape, in an intermediate state of ambiguous existence for an indefinite period; and, more than that, that after it has been called from that limbo, commerce with it is absolutely subject to the will of Congress, irrespective of constitutional provisions." But a more candid summary of the Court's attitude was expressed in the *Review of Reviews:* "The decision of the Supreme Court means that we are not to be hampered in our serious policies by the ingenious use of logic in the interpretation of an ancient document that was not intended to hamper posterity."

Thus far, at least, the Court has been content to avoid a definition of "incorporation," preferring instead to settle each question separately after considering the specifications and intentions of congressional enactments. The Mankichi case (No. 146) raised the question of whether guarantees of grand jury indictment and jury trial, in the Bill of Rights, extended to Hawaii. The Court decided that since the annexation of Hawaii did not make it an incorporated territory, these formal rights did not apply. In *Dorr v. U.S.*, the Court reached a similar decision for the Philippines, disregarding, as it had in Mankichi, a vigorous dissent by Justice Harlan (No. 147). As for Alaska, the Rassmussen case extended these guarantees, maintaining that Congress had incorporated that territory by the treaty of acquisition and subsequent legislation (No. 148). A similar issue in Puerto Rico was complicated by the passage of the Organic Act of 1917 conferring citizenship on the inhabitants. Balzac, a newspaper editor convicted of criminal libel, contended that this Act incorporated the island, and hence established jury trial. This fact the Court denied (*Balzac v. Puerto Rico*, 1922).

145. *Status of Non-contiguous Territories*

Downes v. Bidwell, 182 U.S. 244 (1901).

BROWN, J.: This case involves the question whether merchandise brought into the port of New York from Porto Rico, since the passage of the Foraker act, is exempt from duty, notwithstanding the third section of that act, which requires the payment of "fifteen per centum of the duties which are required to be levied, collected and paid upon like articles of merchandise imported from foreign countries." . . .

In the case of *De Lima v. Bidwell* just decided, we held that upon the ratification of the treaty of peace with Spain, Porto Rico ceased to be a foreign country, and became a territory of the United States, and that duties were no longer collectible upon merchandise brought from that island. We are now asked to hold that it became a part of the *United States* within that provision of the Constitution which declares that "all duties, imposts and excises shall be uniform throughout the United States." . . . If Porto Rico be a

part of the United States, the Foraker act imposing duties upon its products is unconstitutional, not only by reason of a violation of the uniformity clause, but because by section 9 "vessels bound to or from one State" cannot "be obliged to enter, clear or pay duties in another."

The case also involves the broader question whether the revenue clauses of the Constitution extend of their own force to our newly acquired territories. The Constitution itself does not answer the question. Its solution must be found in the nature of the government created by that instrument, in the opinion of its contemporaries, in the practical construction put upon it by Congress and in the decisions of this court. . . .

To sustain the judgment in the case under consideration it by no means becomes necessary to show that none of the articles of the Constitution apply to the Island of Porto Rico. There is a clear distinction between such prohibitions as go to the very root of the power of Congress to act at all, irrespective of time or place, and such as are operative only "throughout the United States" or among the several States.

Thus, when the Constitution declares that "no bill of attainder or *ex post facto* law shall be passed," and that "no title of nobility shall be granted by the United States," it goes to the competency of Congress to pass a bill *of that description.* Perhaps the same remark may apply to the First Amendment. . . . We do not wish, however, to be understood as expressing an opinion how far the bill of rights contained in the first eight amendments is of general and how far of local application.

Upon the other hand, when the Constitution declares that all duties shall be uniform "throughout the United States," it becomes necessary to inquire whether there be any territory over which Congress has jurisdiction which is not a part of the "United States," by which term we understand the *States* whose people *united* to form the Constitution, and such as have since been admitted to the Union upon an equality with them. Not only did the people in adopting the Thirteenth Amendment thus recognize a distinction between the United States and "any place subject to their jurisdiction," but Congress itself, in the Act of March 27, 1804, . . . providing for the proof of public records, applied the provisions of the act, not only to "every court and office within the United States," but to the "courts and offices of the respective territories of the United States and countries subject to the jurisdiction of the United States." . . .

Unless these words are to be rejected as meaningless, we must treat them as a recognition by Congress of the fact that there may be territories subject to the jurisdiction of the United States, which are not *of* the United States. . . .

Indeed, the practical interpretation put by Congress upon the Constitution has been long continued and uniform to the effect that the Constitution is applicable to territories acquired by purchase or conquest only when and so far as Congress shall so direct. . . .

We are also of opinion that the power to acquire territory by treaty implies, not only the power to govern such territory, but to prescribe upon what terms the United States will receive its inhabitants, and what their *status* shall be in what Chief Justice Marshall termed the "American Empire." . . .

It is obvious that in the annexation of outlying and distant possessions grave questions will arise from differences of race, habits, laws and customs of the people, and from differences of soil, climate and production, which may require action on the part of Congress that would be quite unnecessary in the annexation of contiguous territory inhabited only by people of the same race, or by scattered bodies of native Indians.

We suggest, without intending to decide, that there may be a distinction between certain natural rights enforced in the Constitution by prohibitions against interference with them, and what may be termed artificial or remedial rights which are peculiar to our own system of jurisprudence. Of the former class are the rights to one's own religious opinions and to a public expression of them, or, as sometimes said, to worship God according to the dictates of one's own conscience; the right to personal liberty and individual property; to freedom of speech and of the press; to free access to courts of justice, to due process of law, and to an equal protection of the laws; to immunities from unreasonable searches and seizures, as well as cruel and unusual punishments; and to such other immunities as are indispensable to a free government. Of the latter case are the rights to citizenship, to suffrage, *Minor v. Happersett,* . . . and to the particular methods of procedure pointed out in the Constitution, which are peculiar to Anglo-Saxon jurisprudence, and some of which have already been held by the States to be unnecessary to the proper protection of individuals.

Whatever may be finally decided by the American people as to the *status* of these islands and their inhabitants—whether they shall be introduced into the sisterhood of States or be permitted to form independent governments—it does not follow that, in the meantime, awaiting that decision, the people are in the matter of personal rights unprotected by the provisions of our Constitution and subject to the merely arbitrary control of Congress. Even if regarded as aliens, they are entitled under the principles of the Constitution to be protected in life, liberty and property. This has been frequently held by this court in respect to the Chinese, even when aliens, not possessed of the political rights of citizens of the United States. . . . We do not desire, however, to anticipate the difficulties which would naturally arise in this connection, but merely to disclaim any intention to hold that the inhabitants of these territories are subject to an unrestrained power on the part of Congress to deal with them upon the theory that they have no rights which it is bound to respect. . . .

The liberality of Congress in legislating the Constitution into all our contiguous territories has undoubtedly fostered the impression that it went there by its own force, but there is nothing in the Constitution itself, and little in the interpretation put upon it, to confirm that impression. . . . The executive and legislative departments of the government have for more than a century interpreted this silence as precluding the idea that the Constitution attached to these territores as soon as acquired, and unless such interpretation be manifestly contrary to the letter or spirit of the Constitution, it should be followed by the judicial department. . . .

Patriotic and intelligent men may differ widely as to the desirableness of this or that acquisition, but this is solely a political question. We can only consider this aspect of the case so far as to say that no construction of the Constitution should be adopted which would prevent Congress from considering each case upon its merits, unless the language of the instrument imperatively demand it. A false step at this time might be fatal to the development of what Chief Justice Marshall called the American Empire. Choice in some cases, the natural gravitation of small bodies towards large ones in others, the result of a successful war in still others, may bring about conditions which would render the annexation of distant possessions desirable. If those possessions are inhabited by alien races, differing from us in religion, customs, laws, methods of taxation and modes of thought, the administration of government and justice, according to Anglo-Saxon principles, may for a time be impossible; and the question at once arises whether large concessions ought not to be made for a time, that, ultimately, our own theories may be carried out, and the blessings of a free government under the Constitution extended to them. We decline to hold that there is anything in the Constitution to forbid such action.

We are therefore of opinion that the Island of Porto Rico is a territory appurtenant and belonging to the United States, but not a part of the United States within the revenue clauses of the Constitution; that the Foraker act is constitutional, so far as it imposes duties upon imports from such island, and that the plaintiff cannot recover back the duties exacted in this case.

146. *Fundamental and Procedural Rights in Unincorporated Territories*

Hawaii v. Mankichi, 190 U.S. 197 (1903).

BROWN, J.: The question involved in this case is an extremely simple one. The difficulty is in fixing upon the principles applicable to its solution. By a joint resolution adopted by Congress, July 7, 1898 . . . and with the consent of the Republic of Hawaii, . . . the Hawaiian Islands and their dependencies were annexed "as a part of the Territory of the United States, and subject to the sovereign dominion thereof," with the following condition: "The municipal legislation of the Hawaiian Islands, not enacted for the fulfillment of the treaties so extinguished, and not inconsistent with this joint resolution *nor contrary to the Constitution of the United States,* nor to any existing treaty of the United States, shall remain in force until the Congress of the United States shall otherwise determine." . . . Under the conditions named in this resolution, the Hawaiian Islands remained under the name of the "Republic of Hawaii" until June 14, 1900, when they were formally incorporated by act of Congress under the name of the "Territory of Hawaii." . . . By this act the Constitution was formally extended to these islands, Sec. 5, and special provisions made for empanelling grand juries, and for unanimous verdicts of petty juries. Sec. 83.

The question is whether, in continuing the municipal legislation of the islands not contrary to the Constitution of the United States, it was intended to abolish at once the criminal procedure theretofore in force upon the islands, and to substitute immediately, and without new legislation, the common law proceedings by grand and petit jury, which had been held applicable to other organized Territories. . . .

By a law passed in 1847, the number of a jury was fixed at twelve, but a verdict might be rendered upon the agreement of nine jurors. The question involved in this case is whether it was intended that this practice should be instantly changed, and the criminal procedure embodied in the Fifth and Sixth Amendments to the Constitution be adopted as of August 12, 1898, when the Hawaiian flag was hauled down and the American flag hoisted in its place.

If the words of the Newlands resolution, adopting the municipal legislation of Hawaii *not contrary to the Constitution of the United States,* be literally applied, the petitioner is entitled to his discharge, since that instrument expressly requires, Amendment 5, that "no person shall be held to answer for a capital or otherwise infamous crime, unless on a presentment or indictment of a grand jury"; and, Amendment 6, that "in all criminal prosecutions the accused shall enjoy the right to a speedy and public trial by an impartial jury of the State and district wherein the crime shall have been committed." But there is another question underlying this and all other rules for the interpretation of statutes, and that is, What was the intention of the legislative body? . . .

If the negative words of the resolution, "nor contrary to the Constitution of the United States," be construed as imposing upon the islands every provision of a Constitution which must have been unfamiliar to a large number of their inhabitants, and for which no previous preparation had been made, the consequences in this particular connection would be that every criminal in the Hawaiian Islands convicted of an infamous offense between August 12, 1898, and June 14, 1900, when the act organizing the territorial government took effect, must be set at large; and every verdict in a civil case rendered by less than a unanimous jury held for naught. Surely, such a result could not have been within the contemplation of Congress. It is equally manifest that such could not have been the intention of the Republic of Hawaii in surrendering its autonomy. Until then it was an independent nation, exercising all the powers and prerogatives of complete sovereignty. It certainly could not have anticipated that, in dealing with another independent nation, and yielding up its sovereignty, it had denuded itself, by a negative pregnant, of all powers of enforcing its criminal laws according to the methods which had been in vogue for sixty years, and was adopting a new procedure for which it had had no opportunity of making preparation. The legislature of the Republic had just adjourned, not to convene again until some time in 1900, and not actually convening until 1901. The resolution on its face bears evidence of having been intended merely for a temporary purpose, and to give time to the Republic to adapt itself to such form of territorial government as should afterwards be adopted in its organic act. . . .

It is not intended here to decide that the words "nor contrary to the Constitution of the United States" are meaningless. Clearly, they would be operative upon any municipal legislation thereafter adopted, and upon any proceedings thereafter had, when the application of the Constitution would not result in the destruction of existing provisions conducive to the peace and good order of the community. . . . Most, if not all, the privileges and immunities contained in the bill of rights of the Constitution were intended to apply from the moment of annexation; but we place our decision of this case upon the ground that the two rights alleged to be violated in this case are not fundamental in their nature, but concern merely a method of procedure which sixty years of practice had shown to be suited to the conditions of the islands, and well calculated to conserve the rights of their citizens to their lives, their property, and their well being. . . .

147. *Justice Harlan Dissents in the Insular Cases*

Insular Cases, 190 U.S. 197, 195 U.S. 138 (1903-04).

HARLAN, J., dissenting in *Mankichi:* I am of the opinion: 1. That when the annexation of Hawaii was completed, the Constitution—without any declaration to that effect by Congress, and without any power of Congress to prevent it—became the supreme law for that country, and, therefore, it forbade the trial and conviction of the accused for murder otherwise than upon a presentment or indictment of a grand jury, and by the unanimous verdict of a petit jury. 2. That if the legality of such trial and conviction is to be tested alone by the Joint Resolution of 1898, then the law is for the accused, because Congress, by that Resolution, abrogated or forbade the enforcement of any municipal law of Hawaii so far as it authorized a trial for an infamous crime otherwise than in the mode prescribed by the Constitution of the United States; and that any other construction of the Resolution is forbidden by its clear, unambiguous words, and is to make, not to interpret, the law.

HARLAN, J., dissenting in *Dorr:* I do not believe now any more than I did when *Hawaii v. Mankichi* . . . was decided, that the provisions of the Federal Constitution as to grand and petit juries relate to mere methods of procedure and are not fundamental in their nature. In my opinion, guaranties for the protection of life, liberty and property, as embodied in the Constitution, are for the benefit of all, of whatever race or nativity, in the States composing the Union, or in any territory, however acquired, over the inhabitants of which the Government of the United States may exercise the powers conferred upon it by the Constitution.

The Constitution declares that *no* person, except in the land or naval forces, shall be held to answer for a capital or otherwise infamous crime, except on the presentment or indictment of a grand jury; and forbids the conviction, in a criminal prosecution, of any person, for any crime, except on the unanimous verdict of a petit jury composed of twelve persons. Necessarily, that mandate was addressed to every one committing crime punishable by the United States. This court, however, holds that these provisions are not fundamental and may be disregarded in any territory acquired in the manner the Philippine Islands were acquired, although, as heretofore decided by this court, they could not be disregarded in what are commonly called the organized territories of the United States. . . . I cannot assent to this interpretation of the Constitution. It is, I submit, so obviously inconsistent with the Constitution that I cannot regard the judgment of the court otherwise than as an amendment of that instrument by judicial construction. . . . No power exists in the judiciary to suspend the operation of the Constitution in any territory governed, as to its affairs and people, by authority of the United States. . . . It is now adjudged that . . . [the jury trial] provision is not fundamental in respect of a part of the people over whom the United States may exercise full legislative, judicial and executive power. . . . Such a mode of constitutional interpretation plays havoc with the old-fashioned ideas of the fathers, who took care to say that the Constitution was the supreme law—supreme everywhere, at all times, and over all persons who are subject to the authority of the United States. . . .

148. *Fundamental and Procedural Rights in Incorporated Territories*

Rassmussen v. U.S., 197 U.S. 516 (1905).

WHITE, J.: The plaintiff in error was indicted for violating section 127 of the Alaska Code, prohibiting the keeping of a disreputable house and punishing the offense by a fine or imprisonment in the county jail. . . .

When the case was called the court announced "that the cause would be tried before a jury composed of six jurors," in accordance with section 171 of the Code for Alaska adopted by Congress. . . .

At the threshold of the case lies the constitutional question whether . . . the provision of the act of Congress in question was repugnant to the Sixth Amendment to the Constitution of the United States. . . .

The validity of the provision in question is . . . sought to be sustained upon the proposition that the Sixth Amendment to the Constitution did not apply to Congress in legislating for Alaska. And this rests upon two contentions which we proceed separately to consider.

1. *Alaska was not incorporated into the United States, and therefore the Sixth Amendment did not control Congress in legislating for Alaska.* . . .

We are brought, then, to determine whether Alaska has been incorporated into the United States as a part thereof, or is simply held, as the Philippine Islands are held, under the sovereignty of the United States as a possession or dependency. . . .

The treaty concerning Alaska, instead of exhibiting, as did the treaty respecting the Philippine Islands, the determination to reserve the question of the status of the acquired territory for ulterior action by Congress, manifested a contrary intention, since it is therein expressly declared . . . that:

"The inhabitants of the ceded territory shall be admitted to the enjoyment of all the rights, advantages, and immunities of citizens of the United States; and shall be maintained and protected in the free enjoyment of their liberty, property and religion."

This declaration, although somewhat changed in phraseology, is the equivalent, as pointed out in *Downes v. Bidwell,* of the formula employed from the beginning to express the purpose to incorporate acquired territory into the United States, especially in the absence of other provisions showing an intention to the contrary. . . .

It follows, then, from the text of the treaty by which Alaska was acquired, from the action of Congress thereunder, and the reiterated decisions of this court, that the proposition that Alaska is not incorporated into and a part of the United States is devoid of merit, and therefore the doctrine settled as to unincorporated territory is inapposite and lends no support to the contention that Congress in legislating for Alaska had authority to violate the express commands of the Sixth Amendment.

This brings us to the second proposition, which is—

2. *That even if Alaska was incorporated into the United States, as it was not an organized territory, therefore the provisions of the Sixth Amendment were not controlling on Congress when legislating for Alaska.*

We do not stop to demonstrate from original considerations the unsoundness of this contention and its irreconcilable conflict with the essential principles upon which our constitutional system of government rests. Nor do we think it is required to point out the inconsistency which would arise between various provisions of the Constitution if the proposition was admitted, or the extreme extension on the one hand, and the undue limitation on the other, of the powers of Congress which would be occasioned by conceding it. This is said, because, in our opinion, the unsoundness of the proposition is conclusively established by a long line of decisions. . . .

The argument by which the decisive force of the cases just cited is sought to be escaped is that, as when the cases were decided there was legislation of Congress extending the Constitution to the District of Columbia or to the particular territory to which a case may have related, therefore the decisions must be taken to have proceeded alone upon the statutes, and not upon the inherent application of the provisions of the Fifth, Sixth, and Seventh Amendments to the District of Columbia or to an incorporated Territory. And, upon the assumption that the cases are distinguishable from the present one upon the basis just stated, the argument proceeds to insist that the Sixth Amendment does not apply to the Territory of Alaska, because section 1891 of the Revised Statutes only extends the Constitution to the organized Territories, in which, it is urged, Alaska is not embraced.

Whilst the premise as to the existence of legislation declaring the extension of the Constitution to the Territories with which the cases were respectively concerned is well founded, the conclusion drawn from that fact is not justified. Without attempting to examine in detail the opinions in the various cases, in our judgment it clearly results from them that they substantially rested upon the proposition that where territory was a part of the United States the inhabitants thereof were entitled to the guarantees of the Fifth, Sixth and Seventh Amendments, and that the act or acts of Congress purporting to extend the Constitution were considered as declaratory merely of a result which existed independently by the inherent operation of the Constitution. . . .

As it conclusively results from the foregoing considerations that the Sixth Amendment to the Constitution was applicable to Alaska, and as of course, being applicable, it was controlling upon Congress in legislating for Alaska, it follows that the provision of the act of Congress under consideration, depriving persons accused of a misdemeanor in Alaska of a right to trial by a common law jury, was repugnant to the Constitution and void. . . .

CHAPTER XVII

Governmental Efforts to Restore Competition

OR nearly fifty years following the Civil War amendments, no basic alterations were made in the form of the federal government. However, constitutional developments of major importance were taking place by the turn of the century. Not the least of these was the revolt against mechanistic concepts of law and the attempt to supplant fixed doctrines with a jurisprudence that combined pragmatic insights and social conscience in dealing with economic and social problems. The shift from the theory that the Constitution belonged to the professional lawyer and the judges to the view that it was everyman's property can be well illustrated by contrasting the remarks of E. J. Phelps, one of the early presidents of the American Bar Association, and Oliver Wendell Holmes, Jr., Theodore Roosevelt's first appointee to the Supreme Court.

In 1879 Phelps declared that the sacred Constitution should not be profaned by public discussion; it should not be "hawked about the country, debated in the newspapers, discussed from the stump, elucidated by pot-house politicians and dunghill editors, or by scholars . . . who have never found leisure for the grace of English grammar or the embellishment of correct spelling." Obviously, the logic of the law could be discovered only by members of bench and bar. To the high priests of the old jurisprudence, the criticism from within the guild by Holmes was heresy. "The life of law," he said as early as 1880, "has not been logic; it has been experience. The felt necessities of the time, the prevalent moral and

political theories, intuitions of public policy, avowed or unconscious, even the prejudices which judges share with their fellow-men, have had a good deal more to do
than the syllogism in determining the rules by which men should be governed."

By 1900 the problem of interpreting the Constitution in dealing with the
complex problems of industrialization was critical. A deep-rooted demand for reform and regulation found a unifying figure in Theodore Roosevelt, who dominated
the national scene from 1901 until 1909. Like Holmes, the new President declared
that the Constitution "must be interpreted, not as a strait-jacket, not as laying the
hand of death upon our development, but as an instrument designed for the life
and healthy growth of the Nation." In reasserting national authority, Roosevelt
stressed the executive branch of the government as the agency of reform, and
utilized executive commissions to curb corporate power. By 1911 the Supreme
Court accepted the doctrine of "administrative discretion" and acknowledged that
commission rulings had the force of law (*U.S. v. Grimaud*).

A revitalized I. C. C. was one of the first results of the Roosevelt leadership.
The Elkins Act of 1903 strengthened the Commission's control over rebates, and
the Hepburn Act of 1906 gave authority to fix just and reasonable maximum railroad rates, which were binding on the carriers. No longer did the Commission have
to go to court to enforce its order. In two early cases involving the Illinois Central
Railroad, the Court first upheld the Commission's fact-finding authority (*Illinois
Central v. I. C. C.*, 1907) and later refused to interfere with the Commission's
policy-making discretion (*I. C. C. v. Illinois Central* [No. 149]). In 1910 Congress
bolstered the Commission's authority by granting it original rate-making power,
and the Court approved this delegation in 1914 (*U.S. v. Atchison, Topeka, and
Santa Fe*).

With the development of effective federal control of railroad rates, railroad lawyers argued that federal regulation excluded state authority over intrastate rates. In the Minnesota Rate Cases (1913), the Court rejected this contention, asserting that a state might properly act in a field where it did not conflict
with federal laws. A year later, in the Shreveport Rate Case (No. 150), Justice
Charles Evans Hughes ruled that the Commission's power extended to intrastate
rates, arguing that local activity affecting interstate commerce came within the
scope of federal power. This "affect" doctrine became a key constitutional device
for extending national authority over widely divergent areas of local economic
activity.

Perhaps Teddy Roosevelt's most widely remembered sobriquet was that of
"Trust Buster." His ambivalence hardly justified this title, as Mr. Dooley in-
cisively pointed out: "Th' trusts, says he [Tiddy] are heejoous monsthers built up
by th' inlightened intherprise ov th' men that have done so much to advance progress in our beloved counthry. . . . On wan hand I wud stamp them undher fut;
on th' other hand, not so fast." Certainly the Court had moved lethargically
enough in the Knight case (Chapter XV). But in two later cases, clearly involving
interstate commerce, it had applied the Sherman Act positively. In the Trans-
Missouri Freight Association case (1897), the Court ruled that a combination of
eighteen competitive railroads which existed to fix rates violated the antitrust law.
Rejecting the "rule of reason," it held that whether or not the rates were reason-

able, the act applied to any combination in restraint of trade. In the field of manufacture, a unanimous Court partially revitalized the Sherman Act in the Addystone Pipe and Steel Company case (1899), distinguishing it from the Knight case on the ground that in this instance the combination not only manufactured items but also directly controlled prices in interstate commerce.

Roosevelt's reputation as a "Trust Buster" can be measured by his successful attack on the Northern Securities Company, a holding company uniting the Northern Pacific and the Great Northern Railroads. A 5 to 4 Court ruled that the acquisition by a holding company of stock control of competing carriers, even though reasonable, constituted an illegal monopoly (No. 151). In a surprise dissent, Holmes pleaded for the "rule of reason" (No. 152). The next year, however, Holmes wrote a unanimous opinion upholding the government's antitrust prosecution of the "Beef Trust." He first expanded the commerce clause by formulating the "stream of commerce" concept, and then applied the Sherman Act literally to the meat-packers' combination in Chicago (Swift case [No. 153]).

The direct effect of Roosevelt's two major victories was virtually nil. The Beef Trust was dissolved, but managed to reintegrate sufficiently to circumvent the government's injunction in the Swift case, and the Northwestern railroads established an effective community of interest for directing their policies. Although Roosevelt continued to press the prosecution of monopolistic giants, particularly against the unpopular Standard Oil and American Tobacco combines, he popularized a distinction between "good" and "bad" trusts, conceding that the size and power of a consolidation did not necessarily render it illegal. When the Standard Oil and American Tobacco companies were dissolved in 1911, the Supreme Court elevated Roosevelt's ethical distinction to a legal doctrine. This differentiation between "reasonableness" and "unreasonableness" amended the Sherman Act by judicial interpretation (No. 154), thus giving the statute new meaning and less authority. Justice Harlan considered the "rule of reason" nothing more than judicial usurpation (No. 155).

President Woodrow Wilson also opposed the rule. In 1912 the Democratic platform condemned private monopoly as "indefensible and intolerable," and demanded "the enactment of such additional legislation as may be necessary to make it impossible for a private monopoly to exist in the United States." In his acceptance speech, Wilson emphatically endorsed this plank, and called for new laws to meet "conditions which menace our civilization." In 1914 Congress passed an act establishing the Federal Trade Commission, outlawing unfair methods of competition, and authorizing the issuance of "cease and desist" orders. A companion measure, enacted a month later, was specifically designed to strengthen the Sherman Act. The Clayton Anti-Trust Act prohibited a number of abuses of "big business," and specifically exempted labor unions and farmer organizations from its terms.

The latter provision was a direct outgrowth of the Danbury Hatter's Case (*Loewe v. Lawlor* [No. 156]), and the opinion in *Buck Stove Company v. Gompers* (1914). Both cases involved attempts by the American Anti-Boycott Association to outlaw the boycott by bringing it within the purview of the Sherman Act as a conspiracy in restraint of trade. In both, the Court applied the antitrust statute against labor unions. The personal involvement of Samuel Gompers, the president of the American Federation of Labor, in the Buck Stove Case brought home to organized labor the necessity of congressional repeal of "judicial legislation." The Clayton Anti-Trust Act (No. 157), therefore, was hailed as the "Magna Charta" of labor since it limited "government by injunction," and legalized strikes, peaceful picketing, and boycotts. Judicial interpretation, however, subsequently restricted these new guarantees.

Congress and the courts consistently dealt with railroad labor in a separate category because of its intimate connection with interstate commerce. The Erdman Act of 1898, a result of the vicious labor disputes of that decade, stated that railroads could not prevent their employees from joining a union. Ten years later the Court invalidated this Act, upholding the use of "yellow-dog contracts." (Adair v. U.S. [No. 158]). Important as a leading labor case, the decision was also a landmark in constitutional law; for the first time an act of Congress was ruled unconstitutional for violating the due process clause of the Fifth Amendment. Not until 1917, when the prewar emergency forced the hand of a reluctant Court, was a railroad labor law regulating hours approved by the federal judiciary. To prevent a nation-wide railroad strike on the eve of America's entry into World War I, Congress in 1916 passed the Adamson Act, specifying eight hours as a day's work on interstate railroads. In Wilson v. New (No. 159), a bare majority of the Court upheld the establishment of a temporary standard of wages and hours as an emergency measure.

Despite the concentrated efforts of both Republicans and Democrats during the Progressive Era, government regulations designed to restore competition and to improve industrial and labor relations frequently fell short of progressive reform ideals. In his testimony before the United States Commission on Industrial Relations in 1915, Louis D. Brandeis, a leading reformer later appointed to the Supreme Court, painted a Progressive portrait of the American economy which contrasted the dull industrial absolutism of the period to the bright achievements in political democracy (No. 160),

Revival of the Interstate Commerce Commission

149. The Court May Not Usurp Administrative Functions of the I. C. C.

I. C. C. v. Illinois Central Railroad Company, 215 U.S. 452 (1910).

WHITE, J.: Whether a duty rested upon the Illinois Central Railroad Company to obey an order made by the Interstate Commerce Commission is the question here to be decided. . . .

In determining whether an order of the

commission shall be suspended or set aside, we must consider, *a,* all relevant questions of constitutional power or right; *b,* all pertinent questions as to whether the administrative order is within the scope of the delegated authority under which it purports to have been made; and, *c,* a proposition which we state independently, although in its essence it may be contained in the previous one, viz., whether, even although the order be in form within the delegated power, nevertheless it must be treated as not embraced therein, because the exertion of authority which is questioned has been manifested in such an unreasonable manner as to cause it, in truth, to be within the elementary rule that the substance, and not the shadow, determines the validity of the exercise of the power. . . . Plain as it is that the powers just stated are of the essence of judicial authority, and which, therefore, may not be curtailed, and whose discharge may not be by us in a proper case avoided, it is equally plain that such perennial powers lend no support whatever to the proposition that we may, under the guise of exerting judicial power, usurp merely administrative functions by setting aside a lawful administrative order upon our conception as to whether the administrative power has been wisely exercised. . . .

In view, however, of the great importance of the questions directly arising for decision, . . . we shall . . . come at once to the propositions of power previously stated.

First. *That the act to regulate commerce has not delegated to the commission authority to regulate the distribution of company fuel cars in times of car shortage as a means of prohibiting unjust preferences or undue discrimination.* . . .

The deduction from the proposition is, as the movement of coal under the conditions stated is not commerce, it is therefore not within the authority delegated to the commission by the act of Congress, as all such acts have relation to the regulation of commerce, and do not, therefore, embrace that which is not commerce. . . .

When the erroneous assumption upon which the proposition must rest is considered, its unsoundness is readily demonstrable. That assumption is this, that commerce in the constitutional sense only embraces shipment in a technical sense, and does not, therefore, extend to carriers engaged in interstate commerce, certainly in so far as so engaged, and the instrumentalities by which such commerce is carried on, a doctrine the unsoundness of which has been apparent ever since the decision in *Gibbons v. Ogden,* . . . and which has not since been open to question. It may not be doubted that the equipment of a railroad company engaged in interstate commerce, included in which are its coal cars, are instruments of such commerce. From this it necessarily follows that such cars are embraced within the governmental power of regulation which extends, in time of car shortage, to compelling a just and equal distribution and the prevention of an unjust and discriminatory one.

The corporation as a carrier engaged in interstate commerce being then, as to its interstate commerce business, subject to the control exerted by the act to regulate commerce, and the instrumentalities employed for the purpose of such commerce, being likewise so subject to control, we are brought to consider the remaining proposition, which is,

Second. *That even if power has been delegated to the commission by the act to regulate commerce, the order whose continued enforcement was enjoined by the court below was beyond the authority delegated by the statute.*

In view of the facts found by the commission as to preferences and discriminations resulting from the failure to count the company fuel cars in the daily distribution in times of car shortage, and in further view of the far-reaching preferences and discriminations alleged in the answer of the commission in this case, and which must be taken as true, as the cause was submitted on bill and answer, it is beyond controversy that the subject with which the order dealt was within the sweeping provisions of §3 of the act to regulate commerce, prohibiting preferences and discriminations. . . .

It follows from what we have said that the court below erred in enjoining the order of the commission, in so far as it related to company fuel cars, and its decree is therefore reversed, and the case remanded for further proceedings in conformity with this opinion.

150. When intrastate transactions affect interstate commerce, Congress may prescribe the final rule.

The Shreveport Rate Case, 234 U.S. 342 (1914).

HUGHES, C.J.: These suits were brought in the Commerce Court . . . to set aside an order of the Interstate Commerce Commission, dated March 11, 1912, upon the ground that it exceeded the Commission's authority. . . .

The gravamen of the complaint, said the Interstate Commerce Commission, was that the carriers made rates out of Dallas and other Texas points into eastern Texas which were much lower than those which they extended into Texas from Shreveport. The situation may be briefly described: Shreveport, Louisiana, is about 40 miles from the Texas state line, and 231 miles from Houston, Texas, on the line of the Houston, East & West Texas and Houston and Shreveport Companies . . . ; it is 189 miles from Dallas, Texas, on the line of the Texas & Pacific. Shreveport competes with both cities for the trade of the intervening territory. The rates on these lines from Dallas and Houston, respectively, eastward to intermediate points, in Texas, were much less, according to distance, than from Shreveport westward to the same points. It is undisputed that the difference was substantial, and injuriously affected the commerce of Shreveport. . . .

The Interstate Commerce Commission found that the interstate class rates out of Shreveport to named Texas points were unreasonable, and it established maximum class rates for this traffic. . . .

The point of the objection to the order is that, as the discrimination found by the Commission to be unjust arises out of the relation of intrastate rates, maintained under state authority, to interstate rates that have been upheld as reasonable, its correction was beyond the Commission's power. . . . The invalidity of the order is challenged upon two grounds:

(1.) That Congress is impotent to control the intrastate charges of an interstate carrier even to the extent necessary to prevent injurious discrimination against interstate traffic. . . .

Congress is empowered to regulate,— that is, to provide the law for the government of interstate commerce; to enact 'all appropriate legislation' for its 'protection and advancement' . . . As it is competent for Congress to legislate to these ends, unquestionably it may seek their attainment by requiring that the agencies of interstate commerce shall not be used in such manner as to cripple, retard, or destroy it. The fact that carriers are instruments of intrastate commerce, as well as of interstate commerce, does not derogate from the complete and paramount authority of Congress over the latter, or preclude the Federal power from being exerted to prevent the intrastate operations of such carriers from being made a means of injury to that which has been confided to Federal care. Wherever the interstate and intrastate transactions of carriers are so related that the government of the one involves the control of the other, it is Congress, and not the state, that is entitled to prescribe the final and dominant rule, for otherwise Congress would be denied the exercise of its constitutional authority, and the state, and not the nation, would be supreme within the national field. . . .

It is for Congress to supply the needed correction where the relation between intrastate and interstate rates presents the evil to be corrected, and this it may do completely by reason of its control over the interstate carrier in all matters having such a close and substantial relation to interstate commerce that it is necessary or appropriate to exercise the control for the effective government of that commerce.

It is also clear that, in removing the injurious discriminations against interstate traffic arising from the relation of intra-

state to interstate rates, Congress is not bound to reduce the latter below what it may deem to be a proper standard fair to the carrier and to the public. Otherwise, it could prevent the injury to interstate commerce only by the sacrifice of its judgment as to interstate rates. Congress is entitled to maintain its own standard as to these rates, and to forbid any discriminatory action by interstate carriers which will obstruct the freedom of movement of interstate traffic over their lines in accordance with the terms it establishes.

Having this power, Congress could provide for its execution through the aid of a subordinate body; and we conclude that the order of the Commission now in question cannot be held invalid upon the ground that it exceeded the authority which Congress could lawfully confer. . . .

Reinvigoration of the Sherman Act

BEGINNINGS OF EFFECTIVE REGULATION

151. *The Court "Busts" a Trust*

Northern Securities Company v. U.S., 193 U.S. 197 (1904).

HARLAN, J.: . . . The Government charges that if the combination was held not to be in violation of the act of Congress, then all efforts of the National Government to preserve to the people the benefits of free competition among carriers engaged in interstate commerce will be wholly unavailing, and all transcontinental lines, indeed the entire railway systems of the country, may be absorbed, merged and consolidated, thus placing the public at the absolute mercy of the holding corporation. . . .

From the decisions in . . . [previous] cases certain propositions are plainly deducible and embrace the present case. Those propositions are:

That although the act of Congress known as the Anti-Trust Act has no reference to the mere manufacture or production of articles or commodities within the limits of the several States, it does embrace and declare to be illegal every contract, combination or conspiracy, in whatever form, or whatever nature, and whoever may be parties to it, which directly or necessarily operates *in restraint* of trade or commerce *among the several States or with foreign nations;*

That the act is not limited to restraints of interstate and international trade or commerce that are unreasonable in their nature, but embraces *all* direct *restraints* imposed by any combination, conspiracy or monopoly upon such trade or commerce;

That railroad carriers engaged in interstate or international commerce are embraced by the act;

That combinations even among *private* manufacturers or dealers whereby *interstate or international commerce* is restrained are equally embraced by the act;

That Congress has the power to establish *rules* by which *interstate and international* commerce shall be governed, and, by the Anti-Trust Act, has prescribed the rule of free competition among those engaged in such commerce;

That *every* combination or conspiracy which would extinguish competition between otherwise competing railroads engaged in *interstate trade or commerce,* and which would *in that way* restrain *such* trade or commerce, is made illegal by the act;

That the natural effect of competition is to increase commerce, and an agreement whose direct effect is to prevent this play of competition restrains instead of promotes trade and commerce;

That to vitiate a combination, such as the act of Congress condemns, it need not be shown that the combination, in fact, results or will result in a total suppression of trade or in a complete monopoly, but it is only essential to show that by its necessary operation it tends to restrain interstate or international trade or commerce and to deprive the public of the advantages that flow from free competition;

That the constitutional guarantee of liberty of contract does not prevent Congress from prescribing the rule of free competition for those engaged in *interstate and international* commerce; and,

That under its power to regulate commerce among the several States and with foreign nations, Congress had authority to enact the statute in question. . . .

What the Government particularly complains of, indeed, all that it complains of here, is the existence of a combination among the stockholders of competing railroad companies which in violation of the act of Congress restrains interstate and international commerce through the agency of a common corporate trustee designated to act for both companies in repressing free competition between them. . . .

Whether the free operation of the normal laws of competition is a wise and wholesome rule for trade and commerce is an economic question which this court need not consider or determine. Undoubtedly, there are those who think that the general business interests and prosperity of the country will be best promoted if the rule of competition is not applied. But there are others who believe that such a rule is more necessary in these days of enormous wealth than it ever was in any former period of our history. Be all this as it may, Congress has, in effect, recognized the rule of free competition by declaring illegal every combination or conspiracy in restraint of interstate and international commerce. . . .

Guided by these long-established rules of construction, it is manifest that if the Anti-Trust Act is held not to embrace a case such as is now before us, the plain intention of the legislative branch of the Government will be defeated. If Congress has not, by the words used in the act, described this and like cases, it would, we apprehend, be impossible to find words that would describe them. . . .

152. *"Great cases like hard cases make bad law."*

Northern Securities Company v. U.S., 193 U.S. 197 (1904).

HOLMES, J., dissenting: . . . Great cases like hard cases make bad law. For great cases are called great, not by reason of their real importance in shaping the law of the future, but because of some accident of immediate overwhelming interest which appeals to the feelings and distorts the judgment. These immediate interests exercise a kind of hydraulic pressure which makes what previously was clear seem doubtful, and before which even well settled principles of law will bend. What we have to do in this case is to find the meaning of some not very difficult words. . . .

In my opinion there is no attempt to monopolize, and what, as I have said, in my judgment amounts to the same thing, that there is no combination in restraint of trade, until something is done with the intent to exclude strangers to the combination from competing with it in some part of the business which it carries on.

Unless I am entirely wrong in my understanding of what a "combination in restraint of trade" means, then the same monopoly may be attempted and effected by an individual, and is made equally illegal in that case by §2. . . .

A partnership is not a contract or combination in restraint of trade between the partners unless the well known words are to be given a new meaning invented for the purpose of this act. . . . The law, I repeat, says nothing about competition, and only prevents its suppression by contracts or combinations in restraint of trade, and such contracts or combinations derive their character as restraining trade from other features than the suppression of competition alone. . . . If the restraint on the freedom of the members of a combination caused by their entering into partnership is a restraint of trade, every such combination, as well the small as the great, is within the act. . . .

I am happy to know that only a minority of my brethren adopt an interpretation of the law which in my opinion would make eternal the *bellum omnium contra omnes* and disintegrate society so far as it could into individual atoms. If that were its intent I should regard calling such a law a regulation of commerce as a mere pretense. It would be an attempt to reconstruct society. I am not concerned with the wisdom of such an an attempt, but I believe that Congress was not entrusted by the Constitution with the power to make it and I am deeply persuaded that it has not tried.

153. *The "Stream of Commerce" Doctrine*

Swift and Company v. U.S., 196 U.S. 375 (1905).

HOLMES, J.: . . . Although the combination alleged embraces restraint and monopoly of trade within a single State, its effect upon commerce among the States is not accidental, secondary, remote or merely probable. On the allegations of the bill the latter commerce no less, perhaps even more, than commerce within a single State is an object of attack. . . .

Moreover, it is a direct object, it is that for the sake of which the several specific acts and courses of conduct are done and adopted. Therefore the case is not like *United States v. E. C. Knight Co.*, . . . where the subject matter of the combination was manufacture and the direct object monopoly of manufacture within a State. However likely a monopoly of commerce among the States in the article manufactured was to follow from the agreement it was not a necessary consequence nor a primary end. Here the subject matter is sales and the very point of the combination is to restrain and monopolize commerce among the States in respect to such sales. . . .

Commerce among the States is not a technical legal conception, but a practical one, drawn from the course of business. When cattle are sent for sale from a place in one State, with the expectation that they will end their transit, after purchase, in another, and when in effect they do so, with only the interruption necessary to find a purchaser at the stock yards, and when this is a typical, constantly recurring course, the current thus existing is a current of commerce among the States, and the purchase of the cattle is a part and incident of such commerce. What we say is true at least of such a purchase by residents in another State from that of the seller and of the cattle. And we need not trouble ourselves at this time as to whether the statute could be escaped by any arrangement as to the place where the sale in point of law is consummated. . . .

The injunction against taking part in a combination, the effect of which will be a restraint of trade among the States by directing the defendants' agents to refrain from bidding against one another at the sales of live stock, is justified so far as the subject matter is concerned. . . .

TRIUMPH OF THE RULE OF REASON

154. *Amending the Anti-Trust Act by "Judicial Legislation"*

Standard Oil Company v. U.S., 221 U.S. 1 (1911).

WHITE, C.J.: . . . It is certain that only one point of concord between the parties is discernible, which is, that the controversy in every aspect is controlled by a correct conception of the meaning of the first and second sections of the Anti-trust Act. . . . We shall make our investigation under four separate headings: First. The text of the first and second sections of the act originally considered and its meaning in the light of the common law and the law of this country at the time of its adoption. Second. The contentions of the parties concerning the act, and the scope and effect of the decisions of this court upon which they rely. . . .

In view of the common law and the law in this country as to restraint of trade, which we have reviewed, and the illuminating effect which that history must have under the rule to which we have referred, we think it results:

a. That the context manifests that the statute was drawn in the light of the existing practical conception of the law of restraint of trade, because it groups as within that class, not only contracts which were in restraint of trade in the subjective sense, but all contracts or acts which theoretically were attempts to monopolize, yet which in practice had come to be considered as in restraint of trade in a broad sense.

b. That in view of the many new forms of contracts and combinations which were being evolved from existing economic conditions, it was deemed essential by an all-embracing enumeration to make sure that no form of contract or combination by which an undue restraint of interstate or foreign commerce was brought about could save such restraint from condemnation. The statute under this view evidenced the intent not to restrain the right to make and enforce contracts, whether resulting from combination or otherwise, which did not unduly restrain interstate or foreign commerce, but to protect that commerce from being restrained by methods, whether old or new, which would constitute an interference that is an undue restraint.

c. And as the contracts or acts embraced in the provision were not expressly defined, since the enumeration addressed itself simply to classes of acts, those classes being broad enough to embrace every conceivable contract or combination which could be made concerning trade or commerce or the subjects of such commerce, and thus caused any act done by any of the enumerated methods anywhere in the whole field of human activity to be illegal if in restraint, it inevitably follows that the provision necessarily called for

the exercise of judgment which required that some standard should be resorted to for the purpose of determining whether the prohibitions contained in the statute had or had not in any given case been violated. Thus not specifying but indubitably contemplating and requiring a standard, it follows that it was intended that the standard of reason which had been applied at the common law and in this country in dealing with subjects of the character embraced by the statute, was intended to be the measure used for the purpose of determining whether in a given case a particular act had or had not brought about the wrong against which the statute provided. . . .

155. *Courts "have no function to declare a public policy, nor to amend legislative enactments."*

Standard Oil Co. v. U.S., 221 U.S. 1 (1911).

HARLAN, J., dissenting in part: . . . In order that my objections to certain parts of the court's opinion may distinctly appear, I must state the circumstances under which Congress passed the Anti-trust Act, and trace the course of judicial decisions as to its meaning and scope. . . .

All who recall the condition of the country in 1890 will remember that there was everywhere, among the people generally, a deep feeling of unrest. The Nation had been rid of human slavery—fortunately, as all now feel—but the conviction was universal that the country was in real danger from another kind of slavery sought to be fastened on the American people, namely, the slavery that would result from aggregations of capital in the hands of a few individuals and corporations controlling, for their own profit and advantage exclusively, the entire business of the country, including the production and sale of the necessaries of life. Such a danger was thought to be then imminent, and all felt that it must be met firmly and by such

statutory regulations as would adequately protect the people against oppression and wrong. Congress therefore took up the matter and gave the whole subject the fullest consideration. . . .

Guided by these considerations, and to the end that the people, *so far as interstate commerce* was concerned, might not be dominated by vast combinations and monopolies, having power to advance their own selfish ends, regardless of the general interests and welfare, Congress passed the Anti-trust Act of 1890. . . .

After what has been adjudged, upon full consideration, as to the meaning and the scope of the Anti-trust Act, and in view of the usages of this court when attorneys for litigants have attempted to reopen questions that have been deliberately decided, I confess to no little surprise as to what has occurred in the present case. The court says that the previous cases, above cited, "cannot by any possible conception be treated as authoritative without the certitude that *reason* was resorted to for the purpose of deciding them." . . . It is more than once intimated, if not suggested, that if the Anti-Trust Act is to be construed as prohibiting *every* contract or combination, of whatever nature, which is in fact in restraint of commerce, regardless of the reasonableness or unreasonableness of such restraint, that fact would show that the court had not proceeded, in its decision, according to "the light of reason," but had disregarded the "rule of reason" . . . Now this court is asked to do that which it has distinctly declared it could not and would not do, and has now done what it then said it could not constitutionally do. It has, by mere interpretation, modified the act of Congress, and deprived it of practical value as a defensive measure against the evils to be remedied. . . . In effect, the court says, that it will now, for the first time, bring the discussion under the "light of reason" and apply the "rule of reason" to the questions to be decided. I have the authority of this court for saying that such a course of proceeding on its part would be "judicial legislation." . . .

But my brethren, in their wisdom, have deemed it best to pursue a different course. They have now said to those who condemn our former decisions and who object to all legislative prohibitions of contracts, combinations, and trusts in restraint of interstate commerce, "You may *now* restrain such commerce, provided you are reasonable about it; only take care that the restraint is not undue." . . .

It remains for me to refer, more fully than I have heretofore done, to another, and, in my judgment—if we look to the future—the most important aspect of this case. That aspect concerns the usurpation by the judicial branch of the Government

of the functions of the legislative department. . . .

I said at the outset that the action of the court in this case might well alarm thoughtful men who revered the Constitution. I meant by this that many things are intimated and said in the court's opinion which will not be regarded otherwise than as sanctioning an invasion by the judiciary of the constitutional domain of Congress —an attempt by interpretation to soften or modify what some regard as a harsh public policy. This court, let me repeat, solemnly adjudged many years ago that it could not, except by *"judicial legislation"* read words into the Anti-trust Act not put there by Congress, and which, being inserted, give it a meaning which the words of the act, as passed, if properly interpreted, would not justify. The court has decided that it could not thus change a public policy formulated and declared by Congress; that Congress has paramount authority to regulate interstate commerce, and that it alone can change a policy once inaugurated by legislation. The courts have nothing to do with the wisdom or policy of an act of Congress. Their duty is to ascertain the will of Congress, and if the statute embodying the expression of that will is constitutional, the courts must respect it. They have no function to declare a public policy, nor to *amend* legislative enactments. . . . Nevertheless, if I do not misapprehend its opinion, the court has now read into the act of Congress words which are not to be found there, and has thereby done that which it adjudged in 1896 and in 1898 could not be done without violating the Constitution, namely, by interpretation of a statute, changed a public policy declared by the legislative department. . . .

Federal Regulation of Labor

LABOR AS A COMBINATION IN RESTRAINT OF TRADE

156. *The Danbury Hatters Encounter the Sherman Act*

Loewe v. Lawlor, 208 U.S. 274 (1908).

FULLER, C.J.: . . . The combination charged falls within the class of restraints of trade aimed at compelling third parties and strangers involuntarily not to engage in the course of trade except on conditions that the combination imposes; and there is no doubt that . . . "at common law every person has individually, and the public also has collectively, a right to require that the course of trade should be kept free from unreasonable obstruction." But the objection here is to the jurisdiction, because, even conceding that the declaration states a case good at common law, it is contended that it does not state one within the statute. Thus, it is said, that the restraint alleged would operate to entirely destroy plaintiffs' business and thereby include intrastate trade as well; that physical obstruction is not alleged as contemplated; and that defendants are not themselves engaged in interstate trade.

We think none of these objections are tenable, and that they are disposed of by previous decisions of this court. . . .

The [Sherman] act made no distinction between classes. It provided that "every" contract, combination or conspiracy in restraint of trade was illegal. The records of Congress show that several efforts were made to exempt, by legislation, organizations of farmers and laborers from the operation of the act and that all these efforts failed, so that the act remained as we have it before us. . . .

The . . . plaintiffs were manufacturers of hats in Danbury, Connecticut, . . . and were then and there engaged in an interstate trade in some twenty States other than . . . Connecticut; that they were practically dependent upon such interstate trade to consume the product of their factory, only a small percentage of their entire output being consumed in . . . Connecticut; that all the time the alleged combination was formed they were in the process of manufacturing a large number of hats for the purpose of fulfilling engagements then actually made with consignees and wholesale dealers in States other than Connecticut, and that if prevented from carrying on the work of manufacturing these hats they would be unable to complete their engagements.

That defendants were members of a vast combination called the United Hatters of North America, comprising about 9,000 members and including a large number of subordinate unions, and that they were combined with some 1,400,000 others into another association known as The American Federation of Labor. . . ; that defendants were "engaged in a combined scheme and effort to force all manufacturers of fur hats in the United States, including the plaintiffs, against their will and their previous policy of carrying on their business, to organize their workmen in the departments of making and finishing, in each of their factories, into an organization . . . or as the defendants and their confederates term it, to unionize their shops, with the intent thereby to control the employment of labor in and the operation of said factories, and to subject the same to the direction and control of persons, other than the owners of the same, in a manner extremely onerous and distasteful to such owners, and to carry out such scheme, effort and purpose, by restraining and destroying the interstate trade and commerce of such manufacturers, by means of intimidation of and threats made to such manufacturers and their customers in the several States, or boycotting them, their product and their customers, using therefor all the powerful means at their command, . . . until such time as, from the damage and loss of business . . . , the said manufacturers should yield to the said demand to unionize their factories."

That the conspiracy or combination was

so far progressed that out of eighty-two manufacturers of this country engaged in the production of fur hats seventy had accepted the terms and acceded to the demand that the shop should be conducted in accordance, so far as conditions of employment were concerned, with the will of the American Federation of Labor; the local union demanded of plaintiffs that they should unionize their shop under peril of being boycotted by this combination, which demand defendants declined to comply with; thereupon the American Federation of Labor, acting through its official organ and through its organizers, declared a boycott. . . .

We think a case within the statute was set up and that the demurrer should have been overruled. . . .

157. The "Magna Charta" of Labor

Sections 6 and 20, The Clayton Anti-Trust Act, *U.S. Stat. at L.*, XXXVIII, 731, 738 (October 15, 1914).

SEC. 6. That the labor of a human being is not a commodity or article of commerce. Nothing contained in the anti-trust laws shall be construed to forbid the existence and operation of labor, agricultural, or horticultural organizations, instituted for the purposes of mutual help, and not having capital stock or conducted for profit, or to forbid or restrain individual members of such organizations from lawfully carrying out the legitimate objects thereof; nor shall such organizations, or the members thereof, be held or construed to be illegal combinations or conspiracies in restraint of trade, under the anti-trust laws.

SEC. 20. That no restraining order or injunction shall be granted by any court of the United States, or a judge or the judges thereof, in any case between an employer and employees or between employers and employees, or between employees, or between persons employed and persons seeking employment, involving, or growing out of, a dispute concerning terms or conditions of employment, unless

necessary to prevent irreparable injury to property, or to a property right, of the party making the application, for which injury there is no adequate remedy at law, and such property or property right must be described with a particularity in the application, which must be in writing and sworn to by the applicant or by his agent or attorney.

And no such restraining order or injunction shall prohibit any person or persons, whether singly or in concert, from terminating any relation of employment, or from ceasing to perform any work or labor, or from recommending, advising, or persuading others by peaceful means so to do; or from attending at any place where any such person or persons may lawfully be, for the purpose of peacefully obtaining or communicating information, or from peacefully persuading any person to work or to abstain from working; or from ceasing to patronize or to employ any party to such dispute, or from recommending, advising, or persuading others by peaceful and lawful means so to do; or from paying or giving to, or withholding from, any person engaged in such dispute, any strike benefits or other moneys or things of value; or from peaceably assembling in a lawful manner, and for lawful purposes; or from doing any act or thing which might lawfully be done in the absence of such dispute by any party thereto; nor shall any of the acts specified in this paragraph be considered or held to be violations of any law of the United States.

THE FEDERAL GOVERNMENT AND RAILROAD LABOR

158. *The "Yellow-Dog Contract" and Union Membership*

Adair v. U.S., 208 U.S. 161 (1908).

HARLAN, J.: . . . May Congress make it a criminal offense against the United States—as, by the 10th section of the Act of 1898 it does,—for an agent or officer of an interstate carrier, . . . to discharge an employee from service simply because of his membership in a labor organization? . . .

The first inquiry is whether the part of the 10th section of the Act of 1898 upon which the first count of the indictment is based is repugnant to the 5th Amendment of the Constitution, declaring that no person shall be deprived of liberty or property without due process of law. In our opinion that section in the particular mentioned is an invasion of the personal liberty, as well as of the right of property, guaranteed by that Amendment. Such liberty and right embrace the right to make contracts for the purchase of the labor of others, and equally the right to make contracts for the sale of one's own labor; each right, however, being subject to the fundamental condition that no contract, whatever its subject-matter, can be sustained which the law, upon reasonable grounds, forbids as inconsistent with the public interest, or as hurtful to the public order, or as detrimental to the common good. . . . It is sufficient in this case to say that, as agent of the railroad company, and, as such, responsible for the conduct of the business of one of its departments, it was the defendant Adair's right—and that

right inhered in his personal liberty, and was also a right of property—to serve his employer as best he could, so long as he did nothing that was reasonably forbidden by law as injurious to the public interest. It was the right of the defendant to prescribe the terms upon which the services of Coppage would be accepted, and it was the right of Coppage to become or not, as he chose, an employee of the railroad company upon the terms offered to him. . . .

In every case that comes before this court, therefore, where legislation of this character is concerned, . . . the question necessarily arises: Is this a fair, reasonable, and appropriate exercise of the police power of the state, or is it an unreasonable, unnecessary, and arbitrary interference with the right of the individual to his personal liberty or to enter into those contracts in relation to labor which may seem to him appropriate or necessary for the support of himself and his family? . . .

While . . . the right of liberty and property guaranteed by the Constitution against deprivation without due process of law is subject to such reasonable restraints as the common good or the general welfare may require, it is not within the functions of government . . . to compel any person in the course of his business and against his will, to accept or retain the personal services of another, or to compel any person, against his will, to perform personal services for another. . . .

As the relations and the conduct of the parties towards each other was not controlled by any contract other than a general agreement on one side to accept the services of the employee and a general agreement on the other side to render services to the employer,—no term being fixed for the continuance of the employment,—Congress could not, consistently with the 5th Amendment, make it a crime against the United States to discharge the employee because of his being a member of a labor organization.

But it is suggested that the authority to make it a crime . . . can be referred to the power of Congress to regulate interstate commerce, without regard to any question of personal liberty or right of property arising under the 5th Amendment. This suggestion can have no bearing, in the present discussion unless the statute, in the particular just stated, is, within the meaning of the Constitution, a regulation of commerce among the States. If it be not, then clearly the government

cannot invoke the commerce clause of the Constitution as sustaining the indictment against Adair. . . .

Looking alone at the words of the statute for the purpose of ascertaining its scope and effect, and of determining its validity, we hold that there is no such connection between interstate commerce and membership in a labor organization as to authorize Congress to make it a crime against the United States for an agent of an interstate carrier to discharge an employee because of such membership on his part. . . .

It results, on the whole case, that the provision of the statute under which the defendant was convicted must be held to be repugnant to the 5th Amendment and as not embraced by nor within the power of Congress to regulate interstate commerce, but, under the guise of regulating commerce, and as applied to this case, it arbitrarily sanctions an illegal invasion of the personal liberty as well as the right of property of the defendant Adair.

159. *The Court Considers Emergency Wage-and-Hour Legislation*

Wilson v. New, 243 U.S. 332 (1917).

WHITE, C.J.: . . . Did . . . [Congress] have the power in order to prevent the interruption of interstate commerce to exert its will to supply the absence of a wage scale resulting from the disagreement as to wages between the employers and employees and to make its will on that subject controlling for the limited period provided for?

Coming to the general considerations by which both subjects must be controlled, to simplify the analysis for the purpose of considering the question of inherent power, we put the question as to the eight-hour standard entirely out of view on the ground that the authority to permanently establish it is so clearly sus-

tained as to render the subject not disputable. . . .

That the business of common carriers by rail is in a sense a public business because of the interest of society in the continued operation and rightful conduct of such business, and that the public interest begets a public right of regulation to the full extent necessary to secure and protect it, is settled by so many decisions, state and federal, and is illustrated by such a continuous exertion of state and federal legislative power, as to leave no room for question on the subject. It is also equally true that as the right to fix by agreement between the carrier and its employees a standard of wages to control their relations is primarily private, the establishment and giving effect to such agreed-on standard is not subject to be controlled or prevented by public authority. But taking all these propositions as undoubted, if the situation which we have described and with which the act of Congress dealt be taken into view, that is, the dispute between the employers and employees as to a standard of wages, their failure to agree, the resulting absence of such standard, the entire interruption of interstate commerce which was threatened, and the infinite injury to the public interest which was imminent, it would seem inevitably to result that the power to regulate necessarily obtained and was subject to be applied to the extent necessary to provide a remedy for the situation, which included the power to deal with the dispute, to provide by appropriate action for a standard of wages to fill the want of one caused by the failure to exert the private right on the subject, and to give effect by appropriate legislation to the regulations thus adopted. This must be unless it can be said that the right to so regulate as to save and protect the public interest did not apply to a case where the destruction of the public right was imminent as the result of a dispute between the parties and their consequent failure to establish by private agreement the standard of wages which was essential; in other words that the existence of the public right and the public power to preserve it was wholly under the control of the private right to establish a standard by agreement. Nor is it an answer to this view to suggest that the situation was one of emergency and that emergency cannot be made the source of power. . . . The proposition begs the question, since although an emergency may not call into life a power which has never lived, nevertheless emergency may afford a reason for the exertion of a living power already enjoyed. . . .

We are of the opinion that the reasons stated conclusively establish that from the point of view of inherent power the act which is before us was clearly within the legislative power of Congress to adopt, and that in substance and effect it amounted to an exertion of its authority under the circumstances disclosed to compulsorily arbitrate the dispute between the parties by establishing as to the subject matter of that dispute a legislative standard of wages operative and binding as a matter of law upon the parties,—a power none the less efficaciously exerted because exercised by direct legislative act instead of by the enactment of other and appropriate means providing for the bringing about of such result. If it be conceded that the power to enact the statute was in effect the exercise of the right to fix wages where, by reason of the dispute, there had been a failure to fix by agreement, it would simply serve to show the nature and character of the regulation essential to protect the public right and safeguard the movement of interstate commerce, not involving any denial of the authority to adopt it. . . .

A PROGRESSIVE PORTRAIT OF THE INDUSTRIAL SCENE

160. *Louis Brandeis Describes Industrial and Labor Relations, 1916*

U. S. Commission on Industrial Relations, *Final Report and Testimony*, VIII (Sen. Doc. No. 415, 64th Cong., 1st Sess.), 7659-60.

MR. BRANDEIS: My observation leads me to believe that while there are many contributing causes to unrest, that there is one cause which is fundamental. That is the necessary conflict—the contrast between our political liberty and our industrial absolutism. We are as free politically, perhaps, as free as it is possible for us to be. . . .

On the other hand, in dealing with industrial problems the position of the ordinary worker is exactly the reverse. The individual employee has no effective voice or vote. And the main objection, as I see it, to the very large corporation is, that it makes possible—and in many cases makes inevitable—the exercise of industrial absolutism. It is not merely the case of the individual worker against employer which, even if he is a reasonably sized employer, presents a serious situation calling for the interposition of a union to protect the individual. But we have the situation of an employer so potent, so well-organized, with such concentrated forces and with such extraordinary powers of reserve and the ability to endure against strikes and other efforts of a union, that the relatively loosely organized masses of even strong unions are unable to cope with the situation. . . . The result, in the cases of these large corporations, may be to develop a benevolent absolutism, but it is an absolutism all the same; and it is that which makes the great corporation so dangerous. There develops within the State a state so powerful that the ordinary social and industrial forces existing are insufficient to cope with it. . . .

The social justice for which we are striving is an incident of our democracy, not the main end. It is rather the result of democracy—perhaps its finest expression—but it rests upon democracy, which implies the rule by the people. And therefore the end for which we must strive is the attainment of rule by the people, and that involves industrial democracy as well as political democracy.

There must be a division not only of profits, but a division also of responsibilities. The employees must have the opportunity of participating in the decisions as to what shall be their condition and how the business shall be run. They must learn also in sharing that responsibility that they must bear [too] the suffering arising from grave mistakes, just as the employer must. But the right to assist in making the decisions, the right of making their own mistakes, if mistakes there must be, is a privilege which should not be denied to labor. We must insist upon labor sharing the responsibilities for the result of the business. . . .

CHAPTER XVIII

The Police Power and the Progressive Era

RDINARILY laws protecting the public health, safety, morals, and general welfare of a community are prerogatives of the states. None of these "police powers" is delegated by the Constitution to the federal government. Although Chief Justice Marshall referred to a federal police power as early as 1827 (*Brown v. Maryland, Chapter VII*), his casual use of the phrase did not establish such a power, and throughout the nineteenth century it was generally agreed that this general power was reserved to the states exclusively by the Tenth Amendment. During the Progressive Era, however, Congress began using its commerce, taxing, and postal powers as devices for accomplishing purely social ends. In this indirect manner, Congress has expanded its control over social and economic problems in areas where it formerly had no direct authority.

In an important test case in 1903, the Supreme Court gave judicial sanction to the principle of a federal police power. *Champion v. Ames* (No. 161) upheld a federal act of 1895 prohibiting the distribution of lottery tickets through interstate commerce or the mails. The next year the Court sustained the use of the federal taxing power as an instrument of social control (*McCray v. U.S.,* 1904). As a result of these cases, a reform-minded Congress promptly passed new regulatory legislation in areas thus opened to it. Between 1903 and World War I, laws were passed dealing with subjects as diverse as meat inspection and phosphorus matches, narcotics and prostitution. Of major constitutional importance were the cases sustaining the Pure Food and Drug Act of 1906 (*Hipolite Egg Co. v. U.S.,* 1911), the legislation restricting shipment of liquor into dry states (*Clark Distilling Co. v. W. Maryland R.R. Co.,* 1917), and the Mann White Slave Act proscribing the interstate transportation of women for immoral purposes (*Hoke v. U.S.,* [No. 162]). In the latter case, Justice McKenna specifically upheld use of the commerce power "to promote the general welfare, material and moral."

In only one case during this period did the Supreme Court refuse to validate Congress's social measures. Encouraged by the Court's consistent approval of reform legislation based on the commerce power, Congress in 1916 struck at the evil of child labor by excluding from interstate shipment products manufactured by children. When the Court ruled on this law, however, Justice Day, after misquoting the Tenth Amendment, disregarded the ruling in Hoke and reverted to the Knight doctrine that states have the "expressly" reserved power to regulate production and manufacturing (*Hammer v. Dagenhart* [No. 163]). This concept of "dual federalism" was attacked by Justice Holmes who declared that the Child Labor Law was a direct exercise of the commerce power which did "not meddle with anything belonging to the states. They may regulate their internal affairs and their domestic commerce as they like. But when they seek to send their products across the state line they are no longer within their rights." Holmes's dissent indicated that the decision resulted from the difference between the majority's conception of acceptable social policy and Congress's attitude toward "the evil of premature and excessive child labor."

Even before the Supreme Court formulated the doctrine of "dual federalism" as a weapon against federal regulation in areas presumably reserved to the states, it had restricted the police power of the states by using the equally effective principle of substantive due process. The leading refinement of this principle was the evolution of the "liberty of contract" theory. In *Allgeyer v. Louisiana* (No. 164), the Court defined "liberty," as guaranteed by the due process clause of the Fourteenth Amendment, to include the liberty of the individual to enter into contracts without state interference. Although the liberty of contract theory originated in the Allgeyer Insurance case, it became identified chiefly with labor contracts. The Court posited two propositions: (1) an essential equality of bargaining power existed between an individual employee and his employer, and (2) any interference by the state with this equitable arrangement was "unreasonable" and violated the individual's liberty without due process of law. *Coppage v. Kansas* (No. 165) outlawed a state law prohibiting yellow-dog contracts as an illegal restriction upon freedom of contract.

At almost the same time that the Court enunciated the "liberty of contract" theory in *Allgeyer,* it gave the formula a broad enough application to sustain a Utah statute establishing the eight-hour day in the mining industry (*Holden v. Hardy* [No. 166]). Here the Court simply argued that the statute was a legitimate exercise of the state police power to protect the health of workers in a particularly dangerous occupation. Yet the Court, only seven years later, threw out for the first time a state labor statute because it was contrary to the Fourteenth Amendment. Fearful that legislative regulation of labor relations was "on the increase," Justice Peckham rejected the Hardy precedent of 1898 and ruled that the New York statute establishing a sixty-hour week for bakers was not a health law but only "meddlesome interference with the rights of the individual" (*Lochner v. New York* [No. 167]). In one of his more famous statements, Justice Holmes (No. 168) replied that "the Fourteenth Amendment does not enact Mr. Herbert Spencer's *Social Statics*" or any other social or economic theory. For all practical purposes, however, Peckham's opinion did just that, translating the dominant industrial laissez-faire social theory into constitutional law for nearly three decades.

The severe criticism that greeted the Lochner decision seemed to confirm Holmes's contention that the case was decided "upon an economic theory which a large part of the country does not entertain." As Mayor Gaynor of New York once put it, "There were no journeymen bakers that I know of clamoring for any such liberty." Doubtless such widespread criticism was felt by the majority. During this period the "Brandeis Brief," which presented statistical, historical, sociological, and economic data to support social legislation, was introduced (No. 169), and the Court, seemingly reoriented, upheld in 1908 an Oregon law establishing a ten-hour working day for women (*Muller v. Oregon*). In 1917 it went further, validating a general ten-hour statute (*Bunting v. Oregon*).

Judicial tolerance of legislative experimentation with the state police power seemed to be assured by Justice McKenna's statement in Bunting: "There is a contention made that the law, even regarded as regulating hours of service, is not either necessary or useful for the preservation of the health of employees in mills, factories and manufacturing establishments. The record contains no facts to support the contention and against it is the judgment of the legislature and the Supreme Court of Oregon." A similar attitude had been expressed as early as 1905 in a decision sustaining a compulsory vaccination law in Massachusetts. Rejecting the argument that laws against smallpox contagion violated the due process clause of the Fourteenth Amendment, Justice Harlan pointed out the Massachusetts constitution of 1780 had "laid down as a fundamental principle of the social compact that the whole people covenants with each citizen, and each citizen with the whole people, and that all shall be governed by certain laws for 'the common good'. . . . While this court should guard with firmness every right appertaining to life, liberty or property as secured to the individual by the Supreme Law of the Land, it is of the last importance that it should not invade the domain of local authority except when it is plainly necessary to do so in order to enforce that law" (*Jacobson v. Massachusetts* [No. 170]).

The apparent inconsistency in the due process cases can best be explained by frank recognition of the role played by the individual judge's social and economic philosophy. With the Court's acceptance of the "rule of reason" test, judges pitted their concepts of desirable public policy against those of duly elected legislators, accepting regulations which to them seemed reasonable and rejecting as unreasonable those which did not square with their predilections.

Although constitutional reinterpretation during the Progressive Era made it possible to deal with twentieth-century social and industrial problems, the traditional machinery of formal amendment was also utilized as a method of constitutional change. Such reform objectives as a graduated income tax, direct election of Senators, prohibition, and woman suffrage (No. 171A-D) were achieved by adding four amendments between 1913 and 1920. Another constitutional reflection of Progressivism involved the amendment of state constitutions to provide a greater measure of direct democracy. In 1902 the Oregon Constitution was amended to allow the people of the state the right of direct participation in the legislative process through the initiative and the referendum. In *Pacific States Telephone and Telegraph Co. v. Oregon* (No. 172), the Court maintained a hands-off attitude toward these democratic experiments, dismissing as a political question the contention that these reforms destroyed the republican form of government in Oregon. Not so reluctant as the Court in discussing political questions, President William Howard Taft vetoed the Arizona Admission Act because the constitution of the new state provided for judicial recall (No. 173). Sacrificing progressive reform to pragmatic necessity, Arizona removed the objectional constitutional provision and promptly joined the Union as the forty-eighth state. After admission, Arizona reaffirmed its progressivism by restoring judicial recall through the amendment process.

The Development of the Federal Police Power

161. *Federal Power over Health, Welfare, and Morals*

Champion v. Ames, 188 U.S. 321 (1903).

HARLAN, J.: . . . The Constitution does not define what is to be deemed a legitimate regulation of interstate commerce. In *Gibbons v. Ogden* it was said that the power to regulate such commerce is the power to prescribe the rule by which it is to be governed. But this general observation leaves it to be determined, when the question comes before the court, whether Congress in prescribing a particular rule, has exceeded its power under the Constitution. . . .

We have said that the carrying from State to State of lottery tickets constitutes interstate commerce, and that the regulation of such commerce is within the power of Congress under the Constitution. Are we prepared to say that a provision which is, in effect *a prohibition* of the carriage of such articles from State to State

is not a fit or appropriate mode for the *regulation* of that particular kind of commerce? If lottery traffic, *carried on through interstate commerce,* is a matter of which Congress may take cognizance and over which its power may be exerted, can it be possible that it must tolerate the traffic, and simply regulate the manner in which it may be carried on? Or may not Congress, for the protection of the people of all the States, and under the power to regulate interstate commerce, devise such means, within the scope of the Constitution, and not prohibited by it, as will drive that traffic out of commerce among the States? . . .

It must not be forgotten that the power of Congress to regulate commerce among the States is plenary, is complete in itself, and is subject to no limitations except such as may be found in the Constitution. . . .

If it be said that the act of 1895 is inconsistent with the Tenth Amendment, reserving to the States respectively, or to the people, the powers not delegated to the United States, the answer is that the power to regulate commerce among the States has been expressly delegated to Congress. . . .

In legislating upon the subject of the traffic in lottery tickets, as carried on through interstate commerce, Congress only supplemented the action of those States—perhaps all of them—which, for the protection of the public morals, prohibit the drawing of lotteries, as well as the sale or circulation of lottery tickets, within their respective limits. It said, in effect, that it would not permit the declared policy of the States, which sought to protect their people against the mischiefs of the lottery business, to be overthrown or disregarded by the agency of interstate commerce. We should hesitate long before adjudging that an evil of such appalling character, carried on through interstate commerce, cannot be met and crushed by the only power competent to that end. We say competent to that end, because Congress alone has the power to occupy, by legislation, the whole field of interstate commerce. . . .

It is said, however, that if, in order to suppress lotteries carried on through interstate commerce, Congress may exclude lottery tickets from such commerce, that principle leads necessarily to the conclusion that Congress may arbitrarily exclude from commerce among the States any article, commodity, or thing, of whatever kind or nature, or however useful or valuable, which it may choose, no matter with what motive, to declare shall not be carried from one State to another. It will be time enough to consider the constitutionality of such legislation when we must do so. The present case does not require the court to declare the full extent of the power that Congress may exercise in the regulation of commerce among the States. We may, however, repeat, in this connection, what the court has heretofore said, that the power of Congress to regulate commerce among the States, although plenary, cannot be deemed arbitrary, since it is subject to such limitations or restrictions as are prescribed by the Constitution. This power, therefore, may not be exercised so as to infringe rights secured or protected by that instrument. It would not be difficult to imagine legislation that would be justly liable to such an objection as that stated, and be hostile to the objects for the accomplishment of which Congress was invested with the general power to regulate commerce among the several States. But, as often said, the possible abuse of a power is not an argument against its existence. There is probably no governmental power that may not be exerted to the injury of the public. . . .

We decide nothing more in the present case than that lottery tickets are subjects of traffic among those who choose to sell or buy them; that the carriage of such tickets by independent carriers from one State to another is therefore interstate commerce; that under its power to regulate commerce among the several States Congress—subject to the limitations imposed by the Constitution upon the exercise of the powers granted—has plenary authority over such commerce, and may prohibit the carriage of such tickets from State to State; and that legislation to that end, and of that character, is not inconsistent with any limitation or restriction imposed upon the exercise of the powers granted to Congress.

162. *Prostitution and Pure Morals*

Hoke v. U.S., 227 U.S. 308 (1913).

McKENNA, J.: . . . Commerce among the States . . . consists of intercourse and traffic between their citizens, and includes the transportation of persons as well as of property; . . . that is, a person may move or be moved in interstate commerce. And the act under consideration was drawn in view of that possibility. What the act condemns is transportation obtained or aided or transportation induced in interstate commerce for the immoral purposes mentioned. But an objection is made and urged with earnestness. It is said that it is the right and privilege of a person to move between States and that such being the right, another cannot be made guilty of the crime of inducing or assisting or aiding in the exercise of it and "that the motive or intention of the passenger, either before beginning the journey, or during or after completing it, is not a matter of interstate commerce." The contentions confound things important to be distinguished. It urges a right exercised in morality to sustain a right to be exercised in immorality. . . .

Plaintiffs in error admit that the State may control the immoralities of its citizens. Indeed, this is their chief insistence, and they especially condemn the act under review as a subterfuge and an attempt to interfere with the police power of the States to regulate the morals of their citizens and assert that it is in consequence an invasion of the reserved powers of the States. There is unquestionably a control in the States over the morals of their citizens, and, it may be admitted, it extends to making prostitution a crime. It is a control, however, which can be exercised only within the jurisdiction of the States, but there is a domain which the States cannot reach and over which Congress alone has power; and if such power be exerted to control what the States cannot it is an ar-

gument for—not against—its legality. Its exertion does not encroach upon the jurisdiction of the States. We have cited examples; others may be adduced. The Pure Food and Drugs Act . . . is a conspicuous instance. In all other instances a clash of national legislation with the power of the States was urged, and in all rejected.

Our dual form of government has its perplexities, State and Nation having different spheres of jurisdiction, . . . but it must be kept in mind that we are one people; and the powers reserved to the States and those conferred on the Nation are adapted to be exercised, whether independently or concurrently, to promote the general welfare, material and moral. This is the effect of the decisions, and surely if the facility of interstate transportation can be taken away from the demoralization of lotteries, the debasement of obscene literature, the contagion of diseased cattle or persons, the impurity of food and drugs, the like facility can be taken away from the systematic enticement to and the enslavement in prostitution and debauchery of women, and, more insistently, of girls.

This is the aim of the law expressed in broad generalization; and motives are made of determining consequences. Motives executed by actions may make it the concern of Government to exert its powers. Right purpose and fair trading need no restrictive regulation, but let them be transgressed and penalties and prohibitions must be applied. We may illustrate again by the Pure Food and Drugs Act. Let an article be debased by adulteration, let it be misrepresented by false branding, and Congress may exercise its prohibitive power. It may be that Congress could not prohibit the manufacture of the article in a State. It may be that Congress could not prohibit in all of its conditions its sale within a State. But Congress may prohibit its transportation between the States, and by that means defeat the motive and evils of its manufacture. . . .

Of course it will be said that women are not articles of merchandise, but this does not affect the analogy of the cases; the substance of the congressional power is the same, only the manner of its exercise must be accommodated to the difference in its objects. It is misleading to say that men and women have rights. Their rights cannot fortify or sanction their wrongs; and if they employ interstate transporta-

tion as a facility of their wrongs, it may be forbidden to them. . . .

The principle established by the cases is the simple one, when rid of confusing and distracting considerations, that Congress has power over transportation "among the several States"; that the power is complete in itself, and that Congress, as an incident to it may adopt not only means necessary but convenient to its exercise, and the means may have the quality of police regulations. . . .

163. *Child Labor, the Tenth Amendment, and "Dual Federalism"*

Hammer v. Dagenhart, 247 U.S. 251 (1918).

DAY, J.: . . . It is insisted that adjudged cases in this court establish the doctrine that the power to regulate given to Congress incidentally includes the authority to prohibit the movement of ordinary commodities, and therefore that the subject is not open for discussion. The cases demonstrate the contrary. They rest upon the character of the particular subjects dealt with and the fact that the scope of governmental authority, state or national, possessed over them, is such that the authority to prohibit is, as to them, but the exertion of the power to regulate. . . .

In each of these instances the use of interstate transportation was necessary to the accomplishment of harmful results. In other words, although the power over interstate transportation was to regulate, that could only be accomplished by prohibiting the use of the facilities of interstate commerce to effect the evil intended.

This element is wanting in the present case. The thing intended to be accomplished by this statute is the denial of the facilities of interstate commerce to those manufacturers in the States who employ children within the prohibited ages. The act in its effect does not regulate trans-

portation among the States, but aims to standardize the ages at which children may be employed in mining and manufacturing within the States. The goods shipped are of themselves harmless. The act permits them to be freely shipped after thirty days from the time of their removal from the factory. When offered for shipment, and before transportation begins, the labor of their production is over, and the mere fact that they were intended for interstate commerce transportation does not make their production subject to federal control under the commerce power.

Commerce "consists of intercourse and traffic . . . and includes the transportation of persons and property, as well as the purchase, sale and exchange of commodities." The making of goods and the mining of coal are not commerce, nor does the fact that these things are to be afterwards shipped, or used in interstate commerce, make their production a part thereof. . . .

Over interstate transportation, or its incidents, the regulatory power of Congress is ample, but the production of articles intended for interstate commerce is a matter of local regulation. . . .

If it were otherwise, all manufacture intended for interstate shipment would be brought under federal control to the practical exclusion of the authority of the States, a result certainly not contemplated by the framers of the Constitution when they vested in Congress the authority to regulate commerce among the States. . . .

The grant of power to Congress over the subject of interstate commerce was to enable it to regulate such commerce, and not to give it authority to control the States in their exercise of the police power over local trade and manufacture.

The grant of authority over a purely federal matter was not intended to destroy the local power always existing and carefully reserved to the States in the Tenth Amendment to the Constitution. . . .

That there should be limitations upon the right to employ children in mines and factories in the interest of their own and the public welfare, all will admit. That such employment is generally deemed to require regulation is shown by the fact that the brief of counsel states that every state in the Union has a law upon the subject, limiting the right to thus employ children. In North Carolina, the State wherein is located the factory in which the employment was had in the present case, no child under twelve years of age is permitted to work.

It may be desirable that such laws be uniform, but our federal government is one of enumerated powers. . . .

In interpreting the Constitution it must never be forgotten that the Nation is made up of States to which are entrusted the powers of local government. And to them

and to the people the powers not expressly delegated to the National Government are reserved. . . . To sustain this statute would not be in our judgment a recognition of the lawful exertion of congressional authority over interstate commerce, but would sanction an invasion by the federal power of the control of a matter purely local in its character, and over which no authority has been delegated to Congress in conferring the power to regulate commerce among the States. . . .

In our view the necessary effect of this act is, by means of a prohibition against the movement in interstate commerce of ordinary commercial commodities, to regulate the hours of labor of children in factories and mines within the States, a purely state authority. Thus the act in a twofold sense is repugnant to the Constitution. It not only transcends the authority delegated to Congress over commerce, but also exerts a power as to a purely local matter to which the federal authority does not extend. The far-reaching result of upholding the act cannot be more plainly indicated than by pointing out that if Congress can thus regulate matters intrusted to local authority by prohibition of the movement of commodities in interstate commerce, all freedom of commerce will be at an end, and the power of the states over local matters may be eliminated, and thus our system of government be practically destroyed.

For these reasons we hold that this law exceeds the constitutional authority of Congress. It follows that the decree of the district court must be affirmed.

Judicial Interpretation of State Police Power

DUE PROCESS AND LIBERTY OF CONTRACT

164. *"Liberty of Contract" and the Scope of Judicial Authority*

Allgeyer v. Louisiana, 165 U.S. 578 (1897).

PECKHAM, J.: . . . The Supreme Court of Louisiana says that the act of writing within that State, the letter of notification, was an act therein done to effect an insurance on property then in the State, in a marine insurance company which had not complied with its laws, and such act was, therefore, prohibited by the statute. As so construed we think the statute is a violation of the Fourteenth Amendment of the Federal Constitution, in that it deprives the defendants of their liberty without due process of law. The statute which forbids such act does not become due process of law, because it is inconsistent with the provisions of the Constitution of the Union. The liberty mentioned in that amendment means not only the right of the citizen to be free from the more physical restraint of his person, as by incarceration, but the term is deemed to embrace the right of the citizen to be free in the enjoyment of all his faculties; to be free to use them in all lawful ways; to live and work where he will; to earn his livelihood by any lawful calling; to pursue any livelihood or avocation, and for that purpose to enter into all contracts which may be proper, necessary and essential to his carrying out to a successful conclusion the purposes above mentioned.

It was said by Mr. Justice Bradley, in *Butchers' Union Company v. Crescent City Company* . . . "The right to follow any of the common occupations of life is an inalienable right. It was formulated as

such under the phrase 'pursuit of happiness' in the Declaration of Independence. . . . This right is a large ingredient in the civil liberty of the citizen." Again, . . . the learned justice said: "I hold that the liberty of pursuit—the right to follow any of the ordinary callings of life—is one of the privileges of a citizen of the United States." And again, . . . "But if it does not abridge the privileges and immunities of a citizen of the United States to prohibit him from pursuing his chosen calling, and giving to others the exclusive right of pursuing it, it certainly does deprive him (to a certain extent) of his liberty; for it takes from him the freedom of adopting and following the pursuit which he prefers; which, as already intimated, is a material part of the liberty of the citizen." It is true that these remarks were made in regard to questions of monopoly, but they well describe the rights which are covered by the word "liberty" as contained in the Fourteenth Amendment. . . .

The foregoing extracts have been made for the purpose of showing what general definitions have been given in regard to the meaning of the word "liberty" as used in the amendment, but we do not intend to hold that in no such case can the State exercise its police power. When and how far such power may be legitimately exercised with regard to these subjects must be left for determination to each case as it arises.

Has not a citizen of a State, under the

provisions of the Federal Constitution above mentioned, a right to contract outside of the State for insurance on his property—a right of which state legislation cannot deprive him? We are not alluding to acts done within the State by an insurance company or its agents doing business therein, which are in violation of the state statutes. . . . When we speak of the liberty to contract for insurance or to do an act to effectuate such a contract already existing, we refer to and have in mind the facts of this case, where the contract was made outside the State, and as such was a valid and proper contract. The act done within the limits of the State under the circumstances of this case and for the purpose therein mentioned, we hold a proper act, one which the defendants were at liberty to perform and which the state legislature had no right to prevent, at least with reference to the Federal Constitution. To deprive the citizen of such a right as herein described without due process of law is illegal. Such a statute as this in question is not due process of law, because it prohibits an act which under the Federal Constitution the defendants had a right to perform. This does not interfere in any way with the acknowledged right of the State to enact such legislation in the legitimate exercise of its police or other powers as to it may seem proper. In the exercise of such right, however, care must be taken not to infringe upon those other rights of the citizen which are protected by the Federal Constitution.

In the privileges of pursuing an ordinary calling or trade and of acquiring, holding and selling property must be embraced the right to make all proper contracts in relation thereto, and although it may be conceded that this right to contract in relation to persons or property or to do business within the jurisdiction of the State may be regulated and sometimes prohibited when the contracts or business conflict with the policy of the State as contained in its statutes, yet the power does not and cannot extend to prohibiting a citizen from making contracts of the nature involved in this case outside of the limits and jurisdiction of the State, and which are also to be performed outside of such jurisdiction; nor can the State legally prohibit its citizens from doing such an act as writing this letter of notification, even though the property which is the subject of the insurance may at the time when such insurance attaches be within the limits of the State. . . .

165. *Freedom of Contract and Yellow-Dog Contracts*

Coppage v. Kansas, 236 U.S. 1 (1915).

PITNEY, J: . . . Unless it is to be overruled, . . . [*Adair v. U.S.*] is controlling upon the present controversy; for if Congress is prevented from arbitrary interference with the liberty of contract because of the "due process" provisions of the Fifth Amendment, it is too clear for argument that the States are prevented from the like interference by virtue of the corresponding clause of the Fourteenth Amendment; and hence if it be unconstitutional for Congress to deprive an employer of liberty or property for threatening an employee with loss of employ-ment or discriminating against him because of his membership in a labor organization, it is unconstitutional for a State to similarly punish an employer for requiring his employee, as a condition of securing or retaining employment, to agree not to become or remain a member of such an organization while so employed. . . .

Included in the right of personal liberty and the right of private property—partaking of the nature of each—is the right to make contracts for the acquisition of property. Chief among such contracts is that of personal employment, by which labor and other services are exchanged for money or other forms of property. If this right be struck down or arbitrarily interfered with, there is a substantial impairment of liberty in the long-established constitutional sense. The right is as essential to the laborer as to the capitalist, to the poor as to the rich; for the vast majority or persons have no other honest way to begin to acquire property, save by working for money.

An interference with this liberty so serious as that now under consideration, and so disturbing of equality of right, must be deemed to be arbitrary, unless it be supportable as a reasonable exercise of the police power of the State. But, notwithstanding the strong general presumption in favor of the validity of state laws, we do not think the statute in question, as construed and applied in this case, can be sustained as a legitimate exercise of that power. . . .

As to the interest of the employed, it is said by the Kansas Supreme Court . . . to be a matter of common knowledge that "employees, as a rule, are not financially able to be as independent in making contracts for the sale of their labor as are employers in making a contract of purchase thereof." No doubt, wherever the right of private property exists, there must and will be inequalities of fortune; and thus it naturally happens that parties negotiating about a contract are not equally unhampered by circumstances. This applies to all contracts, and not merely to that between employer and employee. Indeed, a little reflection will show that wherever the right of private property and the right of free contract co-exist, each party when contracting is inevitably more or less influenced by the question whether he has much property, or little, or none; for the contract is made to the very end that each may gain something that he needs or desires more urgently than that which he proposes to give in exchange. And, since it is self-evident

that, unless all things are held in common, some persons must have more property than others, it is from the nature of things impossible to uphold freedom of contract and the right of private property without at the same time recognizing as legitimate those inequalities of fortune that are the necessary result of the exercise of those rights. But the Fourteenth Amendment, in declaring that a State shall not "deprive any person of life, liberty, or property without due process of law," gives to each of these an equal sanction; it recognizes "liberty" and "property" as co-existent human rights, and debars the States from any unwarranted interference with either.

And since a State may not strike them down directly, it is clear that it may not do so indirectly, as by declaring in effect that the public good requires the removal of those inequalities that are but the normal and inevitable result of their exercise, and then invoking the police power in order to remove the inequalities, without other object in view. The police power is broad, and not easily defined, but it cannot be given the wide scope that is here asserted for it, without in effect nullifying the constitutional guaranty. . . .

It is said in the opinion of the state court that membership in a labor organization does not necessarily affect a man's duty to his employer; that the employer has no right, by virtue of the relation, "to dominate the life nor to interfere with the liberty of the employee in matters that do not lessen or deteriorate the service"; and that "the statute implies that labor unions are lawful and not inimical to the rights of employers." The same view is presented in the brief of counsel for the State, where it is said that membership in a labor organization is the "personal and private affair" of the employee. To this line of argument it is sufficient to say that it cannot be judicially declared that membership in such an organization has no relation to a member's duty to his employer; and therefore, if freedom of contract is to be preserved, the employer must be left at liberty to decide for himself whether such membership by his employee is consistent with the satisfactory performance of the duties of the employment. . . .

Of course we do not intend to say, nor to intimate, anything inconsistent with the right of individuals to join labor unions, nor do we question the legitimacy of such organizations so long as they conform to the laws of the land as others are required to do. Conceding the full right of the individual to join the union, he has no inherent right to do this and still remain in the employ of one who is unwilling to employ a union man, any more than the same individual has a right to join the union without the consent of the organization. . . .

DUE PROCESS AND REGULATION OF THE HOURS OF LABOR

166. *"The right of contract is . . . subject to certain limitations which the state may lawfully impose."*

Holden v. Hardy, 169 U.S. 366 (1898).

BROWN, J.: This case involves the constitutionality of an act of the legislature of Utah of March 30, 1896, chap. 72, entitled "An Act Regulating the Hours of Employment in Underground Mines and in Smelters and Ore Reduction Works." . . .

The validity of the statute in question is . . . challenged upon the ground of an alleged violation of the Fourteenth Amendment to the Constitution of the United States, in that it abridges the privileges or immunities of citizens of the United States; deprives both the employer and the laborer of his property without due process of law, and denies to them the equal protection of the laws. . . .

While the cardinal principles of justice are immutable, the methods by which justice is administered are subject to constant fluctuation, and the Constitution of the United States, which is necessarily and to a large extent inflexible and exceedingly difficult of amendment, should not be so construed as to deprive the states of the power to so amend their laws as to make them conform to the wishes of the citizens as they may deem best for the public welfare without bringing them into conflict with the supreme law of the land. . . .

This right of contract, however, is itself subject to certain limitations which the state may lawfully impose in the exercise of its police powers. While this power is inherent in all governments, it has doubtless been greatly expanded in its application during the past century, owing to an enormous increase in the number of occupations which are dangerous, or so far detrimental to the health of employees as to demand special precaution for their well-being and protection, or the safety of adjacent property. While this court has held . . . that the police power cannot be put forward as an excuse for oppressive and unjust legislation, it may be lawfully resorted to for the purpose of preserving the public health, safety, or morals, or the abatement of public nuisances, and a large discretion "is necessarily vested in the legislature to determine, not only what the interests of the public require, but what measures are necessary for the protection of such interests." . . .

Upon the principles above stated, we think the act in question may be sustained as a valid exercise of the police power of the State. The enactment does not profess to limit the hours of all workmen, but merely those who are employed in underground mines, or in the smelting, reduction, or refining of ores or metals. These employments when too long pursued the legislature has judged to be detrimental to the health of the employees, and, so long as there are reasonable grounds for believing that this is so, its decision upon this subject cannot be reviewed by the Federal courts.

While the general experience of mankind may justify us in believing that men may engage in ordinary employments more than eight hours per day without injury to their health, it does not follow that labor for the same length of time is innocuous when carried on beneath the surface of the earth, where the operative is deprived of fresh air and sunlight, and is frequently subjected to foul atmosphere and a very high temperature, or to influence of noxious gases, generated by the processes of refining or smelting. . . .

It may not be improper to suggest in this connection that although the prosecution in this case was against the employer of labor, who apparently under the statute is the only one liable, his defence is not so much that his right to contract has been infringed upon, but that the act works a peculiar hardship to his employees, whose right to labor as long as they please is alleged to be thereby violated. The argument would certainly come with better grace and greater cogency from the latter class. But the fact that both parties are of full age and competent to contract does not necessarily deprive the State of the power to interfere where the parties do not stand upon an equality, or where the public health demands that one party to the contract shall be protected against himself. "The State still retains an interest in his welfare, however reckless he may be. The whole is no greater than the sum of all the parts, and when the individual health, safety, and welfare are sacrificed or neglected, the state must suffer."

We have no disposition to criticise the many authorities which hold that state statutes restricting the hours of labor are unconstitutional. Indeed, we are not called upon to express an opinion upon this subject. It is sufficient to say of them that they have no application to cases where the legislature had adjudged that a limitation is necessary for the preservation of the health of employees, and there are reasonable grounds for believing that such determination is supported by the facts. The question in each case is whether the legislature has adopted the statute in exercise of a reasonable discretion, or whether its action be a mere excuse for an unjust discrimination, or the oppression, or spoliation of a particular class. . . .

167. *"Meddlesome interference with the rights of the individual."*

Lochner v. New York, 198 U.S. 45 (1905).

PECKHAM, J.: . . . The State . . . has power to prevent the individual from making certain kinds of contracts, and in regard to them the Federal Constitution offers no protection. If the contract be one which the State, in the legitimate exercise of its police power, has the right to prohibit, it is not prevented from prohibiting it by the Fourteenth Amendment. . . .

This court has recognized the existence and upheld the exercise of the police powers of the States in many cases which might fairly be considered as border ones, and it has, in the course of its determination of questions regarding the asserted invalidity of such statutes, on the ground of their violation of the rights secured by the federal Constitution, been guided by rules of a very liberal nature, the application of which has resulted, in numerous instances, in upholding the validity of state statutes thus assailed. . . .

It must, of course, be conceded that there is a limit to the valid exercise of the police power by the State. There is no dispute concerning this general proposition. Otherwise the Fourteenth Amendment would have no efficacy and the legislatures of the States would have unbounded power, and it would be enough to say that any piece of legislation was enacted to conserve the morals, the health, or the safety of the people; such legislation would be valid, no matter how absolutely without foundation the claim might be. . . . In every case that comes before this court, therefore, where legislation of this character is concerned, and where the protection of the federal Constitution is sought, the question necessarily arises: Is this a fair, reasonable, and appropriate exercise of the police power of the State, or is it an unreasonable, unnecessary, and arbitrary interference with the right of the individual to his personal liberty or to enter into those contracts in relation to labor which may seem to him appropriate or necessary for the support of himself and his family? Of course the liberty of contract relating to labor includes both parties to it. The one has as much right to purchase as the other to sell labor. . . .

The question whether this act is valid as a labor law, pure and simple, may be dismissed in a few words. There is no reasonable ground for interfering with the liberty of person or the right of free contract, by determining the hours of labor, in the occupation of a baker. There is no contention that bakers as a class are not equal in intelligence and capacity to men in other trades or manual occupations, or that they are not able to assert their rights and care for themselves without the protecting arm of the State, interfering with their independence of judgment and of action. They are in no sense wards of the State. Viewed in the light of a purely labor law, with no reference whatever to the question of health, we think that a law like the one before us involves neither the safety, the morals, nor the welfare, of the public, and that the interest of the public is not in the slightest degree affected by such an act. The law must be upheld, if at all, as a law pertaining to the health of the individual engaged in the occupation of a baker. It does not affect any other portion of the public than those who who engaged in that occupation. Clean and wholesome bread does not depend upon whether the baker works but ten hours per day or only sixty hours a week. The limitation of the hours of labor does not come within the police power on that ground.

It is a question of which of two powers or rights shall prevail—the power of the State to legislate or the right of the individual to liberty of person and freedom of contract. The mere assertion that the subject relates, though but in a remote degree, to the public health, does not necessarily render the enactment valid. The act must have a more direct relation, as a means to an end, and the end itself must be appropriate and legitimate, before an act can be held to be valid which interferes with the general right of an individual to be free in his person and in his power to contract in relation to his own labor. . . .

We think the limit of the police power has been reached and passed in this case. . . . Statutes of the nature of that under review, limiting the hours in which grown and intelligent men may labor to earn their living, are mere meddlesome interferences with the rights of the individual. . . .

It is manifest to us that the limitation of the hours of labor as provided for in this section of the statute . . . has no such direct relation to and no such substantial effect upon the health of the employee, as to justify us in regarding the section as really a health law. It seems to us that the real object and purpose were simply to regulate the hours of labor between the master and his employees . . .

in a private business, not dangerous in any degree to morals or in any real and substantial degree, to the health of the employees. Under such circumstances the freedom of master and employee to contract with each other in relation to their employment, and in defining the same, cannot be prohibited or interfered with, without violating the Federal Constitution.

168. *"The Fourteenth Amendment does not enact Spencer's Social Statics."*

Lochner v. New York, 198 U.S. 45 (1905).

HOLMES, J., dissenting: . . . This case is decided upon an economic theory which a large part of the country does not entertain. If it were a question whether I agreed with that theory, I should desire to study it further and long before making up my mind. But I do not conceive that to be my duty, because I strongly believe that my agreement or disagreement has nothing to do with the right of a majority to embody their opinions in law. It is settled by various decisions of this court that state constitutions and state laws may regulate life in many ways which we as legislators might think as injudicious or if you like as tyrannical as this, and which equally with this, interfere with the liberty to contract. Sunday laws and usury laws are ancient examples. A more modern one is the prohibition of lotteries. The liberty of the citizen to do as he likes so long as he does not interfere with the liberty of others to do the same, which has been a shibboleth for some well-known writers, is interfered with by school laws, by the post-office, by every state or municipal institution which takes his money for purposes thought desirable, whether he likes it or not. The Fourteenth Amendment does not enact Mr. Herbert Spencer's Social Statics. . . . United States and state statutes and decisions cutting down the liberty to contract by way of combination are familiar to this court. . . . Some of these laws embody convictions or prejudices which judges are likely to share. Some may not. But a constitution is not intended to embody a particular economic theory, whether of paternalism and the organic relation of the citizen to the state or of *laissez faire*. It is made for people of fundamentally differing views, and the accident of our finding certain opinions natural and familiar or novel and even shocking ought not to conclude our judgment upon the question whether statutes embodying them conflict with the Constitution of the United States.

General propositions do not decide concrete cases. The decision will depend on a judgment or intuition more subtle than any articulate major premise. But I think that the proposition just stated, if it is accepted, will carry us far toward the end. Every opinion tends to become a law. I think that the word liberty in the Fourteenth Amendment, is perverted when it is held to prevent the natural outcome of a dominant opinion, unless it can be said that a rational and fair man necessarily would admit that the statute proposed would infringe fundamental principles as they have been understood by the traditions of our people and our law. It does not need research to show that no such sweeping condemnation can be passed upon the statute before us. A reasonable man might think it a proper measure on the score of health. Men whom I certainly could not pronounce unreasonable would uphold it as a first instalment of a general regulation of the hours of work. Whether in the latter aspect it would be open to the charge of inequality I think it unnecessary to discuss.

169. *The "Brandeis Brief" Adds a New Dimension to Legal Argument*

Louis D. Brandeis, Brief for Defendant in Error, *Muller v. Oregon, Transcripts of Records and File Copies of Briefs*, 1907, XXIV (Cases 102-7), Library of the Supreme Court, Washington, D.C.

This case presents the single question whether the Statute of Oregon, . . . which provides that "no female [shall] be employed in any mechanical establishment or factory or laundry" "more than ten hours during any one day," is unconstitutional and void as violating the Fourteenth Amendment of the Federal Constitution.

The decision in this case will, in effect, determine the constitutionality of nearly all the statutes in force in the United States, limiting the hours of labor of adult women. . . .

The facts of common knowledge of which the Court may take judicial notice . . . establish, we submit, conclusively, that there is reasonable ground for holding that to permit women in Oregon to work in a "mechanical establishment, or factory, or laundry" more than ten hours in one day is dangerous to the public health, safety, morals, or welfare. . . .

The leading countries in Europe in which women are largely employed in factory or similar work have found it necessary to take action for the protection of their health and safety and the public welfare, and have enacted laws limiting the hours of labor for adult women. . . .

Twenty States of the Union . . . have [also] enacted laws limiting the hours of labor for adult women. . . .

In the United States, as in foreign countries, there has been a general movement to strengthen and to extend the operation of these laws. In no State has any such law been held unconstitutional, except in Illinois. . . .

I. THE DANGER OF LONG HOURS
A. *Causes*

(1) Physical Differences Between Men and Women. . . .
Report of Select Committee on Shops Early Closing Bill, British House of Commons, 1895.

Dr. Percy Kidd, physician in Brompton and London Hospitals:

The most common effect I have noticed of the long hours is general deterioration of health; very general symptoms which we medically attribute to over-action, and debility of the nervous system; that includes a great deal more than what is called nervous disease, such as indigestion, constipation, a general slackness, and a great many other indefinite symptoms.

Are those symptoms more marked in women than in men?

I think they are much more marked in women. I should say one sees a great many more women of this class than men; but I have seen precisely the same symptoms in men, I should not say in the same proportion, because one has not been able to make anything like a statistical inquiry. There are other symptoms, but I mention those as being the most common. Another symptom especially among women is anemia, bloodlessness or pallor, that I have no doubt is connected with long hours indoors. . . .

Report of the Maine Bureau of Industrial and Labor Statistics, 1888.

Let me quote from Dr. Ely Von der Warker (1875):

Woman is badly constructed for the purposes of standing eight or ten hours upon her feet. I do not intend to bring into evidence the peculiar position and nature of the organs contained in the pelvis, but to call attention to the peculiar construction of the knee and the shallowness of the pelvis, and the delicate nature of the foot as part of a sustaining column. The knee joint of woman is a sexual characteristic. Viewed in front and extended, the joint in but a slight degree interrupts the gradual taper of the thigh into the leg. Viewed in a semi-flexed position, the joint forms a smooth ovate spheriod. The reason of this lies in the smallness of the patella in front, and the narrowness of the articular surfaces of the tibia and femur, and which in man form the lateral prominences, and thus is much more perfect as a sustaining column than that of a woman. The muscles which keep the body fixed upon the thighs in the erect position labor under the disadvantage of shortness of purchase, owing to the short distance, compared to that of men, between the crest of the ilium and the great trochanter of the femur, thus giving to man a much larger purchase in the leverage existing between the trunk and the extremities. Comparatively the foot is less able to sustain weight than that of man, owing to its shortness and the more delicate formation of the tarsus and metatarsus. . . .

Infant Mortality: A Social Problem. George Newman, M.D., *London*, 1906.

The results of fatigue become manifest in various ways, not the least being the occurrence of accidents or of physical breakdown. The former, as is now well recognized, occur most frequently in fatigued workers. For example, since 1900 there has been a steady, though not marked, increase in the number of accidents to women over eighteen years of age in laundries. In 1900 such accidents numbered 131; in 1904, 157. Now it has been shown that whilst the first half of the day yields about the same number of accidents as the second half, more accidents, amounting to nearly double the number, occur between the hours of 11

A.M. and 1 P.M., and between 4 P.M. and 7 P.M. than at any other time of the day. . . .

Relations between Labor and Capital. United States Senate Committee, 1883.

Vol. I. *Testimony of* Robert Howard, *Mule-Spinner in Fall River Cotton Mills.*

I have noticed that the hard, slavish overwork is driving those girls into the saloons, after they leave the mills evenings . . . good, respectable girls, but they come out so tired and so thirsty and so exhausted . . . from working along steadily from hour to hour and breathing the noxious effluvia from the grease and other ingredients used in the mill. . . .

Drinking is most prevalent among working people where the hours of labor are long. . . .

President Roosevelt's Annual Message delivered to the Second Session of the 59th Congress, December 4, 1906.

More and more [of] our people are growing to recognize the fact that the questions which are not merely of industrial but of social importance outweigh all others; and these two questions (labor of women and children) most emphatically come in the category of those which affect in the most far-reaching way the home-life of the nation. . . .

Industrial Conference National Civic Federation, 1902.

The most striking fact about this question of hours of labor seems to be its universality. In virtually every country dominated by Western civilization the daily work-time in mechanical industries is being cut down by successive movements that appear to be as inevitable as the tide, and that have the appearance of steps in the path of human progress. . . . (George Gunton, page 190).

That the time is now ripe for another

general reduction in the daily working time is indicated by the testimony of physicians and the mortality statistics of occupations. . . . (A. J. Weber, Chief Statistician, New York Department of Labor, page 200). . . .

LAUNDRIES

The special prohibition in the Oregon Act of more than ten hours' work in laundries is not an arbitrary discrimination against that trade. Laundries would probably not be included under the general term of "manufacturing" or "mechanical establishments"; and yet the special dangers of long hours in laundries, as the business is now conducted, present strong reasons for providing a legal limitation of the hours of work in that business. . . .

CONCLUSION

We submit that in view of the facts above set forth and of legislative action extending over a period of more than sixty years in the leading countries in Europe, and in twenty of our States, it cannot be said that the Legislature of Oregon has no reasonable ground for believing that the public health, safety, or welfare did not require a legal limitation on women's work in manufacturing and mechanical establishments and laundries to ten hours in one day.

DUE PROCESS AND PUBLIC HEALTH

170. Is Smallpox Contagion Guaranteed by the Fourteenth Amendment?

Jacobson v. Massachusetts, 197 U.S. 11 (1905).

HARLAN, J.: . . . The authority of the State to enact this statute is to be referred to what is commonly called the police power—a power which the State did not surrender when becoming a member of the Union under the Constitution. Although this court has refrained from any attempt to define the limits of that power, yet it has distinctly recognized the authority of a State to enact quarantine laws and "health laws of every description"; indeed, all laws that relate to matters completely within its territory and which do not by their necessary operation affect the people of other States. According to settled principles the police power of a State must be held to embrace, at least, such reasonable regulations established directly by legislative enactment as will protect the public health and the public safety. . . . It is equally true that the State may invest local bodies called into existence for purposes of local administration with authority in some appropriate way to safeguard the public health and the public safety. . . .

The defendant insists that his liberty is invaded when the State subjects him to fine or imprisonment for neglecting or refusing to submit to vaccination; that a compulsory vaccination law is unreasonable, arbitrary and oppressive, and, therefore, hostile to the inherent right of every freeman to care for his own body and health in such way as to him seems best; and that the execution of such a law against one who objects to vaccination, no matter for what reason, is nothing short of an assault upon his person. But the liberty secured by the Constitution of the United States to every person within its jurisdiction does not import an absolute right in each person to be, at all times and in all circumstances, wholly freed from restraint. There are manifold restraints to which every person is necessarily subject for the common good. On any other basis organized society could not exist with safety to its members. Society based on the rule that each one is a law unto himself would soon be confronted with disorder and anarchy. Real liberty for all could not exist under the operation of a principle which recognizes the right of each individual person to use his own, whether in respect of his person or his property, regardless of the injury that may be done to others. . . .

The defendant did not offer to prove that, by reason of his then condition, he was in fact not a fit subject of vaccination. . . .

We are unwilling to hold it to be an element in the liberty secured by the Constitution of the United States that one

person, or a minority of persons, residing in any community and enjoying the benefits of its local government, should have the power thus to dominate the majority when supported in their action by the authority of the State. While this court should guard with firmness every right appertaining to life, liberty or property as secured to the individual by the Supreme Law of the Land, it is of the last importance that it should not invade the domain of local authority except when it is plainly necessary to do so in order to enforce that law. The safety and the health of the people of Massachusetts are, in the first instance, for that Commonwealth to guard and protect. . . .

Constitutional Reflections of Progressivism

PROGRESSIVISM AND REFORM AMENDMENTS

171. Changing the Constitution

A. THE SIXTEENTH AMENDMENT: INCOME TAX

Proposed July 12, 1909; adopted February 25, 1913.

The Congress shall have power to lay and collect taxes on incomes, from whatever source derived, without apportionment among the several States, and without regard to any census or enumeration.

B. THE SEVENTEENTH AMENDMENT: DIRECT ELECTION OF SENATORS

Proposed May 16, 1912; adopted May 31, 1913.

The Senate of the United States shall be composed of two Senators from each State, elected by the people thereof, for six years; and each Senator shall have one vote. The electors in each State shall have the qualifications requisite for electors of the most numerous branch of the State legislature.

When vacancies happen in the representation of any State in the Senate, the executive authority of such State shall issue writs of election to fill such vacancies: *Provided,* That the legislature of any State may empower the executive thereof to make temporary appointment until the people fill the vacancies by election as the legislature may direct.

This amendment shall not be so construed as to affect the election or term of any Senator chosen before it becomes valid as part of the Constitution.

C. THE EIGHTEENTH AMENDMENT: PROHIBITION

Proposed December 18, 1917; adopted January 29, 1919.

1. After one year from the ratification of this article the manufacture, sale, or transportation of intoxicating liquors within, the importation thereof into, or the exportation thereof from the United States and all territory subject to the jurisdiction thereof for beverage purposes is hereby prohibited.

2. The Congress and the several States shall have concurrent power to enforce this article by appropriate legislation.

3. This article shall be inoperative unless it shall have been ratified as an amendment to the Constitution by the Legislatures of the several States, as provided in the Constitution, within seven years from the date of the submission hereof to the States by the Congress.

D. THE NINETEENTH AMENDMENT: WOMAN SUFFRAGE

Proposed June 4, 1919; adopted August 26, 1920.

1. The right of citizens of the United States to vote shall not be denied or abridged by the United States or by any State on account of sex.

2. Congress shall have power, by appropriate legislation, to enforce the provisions of this article.

THE PREROGATIVES OF STATEHOOD

172. *Direct Democracy and a Republican Form of Government*

Pacific States Telephone and Telegraph Co. v. Oregon, 223 U.S. 118 (1912).

WHITE, C.J.: . . . The assignments of error filed on the allowance of the writ of error are numerous. The entire matters covered by each and all of them in the argument, however, are reduced to six propositions, which really amount to but one, since they are all based upon the single contention that the creation by a State of the power to legislate by the initiative and referendum causes the prior lawful state government to be bereft of its lawful character as the result of the provisions of §4 of Art. IV of the Constitution, that "The United States shall guarantee to every State in this Union, a Republican Form of Government. . . ." This being the basis of all the contentions, the case comes to the single issue whether the enforcement of that provision, because of its political character, is exclusively committed to Congress or is judicial in its character. . . .

Do the provisions of . . . [§4, Art. iv] obliterate the division between judicial authority and legislative power upon which the Constitution rests? In other words, do they authorize the judiciary to substitute its judgment as to a matter purely political for the judgment of Congress on a subject committed to it and thus overthrow the Constitution upon the ground that thereby the guarantee to the States of a government republican in form may be secured, a conception which after all rests upon the assumption that the States are to be guaranteed a government republican in form by destroying the very existence of a government republican in form in the Nation.

We shall not stop to consider the text to point out how absolutely barren it is of support for the contentions sought to be based upon it, since the repugnancy of those contentions to the letter and spirit of that text is so conclusively established by prior decisions of this court as to cause the matter to be absolutely foreclosed. . . .

The court, speaking through Mr. Chief Justice Fuller, in *Taylor v. Beckham,* No. 1, . . . said:

"But it is said that the Fourteenth Amendment must be read with §4 of Art. iv, of the Constitution, providing that: 'the United States shall guarantee to every State in this Union a republican form of government. . . .'"

"It was long ago settled that the enforcement of this guarantee belonged to the political department. *Luther v. Bor-*den. . . . In that case it was held that the question, which of the two opposing governments of Rhode Island, namely, the charter government or the government established by a voluntary convention, was the legitimate one, was a question for the determination of the political department; and when that department had decided, the courts were bound to take notice of the decision and follow it. . . ."

It is indeed a singular misconception of the nature and character of our constitutional system of government to suggest that the settled distinction which the doctrine just stated points out between judicial authority over justiciable controversies and legislative power as to purely political questions tends to destroy the duty of the judiciary in proper cases to enforce the Constitution. The suggestion but results from failing to distinguish between things which are widely different, that is, the legislative duty to determine the political questions involved in deciding whether a state government republican in form exists, and the judicial power and ever-present duty whenever it becomes necessary, in a controversy properly submitted, to enforce and uphold the applicable provisions of the Constitution as to each and every exercise of governmental power. . . .

As the issues presented, in their very essence, are, and have long since by this court been, definitely determined to be political and governmental, and embraced within the scope of the powers conferred upon Congress, and not, therefore, within the reach of judicial power, it follows that the case presented is not within our jurisdiction, and the writ of error must therefore be, and it is, dismissed for want of jurisdiction.

173. *President Taft's Veto of the Arizona Enabling Act, August 22, 1911*

Richardson, ed., *Messages and Papers of the Presidents*, XI, 7636-44.

I return herewith, without my approval, House joint resolution No. 14, "To admit the Territories of New Mexico and Arizona as States into the Union on an equal footing with the original States." . . .

If I sign this joint resolution, I do not see how I can escape responsibility for the judicial recall of the Arizona constitution. . . .

This provision of the Arizona constitution, in its application to county and State judges, seems to me so pernicious in its effect, so destructive of independence in the judiciary, so likely to subject the rights of the individual to the possible tyranny of a popular majority, and, therefore, to be so injurious to the cause of free government, that I must disapprove a constitution containing it. . . .

A government is for the benefit of all the people. . . . Now, as the government is for all the people, and is not solely for a majority of them, the majority in exercising control either directly or through its agents is bound to exercise the power for the benefit of the minority as well as the majority. . . . No honest, clear-headed man, however great a lover of popular government, can deny that the unbridled expression of the majority of a community converted hastily into law or action would sometimes make a government tyrannical and cruel. Constitutions are checks upon the hasty action of the majority. They are the self-imposed restraints of a whole people upon a majority of them to secure sober action and a respect for the rights of the minority, and of the individual in his relation to other individuals, and in his relation to the whole people in their character as a state or government. . . .

By the recall in the Arizona constitution it is proposed to give to the majority power to remove arbitrarily, and without delay, any judge who may have the courage to render an unpopular decision. . . . Could there be a system more ingeniously devised to subject judges to momentary gusts of popular passion than this? We cannot be blind to the fact that often an intelligent and respectable electorate may be so roused upon an issue that it will visit with condemnation the decision of a just judge, though exactly in accord with the law governing the case, merely because it affects unfavorably their contest. . . .

Judicial recall is advocated on the ground that it will bring the judges more into sympathy with the popular will and the progress of ideas among the people. It is said that now judges are out of touch with the movement toward a wider democracy and a greater control of governmental agencies in the interest and for the benefit of the people. The righteous and just course for a judge to pursue is ordinarily fixed by statute or clear principles of law, and the cases in which his judgment may be affected by his political, economic, or social views are infrequent. But even in such cases, judges are not removed from the people's influence. Surround the judiciary with all the safeguards possible, create judges by appointment, make their tenure for life, forbid diminution of salary during their term, and still it is impossible to prevent the influence of popular opinion from coloring judgments in the long run. Judges are men, intelligent, sympathetic men, patriotic men, and in those fields of the law in which the personal equation unavoidably plays a part, there will be found a response to sober popular opinion as it changes to meet the exigency of social, political, and economic changes. Indeed this should be so. Individual instances of a hidebound and retrograde conservatism on the part of courts in decisions which turn on the individual economic or sociological views of the judges may be pointed out; but they are not many, and do not call for radical action. . . .

But it is said that the people of Arizona are to become an independent State when created, and even if we strike out judicial recall now, they can reincorporate it in their constitution after statehood.

To this I would answer that in dealing with the courts, which are the cornerstone of good government, and in which not only the voters, but the nonvoters and nonresidents, have a deep interest as a security for their rights of life, liberty, and property, no matter what the future action of the State may be, it is necessary for the authority which is primarily responsible for its creation to assert in no doubtful tones the necessity for an independent and untrammeled judiciary. . . .

CHAPTER XIX

World War I

EVEN though the United States entered the World War on a note of Wilsonian idealism, the shattering experience of total war ended the era of Progressivism. In shifting to wartime mobilization, however, broad federal powers, which had been utilized to further domestic reforms, were expanded to meet the overwhelming demands of international conflict, accelerating the trend towards national centralization and executive leadership. The extent of federal power and presidential control raised formidable constitutional issues. The Lever Act (No. 174), one of the most important war measures, was a drastic enactment authorizing federal control of the domestic economy, a sphere normally reserved for the states. Only one feature of this law, as subsequently amended, was declared unconstitutional. In *U.S. v. Cohen Grocery* (1921), the Court voided the price-fixing provisions that failed to specify what constituted unjust prices. By concentrating on the detailed phrasing of only one section of the statute, the Court implicitly accepted the broad grant of power. In *Matthew Addy Co. v. U.S.* (1924), the Court also decided a similar case on narrow technical grounds, thus avoiding an adverse decision on a war measure, even though hostilities had ceased nearly six years earlier.

Another example of expanding federal power and increased executive authority was presidential seizure and government operation of the nation's rail network. As early as 1916, an Army Appropriation Act had authorized the President "in time of war . . . to take possession and assume control of any system . . . of transportation." After presidential seizure in 1917, Congress passed the Railway Administration Act (1918) providing for government operation of the roads and compensation of their owners. The Court upheld executive seizure in *Northern Pacific Railway Co. v. North Dakota* (No. 175).

Prohibition of the manufacture and sale of alcoholic beverages also extended federal powers. The Selective Service Law of 1917 had forbidden the sale of liquor on military posts or to military personnel in uniform. In 1918 Congress empowered the President to prohibit the sale of liquor near coal mines, munition factories, shipbuilding and other war plants. Ironically, however, complete prohibition was not established until ten days after the signing of the Armistice. In the so-called Wartime Prohibition Cases (1918), Justice Brandeis upheld the act under the federal war power, ruling that the conflict had not been officially terminated.

One of the most sweeping delegations of legislative authority to the executive came in the Overman Act (No. 176), which gave the President almost unlimited power to reorganize federal agencies directing the nation's resources in wartime. The broad scope of the measure aroused bitter opposition, and Senator Frank B. Brandagee caustically proposed that "if any power, constitutional or not, has been inadvertently omitted from this bill, it is hereby granted in full." Passed by a wide margin, the Act never came before the Court for adjudication.

Despite the limitations imposed by the first ten amendments on governmental interference with individual liberties, federal authority was expanded at the expense of traditional civil rights. Although Congress had passed a conscription act during the Civil War, the Court had not reviewed its constitutionality. It was not until 1918 that Chief Justice White ruled in the Selective Draft Law Cases (No. 177) that the power of conscription was implied by the provision authorizing Congress to declare war and to raise and support armies.

The most drastic abrogation of civil liberties during the war came as a result of the Espionage Act (1917) and the Sedition Act (1918). The first measure contained two sections dealing with freedom of speech and of the press. One punished attempts to cause disobedience or insubordination in the armed forces, to obstruct enlistments, or to make false reports intended to obstruct military operations. Postal censorship was established by Title 12 which banned treasonable or seditious material from the mails. Both sections were so loosely phrased as to constitute severe threats to basic freedoms, if interpreted as broadly as other wartime legislation. In *Schenck v. U.S.* (No. 178), Justice Holmes enunciated the "clear and present danger" doctrine as the proper standard by which to measure the extent of freedom of speech. Applying this rule, Holmes ruled that Schenck's antidraft pamphlets constituted an immediate danger to the recruiting service, amounting to a violation of the Espionage Act.

It was the Sedition Act, however, which lent itself most readily to regimentation of speech and press. In the Abrams case (No. 179), the defendants were charged with using "disloyal, scurrilous, and abusive language about the form of government of the United States" and opposing the "cause of the United States" in their denunciation of its expeditionary force to Russia. Two aspects of the case have had continuing significance: (1) in upholding the Sedition statute, the majority established the principle of curtailment of free speech despite the

First Amendment guarantees, and (2) Holmes' eloquent dissent (No. 180) elaborated the "clear and present danger" rule as the leading defense against overzealous enforcement of such a law.

Wartime Economic Controls

CONGRESS ENACTS EMERGENCY LEGISLATION

174. *The National Security and Internal Controls*

Lever Act, *U. S. Stat. at L.*, XL, 276-87 (August 10, 1917).

Be it enacted, That by reason of the existence of a state of war, it is essential to the national security and defense, for the successful prosecution of the war, and for the support and maintenance of the Army and Navy, to assure an adequate supply and equitable distribution, and to facilitate the movement, of foods, feeds, fuel . . . and equipment required for the actual production of foods, feeds, and fuel, hereafter in this Act called necessaries; to prevent, . . . scarcity, monopolization, hoarding, injurious speculation, manipulations . . . and private controls, affecting such supply, . . . and to establish and maintain governmental control of such necessaries during the war. For such purposes the instrumentalities . . . and prohibitions hereinafter set forth are created. The President is authorized to make such regulations and to issue such orders as are essential effectively to carry out the provisions of this Act. . . .

SEC. 14. That whenever the President shall find that an emergency exists requiring stimulation of the production of wheat and that it is essential that the producers of wheat, produced within the United States, shall have the benefits of the guaranty provided for in this section, he is au-

thorized, . . . to determine and fix and to give public notice of what, under specified conditions, is a reasonable guaranteed price for wheat, in order to assure such producers a reasonable profit. The President shall thereupon fix such guaranteed price. . . . Thereupon, the Government of the United States hereby guarantees every producer of wheat produced within the United States, that, upon compliance by him with the regulations prescribed, he shall receive for any wheat produced in reliance upon this guarantee within the period, not exceeding eighteen months, prescribed in the notice, a price not less than the guaranteed price therefor as fixed pursuant to this section. . . . The guaranteed prices for the several standard grades of wheat for the crop of nineteen hundred and eighteen, shall be based upon number one northern spring or its equivalent at not less than $2 per bushel at the principal interior primary markets. This guaranty shall not be dependent upon the action of the President under the first part of this section, but is hereby made absolute and shall be binding until May first, nineteen hundred and nineteen. . . .

For the purpose of making any guaranteed price effective under this section, or whenever he deems it essential . . . the President is authorized also, in his discretion, to purchase any wheat for which a guaranteed price shall be fixed . . . and to hold, transport, or store it, or to sell, dispose of, and deliver the same. . . .

SEC. 15. That from and after thirty days from the date of the approval of this Act no foods, fruits, food materials, or feeds shall be used in the production of distilled spirits for beverage purposes. . . . Nor shall there be imported into the United States any distilled spirits. Whenever the President shall find that limitation, regulation, or prohibition of the use of foods, fruits, food materials, or feeds in the production of malt or vinous liquors for beverage purposes, or that reduction of the alcoholic content of any such malt or vinous liquor, is essential, in order to assure an adequate and continuous supply of food, or that the national security and defense will be subserved thereby, he is authorized, from time to time, to prescribe and give public notice of the extent of the limitation, regulation, prohibition, or reduction so necessitated. . . .

SEC. 16. That the President is authorized and directed to commandeer any or all distilled spirits in bond or in stock at the date of the approval of this Act for redistillation, in so far as such redistillation may be necessary to meet the requirements of the Government in the manufacture of munitions and other military and hospital supplies. . . .

SEC. 24. That the provisions of this Act shall cease to be in effect when the existing state of war between the United States and Germany shall have terminated. . . .

SEC. 25. That the President of the United States shall be, . . . empowered, whenever and wherever in his judgment necessary for the efficient prosecution of the war, to fix the price of coal and coke, wherever and whenever sold . . . to regulate the method of production, sale, shipment, distribution, apportionment, or storage thereof among dealers and consumers. . . .

175. *"The complete character of the war power is not disputable."*

Northern Pacific Railway Co. v. North Dakota, 250 U.S. 135 (1919).

WHITE, C.J.: . . . No elaboration could make clearer than do the Act of Congress of 1916, the proclamation of the President exerting the powers given, and the Act of 1918 dealing with the situation created by the exercise of such authority, that no divided but a complete possession and control were given the United States for all purposes as to the railroads in question. But if it be conceded that despite the absolute clarity of the provisions concerning the control given the United States, and the all-embracing scope of that control, there is room for some doubt, the consideration of the general context completely dispels hesitancy. . . . There is no basis for the contention that the power to make rates and enforce them which was plainly essential to the authority given was not included in it.

Conclusive as are these inferences, they are superfluous, since . . . §10 . . . confers the complete and undivided power to fix rates. The provision is this: "That during the period of Federal control, whenever in his opinion the public interest requires, the President may initiate rates, fares, charges, classifications, regulations, and practices by filing the same with the Interstate Commerce Commission, which . . . rates . . . and practices shall not be suspended by the commission pending final determination." These quoted words are immediately followed by provisions further defining the power of the Commission and its duty in the premises, so as to enable it beyond doubt to consider the situation resulting from the act and to which the rates were to be applied. The unison between that which is inferable and that which is expressed demonstrates the true significance of the statute. . . .

Besides, the presumption in question but denied the power exerted in the adoption of the statute, and displaced by an imaginary the dominant presumption which arose by operation of the Constitution as an inevitable effect of the adoption of the statute, as shown by the following:

(a) The complete and undivided character of the war power of the United States is not disputable. . . . On the face of the statutes it is manifest that they were in terms based upon the war power, since the authority they gave arose only because of the existence of war, and the right to exert such authority was to cease upon the war's termination. To interpret, therefore, the exercise of the power by a presumption of the continuance of a state power limiting and controlling the national authority was but to deny its existence. It was akin to the contention that the supreme right to raise armies and use them in case of war did not extend to directing where and when they should be used. . . .

(b) The elementary principle that under the Constitution the authority of the Government of the United States is paramount when exerted as to subjects concerning which it has the power to control, is indisputable. This being true, it results that although authority to regulate within a given sphere may exist in both the United States and in the States, when the former calls into play constitutional authority within such general sphere the necessary effect of doing so is, that to the extent that any conflict arises the state power is limited, since in case of conflict that which is paramount necessarily controls that which is subordinate.

Again, as the power which was exerted was supreme, to interpret it upon the basis that its exercise must be presumed to be limited was to deny the power itself. Thus, once more it comes to pass that the application of the assumed presumption was in effect but a form of expression by which the power which Congress had exerted was denied. In fact, error arising from indulging in such erroneous presumption permeates every contention. . . .

The confusion produced is . . . aptly illustrated by the rule of interpretation by which it is insisted that the express power to fix rates conferred by the statute was rightly disregarded. Thus, while admitting that the power which was conferred to initiate rates when considered in and of itself included all rates, it is nevertheless said that such power must be presumed to be limited to the only character of rates which under the prior law the Interstate Commerce Commission had the power to consider, that is, interstate rates, because the new rates when initiated were to be acted upon by that body. As, however, the statute in terms gives power to the Interstate Commerce Commission to consider the new rates in the light of the new and unified control which it creates, the error in the contention becomes manifest. . . .

It follows that the judgment below was erroneous. . . .

EXECUTIVE REORGANIZATION OF WARTIME BUREAUCRACY

176. *Congress Delegates Authority to the President as Commander in Chief*

Overman Act, *U. S. Stat. at L.*, XL, 556-7 (May 20, 1918).

Be it enacted . . . That for the national security and defense, for the successful prosecution of the war, for the support and maintenance of the Army and Navy, for the better utilization of resources and industries, and for the more effective exercise and more efficient administration by the President of his powers as Commander in Chief of the land and naval forces the President is hereby authorized to make such redistribution of functions among executive agencies as he may deem necessary, including any functions, duties, and powers hitherto by law conferred upon any executive department, commission, bureau, agency, office, or officer, in such manner as in his judgment shall seem best fitted to carry out the purposes of this Act, and to this end is authorized to make such regulations and to issue such orders as he may deem necessary, which regulations and orders shall be in writing and shall be filed with the head of the department affected and constitute a public record: *Provided,* . . . That the termination of this Act shall not affect any act done or any right or obligation accruing or accrued pursuant to this Act and during the time that this Act is in force: *Provided further,* That the authority by this Act granted shall be exercised only in matters relating to the conduct of the present war.

SEC. 2. That in carrying out the purposes of this Act the President is authorized to utilize, coordinate, or consolidate any executive or administrative commissions, bureaus, agencies, offices, or officers now existing by law, to transfer any duties or powers from one existing department, commission . . . to another, to transfer the personnel thereof or any part of it either by detail or assignment, together with the whole or any part of the records and public property belonging thereto. . . .

SEC. 5. That should the President, in redistributing the functions among the executive agencies as provided in this Act, conclude that any bureau should be abolished and it or their duties and functions conferred upon some other department or bureau or eliminated entirely, he shall report his conclusions to Congress with such recommendations as he may deem proper.

SEC. 6. That all laws or parts of laws conflicting with the provisions of this Act are to the extent of such conflict suspended while this Act is in force. . . .

Personal Controls: Selective Service, and Civil Liberties

177. Constitutionality of Conscription

Selective Draft Law Cases, *Arver v. U.S.*, 245 U.S. 366 (1918).

WHITE, C.J.: . . . The possession of authority to enact the statute must be found in the clauses of the Constitution giving Congress power "to declare war; . . . to raise and support armies, but no appropriation of money to that use shall be for a longer term than two years; . . . to make rules for the government and regulation of the land and naval forces." Article 1, §8. And of course the powers conferred by these provisions like all other powers given carry with them as provided by the Constitution the authority "to make all laws which shall be necessary and proper for carrying into execution the foregoing powers." Article 1, §8.

As the mind cannot conceive an army without the men to compose it, on the face of the Constitution the objection that it does not give power to provide for such men would seem to be too frivolous for further notice. It is said, however, that since under the Constitution as originally framed state citizenship was primary and United States citizenship but derivative and dependent thereon, therefore the power conferred upon Congress to raise armies was only coterminous with United States citizenship and could not be exerted so as to cause that citizenship to lose its dependent character and dominate state citizenship. But the proposition simply denies to Congress the power to raise armies which the Constitution gives. That power by the very terms of the Constitution, being delegated, is supreme. Article 6. In truth the contention simply assails the wisdom of the framers of the Constitution in conferring authority on Congress and in not retaining it as it was under the Confederation in the several States. Further it is said, the right to provide is not denied by calling for volunteer enlistments, but it does not and cannot include the power to exact enforced military duty by the citizen. This however but challenges the existence of all power, for a governmental power which has no sanction to it and which therefore can only be exercised provided the citizen consents to its exertion is in no substantial sense a power. It is argued, however, that although this is abstractedly true, it is not concretely so because as compelled military service is repugnant to a free government and in conflict with all the great guarantees of the Constitution as to individual liberty, it must be assumed that the authority to raise armies was intended to be limited to the right to call an army into existence counting alone upon the willingness of the citizen to do his duty in time of public need, that is, in time of war. But the premise of this proposition is so devoid of foundation that it leaves not even a shadow of ground upon which to base the conclusion. Let us see if this is not at once demonstrable. It may not be doubted that the very conception of a just government and its duty to the citizen includes the reciprocal obligation of the citizen to render military service in case of need and the right to compel it. . . .

In the Colonies before the separation from England there cannot be the slightest doubt that the right to enforce military service was unquestioned and that practical effect was given to the power in many cases. Indeed the brief of the government contains a list of Colonial acts manifesting the power and its enforcement in more than two hundred cases. And this exact situation existed also after the separation. Under the Articles of Confederation it is true Congress had no such power, as its authority was absolutely limited to making calls upon the States for the military forces needed to create and maintain the army, each State being bound for its quota as called. But it is indisputable that the States in response to the calls made upon them met the situation when they deemed it necessary by directing enforced military service on the part of the citizens. In fact the duty of the citizen to render military service and the power to compel him against his consent to do so was expressly sanctioned by the constitutions of at least nine of the States. . . .

When the Constitution came to be formed it may not be disputed that one of the recognized necessities for its adoption was the want of power in Congress to raise an army and the dependence upon the States for their quotas. In supplying the power it was manifestly intended to give it all and leave none to the States, since besides the delegation to Congress of authority to raise armies the Constitution prohibited the States, without the consent of Congress, from keeping troops in time of peace or engaging in war. Article I, §10. . . .

Thus sanctioned as is the act before us by the text of the Constitution, and by its significance as read in the light of the fundamental principles with which the subject is concerned, by the power recognized and carried into effect in many civilized countries, by the authority and practice of the colonies before the Revolution, of the States under the Confederation and of the Government since the formation of the Constitution, the want of merit in the contentions that the act

in the particulars which we have been previously called upon to consider was beyond the constitutional power of Congress, is manifest. . . .

In reviewing the subject we have hitherto considered it as it has been argued from the point of view of the Constitution as it stood prior to the adoption of the Fourteenth Amendment. But to avoid all misapprehension we briefly direct attention to that Amendment for the purpose of pointing out, as has been frequently done in the past, how completely it broadened the national scope of the Government under the Constitution by causing citizenship of the United States to be paramount and dominant instead of being subordinate and derivative, and therefore, operating as it does upon all the powers conferred by the Constitution, leaves no possible support for the contentions made, if their want of merit was otherwise not so clearly made manifest.

It remains only to consider contentions which, while not disputing power, challenge the act because of the repugnancy to the Constitution supposed to result from some of its provisions. First, we are of opinion that the contention that the act is void as a delegation of federal power to state officials because of some of its administrative features is too wanting in merit to require further notice. Second, we think that the contention that the statute is void because vesting administrative officers with legislative discretion has been so completely adversely settled as to require reference only to some of the decided cases. . . . A like conclusion also adversely disposes of a similar claim concerning the conferring of judicial power. . . . And we pass without anything but statement the proposition that an establishment of a religion or an interference with the free exercise thereof repugnant to the First Amendment resulted from the exemption clauses of the act to which we at the outset referred, because we think its unsoundness is too apparent to require us to do more.

Finally, as we are unable to conceive upon what theory the exaction by government from the citizen of the performance of his supreme and noble duty of contributing to the defense of the rights and honor of the nation, as the result of a war declared by the great representative body of the people, can be said to be the imposition of involuntary servitude in violation of the prohibitions of the Thirteenth Amendment, we are constrained to the conclusion that the contention to that effect is refuted by its mere statement.

Affirmed.

178. The "Clear and Present Danger" Test Qualifies Free Speech

Schenck v. U.S., 249 U.S. 47 (1919).

HOLMES, J.: . . . According to the testimony Schenck said he was general secretary of the Socialist party and had charge of the Socialist headquarters from which the documents were sent. He identified a book found there as the minutes of the Executive Committee of the party. The book showed a resolution of August 13, 1917, that 15,000 leaflets should be printed on the other side of one of them in use, to be mailed to men who had passed exemption boards, and for distribution. Schenck personally attended to the printing. On August 20, the general secretary's report said, "Obtained new leaflets from printer and started work addressing envelopes" &c.; and there was a resolve that Comrade Schenck be allowed $125 for sending leaflets through the mail. He said that he had about fifteen or sixteen thousand printed. There were files of the circular in question in the inner office which he said were printed on the other side of the one sided circular and were there for distribution. Other copies were proved to have been sent through the mails to drafted men. Without going into confirmatory details that were proved, no reasonable man could doubt that the defendant Schenck was largely instrumental in sending the circulars about. . . .

The document in question upon its first printed side recited the first section of the Thirteenth Amendment, said that the idea embodied in it was violated by the Con-

scription Act and that a conscript is little better than a convict. In impassioned language it intimated that conscription was despotism in its worse form and a monstrous wrong against humanity in the interest of Wall Street's chosen few. It said, "Do not submit to intimidation," but in form at least confined itself to peaceful measures such as a petition for the repeal of the act. The other and later printed side of the sheet was headed "Assert Your Rights." It stated reasons for alleging that any one violated the Constitution when he refused to recognize "your right to assert your opposition to the draft," and went on "If you do not assert and support your rights, you are helping to deny or disparage rights which it is the solemn duty of all citizens and residents of the United States to retain." It described the arguments on the other side as coming from cunning politicians and a mercenary capitalist press, and even silent consent to the conscription law as helping to support an infamous conspiracy. It denied the power to send our citizens away to foreign shores to shoot up the people of other lands, and added that words could not express the condemnation such cold-blooded ruthlessness deserves, &c., &c., winding up "You must do your share to maintain, support and uphold the rights of the people of this country." Of course the document would not have been sent unless it had been intended to have some effect, and we do not see what effect it could be expected to have upon persons subject to the draft except to influence them to obstruct the carrying of it out. The defendants do not deny that the jury might find against them on this point.

But it is said, suppose that that was the tendency of this circular, it is protected by the First Amendment to the Constitution. . . . We admit that in many places and in ordinary times the defendants in saying all that was said in the circular would have been within their constitutional rights. But the character of every act depends upon the circumstances in which it is done. . . . The most stringent protection of free speech would not protect a man in falsely shouting fire in a theatre and causing a panic. It does not even protect a man from an injunction against uttering words that may have all the effect of force. . . . The question in every case is whether the words used are used in such circumstances and are of such a nature as to create a clear and present danger that they will bring about the substantive evils that Congress has a right to prevent. It is a question of proximity and degree. When a nation is at war many things that might be said in time of peace are such a hindrance to its effort that their utterance will not be endured so long as men fight and that no Court could regard them as protected by any constitutional right. It seems to be admitted that if an actual obstruction of the recruiting service were proved, liability for words that produced that effect might be enforced. The statute of 1917 in §4 punishes conspiracies to obstruct as well as actual obstruction. If the act, (speaking, or circulating a paper,) its tendency and the intent with which it is done are the same, we perceive no ground for saying that success alone warrants making the act a crime. . . .

Judgments affirmed.

179. *Sedition and Speech in World War I*

Abrams v. U.S., 250 U.S. 616 (1919).

CLARKE, J.: On a single indictment, containing four counts, the five plaintiffs . . . were convicted of conspiring to violate provisions of the [Sedition] Act . . . of May 16, 1918. . . .

Each of the first three counts charged the defendants with conspiring, when the United States was at war with the Imperial Government of Germany, to unlawfully utter, print, write and publish: In the first count, "disloyal, scurrilous and abusive language about the form of Government of the United States;" in the second count, language "intended to bring the form of Government of the United States into contempt, scorn, contumely and disrepute;" and in the third count, language "intended to incite, provoke and encourage resistance to the United States in said war." The charge in the fourth count was that the defendants conspired "when the United States was at war with the Imperial German Government, . . . unlawfully and wilfully, by utterance, writing, printing and publication, to urge, incite and advocate curtailment of production of things and products, to wit, ordinance and ammunition, necessary and essential to the prosecution of the war." The offenses were charged in the language of the act of Congress.

It was charged in each count of the indictment that it was part of the conspiracy that the defendants would attempt to accomplish their unlawful purpose by printing, writing and distributing in the City of New York many copies of a leaflet or circular, printed in the English language, and of another printed in the Yiddish language, copies of which, properly identified, were attached to the indictment.

All of the five defendants were born in Russia. They were intelligent, had considerable schooling, and at the time they were arrested they had lived in the United States terms varying from five to ten years, but none of them had applied for naturalization. Four of them testified as witnesses in their own behalf and of these, three frankly avowed that they were "rebels," "revolutionists," "anarchists," that they did not believe in government in any form, and they declared that they had no interest whatever in the Government of the United States. The fourth defendant testified that he was a "socialist" and believed in "a proper kind of government, not capitalistic," but in his classification the Government of the United States was "capitalistic."

It was admitted on the trial that the defendants had united to print and distribute the described circulars and that five thousand of them had been printed and distributed about the 22d day of August, 1918. The group had a meeting place in New York City, in rooms rented by defendant Abrams, under an assumed name, and there the subject of printing the circulars was discussed about two weeks before the defendants were arrested. The defendant Abrams, although not a printer, on July 27, 1918, purchased the printing outfit with which the circulars were printed and installed it in a basement room where the work was done at night. The circulars were distributed some by throwing them from a window of a building where one of the defendants was employed and others secretly, in New York City.

The defendants pleaded "not guilty," and the case of the Government consisted in showing the facts we have stated, and in introducing in evidence copies of the two printed circulars attached to the indictment, a sheet entitled "Revolutionists Unite for Action," written by the defendant Lipman, and found on him when he was arrested, and another paper, found at the headquarters of the group, and for which Abrams assumed responsibility.

Thus the conspiracy and the doing of

the overt acts charged were largely admitted and were fully established.

On the record thus described it is argued, somewhat faintly, that the acts charged against the defendants were not unlawful because within the protection of that freedom of speech and of the press which is guaranteed by the First Amendment to the Constitution of the United States, and that the entire Espionage Act is unconstitutional because in conflict with that Amendment. . . .

The first of the two articles attached to the indictment is conspicuously headed, "The Hypocrisy of the United States and her Allies." After denouncing President Wilson as a hypocrite and a coward because troops were sent into Russia, it proceeds to assail our Government in general . . .

It will not do to say, as is now argued, that the only intent of these defendants was to prevent injury to the Russian cause. Men must be held to have intended, and to be accountable for, the effects which their acts were likely to produce. Even if their primary purpose and intent was to aid the cause of the Russian Revolution, the plan of action which they adopted necessarily involved, before it could be realized, defeat of the war program of the United States, for the obvious effect of this appeal, if it should become effective, as they hoped it might, would be to persuade persons of character such as those whom they regarded themselves as addressing, not to aid government loans and not to work in ammunition factories, where their work would produce "bullets, bayonets, cannon" and other munitions of war, the use of which would cause the "murder" of Germans and Russians. . . .

That the interpretation we have put upon these articles, circulated in the greatest port of our land, from which great numbers of soldiers were at the time taking ship daily, and in which great quantities of war supplies of every kind were at the time being manufactured for transportation overseas, is not only the fair interpretation of them, but that it is the meaning which their authors consciously intended should be conveyed by them to others is further shown by the additional writings found in the meeting place of the defendant group and on the person of one of them. . . .

These excerpts sufficiently show, that while the immediate occasion for this particular outbreak of lawlessness, on the part of the defendant alien anarchists, may have been resentment caused by our Government sending troops into Russia as a strategic operation against the Germans on the eastern battle front, yet the plain purpose of their propaganda was to excite, at the supreme crisis of the war, disaffection, sedition, riots, and, as they hoped, revolution, in this country for the purpose of embarrassing and if possible defeating the military plans of the Government in Europe. A technical distinction may perhaps be taken between disloyal and abusive language applied to the *form* of our government or language intended to bring the *form* of our government into contempt and disrepute, and language of like

character and intended to produce like results directed against the President and Congress, the agencies through which that form of government must function in time of war. But it is not necessary to a decision of this case to consider whether such distinction is vital or merely formal, for the language of these circulars was obviously intended to provoke and to encourage resistance to the United States in the war, as the third count runs, and, the defendants, in terms, plainly urged and advocated a resort to a general strike of workers in ammunition factories for the purpose of curtailing the production of ordnance and munitions necessary and essential to the prosecution of the war as is charged in the fourth count. Thus it is clear not only that some evidence but that much persuasive evidence was before the jury tending to prove that the defendants were guilty as charged in both the third and fourth counts of the indictment and under the long established rule of law hereinbefore stated the judgment of the District Court must be

Affirmed.

180. "We should be eternally vigilant against attempts to check the expression of opinions."

Abrams v. U.S., 250 U.S. 616 (1919).

HOLMES, J., dissenting: . . . No argument seems to me necessary to show that these pronunciamentos in no way attack the form of government of the United States, or that they do not support either of the first two counts. What little I have to say about the third count may be postponed until I have considered the fourth. With regard to that it seems too plain to be denied that the suggestion to workers in the ammunition factories that they are producing bullets to murder their dearest, and the further advocacy of a general strike, both in the second leaflet, do urge curtailment of production of things necessary to the prosecution of the war within the

meaning of the [Sedition] Act. . . . But to make the conduct criminal that statute requires that it should be "with intent by such curtailment to cripple or hinder the United States in the prosecution of the war." It seems to me that no such intent is proved.

I am aware of course that the word intent as vaguely used in ordinary legal discussion means no more than knowledge at the time of the act that the consequences said to be intended will ensue. Even less than that will satisfy the general principle of civil and criminal liability. A man may have to pay damages, may be sent to prison, at common law might be hanged, if at the time of his act he knew facts from which common experience showed that the consequences would follow, whether he individually could foresee them or not. But, when words are used exactly, a deed is not done with intent to produce a consequence unless that consequence is the aim of the deed. It may be obvious, and obvious to the actor, that the consequence will follow, and he may be liable for it even if he regrets it, but he does not do the act with intent to produce it unless the aim to produce it is the proximate motive of the specific act, although there may be some deeper motive behind.

It seems to me that this statute must be taken to use its words in a strict and accurate sense. They would be absurd in any other. A patriot might think that we were wasting money on aeroplanes, or making more cannon of a certain kind than we needed, and might advocate curtailment with success, yet even if it turned out that the curtailment hindered and was thought by other minds to have been obviously likely to hinder the United States in the prosecution of the war, no one would hold such conduct a crime. I admit that my illustration does not answer all that might be said but it is enough to show what I think and to let me pass to a more important aspect of the case. I refer to the First Amendment to the Constitution that Congress shall make no law abridging the freedom of speech. . . .

I do not doubt for a moment that by the same reasoning that would justify punishing persuasion to murder, the United States constitutionally may punish speech that produces or is intended to produce a clear and imminent danger that it will bring about forthwith certain substantive evils that the United States constitutionally may seek to prevent. The power undoubtedly is greater in time of war than in time of peace because war opens dangers that do not exist at other times.

But as against dangers peculiar to war, as against others, the principle of the right to free speech is always the same. It is only the present danger of immediate evil or an intent to bring it about that warrants Congress in setting a limit to the expression of opinion where private rights are not concerned. Congress certainly cannot forbid all effort to change the mind of the country. Now nobody can suppose that the surreptitious publishing of a silly leaflet by an unknown man, without more, would present any immediate danger that its opinions would hinder the success of the government arms or have any appreciable tendency to do so. Publishing those opinions for the very purpose of obstructing however, might indicate a greater danger and at any rate would have the quality of an attempt. So I assume that the second leaflet if published for the purposes alleged in the fourth count might be punishable. But it seems pretty clear to me that nothing less than that would bring these papers within the scope of this law. An actual intent in the sense that I have explained is necessary to constitute an attempt, where a further act of the same individual is required to complete the substantive crime. . . .

I do not see how anyone can find the intent required by the statute in any of the defendants' words. The second leaflet is the only one that affords even a foundation for the charge, and there, without invoking the hatred of German militarism expressed in the former one, it is evident from the beginning to the end that the only object of the paper is to help Russia and stop American intervention there against the popular government—not to impede the United States in the war that it was carrying on. To say that two phrases taken literally might import a suggestion of conduct that would have interference with the war as an indirect and probably undesired effect seems to me by no means enough to show an attempt to produce that effect. . . .

In this case sentences of twenty years imprisonment have been imposed for the publishing of two leaflets that I believe the defendants had as much right to publish as the Government has to publish the Constitution of the United States now vainly invoked by them. Even if I am technically wrong and enough can be squeezed from these poor and puny anonymities to turn the color of legal litmus paper; I will add, even if what I think the necessary intent were shown; the most nominal punishment seems to me all that possibly could be inflicted, unless the defendants are to be made to suffer not for what the indictment alleges but for the creed that they avow—a creed that I believe to be the creed of ignorance and immaturity when honestly held, as I see no reason to doubt that it was held here, but which, although made the subject of examination at the trial, no one has a right even to consider in dealing with the charges before the Court.

Persecution for the expression of opinions seems to me perfectly logical. If you have no doubt of your premises or your power and want a certain result with all your heart you naturally express your wishes in law and sweep away all opposition. To allow opposition by speech seems to indicate that you think the speech impotent, as when a man says that he has squared the circle, or that you do not care whole-heartedly for the result, or that you doubt either your power or your premises. But when men have realized that time has upset many fighting faiths, they may come to believe even more than they believe the very foundations of their own conduct that the ultimate good desired is better reached by free trade in ideas—that the best test of truth is the power of the thought to get itself accepted in the competition of the market, and that truth is the only ground upon which their wishes safely can be carried out. That at any rate is the theory of our Constitution. It is an experiment, as all life is an experiment. Every year if not every day we have to wager our salvation upon some prophecy based upon imperfect knowledge. While that experiment is part of our system I think that we should be eternally vigilant against attempts to check the expression of opinions that we loathe and believe to be fraught with death, unless they so imminently threaten immediate interference with the lawful and pressing purposes of the law that an immediate check is required to save the country. I wholly disagree with the argument of the Government that the First Amendment left the common law as to seditious libel in force. History seems to me against the notion. I had conceived that the United States through many years had shown its repentence for the Sedition Act of 1798, by repaying fines that it imposed. Only the emergency that makes it immediately dangerous to leave the correction of evil counsels to time warrants making any exception to the sweeping command, "Congress shall make no law . . . abridging the freedom of speech." Of course I am speaking only of expressions of opinion and exhortations, which were all that were uttered here, but I regret that I cannot put into more impressive words my belief that in their conviction upon this indictment the defendants were deprived of their rights under the Constitution of the United States.

Mr. Justice Brandeis concurs with the foregoing opinion.

CHAPTER XX

Diverse Trends of the Twenties

RESIDENT Warren G. Harding's declaration that "what America needs is less government in business and more business in government" heralded a period of "normalcy" which rejected Wilsonian and Progressive idealism in all three branches of government. The solemn averment of Harding's successor, Calvin Coolidge, that "the business of America is business" was an excellent barometer of the climate of opinion of the 1920's. Caught between the new "normalcy" and the expansive constitutional doctrines that had been used to justify wartime measures, the Court tended to vacillate between acquiescence in the constitutional conservatism of the new era and maintenance of the tradition of national supremacy. One of the developments of the 1920's, therefore, was the proclivity of the justices to be consistently inconsistent in defining the scope of national power.

One of the most impressive announcements of national power, for instance, came in 1920 in an unsuspect case involving migratory birds. Interpreting the treaty-making power broadly, Justice Holmes ruled that a treaty, once ratified, could be implemented by legislation that would have been invalid in the absence of the treaty (*Missouri v. Holland* [No. 181]). If the subject matter was sufficiently related to the general welfare, and if it was a national interest that could be protected "only by national action in concert with another power," the treaty-making power could be used to expand the regulatory power of Congress. In an era of *laissez faire*, however, Congress made no effort to extend its regulatory power in this, or any other, way.

On the other hand, Congress did utilize its investigatory powers and in *McGrain v. Daugherty* (No. 182) received strong Court support. Following the scandals of the Harding administration, a congressional committee, seeking an explanation for the activities and inactivities of Harry M. Daugherty, ex-Attorney General, subpoenaed his brother who ignored the order. To obtain information necessary for legislation, the Court ruled, Congress may exercise the judicial power of subpoenaing witnesses and punish them for contempt if they fail to appear. Two years later, the Court upheld the right of congressional committees to punish a witness for contempt if he refuses to answer questions (*Barry v. U.S. ex rel Cunningham*, 1929).

The nation's highest tribunal also continued its broad interpretation of the commerce power, expanded the taxing power, and strengthened the President's right to remove appointive officials. Chief Justice William Howard Taft and a unanimous Court upheld the Transportation Act of 1920 and justified federal intervention to alter intrastate rail rates fixed by a state commission, arguing that "the Nation cannot exercise complete effective control over interstate commerce without incidental regulation of intrastate commerce" (*Railroad Commission of Wisconsin v. C. B. & Q. R.R. Co.* [No. 183]). In *Stafford v. Wallace* (1922), Taft also gave new emphasis to the "current of commerce" doctrine enunciated in the Swift case (Chapter XVII). Upholding a federal statute regulating stockyards and meat packing, the Chief Justice indicated that the Court would not invalidate the measure "by a nice and technical inquiry into the non-interstate character of some of its necessary incidents and facilities." Federal taxing power received a similar sanction when, in *Massachusetts v. Mellon* (1923), the Court implied that revenue raised by national taxation could be used for economic and social purposes that were usually within the domain of the states. In a final important area, former President Taft upheld the power of the Chief Executive to remove appointive officers, thus vindicating Andrew Johnson posthumously by ruling unconstitutional that portion of the Tenure of Office Act of 1867 which required the President to obtain Senate approval before removing executive officials appointed by him (*Myers v. U.S.*, 1926).

Despite these examples, the Court during the Twenties generally acquiesced in business domination over regulatory commissions and administrative agencies, thus translating contemporary conservatism into constitutional law. As early as 1920, the Court negated the government's attempt to dissolve the United States Steel Corporation (No. 184), which then had the largest capitalization of any American business. Applying the "rule of reason," Justice McKenna denied that the company's monopolistic practices were unlawful; this judicial approval of business amalgamation set in motion an economic movement characteristic of the decade. The period also saw a renewal of the old system of business agreement, which now took the form of price and policy arrangements by trade associations. Originally hostile, the Court soon followed the lead of Secretary of Commerce Herbert Hoover, who was persuading businessmen to standardize their products and adopt codes of fair practice. In 1925, six of the Justices agreed that such activities, rather than fostering commercial restraints, tended "to stabilize trade and industry . . . and to avoid the waste which inevitably attends the unintelligent conduct of economic enterprise" (*Maple Flooring Manufacturers Association v. U.S.* [No. 185]). At the same time, the Court curtailed the Federal Trade Commission's right to define unfair trade practices (*F. T. C. v. Gratz* [No. 186]), and severely restricted its fact-finding authority (*F. T. C. v. Curtis Publishing Co., 1923*).

Despite an apparent inconsistency at the constitutional level, there was something of a pattern of consistency in the economics of the Court's decisions: business ordinarily won and labor usually lost. At the very moment that the Court limited federal regulatory power over business, it utilized federal legislation to protect employers and curtail trade-union practices. In 1921, the anti-injunction provisions of the Clayton Act (Chapter XVII) were virtually emasculated, and the way paved for the renewed use of the federal antitrust laws against unions (*Duplex Printing Press Co. v. Deering* [No. 187]). After a campaign of eleven years, however, a combination of liberal Republicans and Democrats pushed through the Norris-LaGuardia Act (1932) in an attempt to limit the issuance of labor injunctions.

During the decade, the Court struck down a child-labor law for the second time. In reframing that measure, care had been taken to avoid the commerce base proscribed by the Court in *Hammer v. Dagenhart* (Chapter XVIII); instead, the new statute proposed to eliminate the evil by levying a tax upon the profits of firms employing children. Such a use of the taxing power had strong precedents, and only one month after the passage of this measure, the Court sustained a similar prohibitive tax on the sale of narcotics (*U.S. v. Doremus*, 1919). But in *Bailey v. Drexel Furniture Co.* (No. 188), Chief Justice Taft condemned the child-labor law as an illegal use of the taxing power and an interference by Congress with matters reserved to the states by the Tenth Amendment. Thus, the "dual federalism" concept of *Hammer v. Dagenhart* again was employed to curtail national authority. Conceding their failure to achieve their purposes through legislation, the opponents of child labor wrote their desires into an amendment (No. 189), but it was never adopted.

The property-conscious majority of the Court also refused to accept state economic and social controls. Although a militant minority condemned the "use of the Fourteenth Amendment . . . to prevent the making of social experiments that an important part of the community desires, in the insulated chambers afforded by the several states," Justice Sutherland set the tone for the decade by overruling a minimum wage law for women in the District of Columbia (*Adkins v. Children's Hospital* [No. 190]). Despite the fact that similar state laws had previously received judicial sanction in *Bunting v. Oregon* and *Muller v. Oregon* (Chapter XVIII), Sutherland distinguished those precedents on the grounds that they dealt with hours of labor and not minimum wages, and returned to the Lochner concept of "freedom of contract." He condemned wage legislation as economically and socially unsound and a denial of due process of law, maintaining that "the good of society as a whole cannot be better served than by the preservation against arbitrary restraint of the liberties of its constituent members."

Following this precedent, the Court overruled a wide variety of state regulatory laws. Over the strong protests of four of the justices, the majority used both

the due process and equal protection clauses of the Fourteenth Amendment to
upset an Arizona anti-injunction law (*Truax v. Corrigan*, 1921). Brandeis and
Holmes dissented, arguing that the majority would have upheld the legislation as
a reasonable legal experiment if the "contemporary conditions, social, industrial and
political, of the community to be affected" had been given as much consideration
as the legal factors (No. 191).

Typical of the Court's laissez-faire attitude toward public regulation was
the sharp curtailment of the scope of the "public interest" doctrine, which had
first been set forth in *Munn v. Illinois* (Chapter XV). In *Wolff Packing Co. v.
Court of Industrial Relations of Kansas* (No. 192), Chief Justice Taft ruled that
a mere declaration by a state legislature that a business is "affected with a public
interest" does not justify regulation. Concerning what types of businesses might be
regulated, Taft was clear only on public utilities. He included businesses "which
though not public at their inception may be said to have risen to be such," but
that definition was sufficiently indefinite to require judicial evaluation of cases as
they arose. The Court repeatedly struck down state laws that it believed fell outside this category. Again a minority protested. When a New York statute designed to protect the public against theater ticket "scalpers" was ruled out as a
violation of the Fourteenth Amendment, Holmes registered an eloquent protest,
contending that a legislature "can do whatever it sees fit to do unless it is restrained
by some express prohibition in the Constitution of the United States or of the
state" (*Tyson v. Banton* [No. 193]).

It was not until the 1930's, however, that the Court acknowledged the un-
workability of its standard. In *Nebbia v. New York* (No. 194), Justice Roberts not
only reversed the trend of the previous decade, but virtually eliminated the "affection with a public interest" doctrine as a constitutional concept. "There is no
closed class or category of businesses affected with a public interest," he stated.
"The States' power extends to every regulation of any business reasonably required and appropriate for the public protection."

In an interesting ruling that did not involve economic affairs, the Court of
the Twenties took a far more liberal view of state legislative authority. Upholding
a Virginia statute permitting sterilization of inmates in institutions for the feeble-
minded, Holmes ruled that the needs of society superceded the invasion of individual liberty: "We have seen more than once that the public welfare may
call upon the best citizens for their lives. It would be strange if it could not call
upon those who already sap the strength of the state for . . . lesser sacrifices"
(*Buck v. Bell* [No. 195]).

The Maintenance of the Tradition of National Supremacy

EXTENSION OF GOVERNMENTAL AUTHORITY

181. Is the Treaty Power Limited by the Tenth Amendment?

Missouri v. Holland, 252 U.S. 416 (1920).

HOLMES, J.: . . . The question raised is the general one whether the treaty and statute are void as an interference with the rights reserved to the States.

To answer this question it is not enough to refer to the Tenth Amendment, reserving the powers not delegated to the United States, because by Article II, §2, the power to make treaties is delegated expressly, and by Article VI treaties made under the authority of the United States, along with the Constitution and laws of the United States made in pursuance thereof, are declared the supreme law of the land. If the treaty is valid there can be no dispute about the validity of the statute under Article I, §8, as a necessary and proper means to execute the powers of the Government. The language of the Constitution as to the supremacy of treaties being general, the question before us is narrowed to an inquiry into the ground upon which the present supposed exception is placed.

It is said that a treaty cannot be valid if it infringes the Constitution, that there are limits, therefore, to the treaty-making power, and that one such limit is that what an act of Congress could not do unaided, in derogation of the powers reserved to the States, a treaty cannot do. An earlier act of Congress that attempted by itself and not in pursuance of a treaty to regulate the killing of migratory birds within the States had been held bad in

the District Court. . . . Those decisions were supported by arguments that migratory birds were owned by the States in their sovereign capacity for the benefit of their people, and that under cases like *Geer v. Connecticut,* . . . this control was one that Congress had no power to displace. The same argument is supposed to apply now with equal force.

Whether the two cases cited were decided rightly or not they cannot be accepted as a test of the treaty power. Acts of Congress are the supreme law of the land only when made in pursuance of the Constitution, while treaties are declared to be so when made under the authority of the United States. It is open to question whether the authority of the United States means more than the formal acts prescribed to make the convention. We do not mean to imply that there are no qualifications to the treaty-making power; but they must be ascertained in a different way. It is obvious that there may be matters of the sharpest exigency for the national well being that an act of Congress could not deal with but that a treaty followed by such an act could, and it is not lightly to be assumed that, in matters requiring national action, "a power which must belong to and somewhere reside in every civilized government" is not to be found. *Andrews v. Andrews.* . . . What was said in that case with regard to the powers of the States applies with equal force to the powers of the nation in cases where the States individually are incompetent to act. We are not yet discussing the particular case before us but only are considering the validity of the test proposed. With regard to that we may add that when we are dealing with words that also are a constituent act, like the Constitution of the United States, we must realize that they have called into life a being the development of which could not have been foreseen completely by the most gifted of its begetters. It was enough for them to realize or to hope that they had created an organism; it has taken a century and has cost their successors much sweat and blood to prove that they created a nation. The case before us must be considered in the light of our whole experience and not merely in that of what was said a hundred years ago. The treaty in question does not contravene any prohibitory words to be found in the Constitution. The only question is whether it is forbidden by some invisible radiation from the general terms of the Tenth Amendment. We must consider what this country has become in deciding what that amendment has reserved.

The State as we have intimated founds its claim of exclusive authority upon an assertion of title to migratory birds, an assertion that is embodied in statute. No doubt it is true that as between a State and its inhabitants the State may regulate the killing and sale of such birds, but it does not follow that its authority is exclusive of

paramount powers. To put the claim of the State upon title is to lean upon a slender reed. Wild birds are not in the possession of anyone; and possession is the beginning of ownership. The whole foundation of the State's rights is the presence within their jurisdiction of birds that yesterday had not arrived, tomorrow may be in another State and in a week a thousand miles away. If we are to be accurate we cannot put the case of the State upon higher ground than that the treaty deals with creatures that for the moment are within the state borders, that it must be carried out by officers of the United States within the same territory, and that but for the treaty the State would be free to regulate this subject itself. . . .

Here a national interest of very nearly the first magnitude is involved. It can be protected only by national action in concert with that of another power. The subject-matter is only transitorily within the State and has no permanent habitat therein. But for the treaty and the statute there soon might be no birds for any powers to deal with. We see nothing in the Constitution that compels the government to sit by while a food supply is cut off and the protectors of our forests and our crops are destroyed. It is not sufficient to rely upon the States. The reliance is vain, and were it otherwise, the question is whether the United States is forbidden to act. We are of opinion that the treaty and statute must be upheld. . . .

182. "The power of inquiry . . . is an essential . . . auxiliary to the legislative function."

McGrain v. Daugherty, 273 U.S. 135 (1927).

VAN DEVANTER, J.: . . . The first of the principal questions . . . is . . . whether the Senate—or the House of Representatives . . . has power, through its own process, to compel a private individual to appear before it or one of its committees

and give testimony needed to enable it efficiently to exercise a legislative function belonging to it under the Constitution.

The Constitution provides for a Congress consisting of a Senate and House of Representatives and invests it with "all legislative powers" granted to the United States, and with power "to make all laws which shall be necessary and proper" for carrying into execution these powers and "all other powers" vested by the Constitution in the United States or in any department or officer thereof. . . . But there is no provision expressly investing either house with power to make investigations and exact testimony to the end that it may exercise its legislative function advisedly and effectively. So the question arises whether this power is so far incidental to the legislative function as to be implied.

In actual legislative practice power to secure needed information by such means has long been treated as an attribute of the power to legislate. It was so regarded in the British Parliament and in the Colonial legislatures before the American Revolution; and a like view has prevailed and been carried into effect in both houses of Congress and in most of the state legislatures.

This power was both asserted and exerted by the House of Representatives in 1792, when it appointed a select committee to inquire into the St. Clair expedition and authorized the committee to send for necessary persons, papers and records. Mr. Madison, who had taken an important part in framing the Constitution only five years before, and four of his associates in that work, were members of the House of Representatives at the time, and all voted for the inquiry. . . . Other exertions of the power by the House of Representatives, as also by the Senate, are shown in the citations already made. Among those by the Senate, the inquiry ordered in 1859 respecting the raid by John Brown and his adherents on the armory and arsenal of the United States at Harper's Ferry is of special significance. The resolution directing the inquiry authorized the committee to send for persons and papers, to inquire into the facts pertaining to the raid and the means by which it was organized and supported, and to report what legislation, if any, was necessary to preserve the peace of the country and protect the public property. The resolution was briefly discussed and adopted without opposition. . . .

The state courts quite generally have held that the power to legislate carries with it by necessary implication ample authority to obtain information needed in the rightful exercise of that power, and to employ compulsory process for the purpose. . . .

We have referred to the practice of the two houses of Congress; and we now shall notice some significant congressional enactments. . . . They show very plainly that Congress intended thereby (a) to recognize the power of either house to institute inquiries and exact evidence touching subjects within its jurisdiction and on which it was disposed to act; (b) to recognize that such inquiries may be conducted through committees; (c) to subject defaulting and contumacious witnesses to indictment and punishment in the courts, and thereby to enable either house to exert the power of inquiry "more effectually"; and (d) to open the way for obtaining evidence in such an inquiry, which otherwise could not be obtained, by exempting witnesses required to give evidence therein from criminal and penal prosecutions in respect of matters disclosed by their evidence.

Four decisions of this Court are cited and more or less relied on. . . .

While these cases are not decisive of the question we are considering, they definitely settle two propositions which we recognize as entirely sound and having a bearing on its solution: One, that the two houses of Congress, in their separate relations, possess not only such powers as are expressly granted to them by the Constitution, but such auxiliary powers as are necessary and appropriate to make the express powers effective; and, the other, that neither house is invested with "general" power to inquire into private affairs and compel disclosures, but only with such limited power of inquiry as is shown to exist when the rule of constitutional interpretation just stated is rightly applied. . . .

We are of opinion that the power of inquiry—with process to enforce it—is an essential and appropriate auxiliary to the legislative function. It was so regarded and employed in American legislatures before the Constitution was framed and ratified. Both houses of Congress took this view of it early in their history . . .

We come now to the question whether it sufficiently appears that the purpose for which the witness's testimony was sought was to obtain information in aid of the legislative function. The court below answered the question in the negative, and put its decision largely on this ground. . . .

We are of opinion that the court's ruling on this question was wrong, and that it sufficiently appears, when the proceedings are rightly interpreted, that the object of the investigation and of the effort to secure the witness's testimony was to obtain information for legislative purposes.

It is quite true that the resolution directing the investigation does not in terms avow that it is intended to be in aid of legislation; but it does show that the subject to be investigated was the administration of the Department of Justice—whether its functions were being properly discharged or were being neglected or misdirected, and particularly whether the Attorney General and his assistants were performing or neglecting their duties in respect of the institution and prosecution of proceedings to punish crimes and enforce appropriate remedies against the wrongdoers—specific instances of alleged neglect being recited. Plainly the subject was one on which legislation could be had and would be materially aided by the information which the investigation was calculated to elicit. This becomes manifest when it is reflected that the functions of the Department of Justice, the powers and duties of the Attorney General and the duties of his assistants, are all subject to regulation by congressional legislation, and that the department is maintained and its activities are carried on under such appropriations as in the judgment of Congress are needed from year to year.

The only legitimate object the Senate could have in ordering the investigation was to aid it in legislating; and we think the subject-matter was such that the presumption should be indulged that this was the real object. An express avowal of the object would have been better; but in view of the particular subject-matter was not indispensable. . . .

We conclude that the investigation was ordered for a legitimate object; that the witness wrongfully refused to appear and testify before the committee and was lawfully attached; that the Senate is entitled to have him give testimony pertinent to the inquiry, either at its bar or before the committee; and that the district court erred in discharging him from custody under the attachment. . . .

BROAD CONSTRUCTION OF REGULATORY POWER

183. *The Paramount Power of Congress over Commerce*

Wisconsin Railroad Fares Case, 257 U.S. 563 (1922).

TAFT, C.J.: The Commission's order, interference with which was enjoined by the District Court, effects the removal of the unjust discrimination found to exist against persons in interstate commerce, and against interstate commerce, by fixing a minimum for intrastate passenger fares in Wisconsin at 3.6 cents per mile. . . .

We have two questions to decide.

First. Do the intrastate passenger fares

work undue prejudice against persons in interstate commerce, such as to justify a horizontal increase of them all?

Second. Are these intrastate fares an undue discrimination against interstate commerce as a whole which it is the duty of the Commission to remove? . . .

The order in this case . . . is much wider than the orders made in the proceedings following the *Shreveport* and *Illinois Central Cases*. There, as here, the report of the Commission showed discrimination against persons and localities at border points and the orders were extended to include all rates or fares from all points in the State to border points. But this order is not so restricted. It includes fares between all interior points, although neither may be near the border, and the fares between them may not work a discrimination against interstate travelers at all. Nothing in the precedents cited justifies an order affecting all rates of a general description when it is clear that this would include many rates not within the proper class or reason of the order. . . .

Intrastate rates and the income from them must play a most important part in maintaining an adequate national railway system. Twenty per cent. of the gross freight receipts of the railroads of the country are from intrastate traffic, and fifty per cent. of the passenger receipts. The ratio of the gross intrastate revenue to the interstate revenue is a little less than one to three. If the rates, on which such receipts are based, are to be fixed at a substantially lower level than in interstate traffic, the share which the intrastate traffic will contribute will be proportionately less. . . .

It is objected here, as it was in the Shreveport Case, that orders of the Commission which raise the intrastate rates to a level of the interstate structure violate the specific proviso of the original Interstate Commerce Act . . . that the Commission is not to regulate traffic wholly within a State. To this the same answer must be made as was made in the Shreveport Case, . . . that such orders as to intrastate traffic are merely incidental to the regulation of interstate commerce, and necessary to its efficiency. Effective control of the one must embrace some control over the other, in view of the blending of both in actual operation. The same rails and the same cars carry both. The same men conduct them. Commerce is a unit and does not regard state lines, and while, under the Constitution, interstate and intrastate commerce are ordinarily subject to regulation by different sovereignties, yet when they are so mingled together that the supreme authority, the Nation, cannot exercise complete effective control over interstate commerce without incidental regulation of intrastate commerce, such incidental regulation is not an invasion of state authority or a violation of the proviso. . . .

Congress in its control of its interstate commerce system, is seeking in the Transportation Act to make the system adequate to the needs of the country by securing for it a reasonably compensatory return for all the work it does. The States are seeking to use that same system for intrastate traffic. That entails large duties and expenditures on the interstate commerce which may burden it unless compensation is received for the intrastate business reasonably proportionate to that for the interstate business. Congress as the dominant controller of interstate commerce may, therefore, restrain undue limitations of the earning power of the interstate commerce system in doing state work. The affirmative power of Congress in developing interstate commerce agencies is clear. . . . In such development, it can impose any reasonable condition on a State's use of interstate carriers for intrastate commerce it deems necessary or desirable. This is because of the supremacy of the national power in this field. . . .

Conservatism and Constitutional Law

CORPORATIONS, TRADE ASSOCIATIONS, AND COMPETITION

184. *Judicial Limitations of Regulatory Power*

U.S. v. United States Steel Corporation, 251 U.S. 417 (1920).

McKENNA, J.: . . . [In the opinion of two judges in a lower court] testimony did "not show that the corporation in and of itself ever possessed or exerted sufficient power when acting alone to control prices of the products of the industry." Its power was efficient only when in cooperation with its competitors, and hence it concerted with them in the expedients of pools, associations, trade meetings, and finally in a system of dinners inaugurated in 1907 by the president of the company, E. H. Gary, and called "the Gary Dinners." The dinners were congregations of producers and "were nothing but trade meetings," successors of the other means of associated action and control through such action. They were instituted first in "stress of panic," but, their potency being demonstrated, they were afterwards called to control prices "in periods of industrial calm." "They were pools without penalties" and more efficient in stabilizing prices. But it was the further declaration that "when joint action was either refused or withdrawn the Corporation's prices were controlled by competition."

The Corporation, it was said, did not at any time abuse the power or ascendency it possessed. It resorted to none of the brutalities or tyrannies that the cases illustrate of other combinations. It did not secure freight rebates; it did not increase its profits by reducing the wages of its employees—whatever it did was not at the expense of labor; it did not increase its profits by lowering the quality of its prod-

ucts, nor create an artificial scarcity of them; it did not oppress or coerce its competitors—its competition, though vigorous, was fair; it did not undersell its competitors in some localities by reducing its prices there below those maintained elsewhere, or require its customers to enter into contracts limiting their purchases or restricting them in resale prices; it did not obtain customers by secret rebates or departures from its published prices; there was no evidence that it attempted to crush its competitors or drive them out of the market, nor did it take customers from its competitors by unfair means, and in its competition it seemed to make no difference between large and small competitors. Indeed it is said in many ways and illustrated that "instead of relying upon its own power to fix and maintain prices, the corporation, at its very beginning sought and obtained the assistance of others." It combined its power with that of its competitors. It did not have power in and of itself, and the control it exerted was only in and by association with its competitors. Its offense, therefore, such as it was, was not different from theirs and was distinguished from "theirs only in the leadership it assumed in promulgating and perfecting the policy." This leadership it gave up and it had ceased to offend against the law before this suit was brought. It was hence concluded that it should be distinguished from its organizers and that their intent and unsuccessful attempt should not be attributed to it, that it "in and of itself is not now and has never been a monopoly or a combination in restraint of trade," and a decree of dissolution should not be entered against it. . . .

We have seen that the judges of the District Court unanimously concurred in the view that the Corporation did not achieve monopoly, and such is our deduction. . . . Monopoly, therefore, was not achieved, and competitors had to be persuaded by pools, associations, and trade meetings, all of them, it may be, violations of the law. . . . They were scattered through the years from 1901 . . . until 1911, but . . . abandoned nine months before this suit. . . .

What, then, can now be urged against the Corporation? . . .

The company's officers, and, as well, its competitors and customers, testified that its competition was genuine. . . . No practical witness was produced by the Government in opposition. . . . Counsel say, "They [the Corporation is made a plural] called . . . two hundred witnesses out of some forty thousand customers, and they expect with that evidence to overcome the whole train of price movement since the Corporation was formed." . . .

The opinion of an editor of a trade journal is adduced, and that of an author and teacher of economics whose philosophical deductions had, perhaps, fortification from experience as Deputy Commissioner of Corporations and as an employee in the Bureau of Corporations. His deduction was that when prices are constant through a definite period an artificial influence is indicated. . . . It has become an aphorism that there is danger of deception in generalities, and in a case of this importance we should have something surer for judgment than speculation,—something more than a deduction . . . even though the facts it rests on or asserts were not contradicted. . . .

Against it competitors, dealers, and customers of the Corporation testify in multitude that . . . prices . . . varied according to natural conditions. . . .

The Corporation is undoubtedly of impressive size, and it takes an effort of resolution not to be affected by it or to exaggerate its influence. But . . . the law does not make mere size an offense or the existence of unexerted power an offense. . . .

The Steel Corporation by its formation united under one control competing companies, and thus, it is urged, a condition was brought about in violation of the statute. . . .

We have seen whatever there was of wrong intent could not be executed; whatever there was of evil effect was discontinued before this suit was brought; and this, we think, determines the decree.

185. Trade associations tend "to stabilize trade and industry."

Maple Flooring Manufacturers Association v. U.S., 268 U.S. 563 (1925).

STONE, J.: . . . In March, 1922, the corporate defendants organized the defendant Maple Flooring Manufacturers Association, but for many years prior to that time and certainly since 1913 a substantial number of the corporate defendants have participated actively in maintaining numerous successive trade associations of the same name, which were predecessors of the present association. . . . The defendants have engaged in many activities to which no exception is taken by the Government and which are admittedly beneficial to the industry and to consumers; such as co-operative advertising and the standardization and improvement of the product. The activities . . . of the present Association of which the Government complains may be summarized as follows:

(1) The computation and distribution among the members of the association of the average cost to association members of all dimensions and grades of flooring.

(2) The compilation and distribution among members of a booklet showing freight rates on flooring from Cadillac, Michigan, to between five and six thousand points of shipment in the United States.

(3) The gathering of statistics which at frequent intervals are supplied by each member of the Association to the Secretary of the Association giving complete information as to the quantity and kind of flooring sold and prices received by the reporting members, and the amount of stock on hand, which information is summarized by the Secretary and transmitted to members without, however, revealing the identity of the members in connection with any specific information thus transmitted.

(4) Meetings at which the representatives of members congregate and discuss the industry and exchange views as to its problems. . . .

We think it might be urged, on the basis of this record that the defendants, by their course of conduct, instead of evidencing the purpose of persistent violators of law, had steadily indicated a purpose to keep within the boundaries of legality as rapidly as those boundaries were marked out by the decisions of courts interpreting the Sherman Act. . . .

It is not, we think, open to question that the dissemination of pertinent information concerning any trade or business tends to stabilize that trade or business and to produce uniformity of price and trade practice. Exchange of price quotations of market commodities tends to produce uniformity of prices in the markets of the world. Knowledge of the supplies of available merchandise tends to prevent over-production and to avoid the economic disturbances produced by business crises resulting from over-production. But the

natural effect of the acquisition of wider and more scientific knowledge of business conditions, on the minds of the individuals engaged in commerce, and its consequent effect in stabilizing production and price, can hardly be deemed a restraint of commerce or if so it cannot, we think be said to be an unreasonable restraint, or in any respect unlawful.

It is the consensus of opinion of economists and of many of the most important agencies of Government that the public interest is served by the gathering and dissemination, in the widest possible manner, of information with respect to the production and distribution, cost and prices in actual sales, of market commodities, because the making available of such information tends to stabilize trade and industry, to produce fairer price levels and to avoid the waste which inevitably attends the unintelligent conduct of economic enterprise. Free competition means a free and open market among both buyers and sellers for the sale and distribution of commodities. Competition does not become less free merely because the conduct of commercial operations becomes more intelligent through the free distribution of knowledge of all the essential factors entering into the commercial transaction. . . .

It was not the purpose or the intent of the Sherman Anti-Trust Law to inhibit the intelligent conduct of business operations, nor do we conceive that its purpose was to suppress such influences as might affect the operations of interstate commerce through the application to them of the individual intelligence of those engaged in commerce, enlightened by accurate information as to the essential elements of the economics of a trade or business, however gathered or disseminated. . . .

We decide only that trade associations or combinations of persons or corporations which openly and fairly gather and disseminate information . . . as did these defendants, and who . . . meet and dis-

cuss such information and statistics without however reaching or attempting to
reach any agreement or any concerted action with respect to prices or restraining
competition, do not thereby engage in unlawful restraint of commerce. . . .

JUDICIAL RESTRICTIONS ON FEDERAL ADMINISTRATIVE COMMISSIONS

186. *The Courts, the F. T. C., and Unfair Competition*

F. T. C. v. Gratz, 253 U.S. 421 (1920).

MCREYNOLDS, J.: . . . It is unnecessary . . . to discuss conflicting views concerning validity and meaning of the act
creating the [Federal Trade] commission
and effect of the evidence presented. The
judgment below must be affirmed since,
in our opinion, the first count of the complaint is wholly insufficient to charge respondents with practicing "unfair methods
of competition in commerce" within the
fair intendment of those words. We go no
further and confine this opinion to the
point specified. . . .

The words "unfair method of competition" are not defined by the statute and
their exact meaning is in dispute. It is for
the courts, not the commission, ultimately
to determine as matter of law what they
include. They are clearly inapplicable to
practices never heretofore regarded as opposed to good morals because characterized by deception, bad faith, fraud or oppression, or as against public policy because of their dangerous tendency unduly
to hinder competition or create monopoly. The act was certainly not intended to
fetter free and fair competition as commonly understood and practiced by honorable opponents in trade.

Count one alleges . . . that Warren,
Jones & Gratz are engaged in selling,
either directly to the trade or through
their co-respondents, cotton ties . . . and
also jute bagging. . . . [Two concerns]
are the selling and distributing agents of
Warren, Jones & Gratz, and as such sell
and distribute their ties and bagging to
jobbers and dealers who resell them to retailers, ginners, and farmers. That with
the purpose and effect of discouraging and
stifling competition in the sale of such
bagging all the respondents for more than
a year have refused to sell any of such
ties unless the purchaser would buy from
them a corresponding amount of bagging
—six yards with as many ties.

The complaint contains no intimation
that Warren, Jones & Gratz did not properly obtain their ties and bagging as merchants usually do; the amount controlled
by them is not stated; nor is it alleged
that they held a monopoly of either ties
or bagging or had ability, purpose or intent to acquire one. So far as appears, acting independently, they undertook to sell
their lawfully acquired property in the ordinary course, without deception, misrep-
resentation, or oppression, and at fair
prices, to purchasers willing to take it
upon terms openly announced.

Nothing is alleged which would justify
the conclusion that the public suffered
injury or that competitors had reasonable
ground for complaint. All question of
monopoly or combination being out of the
way, a private merchant, acting with entire
good faith, may properly refuse to sell except in conjunction, such closely associated
articles as ties and bagging. If real competition is to continue the right of the individual to exercise reasonable discretion
in respect of his own business methods
must be preserved. . . .

ADULT AND CHILD LABOR

187. *Labor, the Injunction, and the Anti-Trust Acts*

Duplex Printing Press Co. v. Deering, 254 U.S. 443
(1921).

PITNEY, J.: . . . That . . . [the] complainant has sustained substantial damage to its interstate trade, and is threatened with further and irreparable loss and damage in the future, is proved by clear and undisputed evidence. Hence the right to an injunction is clear if the threatened loss is due to a violation of the Sherman Act, as amended by the Clayton Act. . . .

The substance of the matters here complained of is an interference with complainant's interstate trade intended to have coercive effect upon complainant, and produced by what is commonly known as a "secondary boycott," that is, a combination not merely to refrain from dealing with complainant, or to advise or by peaceful means persuade complainant's customers to refrain ("primary boycott") but to exercise coercive pressure upon such customers . . . in order to cause them to withhold . . . patronage. . . .

As we shall see, the recognized distinction between a primary and a secondary boycott is material to be considered upon the question of a proper construction of the Clayton Act. . . .

The principal reliance is upon §20. . . . The second paragraph declares that "no *such* restraining order or injunction" shall prohibit certain conduct specified— manifestly still referring to a "case between an employer and employees, . . . involving, or growing out of, a dispute concerning terms or conditions of employment," as designated in the first paragraph. It is very clear that the restriction upon the use of the injunction is in favor only of those concerned as parties to such a dispute as is described. . . .

The majority of the Circuit Court of Appeals appear to have entertained the view that the words "employers and employees," as used in §20, should be treated as referring to "the business class or clan to which the parties ligitant respectively belong;" and that, . . . §20 operated to permit members of the Machinists' Union elsewhere—some 60,000 in number—although standing in no relation of employment under complainant, past, present, or prospective, to make that dispute their own, and proceed to instigate sympathetic strikes, picketing, and boycotting against employers wholly unconnected with complainant's factory, and having relations with complainant only in the way of purchasing its product in the ordinary course of interstate commerce—and this where there was no dispute between such employers and their employees respecting terms or conditions of employment.

We deem this construction altogether inadmissible. . . .

The emphasis placed on the words "lawful" and "lawfully," "peaceful" and "peacefully," and the references to the dispute and the parties to it, strongly rebut a legislative intent to confer a general immunity for conduct violative of the antitrust laws, or otherwise unlawful. The subject of the boycott is dealt with specifically in the "ceasing to patronize" provision, and by the clear force of the language employed the exemption is limited to pressure exerted upon a "party to such dispute" by means of "peaceful and *lawful*" influence upon neutrals. There is nothing here to justify defendants or the organizations they represent in using either threats or persuasion to bring about strikes or a cessation of work on the part of employees of complainant's customers or prospective customers, or of the trucking company employed by the customers, with the object of compelling such customers to withdraw or refrain from commercial relations with complainant, and of thereby constraining complainant to yield the matter in dispute. To instigate a sympathetic strike in aid of a secondary boycott cannot be deemed "peaceful and lawful" persuasion. . . .

The question whether the bill legalized a secondary boycott . . . was emphatically and unequivocally answered [in the debates in the House] . . . in the negative. The subject . . . was under consideration when the bill was framed, and the section as reported was carefully prepared with the settled purpose of excluding the sec-ondary boycott, and confining boycotting to the parties to the dispute, allowing parties to cease to patronize and to ask others to cease to patronize a party to the dispute; it was the opinion of the committee that it did not legalize the secondary boycott; it was not their purpose to authorize such a boycott; not a member of the committee would vote to do so; clarifying amendment was unnecessary; the section as reported expressed the real purpose so well that it could not be tortured into a meaning authorizing the secondary boycott. . . .

There should be an injunction against defendants and the associations represented by them. . . .

188. *Child Labor and Federal Taxation*

Bailey v. Drexel Furniture Co., 259 U.S. 20 (1922).

TAFT, C.J.: . . . The law is attacked on the ground that it is a regulation of the employment of child labor in the States—an exclusively state function under the Federal Constitution and within the reservations of the Tenth Amendment. It is defended on the ground that it is a mere excise tax levied by the Congress of the United States under its broad power of taxation conferred by §8, Article I, of the federal Constitution. We must construe the law and interpret the intent and meaning of Congress from the language of the act. The words are to be given their ordinary meaning unless the context shows that they are differently used. Does this law impose a tax with only that incidental restraint and regulation which a tax must inevitably involve? Or does it regulate by the use of the so-called tax as a penalty? If a tax, it is clearly an excise. If it were an excise on a commodity or other thing of value we might not be permitted under previous decisions of this court to infer solely from its heavy burden that the act intends a prohibition instead of a tax. But this act is more. It provides a heavy exaction for a departure from a detailed and specified course of conduct in business. That course of business is that employers shall employ in mines and quarries, children of an age greater than sixteen years; in mills and factories, children of an age greater than fourteen years, and shall prevent children of less than sixteen years in mills and factories from working more than eight hours a day or six days in the week. If an employer departs from this prescribed course of business, he is to pay to the Government one-tenth of his entire net income in the business for a full year. The amount is not to be proportioned in any degree to the frequency of the departures, but is to be paid by the employer in full measure whether he employs five hundred children for a year, or employs only one for a day. Moreover, if he does not know the child is within the named age limit, he is not to pay; that is to say, it is only where he knowingly departs from the prescribed course that payment is to be exacted. . . .

In the light of these features of the act, a court must be blind not to see that the so-called tax is imposed to stop the employment of children within the age limits prescribed. Its prohibitory and regulatory effect and purpose are palpable. All others can see and understand this. How can we properly shut our minds to it?

It is the high duty and function of this court in cases regularly brought to its bar to decline to recognize or enforce seeming laws of Congress, dealing with subjects not entrusted to Congress but left or committed by the supreme law of the land to the control of the States. We can not avoid the duty even though it requires us to refuse to give effect to legislation designed to promote the highest good. The good sought in unconstitutional legislation is an insidious feature because it leads citizens and legislators of good purpose to promote it without thought of the serious breach it will make in the ark of our covenant or the harm which will come from breaking down recognized standards. In the maintenance of local self government, on the one hand, and the national power on the other, our country has been able to endure and prosper for near a century and a half.

Out of a proper respect for the acts of a coördinate branch of the Government, this court has gone far to sustain taxing acts as such, even though there has been ground for suspecting from the weight of the tax it was intended to destroy its subject. But, in the act before us, the presumption of validity cannot prevail, because the proof of the contrary is found on the very face of its provisions. Grant the validity of this law, and all that Congress would need to do, hereafter, in seeking to take over to its control any one of the great number of subjects of public interest, jurisdiction of which the States have never parted with, and which are reserved to them by the Tenth Amendment, would be to enact a detailed measure of complete regulation of the subject and enforce it by a so-called tax upon departures from it. To give such magic to the word "tax" would be to break down all constitutional limitation of the powers of Congress and completely wipe out the sovereignty of the States. . . .

For the reasons given, we must hold the Child Labor Tax Law invalid and the judgment of the district court is Affirmed.

189. *Child Labor Amendment, Proposed June 4, 1924*

U. S. Stat. at L., XLIII, 670.

SECTION 1. The Congress shall have power to limit, regulate, and prohibit the labor of persons under eighteen years of age.

SECTION 2. The power of the several States is unimpaired by this Article except that the operation of State laws shall be suspended to the extent necessary to give effect to legislation enacted by the Congress.

The Extent of State Regulation Under the Fourteenth Amendment

THE POLICE POWER AND WORKING CONDITIONS

190. *"Freedom of contract is . . . the general rule and restraint the exception."*

Adkins v. Children's Hospital, 261 U.S. 525 (1923).

SUTHERLAND, J.: . . . The statute now under consideration is attacked upon the ground that it authorizes an unconstitutional interference with the freedom of contract included within the guaranties of the due process clause of the Fifth Amendment. That the right to contract about one's affairs is a part of the liberty of the individual protected by this clause is settled by the decisions of this Court and is no longer open to question. . . . Within this liberty are contracts of employment of labor. In making such contracts, generally speaking, the parties have an equal right to obtain from each other the best terms they can as the result of private bargaining. . . .

There is, of course, no such thing as absolute freedom of contract. It is subject to a great variety of restraints. But freedom of contract is, nevertheless, the general rule and restraint the exception; and the exercise of legislative authority to abridge it can be justified only by the existence of exceptional circumstances. . . .

[The present law] is simply and exclusively a price-fixing law, confined to adult women (for we are not now considering the provisions relating to minors), who are legally as capable of contracting for themselves as men. It forbids two parties having lawful capacity—under penalties as to the employer—to freely contract with one another in respect of the price for which

one shall render service to the other in a purely private employment where both are willing, perhaps anxious, to agree, even though the consequence may be to oblige one to surrender a desirable engagement and the other to dispense with the services of a desirable employee. . . .

The standard furnished by the statute for the guidance of the board is so vague as to be impossible of practical application with any reasonable degree of accuracy. What is sufficient to supply the necessary cost of living for a woman worker and maintain her in good health and protect her morals is obviously not a precise or unvarying sum—not even approximately so. The amount will depend upon a variety of circumstances: the individual temperament, habits of thrift, care, ability to buy necessaries intelligently, and whether the woman live alone or with her family. To those who practice economy, a given sum will afford comfort, while to those of a contrary habit the same sum will be wholly inadequate. The coöperative economies of the family group are not taken into account though they constitute an important consideration in estimating the cost of living, for it is obvious that the individual expense will be less in the case of a member of a family than in the case of one living alone. The relation between earnings and morals is not capable of standardization. It cannot be shown that well paid women safe-guard their morals more carefully than those who are poorly paid. Morality rests upon other considerations than wages; and there is, certainly, no such prevalent connection between the two as to justify a broad attempt to adjust the latter with reference to the former. . . .

The feature of this statute which, perhaps more than any other, puts upon it the stamp of invalidity is that it exacts from the employer an arbitrary payment for a purpose and upon a basis having no causal connection with his business, or the contract or the work the employee engages to do. The declared basis, as already pointed out, is not the value of the service rendered but the extraneous circumstances that the employee needs to get a prescribed sum of money to insure her subsistence, health and morals. The ethical right of every worker, man or woman, to a living wage, may be conceded. One of the declared and important purposes of trade organizations is to secure it. And with that principle and with every legitimate effort to realize it in fact, no one can quarrel; but the fallacy of the proposed method of attaining it is that it assumes that every employer is bound at all events to furnish it. . . .

Finally, it may be said that if, in the interest of the public welfare, the police power may be invoked to justify the fixing of a minimum wage, it may, when the public welfare is thought to require it, be invoked to justify a maximum wage. The power to fix high wages connotes, by like reasoning, the power to fix low wages. If, in the face of the guaranties of the Fifth Amendment, this form of legislation shall be legally justified, the field for the operation of the police power will have been widened to a great and dangerous degree. If, for example, in the opinion of future lawmakers, wages in the building trades shall become so high as to preclude people of ordinary means from building and owning homes, an authority which sustains the minimum wage will be invoked to support a maximum wage for building laborers and artisans, and the same argument which has been here urged to strip the employer of his constitutional liberty of contract in one direction will be utilized to strip the employee of his constitutional liberty of contract in the opposite direction. A wrong decision does not end with itself: it is a precedent, and, with the swing of sentiment, its bad influence may run from one extremity of the arc to the other.

It has been said that legislation of the kind now under review is required in the interest of social justice, for whose ends freedom of contract may lawfully be subjected to restraint. The liberty of the individual to do as he pleases, even in innocent matters, is not absolute. It must frequently yield to the common good, and the line beyond which the power of interference may not be pressed is neither definite nor unalterable but may be made to move, within limits not well defined, with changing need and circumstance. Any attempt to fix a rigid boundary would be unwise and futile. But, nevertheless, there are limits to the power, and when these have been passed, it becomes the plain duty of the courts in the proper exercise of their authority to so declare. To sustain the individual freedom of action contemplated by the Constitution, is not to strike down the common good but to exalt it; for surely the good of society as a whole cannot be better served than by the preservation against arbitrary restraint of the liberties of its constituent members.

It follows from what has been said that the act in question passes the limit prescribed by the Constitution . . .

191. *"The law of property . . . is not appropriate for dealing with the forces beneath social unrest."*

Truax v. Corrigan, 257 U.S. 312 (1921).

BRANDEIS, J., dissenting: . . . Few laws are of universal application. It is of the nature of our law that it has dealt not with man in general, but with him in relationships. That a peculiar relationship of individuals may furnish legal basis for the classification which satisfies the requirement of the Fourteenth Amendment is clear. That the relation of employer and employee affords a constitutional basis for legislation applicable only to persons standing in that relation has been repeatedly held by this court. The questions submitted are whether this statutory prohibition of the remedy by injunction is in itself arbitrary and so unreasonable as to deprive the employer of liberty or property without due process of law;— and whether limitation of this prohibition to controversies involving employment denies him equal protection of the laws.

Whether a law enacted in the exercise of the police power is justly subject to the charge of being unreasonable or arbitrary, can ordinarily be determined only by a consideration of the contemporary conditions, social, industrial and political, of the community to be affected thereby. Resort to such facts is necessary, among other things, in order to appreciate the evils sought to be remedied and the possible effects of the remedy proposed. Nearly all legislation involves a weighing of public needs as against private desires; and likewise a weighing of relative social values. Since government is not an exact science, prevailing public opinion concerning the evils and the remedy is among the important facts deserving consideration; particularly, when the public conviction is both deep-seated and widespread and has been reached after deliberation. What, at any particular time, is the paramount public need is, necessarily,

largely a matter of judgment. Hence, in passing upon the validity of a law challenged as being unreasonable, aid may be derived from the experience of other countries and of the several States of our Union in which the common law and its conceptions of liberty and of property prevail. The history of the rules governing contests between employer and employed in the several English-speaking countries illustrates both the susceptibility of such rules to change and the variety of contemporary opinion as to what rules will best serve the public interest. . . .

In England, observance of the rules of the contest has been enforced by the courts almost wholly through the criminal law or through actions at law for compensation. . . . Resort to the injunction has not been frequent and it has played no appreciable part there in the conflict between capital and labor. In America the injunction did not secure recognition as a possible remedy until 1888. When a few years later its use became extensive and conspicuous, the controversy over the remedy overshadowed in bitterness the question of the relative substantive rights of the parties. In the storms of protest against this use many thoughtful lawyers joined. . . .

It was urged that the real motive in seeking the injunction was not ordinarily to prevent property from being injured nor to protect the owner in its use, but to endow property with active, militant power which would make it dominant over men. In other words, that under the guise of protecting property rights, the employer was seeking sovereign power. And many disinterested men, solicitous only for the public welfare, believed that the law of property was not appropriate for dealing with the forces beneath social unrest; that in this vast struggle it was unwise to throw the power of the State on one side or the other according to principles deduced from that law; that the problem of the control and conduct of industry demanded a solution of its own; and that, pending the ascertainment of new principles to govern industry, it was wiser for the State not to interfere in industrial struggles by the issuance of an injunction.

After the constitutionality and the propriety of the use of the injunction in labor disputes was established judicially, those who opposed the practice sought the aid of Congress and state legislatures. . . . These legislative proposals occupied the attention of Congress during every session but one in the twenty years between 1894 and 1914. Reports recommending such legislation were repeatedly made. . . . [In 1914] Congress passed and the President approved the Clayton Act, §20 of which is substantially the same as Paragraph 1464 of the Arizona Civil Code. . . .

The acknowledged legislative discretion exerted in classification, so frequently applied in defining rights, extends equally to the grant of remedies. It is for the legislature to say—within the broad limits of the discretion which it possesses—whether or not the remedy for a wrong shall be both criminal and civil and whether or not it shall be both at law and in equity. . . .

For these reasons, as well as for others . . . , the judgment of the Supreme Court of Arizona should, in my opinion, be affirmed:—first, because in permitting damage to be inflicted by means of boycott and peaceful picketing Arizona did not deprive the plaintiffs of property without due process of law or deny them equal protection of the laws; and secondly, because, if Arizona was constitutionally prohibited from adopting this rule of substantive law, it was still free to restrict the extraordinary remedies of equity where it considered their exercise to be detrimental to the public welfare, since such restriction was not a denial to the employer either of due process or of equal protection of the laws.

SOCIAL LEGISLATION AND THE PUBLIC WELFARE

192. *The Court Narrows the Public Interest Doctrine to Restrict State Regulation*

Wolff Packing Co. v. Court of Industrial Relations of Kansas, 262 U.S. 522 (1923).

TAFT, C.J.: . . . The necessary postulate of the Industrial Court Act is that the State, representing the people, is so much interested in their peace, health, and comfort, that it may compel those engaged in the manufacture of food and clothing, and the production of fuel, whether owners or workers, to continue in their business and employment on terms fixed by an agency of the State, if they cannot agree. Under the construction adopted by the State Supreme Court, the act gives the Industrial Court authority to permit the owner or employer to go out of the business if he shows that he can only continue on the terms fixed at such heavy loss that collapse will follow; but this privilege, under the circumstances, is generally illusory. . . . A laborer dissatisfied with his wages is permitted to quit, but he may not agree with his fellows to quit, or combine with others to induce them to quit.

These qualifications do not change the essence of the act. It curtails the right of the employer, on the one hand, and that of the employee, on the other, to contract about his affairs. This is part of the liberty of the individual protected by the guaranty of the due process clause of the Fourteenth Amendment. . . .

It is manifest from an examination of the cases cited . . . that the mere declaration by a legislature that a business is affected with a public interest is not conclusive of the question whether its attempted regulation on that ground is justified. The circumstances of its alleged change from the status of a private business and its freedom from regulation into one in which the public have come to have an interest, are always a subject of judicial inquiry. . . .

It has never been supposed, since the adoption of the Constitution, that the business of the butcher, or the baker, the tailor, the woodchopper, the mining operator, or the miner, was clothed with such a public interest that the price of his product or his wages could be fixed by State regulation. . . .

To say that a business is clothed with a public interest is not to determine what regulation is permissible in view of the private rights of the owner. The extent to which an inn or a cab system may be regulated may differ widely from that allowable as to a railroad or other common carrier. It is not a matter of legislative discretion solely. It depends upon the nature of the business, on the feature which touches the public, and on the abuses reasonably to be feared. To say that business is clothed with a public interest is not to import that the public may take over its entire management and run it at the expense of the owner. The extent to which regulation may reasonably go varies with different kinds of business. The regulation of rates to avoid monopoly, is one thing. The regulation of wages is another. A business may be of such character that only the first is permissible, while another may involve such a possible danger of monopoly on the one hand, and such dis-

aster from stoppage on the other, that both come within the public concern and power of regulation.

If, as, in effect, contended by counsel for the State, the common callings are clothed with a public interest by a mere legislative declaration, which necessarily authorizes full and comprehensive regulation within legislative discretion, there must be a revolution in the relation of government to general business. This will be running the public-interest argument into the ground. . . . It will be impossible to reconcile such result with the freedom of contract and of labor secured by the Fourteenth Amendment.

This brings us to the nature and purpose of the regulation under the Industrial Court Act. The avowed object is continuity of food, clothing, and fuel supply. By §6 reasonable continuity and efficiency of the industries specified are declared to be necessary for the public peace, health, and general welfare, and all are forbidden to hinder, limit, or suspend them. Section 7 gives the Industrial Court power, in case of controversy between employers and workers which may endanger the continuity or efficiency of service, to bring the employer and employee before it, and after hearing and investigation, to fix the terms and conditions between them. The employer is bound by this act to pay the wages fixed; and while the worker is not required to work at the wages fixed, he is forbidden on penalty of fine or imprisonment, to strike against them, and thus is compelled to give up that means of putting himself on an equality with his employer which action in concert with his fellows gives him. . . .

The minutely detailed government supervision, including that of their relations to their employees, to which the railroads of the country have been gradually subjected by Congress through its power over interstate commerce, furnishes no precedent for regulation of the business of the plaintiff, whose classification as public is, at the best, doubtful. It is not too much to say that the ruling in *Wilson v. New* went to the borderline, although it concerned an interstate common carrier in the presence of a nation-wide emergency and the possibility of great disaster. Certainly there is nothing to justify extending the drastic regulation sustained in that exceptional case to the one before us.

We think the Industrial Court Act . . . is in conflict with the Fourteenth Amendment and deprives it [the packing house] of its property and liberty of contract without due process of law.

The judgment of the court below is reversed.

193. *"Government does not go beyond its sphere in attempting to make life livable."*

Tyson v. Banton, 273 U.S. 418 (1927).

HOLMES, J., dissenting: We fear to grant power and are unwilling to recognize it when it exists. The States very generally have stripped jury trials of one of their most important characteristics by forbidding the judges to advise the jury upon the facts, . . . and when legislatures are held to be authorized to do anything considerably affecting public welfare, it is covered by apologetic phrases like the police power, or the statement that the business concerned has been dedicated to a public use. The former expression is convenient, to be sure, to conciliate the mind to something that needs explanation: the fact that the constitutional requirement of compensation when property is taken cannot be pressed to its grammatical extreme; that property rights may be taken for public purposes without pay if you do not take too much; that some play must be allowed to the joints if the machine is to work. But police power often is used in a wide sense to cover and, as I said, to apologize for the general power of the legislature to make a part of the community uncomfortable by a change.

I do not believe in such apologies. I think the proper course is to recognize that a state legislature can do whatever it sees fit to do unless it is restrained by some express prohibition in the Constitution of the United States or of the State, and that courts should be careful not to extend such prohibitions beyond their obvious meaning by reading into them conceptions of public policy that the particular court may happen to entertain. Coming down to the case before us, I think, as I intimated in *Adkins v. Children's Hospital,* . . . that the notion that a business is clothed with a public interest and has been devoted to the public use is little more than a fiction intended to beautify what is disagreeable to the sufferers. The truth seems to me to be that, subject to compensation when compensation is due, the legislature may forbid or restrict any business when it has a sufficient force of public opinion behind it. Lotteries were thought useful adjuncts of the State a century or so ago; now they are believed to be immoral and they have been stopped. Wine has been thought good for man from the time of the Apostles until recent years. But when public opinion changed it did not need the Eighteenth Amendment, notwithstanding the Fourteenth, to enable a State to say that the business should end. . . . What has happened to lotteries and wine might happen to theatres in some moral storm of the future, not because theatres were devoted to a public use, but because people had come to think that way.

But if we are to yield to fashionable conventions, it seems to me that theatres are as much devoted to public use as anything well can be. We have not that respect for art that is one of the glories of France. But to many people the superfluous is the necessary, and it seems to me that government does not go beyond its sphere in attempting to make life livable for them. I am far from saying that I think this particular law a wise and rational provision. That is not my affair. But if the people of the State of New York speaking by their authorized voice say that they want it, I see nothing in the Constitution of the United States to prevent their having their will.

194. *"There is no closed class or category of businesses affected with a public interest."*

Nebbia v. New York, 291 U.S. 502 (1934).

ROBERTS, J.: . . . We are told that because the law essays to control prices it denies due process. Notwithstanding the admitted power to correct existing economic ills by appropriate regulation of business, even though an indirect result may be a restriction of the freedom of contract or a modification of charges for services or the price of commodities, the appellant urges that direct fixation of prices is a type of regulation absolutely forbidden. His position is that the Fourteenth Amendment requires us to hold the challenged statute void for this reason alone. The argument runs that the public control of rates or prices is *per se* unreasonable and unconstitutional, save as applied to businesses affected with a public interest; that a business so affected is one in which property is devoted to an enterprise of a sort which the public itself might appropriately undertake, or one whose owner relies on a public grant or franchise for the right to conduct the business, or in which he is bound to serve all who apply; in short, such as is commonly called a public utility; or a business in its nature a monopoly. The milk industry, it is said, possesses none of these characteristics, and, therefore, not being affected with a public interest, its charges may not be controlled by the state. Upon the soundness of this contention the appellant's case against the statute depends.

We may as well say at once that the dairy industry is not, in the accepted sense of the phrase, a public utility. We think the appellant is also right in asserting that there is in this case no suggestion of any monopoly or monopolistic practice. It goes without saying that those engaged in the business are in no way dependent upon public grants or franchises for the privilege of conducting their activities. But if, as must be conceded, the industry is subject to regulation in the public interest, what constitutional principle bars the state from correcting existing maladjustments by legislation touching prices? We think there is no such principle. The due process clause makes no mention of sales or of prices any more than it speaks of business or contracts or buildings or other incidents of property. The thought seems nevertheless to have persisted that there is something peculiarly sacrosanct about the price one may charge for what he makes or sells, and that, however able to regulate other elements of manufacture or trade, with incidental effect upon price, the state is incapable of directly controlling the price itself. The view was negatived many years ago. *Munn. v. Illinois.* . . .

It is clear that there is no closed class or category of businesses affected with a public interest, and the function of courts in the application of the Fifth and Fourteenth Amendments is to determine in each case whether circumstances vindicate the challenged regulation as a reasonable exertion of governmental authority or condemn it as arbitrary or discriminatory. . . . The phrase "affected with a public interest" can, in the nature of things, mean no more than that an industry, for adequate reason, is subject to control for the public good. In several of the decisions of this court wherein the expressions "affected with a public interest," and "clothed with a public use," have been brought forward as the criteria of the validity of price control, it has been admitted that they are not susceptible of definition and form an unsatisfactory test of the constitutionality of legislation directed at business practices or prices. These decisions must rest, finally, upon the basis that the requirements of due process were not met because the laws were found arbitrary in their operation and effect. But there can be no doubt that upon proper occasion and by appropriate measures the state may regulate a business in any of its aspects, including the prices to be charged for the products or commodities it sells.

So far as the requirement of due process is concerned, and in the absence of other constitutional restriction, a state is free to adopt whatever economic policy may reasonably be deemed to promote public welfare, and to enforce that policy by legislation adapted to its purpose. The courts are without authority either to declare such policy, or, when it is declared by the legislature, to override it. If the laws passed are seen to have a reasonable relation to a proper legislative purpose, and are neither arbitrary nor discriminatory, the requirements of due process are satisfied, and judicial determination to that effect renders a court *functus officio*. . . . And it is equally clear that if the legislative policy be to curb unrestrained and harmful competition by measures which are not arbitrary or discriminatory it does not lie with the courts to determine that the rule is unwise. With the wisdom of the policy adopted, with the adequacy or practicability of the law enacted to forward it, the courts are both incompetent and unauthorized to deal. . . .

Price control, like any other form of regulation, is unconstitutional only if arbitrary, discriminatory, or demonstrably irrelevant to the policy the legislature is free to adopt, and hence an unnecessary and unwarranted interference with individual liberty.

Tested by these considerations we find no basis in the due process clause of the Fourteenth Amendment for condemning the provisions of the Agriculture and Markets Law here drawn into question.

195. *"Three generations of imbeciles are enough."*

Buck v. Bell, 274 U.S. 200 (1927).

HOLMES, J.: . . . An Act of Virginia . . . recites that the health of the patient and the welfare of society may be promoted in certain cases by the sterilization of mental defectives, under careful safeguard, &c. . . . ; that the Commonwealth is supporting in various institutions many defective persons who if now discharged would become a menace but if incapable of procreating might be discharged with safety and become self-supporting with benefit to themselves and to society. . . .

We have seen more than once that the public welfare may call upon the best citizens for their lives. It would be strange if it could not call upon those who already sap the strength of the State for these lesser sacrifices, often not felt to be such by those concerned, in order to prevent our being swamped with incompetence. It is better for all the world, if instead of waiting to execute degenerate offspring for crime, or to let them starve for their imbecility, society can prevent those who are manifestly unfit from continuing their kind. The principle that sustains compulsory vaccination is broad enough to cover cutting the Fallopian tubes. . . . Three generations of imbeciles are enough.

But, it is said, however it might be if this reasoning were applied generally, it fails when it is confined to the small number who are in the institutions named and is not applied to the multitudes outside. It is the usual last resort of constitutional arguments to point out shortcomings of this sort. But the answer is that the law does all that is needed when it does all that it can, indicates a policy, applies it to all within the lines, and seeks to bring within the lines all similarly situated so far and so fast as its means allow. . . .

CHAPTER XXI

A New Era in Civil Liberties

I T WAS logical that a Court dedicated to a defense of individualism should not concern itself exclusively with protecting property rights but should also examine constitutional guarantees of personal liberties. One of the most spectacular developments in the latter field was the Supreme Court's broadening of the concept of liberty in the Fourteenth Amendment to include the guarantees of the First Amendment, thus protecting basic civil liberties from state, as well as federal, abridgment. Ever since *Barron v. Baltimore* (Chapter IV), the Bill of Rights had been interpreted as a limitation upon the federal government, but not upon the states. "Neither the Fourteenth Amendment," the Court said in 1922, "nor any other provision of the Constitution of the United States imposes upon the states any restrictions about 'freedom of speech.'" In a remarkable reversal less than three years later, the Court casually cast aside this traditional view and effectively nationalized the First Amendment by reading it into the due process clause of the Fourteenth Amendment. The Gitlow case (No. 196), however, was not an unqualified victory in the field of civil liberties, for by reviving the "bad tendency" test as a measure of permissible free speech, it upheld the state legislative restriction.

In *Whitney v. California*, the Court again ruled that the state statute involved did not unduly restrict freedom of speech, but Justice Brandeis wrote a concurring opinion rejecting the Gitlow test and restating the "clear and present danger" test (No. 197). Another California case challenged the validity of a law forbidding the display of a red flag. Yetta Stromberg was convicted for participating in leading a Communist youth-camp group in the following flag salute: "I pledge allegiance to the workers' red flag and to the cause for which it stands, one aim throughout our lives, freedom for the working class." Chief Justice Hughes struck down the state statute on the ground that it was a denial of the liberty guaranteed by the due process clause of the Fourteenth Amendment (*Stromberg v. California* [No. 198]). At the same session, Hughes also invalidated the "Minnesota gag law," ruling that freedom of the press is another of the First Amendment rights protected by the liberty guaranteed by the Fourteenth Amendment (*Near v. Minnesota* [No. 199]).

Another aspect of the Court's concern for fundamental freedoms of the individual was revealed in the highly controversial 5 to 4 decision in *Olmstead v. U.S.* (No. 200). Over the vigorous dissents of Brandeis (No. 201) and Holmes, who branded wire tapping "dirty business," Chief Justice Taft ruled that this practice did not constitute an illegal search or seizure. In 1934, however, Congress passed a law stating that "no person not being authorized by the sender shall intercept any communication and divulge or publish the existence, contents, substance . . . of such intercepted communication to any person." Three years later, in *Nardone v. U.S.*, the Court held that evidence obtained in searches violating the statute was inadmissible in a federal prosecution.

The famous "Scottsboro cases" made two major contributions to American constitutional law. In the first (*Powell v. Alabama*, 1932), a majority agreed that seven Negroes convicted of rape and sentenced to death were deprived of life and liberty without due process of law when they were denied assistance of counsel, thus reading the guarantees of the Sixth Amendment into the Fourteenth Amendment. The second Scottsboro case (*Norris v. Alabama* [No. 202]) raised the question of the guarantee of a fair and impartial jury. As early as 1880 the Court had ruled that a Negro was denied equal protection of the laws when tried by a jury from which Negroes were excluded by law because of their color (*Strauder v. West Virginia*). At the same time, however, the Court decided that a Negro was not denied due process merely because there were no Negroes on his jury (*Virginia v. Rives*). It was not until fifty-five years later that the Norris case challenged the standard southern practice of not calling Negroes for jury service. Then the Court held that systematic exclusion of Negroes by the state violated the Fourteenth Amendment's mandate of equal protection of the laws.

Another minority group for which the Court showed a measure of solicitude was aliens. In *Truax v. Raich* (1915), the Court invalidated, for denying equal protection, an Arizona law that discriminated against aliens in employment. In *Terrance v. Thompson* (1923), however, the Court differentiated between this right and the right to own land. Further manifestations of the xenophobia of the 1920's were the quota provision in the Immigration Act of 1924 and the decision in *Mahler v. Eby* (1924), which upheld a federal statute facilitating the deportation of undesirable aliens. Chief Justice Taft explained that "the right to expel aliens is a sovereign power, necessary to the safety to the country, and only limited by treaty obligations."

Broadening the Concept of Liberty to Protect Freedom of Expression

196. Nationalization of First Amendment Freedoms

Gitlow v. New York, 268 U.S. 652 (1925).

SANFORD, J.: Benjamin Gitlow was indicted in the supreme court of New York, with three others, for the statutory crime of criminal anarchy. . . .

The indictment was in two counts. The first charged that the defendants had advocated, advised, and taught the duty, necessity, and propriety of overthrowing and overturning organized government by force, violence, and unlawful means, by certain writings therein set forth, entitled, "The Left Wing Manifesto"; the second, that the defendants had printed, published, and knowingly circulated and distributed a certain paper called "The Revolutionary Age," containing the writings set forth in the first count, advocating, advising, and teaching the doctrine that organized government should be overthrown by force, violence, and unlawful means. . . .

There was no evidence of any effect resulting from the publication and circulation of the Manifesto.

No witnesses were offered in behalf of the defendant. . . .

The sole contention here is, essentially, that, as there was no evidence of any concrete result flowing from the publication of the Manifesto, or of circumstances showing the likelihood of such result, the statute as construed and applied by the trial court penalizes the mere utterance, as such, of "doctrine" having no quality of incitement, without regard either to the circumstances of its utterance or to the likelihood of unlawful sequences; and that, as the exercise of the right of free expression with relation to government is only punishable "in circumstances involving likelihood of substantive evil," the statute contravenes the due process clause of the Fourteenth Amendment. The argument in support of this contention rests primarily upon the following propositions: first, that the "liberty" protected by the Fourteenth Amendment includes the liberty of speech and of the press; and second, that while liberty of expression "is not absolute," it may be restrained "only in circumstances where its exercise bears a causal relation with some substantive evil, consummated, attempted, or likely"; and as the statute "takes no account of circumstances," it unduly restrains this liberty, and is therefore unconstitutional.

The precise question presented, and the only question which we can consider under this writ of error, then, is whether the statute, as construed and applied in this case by the state courts, deprived the defendant of his liberty of expression, in violation of the due process clause of the Fourteenth Amendment. . . .

For the present purposes we may and do assume that freedom of speech and of the press—which are protected by the First Amendment from abridgment by Congress—are among the fundamental personal rights and "liberties" protected by the due process clause of the Fourteenth Amendment from impairment by the states. . . .

That a state, in the exercise of its police power, may punish those who abuse this freedom by utterances inimical to the public welfare, tending to corrupt public morals, incite to crime, or disturb the public peace, is not open to question. . . .

And, for yet more imperative reasons, a State may punish utterances endangering the foundations of organized government and threatening its overthrow by unlawful means. These imperil its own existence as a constitutional state. Freedom of speech and press, said Story . . . , does not protect disturbances of the public peace or the attempt to subvert the government. It does not protect publications or teachings which tend to subvert or imperil the government, or to impede or hinder it in the performance of its governmental duties. It does not protect publications prompting the overthrow of government by force; the punishment of those who publish articles which tend to destroy organized society being essential to the security of freedom and the stability of the state. And a State may penalize utterances which openly advocate the overthrow of the representative and constitutional form of government of the United States and the several states, by violence or other unlawful means. In short, this freedom does not deprive a State of the primary and essential right of self-preservation, which, so long as human governments endure, they cannot be denied. . . .

By enacting the present statute the State has determined, through its legislative body, that utterances advocating the overthrow of organized government by force, violence, and unlawful means, are so inimical to the general welfare, and involve such danger of substantive evil, that they may be penalized in the exercise of its police power. That determination must be given great weight. Every presumption is to be indulged in favor of the validity of the statute. . . . That utterances inciting to the overthrow of organized government by unlawful means present a sufficient danger of substantive evil to bring their punishment within the range of legislative discretion is clear. Such utterances, by their very nature, involve danger to the public peace and to the security of the state. They threaten breaches of the peace and ultimate revolution. And the immedi-

ate danger is none the less real and substantial because the effect of a given utterance cannot be accurately foreseen. The state cannot reasonably be required to measure the danger from every such utterance in the nice balance of a jeweler's scale. A single revolutionary spark may kindle a fire that, smoldering for a time, may burst into a sweeping and destructive conflagration. It cannot be said that the state is acting arbitrarily or unreasonably when, in the exercise of its judgment as to the measures necessary to protect the public peace and safety, it seeks to extinguish the spark without waiting until it has enkindled the flame or blazed into the conflagration. It cannot reasonably be required to defer the adoption of measures for its own peace and safety until the revolutionary utterances lead to actual disturbances of the public peace or imminent and immediate danger of its own destruction; but it may, in the exercise of its judgment, suppress the threatened danger in its incipiency. . . .

We cannot hold that the present statute is an arbitrary or unreasonable exercise of the police power of the state, unwarrantably infringing the freedom of speech or press; and we must and do sustain its constitutionality.

This being so it may be applied to every utterance—not too trivial to be beneath the notice of the law—which is of such a character and used with such intent and purpose as to bring it within the prohibition of the statute. . . . In other words, when the legislative body has determined generally, in the constitutional exercise of its discretion, that utterances of a certain kind involve such danger of substantive evil that they may be punished, the question whether any specific utterance coming within the prohibited class is likely, in and of itself, to bring about the substantive evil, is not open to consideration. It is sufficient that the statute itself be constitutional, and that the use of the language comes within its prohibition. . . .

197. "It is the function of speech to free men from the bondage of irrational fears."

Whitney v. California, 274 U.S. 357 (1927).

BRANDEIS, J., concurring: . . . The right of free speech, the right to teach and the right of assembly are, of course, fundamental rights. . . . These may not be denied or abridged. But, although the rights of free speech and assembly are fundamental, they are not in their nature absolute. Their exercise is subject to restriction, if the particular restriction proposed is required in order to protect the State from destruction or from serious injury, political, economic or moral. That the necessity which is essential to a valid restriction does not exist unless speech would produce, or is intended to produce, a clear and imminent danger of some substantive evil which the State constitutionally may seek to prevent has been settled. . . .

This Court has not yet fixed the standard by which to determine when a danger shall be deemed clear; how remote the danger may be and yet be deemed present; and what degree of evil shall be deemed sufficiently substantial to justify resort to abridgement of free speech and assembly as the means of protection. To reach sound conclusions on these matters, we must bear in mind why a State is, ordinarily, denied the power to prohibit dissemination of social, economic and political doctrine which a vast majority of its citizens believes to be false and fraught with evil consequence.

Those who won our independence believed that the final end of the State was to make men free to develop their faculties; and that in its government the deliberative forces should prevail over the arbitrary. They valued liberty both as an end and as a means. They believed liberty to be the secret of happiness and courage to be the secret of liberty. They believed that freedom to think as you will and to speak as you think are means indispensable to the discovery and spread of political truth; that without free speech and assembly discussion would be futile; that with them, discussion affords ordinarily adequate protection against the dissemination of noxious doctrine; that the greatest menace to freedom is an inert people; that public discussion is a political duty; and that this should be a fundamental principle of the American government. They recognized the risks to which all human institutions are subject. But they knew that order cannot be secured merely through fear of punishment for its infraction; that it is hazardous to discourage thought, hope and imagination; that fear breeds repression; that repression breeds hate; that hate menaces stable government; that the path of safety lies in the opportunity to discuss freely supposed grievances and proposed remedies; and that the fitting remedy for evil counsels is good ones. Believing in the power of reason as applied through public discussion, they eschewed silence coerced by law—the argument of force in its worst form. Recognizing the occasional tyrannies of governing majorities, they amended the Constitution so that free speech and assembly should be guaranteed.

Fear of serious injury cannot alone justify suppression of free speech and assembly. Men feared witches and burnt women. It is the function of speech to free men from the bondage of irrational fears. To justify suppression of free speech there must be reasonable ground to fear that serious evil will result if free speech is practiced. There must be a reasonable ground to believe that the danger apprehended is imminent. There must be reasonable ground to believe that the evil to be prevented is a serious one. Every denunciation of existing law tends in some measure to increase the probability that there will be violation of it. Condonation of a breach enhances the probability. Propagation of the criminal state of mind by teaching syndicalism increases it. Advocacy of law-breaking heightens it still further. But even advocacy of violation, however reprehensible morally, is not a justification for denying free speech where the advocacy falls short of incitement and there is nothing to indicate that advocacy would be immediately acted on. The wide difference between advocacy and incitement, between preparation and attempt, between assembling and conspiracy, must be borne in mind. In order to support a finding of a clear and present danger it must be shown either that immediate serious violence was to be expected or was advocated, or that the past conduct furnished reason to believe that such advocacy was then contemplated.

Those who won our independence by revolution were not cowards. They did not fear political change. They did not exalt order at the cost of liberty. To courageous, self-reliant men, with confidence in the power of free and fearless reasoning applied through the processes of popular government, no danger flowing from speech can be deemed clear and present, unless the incidence of the evil apprehended is so imminent that it may befall before there is an opportunity for full discussion. If there be time to expose through discussion the falsehood and fallacies, to avert the evil by processes of education, the remedy to be applied is more speech, not enforced silence. Only an emergency can justify repression. Such must be the rule if authority is to be reconciled with freedom. Such, in my opinion, is the command of the Constitution. It is therefore always open to Americans to challenge a law abridging free speech and assembly by showing that there was

no emergency justifying it.

Moreover, even imminent danger cannot justify resort to prohibition of these functions essential to effective democracy, unless the evil apprehended is relatively serious. Prohibition of free speech and assembly is a measure so stringent that it would be inappropriate as the means for averting a relatively trivial harm to society. A police measure may be unconstitutional merely because the remedy, although effective as means of protection, is unduly harsh or oppressive. . . . Among free men, the deterrents ordinarily to be applied to prevent crime are education and punishment for violations of the law, not abridgment of the rights of free speech and assembly. . . .

Whenever the fundamental rights of free speech and assembly are alleged to have been invaded, it must remain open to a defendant to present the issue whether there actually did exist at the time a clear danger; whether the danger, if any, was imminent; and whether the evil apprehended was one so substantial as to justify the stringent restriction interposed by the legislature. . . .

Whether in 1919, when Miss Whitney did the things complained of, there was in California such clear and present danger of serious evil, might have been made the important issue in the case. She might have required that the issue be determined either by the court or the jury. She claimed below that the statute as applied to her violated the Federal Constitution; but she did not claim that it was void because there was no clear and present danger of serious evil, nor did she request that the existence of these conditions of a valid measure thus restricting the rights of free speech and assembly be passed upon by the court or jury. On the other hand, there was evidence on which the court or jury might have found that such danger existed. I am unable to assent to the suggestion in the opinion of the Court that assembling with a political party, formed to advocate the desirability of a proletarian revolution by mass action at some date necessarily far in the future, is not a right within the protection of the Fourteenth Amendment. . . .

198. *Red Flags, Communism, and "Dangerous Tendency"*

Stromberg v. California, 283 U.S. 359 (1931).

HUGHES, C.J.: . . . It appears that the appellant, a young woman of nineteen, a citizen of the United States by birth, was one of the supervisors of a summer camp for children, between ten and fifteen years of age, in the foothills of the San Bernardina mountains. Appellant led the children in their daily study, teaching them history and economics. "Among other things, the children were taught class consciousness, the solidarity of the workers, and the theory that the workers of the world are of one blood and brothers all." Appellant was a member of the Young Communist League, an international organization affiliated with the Communist Party. The charge against her concerned a daily ceremony at the camp, in which the appellant supervised and directed the children in raising a red flag, "a camp-made reproduction of the flag of Soviet Russia, which was also the flag of the Communist Party in the United States." . . . The stipulation further shows that "a library was maintained at the camp containing a large number of books, papers and pamphlets, including much radical communist propaganda, specimens of which are quoted in the opinion of the state court." These quotations abundantly demonstrated that the books and pamphlets contained incitements to violence and to "armed uprisings," teaching "the indispensability of a desperate, bloody, destructive war as the immediate task of the coming action." . . .

It has been determined that the conception of liberty under the due process clause of the Fourteenth Amendment embraces the right of free speech. . . . The right is not an absolute one, and the State in the exercise of its police power may punish the abuse of this freedom. There is no question but that the State may thus provide for the punishment of those who indulge in utterances which incite to violence and crime and threaten the overthrow of organized government by unlawful means. There is no constitutional immunity for such conduct abhorrent to our institutions. . . .

The question is thus narrowed to that of the validity of the first clause, that is, with respect to the display of the flag "as a sign, symbol or emblem of opposition to organized government," and the construction which the state court has placed upon this clause removes every element of doubt. The state court recognized the indefiniteness and ambiguity of the clause. The court considered that it might be construed as embracing conduct which the State could not constitutionally prohibit. Thus it was said that the clause "might be construed to include the peaceful and orderly opposition to a government as organized and controlled by one political party by those of another political party equally high minded and patriotic, which did not agree with the one in power. It might also be construed to include peaceful and orderly opposition to government by legal means and within constitutional limitations." The maintenance of the opportunity for free political discussion to the end that government may be responsive to the will of the people and that changes may be obtained by lawful means, an opportunity essential to the security of the Republic, is a fundamental principle of our constitutional system. A statute which, upon its face, and as authoritatively construed, is so vague and indefinite as to permit the punishment of the fair use of this opportunity is repugnant to the guarantee of liberty contained in the Fourteenth Amendment. The first clause of the statute being invalid upon its face, the conviction of the appellant, which so far as the record discloses may have rested upon that clause exclusively, must be set aside.

199. *The Court Invalidates the Minnesota "Gag Law"*

Near v. Minnesota, 283 U.S. 697 (1931).

HUGHES, C.J.: . . . This statute for the suppression as a public nuisance of a newspaper or periodical, is unusual, if not unique, and raises questions of grave importance transcending the local interests involved in the particular action. It is no longer open to doubt that the liberty of the press, and of speech, is within the liberty safeguarded by the due process clause of the Fourteenth Amendment from invasion by state action. . . . Liberty of speech, and of the press, is also not an absolute right, and the state may punish its abuse. . . . Liberty, in each of its phases, has its history and connotation and, in the present instance, the inquiry is as to the historic conception of the liberty of the press and whether the statute under review violates the essential attributes of that liberty. . . .

If we cut through mere details of procedure, the operation and effect of the statute in substance is that public authorities may bring the owner or publisher of a newspaper or periodical before a judge upon a charge of conducting a business of publishing scandalous and defamatory matter—in particular that the matter consists of charges against public officers of official dereliction—and unless the owner or publisher is able and disposed to bring competent evidence to satisfy the judge that the charges are true and are published with good motives and for justifiable ends, his newspaper or periodical is suppressed and further publication is made punishable as a contempt. This is of the essence of censorship.

The question is whether a statute authorizing such proceedings in restraint of publication is consistent with the conception of the liberty of the press as historically conceived and guaranteed. In determining the extent of the constitutional protection, it has been generally, if not universally, considered that it is the chief purpose of the guaranty to prevent previous restraints upon publication. The struggle in England, directed against the legislative power of the licenser, resulted in renunciation of the censorship of the press. . . . The liberty deemed to be established was thus described by Blackstone: "The liberty of the press is indeed essential to the nature of a free state; but this consists in laying no *previous* restraints upon publications, and not in freedom from censure for criminal matter when published. . . ."

The criticism upon Blackstone's statement has not been because immunity from previous restraint upon publication has not been regarded as deserving of special emphasis, but chiefly because that immunity cannot be deemed to exhaust the conception of the liberty guaranteed by state and federal constitutions. The point of criticism has been "that the mere exemption from previous restraints cannot be all that is secured by the constitutional provisions"; and that "the liberty of the press might be rendered a mockery and a delusion, and the phrase itself a by-word, if, while every man was at liberty to publish what he pleased, the public authorities might nevertheless punish him for harmless publications." . . . But it is recognized that punishment for the abuse of the liberty accorded to the press is essential to the protection of the public, and that the common law rules that subject the libeler to responsibility for the public offense, as well as for the private injury, are not abolished by the protection extended in our constitutions. . . . In the present case, we have no occasion to inquire as to the permissible scope of subsequent punishment. For whatever wrong the appellant has committed or may commit, by his publications, the state appropriately affords both public and private redress by its libel laws. As has been noted, the statute in question does not deal with punishments; it provides for no punishment, except in case of contempt for violation of the court's order, but for suppression and injunction, that is, for restraint upon publication.

The objection has also been made that the principle as to immunity from previous restraint is stated too broadly, if ever such restraint is deemed to be prohibited. That is undoubtedly true; the protection even as to previous restraint is not absolutely unlimited. But the limitation has been recognized only in exceptional cases: "When a nation is at war many things that might be said in time of peace are such a hindrance to its effort that their utterance will not be endured so long as men fight and that no court could regard them as protected by any constitutional right." *Schenck v. United States*. . . .

The exceptional nature of its limitations places in a strong light the general conception that liberty of the press, historically considered and taken up by the federal Constitution, has meant, principally although not exclusively, immunity from previous restraints or censorship. The conception of the liberty of the press in this country had broadened with the exigencies of the colonial period and with the efforts to secure freedom from oppressive administration. That liberty was especially cherished for the immunity it afforded from previous restraint of the publication of censure of public officers and charges of official misconduct. . . .

The importance of this immunity has

not lessened. While reckless assaults upon public men, and efforts to bring obloquy upon those who are endeavoring faithfully to discharge official duties, exert a baleful influence and deserve the severest condemnation in public opinion, it cannot be said that this abuse is greater, and it is believed to be less, than that which characterized the period in which our institutions took shape. Meanwhile, the administration of government has become more complex, the opportunities for malfeasance and corruption have multiplied, crime has grown to most serious proportions, and the danger of its protection by unfaithful officials and of the impairment of the fundamental security of life and property by criminal alliances and official neglect, emphasizes the primary need of a vigilant and courageous press, especially in great cities. The fact that the liberty of the press may be abused by miscreant purveyors of scandal does not make any the less necessary the immunity of the press from previous restraint in dealing with official misconduct. Subsequent punishment for such abuses as may exist is the appropriate remedy, consistent with constitutional privilege. . . .

The statute in question cannot be justified by reason of the fact that the publisher is permitted to show, before injunction issues, that the matter published is true and is published with good motives and for justifiable ends. If such a statute, authorizing suppression and injunction on such a basis, is constitutionally valid, it would be equally permissible for the legislature to provide that at any time the publisher of any newspaper could be brought before a court, or even an administrative officer (as the constitutional protection may not be regarded as resting on mere procedural details) and required to produce proof of the truth of his publication, or of what he intended to publish, and of his motives, or stand enjoined. If this can be done, the legislature may provide machinery for determining in the complete exercise of its discretion what are justifiable ends and restrain publication accordingly. And it would be but a step to a complete system of censorship. The recognition of authority to impose previous restraint upon publication in order to protect the community against the circulation of charges of misconduct, and especially of official misconduct, necessarily would carry with it the admission of the authority of the censor against which the constitutional barrier was erected. The preliminary freedom, by virtue of the very reason for its existence, does not depend, as this Court has said, on proof of truth. . . .

Equally unavailing is the insistence that the statute is designed to prevent the circulation of scandal which tends to disturb the public peace and to provoke assaults and the commission of crime. Charges of reprehensible conduct, and in particular of official malfeasance, unquestionably create a public scandal, but the theory of the constitutional guaranty is that even a more

serious public evil would be caused by authority to prevent publication. . . . There is nothing new in the fact that charges of reprehensible conduct may create resentment and the disposition to resort to violent means of redress, but this well-understood tendency did not alter the determination to protect the press against censorship and restraint upon publication. . . . The danger of violent reactions becomes greater with effective organization of defiant groups resenting exposure, and if this consideration warranted legislative interference with the initial freedom of publication, the constitutional protection would be reduced to a mere form of words.

For these reasons we hold the statute, so far as it authorized the proceedings in this action under clause (b) of section one, to be an infringement of the liberty of the press guaranteed by the Fourteenth Amendment. . . .

Due Process and the Rights of Accused

SEARCHES AND SEIZURES

200. Is Wire Tapping an Illegal Search and Seizure?

Olmstead v. U.S., 277 U.S. 438 (1928).

TAFT, C.J.: . . . The Fourth Amendment provides: "The right of the people to be secure in their persons, houses, papers, and effects, against unreasonable searches and seizures, shall not be violated. . . ." And the Fifth: "No person . . . shall be compelled in any criminal case to be a witness against himself. . . ."

There is no room in the present case for applying the Fifth Amendment un-

less the Fourth Amendment was first violated. There was no evidence of compulsion to induce the defendants to talk over their many telephones. They were continually and voluntarily transacting business without knowledge of the interception. Our consideration must be confined to the Fourth Amendment. . . .

The well known historical purpose of the Fourth Amendment, directed against general warrants and writs of assistance, was to prevent the use of governmental force to search a man's house, his person, his papers, and his effects, and to prevent their seizure against his will. . . .

The Amendment itself shows that the search is to be of material things—the person, the house, his papers or his effects. The description of the warrant necessary to make the proceeding lawful is that it must specify the place to be searched and the person or *things* to be seized. . . .

The language of the Amendment can not be extended and expanded to include telephone wires reaching to the whole world from the defendant's house or office. The intervening wires are not part of his house or office, any more than are the highways along which they are stretched. . . .

Congress may, of course, protect the secrecy of telephone messages by making them, when intercepted, inadmissible in evidence in federal criminal trials, by direct legislation, and thus depart from the common law of evidence. But the courts may not adopt such a policy by attributing an enlarged and unusual meaning to the Fourth Amendment. The reasonable view is that one who installs in his house a telephone instrument with connecting wires intends to project his voice to those quite outside, and that the wires beyond his house and messages while passing over them are not within the protection of the Fourth Amendment. Here those who intercepted the projected voices were not in the house of either party to the conversation.

Neither the cases we have cited nor any of the many federal decisions brought to our attention hold the Fourth Amendment to have been violated as against a defendant unless there has been an official search and seizure of his person or such a seizure of his papers or his tangible material effects or an actual physical invasion of his house "or curtilage" for the purpose of making a seizure.

We think, therefore, that the wire-tapping here disclosed did not amount to a search or seizure within the meaning of the Fourth Amendment. . . .

Some of our number . . . have concluded that there is merit in the twofold objection overruled in both courts below that evidence obtained through intercepting of telephone messages by government agents was inadmissible because the mode of obtaining it was unethical and a misdemeanor under the law of Washington. To avoid any misapprehension of our views of that objection, we shall deal with it in both of its phases. . . .

The common law rule is that the admissibility of evidence is not affected by the illegality of the means by which it was obtained. . . .

Nor can we, without the sanction of congressional enactment, subscribe to the suggestion that the courts have a discretion to exclude evidence, the admission of which is not unconstitutional, because unethically secured. This would be at variance with the common law doctrine generally supported by authority. There is no case that sustains, nor any recognized text book that gives color to such a view. Our general experience shows that much evidence has always been receivable although not obtained by conformity to the highest ethics. The history of criminal trials shows numerous cases of prosecutions of oathbound conspiracies for murder, robbery, and other crimes where officers of the law have disguised themselves and joined the organizations, taken the oaths and given themselves every appearance of active members engaged in the promotion of crime for the purpose of securing evidence. Evidence secured by such means has always been received.

A standard which would forbid the reception of evidence if obtained by other than nice ethical conduct by government officials would make society suffer and give criminals greater immunity than has been known heretofore. In the absence of controlling legislation by Congress, those who realize the difficulties in bringing offenders to justice may well deem it wise that the exclusion of evidence should be confined to cases where rights under the Constitution would be violated by admitting it. . . .

201. *"If the Government becomes a law-breaker, it breeds contempt for law."*

Olmstead v. U.S. (1928).

BRANDEIS, J., dissenting: . . . The government makes no attempt to defend the methods employed by its officers. Indeed, it concedes that if wire-tapping can be deemed a search and seizure within the Fourth Amendment, such wire-tapping as was practised in the case at bar was an unreasonable search and seizure, and that the evidence thus obtained was inadmissible. But it relies on the language of the amendment; and it claims that the protection given thereby cannot properly be held to include a telephone conversation. . . .

When the Fourth and Fifth Amendments were adopted, "the form that evil had theretofore taken" had been necessarily simple. Force and violence were then the only means known to man by which a government could directly effect self-incrimination. It could compel the individual to testify—a compulsion effected, if need be, by torture. It could secure possession of his papers and other articles incident to his private life—a seizure effected, if need be, by breaking and entry. Protection against such invasion of "the sanctities of a man's home and the privacies of life" was provided in the Fourth and Fifth Amendments, by specific language. . . . But "time works changes, brings into existence new conditions and purposes." Subtler and more far-reaching means of invading privacy have become available to the government. Discovery and invention have made it possible for the government, by means far more effective than stretching upon the rack, to obtain disclosure in court of what is whispered in the closet. . . .

The progress of science in furnishing the government with means of espionage is not likely to stop with wire-tapping. Ways may some day be developed by which the government, without removing papers from secret drawers, can reproduce them in court, and by which it will be enabled to expose to a jury the most intimate occurrences of the home. Advances in the psychic and related sciences may bring means of exploring unexpressed beliefs, thoughts and emotions. . . . Can it be that the Constitution affords no protection against such invasions of individual security? . . .

Applying to the Fourth and Fifth Amendments the established rule of construction, the defendants' objections to the evidence obtained by a wire-tapping must, in my opinion, be sustained. It is, of course, immaterial where the physical connection with the telephone wires leading into the defendants' premises was made. And it is also immaterial that the intrusion was in aid of law enforcement. Experience should teach us to be most on our guard to protect liberty when the government's purposes are beneficent. Men born to freedom are naturally alert to repel invasion of their liberty by evil-minded rulers. The greatest dangers to liberty lurk in insidious encroachment by men of zeal, well-meaning, but without understanding.

Independently of the constitutional question, I am of opinion that the judgment should be reversed. By the laws of Washington, wire-tapping is a crime. . . . To prove its case, the government was obliged to lay bare the crimes committed by its officers on its behalf. A federal court should not permit such a prosecution to continue. . . .

Decency, security, and liberty alike demand that government officials shall be subjected to the same rules of conduct that are commands to the citizen. In a government of laws, existence of the government will be imperiled if it fails to observe the law scrupulously. Our government is the potent, the omnipresent, teacher. For good or for ill, it teaches the whole people by its example. Crime is contagious. If the government becomes a law-breaker, it breeds contempt for law; it invites every man to become a law unto himself; it invites anarchy. To declare that in the administration of the criminal law the end justifies the means—to declare that the government may commit crimes in order to secure the conviction of a private criminal—would bring terrible retribution. Against that pernicious doctrine this Court should resolutely set its face.

202. *Jury Trial and the Right to Counsel: The Scottsboro Cases*

Norris v. Alabama, 294 U.S. 587 (1935).

Hughes, C.J.: . . . There is no controversy as to the constitutional principle involved . . . this Court thus stated the principle in *Carter v. Texas* . . . in relation to exclusion from service on grand juries: "Whenever by any action of a state, whether through its legislature, through its courts, or through its executive or administrative officers, all persons of the African race are excluded, solely because of their race or color, from serving as grand jurors in the criminal prosecution of a person of the African race, the equal protection of the laws is denied to him, contrary to the Fourteenth Amendment.["] . . . The principle is equally applicable to a similar exclusion of negroes from service on petit juries. . . . And although the state statute defining the qualifications of jurors may be fair on its face, the constitutional provision affords protection against action of the state through its administrative officers in effecting the prohibited discrimination. . . . The testimony, as the state court said, tended to show that "in a long number of years no negro had been called for jury service in that county." It appeared that no negro had served on any grand or petit jury in that county within the memory of witnesses who had lived there all their lives. Testimony to that effect was given by men whose ages ran from fifty to seventy-six years. Their testimony was uncontradicted. It was supported by the testimony of officials. The clerk of the jury commission and the clerk of the circuit court had never known of a negro serving on a grand jury in Jackson County. The court reporter, who had not missed a session in that county in twenty-four years, and two jury commissioners testified to the same effect. One of the latter, who was a member of the commission which made up the jury roll for the grand jury which found the indictment, testified that he had "never known of a single instance where any negro sat on any grand or petit jury in the entire history of that county."

That testimony in itself made out a *prima facie* case of the denial of the equal protection which the Constitution guarantees. . . . The case thus made was supplemented by direct testimony that specified negroes, thirty or more in number, were qualified for jury service. Among these were negroes who were members of school boards, or trustees, of colored schools, and property owners and householders. It also appeared that negroes from that county had been called for jury service in the federal court. Several of those who were thus described as qualified were witnesses. While there was testimony which cast doubt upon the qualifications of some of the negroes who had been named, and there was also general testimony by the editor of a local newspaper who gave his opinion as to the lack of "sound judgment" of the "good negroes" in Jackson County, we think that the definite testimony as to the actual qualifications of individual negroes, which was not met by any testimony equally direct, showed that there were negroes in Jackson County qualified for jury service. . . .

We are of the opinion that the evidence required a different result from that reached in the state court. We think that the evidence that for a generation or longer no negro had been called for service on any jury in Jackson County, that there were negroes qualified for jury service, that according to the practice of the jury commission their names would normally appear on the preliminary list of male citizens of the requisite age but that no names of negroes were placed on the jury roll, and the testimony with respect to the lack of appropriate consideration of the qualifications of negroes, established the discrimination which the Constitution forbids. The motion to quash the indictment upon that ground should have been granted. . . .

The evidence that for many years no negro had been called for jury service itself tended to show the absence of the names of negroes from the jury rolls, and the state made no effort to prove their presence. . . .

That showing as to the long-continued exclusion of negroes from jury service, and as to the many negroes qualified for that service, could not be met by mere generalities. If, in the presence of such testimony as defendant adduced, the mere general assertions by officials of their performance of duty were to be accepted as an adequate justification for the complete exclusion of negroes from jury service, the constitutional provision—adopted with special reference to their protection—would be but a vain and illusory requirement. . . .

We are concerned only with the federal question which we have discussed, and in view of the denial of the federal right suitably asserted, the judgment must be reversed and the cause remanded for further proceedings not inconsistent with this opinion. . . .

CHAPTER XXII

The New Deal and the Old Supreme Court

To cope with the most disastrous economic emergency which the American people had ever faced, President Franklin D. Roosevelt launched a vigorous New Deal, predicated on the proposition that drastic federal control over banking and finance, labor, manufacturing, and agriculture could be effected within the American constitutional framework. "Our Constitution," the new President declared in his inaugural address, "is so simple, so practical that it is possible always to meet extraordinary needs by changes in emphasis and arrangement without loss of essential form." Unless this view was shared by the Supreme Court, however, New Deal legislation would have to travel a rough road, for never before in the country's history had federal authority over national economic life been asserted as extensively as it was under Roosevelt's leadership.

The fate of the relief, recovery, and reform programs depended in the final analysis on which set of judicial precedents the Supreme Court applied—that which stressed broad commerce and taxing powers to control industry, or that which relied on a definition of federal authority as narrow as the Knight (Chapter XV) and Dagenhart (Chapter XVIII) rules. Unfortunately for the New Deal, the Court of the early 1930's was composed of four justices highly conservative in their economic views and bitterly opposed to any extension of governmental power over the nation's social and economic life. This solid phalanx of Justices Butler, McReynolds, Sutherland, and Van Devanter was frequently joined by either Justice Roberts or Chief Justice Hughes, or both, enabling it to dominate judicial action. Only Justices Brandeis, Cardozo, and Stone consistently displayed a social consciousness and a willingness to experiment with new approaches to pressing economic problems.

During Roosevelt's first term, his administration won but two limited victories in the constitutional warfare. In the "Gold Clause" cases, the Court accepted the Congressional resolution of 1933 which nullified the gold clause in public and private contracts. Although the four conservative justices dissented bitterly—McReynolds, visibly shaken, muttered, "The Constitution is gone!"— these technical decisions established no important precedents for expanded federal power, merely implementing the long-established national authority over monetary matters. In considering a challenge to the constitutionality of the Tennessee Valley Authority, the Court carefully limited its ruling to uphold only the construction of the Wilson Dam and the sale of its surplus power (*Ashwander v. T. V. A.* [No. 203]). Because the dam had been built under the National Defense Act, the ruling was based primarily upon the war power and did not deal with the constitutionality of the whole T. V. A. The decision therefore left the door open for a variety of challenges on other grounds by opponents of T. V. A.

These minor victories were more than offset by a stunning series of defeats. Between January, 1935, and May, 1936, twelve major statutes were ruled unconstitutional in decisions which frequently involved a return to nineteenth-century legal concepts, rejected by the Court even during the "normalcy" of the 1920's. The measures invalidated were of such wide application that the principal programs of the early New Deal were sapped of all vitality. Significantly, the first attack was on the National Industrial Recovery Act. This measure provided for federal control of the entire industrial structure of the country through the enforcement of codes of fair practice and procedure. In the "Hot Oil" case (*Panama Refining Co. v. Ryan,* 1935), the Court upset the provision that granted the President power to control interstate oil shipments, on the ground, never stated previously, that such extensive executive authority resulted from an unconstitutional delegation of legislative power. Although Congress hastened to revise the statute to alleviate judicial misgivings, the oil decision was a portent of things to come. Five months later, the Court relied on the same constitutional concept, plus an extremely narrow interpretation of the commerce clause, and invalidated the entire N. I. R. A. in the famous "sick chicken" case (*Schechter Poultry Corporation v. U.S.* [No. 204]). Asked to comment on the ruling in a press conference, the President responded bitterly: "We have been relegated to the horse-and-buggy definition of interstate commerce."

In 1936, a series of fateful decisions confirmed the Schechter doctrine and created a constitutional dilemma for the administration. The Agricultural Adjustment Act was the next to fall. Based on the assumption that the farmer's plight was caused by overproduction, the A. A. A. of 1933 provided benefit payments for acreage reduction; the amount paid was to be recovered by the government through a general tax on the processing of the commodity. In *U.S. v. Butler* (No. 205), Justice Roberts, speaking for six of the Justices, overruled the measure as "a scheme for purchasing with Federal Funds submission to Federal Regulation of a subject reserved to the States." The opinion was noteworthy both for Roberts's contention that the Court's work was purely mechanical, and for his deep probing into the meaning of the general welfare clause. He concluded that the federal government possessed the power to tax and appropriate for the general welfare apart from the other enumerated powers of Congress, but then ruled that even this expansive authority could not justify the processing tax since it was not really a tax but a part of an illegal system for regulating agricultural production. In a stinging dissent, Justice Stone berated the inconsistency of the majority's position and warned against a "tortured construction of the Constitution."

Following the death of the N. I. R. A., the government did not again seek to control the nation's economy through one omnibus law. Instead, its programs were carefully limited to specific areas and groups. Typical was the Bituminous Coal Act of 1935, which enjoyed the support of both miners and operators. The measure was intended to control prices and wages and enforce collective bargaining in the "sick" coal industry; it sought constitutional justification in the commerce clause. President Roosevelt requested Congress to pass the bill "despite admitted doubts as to whether the Supreme Court would uphold it." Strengthened by the growing Liberty League and viewing the Supreme Court as a partner, business began a test case against the law the day it was passed. When the case reached the Supreme Court, the conservative majority, consistent with its Schechter ruling, nullified the entire act, reverting to the "direct-indirect" concept of the Knight and Dagenhart cases (*Carter v. Carter Coal Company* [No. 206]). Although many agreed with Justice Cardozo that "a great principle of constitutional law is not susceptible of comprehensive statement in an adjective," the ruling stood as an ominous threat to other recently passed legislation, such as the National Labor Relations Act, the Social Security Act, and the Public Utility Holding Company Act.

Bolstered by a smashing election victory in 1936, President Roosevelt set out to "save the Constitution from the Court and the Court from itself." In February, 1937, a bill was submitted to Congress for reorganizing the federal judiciary. Reminiscent of a measure proposed by Justice McReynolds while Attorney General under Woodrow Wilson, the act's most controversial provision would have increased the membership of the Supreme Court from nine to a maximum of fifteen, if judges reaching the age of seventy refused to retire. Other provisions would have reorganized lower federal courts and modified judicial procedure. The original measure gave no indication of motive, carefully avoiding any suggestion of the desire to alter "reactionary" court decisions, but in a "fireside chat" on March 9, the President left no doubts as to his purposes and goals (No. 207).

The "court-packing" bill precipitated the bitterest domestic controversy of Roosevelt's long Presidency. Attacked as executive usurpation and an attempt to destroy judicial independence, the measure became a political rallying point for Republicans and dissident Democrats, who until that time had been hesitant to launch a head-on attack on the popular Chief Executive. Following heated hearings, the Senate Judiciary Committee in June rejected the proposal in a report which insinuated that the President was trying to subvert American institutions and overturn the Constitution by questionable methods (No. 208).

Although this report deplored any attempt to make the federal judiciary "subservient to the pressures of public opinion of the hour," the Court, unaltered in personnel, had already been responding to such pressures in a series of decisions validating New Deal legislation. The first of these was indicative of the Court's changed attitude. Federal minimum wage legislation had been precluded for years by the Adkins ruling (Chapter XX), and when a New York State minimum wage law was challenged in 1936, the Justices had held, in a 5 to 4 decision (*Morehead v. N.Y. ex rel. Tipaldo*), that such legislation was also beyond the authority of the states. At the height of the judiciary controversy, Justice Roberts reversed his stand of ten months earlier and joined a majority of five, led by Chief Justice Hughes, in upholding a similar minimum wage statute of the State of Washington (*West Coast Hotel Co. v. Parrish* [No. 209]). The opinion specifically overruled the Adkins case, and although Hughes carefully avoided a positive reversal of the New York decision, constitutional lawyers agreed that this was done primarily to save embarrassment; it certainly did not hide the clear implication that the latter was also invalid.

The Parrish decision inaugurated a general reappraisal of New Deal legislation, and Court approval removed the administration's chief cause of concern over the high tribunal. Thus, as a journalist of the day put it, "a switch in time saved nine." Roosevelt had accomplished his original desire to remove the judicial roadblock to his programs. The subsequent defeat of the "court-packing" plan was accepted with reluctance but with a knowledge that a chastened judiciary had now heeded Justice Stone's admonition in his Butler dissent: "For the removal of unwise laws from the statute books, appeal lies not to the courts but to the ballot and to the processes of democratic government."

Judicial Review of National Control over Economic Regulation

203. *The New Deal Wins a Limited Judicial Victory*

Ashwander v. T. V. A., 297 U.S. 288 (1936).

HUGHES, C.J.: . . . The Government's contention is that the Wilson Dam was constructed, and the power plant connected with it was installed, in the exercise by the Congress of its war and commerce powers, that is, for the purposes of national defense and the improvement of navigation. . . .

We may take judicial notice of the international situation at the time the Act of 1916 was passed, and it cannot be successfully disputed that the Wilson Dam and its auxiliary plants, including the hydro-electric power plant, are, and were intended to be, adapted to the purposes of national defense. While the District Court found that there is no intention to use the nitrate plants or the hydro-electric units installed at Wilson Dam for the production of war materials in time of peace, "the maintenance of said properties in operating condition and the assurance of an abundant supply of electric energy in the event of war, constitute national defense assets." This finding has ample support.

The Act of 1916 also had in view "improvements to navigation." Commerce includes navigation. "All America understands, and has uniformly understood," said Chief Justice Marshall in *Gibbons v. Ogden*, . . . "the word 'commerce,' to comprehend navigation." The power to regulate interstate commerce embraces the power to keep the navigable rivers of the United States free from obstructions to navigation and to remove such obstructions when they exist. . . .

The Government acquired full title to the dam site, with all riparian rights. The power of falling water was an inevitable incident of the construction of the dam. That water power came into the exclusive control of the Federal Government. The mechanical energy was convertible into electric energy, and the water power, the right to convert it into electric energy, and the electric energy thus produced, constitute property belonging to the United States. . . .

Authority to dispose of property constitutionally acquired by the United States is expressly granted to the Congress by §3 of Article IV of the Constitution. This section provides:

The Congress shall have Power to dispose of and make all needful Rules and Regulations respecting the Territory or other Property belonging to the United States; and nothing in this Constitution shall be so construed as to Prejudice any Claims of the United States, or of any particular State.

To the extent that the power of disposition is thus expressly conferred, it is manifest that the Tenth Amendment is not applicable. And the Ninth Amendment (which petitioners also invoke) in insuring the maintenance of the rights retained by the people does not withdraw the rights which are expressly granted to the Federal Government. . . .

As to the mere sale of surplus energy, nothing need be added to what we have said as to the constitutional authority to dispose. The Government could lease or sell and fix the terms. Sales of surplus energy to the Power Company by the Authority continued a practice begun by the Government several years before. The contemplated interchange of energy is a form of disposition and presents no questions which are essentially different from those that are pertinent to sales.

The transmission lines which the Authority undertakes to purchase from the Power Company lead from the Wilson Dam to a large area within about fifty miles of the dam. These lines provide the means of distributing the electric energy, generated at the dam, to a large population. They furnish a method of reaching a market. The alternative method is to sell the surplus energy at the dam, and the market there appears to be limited to one purchaser, the Alabama Power Company, and its affiliated interests. We know of no constitutional ground upon which the Federal Government can be denied the right to seek a wider market. We suppose that in the early days of mining in the West, if the Government had undertaken to operate a silver mine on its domain, it could have acquired the mules or horses and equipment to carry its silver to market. And the transmission lines for electric energy are but a facility for conveying to market that particular sort of property, and the acquisition of these lines raises no different constitutional question, unless in some way there is an invasion of the rights reserved to the State or to the people. We find no basis for concluding that the limited undertaking with the Alabama Power Company amounts to such an invasion. Certainly, the Alabama Power Company has no constitutional right to insist that it shall be the sole purchaser of the energy generated at the Wilson Dam; that the energy shall be sold to it or go to waste.

We limit our decision to the case before us, as we have defined it. The argument is earnestly presented that the Government by virtue of its ownership of the dam and power plant could not establish a steel mill and make and sell steel products, or a factory to manufacture clothing or shoes for the public, and thus attempt to make its ownership of energy, generated at its dam, a means of carrying on competitive commercial enterprises and thus drawing to the Federal Government the conduct and management of business having no relation to the purposes for which the Federal Government was established. The picture is eloquently drawn but we deem it to be irrelevant to the issue here. The Government is not using the water power at the Wilson Dam to establish any industry or business. It is not using the energy generated at the dam to manufac-ture commodities of any sort for the public. The Government is disposing of the energy itself which simply is the mechanical energy, incidental to falling water at the dam, converted into the electric energy which is susceptible of transmission. The question here is simply as to the acquisition of the transmission lines as a facility for the disposal of that energy. And the Government rightly conceded at the bar, in substance, that it was without constitutional authority to acquire or dispose of such energy except as it comes into being in the operation of works constructed in the exercise of some power delegated to the United States. As we have said, these transmission lines lead directly from the dam, which has been lawfully constructed, and the question of the constitutional right of the Government to acquire or operate local or urban distribution systems is not involved. We express no opinion as to the validity of such an effort, as to the status of any other dam or power development in the Tennessee Valley, whether connected with or apart from the Wilson Dam, or as to the validity of the Tennessee Valley Authority Act or of the claims made in the pronouncements and program of the Authority apart from the questions we have discussed in relation to the particular provisions of the contract of January 4, 1934, affecting the Alabama Power Company.

204. *The N. I. R. A. and the "Sick Chicken" Case*

Schechter Poultry Corporation v. U.S., 295 U.S. 495 (1935).

HUGHES, C.J.: . . . Two preliminary points are stressed by the Government with respect to the appropriate approach to the important questions presented. We are told that the provision of the statute authorizing the adoption of codes must be viewed in the light of the grave national crisis with which Congress was confronted. Undoubtedly, the conditions to which power is addressed are always to be considered when the exercise of power is challenged. Extraordinary conditions may call for extraordinary remedies. But the argument necessarily stops short of an attempt to justify action which lies outside the sphere of constitutional authority. Extraordinary conditions do not create or enlarge constitutional power. The Constitution established a national government with powers deemed to be adequate, as they have proved to be both in war and peace, but these powers of the national government are limited by the constitutional grants. Those who act under these grants are not at liberty to transcend the imposed limits because they believe that more or different power is necessary. Such assertions of extraconstitutional authority were anticipated and precluded by the explicit terms of the Tenth Amendment. . . .

The further point is urged that the national crisis demanded a broad and intensive coöperative effort by those engaged in trade and industry, and that this necessary cooperation was sought to be fostered by permitting them to initiate the adoption of codes. But the statutory plan is not simply one for voluntary effort. It does not seek merely to endow voluntary trade or industrial associations or groups with privileges or immunities. It involves the coercive exercise of the lawmaking power. The codes of fair competition, which the statute attempts to authorize, are codes of laws. If valid, they place all persons within their reach under the obligation of positive law, binding equally those who assent and those who do not assent. Violations of the provisions of the codes are punishable as crimes. . . .

The question of the delegation of legislative power. . . . The Congress is not permitted to abdicate or to transfer to others the essential legislative functions with which it is thus vested. We have repeatedly recognized the necessity of adapting legislation to complex conditions involving a host of details with which the national legislature cannot deal directly. We pointed out in the Panama Company case that the Constitution has never been regarded as denying to Congress the necessary resources of flexibility and practicality, which will enable it to perform its function in laying down policies and establishing standards, while leaving to selected instrumentalities the making of subordinate rules within prescribed limits and the determination of facts to which the policy as declared by the legislature is to apply. But we said that the constant recognition of the necessity and validity of such provisions, and the wide range of administrative authority which has been developed by means of them, cannot be allowed to obscure the limitations of the authority to delegate, if our constitutional system is to be maintained. . . .

Such a sweeping delegation of legislative power [as that in the National Industrial Recovery Act] finds no support in the decisions upon which the Government especially relies. . . .

To summarize and conclude upon this point: Section 3 of the Recovery Act is without precedent. It supplies no standards for any trade, industry or activity. It does not undertake to prescribe rules of conduct to be applied to particular states of fact determined by appropriate administrative procedure. Instead of prescribing rules of conduct, it authorizes the making of codes to prescribe them. For that legislative undertaking, §3 sets up no standards, aside from the statement of the general aims of rehabilitation, correction and expansion described in section one. In view of the scope of that broad declaration, and of the nature of the few restrictions that are imposed, the discretion of the President in approving or prescribing codes, and thus enacting laws for the government of trade and industry throughout the country, is virtually unfettered. We think that the code-making authority thus conferred is an unconstitutional delegation of legislative power. . . .

The question of the application of the provisions of the Live Poultry Code to intrastate transactions. . . . This aspect of the case presents the question whether the particular provisions of the Live Poultry Code, which the defendants were convicted for violating and for having conspired to violate, were within the regulating power of Congress.

These provisions relate to the hours and wages of those employed by defendants in their slaughterhouses in Brooklyn and to the sales there made to retail dealers and butchers.

(1) Were these transactions *"in"* interstate commerce? . . .

The undisputed facts . . . afford no warrant for the argument that the poultry handled by defendants at their slaughterhouse markets was in a *"current"* or *"flow"* of interstate commerce and was thus subject to congressional regulation. The mere fact that there may be a constant flow of commodities into a State does not mean that the flow continues after the property has arrived and has become commingled with the mass of property within the State and is there held solely for local disposition and use. So far as the poultry here in question is concerned, the flow in interstate commerce had ceased. The poultry had come to a permanent rest within the State. It was not held, used, or sold by defendants in relation to any further transactions in interstate commerce and was not destined for transportation to other states. Hence, decisions which deal with a stream of interstate commerce—where goods come to rest within a State temporarily and are later to go forward in interstate commerce—and with the regulations of transactions involved in that practical continuity of movement, are not applicable here. . . .

(2) Did the defendants' transactions directly *"affect"* interstate commerce so as to be subject to federal regulation? The power of Congress extends not only to the regulation of transactions which are part of interstate commerce, but to the protection of that commerce from injury. . . .

In determining how far the federal government may go in controlling intrastate transactions upon the ground that they "affect" interstate commerce, there is a necessary and well-established distinction between direct and indirect effects. The precise line can be drawn only as individual cases arise, but the distinction is clear in principle. . . .

The question of chief importance relates to the provisions of the Code as to the hours and wages of those employed in defendants' slaughterhouse markets. It is plain that these requirements are imposed in order to govern the details of defendants' management of their local business. The persons employed in slaughtering and selling in local trade are not employed in interstate commerce. Their hours and wages have no direct relation to interstate commerce. . . . If the federal government may determine the wages and hours of employees in the internal commerce of a State, because of their relation to cost and prices and their indirect effect upon interstate commerce, it would seem that a similar control might be exerted over other elements of cost, also affecting prices, such as the number of employees, rents, advertising, methods of doing business, etc. All the processes of production and distribution that enter into cost could likewise be controlled. If the cost of doing an intrastate business is in itself the permitted object of federal control, the extent of the regulation of cost would be a question of discretion and not of power.

The Government also makes the point that efforts to enact state legislation establishing high labor standards have been impeded by the belief that unless similar action is taken generally, commerce will be diverted from the States adopting such standards, and that this fear of diversion has led to demands for federal legislation on the subject of wages and hours. The apparent implication is that the federal authority under the commerce clause should be deemed to extend to the establishment of rules to govern wages and hours in intrastate trade and industry generally throughout the country, thus overriding the authority of the States to deal with domestic problems arising from labor conditions in their internal commerce.

It is not the province of the Court to consider the economic advantages or disadvantages of such a centralized system. It is sufficient to say that the Federal Constitution does not provide for it. Our growth and development have called for wide use of the commerce power of the federal government in its control over the expanded activities of interstate commerce, and in protecting that commerce from burdens, interferences, and conspiracies to restrain and monopolize it. But the authority of the federal government may not be pushed to such an extreme as to destroy the distinction, which the commerce clause itself establishes, between commerce "among the several States" and the internal concerns of a State. The same answer must be made to the contention that is based upon the serious economic situation which led to the passage of the Recovery Act,—the fall in prices, the decline in wages and employment, and the curtailment of the market for commodities. Stress is laid upon the great importance of maintaining wage distributions which would provide the necessary stimulus in starting "the cumulative forces making for expanding commercial activity." Without in any way disparaging this motive, it is enough to say that the recuperative efforts of the federal government must be made in a manner consistent with the authority granted by the Constitution.

We are of the opinion that the attempt through the provisions of the Code to fix the hours and wages of employees of defendants in their intrastate business was not a valid exercise of federal power. . . .

205. *The First Triple A and "Coercion by Economic Pressure"*

U.S. v. Butler, 297 U.S. 1 (1936).

ROBERTS, J.: . . . It is inaccurate and misleading to speak of the exaction from processors prescribed by the challenged act as a tax, or to say that as a tax it is subject to no infirmity. A tax, in the general understanding of the term, and as used in the Constitution, signifies an exaction for the support of the Government. The word has never been thought to connote the expropriation of money from one group for the benefit of another. We may concede that the latter sort of imposition is constitutional when imposed to effectuate regulation of a matter in which both groups are interested and in respect of which there is a power of legislative regulation. But manifestly no justification for it can be found unless as an integral part of such regulation. . . .

We conclude that the act is one regulating agricultural production; that the tax is a mere incident of such regulation and that the respondents have standing to challenge the legality of the exaction. . . .

The Government asserts that even if the respondents may question the propriety of the appropriation embodied in the statute their attack must fail because Article I, §8 of the Constitution authorizes the contemplated expenditure of the funds raised by the tax. This contention presents the great and the controlling question in the case. . . .

There should be no misunderstanding as to the function of this court in such a case. It is sometimes said that the court assumes a power to overrule or control the action of the people's representatives. This is a misconception. The Constitution is the supreme law of the land ordained and established by the people. All legislation must conform to the principles it lays down. When an act of Congress is appropriately challenged in the courts as not conforming to the constitutional mandate the judicial branch of the Government has only one duty,—to lay the article of the Constitution which is invoked beside the statute which is challenged and to decide whether the latter squares with the former. All the court does, or can do, is to announce its considered judgment upon the question. The only power it has, if such it may be called, is the power of judgment. This court neither approves nor condemns any legislative policy. Its delicate and difficult office is to ascertain and declare whether the legislation is in accordance with, or in contravention of, the provisions of the Constitution; and, having done that, its duty ends. . . .

Article I, §8, of the Constitution vests sundry powers in the Congress. But two of its clauses have any bearing upon the validity of the statute under review.

The third clause endows the Congress with power "to regulate Commerce . . . among the several States." Despite a reference in its first section to a burden upon, and an obstruction of the normal currents of commerce, the act under review does not purport to regulate transactions in interstate or foreign commerce. Its stated purpose is the control of agricultural production, a purely local activity in an effort to raise the prices paid the farmer. Indeed, the Government does not attempt to uphold the validity of the act on the basis of the commerce clause, which, for the purpose of the present case, may be put aside as irrelevant.

The clause thought to authorize the legislation,—the first,—confers upon the Congress power "to lay and collect Taxes, Duties, Imposts and Excises, to pay the Debts and provide for the common Defence and general Welfare of the United States." . . . The Government asserts that warrant is found in this clause for the adoption of the Agricultural Adjustment Act. The argument is that Congress may appropriate and authorize the spending of moneys for the "general welfare"; that the phrase should be liberally construed to cover anything conducive to national welfare; that decision as to what will promote such welfare rests with Congress alone, and the courts may not review its deter-

mination; and finally that the appropriation under attack was in fact for the general welfare of the United States. . . .

Since the foundation of the Nation sharp differences of opinion have persisted as to the true interpretation of the phrase. Madison asserted it amounted to no more than a reference to the other powers enumerated in the subsequent clauses of the same section; that, as the United States is a government of limited and enumerated powers, the grant of power to tax and spend for the general national welfare must be confined to the enumerated legislative fields committed to the Congress. In this view the phrase is mere tautology, for taxation and appropriation are or may be necessary incidents of the exercise of any of the enumerated legislative powers. Hamilton, on the other hand, maintained the clause confers a power separate and distinct from those later enumerated, is not restricted in meaning by the grant of them, and Congress consequently has a substantive power to tax and to appropriate, limited only by the requirement that it shall be exercised to provide for the general welfare of the United States. Each contention has had the support of those whose views are entitled to weight. This court has noticed the question, but has never found it necessary to decide which is the true construction. Mr. Justice Story, in his Commentaries, espouses the Hamiltonian position. . . . While, therefore, the power to tax is not unlimited, its confines are set in the clause which confers it, and not in those of §8 which bestow and define the legislative powers of the Congress. It results that the power of Congress to authorize expenditure of public moneys for public purposes is not limited by the direct grants of legislative power found in the Constitution.

But the adoption of the broader construction leaves the power to spend subject to limitations. . . .

That the qualifying phrase must be given effect all advocates of broad construction admit. Hamilton, in his well known Report on Manufactures, states that the purpose must be "general, and not local." . . .

We are not now required to ascertain the scope of the phrase "general welfare of the United States" or to determine whether an appropriation in aid of agriculture falls within it. Wholly apart from that question, another principle embedded in our Constitution prohibits the enforcement of the Agricultural Adjustment Act. The act invades the reserved rights of the states. It is a statutory plan to regulate and control agricultural production, a matter beyond the powers delegated to the federal government. The tax, the appropriation of the funds raised, and the direction for their disbursement, are but parts of the plan. They are but means to an unconstitutional end. . . .

The power of taxation, which is expressly granted, may, of course, be adopted as a means to carry into operation another power also expressly granted. But resort to the taxing power to effectuate an end which is not legitimate, not within the scope of the Constitution, is obviously inadmissible. . . .

If the taxing power may not be used as the instrument to enforce a regulation of matters of state concern with respect to which the Congress has no authority to interfere, may it, as in the present case, be employed to raise the money necessary to purchase a compliance which the Congress is powerless to command? The Government asserts that whatever might be said against the validity of the plan, if compulsory, it is constitutionally sound because the end is accomplished by voluntary cooperation. There are two sufficient answers to the contention. The regulation is not in fact voluntary. The farmer, of course, may refuse to comply, but the price of such refusal is the loss of benefits. The amount offered is intended to be sufficient to exert pressure on him to agree to the proposed regulation. The power to confer or withhold unlimited benefits is the power to coerce or destroy. If the cotton grower elects not to accept the benefits, he will receive less for his crops; those who receive payments will be able to undersell him. The result may well be financial ruin. . . . The Department of Agriculture has properly described the plan as one to keep a non-cooperating minority in line. This is coercion by economic pressure. The asserted power of choice is illusory. . . .

Congress has no power to enforce its commands on the farmer to the ends sought by the Agricultural Adjustment Act. It must follow that it may not indirectly accomplish those ends by taxing and spending to purchase compliance. The Constitution and the entire plan of our government negative any such use of the power to tax and to spend as the act undertakes to authorize. It does not help to declare that local conditions throughout the nation have created a situation of national concern; for this is but to say that whenever there is a widespread similarity of local conditions, Congress may ignore constitutional limitations upon its own powers and usurp those reserved to the states. If, in lieu of compulsory regulation of subjects within the states' reserved jurisdiction, which is prohibited, the Congress could invoke the taxing and spending power as a means to accomplish the same end, clause 1 of §8 of Article I would become the instrument for total subversion of the governmental powers reserved to the individual states. . . .

206. *Industry and Labor: The Second Phase*

Carter v. Carter Coal Company, 298 U.S. 238 (1936).

SUTHERLAND, J.: . . . The position of the Government, as we understand it, is that the validity of the exaction does not rest upon the taxing power but upon the power of Congress to regulate interstate commerce; and that if the act in respect of the labor and price-fixing provisions be not upheld, the "tax" must fall with them. With that position we agree and confine our consideration accordingly. . . .

Since the validity of the act depends upon whether it is a regulation of interstate commerce, the nature and extent of the power conferred upon Congress by the commerce clause becomes the determinative question in this branch of the case. . . . We first inquire, then—What is commerce? The term, as this court many times has said, is one of extensive import. No all-embracing definition has ever been formulated. The question is to be approached both affirmatively and negatively —that is to say, from the points of view as to what it includes and what it excludes. . . .

That commodities produced or manufactured within a state are intended to be sold or transported outside the state does not render their production or manufacture subject to federal regulation under the commerce clause. . . .

We have seen that the word "commerce" is the equivalent of the phrase "intercourse for the purposes of trade." Plainly, the incidents leading up to and culminating in the mining of coal do not constitute such intercourse. The employment of men, the fixing of their wages, hours of labor and working conditions, the bargaining in respect to these things —whether carried on separately or collectively—each and all constitute intercourse for the purposes of production, not of trade. The latter is a thing apart from the relation of employer and employee, which

in all producing occupations is purely local in character. Extraction of coal from the mine is the aim and the completed result of local activities. Commerce in the coal mined is not brought into being by force of these activities, but by negotiations, agreements, and circumstances entirely apart from production. Mining brings the subject matter of commerce into existence. Commerce disposes of it.

A consideration of the foregoing, and of many cases which might be added to those already cited, renders inescapable the conclusion that the effect of the labor provisions of the act, including those in respect of minimum wages wage agreements, collective bargaining, and the Labor Board and its powers, primarily falls upon production and not upon commerce; and confirms the further resulting conclusion that production is a purely local activity. It follows that none of these essential antecedents of production constitutes a transaction in or forms any part of interstate commerce. . . . Everything which moves in interstate commerce has had a local origin. Without local production somewhere, interstate commerce, as now carried on, would practically disappear. Nevertheless, the local character of mining, of manufacturing and of crop growing is a fact, and remains a fact, whatever may be done with the products. . . .

But §1 (the preamble) of the act now under review declares that all production and distribution of bituminous coal "bear upon and directly affect its interstate commerce"; and that regulation thereof is imperative for the protection of such commerce. The contention of the government is that the labor provisions of the act may be sustained in that view.

That the production of every commodity intended for interstate sale and transportation has some effect upon interstate commerce may be, if it has not already been, freely granted; and we are brought to the final and decisive inquiry, whether here that effect is direct, as the "preamble" recites, or indirect. The distinction is not formal, but substantial in the highest degree, as we pointed out in the *Schechter* case. . . .

Whether the effect of a given activity or condition is direct or indirect is not always easy to determine. The word "direct" implies that the activity or condition invoked or blamed shall operate proximately —not mediately, remotely, or collaterally —to produce the effect. It connotes the absence of an efficient intervening agency or condition. And the extent of the effect bears no logical relation to its character. The distinction between a direct and an indirect effect turns, not upon the magnitude of either the cause or the effect, but entirely upon the manner in which the effect has been brought about. If the production by one man of a single ton of coal intended for interstate sale and shipment, and actually so sold and shipped, affects interstate commerce indirectly, the effect does not become direct by multiplying the tonnage, or increasing the number of men employed, or adding to the expense or complexities of the business, or by all combined. It is quite true that rules of law are sometimes qualified by considerations of degree, as the government argues. But the matter of degree has no bearing upon the question here, since that question is not— What is the *extent* of the local activity or condition, or the *extent* of the effect produced upon interstate commerce? but— What is the *relation* between the activity or condition and the effect?

Much stress is put upon the evils which come from the struggle between employers and employees over the matter of wages, working conditions, the right of collective bargaining, etc., and the resulting strikes, curtailment and irregularity of production and effect on prices; and it is insisted that interstate commerce is *greatly* affected thereby. But, in addition to what has just been said, the conclusive answer is that the evils are all local evils over which the federal government has no legislative control. The relation of employer and employee is a local relation. At common law, it is one of the domestic relations. The wages are paid for the doing of local work. Working conditions are obviously local conditions. The employees are not engaged in or about commerce, but exclusively in producing a commodity. And the controversies and evils, which it is the object of the act to regulate and minimize, are local controversies and evils affecting local work undertaken to accomplish that local result. Such effect as they may have upon commerce, however extensive it may be, is secondary and indirect. An increase in the greatness of the effect adds to its importance. It does not alter its character. . . .

The want of power on the part of the federal government is the same whether the wages, hours of service, and working conditions, and the bargaining about them, are related to production before interstate commerce has begun, or to sale and distribution after it has ended. . . .

Wages, hours of labor, and working conditions are to be so adjusted as to effectuate the purposes of the act; and prices are to be so regulated as to *stabilize* wages, working conditions, and hours of labor which have been or are to be fixed under the labor provisions. The two are so woven together as to render the probability plain enough that uniform prices, in the opinion of Congress, could not be fairly fixed or effectively regulated, without also regulating these elements of labor which enter so largely into the cost of production. . . .

The conclusion is unavoidable that the price-fixing provisions of the code are so related to and dependent upon the labor provisions as conditions, considerations or compensations, as to make it clearly probable that the latter being held bad, the former would not have been passed. The fall of the latter, therefore, carries down with it the former. . . .

The price-fixing provisions of the code are thus disposed of without coming to the question of their constitutionality; but neither this disposition of the matter, nor anything we have said, is to be taken as indicating that the court is of opinion that these provisions, if separately enacted, could be sustained. . . .

The Court Crisis of 1936-37

207. Franklin D. Roosevelt, Radio Address on Judicial Reform, March 9, 1937

Senate Reports, 75th Cong., 1st Sess., Jan. 5–Aug. 21, 1937, Report No. 711, I, 41-4.

Since the rise of the modern movement for social and economic progress through legislation, the Court has more and more often and more and more boldly asserted a power to veto laws passed by the Congress and State legislatures in complete disregard of this original limitation.

In the last 4 years the sound rule of giving statutes the benefit of all reasonable doubt has been cast aside. The Court has been acting not as a judicial body, but as a policy-making body.

When the Congress has sought to stabilize national agriculture, to improve the conditions of labor, to safeguard business against unfair competition, to protect our national resources, and in many other ways to serve our clearly national needs, the majority of the Court has been assuming the power to pass on the wisdom of these acts of the Congress—and to approve or disapprove the public policy written into these laws.

That is not only my accusation. It is the accusation of most distinguished Justices of the present Supreme Court. I have not the time to quote to you all the language used by dissenting Justices in many of these cases. But in the case holding the Railroad Retirement Act unconstitutional, for instance, Chief Justice Hughes said in a dissenting opinion that the majority opinion was "a departure from sound principles," and placed "an unwarranted limitation upon the commerce clause." And three other Justices agree with him.

In the case holding the A. A. A. unconstitutional, Justice Stone said of the majority opinion that it was a "tortured construction of the Constitution." And two other Justices agreed with him.

In the case holding the New York Minimum Wage Law unconstitutional, Justice Stone said that the majority were actually reading into the Constitution their own "personal economic predilections," and that if the legislative power is not left free to choose the methods of solving the problems of poverty, subsistence, and health of large numbers in the community, then "government is to be rendered impotent." And two other Justices agreed with him.

In the face of these dissenting opinions, there is no basis for the claim made by some members of the Court that something in the Constitution has compelled them regretfully to thwart the will of the people.

In the face of such dissenting opinions, it is perfectly clear that as Chief Justice Hughes has said, "We are under a Constitution, but the Constitution is what the judges say it is."

The Court in addition to the proper

use of its judicial functions has improperly set itself up as a third House of the Congress—a super-legislature, as one of the Justices has called it—reading into the Constitution words and implications which are not there, and which were never intended to be there.

We have, therefore, reached the point as a Nation where we must take action to save the Constitution from the Court and the Court from itself. We must find a way to take an appeal from the Supreme Court to the Constitution itself. We want a Supreme Court which will do justice under the Constitution—not over it. In our courts we want a government of laws and not of men.

I want—as all Americans want—an independent judiciary as proposed by the framers of the Constitution. That means a Supreme Court that will enforce the Constitution as written—that will refuse to amend the Constitution by the arbitrary exercise of judicial power—amendment by judicial say-so. It does not mean a judiciary so independent that it can deny the existence of facts universally recognized.

How, then, could we proceed to perform the mandate given us? It was said in last year's Democratic platform, "If these problems cannot be effectively solved within the Constitution, we shall seek such clarifying amendment as will assure the power to enact those laws, adequately to regulate commerce, protect public health and safety, and safeguard economic security." In other words, we said we would seek an amendment only if every other possible means by legislation were to fail. . . .

Whenever a judge or justice of any Federal court has reached the age of 70 and does not avail himself of the opportunity to retire on a pension, a new member shall be appointed by the President then in office, with the approval, as required by the Constitution, of the Senate of the United States.

That plan has two chief purposes: By bringing into the judicial system a steady and continuing stream of new and younger blood, I hope, first, to make the administration of all Federal justice speedier and therefore less costly; secondly, to bring to the decision of social and economic problems younger men who have had personal experience and contact with modern facts and circumstances under which average men have to live and work. This plan will save our National Constitution from hardening of the judicial arteries. . . .

Those opposing this plan have sought to arouse prejudice and fear by crying that I am seeking to "pack" the Supreme Court and that a baneful precedent will be established.

What do they mean by the words "packing the Court?"

Let me answer this question with a bluntness that will end all honest misunderstanding of my purposes.

If by that phrase "packing the Court" it is charged that I wish to place on the bench spineless puppets who would disregard the law and would decide specific cases as I wished them to be decided, I make this answer: That no President fit for his office would appoint, and no Senate of honorable men fit for their office would confirm, that kind of appointees to the Supreme Court.

But if by that phrase the charge is made that I would appoint and the Senate would confirm Justices worthy to sit beside present members of the Court who understand those modern conditions; that I will appoint Justices who will not undertake to override the judgment of the Congress on legislative policy; that I will appoint Justices who will act as Justices and not as legislators—if the appointment of such Justices can be called "packing the Courts" —then I say that I, and with me the vast majority of the American people, favor doing just that thing—now. . . .

Like all lawyers, like all Americans, I regret the necessity of this controversy. But the welfare of the United States, and indeed of the Constitution itself, is what we all must think about first. Our difficulty with the Court today rises not from the Court as an institution but from human beings within it. But we cannot yield our constitutional destiny to the personal judgment of a few men who, being fearful of the future, would deny us

the necessary means of dealing with the present.

This plan of mine is no attack on the Court; it seeks to restore the Court to its rightful and historic place in our system of constitutional government and to have it resume its high task of building anew on the Constitution "a system of living law." . . .

208. *Adverse Report of the Senate Judiciary Committee,* 1937

Senate Reports, 75th Cong., 1st Sess., Jan. 5–Aug. 21, 1937, Report No. 711, I, 1-23 *passim.*

The effect of this bill is not to provide for an increase in the number of Justices composing the Supreme Court. The effect is to provide a forced retirement or, failing in this, to take from the Justices affected a free exercise of their independent judgment. . . .

Let us, for the purpose of the argument, grant that the Court has been wrong, wrong not only in that it has rendered mistaken opinions but wrong in the far more serious sense that it has substituted its will for the congressional will in the matter of legislation. May we nevertheless safely punish the Court?

Today it may be the Court which is charged with forgetting its constitutional duties. Tomorrow it may be the Congress. The next day it may be the Executive. If we yield to temptation now to lay the lash upon the Court, we are only teaching others how to apply it to ourselves and to the people when the occasion seems to warrant. Manifestly, if we may force the hand of the Court to secure our interpretation of the Constitution, then some succeeding Congress may repeat the process to secure another and a different interpretation and one which may not sound so pleasant in our ears as that for which we now contend.

There is a remedy for usurpation or other judicial wrongdoing. If this bill be supported by the toilers of this country upon the ground that they want a Court which will sustain legislation limiting

hours and providing minimum wages, they must remember that the procedure employed in the bill could be used in another administration to lengthen hours and to decrease wages. If farmers want agricultural relief and favor this bill upon the ground that it gives them a Court which will sustain legislation in their favor, they must remember that the procedure employed might some day be used to deprive them of every vestige of a farm relief.

When members of the Court usurp legislative powers or attempt to exercise political power, they lay themselves open to the charge of having lapsed from that "good behavior" which determines the period of their official life. But, if you say, the process of impeachment is difficult and uncertain, the answer is, the people made it so when they framed the Constitution. It is not for us, the servants of the people, the instruments of the Constitution, to find a more easy way to do that which our masters made difficult.

But, if the fault of the judges is not so grievous as to warrant impeachment, if their offense is merely that they have grown old, and we feel, therefore, that there should be a "constant infusion of new blood," then obviously the way to achieve that result is by constitutional amendment fixing definite terms for the members of the judiciary or making mandatory their retirement at a given age. Such a provision would indeed provide for the constant infusion of new blood, not only now but at all times in the future. The plan before us is but a temporary expedient which operates once and then never again, leaving the Court as permanently expanded to become once more a court of old men, gradually year by year falling behind the times. . . .

We are told that a reactionary oligarchy defies the will of the majority, that this is a bill to "unpack" the Court and give effect to the desires of the majority; that is to say, a bill to increase the number of Justices for the express purpose of neutralizing the views of some of the present members. In justification we are told, but without authority, by those who would rationalize this program, that Congress was given the power to determine the size of the Court so that the legislative branch would be able to impose its will upon the judiciary. This amounts to nothing more than the declaration that when the Court stands in the way of a legislative enactment, the Congress may reverse the ruling by enlarging the Court. When such a principle is adopted, our constitutional system is overthrown! . . .

Even if every charge brought against the so-called "reactionary" members of this Court be true, it is far better that we await orderly but inevitable change of personnel than that we impatiently overwhelm them with new members. Exhibiting this restraint, thus demonstrating our faith in the American system, we shall set an example that will protect the independent American judiciary from attack as long as this Government stands. . . .

True it is, that courts like Congresses, should take account of the advancing strides of civilization. True it is that the law, being a progressive science, must be pronounced progressively and liberally; but the milestones of liberal progress are made to be noted and counted with caution rather than merely to be encountered and passed. Progress is not a mad mob march; rather, it is a steady, invincible stride. . . .

If, under the "hydraulic pressure" of our present need for economic justice, we destroy the system under which our people have progressed to a higher degree of justice and prosperity than that ever enjoyed by any other people in all the history of the human race, then we shall destroy not only all opportunity for further advance but everything we have thus far achieved. . . .

Even if the case were far worse than it is alleged to be, it would still be no argument in favor of this bill to say that the courts and some judges have abused their power. The courts are not perfect, nor are the judges. The Congress is not perfect, nor are Senators and Representatives. The Executive is not perfect. These branches of government and the offices under them are filled by human beings who for the most part strive to live up to the dignity and idealism of a system that was designed to achieve the greatest possible measure of justice and freedom for all the people. We shall destroy the system when we reduce it to the imperfect standards of the men who operate it. We shall strengthen it and ourselves, we shall make justice and liberty for all men more certain when, by patience and self-restraint, we maintain it on the high plane on which it was conceived.

Inconvenience and even delay in the enactment of legislation is not a heavy price to pay for our system. Constitutional democracy moves forward with certainty rather than with speed. The safety and the permanence of the progressive march of our civilization are far more important to us and to those who are to come after us than the enactment now of any particular law. The Constitution of the United States provides ample opportunity for the expression of popular will to bring about such reforms and changes as the people may deem essential to their present and future welfare. It is the people's charter of the powers granted those who govern them. . . .

SUMMARY

We recommend the rejection of this bill as a needless, futile, and utterly dangerous abandonment of constitutional principle.

It was presented to the Congress in a most intricate form and for reasons that obscured its real purpose.

It would not banish age from the bench nor abolish divided decisions.

It would not affect the power of any court to hold laws unconstitutional nor withdraw from any judge the authority to issue injunctions.

It would not reduce the expense of litigation nor speed the decision of cases.

It is a proposal without precedent and without justification.

It would subjugate the courts to the will of Congress and the President and thereby destroy the independence of the judiciary, the only certain shield of individual rights.

It contains the germ of a system of centralized administration of law that would enable an executive so minded to send his judges into every judicial district in the land to sit in judgment on controversies between the Government and the citizen.

It points the way to the evasion of the Constitution and establishes the method whereby the people may be deprived of their right to pass upon all amendments of the fundamental law.

It stands now before the country, acknowledged by its proponents as a plan to force judicial interpretation of the Constitution, a proposal that violates every sacred tradition of American democracy.

Under the form of the Constitution it seeks to do that which is unconstitutional.

Its ultimate operation would be to make this Government one of men rather than one of law, and its practical operation would be to make the Constitution what the executive or legislative branches of the Government choose to say it is—an interpretation to be changed with each change of administration.

It is a measure which should be so emphatically rejected that its parallel will never again be presented to the free representatives of the free people of America.

209. *The Court Reverses Itself on Minimum Wage Legislation*

West Coast Hotel Co. v. Parrish, 300 U.S. 379 (1937).

HUGHES, C.J.: This case presents the question of the constitutional validity of the minimum wage law of the State of Washington.

The Act, entitled "Minimum Wages for Women," authorizes the fixing of minimum wages for women and minors. . . .

The appellant conducts a hotel. The appellee Elsie Parrish was employed as a chambermaid and (with her husband) brought this suit to recover the difference between the wages paid her and the minimum wage fixed pursuant to the state law. The minimum wage was $14.50 per week of 48 hours. The appellant challenged the act as repugnant to the due process clause of the Fourteenth Amendment of the Constitution of the United States. . . .

The appellant relies upon the decision of this Court in *Adkins v. Children's Hospital,* . . . which held invalid the District of Columbia Minimum Wage Act which was attacked under the due process clause of the Fifth Amendment. . . .

We think that the question which was not deemed to be open in the *Morehead* case is open and is necessarily presented here. The Supreme Court of Washington has upheld the minimum wage statute of that State. It has decided that the statute is a reasonable exercise of the police power of the State. In reaching that conclusion the state court has invoked principles long established by this Court in the application of the Fourteenth Amendment. The state court has refused to regard the decision in the *Adkins* case as deterninative and has pointed to our decisions both before and since that case as justifying its position. We are of the opinion that this ruling of the state court demands on our part a reexamination of the *Adkins* case. The importance of the question, in which many States having similar laws are concerned, the close division by which the decision in the *Adkins* case was reached, and the economic conditions which have supervened, and in the light of which the reasonableness of the exercise of the protective power of the State must be considered, make it not only appropriate, but we think imperative, that in deciding the present case the subject should receive fresh consideration. . . .

The principle which must control our decision is not in doubt. The constitutional provision invoked is the due process clause of the Fourteenth Amendment governing the States, as the due process clause invoked in the *Adkins* case governed Congress. In each case the violation alleged by those attacking minimum wage regulation for women is deprivation of freedom of contract. What is this freedom? The Constitution does not speak of freedom of contract. It speaks of liberty and prohibits the deprivation of liberty without due process of law. In prohibiting that deprivation the Constitution does not recognize an absolute and uncontrollable liberty. Liberty in each of its phases has its history and connotation. But the liberty safeguarded is liberty in a social organization which requires the protection of law against the evils which menace the health, safety, morals and welfare of the people. Liberty under the Constitution is thus necessarily subject to the restraints of due process, and regulation which is reasonble in relation to its subject and is adopted in the interests of the community is due process. . . .

The minimum wage to be paid under the Washington statute is fixed after full consideration by representatives of employers, employees and the public. It may be assumed that the minimum wage is fixed in consideration of the services that are performed in the particular occupations under normal conditions. Provision is made for special licenses at less wages in the case of women who are incapable of full service. The statement of Mr. Justice Holmes in the *Adkins* case is pertinent: . . . . [Holmes is then cited to the effect that the law does not coerce specific payments or employment, but like any police law, establishes a minimum standard which, if not adhered to, will warrant federal action.]

What can be closer to the public interest than the health of women and their protection from unscrupulous and overreaching employers? And if the protection of women is a legitimate end of the exercise of state power, how can it be said that the requirement of the payment of a minimum wage fairly fixed in order to meet the very necessities of existence is not an admissible means to that end? The legislature of the State was clearly entitled to consider the situation of women in employment, the fact that they are in the class receiving the least pay, that their bargaining power is relatively weak, and that they are the ready victims of those who would take advantage of their necessitous circumstances. The legislature was entitled to adopt measures to reduce the evils of the "sweating system," the exploiting of workers at wages so low as to be insufficient to meet the bare cost of living thus making their very helplessness the occasion of a most injurious competition. The legislature had the right to consider that its minimum wage requirements would be an important aid in carrying out its policy of protection. The adoption of similar requirements by many States evidences a deep-seated conviction both as to the presence of the evil and as to the means adapted to check it. Legislative response to that conviction cannot be regarded as arbitrary or capricious and that is all we have to decide. Even if the wisdom of the policy be regarded as debatable and its effects uncertain, still the legislature is entitled to its judgment.

There is an additional and compelling consideration which recent economic experience has brought into a strong light. The exploitation of a class of workers who are in an unequal position with respect to bargaining power and are thus relatively defenceless against the denial of a living wage is not only detrimental to their health and well being but casts a direct burden for their support upon the community. What these workers lose in wages the taxpayers are called upon to pay. The bare cost of living must be met. We may take judicial notice of the unparalleled demands for relief which arose during the recent period of depression and still continue to an alarming extent despite the degree of economic recovery which has been achieved. It is unnecessary to cite official statistics to establish what is of common knowledge through the length and breadth of the land. While in the instant case no factual brief has been presented, there is no reason to doubt that the State of Washington has encountered the same social problem that is present elsewhere. The community is not bound to provide what is in effect a subsidy for unconscionable employers. The community may direct its law-making power to correct the abuse which springs from their selfish disregard of the public interest. . . .

CHAPTER XXIII

The Revolution in Constitutional Law

IF EVER the platitude about losing the battle and winning the war applied to constitutional controversies, it did in 1936-37. After the initial concession toward expanded state authority in the Parrish case (Chapter XXII), the new majority proceeded to broaden the permissible areas of federal regulation so extensively that a "Constitutional Revolution, Ltd.," in the words of Professor Edward S. Corwin, was the result.

During the 168 days that Congress devoted to Roosevelt's reorganization proposal, the Court applied its newly discovered nationalism to uphold extensive labor-management regulations, unemployment and old-age benefits under the Social Security Act, mortgage moratoriums, agricultural controls, and a wide variety of similiar federal measures. The case which broke the log jam of narrow precedents was *N. L. R. B. v. Jones & Laughlin Steel Corporation* (No. 210), decided early in April, 1937. In upholding the National Labor Relations Act, Chief Justice Hughes not only validated the most favorable law that American labor had ever won, but so broadened the interpretation of what constituted interstate commerce that the main doubt in later cases became not so much what was included under the controlling power of the national government as what was not. Of necessity, the decision repudiated the rulings in the Schechter and Carter cases, although not without the bitter protests of Justices Butler, McReynolds, Sutherland, and Van Devanter. Hughes also sanctioned a broad jurisdiction for the National Labor

Relations Board and consistently upheld the Board's authority, even when the local production being supervised had only the remotest effect upon interstate commerce (*N. L. R. B. v. Fainblatt*, 1939).

The Court also broadened its interpretation of the federal taxing power. The Social Security Act of 1935 had been passed in answer to demands for national assistance to protect individuals against the hazards of sickness, old age, and unemployment. Its constitutional base was Congress's broad power to tax for the general welfare. In *Stewart Machine Co. v. Davis* (1937), Justice Cardozo upheld the tax that the measure imposed upon employers and ruled that the program of conditional Federal grants-in-aid was not illegal coercion of the states. In *Helvering et al. v. Davis* (No. 211), he upheld the old-age tax and benefit provisions of the act, while setting forth a strongly nationalistic theory of taxing power, based, ironically, upon Roberts's opinion in *U.S. v. Butler*.

These commerce and taxing decisions were handed down before any change in Court membership. By the middle of 1937, older justices began retiring and within three years, five of the judges were Roosevelt appointees. This "Roosevelt Court" continued to sustain New Deal measures and also reinterpreted broadly a variety of older statutes. Typical were laws dealing with labor activities. For many years the Sherman and Clayton Anti-Trust Acts had been used as restraints on labor unions. In a 1940 case involving sit-down strikers in a Philadelphia hosiery plant, Justice Stone sharply curtailed this application (*Apex Hosiery Co. v. Leader* [No. 212]). Previously it had been necessary, in order to establish the liability of unions under the measures, to prove only that there existed an intent to restrain interstate commerce, coupled with a direct and substantial restraint. But now Stone ruled that it had to be shown that the union's activities had the effect of suppressing a free competitive market, either by monopolizing the supply, controlling the prices, or discriminating between would-be purchasers. Similarly, in a case involving the Norris-LaGuardia Act of 1932 (*U.S. v. Hutcheson* [No. 213]), the Court ruled that within the Act's definition of a permissible labor dispute, a union might strike, picket, and engage in all the other acts specifically enumerated in section 20 of the Clayton Act without fear of injunction, damage suit, or prosecution, as far as the antitrust laws were concerned. Thus, the Hutcheson and Apex decisions seemed virtually to remove union activity from the threat of liability under the antitrust laws. In *Phelps Dodge v. N. L. R. B.*, decided in 1941, the Court struck at "yellow-dog contracts," ruling that an employer was engaging in an unfair labor practice by refusing to hire workmen because of their labor-union affiliations.

Federal wage and hour legislation also received judicial sanction in 1941 in a decision with important constitutional implications (*U.S. v. Darby* [No. 214]). Relying upon Holmes's dissent in *Hammer v. Dagenhart*, Justice Stone specifically overruled that precedent and returned to the *McCulloch v. Maryland* principle that the enumerated powers of the national government can be implemented by Congress through whatever necessary and proper means Congress may determine. In the commerce field, this doctrine meant a return to the *Gibbons v. Ogden* principle: when intrastate activities are so commingled with or related to interstate commerce as to demand uniform regulation, the commerce clause applies. Justice Jackson went even further. In upholding the validity of the wheat-marketing provisions of the 1938 A. A. A.—the Court had earlier sustained the general provisions of the measure in *Mulford v. Smith*, 1939—Jackson threw out all distinctions such as "direct" and "indirect," "production" and "commerce," and emphasized the economic effect upon interstate commerce as the true test of whether local activities could be regulated by Congress under the commerce power (*Wickard v. Filburn* [No. 215]). The ruling left doubt as to whether there was any limit to the commerce power as a tool for federal regulation, a view confirmed by Justice Murphy's 1945 statement that "the commerce power is as broad as the economic needs of the nation." Thus nearly forty years of constitutional strictures on federal authority under the commerce clause seemed at an end. Implementing its new interpretation of the commerce clause, the Court upheld federal authority over the coal and natural gas industries, navigable streams, and public utilities.

The new constitutional nationalism which characterized the Roosevelt Court did not necessarily imply that state power was curtailed. On the contrary, state governments collected and spent more money, employed more people, and engaged in more activities than ever before in their history, evolving a remarkable adjustment of federal-state authority in an era of expanding governmental power. The Roosevelt Court reversed the long-standing practice of intergovernmental tax immunity and upheld a state income tax levied on a federal employee (*Graves v. New York ex rel. O'Keefe* [No. 216]). In succeeding cases, the Court also looked with general favor on a variety of new types of state taxation. Moreover, permissible areas of state police power were expanded when the Court took a long step backward toward the old Cooley doctrine of "selective exclusiveness" (see Chapter IX). In the same vein, *Swift v. Tyson*, which for a century had permitted the federal courts to disregard decisions of the state courts on matters of state law, was formally overruled in 1938 (*Erie Railroad v. Tompkins*).

The 1930's also saw new approaches to major constitutional problems involving the legislative and executive departments of the government. The Twentieth Amendment eliminated the "lame duck" session of Congress (No. 217A), and the Twenty-first ended the "noble experiment" with prohibition (No. 217B). Two important decisions illustrate the contradictory attitudes of the "old court" toward Presidential authority. In 1935, *Humphrey's Executor* (*Rathbun*) *v. U.S.* (No. 218) sharply curtailed the Chief Executive's power to remove appointive officers vested with judicial and legislative powers (in this case a member of an independent regulatory commission), thus modifying Taft's decision in the Myers case (see Introduction to Chapter XX). In 1936, however, Justice Sutherland ruled that the President, by virtue of the inherent authority of his office, possessed "plenary and exclusive power" over all international affairs, and that this power did not require an act of Congress as a basis for its exercise (*U.S. v. Curtiss-Wright Export Corporation* [No. 219]). Sutherland also ruled (*U.S. v. Belmont,* 1937) that executive agreements on foreign issues have the same legal effect as treaties. Since these can be negotiated independently, they further strengthen the President's position in the handling of foreign affairs. Although this procedure had early critics, it was President Roosevelt's wartime usages, particularly at Yalta, which aroused the most opposition, culminating in a postwar effort to curb presidential authority by the amendment process (Chapter XXVI).

The New Deal and the Court's New Attitude

210. The Court Reconsiders Federal Regulation of Industrial and Labor Relations

N. L. R. B. v. Jones & Laughlin Steel Corporation,
301 U.S. 1 (1937).

HUGHES, C.J.: . . . *The scope of the Act.*—The Act is challenged in its entirety as an attempt to regulate all industry, thus invading the reserved powers of the States over their local concerns. It is asserted that the references in the Act to interstate and foreign commerce are colorable at best; that the Act is not a true regulation of such commerce or of matters which directly affect it but on the contrary has the fundamental object of placing under the compulsory supervision of the federal government all industrial labor relations within the nation. The argument seeks support in the broad words of the preamble and in the sweep of the provisions of the Act, and it is further insisted that its legislative history shows an essential universal purpose in the light of which its scope cannot be limited by either construction or by the application of the separability clause.

If this conception of terms, intent and consequent inseparability were sound, the Act would necessarily fall by reason of the limitation upon the federal power which inheres in the constitutional grant, as well as because of the explicit reservation of the Tenth Amendment. *Schechter Corporation v. United States.* . . . The authority of the federal government may not be pushed to such an extreme as to destroy the distinction, which the commerce clause itself establishes, between commerce "among the several States" and the internal concerns of a State. That distinction between what is national and what is local in the activities of commerce is vital

to the maintenance of our federal system. . . .

But we are not at liberty to deny effect to specific provisions, which Congress has constitutional power to enact, by superimposing upon them inferences from general legislative declarations of an ambiguous character, even if found in the same statute. The cardinal principle of statutory construction is to save and not to destroy. We have repeatedly held that as between two possible interpretations of a statute, by one of which it would be unconstitutional and by the other valid, our plain duty is to adopt that which will save the act. Even to avoid a serious doubt the rule is the same. . . .

We think it clear that the National Labor Relations Act may be construed so as to operate within the sphere of constitutional authority. The jurisdiction conferred upon the Board, and invoked in this instance, is found in §10 (a), which provides:

> Sec. 10 (a). The Board is empowered, as hereinafter provided, to prevent any person from engaging in any unfair labor practice (listed in section 8) affecting commerce.

The critical words of this provision, prescribing the limits of the Board's authority in dealing with the labor practices, are "affecting commerce." The Act specifically defines the "commerce" to which it refers (§2 (6)). . . .

There can be no question that the commerce thus contemplated by the Act (aside from that within a Territory or the District of Columbia) is interstate and foreign commerce in the constitutional sense. The Act also defines the term "affecting commerce" (§2 (7)). . . .

This definition is one of exclusion as well as inclusion. The grant of authority to the Board does not purport to extend to the relationship between all industrial employees and employers. Its terms do not impose collective bargaining upon all industry regardless of effects upon interstate or foreign commerce. It purports to reach only what may be deemed to burden or obstruct that commerce and, thus qualified, it must be construed as contemplating the exercise of control within constitutional bounds. It is a familiar principle that acts which directly burden or obstruct interstate or foreign commerce, or its free flow, are within the reach of the congressional power. Acts having that effect are not rendered immune because they grow out of labor disputes. . . . It is the effect upon commerce, not the source of the injury, which is the criterion. . . . Whether or not particular action does affect commerce in such a close and intimate fashion as to be subject to federal control, and hence to lie within the authority conferred upon the Board, is left by the statute to be determined as individual cases arise. We are thus to inquire whether in the instant case the constitutional boundary has been passed. . . .

The application of the Act to employees engaged in production.—The principle involved.—Respondent says that whatever may be said of employees engaged in interstate commerce, the industrial relations and activities in the manufacturing department of respondent's enterprise are not subject to federal regulation. The argument rests upon the proposition that manufacturing in itself is not commerce. . . .

The Government distinguishes these cases. The various parts of respondent's enterprise are described as interdependent and as thus involving "a great movement of iron ore, coal and limestone along well-defined paths to the steel mills, thence through them, and thence in the form of steel products into the consuming centers of the country—a definite and well-understood course of business." It is urged that these activities constitute a "stream" or "flow" of commerce, of which the Aliquippa manufacturing plant is the focal point, and that industrial strife at that point would cripple the entire movement. Reference is made to our decision sustaining the Packers and Stockyards Act. . . . The Court found that the stockyards were but a "throat" through which the current of commerce flowed and the transactions which there occurred could not be separated from that movement. . . .

Respondent contends that the instant case presents material distinctions. . . .

We do not find it necessary to determine whether these features of defendant's business dispose of the asserted analogy to the "stream of commerce" cases. The congressional authority to protect interstate commerce from burdens and obstructions is not limited to transactions which can be deemed to be an essential part of a "flow" of interstate or foreign commerce. Burdens and obstructions may be due to injurious action springing from other sources. The fundamental principle is that the power to regulate commerce is the power to enact "all appropriate legislation" for "its protection and advancement" . . . ; to adopt measures "to promote its growth and insure its safety" . . . ; "to foster, protect, control and restrain." . . . That power is plenary and may be exerted to protect interstate commerce "no matter what the source of the dangers which threaten it." . . . Although activities may be intrastate in character when separately considered, if they have such a close and substantial relation to interstate commerce that their control is essential or appropriate to protect that commerce from burdens and obstructions, Congress cannot be denied the power to exercise that control. . . . Undoubtedly the scope of this power must be considered in the light of our dual system of government and may not be extended so as to embrace effects upon interstate commerce so indirect and remote that to embrace them, in view of our complex society, would effectually obliterate the distinction between what is national and what is local and create a completely centralized government. . . . The question is necessarily one of degree. . . .

It is thus apparent that the fact that the employees here concerned were engaged in production is not determinative. The question remains as to the effect upon interstate commerce of the labor practice involved. . . .

Effects of the unfair labor practice in respondent's enterprise.—Giving full weight to respondent's contention with respect to a break in the complete continuity of the "stream of commerce" by reason of respondent's manufacturing operations, the fact remains that the stoppage of those operations by industrial strife would have a most serious effect upon interstate commerce. In view of respondent's far-flung activities, it is idle to say that the effect would be indirect or remote. It is obvious that it would be immediate and might be catastrophic. We

are asked to shut our eyes to the plainest facts of our national life and to deal with the question of direct and indirect effects in an intellectual vacuum. Because there may be but indirect and remote effects upon interstate commerce in connection with a host of local enterprises throughout the country, it does not follow that other industrial activities do not have such a close and intimate relation to interstate commerce as to make the presence of industrial strife a matter of the most urgent national concern. When industries organize themselves on a national scale, making their relation to interstate commerce the dominant factor in their activities, how can it be maintained that their industrial labor relations constitute a forbidden field into which Congress may not enter when it is necessary to protect interstate commerce from the paralyzing consequences of industrial war? We have often said that interstate commerce itself is a practical conception. It is equally true that interferences with that commerce must be appraised by a judgment that does not ignore actual experience. . . .

Our conclusion is that the order of the Board was within its competency and that the Act is valid as here applied. . . .

211. *Promoting the General Welfare through Social Security*

Helvering et al. v. Davis, 301 U.S. 619 (1937).

CARDOZO, J.: The Social Security Act . . . is challenged once again. . . .

In this case Titles VIII and II are the subject of attack. Title VIII. . . . lays a special income tax upon employees to be deducted from their wages and paid by the employers. Title II provides for the payment of Old Age Benefits, and supplies the motive and occasion, in the view of the assailants of the statute, for the levy of the taxes imposed by Title VIII. . . .

The [district] court held that Title II was void as an invasion of powers reserved

by the Tenth Amendment to the states or to the people, and that Title II in collapsing carried Title VIII along with it. . . .

The scheme of benefits created by the provisions of Title II is not in contravention of the limitations of the Tenth Amendment.

Congress may spend money in aid of the "general welfare." Constitution, Art. I, section 8; *United States v. Butler* . . . ; *Steward Machine Co. v. Davis*. . . . There have been great statesmen in our history who have stood for other views. We will not resurrect the contest. It is now settled by decision. *United States v. Butler.* . . . The conception of the spending power advocated by Hamilton and strongly reinforced by Story has prevailed over that of Madison, which has not been lacking in adherents. Yet difficulties are left when the power is conceded. The line must still be drawn between one welfare and another, between particular and general. Where this shall be placed cannot be known through a formula in advance of the event. There is a middle ground or certainly a penumbra in which discretion is at large. The discretion, however, is not confided to the courts. The discretion belongs to Congress, unless the choice is clearly wrong, a display of arbitrary power, not an exercise of judgment. This is now familiar law. "When such a contention comes here we naturally require a showing that by no reasonable possibility can the challenged legislation fall within the wide range of discretion permitted to the Congress." *United States v. Butler.* . . . Nor is the concept of the general welfare static. Needs that were narrow or parochial a century ago may be interwoven in our day with the well-being of the nation. What is critical or urgent changes with the times.

The purge of nation-wide calamity that began in 1929 has taught us many lessons. Not the least is the solidarity of interests that may once have seemed to be divided. Unemployment spreads from state to state, the hinterland now settled that in pioneer days gave an avenue of escape. . . . Spreading from State to State, unemployment is an ill not particular but general, which may be checked, if Congress so determines, by the resources of the Nation. If this can have been doubtful until now, our ruling today in the case of the *Steward Machine Co.* . . . has set the doubt at rest. But the ill is all one or at least not greatly different whether men are thrown out of work because there is no longer work to do or because the disabilities of age make them incapable of doing it. Rescue becomes necessary irrespective

of the cause. The hope behind this statute is to save men and women from the rigors of the poor house as well as from the haunting fear that such a lot awaits them when journey's end is near. . . .

A recent study of the Social Security Board informs us that "one-fifth of the aged in the United States were receiving old-age assistance, emergency relief, institutional care, employment under the works program, or some other form of aid from public or private funds; two-fifths to one-half were dependent on friends and relatives, one-eighth had some income from earnings; and possibly one-sixth had some savings or property. Approximately three out of four persons 65 or over were probably dependent wholly or partially on others for support." We summarize in the margin the results of other studies by state and national commissions. They point the same way.

The problem is plainly national in area and dimensions. Moreover, laws of the separate states cannot deal with it effectively. Congress, at least, had a basis for that belief. States and local governments are often lacking in the resources that are necessary to finance an adequate program of security for the aged. This is brought out with a wealth of illustration in recent studies of the problem. Apart from the failure of resources, states and local governments are at times reluctant to increase so heavily the burden of taxation to be borne by their residents for fear of placing themselves in a position of economic disadvantage as compared with neighbors or competitors. We have seen this in our study of the problem of unemployment compensation. *Steward Machine Co. v. Davis.* . . . A system of old age pensions has special dangers of its own, if put in force in one state and rejected in another. The existence of such a system is a bait to the needy and dependent elsewhere, encouraging them to migrate and seek a haven of repose. Only a power that is national can serve the interests of all.

Whether wisdom or unwisdom resides

in the scheme of benefits set forth in Title II, it is not for us to say. The answer to such inquiries must come from Congress, not the courts. Our concern here, as often, is with power, not with wisdom. Counsel for respondent has recalled to us the virtues of self-reliance and frugality. There is a possibility, he says, that aid from a paternal government may sap those sturdy virtues and breed a race of weaklings. If Massachusetts so believes and shapes her laws in that conviction, must her breed of sons be changed, he asks, because some other philosophy of government finds favor in the halls of Congress? But the answer is not doubtful. One might ask with equal reason whether the system of protective tariffs is to be set aside at will in one state or another whenever local policy prefers the rule of *laissez faire*. The issue is a closed one. It was fought out long ago. When money is spent to promote the general welfare, the concept of welfare or the opposite is shaped by Congress, not the states. So the concept be not arbitrary, the locality must yield. Constitution, Art. VI, Par. 2.

The New Deal and the Roosevelt Court

212. The Reassessment of Labor Under the Sherman Act

Apex Hosiery Co. v. Leader, 310 U.S. 469 (1940).

STONE, J.: . . . Only a single question is presented by the record for our decision, whether the evidence . . . whose verity must be taken to be established by the jury's verdict, establishes a restraint of trade or commerce which the Sherman Act condemns. . . .

The Sherman Act admittedly does not condemn all combinations and conspiracies which interrupt interstate transportation . . .

This Court has never applied the Act to laborers or to others as a means of policing interstate transportation, and so the question to which we must address ourselves is whether a conspiracy of strikers in a labor dispute to stop the operation of the employer's factory in order to enforce their demands against the employer is the kind of restraint of trade or commerce at which the Act is aimed, even though a natural and probable consequence of their acts and the only effect on trade or commerce was to prevent substantial shipments interstate by the employer.

A point strongly urged in behalf of respondents in brief and argument before us is that Congress intended to exclude labor organizations and their activities wholly from the operation of the Sherman Act. To this the short answer must be made that for the thirty-two years which have elapsed since the decision in *Loewe v. Lawlor* . . . this Court, in its efforts to determine the true meaning and application of the Sherman Act has repeatedly held that the words of the act, "Every contract, combination . . . or conspiracy in restraint of trade or commerce" do embrace to some extent and in some circumstances labor unions and their activities; and that during that period Congress, although often asked to do so, has passed no act purporting to exclude labor unions wholly from the operation of the Act. On the contrary Congress has repeatedly enacted laws restricting or purporting to curtail the application of the Act to labor organizations and their activities, thus recognizing that to some extent not defined they remain subject to it. . . .

While we must regard the question whether labor unions are to some extent and in some circumstances subject to the Act as settled in the affirmative, it is equally plain that this Court has never thought the Act to apply to all labor union activities affecting interstate commerce. . . .

The question remains whether the effect of the combination or conspiracy among respondents was a restraint of trade within the meaning of the Sherman Act. This is not a case of a labor organization being used by combinations of those engaged in an industry as the means or instrument for suppressing competition or fixing prices. . . . Here it is plain that the combination or conspiracy did not have as its purpose restraint upon competition in the market for petitioner's product. Its object was to compel petitioner to accede to the union demands and an effect of it, in consequence of the strikers' tortious acts, was the prevention of the removal of petitioner's product for interstate shipment. So far as appears the delay of these shipments was not intended to have and had no effect on prices of hosiery in the market. . . .

Since the enactment of the declaration in §6 of the Clayton Act . . . , it would seem plain that restraints on the sale of the employee's services to the employer, however much they curtail the competition among employees, are not in themselves combinations or conspiracies in restraint of trade or commerce under the Sherman Act.

Strikes or agreements not to work, entered into by laborers to compel employers to yield to their demands, may restrict to some extent the power of employers who are parties to the dispute to compete in the market with those not subject to such demands. But under the doctrine applied to non-labor cases, the mere fact of such restrictions on competition does not in itself bring the parties to the agreement within the condemnation of the Sherman Act. . . .

These cases show that activities of labor organizations not immunized by the Clayton Act are not necessarily violations of the Sherman Act. Underlying and implicit in all of them is recognition that the Sherman Act was not enacted to police interstate transportation, or to afford a remedy for wrongs, which are actionable under state law, and result from combinations and conspiracies which fall short, both in their purpose and effect, of any form of market control of a commodity, such as to "monopolize the supply, control its price, or discriminate between its would-be purchasers. . . ." We do not hold that conspiracies to obstruct or prevent transportation in interstate commerce can in no circumstances be violations of the Sherman Act. Apart from the Clayton Act it makes no distinction between labor and non-labor cases. . . .

If, without such effects on the market, we were to hold that a local factory strike, stopping production and shipment of its product interstate, violates the Sherman law, practically every strike in modern industry would be brought within the jurisdiction of the federal courts, under the Sherman Act to remedy local law violations. The Act was plainly not intended to reach such a result, its language does not require it, and the course of our decision precludes it. The maintenance in our federal system of a proper distribution between state and national governments of police authority and of remedies private and public for public wrongs is of far-reaching importance. An intention to disturb the balance is not lightly to be imputed to Congress. The Sherman Act is concerned with the character of the prohibited restraints effected by violence and those achieved by peaceful but oftentimes quite as effective means. Restraints not within the Act, when achieved by peace-ful means, are not brought within its sweep merely because, without other differences, they are attended by violence. . . .

213. *The Norris–LaGuardia Act, Unions, and Federal Antitrust Legislation*

U.S. v. Hutcheson, 312 U.S. 219 (1941).

FRANKFURTER, J.: Whether the use of conventional, peaceful activities by a union in controversy with a rival union over certain jobs is a violation of the Sherman Act . . . is the question. . . .

Whether trade union conduct constitutes a violation of the Sherman Law is to be determined only by reading the Sherman Law and §20 of the Clayton Act and the Norris-LaGuardia Act as a harmonizing text of outlawry of labor conduct. . . .

There is nothing remotely within the terms of §20 that differentiates between trade union conduct directed against an employer because of a controversy arising in the relation between employer and employee, as such, and conduct similarly directed but ultimately due to an internecine struggle between two unions seeking the favor of the same employer. Such strife between competing unions has been an obdurate conflict in the evolution of so-called craft unionism and has undoubtedly been one of the potent forces in the modern development of industrial unions. These conflicts have intensified industrial tension but there is not the slightest warrant for saying that Congress has made §20 applicable to trade union conduct resulting from them. . . .

It is at once apparent that the acts with which the defendants are charged are the kind of acts protected by §20 of the Clayton Act. The refusal of the Carpenters to work for Anheuser-Busch or on construction work being done for it and its adjoining tenant, and the peaceful attempt to get members of other unions similarly to refuse to work, are plainly within the free scope accorded to workers by §20 for "terminating any relation of employment," or "ceasing to perform any work or labor," or "recommending, advising, or persuading others by peaceful means so to do." The picketing of Anheuser-Busch premises with signs to indicate that Anheuser-Busch was unfair to organized labor, a familiar practice in these situations, comes within the language "attending at any place where any such person or persons may lawfully be, for the purpose of peacefully obtaining or communicating information, or from peacefully persuading any person to work or to abstain from working." Finally, the recommendation to union members and their friends not to buy or use the product of Anheuser-Busch is explicitly covered by "ceasing to patronize . . . any party to such dispute, or from recommending, advising, or persuading others by peaceful and lawful means so to do."

Clearly, then, the facts here charged constitute lawful conduct under the Clayton Act unless the defendants cannot invoke that Act because outsiders to the immediate dispute also shared in the conduct. But we need not determine whether the conduct is legal within the restrictions which *Duplex Co. v. Deering* gave to the immunities of §20 of the Clayton Act. Congress in the Norris-LaGuardia Act has expressed the public policy of the United States and defined its conception of a "labor dispute" in terms that no longer leave room for doubt. . . .

The relation of the Norris-LaGuardia

Act to the Clayton Act is not that of a tightly drawn amendment to a technically phrased tax provision. The underlying aim of the Norris-LaGuardia Act was to restore the broad purpose which Congress thought it had formulated in the Clayton Act but which was frustrated, so Congress believed, by unduly restrictive judicial construction. . . .

The Norris-LaGuardia Act reasserted the original purpose of the Clayton Act by infusing into it the immunized trade union activities as redefined by the later Act. In this light §20 removes all such allowable conduct from the taint of being a "violation of any law of the United States," including the Sherman Law. . . .

214. *"It is within the legislative power to fix maximum hours" and minimum wages.*

U.S. v. Darby, 312 U.S. 100 (1941).

STONE, C.J.: The two principal questions raised by the record in this case are, *first,* whether Congress has constitutional power to prohibit the shipment in interstate commerce of lumber manufactured by employees whose wages are less than a prescribed minimum or whose weekly hours of labor at that wage are greater than a prescribed maximum, and, *second,* whether it has power to prohibit the employment of workmen in the production of goods "for interstate commerce" at other than prescribed wages and hours. . . .

While manufacture is not of itself interstate commerce, the shipment of manufactured goods interstate is such commerce and the prohibition of such shipment by Congress is indubitably a regulation of the commerce. The power to regulate commerce is the power "to prescribe the rule by which commerce is governed." *Gibbons v. Ogden.* . . . It extends not only to those regulations which aid, foster and protect the commerce, but embraces those which prohibit it. . . . It is conceded that the power of Congress to prohibit transportation in interstate commerce includes noxious articles, . . . stolen articles, . . . kidnapped persons, . . . and articles such as intoxicating liquor or convict made goods, traffic in which is forbidden or restricted by the laws of the state of destination. . . .

But it is said that the present prohibition falls within the scope of none of these categories; that while the prohibition is nominally a regulation of the commerce its motive or purpose is regulation of wages and hours of persons engaged in manufacture, the control of which has been reserved to the states and upon which Georgia and some of the states of destination have placed no restriction; that the effect of the present statute is not to exclude the prescribed articles from interstate commerce in aid of state regulation as in *Kentucky Whip & Collar Co. v. Illinois Central Railroad Co.* . . . but instead, under the guise of a regulation of interstate commerce, it undertakes to regulate wages and hours within the state contrary to the policy of the state which has elected to leave them unregulated.

The power of Congress over interstate commerce "is complete in itself, may be exercised to its utmost extent, and acknowledges no limitations other than are prescribed in the Constitution." . . . That power can neither be enlarged nor diminished by the exercise or non-exercise of state power. . . . Congress, following its own conception of public policy concerning the restrictions which may appropriately be imposed on interstate commerce, is free to exclude from the commerce articles whose use in the states for which they are destined it may conceive to be injurious to the public health, morals or welfare, even though the state has not sought to regulate their use. . . .

Such regulation is not a forbidden invasion of state power merely because either its motive or its consequence is to restrict the use of articles of commerce within the states of destination; and is not prohibited unless by other constitutional provisions. It is no objection to the assertion of the power to regulate interstate commerce that its exercise is attended by the same incidents which attend the exercise of the police power of the states. . . .

The motive and purpose of the present regulation are plainly to make effective the Congressional conception of public policy that interstate commerce should not be made the instrument of competition in the distribution of goods produced under substandard labor conditions, which competition is injurious to the commerce and to the states from and to which the commerce flows. The motive and purpose of a regulation of interstate commerce are matters for the legislative judgment upon the exercise of which the Constitution places no restriction and over which the courts are given no control. . . . Whatever their motive and purpose, regulations of commerce which do not infringe some constitutional prohibition are within the plenary power conferred on Congress by the Commerce Clause. Subject only to that limitation, presently to be considered, we conclude that the prohibition of the shipment interstate of goods produced under the forbidden substandard labor conditions is within the constitutional authority of Congress.

In the more than a century which has elapsed since the decision of *Gibbons v. Ogden,* these principles of constitutional interpretation have been so long and repeatedly recognized by this Court as applicable to the Commerce Clause, that there would be little occasion for repeating them now were it not for the decision of this Court twenty-two years ago in *Hammer v. Dagenhart.* . . . In that case

it was held by a bare majority of the Court over the powerful and now classic dissent of Mr. Justice Holmes setting forth the fundamental issues involved, that Congress was without power to exclude the products of child labor from interstate commerce. The reasoning and conclusion of the Court's opinion there cannot be reconciled with the conclusion which we have reached, that the power of Congress under the Commerce Clause is plenary to exclude any article from interstate commerce subject only to the specific prohibitions of the Constitution.

Hammer v. Dagenhart has not been followed. The distinction on which the decision was rested that Congressional power to prohibit interstate commerce is limited to articles which in themselves have some harmful or deleterious property—a distinction which was novel when made and unsupported by any provision of the Constitution—has long since been abandoned. . . .

The conclusion is inescapable that *Hammer v. Dagenhart,* was a departure from the principles which have prevailed in the interpretation of the commerce clause both before and since the decision and that such vitality, as a precedent, as it then had has long since been exhausted. It should be and now is overruled.

Validity of the wage and hour requirements. Section 15(a) (2) and §§6 and 7 require employers to conform to the wage and hour provisions with respect to all employees engaged in the production of goods for interstate commerce. As appellee's employees are not alleged to be "engaged in interstate commerce" the validity of the prohibition turns on the question whether the employment, under other than the prescribed labor standards, of employees engaged in the production of goods for interstate commerce is so related to the commerce and so affects it as to be within the reach of the power of Congress to regulate it. . . .

Congress, having by the present Act adopted the policy of excluding from interstate commerce all goods produced for the commerce which do not conform to the specified labor standards, it may choose the means reasonably adapted to the attainment of the permitted end, even though they involve control of intrastate activities. . . . A familiar like exercise of power is the regulation of intrastate transactions which are so commingled with or related to interstate commerce that all must be regulated if the interstate commerce is to be effectively controlled. . . .

So far as *Carter v. Carter Coal Co.* . . . is inconsistent with this conclusion, its doctrine is limited in principle by the decisions under the Sherman Act and the National Labor Relations Act, which we have cited and which we follow. . . .

Our conclusion is unaffected by the Tenth Amendment. . . . The amendment states but a truism that all is retained which has not been surrendered. There is nothing in the history of its adoption to suggest that it was more than declaratory of the relationship between the national and state governments as it had been established by the Constitution before the amendment or that its purpose was other than to allay fears that the new national government might seek to exercise powers not granted, and that the states might not be able to exercise fully their reserved powers. . . .

The Act is sufficiently definite to meet constitutional demands. One who employs persons, without conforming to the prescribed wage and hour conditions, to work on goods which he ships or expects to ship across state lines, is warned that he may be subject to the criminal penalties of the Act. No more is required. . . .

215. *The New Interpretation of Legislation on Agriculture*

Wickard v. Filburn, 317 U.S. 111 (1942).

JACKSON, J.: . . . Appellee says that this is a regulation of production and consumption of wheat. Such activities are, he urges, beyond the reach of Congressional power under the Commerce Clause, since they are local in character, and their effects upon interstate commerce are at most "indirect." In answer the Government argues that the statute regulates neither production nor consumption, but only marketing; and, in the alternative, that if the Act does go beyond the regulation of marketing it is sustainable as a "necessary and proper" implementation of the power of Congress over interstate commerce.

The Government's concern lest the Act be held to be a regulation of production or consumption, rather than of marketing, is attributable to a few dicta and decisions of this Court which might be understood to lay it down that activities such as "production," "manufacturing," and "mining" are strictly "local" and, except in special circumstances which are not present here, cannot be regulated under the commerce power because their effects upon interstate commerce are, as matter of law, only "indirect." Even today, when this power has been held to have great latitude, there is no decision of this Court that such activities may be regulated where no part of the product is intended for interstate commerce or intermingled with the subjects thereof. We believe that a review of the course of decision under the Commerce Clause will make plain, however, that questions of the power of Congress are not to be decided by reference to any formula which would give controlling force to nomenclature such as "production" and "indirect" and foreclose consideration of the actual effects of the activity in question upon interstate commerce. . . .

The Court's recognition of the relevance of the economic effects in the application of the Commerce Clause . . . has made the mechanical application of legal formulas no longer feasible. Once an economic measure of the reach of the power granted to Congress in the Commerce Clause is accepted, questions of federal power cannot be decided simply by finding the activity in question to be "production," nor can consideration of its economic effects be foreclosed by calling them "indirect. . . ."

Whether the subject of the regulation in question was "production," "consumption," or "marketing" is, therefore, not material for purposes of deciding the question of federal power before us. That an activity is of local character may help in a doubtful case to determine whether Congress intended to reach it. The same consideration might help in determining whether in the absence of Congressional action it would be permissible for the state to exert its power on the subject matter, even though in so doing it to some degree affected interstate commerce. But even if appellee's activity be local and though it may not be regarded as commerce, it may still, whatever its nature, be reached by Congress if it exerts a substantial economic effect on interstate commerce, and this irrespective of whether such effect is what might at some earlier time have been defined as "direct" or "indirect." . . .

The effect of consumption of home-grown wheat on interstate commerce is due to the fact that it constitutes the most variable factor in the disappearance of the wheat crop. Consumption on the farm where grown appears to vary in an amount greater than 20 per cent of average production. The total amount of wheat consumed as food varies but relatively little, and use as seed is relatively constant. . . .

It is well established by decisions of this Court that the power to regulate commerce includes the power to regulate the prices at which commodities in that commerce are dealt in and practices affecting such prices. One of the primary purposes of the Act in question was to increase the market price of wheat, and to that end to limit the volume thereof that could affect the market. It can hardly be denied that a factor of such volume and variability as home-consumed wheat would have a substantial influence on price and market conditions. This may arise because being in marketable condition such wheat overhangs the market and, if induced by rising prices, tends to flow into the market and check price increases. But if we assume that it is never marketed, it supplies a need of the man who grew it which would otherwise be reflected by purchases in the open market. Home-grown wheat in this sense competes with wheat in commerce. The stimulation of commerce is a use of the regulatory function quite as definitely as prohibitions or restrictions thereon. This record leaves us in no doubt that Congress may properly have considered that wheat consumed on the farm where grown, if wholly outside the scheme of regulation, would have a substantial effect in defeating and obstructing its purpose to stimulate trade therein at increased prices.

It is said, however, that this Act, forcing some farmers into the market to buy what they could provide for themselves, is an unfair promotion of the markets and prices of specializing wheat growers. It is of the essence of regulation that it lays a restraining hand on the self-interest of the regulated and that advantages from the regulation commonly fall to others. The conflicts of economic interest between the regulated and those who advantage by it are wisely left under our system to resolution by the Congress under its more flexible and responsible legislative process. Such conflicts rarely lend themselves to judicial determination. And with the wisdom, workability, or fairness, of the plan of regulation we have nothing to do. . . .

216. *Intergovernmental Tax Immunity*

Graves v. New York ex rel. O'Keefe, 306 U.S. 466 (1939).

STONE, J.: . . . The single question with which we are now concerned is whether the tax laid by the state upon the salary of respondent, employed by a corporate instrumentality of the federal government, imposes an unconstitutional burden upon that government. . . .

Congress has declared . . . that the Home Owners' Loan Corporation is an instrumentality of the United States and that its bonds are exempt, as to principal and interest, from federal and state taxation, except surtaxes, estate, inheritance and gift taxes. The corporation itself, "including its franchise, its capital, reserves and surplus, and its loans and income," is likewise exempted from taxation; its real property is subject to tax to the same extent as other real property. But Congress has given no intimation of any purpose either to grant or withhold immunity from state taxation of the salary of the corporation's employees, and the Congressional intention is not to be gathered from the statute by implication. . . .

It is true that the silence of Congress, when it has authority to speak, may sometimes give rise to an implication as to the Congressional purpose. The nature and extent of that implication depend upon the nature of the Congressional power and the effect of its exercise. But there is little scope for the application of that doctrine to the tax immunity of governmental instrumentalities. The constitutional immunity of either government from taxation by the other, where Congress is silent, has its source in an implied restriction upon the powers of the taxing government. So far as the implication rests upon the purpose to avoid interference with the functions of the taxed government or the imposition upon it of the economic burden of the tax, it is plain that there is no basis for implying a purpose of Congress to exempt the fed-

eral government or its agencies from tax burdens which are unsubstantial or which courts are unable to discern. Silence of Congress implies immunity no more than does the silence of the Constitution. It follows that when exemption from state taxation is claimed on the ground that the federal government is burdened by the tax, and Congress has disclosed no intention with respect to the claimed immunity, it is in order to consider the nature and effect of the alleged burden, and if it appears that there is no ground for implying a constitutional immunity, there is equally a want of any ground for assuming any purpose on the part of Congress to create an immunity.

The present tax is a non-discriminatory tax on income applied to salaries at a specified rate. It is not in form or substance a tax upon the Home Owners' Loan Corporation or its property or income, nor is it paid by the corporation or the government from their funds. It is laid upon income which becomes the property of the taxpayer when received as compensation for his services; and the tax laid upon the privilege of receiving it is paid from his private funds and not from the funds of the government, either directly or indirectly. The theory, which once won a qualified approval, that a tax on income is legally or economically a tax on its source, is no longer tenable, . . . and the only possible basis for implying a constitutional immunity from state income tax of the salary of an employee of the national government or of a governmental agency is that the economic burden of the tax is in some way passed on so as to impose a burden on the national government tantamount to an interference by one government with the other in the performance of its functions. . . .

Assuming, as we do, that the Home

Owners' Loan Corporation is clothed with the same immunity from state taxation as the government itself, we cannot say that the present tax on the income of its employees lays any unconstitutional burden upon it. All the reasons for refusing to imply a constitutional prohibition of federal income taxation of salaries of state employees, stated at length in the Gerhardt case, are of equal force when immunity is claimed from state income tax on salaries paid by the national government or its agencies. In this respect we perceive no basis for a difference in result whether the taxed income be salary or some other form of compensation, or whether the taxpayer be an employee or an officer of either a state or the national government, or of its instrumentalities. In no case is there basis for the assumption that any such tangible or certain economic burden is imposed on the government concerned as would justify a court's declaring that the taxpayer is clothed with the implied constitutional tax immunity of the government by which he is employed. That assumption, made in *Collector v. Day, . . .* and in *New York ex rel. Rogers v. Graves, . . .* is contrary to the reasoning and to the conclusions reached in the *Gerhardt* case. . . . In their light the assumption can no longer be made. *Collector v. Day, . . .* and *New York ex rel. Rogers v. Graves, . . .* are overruled so far as they recognize an implied constitutional immunity from income taxation of the salaries of officers or employees of the national or a state government or their instrumentalities.

So much of the burden of a non-discriminatory general tax upon the incomes of employees of a government, state or national, as may be passed on economically to that government, through the effect of the tax on the price level of labor or materials, is but the normal incident of the organization within the same territory of two governments, each possessing the taxing power. The burden, so far as it can be said to exist or to affect the government in any indirect or incidental way, is one which the Constitution presupposes, and hence it cannot rightly be deemed to be within an implied restriction upon the taxing power of the national and state governments which the Constitution has expressly granted to one and has confirmed to the other. The immunity is not one to be implied from the Constitution, because if allowed it would impose to an inadmissible extent a restriction on the taxing power which the Constitution has reserved to the state governments.

Shifting Areas of National Authority

THE AMENDING PROCESS

217. *"Lame Ducks" and Liquor*

A. THE TWENTIETH AMENDMENT

Proposed March 2, 1932; adopted February 6, 1933.

SECTION 1. The terms of the President and Vice-President shall end at noon on the twentieth day of January, and the terms of Senators and Representatives at noon on the third day of January of the years in which such terms would have ended if this article had not been ratified; and the terms of their successors shall then begin.

SECTION 2. The Congress shall assemble at least once in every year, and such meeting shall begin at noon on the third day of January, unless they shall by law appoint a different day.

SECTION 3. If, at the time fixed for the beginning of the term of the President the President-elect shall have died, the Vice-President-elect shall become President. If a President shall not have been chosen before the time fixed for the beginning of his term, or if the President-elect shall have failed to qualify, then the Vice-President-elect shall act as President until a President shall have qualified; and the Congress may by law provide for the case wherein neither a President-elect nor a Vice-President-elect shall have qualified, declaring who shall then act as President, or the manner in which one who is

to act shall be selected, and such person shall act accordingly until a President or Vice-President shall have qualified.

SECTION 4. The Congress may by law provide for the case of the death of any of the persons from whom the House of Representatives may choose a President whenever the right of choice shall have devolved upon them, and for the case of the death of any of the persons from whom the Senate may choose a Vice-President whenever the right of choice shall have devolved upon them.

SECTION 5. Sections 1 and 2 shall take effect on the Fifteenth day of October following the ratification of this article.

SECTION 6. This article shall be inoperative unless it shall have been ratified as an amendment to the Constitution by the legislatures of three-fourths of the several states within seven years from the date of its submission.

B. THE TWENTY-FIRST AMENDMENT

Proposed February 20, 1933; adopted December 5, 1933.

SECTION 1. The eighteenth article of amendment to the Constitution of the United States is hereby repealed.

SECTION 2. The transportation or importation into any state, territory, or possession of the United States for delivery or use therein of intoxicating liquors, in violation of the laws thereof, is hereby

prohibited.

SECTION 3. This article shall be inoperative unless it shall have been ratified as an amendment to the Constitution by conventions in the several states, as provided in the Constitution, within seven years from the date of the submission hereof to the states by the Congress.

THE REMOVAL POWER OF THE PRESIDENT

218. *"Illimitable power of removal is not possessed by the President."*

Humphrey's Executor (Rathbun) v. U.S., 295 U.S. 602 (1935).

SUTHERLAND, J.: . . . "Do the provisions of §1 of the Federal Trade Commission Act, stating that 'any commissioner may be removed by the President for inefficiency, neglect of duty or malfeasance in office,' restrict or limit the power of the President to remove a commissioner except upon one or more of the causes named?

"If the foregoing question is answered in the affirmative, then—

"2. If the power of the President to remove a commissioner is restricted or limited as shown by the foregoing interrogatory and the answer made thereto, is such a restriction or limitation valid under the Constitution of the United States?" . . .

The commission is to be nonpartisan; and it must, from the very nature of its duties, act with entire impartiality. It is charged with the enforcement of no policy except the policy of the law. Its duties are neither political nor executive, but predominantly quasi-legislative. Like the Interstate Commerce Commission, its members are called upon to exercise the trained judgment of a body of experts "appointed by law and informed by experience." . . .

The legislative reports in both houses of Congress clearly reflect the view that a fixed term was necessary to the effective and fair administration of the law. . . .

The debates in both houses demonstrate that the prevailing view was that the commission was not to be "subject to anybody in the government but only to the people of the United States," free from "political domination or control," or the "probability or possibility of such a thing," to be "separate and apart from any existing department of the government—not subject to the orders of the President." . . .

Thus the language of the act, the legislative reports and the general purposes of the legislation as reflected by the debates, all combine to demonstrate the congressional intent to create a body of experts who shall gain experience by length of service—a body which shall be independent of executive authority, *except in its selection,* and free to exercise its judgment without the leave or hindrance of any other official or any department of the government. To the accomplishment of these purposes it is clear that Congress

was of opinion that length and certainty of tenure would vitally contribute. And to hold that, nevertheless, the members of the commission continue in office at the mere will of the President, might be to thwart, in large measure, the very ends which Congress sought to realize by definitely fixing the term of office.

We conclude that the intent of the act is to limit the executive power of removal to the causes enumerated, the existence of none of which is claimed here; and we pass to the second question.

Second. To support its contention that the removal provision of §1, as we have just construed it, is an unconstitutional interference with the executive powers of the President, the government's chief reliance is *Myers v. U.S.* . . . Nevertheless, the narrow point actually decided was only that the President had power to remove a postmaster of the first class, without the advice and consent of the Senate, as required by act of Congress. . . .

The office of postmaster is so essentially unlike the office now involved that the decision in the Myers case cannot be accepted as controlling our decision here. A postmaster is an executive officer restricted to the performance of executive functions. He is charged with no duty at all related to either the legislative or judicial power. . . . The necessary reach of the decision goes far enough to include all purely executive officers. It goes no farther; much less does it include an officer who occupies no place in the executive department and who exercises no part of the executive power vested by the Constitution in the President.

The Federal Trade Commission is an administrative body created by Congress to carry into effect legislative policies embodied in the statute in accordance with the legislative standard therein prescribed, and to perform other specified duties as a legislative or as a judicial aid. Such a body cannot in any proper sense be characterized as an arm or an eye of the executive. Its duties are performed without executive leave and, in the contemplation of the statute, must be free from executive control. . ; .

We think it plain under the Constitution that illimitable power of removal is not possessed by the President in respect of officers of the character of those just named. The authority of Congress, in creating quasi-legislative or quasi-judicial agencies, to require them to act in discharge of their duties independently of executive control, cannot well be doubted; and that authority includes, as an appropriate incident, power to fix the period during which they shall continue, and to forbid their removal except for cause in the meantime. For it is quite evident that one who holds his office only during the pleasure of another cannot be depended upon to maintain an attitude of independence against the latter's will.

The fundamental necessity of maintaining each of the three general departments of government entirely free from the control or coercive influence, direct or indirect, of either of the others, has often been stressed and is hardly open to serious question. So much is implied in the very fact of the separation of the powers of these departments by the Constitution, and in the rule which recognizes their es-

sential coequality. The sound application of a principle that makes one master in his own house precludes him from imposing his control in the house of another who is master there. . . .

Whether the power of the President to remove an officer shall prevail over the authority of Congress to condition the power by fixing a definite term and precluding a removal except for cause will depend upon the character of the office; the Myers decision, affirming the power of the President alone to make the removal, is confined to purely executive officers; and as to officers of the kind here under consideration, we hold that no removal can be made during the prescribed term for which the officer is appointed, except for one or more of the causes named in the applicable statute.

To the extent that, between the decision in the Myers case, which sustains the unrestrictable power of the President to remove purely executive officers, and our present decision that such power does not extend to an office such as that here involved, there shall remain a field of doubt, we leave such cases as may fall within it for future consideration and determination as they arise.

THE TREATY POWER AND EXECUTIVE AGREEMENTS

219. *The President's Plenary Power over International Affairs*

U.S. v. Curtiss-Wright Export Corporation, 299 U.S. 304 (1936).

SUTHERLAND, J.: . . . *First.* It is contended that by the Joint Resolution, the going into effect and continued operation of the resolution was conditioned (a) upon the President's judgment as to its beneficial effect upon the reestablishment of peace between the countries engaged in armed conflict in the Chaco; (b) upon the making of a proclamation, which was left to his unfettered discretion, thus con-

stituting an attempted substitution of the President's will for that of Congress; (c) upon the making of a proclamation putting an end to the operation of the resolution, which again was left to the President's unfettered discretion; and (d) further, that the extent of its operation in particular cases was subject to limitation and exception by the President, controlled by no standard. In each of these particulars, appellees urge that Congress abdicated its essential functions and delegated them to the Executive.

Whether, if the Joint Resolution had related solely to internal affairs it would be open to the challenge that it constituted an unlawful delegation of legislative power to the Executive, we find it unnecessary to determine. The whole aim of the resolution is to affect a situation entirely external to the United States, and falling within the category of foreign affairs. The determination which we are called to make, therefore, is whether the Joint Resolution, as applied to that situation, is vulnerable to attack under the rule that forbids a delegation of the law-making power. In other words, assuming (but not deciding) that the challenged delegation, if it were confined to internal affairs, would be invalid, may it nevertheless be sustained on the ground that its exclusive aim is to afford a remedy for a hurtful condition within foreign territory?

It will contribute to the elucidation of the question if we first consider the differences between the powers of the federal government in respect of foreign or external affairs and those in respect of domestic or internal affairs. That there are differences between them, and that these differences are fundamental, may not be doubted.

The two classes of powers are different, both in respect of their origin and their nature. The broad statement that the federal government can exercise no powers except those specifically enumerated in the Constitution, and such implied powers as are necessary and proper to carry into effect the enumerated powers, is categorically true only in respect of our internal affairs. In that field, the primary purpose of the Constitution was to carve from the general mass of legislative powers *then possessed by the states* such portions as it was thought desirable to vest in the federal government, leaving those not included in the enumeration still in the States. *Carter v. Carter Coal Co.* . . .

That this doctrine applies only to powers which the states had, is self evident. And since the states severally never possessed international powers, such powers could not have been carved from the mass of state powers but obviously were transmitted to the United States from some other source. . . . [There follows a detailed discussion of the historical sources of the federal government's exclusive power over foreign relations.]

It results that the investment of the federal government with the powers of external sovereignty did not depend upon the affirmative grants of the Constitution. The powers to declare and wage war, to conclude peace, to make treaties, to maintain diplomatic relations with other sovereignties, if they had never been mentioned in the Constitution, would have vested in the federal government as necessary concomitants of nationality. Neither the Constitution nor the laws passed in pursuance of it have any force in foreign territory unless in respect of our own citizens . . . ; and operations of the nation in such territory must be governed by treaties, international understandings and compacts, and the principles of international law. As a member of the family of nations, the right and power of the United States in that field are equal to the right and power of the other members of the international family. Otherwise, the United States is not completely sovereign. . . .

Not only, as we have shown, is the federal power over external affairs in origin and essential character different from that over internal affairs, but participation in the exercise of the power is significantly limited. In this vast external realm, with its important, complicated, delicate and manifold problems, the President alone has the power to speak or listen as a representative of the nation. He *makes* treaties with the advice and consent of the Senate; but he alone negotiates. Into the field of negotiation the Senate cannot intrude; and Congress itself is powerless to invade it. . . .

It is important to bear in mind that we are here dealing not alone with an authority vested in the President by an exertion of legislative power, but with such an authority plus the very delicate, plenary and exclusive power of the President as the sole organ of the federal government in the field of international relations—a power which does not require as a basis for its exercise an act of Congress, but which, of course, like every other governmental power, must be exercised in subordination to the applicable provisions of the Constitution. It is quite apparent that if, in the maintenance of our international relations, embarrassment—perhaps serious embarrassment—is to be avoided and success for our aims achieved, congressional legislation which is to be made effective through negotiation and inquiry within the international field must often accord to the President a degree of discretion and freedom from statutory restriction which would not be admissible were domestic affairs alone involved. Moreover he, not Congress, has the better opportunity of knowing the conditions which prevail in foreign countries, and especially is this true in time of war. He has his confidential sources of information. He has his agents in the form of diplomatic, consular and other officials. Secrecy in respect of information gathered by them may be highly necessary, and the premature disclosure of it productive of harmful results. Indeed, so clearly is this true that the first President refused to accede to a request to lay before the House of Representatives the instructions, correspondence and documents relating to the negotiation of the Jay Treaty. . . .

In the light of the foregoing observations, it is evident that this court should not be in haste to apply a general rule which will have the effect of condemning legislation like that under review as constituting an unlawful delegation of legislative power. The principles which justify such legislation find overwhelming support in the unbroken legislative practice which has prevailed almost from the inception of the national government to the present day. . . .

The result of holding that the joint resolution here under attack is void and unenforceable as constituting an unlawful delegation of legislative power would be to stamp this multitude of comparable acts and resolutions as likewise invalid. And while this court may not, and should not, hesitate to declare acts of Congress, however many times repeated, to be unconstitutional if beyond all rational doubt it finds them to be so, an impressive array of legislation such as we have just set forth, enacted by nearly every Congress from the beginning of our national existence to the present day, must be given unusual weight in the process of reaching a correct determination of the problem. A legislative practice such as we have here, evidenced not by only occasional instances, but marked by the movement of a steady stream for a century and a half of time, goes a long way in the direction of proving the presence of unassailable ground for the constitutionality of the practice, to be found in the origin and history of the power involved, or in its nature or in both combined. . . .

The uniform, long-continued and undisputed legislative practice just disclosed rests upon an admissible view of the Constitution which, even if the practice found far less support in principle than we think it does, we should not feel at liberty at this late day to disturb. . . .

CHAPTER XXIV

The Roosevelt Court and Civil Liberties

FULLY as important as the Roosevelt Court's expansion of governmental authority in the economic realm were the restraints imposed on federal and state power in order to protect civil liberty. In the late 1930's and early 1940's, judicial supervision of civil liberties created a body of constitutional law unique in the annals of American history. The chief constitutional basis for this rapid development of new safeguards was the expanded concept of basic liberties guaranteed by the Fourteenth Amendment, begun in the Gitlow case in 1925 and strengthened in the Stromberg and Near decisions in 1931 (Chapter XXI).

By 1937 various First and Sixth Amendment guarantees had been held to comprise part of the "liberty" that the Fourteenth Amendment forbids the states to abridge without due process of law. However, the question of whether all the guarantees of the first eight amendments were applicable to the states still needed settlement. In *Palko v. Connecticut* (No. 220), the Court set forth a standard reminiscent of the distinction in the Insular Cases (Chapter XVI). Employing selective natural law principles, Justice Cardozo drew a line between those rights "implicit in the concept of ordered liberty," such as the First Amendment freedoms of speech, assembly, press, and religion, and rights merely procedural or remedial, and he ruled in the immediate case that the Fourteenth Amendment did not include the double jeopardy provision of the Fifth Amendment. Although the decision clearly avoided making all the guarantees of the Bill of Rights applicable to the states, it opened the door for judicial development of a wide variety of constitutional rights, creating a new area of substantive due process in the field of civil liberties at almost the same moment that the Court rejected this concept in the area of economic and social legislation.

The expansion was especially noteworthy in its relation to First Amendment freedoms. In the field of freedom of the press, it made possible a notable ruling against indirect censorship by the Huey Long government in Louisiana (*Grosjean v. American Press Company* [No. 221]). For a unanimous Court, Justice Sutherland announced that "the states are precluded from abridging the freedom of speech or of the press by force of the due process clause of the Fourteenth Amendment." In *DeJonge v. Oregon* (No. 222), freedom of assembly was held to be a Fourteenth Amendment liberty protected from state encroachment. Chief Justice Hughes therefore voided the conviction of a Communist who had been prosecuted under a state criminal syndicalism law for having spoken at a peaceable public meeting. Although the majority could not agree about which clause of the Fourteenth Amendment applied, they did invalidate Jersey City's restrictions on public meetings in *Hague v. C. I. O.* (1939). Some of the justices thought that Boss Hague's machine had abridged the privileges and immunities of United States citizens, but Justice Stone, who wrote the opinion, held to the more conventional view that the municipal ordinance deprived persons of their liberty without due process of law.

In other speech and press cases, the Court revived the Holmes-Brandeis "clear and present danger" rule as a standard by which to measure state denial of due process. In upholding the legality of speeches and printed material disseminated by a Negro Communist organizer, the Court rejected the Gitlow "bad tendency" test, pointing out that the Georgia syndicalist statute against incitement to insurrection "has not made membership in the Communist Party unlawful by reason of its supposed dangerous tendency even in the remote future" (*Herndon v. Lowry*, 1937). Begining in 1941, the Court also applied the "clear and present danger" rule in voiding, as a denial of due process, contempts of court by publication (*Bridges v. California*, 1941; *Pennekamp v. Florida*, 1946). At the same time, the Court made it clear that freedom of the press does not exempt newspapers from government regulation of their business activities and labor relations (*Associated Press v. U.S.*, 1945).

In expanding the area of protected speech, the Roosevelt Court in 1940 brought peaceful picketing in labor disputes under the liberty guarantees of the Fourteenth Amendment. As early as 1937, Justice Brandeis had linked picketing to speech (*Senn v. Tile Layers Protective Union*), and *Thornhill v. Alabama* (No. 223) elevated that dictum to ruling law. In striking down an antipicketing statute, the Court said: "The dissemination of information concerning the facts of a labor dispute must be regarded as within that area of free discussion that is guaranteed by the Constitution." The public display of placards by pickets was interpreted as a legitimate exercise of free speech. Later decisions indicated that picketing accompanied by violence or intimidation does not enjoy the same protection.

Another important labor union case invalidated a Texas statute requiring union organizers to register with city authorities before soliciting union memberships (*Thomas v. Collins* [No. 224]). "Lawful public assemblies, involving no element of grave and immediate danger to an interest the state is entitled to protect," Justice Rutledge observed for a 5 to 4 majority, "are not instruments of harm which require previous identification of the speaker." In both Thornhill and Thomas, the "clear and present danger" doctrine was invoked, but it was used to void state statutes rather than test their applicability. In the Thomas case, moreover, the Court combined this doctrine with its "preferred position" theory, asserting that the "indispensable democratic freedoms secured by the First Amendment" are so basic that any attempt to restrict them "must be justified by clear public interest, threatened not doubtfully or remotely, but by clear and present danger."

The solicitude of the Roosevelt Court for civil liberties resulted in a rash of cases dealing with state and local ordinances directed at the militant techniques of an unorthodox religious group, the Jehovah Witnesses. In their legal fight against restrictions on their liberty, the Witnesses brought nearly two dozen cases to the Court which clarified broad areas of constitutional law relating to the First Amendment freedoms of religion, assembly, speech, and press. In the first of this series, *Lovell v. Griffin* (1938), a unanimous Court struck down a Georgia city ordinance forbidding the distribution of pamphlets, handbills, and other literature without prior permission from the city manager. Such a rule subjected the press to "license and censorship" and constituted a denial of due process of law. In *Cantwell v. Connecticut* (1940), the Court invalidated, as a "censorship of religion" that denied due process, a statute requiring a permit for all solicitors for religious or charitable causes. Although both of these opinions were unanimous, the Court split sharply in *Jones v. Opelika* (1942), upholding a nondiscriminatory tax on peddling or canvassing which placed no special burden on those selling religious books. When Justice Rutledge replaced Justice Byrnes in 1943, a new 5 to 4 majority reversed the Opelika decision, interpreting door-to-door book sales by Witnesses as a religious rather than a commercial venture (*Murdock v. Pennsylvania* [No. 225]). This tax immunity for vendors of religious books was made complete in *Follett v. McCormick* (1944).

Other claims by the Witnesses have not received judicial blessing. The Court sustained the conviction of a Witness who created a breach of the peace by using libelous and "fighting words," held that Witnesses who allow children to sell religious literature violate state child labor laws, and upheld a fee to cover the cost of extra police for parade duty, even though the procession was a religious one. But the most spectacular reversal for the Witnesses came in the compulsory flag-salute case in 1940. In *Minersville School District v. Gobitis*, Justice Frankfurter sustained a Pennsylvania statute that directed the expulsion of children who refused to salute the flag in school ceremonies. Abandoning the "clear and present danger" test, the majority ruled that such a law did not restrict freedom of religion unconstitutionally. But a change of Court personnel and strong misgivings on the part of some of the majority made it possible for the Court to overrule Gobitis in *West Virginia State Board v. Barnette*. Stressing that the refusal to salute did not interfere with the rights of other individuals, Justice Jackson made an eloquent defense of nonconformity in all areas (No. 226). Frankfurter reaffirmed his original position in an equally brilliant plea for judicial acknowledgment of the competence of legislatures to deal with questions of local educational policy.

Despite the Court's reluctance to apply all the procedural rights of the first eight amendments to the states, the justices did develop many limitations on state criminal procedure. Although the elements of a fair and decent trial have been spelled out piecemeal, the Court has been consistent in proscribing actual brutality and flagrant intimidation to secure confessions. In 1940, Justice Black, speaking for a unanimous Court, wrote a dramatic decision that struck at more subtle means of pressure in invalidating a conviction of four Negroes obtained by ceaseless "grilling" by state officials (*Chambers v. Florida* [No. 227]). During the same period, the McNabb case set down a rule to guide federal courts in deciding on the admissibility of confessions, whether obtained by coercion or not. In this case a confession to murder was secured without coercion, but before the prisoner was arraigned; the Court stated flatly that "a confession is inadmissible if made during illegal detention due to a failure promptly to carry a prisoner before a committing magistrate, whether or not the 'confession is the result of torture, physical or psychological.'" On the other hand, the Court, in its consideration of the rights of accused persons, retreated from its earlier ruling (*Powell v. Alabama,* 1932) that the absence of adequate counsel deprived a person of life or liberty without due process of law. For a decade it was presumed that this first Scottsboro case had nailed down the right to counsel in criminal trials as one of the due process requirements. But in *Betts v. Brady* (1942) the majority ruled that in noncapital cases the right was not a fundamental one, since a number of state constitutions did not recognize it, nor was it required by common law. Protest against this ruling was strong, both on and off the bench; to many it seemed to tilt "the scales against the safeguarding of one of the most precious rights of man" (No. 228).

Federal protection of the rights of accused persons, of militant minority religious sects, and of labor was paralleled by an almost revolutionary reversal of the status of the Negro in American constitutional law. The attitude of the nation's highest tribunal always has been of supreme importance in determining the legal position of the Negro, for court consent has been necessary to legalize his subordinate status. For the Negro, the suffrage issue has been a key consideration, and the Court generally has nullified state legislation clearly inconsistent with the Fifteenth Amendment. In 1915 the "grandfather clause" was outlawed as a violation of that provision (*Guinn v. U.S.*). In 1916 Oklahoma replaced this law with a more subtle code that effectively disfranchised Negroes. Not until 1939 did this law come up for decision, and the Roosevelt Court promptly canceled it, observing that the Fifteenth Amendment "nullifies sophisticated as well as simpleminded modes of discrimination" (*Lane v. Wilson*).

The white primary question first received judicial interpretation in 1927, when a Texas law excluding Negroes from participating in primaries was struck down as an infringement of the Fourteenth Amendment (*Nixon v. Herndon*). Disfranchisement was then achieved when the Democratic Party in Texas, without legislative assistance, organized as a "private club," restricted its membership to whites, and thus barred Negroes from party primary elections. The "old Court" upheld this device in 1935 on the grounds that the political party was a private and not a governmental body, and private persons or groups could not violate the Fourteenth Amendment (*Grovey v. Townsend*). In 1941, however, a case came before the Roosevelt Court involving the failure of state officials, acting under "color" of state law, to count primary election ballots properly (*U.S. v. Classic*, 1941). Justice Stone ruled that the federal government could guarantee the right to vote in a primary in a one-party state where the primary was obviously an integral step in the election of members of Congress. The opinion did not mention the Grovey precedent, but the two were clearly in conflict and three years later the Court formally overruled Grovey and outlawed the Texas ruse as a violation of the Fifteenth Amendment (*Smith v. Allwright* [No. 229]). "Constitutional rights would be of little value," said Justice Rutledge, "if they could be thus indirectly denied." The Smith case did not end Southern efforts to disfranchise the Negro (Chapter XXVIII, No. 270) but the impressive growth of Negro voting in every Southern state indicates the gradual improvement of the political status of the Negro.

The judicial attack on discrimination by the Roosevelt Court also led to the first serious reconsideration of the "separate but equal" doctrine in 1938. The University of Missouri Law School had refused to admit a Negro student even though there were no separate or equal facilities in the state. This, said Chief Justice Hughes, was a violation of the equal protection clause of the Fourteenth Amendment. Carefully avoiding explicit conflict with the Plessy doctrine, Hughes insisted only that equality meant what it said: "The admissibility of laws separating the races . . . rests wholly upon the equality of the privileges which the laws give to the separated groups within the State" (*Missouri ex rel. Gaines v. Canada* [No. 230]). Subsequent cases applied the same principle to transportation facilities (*Mitchell v. U.S.*, 1941; *Morgan v. Virginia*, 1945), and the whole series of rulings posed a threat to the entire legal pattern of segregation in the South.

To its contribution to the constitutional doctrine of liberty the Roosevelt Court also added a unique footnote. Instances of legislative punishment have been rare in American history, but in 1946 the liberty-minded justices had an opportunity to rule on this almost unprecedented issue. To strike at three executive officials who had been attacked by the House UnAmerican Activities Committee, Congress, through a rider to an appropriations bill, had cut off their salaries and thus forced their removal from the federal payroll. When the trio sued for their back salaries, Justice Black branded the congressional action illegal as a bill of attainder (*U.S. v. Lovett, Watson, and Dodd* [No. 231]), ruling an act of Congress unconstitutional in one of the few occasions since the "Court-packing" fight.

The Scope and Theory of Federal Protection

220. *Freedoms "implicit in the concept of ordered liberty."*

Palko v. Connecticut, 302 U.S. 319 (1937).

CARDOZO, J.: . . . The argument for appellant is that whatever is forbidden by the Fifth Amendment is forbidden by the Fourteenth also. The Fifth Amendment, which is not directed to the states, but solely to the federal government, creates immunity from double jeopardy. No person shall be "subject for the same offense to be twice put in jeopardy of life or limb." The Fourteenth Amendment ordains, "nor shall any State deprive any person of life, liberty, or property, without due process of law." To retry a defendant, though under one indictment and only one, subjects him, it is said, to double jeopardy in violation of the Fifth Amendment, if the prosecution is one on behalf of the United States. From this the consequence is said to follow that there is a denial of life or liberty without due process of law, if the prosecution is one on behalf of the people of a state. . . .

This thesis is even broader. Whatever would be a violation of the original Bill of Rights (Amendments 1 to 8) if done by the federal government is now equally unlawful by force of the Fourteenth Amendment if done by a state. There is no such general rule.

The Fifth Amendment provides, among other things, that no person shall be held to answer for a capital or otherwise infamous crime unless on presentment or indictment of a grand jury. This Court has held that, in prosecutions by a state, presentment or indictment by a grand jury may give way to informations at the instance of a public officer. *Hurtado v. California.* . . . The Fifth Amendment provides also that no person shall be com-

pelled in any criminal case to be a witness against himself. This Court has said that, in prosecutions by a state, the exemption will fail if the state elects to end it. *Twining v. New Jersey.* . . . The Sixth Amendment calls for a jury trial in criminal cases and the Seventh for a jury trial in civil cases at common law where the value in controversy shall exceed twenty dollars. This Court has ruled that consistently with those amendments trial by jury may be modified by a state or abolished altogether. . . .

On the other hand, the due process clause of the Fourteenth Amendment may make it unlawful for a state to abridge by its statutes the freedom of speech which the First Amendment safeguards against encroachment by the Congress . . . or the like freedom of the press . . . or the free exercise of religion . . . or the right of peaceable assembly, without which speech would be unduly trammeled . . . or the right of one accused of crime to the benefit of counsel. . . . In these and other situations immunities that are valid as against the federal government by force of the specific pledges of particular amendments have been found to be implicit in the concept of ordered liberty, and thus, through the Fourteenth Amendment, become valid as against the states.

The line of division may seem to be wavering and broken if there is a hasty catalogue of the cases on the one side and the other. Reflection and analysis will induce a different view. There emerges the perception of a rationalizing principle which gives to discrete instances a proper order and coherence. The right to trial by jury and the immunity from prosecution except as the result of an indictment may have value and importance. Even so, they are not of the very essence of a scheme of ordered liberty. To abolish them is not to violate a "principle of justice so rooted in the traditions and conscience of our people as to be ranked as fundamental." . . . Few would be so narrow or provincial as to maintain that a fair and enlightened system of justice would be impossible without them. What is true of jury trials and indictments is true also, as the cases show, of the immunity from compulsory self-incrimination. . . . This too might be lost, and justice still be done. Indeed, today as in the past there are students of our penal system who look upon the immunity as a mischief rather than a benefit, and who would limit its scope or destroy it altogether. . . . The exclusion of these immunities and privileges from the privileges and immunities protected against the action of the states has not been arbitrary or casual. It has been dictated by a study and appreciation of the meaning, the essential implications, of liberty itself.

We reach a different plane of social and moral values when we pass to the privileges and immunities that have been taken over from the earlier articles of the federal Bill of Rights and brought within the Fourteenth Amendment by a process of absorption. These in their origin were effective against the federal government alone. If the Fourteenth Amendment has absorbed them, the process of absorption has had its source in the belief that neither liberty nor justice would exist if they were sacrificed. . . . This is true, for illustration, of freedom of thought and speech. Of that freedom one may say that it is the matrix, the indispensable condition, of nearly every other form of freedom. With rare aberrations a pervasive recognition of that truth can be traced in our history, political and legal. So it has come about that the domain of liberty, withdrawn by the Fourteenth Amendment from encroachment by the states, has been enlarged by latter-day judgments to include liberty of the mind as well as liberty of action. . . .

Our survey of the cases serves, we think, to justify the statement that the dividing line between them, if not unfaltering throughout its course, has been true for the most part to a unifying principle. On which side of the line the case made out by the appellant has appropriate location must be the next inquiry and the final one. Is that kind of double jeopardy to which the statute has subjected him a hardship so acute and shocking that our polity will not endure it? Does it violate those "fundamental principles of liberty and justice which lie at the base of all our civil and political institutions?" . . . The answer surely must be "no." . . . The state is not attempting to wear the accused out by a multitude of cases with accumulated trials. It asks no more than this, that the case against him shall go on until there shall be a trial free from the corrosion of substantial legal error. . . . This is not cruelty at all, nor even vexation in any immoderate degree. If the trial had been infected with error adverse to the accused, there might have been review at his instance, and as often as necessary to purge the vicious taint. A reciprocal privilege, subject at all times to the discretion of the presiding judge . . . , has now been granted to the state. There is here no seismic innovation. The edifice of justice stands, in its symmetry, to many, greater than before.

Freedom Under the First Amendment

FREEDOM OF SPEECH, PRESS, AND ASSEMBLY

221. *Informed Public Opinion Restrains Misgovernment*

Grosjean v. American Press Company, 297 U.S. 233 (1936).

SUTHERLAND, J.: This suit was brought by appellees, nine publishers of newspapers in the State of Louisiana, to enjoin the enforcement against them of the Provisions of . . . [an act] of Louisiana as follows:

"That every person, firm, association, or corporation, domestic or foreign, engaged in the business of selling, or making any charge for, advertising or for advertisements, whether printed or published, or to be printed or published, in any newspaper, magazine, periodical or publication whatever having a circulation of more than 20,000 copies per week, or displayed and exhibited, or to be displayed and exhibited by means of moving pictures, in the State of Louisiana, shall, in addition to all other taxes and licenses levied and assessed in this State, pay a license tax for the privilege of engaging in such business in this State of two per cent. of the gross receipts of such business." . . .

The validity of the act is assailed as violating the Federal Constitution in two particulars—(1) that it abridges the freedom of the press in contravention of the due process clause contained in §1 of the Fourteenth Amendment; (2) that it denies appellees the equal protection of the laws in contravention of the same Amendment. . . .

1. The first point presents a question of the utmost gravity and importance; for, if well made, it goes to the heart of the natural right of the members of an or-

ganized society, united for their common good, to impart and acquire information about their common interests. The First Amendment to the Federal Constitution . . . is not a restraint upon the powers of the states, [but] the states are precluded from abridging the freedom of speech or of the press by force of the due process clause of the Fourteenth Amendment. . . .

That freedom of speech and of the press are rights of the same fundamental character, safeguarded by the due process of law clause of the Fourteenth Amendment against abridgement by state legislation, has likewise been settled by a series of decisions of this Court beginning with *Gitlow v. New York* . . . and ending with *Near v. Minnesota.* . . . The word "liberty" contained in that amendment embraces not only the right of a person to be free from physical restraint, but the right to be free in the enjoyment of all his faculties as well. . . .

The tax imposed is designated a "license tax for the privilege of engaging in such business"—that is to say, the business of selling, or making any charge for, advertising. As applied to appellees, it is a tax of two per cent. on the gross receipts derived from advertisements. . . . It thus operates as a restraint in a double sense. First, its effect is to curtail the amount of revenue realized from advertising, and, second, its direct tendency is to restrict circulation. This is plain enough when we consider that, if it were increased to a high degree, as it could be if valid, it well might result in destroying both advertising and circulation.

A determination of the question whether the tax is valid in respect of the point now under review, requires an examination of the history and circumstances which antedated and attended the adoption of the abridgement clause of the First Amendment, since that clause expresses one of those "fundamental principles of liberty and justice which lie at the base of all our civil and political institutions," and, as such, is embodied in the concept "due process of law," and, therefore, protected against hostile state invasion by the due process clause of the Fourteenth Amendment. . . .

It is impossible to concede that by the words "freedom of the press" the framers of the amendment intended to adopt merely the narrow view then reflected by the law of England that such freedom consisted only in immunity from previous censorship; for this abuse had then permanently disappeared from English practice. It is equally impossible to believe that it was not intended to bring within the reach of these words such modes of restraint as were embodied in the two forms of taxation already described. . . .

This court had occasion in *Near v. Minnesota* . . . to discuss at some length the subject in its general aspect. . . . Liberty of the press within the meaning of the constitutional provision, it was broadly said, meant "principally although not exclusively, immunity from previous restraints or [from] censorship."

Judge Cooley has laid down the test to be applied—"The evils to be prevented were not the censorship of the press merely, but any action of the government by means of which it might prevent such free and general discussion of public matters as seems absolutely essential to prepare the people for an intelligent exercise of their rights as citizens." . . .

It is not intended by anything we have said to suggest that the owners of newspapers are immune from any of the ordinary forms of taxation for support of the government. But this is not an ordinary form of tax, but one single in kind, with a long history of hostile misuse against the freedom of the press.

The predominant purpose of the grant of immunity here invoked was to preserve an untrammeled press as a vital source of public information. The newspapers, magazines and other journals of the country, it is safe to say, have shed and continue to shed, more light on the public and business affairs of the nation than any other instrumentality of publicity; and since informed public opinion is the most potent of all restraints upon misgovernment, the suppression or abridgement of the publicity afforded by a free press cannot be regarded otherwise than with grave concern. The tax here involved is bad not because it takes money from the pockets of the appellees. If that were all, a wholly different question would be presented. It is bad because, in the light of its history and of its present setting, it is seen to be a deliberate and calculated device in the guise of a tax to limit the circulation of information to which the public is entitled in virtue of the constitutional guaranties. A free press stands as one of the great interpreters between the government and the people. To allow it to be fettered is to fetter ourselves. . . .

222. *"Peaceable assembly for lawful discussion cannot be made a crime."*

DeJonge v. Oregon, 299 U.S. 353 (1937).

HUGHES, C.J.: . . . Appellant moved for a direction of acquittal, contending that the statute as applied to him, for merely assisting at a meeting called by the Communist party at which nothing unlawful was done or advocated, violated the due process clause of the Fourteenth Amendment of the Constitution of the United States. . . . Having limited the charge to defendant's participation in a meeting called by the Communist party, the State Court sustained the conviction upon that basis regardless of what was said or done at the meeting. . . .

The broad reach of the statute as thus applied is plain. While defendant was a member of the Communist party, that membership was not necessary to conviction on such a charge. A like fate might have attended any speaker, although not a member who "assisted in the conduct" of the meeting. However innocuous the object of the meeting, however lawful the subjects and tenor of the addresses, however reasonable and timely the discussion, all those assisting in the conduct of the meeting would be subject to imprisonment as felons if the meeting were held by the Communist party. . . .

Thus if the Communist party had called a public meeting in Portland to discuss the tariff, or the foreign policy of the government, or taxation, or relief, or candidacies for the offices of President, members of Congress, Governor or State legislators, every speaker who assisted in the conduct of the meeting would be equally guilty with the defendant in this case, upon the charge as here defined and sustained. . . .

While the States are entitled to protect themselves from the abuse of the privileges of our institutions through an attempted substitution of force and violence

in the place of peaceful political action in order to effect revolutionary changes in government, none of our decisions go to the length of sustaining such a curtailment of the right of free speech and assembly as the Oregon statute demands in its present application.

Freedom of speech and of the press are fundamental rights which are safeguarded by the due process clause of the Fourteenth Amendment of the Federal Constitution. The right of peaceable assembly is a right cognate to those of free speech and free press and is equally fundamental. . . .

The First Amendment of the Federal Constitution expressly guarantees that right against abridgment by Congress. But explicit mention there does not argue exclusion elsewhere. For the right is one that cannot be denied without violating those fundamental principles of liberty and justice which lie at the base of all civil and political institutions, principles which the Fourteenth Amendment embodies in the general terms of its due process clause.

These rights may be abused by using speech or press or assembly in order to incite to violence and crime. The people, through their Legislatures, may protect themselves against that abuse. But the legislative intervention can find constitutional justification only by dealing with the abuse. The rights themselves must not be curtailed.

The greater the importance of safeguarding the community from incitements to the overthrow of our institutions by force and violence, the more imperative is the need to preserve inviolate the constitutional rights of free speech, free press and free assembly in order to maintain the opportunity for free political discussion, to the end that government may be responsive to the will of the people and that changes, if desired, may be obtained by peaceful means. Therein lies the security of the republic, the very foundation of constitutional government.

It follows from these considerations that, consistently with the Federal Constitution, peaceable assembly for lawful discussion cannot be made a crime. The holding of meetings for peaceable political action cannot be proscribed. Those who assist in the conduct of such meetings cannot be branded as criminals on that score. The question, if the rights of free speech and peaceable assembly are to be preserved, is not as to the auspices under which the meeting is held, but as to its purpose; not as to the relations of the speakers, but whether their utterances transcend the bounds of the freedom of speech which the Constitution protects.

If the persons assemblying have committed crimes elsewhere, if they have formed or are engaged in a conspiracy against the public peace and order, they may be prosecuted for their conspiracy or other violation of valid laws.

But it is a different matter when the State, instead of prosecuting them for such offenses, seizes upon mere participation in a peaceable assembly and a lawful public discussion as the basis for a criminal charge.

We are not called upon to review the findings of the State court as to the objectives of the Communist party. Notwithstanding those objectives, the defendant still enjoyed his personal right of free speech and to take part in a peaceable assembly having a lawful purpose, although called by that party. The defendant was none the less entitled to discuss the public issues of the day and thus in a lawful manner, without incitement to violence or crime, to seek redress of alleged grievances. That was of the essence of his guaranteed personal liberty.

We hold that the Oregon statute as applied to the particular charge as defined by the State court is repugnant to the due process clause of the Fourteenth Amendment.

FREEDOM OF SPEECH, AND LABOR RELATIONS

223. *Is Picketing Speech?*

Thornhill v. Alabama, 310 U.S. 88 (1940).

MURPHY, J.: . . . The freedom of speech and of the press, which are secured by the First Amendment against abridgment by the United States, are among the fundamental personal rights and liberties which are secured to all persons by the Fourteenth Amendment against abridgment by a State.

The safeguarding of these rights to the ends that men may speak as they think on matters vital to them and that falsehoods may be exposed through the processes of education and discussion is essential to free government. Those who won our independence had confidence in the power of free and fearless reasoning and communication of ideas to discover and spread political and economic truth. Noxious doctrines in those fields may be refuted and their evil averted by the courageous exercise of the right of free discussion. Abridgment of freedom of speech and of the press, however, impairs those opportunities for public education that are essential to effective exercise of the power of correcting error through the processes of popular government. . . . Mere legislative preference for one rather than another means for combatting substantive evils, therefore, may well prove an inadequate foundation on which to rest regulations which are aimed at or in their operation diminish the effective exercise of rights so necessary to the maintenance of democratic institutions. It is imperative that, when the effective exercise of these rights is claimed to be abridged, the courts should "weigh the circumstances" and "appraise the substantiality of the reasons advanced" in support of the challenged regulations. . . .

Proof of an abuse of power in the particular case has never been deemed a requisite for attack on the constitutionality of a statute purporting to license the dissemination of ideas. . . . The cases when interpreted in the light of their facts indicate that the rule is not based upon any assumption that application for the license would be refused or would result in the imposition of other unlawful regulations. Rather it derives from an appreciation of the character of the evil inherent in a licensing system. The power of the licensor against which John Milton directed his assault by his "Appeal for the Liberty of Unlicensed Printing" is pernicious not merely by reason of the censure of particular comments but by reason of the threat to censure comments on matters of public concern. It is not merely the sporadic abuse of power by the censor but the pervasive threat inherent in its very existence that constitutes the danger to freedom of discussion. See *Near v. Minnesota.* . . . A like threat is inherent in a penal statute, like that in question here, which does not aim specifically at evils within the allowable area of state control but, on the contrary, sweeps within its ambit other activities that in ordinary circumstances constitute an exercise of freedom of speech or of the press. The existence of such a statute, which readily lends itself to harsh and discriminatory enforcement by local prosecuting officials, against particular groups deemed to merit their displeasure, results in a continuous and pervasive restraint on all freedom of discussion that might reasonably be regarded as within

its purview. It is not any less effective or, if the restraint is not permissible, less pernicious than the restraint on freedom of discussion imposed by the threat of censorship. An accused, after arrest and conviction under such a statute, does not have to sustain the burden of demonstrating that the State could not constitutionally have written a different and specific statute covering his activities as disclosed by the charge and the evidence introduced against him. . . . Where regulations of the liberty of free discussion are concerned, there are special reasons for observing the rule that it is the statute, and not the accusation or the evidence under it, which prescribes the limits of permissible conduct and warns against transgression. . . .

The Alabama statute has been applied by the state courts so as to prohibit a single individual from walking slowly and peacefully back and forth on the public sidewalk in front of the premises of an employer, without speaking to anyone, carrying a sign or placard on a staff above his head stating only the fact that the employer did not employ union men affiliated with the American Federation of Labor; the purpose of the described activity was concededly to advise customers and prospective customers of the relationship existing between the employer and its employees and thereby to induce such customers not to patronize the employer. . . . The statute as thus authoritatively construed and applied leaves room for no exceptions based upon either the number of persons engaged in the proscribed activity, the peaceful character of their demeanor, the nature of their dispute with an employer, or the restrained character and the accurateness of the terminology used in notifying the public of the facts of the dispute. . . .

In sum, whatever the means used to publicize the facts of a labor dispute, whether by printed sign, by pamphlet, by word of mouth or otherwise, all such activity without exception is within the inclusive prohibition of the statute so long as it occurs in the vicinity of the scene of the dispute. . . .

We think that §3448 is invalid on its face.

The freedom of speech and of the press guaranteed by the Constitution embraces at the least the liberty to discuss publicly and truthfully all matters of public concern without previous restraint or fear of subsequent punishment. . . .

Free discussion concerning the conditions in industry and the causes of labor disputes appears to us indispensable to the effective and intelligent use of the processes of popular government to shape the destiny of modern industrial society. . . .

The range of activities proscribed by §3448, whether characterized as picketing or loitering or otherwise, embraces nearly every practicable, effective means whereby those interested—including the employees directly affected—may enlighten the public on the nature and causes of a labor dispute. The safeguarding of these means is essential to the securing of an informed and educated public opinion with respect to a matter which is of public concern. It may be that effective exercise of the means of advancing public knowledge may persuade some of those reached to refrain from entering into advantageous relations with the business establishment which is the scene of the dispute. Every expression of opinion on matters that are important has the potentiality of inducing action in the interests of one rather than another group in society. But the group in power at any moment may not impose penal sanctions on peaceful and truthful discussion of matters of public interest merely on a showing that others may thereby be persuaded to take action inconsistent with its interests. Abridgment of the liberty of such discussion can be justified only where the clear danger of substantive evils arises under circumstances affording no opportunity to test the merits of ideas by competition for acceptance in the market of public opinion. We hold that the danger of injury to an industrial concern is neither so serious nor so imminent as to justify the sweeping proscription of freedom of discussion embodied in §3448. . . .

224. *The Right of Workmen to Discuss Their Affairs*

Thomas v. Collins, 323 U.S. 516 (1944).

RUTLEDGE, J.: . . . The case confronts us again with the duty our system places on this Court to say where the individual's freedom ends and the State's power begins. Choice on that border, now as always delicate, is perhaps more so where the usual presumption supporting legislation is balanced by the preferred place given in our scheme to the great, the indispensable democratic freedoms secured by the First Amendment. . . .

That the State has power to regulate labor unions with a view to protecting the public interest is, as the Texas court said, hardly to be doubted. They cannot claim special immunity from regulation. Such regulation however, whether aimed at fraud or other abuses, must not trespass upon the domain set apart for free speech and free assembly. . . . The right thus to discuss, and inform people concerning, the advantages and disadvantages of unions and joining them is protected not only as part of free speech, but as part of free assembly. . . .

These rights of assembly and discussion are protected by the First Amendment. Whatever would restrict them, without sufficient occasion, would infringe its safeguards. The occasion was clearly protected. The speech was an essential part of the occasion, unless all meaning and purpose were to be taken from it. And the invitations, both general and particular, were parts of the speech, inseparable incidents of the occasion and of all that was said or done.

That there was restriction upon Thomas' right to speak and the rights of the workers to hear what he had to say, there can be no doubt. The threat of the restraining order, backed by the power of contempt, and of arrest for crime, hung over every word. . . .

No speaker, in such circumstances, safely could assume that anything he might say upon the general subject would not be understood by some as an invitation. In short, the supposedly clear-cut distinction between discussion, laudation, general advocacy, and solicitation puts the speaker in these circumstances wholly at the mercy of the varied understanding of his hearers and consequently of whatever inference may be drawn as to his intent and meaning.

Such a distinction offers no security for free discussion. In these conditions it blankets with uncertainty whatever may be said. It compels the speaker to hedge and trim. He must take care in every word to create no impression that he means, in advocating unionism's most central principle, namely, that workingmen should unite for collective bargaining, to urge those present to do so. The vice is not merely that invitation, in the circumstances shown here, is speech. It is also that its prohibition forbids or restrains discussion which is not or may not be invitation. The sharp line cannot be drawn surely or securely. The effort to observe it could not be free speech, free press, or free assembly, in any sense of free advocacy of principle or cause. The restriction's effect, as applied, in a very practical sense was to prohibit Thomas not only to solicit members and memberships, but also to speak in advocacy of the cause of trade unionism in Texas, without having first procured the card. Thomas knew this and faced the alternatives it presented. When served with the order he had three choices: (1) to stand on his right and speak freely; (2) to quit, refusing entirely to speak; (3) to trim, and even thus to risk the penalty. He chose the first alternative. We think he was within his rights in doing so.

The assembly was entirely peaceable, and had no other than a wholly lawful purpose. The statements forbidden were not in themselves unlawful, had no tendency to incite to unlawful action, involved no element of clear and present, grave and immediate danger to the public welfare. Moreover, the State has shown no justification for placing restrictions on the use of the word "solicit." We have here nothing comparable to the case where use of the word "fire" in a crowded theater creates a clear and present danger which the State may undertake to avoid or against which it may protect. *Schenck v. United States.* . . . We cannot say that "solicit" in this setting is such a dangerous word. So far as free speech alone is concerned, there can be no ban or restriction or burden placed on the use of such a word except on showing of exceptional circumstances where the public safety, morality or health is involved or some other substantial interest of the community is at stake.

If therefore use of the word or language equivalent in meaning was illegal here, it was so only because the statute and the order forbade the particular speaker to utter it. When legislation or its application can confine labor leaders on such occasions to innocuous and abstract discussion of the virtues of trade unions and so becloud even this with doubt, uncertainty and the risk of penalty, freedom of speech for them will be at an end. A restriction so destructive of the right of public discussion, without greater or more imminent danger to the public interest than existed in this case, is incompatible with the freedoms secured by the First Amendment. . . .

Apart from its "business practice" theory, the State contends that Section 5 is not inconsistent with freedom of speech and assembly, since this is merely a previous identification requirement which, according to the State court's decision, gives the Secretary of State only "ministerial, not discretionary" authority.

How far the State can require previous identification by one who undertakes to exercise the rights secured by the First Amendment has been largely undetermined. . . .

As a matter of principle a requirement of registration in order to make a public speech would seem generally incompatible with an exercise of the rights of free speech and free assembly. Lawful public assemblies, involving no element of grave and immediate danger to an interest the state is entitled to protect, are not instruments of harm which require previous identification of the speakers. And the right either of workmen or of unions under these conditions to assemble and discuss their own affairs is as fully protected by the Constitution as the right of businessmen, farmers, educators, political party members or others to assemble and discuss their affairs and to enlist the support of others.

We think the controlling principle is stated in *DeJonge v. Oregon.* . . . In that case this Court held that "consistently with the Federal Constitution, peaceable assembly for lawful discussion cannot be made a crime." . . .

If the exercise of the rights of free speech and free assembly cannot be made a crime, we do not think this can be accomplished by the device of requiring previous registration as a condition for exercising them and making such a condition the foundation for restraining in advance their exercise and for imposing a penalty for violating such a restraining order. So long as no more is involved than exercise of the rights of free speech and free assembly, it is immune to such a restriction. If one who solicits support for the cause of labor may be required to register as a condition to the exercise of his right to make a public speech, so may he who seeks to rally support for any social, business, religious or political cause. We think a requirement that one must register before he undertakes to make a public speech to enlist support for a lawful movement is quite incompatible with the requirements of the First Amendment.

Once the speaker goes further, however, and engages in conduct which amounts to more than the right of free discussion comprehends, as when he undertakes the collection of funds or securing subscriptions, he enters a realm where a reasonable registration or identification requirement may be imposed. In that context such solicitation would be quite different from the solicitation involved here. . . .

As we think the requirement of registration, in the present circumstances, was in itself an invalid restriction, we have no occasion to consider whether the restraint as imposed goes beyond merely requiring previous identification or registration. . . .

The restraint is not small when it is considered what was restrained. The right is a national right, federally guaranteed. There is some modicum of freedom of thought, speech and assembly which all citizens of the Republic may exercise throughout its length and breadth, which no State, nor all together, nor the Nation itself, can prohibit, restrain or impede. If the restraint were smaller than it is, it is from petty tyrannies that large ones take root and grow. This fact can be no more plain than when they are imposed on the most basic rights of all. Seedlings planted in that soil grow great and, growing, break down the foundations of liberty. . . .

RELIGION AND SPEECH

225. *Preaching, Pamphlet Peddling, and Privacy*

Murdock v. Pennsylvania, 319 U.S. 105 (1943).

DOUGLAS, J.: . . . The First Amendment, which the Fourteenth makes applicable to the states, declares that "Congress shall make no law respecting an establishment of religion, or prohibiting the free exercise thereof; or abridging the freedom of speech, or of the press. . . ." It could hardly be denied that a tax laid specifically on the exercise of those freedoms would be unconstitutional. Yet the license tax imposed by this ordinance is, in substance, just that.

Petitioners spread their interpretations of the Bible and their religious beliefs largely through the hand distribution of literature by full or part time workers. They claim to follow the example of Paul, teaching "publickly, and from house to house." Acts 20:20. . . .

The hand distribution of religious tracts is an age-old form of missionary evangelism—as old as the history of printing presses. It has been a potent force in various religious movements down through the years. This form of evangelism is utilized today on a large scale by various religious sects whose colporteurs carry the Gospel to thousands upon thousands of homes and seek through personal visitations to win adherents to their faith. It is more than preaching; it is more than distribution of religious literature. It is a combination of both. Its purpose is as evangelical as the revival meeting. This form of religious activity occupies the same high estate under the First Amendment as do worship in the churches and preaching from the pulpits. It has the same claim to protection as the more orthodox and conventional exercises of religion. It also has the same claim as the others to the guarantees of freedom of speech and freedom of the press. . . .

We are concerned, however, in these cases merely with one narrow issue. . . . The cases present a single issue—the constitutionality of an ordinance which as construed and applied requires religious colporteurs to pay a license tax as a condition to the pursuit of their activities.

The alleged justification for the exaction of this license tax is the fact that the religious literature is distributed with a solicitation of funds. . . . But the mere fact that the religious literature is "sold" by itinerant preachers rather than "donated" does not transform evangelism into a commercial enterprise. If it did, then the passing of the collection plate in church would make the church service a commercial project. The constitutional rights of those spreading their religious beliefs through the spoken and printed word are not to be gauged by standards governing retailers or wholesalers of books. The right to use the press for expressing one's views is not to be measured by the protection afforded commercial handbills. It should be remembered that the pamphlets of Thomas Paine were not distributed free of charge. It is plain that a religious organization needs funds to remain a going concern. But an itinerant evangelist, however misguided or intolerant he may be, does not become a mere book agent by selling the Bible or religious tracts to help defray his expenses or to sustain him. Freedom of speech, freedom of the press, freedom of religion are available to all, not merely to those who can pay their own way. As we have said, the problem of drawing the line between a purely commercial activity and a religious one will at times be difficult. On this record it plainly cannot be said that petitioners were engaged in a commercial rather than a religious venture. It is a distortion of the facts of record to describe their activities as the occupation of selling books and pamphlets. . . .

We do not mean to say that religious groups and the press are free from all financial burdens of government. See *Grosjean v. American Press Co.* . . . We have here something quite different, for example, from a tax on the income of one who engages in religious activities or a tax on property used or employed in connection with those activities. It is one thing to impose a tax on the income or property of a preacher. It is quite another thing to exact a tax from him for the privilege of delivering a sermon. The tax imposed by the City of Jeannette is a flat license tax, the payment of which is a condition of the exercise of these constitutional privileges. The power to tax the exercise of a privilege is the power to control or suppress its enjoyment. *Magnano Co. v. Hamilton.* . . . Those who can tax the

exercise of this religious practice can make its exercise so costly as to deprive it of the resources necessary for its maintenance. Those who can tax the privilege of engaging in this form of missionary evangelism can close its doors to all those who do not have a full purse. Spreading religious beliefs in this ancient and honorable manner would thus be denied the needy. Those who can deprive religious groups of their colporteurs can take from them a part of the vital power of the press which has survived from the Reformation.

It is contended, however, that the fact that the license tax can suppress or control this activity is unimportant if it does not do so. But that is to disregard the nature of this tax. It is a license tax—a flat tax imposed on the exercise of a privilege granted by the Bill of Rights. A state may not impose a charge for the enjoyment of a right granted by the Federal Constitution. . . .

226. *Conformity and Liberty: The Flag Salute Cases*

West Virginia State Board v. Barnette, 319 U.S. 624 (1943).

JACKSON, J.: . . . Appellees, citizens of the United States and of West Virginia, brought suit in the United States District Court for themselves and others similarly situated asking its injunction to restrain enforcement of these laws and regulations against Jehovah's Witnesses. The Witnesses are an unincorporated body teaching that the obligation imposed by law of God is superior to that of laws enacted by temporal government. Their religious beliefs include a literal version of Exodus, Chapter 20, verses 4 and 5, which says: "Thou shalt not make unto thee any graven image, or any likeness of anything that is in heaven above, or that is in the earth beneath, or that is in the water under the earth; thou shalt not bow down thyself to them, nor serve them." They consider that the Flag is an "image" within

this command. For this reason they refuse to salute it. . . .

This case calls upon us to reconsider a precedent decision, as the Court throughout its history often has been required to do. Before turning to the Gobitis case, however, it is desirable to notice certain characteristics by which this controversy is distinguished.

The freedom asserted by these appellees does not bring them into collision with rights asserted by any other individual. It is such conflicts which most frequently require intervention of the State to determine where the rights of one end and those of another begin. But the refusal of these persons to participate in the ceremony does not interfere with or deny rights of others to do so. Nor is there any question in this case that their behavior is peaceable and orderly. The sole conflict is between authority and rights of the individual. The State asserts power to condition access to public education on making a prescribed sign and profession and at the same time to coerce attendance by punishing both parent and child. The latter stand on a right of self-determination in matters that touch individual opinion and personal attitude.

As the present Chief Justice said in dissent in the Gobitis case, the State may "require teaching by instruction and study of all in our history and in the structure and organization of our government, including the guaranties of civil liberty, which tend to inspire patriotism and love of country." Here, however, we are dealing with a compulsion of students to declare a belief. They are not merely made acquainted with the flag salute so that they may be informed as to what it is or even what it means. The issue here is whether this slow and easily neglected route to aroused loyalties constitutionally may be short-cut by substituting a compulsory salute and slogan. . . .

There is no doubt that, in connection with the pledges, the flag salute is a form of utterance. Symbolism is a primitive but effective way of communicating ideas. The use of an emblem or flag to symbolize some system, idea, institution, or personality, is a short cut from mind to mind. . . .

It is also to be noted that the compulsory flag salute and pledge requires affirmation of a belief and an attitude of mind. It is not clear whether the regulation contemplates that pupils forego any contrary convictions of their own and become unwilling converts to the prescribed ceremony or whether it will be acceptable if they simulate assent by words without belief and by a gesture barren of meaning. It is now a commonplace that censorship or suppression of expression of opinion is tolerated by our Constitution only when the expression presents a clear and present danger of action of a kind the State is empowered to prevent and pun-

ish. It would seem that involuntary affirmation could be commanded only on even more immediate and urgent grounds than silence. But here the power of compulsion is invoked without any allegation that remaining passive during a flag salute ritual creates a clear and present danger that would justify an effort even to muffle expression. To sustain the compulsory flag salute we are required to say that a Bill of Rights which guards the individual's right to speak his own mind, left it open to public authorities to compel him to utter what is not in his mind.

Whether the First Amendment to the Constitution will permit officials to order observance of ritual of this nature does not depend upon whether as a voluntary exercise we would think it to be good, bad or merely innocuous. . . .

Nor does the issue as we see it turn on one's possession of particular religious views or the sincerity with which they are held. While religion supplies appellees' motive for enduring the discomforts of making the issue in this case, many citizens who do not share these religious views hold such a compulsory rite to infringe constitutional liberty of the individual. It is not necessary to inquire whether non-conformist beliefs will exempt from the duty to salute unless we first find power to make the salute a legal duty.

The Gobitis decision, however, *assumed*, as did the argument in that case and in this, that power exists in the State to impose the flag salute discipline upon school children in general. The Court only examined and rejected a claim based on religious beliefs of immunity from an unquestioned general rule. The question which underlies the flag salute controversy is whether such a ceremony so touching matters of opinion and political attitude may be imposed upon the individual by official authority under powers committed to any political organization under our Constitution. . . .

In weighing arguments of the parties

it is important to distinguish between the due process clause of the Fourteenth Amendment as an instrument for transmitting the principles of the First Amendment and those cases in which it is applied for its own sake. The test of legislation which collides with the Fourteenth Amendment, because it also collides with the principles of the First, is much more definite than the test when only the Fourteenth is involved. Much of the vagueness of the due process clause disappears when the specific prohibitions of the First become its standard. The right of a State to regulate, for example, a public utility may well include, so far as the due process test is concerned, power to impose all of the restrictions which a legislature may have a "rational basis" for adopting. But freedoms of speech and of press, of assembly, and of worship may not be infringed on such slender grounds. They are susceptible of restriction only to prevent grave and immediate danger to interests which the State may lawfully protect. It is important to note that while it is the Fourteenth Amendment which bears directly upon the State it is the more specific limiting principles of the First Amendment that finally govern this case.

Nor does our duty to apply the Bill of Rights to assertions of official authority depend upon our possession of marked competence in the field where the invasion of rights occurs. True, the task of translating the majestic generalities of the Bill of Rights, conceived as part of the pattern of liberal government in the eighteenth century, into concrete restraints on officials dealing with the problems of the twentieth century, is one to disturb self-confidence. These principles grew in soil which also produced a philosophy that the individual was the center of society, that his liberty was attainable through mere absence of governmental restraints, and that government should be entrusted with few controls and only the mildest supervision over men's affairs. We must transplant these rights to a soil in which

the laissez-faire concept or principle of non-interference has withered at least as to economic affairs, and social advancements are increasingly sought through closer integration of society and through expanded and strengthened governmental controls. These changed conditions often deprive precedents of reliability and cast us more than we would choose upon our own judgment. But we act in these matters not by authority of our competence but by force of our commissions. We cannot, because of modest estimates of our competence in such specialties as public education, withhold the judgment that history authenticates as the function of this Court when liberty is infringed. . . .

The case is made difficult not because the principles of its decision are obscure but because the flag involved is our own. Nevertheless, we apply the limitations of the Constitution with no fear that freedom to be intellectually and spiritually diverse or even contrary will disintegrate the social organization. To believe that patriotism will not flourish if patriotic ceremonies are voluntary and spontaneous instead of a compulsory routine is to make an unflattering estimate of the appeal of our institutions to free minds. We can have intellectual individualism and the rich cultural diversities that we owe to exceptional minds only at the price of occasional eccentricity and abnormal attitudes. When they are so harmless to others or to the State as those we deal with here, the price is not too great. But freedom to differ is not limited to things that do not matter much. That would be a mere shadow of freedom. The test of its substance is the right to differ as to things that touch the heart of the existing order.

If there is any fixed star in our constitutional constellation, it is that no official, high or petty, can prescribe what shall be orthodox in politics, nationalism, religion, or other matters of opinion or force citizens to confess by word or act their faith therein. If there are any circumstances which permit an exception, they do not now occur to us.

We think the action of the local authorities in compelling the flag salute and pledge transcends constitutional limitations on their power and invades the sphere of intellect and spirit which it is the purpose of the First Amendment . . . to reserve from all official control. . . .

Procedural Safeguards of Civil Rights

227. *Forced Confessions*

Chambers v. Florida, 309 U.S. 227 (1940).

BLACK, J.: . . . The grave question . . . presented is whether proceedings in which confessions were utilized, and which culminated in sentences of death upon four young negro men in the state of Florida, failed to afford the safeguard of that due process of law guaranteed by the Fourteenth Amendment. . . .

After one week's constant denial of all guilt, petitioners "broke."

Just before sunrise, the state officials got something "worthwhile" from petitioners which the state's attorney would "want"; again he was called; he came; in the presence of those who had carried on and witnessed the all night questioning, he caused his questions and petitioners' answers to be stenographically reported. These are the confessions utilized by the state to obtain the judgments upon which petitioners were sentenced to death. . . . When Chambers was tried, his conviction rested upon his confession and testimony of the other three confessors. The convict guard and the sheriff "were in the court room sitting down in a seat." And from arrest until sentenced to death, petitioners were never—either in jail or in court —wholly removed from the constant observation, influence, custody and control of those whose persistent pressure brought about the sunrise confessions. . . .

The scope and operation of the Four-teenth Amendment have been fruitful sources of controversy in our constitutional history. However, in view of its historical setting and the wrongs which called it into being, the due process provision of the Fourteenth Amendment— just as that in the Fifth—has led few to doubt that it was intended to guarantee procedural standards adequate and appropriate, then and thereafter, to protect, at all times, people charged with or suspected of crime by those holding positions of power and authority. . . .

The determination to preserve an accused's right to procedural due process sprang in large part from knowledge of the historical truth that the rights and liberties of people accused of crime could not be safely entrusted to secret inquisitorial processes. The testimony of centuries, in governments of varying kinds over populations of different races and beliefs, stood as proof that physical and mental torture and coercion had brought about the tragically unjust sacrifices of some who were the noblest and most useful of their generations. The rack, the thumbscrew, the wheel, solitary confinement, protracted questioning and cross questioning, and other ingenious forms of entrapment of the helpless or unpopular had left their wake of mutilated bodies and shattered minds along the way to the cross, the guillotine, the stake and the hangman's noose. And they who have suffered most from secret and dictatorial proceedings have almost always been the poor, the ignorant, the numerically weak, the friendless, and the powerless.

This requirement—of conforming to fundamental standards of procedure in criminal trials—was made operative against the states by the Fourteenth Amendment. . . . To permit human lives to be forfeited upon confessions thus obtained would make of the constitutional requirement of due process of law a meaningless symbol. . . .

We are not impressed by the argument that law enforcement methods such as those under review are necessary to uphold our laws. The Constitution proscribes such lawless means irrespective of the end. And this argument flouts the basic principle that all people must stand on an equality before the bar of justice in every

American court. Today, as in ages past, we are not without tragic proof that the exalted power of some governments to punish manufactured crime dictatorially is the handmaid of tyranny. Under our constitutional system, courts stand against any winds that blow as havens of refuge for those who might otherwise suffer because they are helpless, weak, outnumbered, or because they are non-conforming victims of prejudice and public excitement. Due process of law, preserved for all by our Constitution, commands that no such practice as that disclosed by this record shall send any accused to his death. No higher duty, no more solemn responsibility, rests upon this Court, than that of translating into living law and maintaining this constitutional shield deliberately planned and inscribed for the benefit of every human being subject to our Constitution—of whatever race, creed or persuasion.

228. *The Right to Counsel*

Benjamin V. Cohen and Erwin N. Griswold to *The New York Times*, July 29, 1942; published August 2, 1942, 6E.

The important facts in *Betts v. Brady* were simple and undisputed. Betts, a farm hand, was indicted for robbery, [and] the maximum penalty . . . under the laws of Maryland is twenty years' imprisonment. Having no funds, the accused requested the court to appoint counsel for him. The trial judge refused, asserting that it was not the practice in Carroll County, Md. to appoint counsel for indigent defendants save in prosecutions for murder and rape. . . .

Most Americans—lawyers and laymen alike—before the [Supreme Court's] decision in *Betts v. Brady* would have thought that the right of the accused to counsel in a serious criminal case was un-

questionably a part of our own Bill of Rights. Certainly the majority of the Supreme Court which rendered the decision . . . would not wish their decision to be used to discredit the significance of that right and the importance of its observance.

Yet at a critical period in world history, *Betts v. Brady* dangerously tilts the scales against the safeguarding of one of the most precious rights of man. For in a free world no man should be condemned to penal servitude for years without having the right of counsel to defend him. The right to counsel, for the poor as well as the rich, is an indispensable safeguard of freedom and justice under law.

Suffrage and Segregation

229. The "White Primary" Outlawed

Smith v. Allwright, 321 U.S. 649 (1944).

REED, J.: . . . Texas is free to conduct her elections and limit her electorate as she may deem wise, save only as her action may be affected by the prohibitions of the United States Constitution or in conflict with powers delegated to and exercised by the National Government. The Fourteenth Amendment forbids a State from making or enforcing any law which abridges the privileges or immunities of citizens of the United States and the Fifteenth Amendment specifically interdicts any denial or abridgement by a State of the right of citizens to vote on account of color. Respondents appeared in the District Court and the Circuit Court of Appeals and defended on the ground that the Democratic party of Texas is a voluntary organization with members banded together for the purpose of selecting individuals of the group representing the common political beliefs as candidates in the general election. As such a voluntary organization, it was claimed, the Democratic party is free to select its own membership and limit to whites participation in the party primary. Such action, the answer asserted, does not violate the Fourteenth, Fifteenth or Seventeenth Amendment as officers of government cannot be chosen at primaries and the Amendments are applicable only to general elections where governmental officers are actually elected. Primaries, it is said, are political party affairs, handled by party, not governmental, officers. . . .

Since *Grovey v. Townsend* and prior to the present suit, no case from Texas involving primary elections has been before this Court. We did decide, however,

United States v. Classic. . . . The fusing by the Classic case of the primary and general elections into a single instrumentality for choice of officers has a definite bearing on the permissibility under the Constitution of excluding Negroes from primaries. . . . Classic bears upon *Grovey v. Townsend* not because exclusion of Negroes from primaries is any more or less state action by reason of the unitary character of the electoral process but because the recognition of the place of the primary in the electoral scheme makes clear that state delegation to a party of the power to fix the qualifications of primary elections is delegation of a state function that may make the party's action the action of the State. When *Grovey v. Townsend* was written, the Court looked upon the denial of a vote in a primary, as a mere refusal by a party of party membership. As the Louisiana statutes for holding primaries are similar to those of Texas, our ruling in Classic as to the unitary character of the electoral process calls for a reexamination as to whether or not the exclusion of Negroes from a Texas party primary was state action. . . .

It may now be taken as a postulate that the right to vote in such a primary for the nomination of candidates without discrimination by the State, like the right to vote in a general election, is a right secured by the Constitution. By the terms of the Fifteenth Amendment that right may not be abridged by any State on account of race. Under our Constitution the great privilege of the ballot may not be denied a man by the State because of his color.

We are thus brought to an examination of the qualifications for Democratic primary electors in Texas, to determine whether state action or private action has excluded Negroes from participation. . . . [The Court then summarizes Texas statutes regulating primaries.]

We think that this statutory system for the selection of party nominees for inclusion on the general election ballot makes the party which is required to follow these legislative directions an agency of the State in so far as it determines the participants in a primary election. The party takes its character as a state agency from the duties imposed upon it by state statutes; the duties do not become matters of private law because they are performed by a political party. The plan of the Texas primary follows substantially that of Louisiana, with the exception that in Louisiana the State pays the cost of the primary while Texas assesses the cost against candidates. In numerous instances, the Texas statutes fix or limit the fees to be charged. Whether paid directly by the State or through state requirements, it is state action which compels. When primaries become a part of the machinery for choosing officials, state and national, as they have here, the same tests to determine the character of discrimination or abridgement should be applied to the primary as are applied to the general election. If the State requires a certain electoral procedure, prescribes a general election ballot made up of party nominees so chosen and limits the choice of the electorate in general elections for state offices, practically speaking, to those whose names appear on such a ballot, it endorses, adopts and enforces the discrimination against Negroes, practiced by a party entrusted by Texas law with the determination of the qualifications of participants in the primary. This is state action within the meaning of the Fifteenth Amendment.

The United States is a constitutional democracy. Its organic law grants to all citizens a right to participate in the choice of elected officials without restriction by any State because of race. This grant to the people of the opportunity for choice is not to be nullified by a State through casting its electoral process in a form which permits a private organization to practice racial discrimination in the election. Constitutional rights would be of little value if they could be thus indirectly denied.

The privilege of membership in a party may be, as this Court said in *Grovey v. Townsend*, . . . no concern of a State. But when, as here, that privilege is also the essential qualification for voting in a primary to select nominees for a general election, the State makes the action of the party the action of the State. . . . Here we are applying, contrary to the recent decision in *Grovey v. Townsend*, the well-established principle of the Fifteenth Amendment, forbidding the abridgement by a State of a citizen's right to vote. *Grovey v. Townsend* is overruled.

230. *"Equality" in the "Separate but Equal" Doctrine*

Missouri ex rel. Gaines v. Canada, 305 U.S. 337 (1938).

HUGHES, C.J.: . . . Petitioner is a citizen of Missouri. In August, 1935, he was graduated with the degree of Bachelor of Arts at the Lincoln University, an institution maintained by the State of Missouri for the higher education of negroes. That University has no law school. Upon the filing of his application for admission to the law school of the University of Missouri, the registrar advised him to communicate with the president of Lincoln University and the latter directed petitioner's attention to §9622 of the Revised Statutes of Missouri. . . .

Petitioner was advised to apply to the State Superintendent of Schools for aid under that statute. . . . It appears that there are schools of law in connection with the state universities of four adjacent States, Kansas, Nebraska, Iowa, and Illinois, where nonresident negroes are admitted. . . .

While there is no express constitutional provision requiring that the white and negro races be separated for the purpose of higher education, the state court on a comprehensive review of the state statutes held that it was intended to separate the white and negro races for that purpose also. Referring in particular to Lincoln University, the court deemed it to be clear "that the Legislature intended to bring the Lincoln University up to the standard of the University of Missouri, and give to the whites and negroes an equal opportunity for higher education— the whites at the University of Missouri, and the negroes at Lincoln University." Further, the court concluded that the provisions of §9622 . . . to the effect that negro residents "may attend the university of any adjacent State with their tuition paid, pending the full development of Lincoln University," made it evident "that the Legislature did not intend that negroes and whites should attend the same university in this State." In that view it necessarily followed that the curators of the University of Missouri acted in accordance with the policy of the State in denying petitioner admission to its School of Law upon the sole ground of his race.

In answering petitioner's contention that this discrimination constituted a denial of his constitutional right, the state court has fully recognized the obligation of the State to provide negroes with advantages for higher education substantially equal to the advantages afforded to white students. The State has sought to fulfill that obligation by furnishing equal facilities in separate schools, a method the validity of which has been sustained by our decisions. . . .

The state court stresses the advantages that are afforded by the schools of the adjacent States . . . which admit non-resident negroes. . . . Petitioner insists that for one intending to practice in Missouri there are special advantages in attending a law school there, both in relation to the opportunities for the particular study of Missouri law and for the observation of the local courts, and also in view of the prestige of the Missouri law school among the citizens of the State, his prospective clients. Proceeding with its examination of relative advantages, the state court found that the difference in distances to be traveled afforded no substantial ground of complaint and that there was an adequate appropriation to meet the full tuition fees which petitioner would have to pay.

We think that these matters are beside the point. The basic consideration is not as to what sort of opportunities other States provide, or whether they are as good as those in Missouri, but as to what opportunities Missouri itself furnishes to white students and denies to negroes solely upon the ground of color. The admissibility of laws separating the races in the enjoyment of privileges afforded by the State rests wholly upon the equality of the privileges which the laws give to the separated groups within the State. The question here is not of a duty of the State to supply legal training, or of the quality of the training which it does supply, but of its duty when it provides such training to furnish it to the residents of the State upon the basis of an equality of right. By the operation of the laws of Missouri a privilege has been created for white law students which is denied to negroes by reason of their race. The white resident is afforded legal education within the State; the negro resident having the same qualifications is refused it there and must go outside the State to obtain it. That is a denial of the equality of legal right to the enjoyment of the privilege which the State has set up, and the provision for the payment of tuition fees in another State does not remove the discrimination. . . .

In the instant case, the state court did note that petitioner had not applied to the management of Lincoln University for legal training. But, as we have said, the state court did not rule that it would have been the duty of the curators to grant such an application, but on the contrary took the view, as we understand it, that the curators were entitled under the state law to refuse such an application and in its stead to provide for petitioner's tuition in an adjacent State. That conclusion presented the federal question as to the constitutional adequacy of such a provision while equal opportunity for legal training within the State was not furnished, and this federal question the state court entertained and passed upon. We must conclude that in so doing the court denied the federal right which petitioner set up and the question as to the correctness of that decision is before us. We are of the opinion that the ruling was in error, and that petitioner was entitled to be admitted to the law school of the State University in the absence of other and proper provision for his legal training within the State. . . .

Legislative Punishment

231. Legislative Trials and Bills of Attainder

U.S. v. Lovett, Watson, and Dodd, 328 U.S. 303 (1946).

BLACK, J.: . . . We hold that the purpose of §304 was not merely to cut off respondents' compensation through regular disbursing channels but permanently to bar them from government service, and that the issue of whether it is constitutional is justiciable. The Section's language as well as the circumstances of its passage which we have just described show that no mere question of compensation procedure or of appropriations was involved, but that it was designed to force the employing agencies to discharge respondents and to bar their being hired by any other governmental agency. . . . Any other interpretation of the section would completely frustrate the purpose of all who sponsored §304, which clearly was to "purge" the then existing and all future lists of government employees of those whom Congress deemed guilty of "subversive activi-ties" and therefore "unfit" to hold a federal job. What was challenged, therefore, is a statute which, because of what Congress thought to be their political beliefs, prohibited respondents from ever engaging in any government work, except as jurors or soldiers. . . .

We hold that §304 falls precisely within the category of Congressional actions which the Constitution barred by providing that "No Bill of Attainder or Ex Post Facto Law shall be passed." . . . [Neither Cummings v. Missouri nor Ex parte Garland have] ever been overruled. They stand for the proposition that legislative acts, no matter what their form, that apply either to named individuals or to easily ascertainable members of a group in such a way as to inflict punishment on them without a judicial trial are bills of attainder prohibited by the Constitution.

Adherence to this principle requires invalidation of §304. We do adhere to it.

Section 304 was designed to apply to particular individuals. Just as the statute in the two cases mentioned it "operates as a legislative decree of perpetual exclusion" from a chosen vocation. . . . This permanent proscription from any opportunity to serve the Government is punishment, and of a most severe type. It is a type of punishment which Congress has only invoked for special types of odious and dangerous crimes, such as treason, . . . acceptance of bribes by members of Congress, . . . or by other government officials. . . ; and interference with elections by Army and Navy officers. . . .

Section 304, thus, clearly accomplishes the punishment of named individuals without a judicial trial. The fact that the punishment is inflicted through the instrumentality of an Act specifically cutting off the pay of certain named individuals found guilty of disloyalty, makes it no less galling or effective than if it had been done by an Act which designated the conduct as criminal. . . . The effect was to inflict punishment without the safeguards of a judicial trial and "determined by no previous law or fixed rule." The Constitution declares that that cannot be done either by a State or by the United States.

Those who wrote our Constitution well knew the danger inherent in special legislative acts which take away the life, liberty, or property of particular named persons because the legislature thinks them guilty of conduct which deserves punishment. They intended to safeguard the people of this country from punishment without trial by duly constituted courts. . . . Our ancestors had ample reason to know that legislative trials and punishments were too dangerous to liberty to exist in the nation of free men they envisioned. And so they proscribed bills of attainder. Section 304 is one. Much as we regret to declare that an Act of Congress violates the Constitution, we have no alternative here. . . .

CHAPTER XXV

Total War and the Constitution

THE effort to extend democratic guarantees at home was soon overshadowed by the growing antidemocratic threats abroad. For the third time in less than a century, war created the problem of adapting constitutional processes to cataclysmic national emergency. Precedents set in World War I smoothed the way for prompt mobilization. Indeed, the First War Powers Act of December, 1941, virtually re-enacted the provisions of the Overman Act of 1918 (Chapter XIX). Moreover, the frequent resort to the doctrine of emergency powers during the depression years accustomed Congress, the courts, and the people to acquiesce in plenary executive authority. Like Lincoln and Wilson, Roosevelt often exercised Presidential prerogative prior to congressional approval. Such was the case in the establishment of the Office of Price Administration, the most powerful independent administrative agency in World War II. In April, 1941, long before Congress granted price-fixing powers, the O. P. A. was created by executive order. The crisis of Pearl Harbor brought statutory approval early in 1942, when Congress delegated to this agency virtually unlimited legislative authority over the national economy.

In *Yakus v. U.S.* (No. 232), the Emergency Price Control Act was attacked as an unconstitutional delegation of legislative power without adequate standards for determining "fair and equitable" price ceilings. Following the peacetime rule formulated in a fair labor standards case in 1941 (*Opp Cotton Mills v. Adminis-*

trator), Chief Justice Stone strongly defended broad delegation of discretionary authority. The question of enforcement of administrative orders also reached the Court in 1944 at a critical moment of the war effort. In *Steuart & Bros. v. Bowles,* an O. P. A. order penalizing an oil distributor for violating the rationing system was upheld as a necessary implication of the Second War Powers Act of 1942, even though the O. P. A. order was alleged to be punishment without proper judicial process.

Just as Congress controlled consumer prices during the wartime emergency, so, too, did it move to protect the public from profiteering on government contracts. To curb excessive profits, Congress passed the Renegotiation Act authorizing the reopening of contracts when evidence indicated that the government was being "gouged." The question of the establishment of a sufficient standard for defining excessive profits was raised in *Lichter v. U.S.* (No. 233). Emphasizing "the compelling necessity for the immediate production" of war goods at reasonable prices, Justice Burton upheld the measure as a policy necessary to prosecute "total global warfare."

Wartime curbs on economic activity were accompanied by similar restrictions on individual liberties. Interestingly enough, one of the early questions related not to the protection of the rights of American citizens but to that of enemy military personnel. In 1942 eight Nazi saboteurs sneaked ashore in New York and Florida from a German submarine. Promptly seized by the F. B. I., the Germans were tried by a special military commission. In a spectacular move, the prisoners challenged the military trial and appealed to the Supreme Court for writs of habeas corpus. Although the Court upheld the military proceedings (*Ex parte* Quirin, 1942), the fact that it would consider whether these persons were protected by basic constitutional provisions suggested that the Court would weigh carefully any governmental invasion of individual rights. As Chief Justice Stone stated, "the court's duty . . . in time of war as well as in time of peace [is] to preserve unimpaired the constitutional safeguards of civil liberty." In an important postwar case (*In re* Yamashita [No. 234]), the Court again reviewed the conduct of military trials of enemy personnel. Although some have contended that the Court's willingness to examine the prisoner's protest against summary military conviction alone constituted an important safeguard to civil liberty, others have condemned the failure to adhere to fundamental procedural guarantees.

Of much greater constitutional consequence was the question of military control of American civilians. Only hours after bombs fell on Pearl Harbor, the governor of Hawaii, acting in conformity with the Hawaiian Organic Act of 1900, placed the territory under martial law, and surrendered governing authority to the army. Until 1944 military tribunals replaced civilian courts in the administration of criminal justice. Not until 1946 was there a successful challenge to summary military trials. In a case involving the conviction of a civilian shipfitter for brawling with Marine sentries (*Duncan v. Kahanamoku* [No. 235]), the Court ruled that the Hawaiian Organic Act "was not intended to authorize the supplanting of courts by military tribunals."

World War II also afforded the Supreme Court the first opportunity in the nation's history to define the meaning of the treason clause in the Constitution. The two leading treason trials were an aftermath to the case of the Nazi saboteurs. In *Cramer v. U.S.* (1945), the Court insisted on a narrow definition of treason, and ruled that Cramer's consorting with the saboteurs did not constitute an "overt act" clearly manifesting treasonable intentions. In *Haupt v. U.S.* (No. 236), however, the Supreme Court, for the first time in its history, upheld a treason conviction. Although the case was quite similar to Cramer's, the Court modified its restrictive interpretation of "overt acts," and made possible the subsequent prosecution of several American citizens for giving aid and comfort to the enemy in time of war.

The most drastic invasion of the rights of citizens by the federal government in American history occurred when President Roosevelt issued an executive order in February, 1942, later reinforced by congressional enactment, authorizing exclusion of "any or all persons" from areas designated by local military commanders. Aimed at the Japanese-Americans on the West coast, this program established detention camps into which 112,000 uprooted Japanese were herded. Cases challenging such summary treatment soon reached the Supreme Court, and in 1943 the Justices upheld a military curfew regulation, but avoided consideration of the constitutionality of American detention camps (*Hirabayashi v. U.S.*). This important issue came before the Court the next year in *Korematsu v. U.S.* (No. 237). Once again the Court side-stepped the basic issue, concentrating instead on the legality of the military evacuation program. Although the majority argued that exclusion was based on military necessity rather than racial prejudice, Justice Murphy found that the removal order was justified "upon questionable racial and sociological grounds" which were "utterly revolting to a free people." At the same time, however, the Court ruled that a person whose loyalty had been established could not be detained in relocation camps (*Ex parte* Endo, 1944).

Unlike World War I, restrictions on freedom of expression were few. In only one case was the Supreme Court confronted with a prosecution under the original Espionage Act of 1917. Without specifically overruling Schenck (Chapter XIX), a 5 to 4 majority upheld a citizen's right to express himself "either by temperate reasoning or by immoderate and vicious invective" (*Hartzel v. U.S.* [1944]), even during wartime. An interesting question in time of war was raised in *Girouard v. U.S.* (1946). In the prosperous and peaceful 1920's, a female pacifist had been denied citizenship because she refused to swear that she would bear arms in the country's defense (*Schwimmer v. U.S.*, 1929). During World War II, however, Girouard, a Seventh Day Adventist, was admitted to citizenship, even though he expressed a similar view. Attempts to cancel citizenship papers on the ground that they had been obtained spuriously were also rejected by the high tribunal in two important wartime decisions (*Schneiderman v. U.S.*, 1943, and *Baumgartner v. U.S.*, 1944).

Wartime Economic Regulation

232. The Power to Fix Consumer Prices

Yakus v. U.S., 321 U.S. 414 (1944).

STONE, C.J.: . . . That Congress has constitutional authority to prescribe commodity prices as a war emergency measure, and that the Act was adopted by Congress in the exercise of that power, are not questioned here, and need not now be considered save as they have a bearing on the procedural features of the Act later to be considered, which are challenged on constitutional grounds.

Congress enacted the Emergency Price Control Act in pursuance of a defined policy and required that the prices fixed by the Administrator should further that policy and conform to standards prescribed by the Act. The boundaries of the field of the Administrator's permissible action are marked by the statute. . . . It is enough to satisfy the statutory requirements that the Administrator finds that the prices fixed will tend to achieve that objective and will conform to those standards, and that the courts in an appropriate proceeding can see that substantial basis for those findings is not wanting.

The Act is thus an exercise by Congress of its legislative power. In it Congress has stated the legislative objective, has prescribed the method of achieving that objective—maximum price fixing—, and has laid down standards to guide the administrative determination of both the occasions for the exercise of the price-fixing power, and the particular prices to be established. . . .

The Constitution as a continuously operative charter of government does not demand the impossible or the impracticable. It does not require that Congress find for itself every fact upon which it desires to base legislative action or that it make for itself detailed determinations which it has declared to be prerequisite to the application of the legislative policy to particular facts and circumstances impossible for Congress itself properly to investigate. The essentials of the legislative function are the determination of the legislative policy and its formulation and promulgation as a defined and binding rule of conduct—here the rule, with penal sanctions, that prices shall not be greater than those fixed by maximum price regulations which conform to standards and will tend to further the policy which Congress has established. These essentials are preserved when Congress has specified the basic conditions of fact upon whose existence or occurrence, ascertained from relevant data by a designated administrative agency, it directs that its statutory command shall be effective. It is no objection that the determination of facts and the inferences to be drawn from them in the light of the statutory standards and declaration of policy call for the exercise of judgment, and for the formulation of subsidiary administrative policy within the prescribed statutory framework. . . .

Nor does the doctrine of separation of powers deny to Congress power to direct that an administrative officer properly designated for that purpose have ample latitude within which he is to ascertain the conditions which Congress has made prerequisite to the operation of its legislative command. Acting within its constitutional power to fix prices it is for Congress to say whether the data on the basis of which prices are to be fixed are to be confined within a narrow or a broad range. In either case the only concern of courts is to ascertain whether the will of Congress has been obeyed. This depends not upon the breadth of the definition of the facts or conditions which the administrative officer is to find but upon the determination whether the definition sufficiently marks the field within which the Administrator is to act so that it may be known whether he has kept within it in compliance with the legislative will. . . .

The standards prescribed by the present Act, with the aid of the "statement of considerations" required to be made by the Administrator, are sufficiently definite and precise to enable Congress, the courts and the public to ascertain whether the Administrator, in fixing the designated prices, had conformed to those standards. Compare *Hirabayashi v. United States.* . . . Hence we are unable to find in them an unauthorized delegation of legislative power. The authority to fix prices only when prices have risen or threaten to rise to an extent or in a manner inconsistent with the purpose of the Act to prevent inflation is not broader than the authority to fix maximum prices when deemed necessary to protect consumers against unreasonably high prices, sustained in *Sun-shine Anthracite Coal Co. v. Adkins* . . . or the authority to take possession of and operate telegraph lines whenever deemed necessary for the national security or defense, upheld in *Dakota Cent. Tel. Co. v. South Dakota* . . . or the authority to suspend tariff provisions upon finding that the duties imposed by a foreign state are "reciprocally unequal and unreasonable," held valid in *Field v. Clark.* . . .

Congress, in . . . authorizing consideration by the district court of the validity of the Act alone, gave clear indication that the validity of the Administrator's regulations or orders should not be subject to attack in criminal prosecutions for their violation, at least before their invalidity had been adjudicated by recourse to the protest procedure prescribed by the statute. Such we conclude is the correct construction of the Act. . . .

Our decisions leave no doubt that when justified by compelling public interest the legislature may authorize summary action subject to later judicial review of its validity. . . . Measured by these standards we find no denial of due process under the circumstances in which this Act was adopted and must be applied, in its denial of any judicial stay pending determination of a regulation's validity. . . .

233. *Congressional Control of Prices Paid by the Government*

Lichter v. U.S., 334 U.S. 742 (1948).

BURTON, J.: . . . On the basis of (a) the nature of the particular constitutional powers being employed, (b) the current administrative practice later incorporated into the Act and (c) the adequacy of the statutory term "excessive profits" as used in this context, we hold that the authority granted was a lawful delegation of administrative authority and not an unconstitutional delegation of legislative power.

(a) *A constitutional power implies a power of delegation of authority under it sufficient to effect its purposes.*—This power is especially significant in connection with constitutional war powers under which the exercise of broad discretion as to methods to be employed may be essential to an effective use of its war powers by Congress. The degree to which Congress must specify its policies and standards in order that the administrative authority granted may not be an unconstitutional delegation of its own legislative power is not capable of precise definition. In peace or in war it is essential that the Constitution be scrupulously obeyed, and particularly that the respective branches of the Government keep within the powers assigned to each by the Constitution. On the other hand, it is of the highest importance that the fundamental purposes of the Constitution be kept in mind and given effect in order that, through the Constitution, the people of the United States may in time of war as in peace bring to the support of those purposes the full force of their united action. . . .

In 1942, in the early stages of total global warfare, the exercise of a war power such as the power "To raise and support Armies . . ." and "To provide and maintain a Navy . . . ," called for the production by us of war goods in unprecedented volume with the utmost speed, combined with flexibility of control over the product and with a high degree of initiative on the part of the producers. Faced with the need to exercise that power, the question was whether it was beyond the constitutional power of Congress to delegate to the high officials named therein the discretion contained in the original Renegotiation Act of April 28, 1942, and the amendments of October 21, 1942. We believe that the administrative authority there granted was well within the constitutional war powers then being put to their predestined uses.

(b) *The administrative practices developed under the Renegotiation Act demonstrated the definitive adequacy of the term "excessive profits" as used in the Act.*— The administrative practices currently developed under the Act in interpreting the term "excessive profits" appear to have come well within the scope of the congressional policy. We have referred above to the War Department Directive of August 10, 1942, and to the Joint Departmental Statement of March 31, 1943, both of which were placed before appropriate Congressional Committees. These clearly stated practices are evidence of a current correct understanding of the congressional intent. This appears from the fact that the congressional action of October 21, 1942, made effective as of April 28, 1942, was taken in the light of the above-mentioned directive and without restricting its effect. . . .

(c) *The statutory term "excessive profits" in its context, was a sufficient expression of legislative policy and standards to render it constitutional.*—The fact that this term later was further defined both by administrative action and by statutory amendment indicates the probable desirability of such added definition, but it does not demonstrate that such further definition was a constitutional necessity essential to the validity of the original exercise by Congress of its war powers in initiating a new solution of an unprecedented problem. The fact that the congressional definition confirmed the administrative practice which already was in effect under the original statutory language tends to show that a statutory definition was not necessary in order to give effect to the congressional intent. . . .

It is not necessary that Congress supply administrative officials with a specific formula for their guidance in a field where flexibility and the adaptation of the congressional policy to infinitely variable conditions constitute the essence of the program. . . . Standards prescribed by Congress are to be read in the light of the conditions to which they are to be applied. . . . The purpose of the Renegotiation Act and its factual background establish a sufficient meaning for "excessive profits" as those words are used in practice. . . .

Wartime Civil Liberties

MILITARY TRIALS OF ENEMY MILITARY PERSONNEL

234. *Judicial Review of Decisions of Military Tribunals*

In re Yamashita, 327 U.S. 1 (1946).

STONE, C.J.: . . . Petitioner argues, is ground for the writ of habeas corpus, that Article 25 of the Articles of War prohibited the reception in evidence by the commission of depositions on behalf of the prosecution in a capital case, and that Article 38 prohibited the reception of hearsay and of opinion evidence.

We think that neither Article 25 nor Article 38 is applicable to the trial of an enemy combatant by a military commission for violations of the law of war. Article 2 of the Articles of War enumerates "the persons . . . subject to these articles," who are denominated, for purposes of the Articles, as "persons subject to military law." In general, the persons so enumerated are members of our own Army and of the personnel accompanying the Army. Enemy combatants are not included among them. Articles 12, 13, and 14, before the adoption of Article 15 in 1916, made all "persons subject to military law" amenable to trial by courts-martial for any offense made punishable by the Articles of War. Article 12 makes triable by general court-martial "any other person who by the law of war is subject to trial by military tribunals." Since Article 2, in its 1916 form, includes some persons who, by the law of war, were, prior to 1916, triable by military commission, it was feared by the proponents of the 1916 legislation that in the absence of a saving provision, the authority given by Articles 12, 13 and 14 to try such persons before courts-martial might be construed to de-

prive the non-statutory military commission of a portion of what was considered to be its traditional jurisdiction. To avoid this, and to preserve that jurisdiction intact, Article 15 was added to the Articles. It declared that "The provisions of these articles conferring jurisdiction upon courts-martial shall not be construed as depriving military commissions . . . of concurrent jurisdiction in respect of offenders or offenses that . . . by the law of war may be triable by such military commissions."

By thus recognizing military commissions in order to preserve their traditional jurisdiction over enemy combatants unimpaired by the Articles, Congress gave sanction, as we held in *Ex parte Quirin,* to any use of the military commission contemplated by the common law of war. But it did not thereby make subject to the Articles of War persons other than those defined by Article 2 as being subject to the Articles, nor did it confer the benefits of the Articles upon such persons. The Articles recognized but one kind of military commission, not two. But they sanctioned the use of that one for the trial of two classes of persons, to one of which the Articles do, and to the other of which they do not, apply in such trials. Being of this latter class, petitioner cannot claim the benefits of the Articles, which are applicable only to the members of the other class. Petitioner, an enemy combatant, is therefore not a person made subject to the Articles of War by Article 2, and the military commission before which he was tried, though sanctioned, and its jurisdiction saved, by Article 15, was not convened by virtue of the Articles of War, but pursuant to the common law of war. It follows that the Articles of War, including Articles 25 and 38, were not applicable to petitioner's trial and imposed no restrictions upon the procedure to be followed. The Articles left the control over the procedure in such a case where it had previously been, with the military command. . . .

We cannot say that the commission, in admitting evidence to which objection is now made, violated any act of Congress, treaty or military command defining the commission's authority. For reasons already stated we hold that the commission's rulings on evidence and on the mode of conducting these proceedings against petitioner are not reviewable by the courts, but only by the reviewing military authorities. From this viewpoint it is unnecessary to consider what, in other situations, the Fifth Amendment might require, and as to that no intimation one way or the other is to be implied. Nothing we have said is to be taken as indicating any opinion on the question of the wisdom of considering such evidence, or whether the action of a military tribunal in admitting evidence, which Congress or controlling military command has directed to be excluded, may be drawn in question by petition for habeas corpus or prohibition. . . .

It thus appears that the order convening the commission was a lawful order, that the commission was lawfully constituted, that petitioner was charged with violation of the law of war, and that the commission had authority to proceed with the trial, and in doing so did not violate any military, statutory, or constitutional command. We have considered, but find it unnecessary to discuss, other contentions which we find to be without merit. We therefore conclude that the detention of the petitioner for trial and his detention upon his conviction, subject to the prescribed review by the military authorities, were lawful, and that the petition for certiorari, and leave to file in this Court petitions for writs of habeas corpus and prohibition should be, and they are *Denied.*

MILITARY TRIALS OF AMERICAN CITIZENS

235. *"Civil liberty and . . . martial law cannot endure together."*

Duncan v. Kahanamoku, 327 U.S. 304 (1946).

BLACK, J.: . . . Did the Organic Act during the period of martial law give the armed forces power to supplant all civilian laws and to substitute military for judicial trials under the conditions that existed in Hawaii at the time these petitioners were tried? The relevant conditions, for our purposes, were the same when both petitioners were tried. The answer to the question depends on a correct interpretation of the Act. . . . Both the language of the Organic Act and its legislative history fail to indicate that the scope of "martial law" in Hawaii includes the supplanting of courts by military tribunals, [so] we must look to other sources in order to interpret that term. We think the answer may be found in the birth, development and growth of our governmental institutions up to the time Congress passed the Organic Act. Have the principles and practices developed during the birth and growth of our political institutions been such as to persuade us that Congress intended that loyal civilians in loyal territory should have their daily conduct governed by military orders substituted for criminal laws, and that such civilians should be tried and punished by military tribunals? Let us examine what those principles and practices have been, with respect to the position of civilian government and the courts and compare that with the standing of military tribunals throughout our history.

People of many ages and countries have feared and unflinchingly opposed the kind of subordination of executive, legislative and judicial authorities to complete military rule which according to the government Congress has authorized here. In this country that fear has become part of our cultural and political institutions. The story of that development is well known and we see no need to retell it all. . . .

Courts and their procedural safeguards are indispensable to our system of government. They were set up by our founders to protect the liberties they valued. . . . Our system of government clearly is the antithesis of total military rule and the founders of this country are not likely to have contemplated complete military dominance within the limits of a Territory made part of this country and not recently taken from an enemy. They were opposed to governments that placed in the hands of one man the power to make, interpret and enforce the laws. Their philosophy has been the people's throughout our history. For that reason we have maintained legislatures chosen by citizens or their representatives and courts and juries to try those who violate legislative enactments. We have always been especially concerned about the potential evils of summary criminal trials and have guarded against them by provisions embodied in the Constitution itself. See *Ex parte Milligan*. . . . Legislatures and courts are not merely cherished American institutions; they are indispensable to our Government.

Military tribunals have no such standing. . . . Congress prior to the time of the enactment of the Organic Act had only once authorized the supplanting of the courts by military tribunals. Legislation to that effect was enacted immediately after the South's unsuccessful attempt to secede from the Union. In so far as that legislation applied to the Southern States after the war was at an end it was challenged by a series of Presidential vetoes as vigorous as any in the country's history. And in order to prevent this Court from passing on the constitutionality of this legislation Congress found it necessary to curtail our appellate jurisdiction. Indeed, prior to the Organic Act, the only time this Court had ever discussed the supplanting of courts by military tribunals in a situation other than that involving the establishment of a military government over recently occupied enemy territory, it had emphatically declared that "civil liberty and this kind of martial law cannot endure together; the antagonism is irreconcilable; and, in the conflict, one or the other must perish." *Ex parte Milligan*. . . .

We believe that when Congress passed the Hawaiian Organic Act and authorized the establishment of "martial law" it had in mind and did not wish to exceed the boundaries between military and civilian power, in which our people have always believed, which responsible military and executive officers had heeded, and which had become part of our political philosophy and institutions prior to the time Congress passed the Organic Act. The phrase "martial law" as employed in that Act, therefore, while intended to authorize the military to act vigorously for the maintenance of an orderly civil government and for the defense of the island against actual or threatened rebellion or invasion, was not intended to authorize the supplanting of courts by military tribunals. Yet the government seeks to justify the punishment of both White and Duncan on the ground of such supposed Congressional authorization. We hold that both petitioners are now entitled to be released from custody.

TREASON

236. *Enemy Sabotage and Treason*

Haupt v. U.S., 330 U.S. 631 (1947).

JACKSON, J.: . . . Petitioner is the father of Herbert Haupt, one of the eight saboteurs convicted by a military tribunal. . . . Sheltering his son, assisting him in getting a job, and in acquiring an automobile, all alleged to be with knowledge of the son's mission, involved defendant in the treason charge. . . .

It is urged that the conviction cannot be sustained because there is no sufficient proof of adherence to the enemy, the acts of aid and comfort being natural acts of aid for defendant's own son. Certainly that relationship is a fact for the jury to weigh along with others, and they were correctly instructed that if they found that defendants' intention was not to injure the United States but merely to aid his son "as an individual, as distinguished from assisting him in his purposes, if such existed, of aiding the German Reich, or of injuring the United States, the defendant must be found not guilty." The defendant can complain of no error in such a submission. It was for the jury to weigh the evidence that the acts proceeded from parental solicitude against the evidence of adherence to the German cause. It is argued that Haupt merely had the misfortune to sire a traitor and all he did was to act as an indulgent father toward a dis-

loyal son. In view however of the evidence of defendant's own statements that after the war he intended to return to Germany, that the United States was going to be defeated, that he would never permit his boy to join the American Army, that he would kill his son before he would send him to fight Germany, and others to the same effect, the jury apparently concluded that the son had the misfortune of being a chip off the old block—a tree inclined as the twig had been bent—metaphors which express the common sense observation that parents are as likely to influence the character of their children as are children to shape that of their parents. Such arguments are for the jury to decide. . . .

Haupt has been twice tried and twice found guilty. The law of treason makes, and properly makes, conviction difficult but not impossible. His acts aided an enemy of the United States toward accomplishing his mission of sabotage. The mission was frustrated but defendant did his best to make it succeed. His overt acts were proved in compliance with the hard test of the Constitution, are hardly denied, and the proof leaves no reasonable doubt of the guilt.

THE JAPANESE MINORITY AND EMERGENCY DETENTION

237. *Forced Exclusion, Racism, and Concentration Camps*

Korematsu v. U.S., 323 U.S. 214 (1944).

BLACK, J.: . . . The petitioner, an American citizen of Japanese descent, was convicted in a federal district court for remaining in San Leandro, California, a

"Military Area," contrary to Civilian Exclusion Order No. 34 of the Commanding General of the Western Command, U.S. Army, which directed that after May 9,

1942, all persons of Japanese ancestry should be excluded from that area. No question was raised as to petitioner's loyalty to the United States. . . .

It should be noted, to begin with, that all legal restrictions which curtail the civil rights of a single racial group are immediately suspect. That is not to say that all such restrictions are unconstitutional. It is to say that courts must subject them to the most rigid scrutiny. Pressing public necessity may sometimes justify the existence of such restrictions; racial antagonism never can. . . .

In the light of the principles we announced in the *Hirabayashi* case, we are unable to conclude that it was beyond the war power of Congress and the Executive to exclude those of Japanese ancestry from the West Coast war area at the time they did. True, exclusion from the area in which one's home is located is a far greater deprivation than constant confinement to the home from 8 p.m. to 6 a.m. Nothing short of apprehension by the proper military authorities of the gravest imminent danger to the public safety can constitutionally justify either. But exclusion from a threatened area, no less than curfew, has a definite and close relationship to the prevention of espionage and sabotage. The military authorities, charged with the primary responsibility of defending our shores, concluded that curfew provided inadequate protection and ordered exclusion. They did so, as pointed out in our *Hirabayashi* opinion, in accordance with Congressional authority to the military to say who should, and who should not, remain in the threatened areas.

In this case the petitioner challenges the assumptions upon which we rested our conclusions in the *Hirabayashi* case. He also urges that by May 1942, when Order No. 34 was promulgated, all danger of Japanese invasion of the West Coast had disappeared. After careful consideration of these contentions we are compelled to reject them. . . .

Like curfew, exclusion of those of Japanese origin was deemed necessary because of the presence of an unascertained number of disloyal members of the group, most of whom we have no doubt were loyal to this country. It was because we could not reject the finding of the military authorities that it was impossible to bring about an immediate segregation of the disloyal from the loyal that we sustained the validity of the curfew order as applying to the whole group. In the instant case, temporary exclusion of the entire group was rested by the military on the same ground. The judgment that exclusion of the whole group was for the same reason a military imperative answers the contention that the exclusion was in the nature of group punishment based on antagonism to those of Japanese origin. That there were members of the group who retained loyalties to Japan has been confirmed by investigations made subsequent to the exclusion. Approximately five thousand American citizens of Japanese ancestry refused to swear unqualified allegiance to the United States and to renounce allegiance to the Japanese Emperor, and several thousand evacuees requested repatriation to Japan.

We uphold the exclusion order as of the time it was made and when the petitioner violated it. . . . In doing so, we are not unmindful of the hardships imposed by it upon a large group of American citizens. . . . But hardships are part of war, and war is an aggregation of hardships. All citizens alike, both in and out of uniform, feel the impact of war in greater or lesser measure. Citizenship has its responsibilities as well as its privileges, and in time of war the burden is always heavier. Compulsory exclusion of large groups of citizens from their homes, except under circumstances of direst emergency and peril, is inconsistent with our basic governmental institutions. But when under conditions of modern warfare our shores are threatened by hostile forces, the power to protect must be commensurate with the threatened danger. . . .

It is now argued that the validity of the exclusion order cannot be considered apart from the orders requiring him, after departure from the area, to report and to remain in an assembly or relocation center. The contention is that we must treat these separate orders as one and inseparable; that, for this reason, if detention in the assembly or relocation center would have illegally deprived the petitioner of his liberty, the exclusion order and his conviction under it cannot stand.

We are thus being asked to pass at this time upon the whole subsequent detention program in both assembly and relocation centers, although the only issues framed at the trial related to petitioner's remaining in the prohibited area in violation of the exclusion order. Had petitioner here left the prohibited area and gone to an assembly center we cannot say either as a matter of fact or law that his presence in that center would have resulted in his detention in a relocation center. Some who did report to the assembly center were not sent to relocation centers, but were released upon condition that they remain outside the prohibited zone until the military orders were modified or lifted. This illustrates that they pose different problems and may be governed by different principles. The lawfulness of one does not necessarily determine the lawfulness of the others. This is made clear when we analyze the requirements of the separate provisions of the separate orders. These separate requirements were that those of Japanese ancestry (1) depart from the area; (2) report to and temporarily remain in an assembly center; (3) go under military control to a relocation center there to remain for an indeterminate period until released conditionally or unconditionally by the military authorities. Each of these requirements, it will be noted, imposed distinct duties in connection with the separate steps in a complete evacuation program. Had Congress directly incorporated into one Act the language of these sepa-

rate orders, and provided sanctions for their violations, disobedience of any one would have constituted a separate offense. . . . There is no reason why violations of these orders, insofar as they were promulgated pursuant to Congressional enactment, should not be treated as separate offenses.

The *Endo* case . . . graphically illustrates the difference between the validity of an order to exclude and the validity of a detention order after exclusion has been effected.

Since the petitioner has not been convicted of failing to report or to remain in an assembly or relocation center, we cannot in this case determine the validity of those separate provisions of the order. It is sufficient here for us to pass upon the order which petitioner violated. To do more would be to go beyond the issues raised, and to decide momentous questions not contained within the framework of the pleadings or the evidence in this case. It will be time enough to decide the serious constitutional issues which petitioner seeks to raise when an assembly or relocation order is applied or is certain to be applied to him, and we have its terms before us. . . .

It is said that we are dealing here with the case of imprisonment of a citizen in a concentration camp solely because of his ancestry, without evidence or inquiry concerning his loyalty and good disposition towards the United States. Our task would be simple, our duty clear, were this a case involving the imprisonment of a loyal citizen in a concentration camp because of racial prejudice. Regardless of the true nature of the assembly and relocation centers—and we deem it unjustifiable to call them concentration camps with all the ugly connotations that term implies—we are dealing specifically with nothing but an exclusion order. To cast this case into outlines of racial prejudice, without reference to the real military dangers which were presented, merely confuses the issue. . . .

CHAPTER XXVI

Recent Constitutional Trends

JUST as Congress had authorized governmental reorganization during wartime by reinstating the Overman Act in 1942, it decided in 1945 that the transition to peace necessitated broad governmental changes in the interest of efficient operation. Congress therefore created a bipartisan Commission on Organization of the Executive Branch of the Government, headed by ex-President Herbert Hoover. The Commission's recommendations when presented, however, involved administrative rather than constitutional alterations, but the Twenty-second Amendment (No. 238), reflecting another aspect of Congress's concern with the American Presidency, clarified a historic constitutional question.

Despite the postwar desire to shake off wartime economic controls, the federal government promptly passed the Employment Act of 1946 (No. 239), which established a new concept of the relation of the government to the national economy. Designed to promote maximum employment, production, and purchasing power, the act signalized the government's acceptance of a continuing responsibility for the economic well-being of the nation. This concern was also indicated when Congress enacted the Housing and Rent Act of 1947, continuing the provisions of the wartime Price Control Act. The legislation raised this important question: Does the war power continue after the shooting has ceased? In *Woods v. Miller* (No. 240), the Supreme Court, not without some soul-searching, answered in the affirmative.

Another manifestation of governmental control over the economy was revealed by increased restraints on organized labor. Despite the protections of the Norris-LaGuardia Act against labor injunctions, a fine of $3,500,000 against the United Mine Workers and $10,000 against John L. Lewis was sustained by the Supreme Court for their contempt of a court order requiring the miners to continue working in the government-held pits until a contract could be negotiated. (*U.S. v. United Mine Workers* [No. 241]). Although the fine was later reduced to $700,000, the decision clearly indicated a changing attitude toward labor. Indeed, the Republican capture of Congress in 1946, for the first time since the passage of the Wagner Act, foreshadowed the drastic revision of labor legislation. The enactment of the Taft-Hartley Act (1947) over President Truman's veto opened a new chapter in the history of labor-management relations in the United States. Unlike the New Deal legislation, the measure sought to eliminate an alleged bias in favor of unions by arming management with new rights and imposing limitations on long-established trade union practices such as the closed shop. During the postwar period, thirty states also enacted a variety of antilabor legislation. In the Lincoln Federal decision (No. 242), the Court upheld state laws forbidding closed-shop contracts and rejected the union's attempt to utilize management's ancient defense against governmental regulation—"liberty of contract." On the other hand, the Warren Court in May, 1956, struck down eighteen states' "right-to-work" laws—laws banning union shops—as they applied to railroad workers.

No major Supreme Court decision or piece of legislation in the postwar era drastically altered antitrust legislation. However, the Court was called on frequently to solve problems of statutory construction. *Kiefer-Stewart Co. v. Seagram* (1951) ruled that the Sherman Act forbids an agreement among competitors to fix maximum as well as minimum resale prices, since any kind of price fixing tends to cripple the freedom of traders. Later in the same term (*Timken Roller Bearing Co. v. U.S.*), Justice Black, in order to strike at international monopolistic practices, ordered an American firm to divest itself of its foreign interests. "The most effective way to suppress further Sherman Act violations is to end the intercorporate relationship which has been the core of the conspiracy." But on this point, the concurring views of Justice Reed prevailed (No. 243). Reed warned against the "harsh remedy" of divestiture and proposed instead use of the injunction. "The injunction leaves power in the courts to enforce divestiture, if the injunction alone fails." This general attitude, quickly adopted by the lower courts, confined the divestiture remedy to major monopolies and seemed to infer that a corporation can commit almost any practice short of complete monopolization with confidence that the most it can suffer is to be told by injunction to stop. The Court did consider the consumer in the case of *Schwegman Brothers v. Calvert* (1951) by invalidating provisions in state "fair trade" acts binding dealers —who had not signed—to the terms of price-fixing contracts between producers and other distributors. The immediate effect was to produce a welcome collapse of so-called "fair trade" prices, but the relief was short lived as Congress moved quickly to substitute federal legislation for invalidated state measures.

The line between public regulation and governmental operation of private business was clearly drawn in *Youngstown Sheet and Tube Co. v. Sawyer* (No.

244), one of the most important postwar constitutional decisions. During the Korean conflict, President Truman authorized Secretary of Commerce Sawyer to seize and operate steel mills to insure production of vital defense materials. The executive order was not based on any statutory authority, but only on the ground that the threatened strike created a national emergency. When the companies sought an injunction against the government, the federal spokesman argued that seizure was based upon Article II of the Constitution, "and whatever inherent, implied or residual powers may flow therefrom." In argument before the Supreme Court, government counsel stressed the concept of an expanded presidential prerogative during national emergencies. In a 6 to 3 decision featuring a sharp dissent by Chief Justice Vinson, the majority dealt decisive blows to the dual doctrines of the president's emergency power and his inherent power in domestic affairs.

Another persistent postwar issue involved tidelands oil. In 1947 the Court ruled that the United States had domination over the resources of the soil under the marginal sea adjoining California (No. 245). That state had maintained that it was entitled, by virtue of the conventional "equal footing" clause in the act admitting it to the Union, to the rights enjoyed by the original states and that those states owned such offshore areas. The Court concluded that such ownership had not been established at the time of the Constitution, and that the interests of sovereignty favored national dominion. Three years later the Court rejected a similar contention by Texas. But following the victorious Eisenhower campaign of 1952, in which the Republicans had courted the South and West with promises of offshore riches, Congress passed the Submerged Lands Act of 1953, vesting in the states the ownership of lands beneath the marginal sea adjacent to the respective states. The Supreme Court subsequently denied leave to file complaints challenging the statute.

Postwar constitutional problems in the international field stemmed from America's participation in the United Nations and its involvement in the cold war. Conscious of its new international responsibilities, the United States took a leading part in the establishment of the United Nations. To assist in the maintenance of peace through collective security—by force if necessary—the United States accepted military commitments which raised fundamental constitutional questions of effective international security action and congressional control of the war-making power. These issues became crucial as international friction intensified into an acknowledged cold war. In a revolutionary reversal, the United States, for the first time in its history, joined a peacetime defensive alliance, the North Atlantic Treaty Organization. The basic issue was raised by Article 5 of the Treaty which pledged the United States, along with other signatories, to automatic intervention in case any member suffered armed attack. It posed this thorny question: Does such a commitment upset the traditional balance between the executive and legislative branches in questions of war and peace? With the invasion of South Korea by Communist forces, presidential discretion rather than congressional action provided a dramatic answer. President Truman, on June 25, 1950, without a formal declaration of war and without consulting Congress, ordered United States air and sea forces "to give the Korean Government troops cover and support," and ordered the Seventh Fleet to prevent any attack on Formosa. This pronouncement quickly involved the United States in large-scale warfare in Korea. The Korean conflict did not attain actual war status because Congress never declared war. Although Congress backed the President's policy with appropriations, there were challenges leveled against Truman's unilateral action without consulting Congress (No. 246).

Since the President had based his move on treaty obligations to the United Nations, a logical point of attack was the treaty-making power of the federal government and the broad implications of that power inherent in Holmes's decision in *Missouri v. Holland* (Chapter XX). Attention had been focused on this power as early as 1948 when the United Nations Charter was cited by four members of the Supreme Court as a yardstick with which to measure the constitutionality of a state statute (*Oyama v. California*). The leader in the movement to curb the treaty-making authority was Senator John W. Bricker of Ohio, who first introduced an amendment to that effect in 1952. Congress defeated both the Bricker Amendment (No. 247) in 1954 and a revision, which was presented in 1956. Neither defeat seemed to daunt the Senator, however, who promised further reworded versions of the amendment in the near future.

Constitutional Change and the Executive

238. *The Twenty-second Amendment: Two-Term Tenure of Office*

Proposed March 24, 1947; adopted February 26, 1951.

SECTION 1. No person shall be elected to the office of the President more than twice, and no person who has held the office of President, or acted as President, for more than two years of a term to which some other person was elected President shall be elected to the office of the President more than once. But this article shall not apply to any person holding the office of President when this article was proposed by the Congress, and shall not prevent any person who may be holding the office of President, or acting as President, during the term within which this article becomes operative from holding the office of President or acting as President during the remainder of such term.

SECTION 2. This article shall be inoperative unless it shall have been ratified as an amendment to the Constitution by the legislatures of three-fourths of the several states within seven years from the date of its submission to the states by the Congress.

Postwar Regulation of the Economy

THE EXTENT OF FEDERAL AUTHORITY OVER THE NATION'S ECONOMY

239. The Employment Act of 1946

U. S. Stat. at L., LX, 23-6.

DECLARATION OF POLICY

SEC. 2. The Congress hereby declares that it is the continuing policy and responsibility of the Federal Government to use all practical means consistent with its needs and obligations and other essential considerations of national policy, with the assistance and cooperation of industry, agriculture, labor, and State and local governments, to coordinate and utilize all its plans, functions, and resources for the purpose of creating and maintaining, in a manner calculated to foster and promote free competitive enterprise and the general welfare, conditions under which there will be afforded useful employment opportunities, including self-employment, for those able, willing, and seeking to work, and to promote maximum employment, production, and purchasing power.

ECONOMIC REPORT OF THE PRESIDENT

SEC. 3. (a) The President shall transmit to the Congress within sixty days after the beginning of each regular session (commencing with the year 1947) an economic report (hereinafter called the "Economic Report") setting forth (1) the levels of employment, production, and purchasing power obtaining in the United States and such levels needed to carry out the policy declared in section 2; (2) current and foreseeable trends in the levels of employment, production, and purchasing power;

(3) a review of the economic program of the Federal Government and a review of economic conditions affecting employment in the United States or any considerable portion thereof during the preceding year and of their effect upon employment, production, and purchasing power; and (4) a program for carrying out the policy declared in section 2, together with such recommendations for legislation as he may deem necessary or desirable. . . .

COUNCIL OF ECONOMIC ADVISERS TO
THE PRESIDENT

SEC. 4. (a) There is hereby created in the Executive Office of the President a Council of Economic Advisers (hereinafter called the "Council"). The Council shall be composed of three members who shall be appointed by the President, by and with the advice and consent of the Senate, and each of whom shall be a person who, as a result of his training, experience, and attainments, is exceptionally qualified to analyze and interpret economic developments, to appraise programs and activities of the Government in the light of the policy declared in section 2, and to formulate and recommend national economic policy to promote employment, production, and purchasing power under free competitive enterprise. . . .

(c) It shall be the duty and function of the Council—(1) to assist and advise the President in the preparation of the Economic Report; (2) to gather timely and authoritative information concerning economic developments and economic trends, both current and prospective, to analyze and interpret such information in the light of the policy declared in section 2 for the purpose of determining whether such developments and trends are interfering, or are likely to interfere, with the achievement of such policy, and to compile and submit to the President studies relating to such developments and trends; (3) to appraise the various programs and activities of the Federal Government in the light of the policy declared in section 2 for the purpose of determining the extent to which such programs and activities are contributing, and the extent to which they are not contributing, to the achievement of such policy, and to make recommendations to the President with respect thereto; (4) to develop and recommend to the President national economic policies to foster and promote free competitive enterprise, to avoid economic fluctuations or to diminish the effects thereof, and to maintain employment, production, and purchasing power. . . .

240. *Rent Control: Does the War Power Continue After the Fighting is Over?*

Woods v. Miller, 333 U.S. 138 (1948).

DOUGLAS, J.: . . . The case is here on a direct appeal . . . from a judgment of the District Court holding unconstitutional Title II of the Housing and Rent Act of 1947. . . .

The Act became effective on July 1, 1947, and the following day the appellee demanded of its tenants increases of 40% and 60% for rental accommodations in the Cleveland Defense-Rental Area, an admitted violation of the act and regulations adopted pursuant thereto. . . .

The District Court was of the view that the authority of Congress to regulate rents by virtue of the war power . . . ended with the Presidential Proclamation terminating hostilities on December 31, 1946, since that proclamation inaugurated "peace-in-fact" though it did not mark termination of the war. It also concluded that, even if the war power continues, Congress did not act under it because it did not say so, and only if Congress says so, or enacts provisions so implying, can it be held that Congress intended to exercise such power. That Congress did not so intend, said the District Court, follows from the provision that the Housing Expediter can end controls in any area with-

out regard to the official termination of the war, and from the fact that the preceding federal rent control laws (which were concededly exercises of the war power) were neither amended nor extended. The District Court expressed the further view that rent control is not within the war power because "the emergency created by housing shortage came into existence long before the war." . . .

We conclude, in the first place, that the war power sustains this legislation. The Court said in *Hamilton v. Kentucky Distilleries Co.*, . . . that the war power includes the power "to remedy the evils which have arisen from its rise and progress" and continues for the duration of that emergency. Whatever may be the consequences when war is officially terminated, the war power does not necessarily end with the cessation of hostilities. . . .

The constitutional validity of the present legislation follows *a fortiori* from such cases. The legislative history of the present Act makes abundantly clear that there has not yet been eliminated the deficit in housing which in considerable measure was caused by the heavy demobilization of veterans and by the cessation or reduction in residential construction during the period of hostilities due to the allocation of building materials to military projects. Since the war effort contributed heavily to that deficit, Congress has the power even after the cessation of hostilities to act to control the forces that a short supply of the needed article created. If that were not true, the Necessary and Proper Clause, . . . would be drastically limited in its application to the several war powers. The Court has declined to follow that course in the past. . . . We decline to take it today. The result would be paralyzing. It would render Congress powerless to remedy conditions the creation of which necessarily followed from the mobilization of men and materials for successful prosecution of the war. So to read the Constitution would be to make it self-defeating.

We recognize the force of the argument that the effects of war under modern conditions may be felt in the economy for years and years, and that if the war power can be used in days of peace to treat all the wounds which war inflicts on our society, it may not only swallow up all other powers of Congress but largely obliterate the Ninth and Tenth Amendments as well. There are no such implications in today's decision. We deal here with the consequences of a housing deficit greatly intensified during the period of hostilities by the war effort. Any power, of course, can be abused. But we cannot assume that Congress is not alert to its constitutional responsibilities. And the question whether the war power has been properly employed in cases such as this is open to judicial inquiry. . . .

The question of the constitutionality of action taken by Congress does not depend on recitals of the power which it undertakes to exercise. Here it is plain from the legislative history that Congress was invoking its war power to cope with a current condition of which the war was a direct and immediate cause. Its judgment on that score is entitled to the respect granted like legislation enacted pursuant to the police power. . . .

POSTWAR LABOR PROBLEMS AND FEDERAL JURISDICTION

241. *John L. Lewis, the Government, and Contempt of Court*

U.S. v. United Mine Workers of America, 330 U.S. 258 (1947).

VINSON, C.J.: . . . Executive Order 9728, in pursuance of which the Government seized possession of the mines, authorized the Secretary of the Interior to negotiate with the representatives of the miners, and thereafter to apply to the National Wage Stabilization Board for appropriate changes in terms and conditions of employment for the period of governmental operation. Such negotiations were undertaken and resulted in the Krug-Lewis agreement. That agreement contains many basic departures from the earlier contract entered into between the mine workers and the private operators on April 11, 1945, which, except as amended and supplemented by the Krug-Lewis agreement, was continued in effect for the period of Government possession. . . .

It should be observed that the Krug-Lewis agreement was one solely between the Government and the union. The private mine operators were not parties to the contract nor were they made parties to any of its subsequent modifications. It should also be observed that the provisions

relate to matters which normally constitute the subject matter of collective bargaining between employer and employee.
Many of the provisions incorporated into
the agreement for the period of Government operation had theretofore been vigorously opposed by the private operators
and have not subsequently received their
approval. . . .

The union has apparently regarded the
Krug-Lewis agreement as a sufficient contract of employment to satisfy the mine
workers' traditional demand of a contract
as a condition precedent to their work.
The defendant Lewis, in responding to a
suggestion of the Secretary of the Interior
that certain union demands should be
taken to the private operators with the
view of making possible the termination
of Government possession, stated in a letter dated November 15, 1946: "The Government of the United States seized the
mines and entered into a contract. The
mine workers do not propose to deal with
parties who have no status under the contract." The defendant Lewis in the same
letter referred to the operators as "strangers to the Krug-Lewis Agreement" and
to the miners as the "400,000 men who
now serve the Government of the United
States in the bituminous coal mines." . . .

We do not find convincing the contention of the defendants that in seizing and
operating the coal mines the government
was not exercising a sovereign function
and that, hence, this is not a situation
which can be excluded from the terms of
the Norris-LaGuardia Act. In the Executive
Order which directed the seizure of the
mines, the President found and proclaimed
that "coal produced by such mines is required for the war effort and is indispensable for the continued operation of
the national economy during the transition from war to peace; that the war effort will be unduly impeded or delayed
by . . . interruptions [in production];
and that the exercise . . . of the powers
vested in me is necessary to insure the operation of such mines in the interest of

the war effort and to preserve the national economic structure in the present
emergency . . ." Under conditions found
by the President to exist, it would be
difficult to conceive a more vital and urgent function of the Government than the
seizure and operation of the bituminous
coal mines. We hold that in a case such as
this, where the Government has seized
actual possession of the mines, or other
facilities, and is operating them, and the
relationship between the Government and
the workers is that of employer and
employee, the Norris-LaGuardia Act does
not apply.

Although we have held that the Norris-
LaGuardia Act did not render injunctive
relief beyond the jurisdiction of the District Court, there are alternative grounds
which support the power of the District
Court to punish violations of its orders as
criminal contempt.

Attention must be directed to the situation obtaining on November 18. The Government's complaint sought a declaratory
judgment in respect to the right of the
defendants to terminate the contract by
unilateral action. What amounted to a
strike call, effective at midnight on November 20, had been issued by the defendant Lewis as an "official notice." Pending a determination of defendants' right
to take this action, the Government requested a temporary restraining order and
injunctive relief. The memorandum in
support of the restraining order seriously
urged the inapplicability of the Norris-
LaGuardia Act to the facts of this case,
and the power of the District Court to
grant the ancillary relief depended in
great part upon the resolution of this
jurisdictional question. In these circumstances, the District Court unquestionably
had the power to issue a restraining order
for the purpose of preserving existing conditions pending a decision upon its own
jurisdiction. . . .

In the case before us, the District Court
had the power to preserve existing conditions while it was determining its own

authority to grant injunctive relief. The defendants, in making their private determination of the law, acted at their peril. Their disobedience is punishable as criminal contempt. . . .

Immediately following the finding of guilty, defendant Lewis stated openly in court that defendants would adhere to their policy of defiance. This policy, as the evidence showed, was the germ center of an economic paralysis which was rapidly extending itself from the bituminous coal mines into practically every other major industry of the United States. It was an attempt to repudiate and override the instrument of lawful government in the very situation in which governmental action was indispensable.

The trial court also properly found the defendants guilty of civil contempt. Judicial sanctions in civil contempt proceedings may, in a proper case, be employed for either or both of two purposes; to coerce the defendant into compliance with the court's order, and to compensate the complainant for losses sustained. *Gompers v. Bucks Stove & Range Co.* . . . Where compensation is intended, a fine is imposed, payable to the complainant. Such fine must of course be based upon evidence of complainant's actual loss, and his right, as a civil litigant, to the compensatory fine is dependent upon the outcome of the basic controversy.

But where the purpose is to make the defendant comply, the court's discretion is otherwise exercised. It must then consider the character and magnitude of the harm threatened by continued contumacy, and the probable effectiveness of any suggested sanction in bringing about the result desired.

It is a corollary of the above principles that a court which has returned a conviction for contempt must, in fixing the amount of a fine to be imposed as a punishment or as a means of securing future compliance, consider the amount of defendant's financial resources and the consequent seriousness of the burden to that particular defendant.

In light of these principles, we think the record clearly warrants a fine of $10,000 against defendant Lewis for criminal contempt. A majority of the Court, however, does not think that it warrants the unconditional imposition of a fine of $3,500,000 against the defendant union. A majority feels that, if the court below had assessed a fine of $700,000 against the defendant union, this, under the circumstances, would not be excessive as punishment for the criminal contempt theretofore committed. . . . Accordingly, the judgment against the defendant union is held to be excessive. It will be modified so as to require the defendant union to pay a fine of $700,000, and further, to pay an additional fine of $2,800,000 unless the defendant union, within five days after the issuance of the mandate herein, shows that it has fully complied with the temporary restraining order . . . and the preliminary injunction. . . . The defendant union can effect full compliance only by withdrawing unconditionally the notice given by it, . . . terminating the Krug-Lewis agreement . . . , and by notifying . . . its members of such withdrawal. . . .

242. *Opening the Gates of the Closed Shop*

Lincoln Federal Labor Union v. Northwestern Iron & Metal Co., 335 U.S. 525 (1949).

BLACK, J.: . . . It is contended that these state laws abridge the freedom of speech and the opportunities of unions and their members "peaceably to assemble, and to petition the Government for a redress of grievances." Under the state policy adopted by these laws, employers must, other considerations being equal, give equal opportunities for remunerative work to union and non-union members without discrimination against either. In order to achieve this objective of equal opportunity for the two groups, employers are forbidden to make contracts which would obligate them to hire or keep none but union members. Nothing in the language of the laws indicates a purpose to prohibit speech, assembly, or petition. Precisely what these state laws do is to forbid employers acting alone or in concert with labor organizations deliberately to restrict employment to none but union members. . . .

We deem it unnecessary to elaborate the numerous reasons for our rejection of this contention of appellants. Nor need we appraise or analyze with particularity the rather startling ideas suggested to support some of the premises on which appellants' conclusions rest. There cannot be wrung from a constitutional right of workers to assemble to discuss improvement of their own working standards, a further constitutional right to drive from remunerative employment all other persons who will not or cannot participate in union assemblies. The constitutional right of workers to assemble, to discuss and formulate plans for furthering their own self-interest in jobs cannot be construed as a constitutional guarantee that none shall get and hold jobs except those who will join in the assembly or will agree to abide by the assembly's plans. For where conduct affects the interests of other individuals and the general public, the legality of that conduct must be measured by whether the conduct conforms to valid law, even though the conduct is engaged in pursuant to plans of an assembly. . . .

It is contended that these state laws deprive appellants of their liberty without due process of law in violation of the Fourteenth Amendment. Appellants argue that the laws are specifically designed to deprive all persons within the two states of "liberty" (1) to refuse to hire

or retain any person in employment because he is or is not a union member, and (2) to make a contract or agreement to engage in such employment discrimination against union or non-union members. . . .

Many cases are cited by appellants in which this Court has said that in some instances the due process clause protects the liberty of persons to make contracts. But none of these cases, even those according the broadest constitutional protection to the making of contracts, ever went so far as to indicate that the due process clause bars a state from prohibiting contracts to engage in conduct banned by a valid state law. So here, if the provisions in the state laws against employer discrimination are valid it follows that the contract prohibition also is valid. . . . We therefore turn to the decisive question under the due process contention, which is: Does the due process clause forbid a state to pass laws clearly designed to safeguard the opportunity of non-union workers to get and hold jobs, free from discrimination against them because they are non-union workers?

There was a period in which labor union members who wanted to get and hold jobs were the victims of widespread employer discrimination practices. Contracts between employers and their employees were used by employers to accomplish this anti-union employment discrimination. Before hiring workers, employers required them to sign agreements stating that the workers were not and would not become labor union members. Such anti-union practices were so obnoxious to workers that they gave these required agreements the name of "yellow dog contracts." This hostility of workers also prompted passage of state and federal laws to ban employer discrimination against union members and to outlaw yellow dog contracts. . . . [There follows a discussion of the Allgeyer, Lochner, Adair and Coppage cases.]

This Court, beginning at least as early

as 1934, when the *Nebbia* case was decided, has steadily rejected the due process philosophy enunciated in the *Adair-Coppage* line of cases. In doing so it has consciously returned closer and closer to the earlier constitutional principle that states have power to legislate against what are found to be injurious practices in their internal commercial and business affairs, so long as their laws do not run afoul of some specific federal constitutional prohibition, or of some valid federal law. . . . Under this constitutional doctrine the due process clause is no longer to be so broadly construed that the Congress and state legislatures are put in a strait jacket when they attempt to suppress business and industrial conditions which they regard as offensive to the public welfare.

Appellants now ask us to return, at least in part, to the due process philosophy that has been deliberately discarded. Claiming that the Federal Constitution itself affords protection for union members against discrimination, they nevertheless assert that the same Constitution forbids a state from providing the same protection for non-union members. Just as we have held that the due process clause erects no obstacle to block legislative protection of union members, we now hold that legislative protection can be afforded non-union workers.

BIG GOVERNMENT AND BIG BUSINESS

243. *The Recurrent Trust Problem*

Timken Roller Bearing Co. v. U.S., 341 U.S. 593 (1951).

REED, J., concurring: . . . There are no specific statutory provisions authorizing courts to employ the harsh remedy of divestiture in civil proceedings to restrain violations of the Sherman Act. Fines and imprisonment may follow criminal convictions . . . and divestiture of property has been used in decrees, not as punishment, but to assure effective enforcement of the laws against restraint of trade.

Since divestiture is a remedy to restore competition and not to punish those who restrain trade, it is not to be used indiscriminately, without regard to the type of violation or whether other effective methods, less harsh, are available. . . . While the decree here does not call for confiscation, it does call for divestiture. I think that requirement is unnecessary. . . .

An injunction was entered by the District Court to prohibit the continuation of the objectionable contracts. Violation of that injunction would threaten the appellant and its officers with civil and criminal contempt. . . . The paucity of cases dealing with contempt of Sherman Act injunctions is, I think, an indication of how carefully the decrees are obeyed. The injunction is a far stronger sanction against further violation than the Sherman Act alone. Once in possession of facts showing violation, the Government would obtain a quick and summary punishment of the violator. Furthermore this case remains on the docket for the purpose of "enforcement of compliance" and "punishment of violations." This provision should leave power in the court to enforce divestiture, if the injunction alone fails. Prompt and full compliance with the decree should be anticipated.

This Court is hesitant, always, to interfere with the scope of the trial court's decree. However, in this case it seems appropriate to indicate my disapproval of the requirement of divestiture and to suggest a direction to the District Court that provisions leading to that result be eliminated from the decree.

244. *The Steel Seizure Case*

Youngstown Sheet and Tube Co. v. Sawyer, 343 U.S. 579 (1952).

BLACK, J.: We are asked to decide whether the President was acting within his constitutional power when he issued an order directing the Secretary of Commerce to take possession of and operate most of the Nation's steel mills. The mill owners argue that the President's order amounts to lawmaking, a legislative function which the Constitution has expressly confided to the Congress and not the President. The Government's position is that the order was made on findings of the President that his action was necessary to avert a national catastrophe which would inevitably result from a stoppage of steel production, and that in meeting this grave emergency the President was acting within the aggregate of his constitutional powers as the Nation's Chief Executive and the Commander in Chief of the Armed Forces of the United States. The issue emerges here from the following series of events:

In the latter part of 1951, a dispute arose between the steel companies and their employees over terms and conditions that should be included in new collective bargaining agreements. Long-continued conferences failed to resolve the dispute. On December 18, 1951, the employees' representative, United Steelworkers of America, C.I.O., gave notice of an intention to strike when the existing bargaining agreements expired on December 31. The Federal Mediation and Conciliation Service then intervened in an effort to get labor and management to agree. This failing, the President on December 22, 1951, referred the dispute to the Federal Wage Stabilization Board to investigate and make recommendations for fair and equitable terms of settlement. This Board's report resulted in no settlement. On April 4, 1952, the Union gave notice of a nation-wide strike called to begin at 12:01 A.M. April 9. The indispensability

of steel as a component of substantially all weapons and other war materials led the President to believe that the proposed work stoppage would immediately jeopardize our national defense and that governmental seizure of the steel mills was necessary in order to assure the continued availability of steel. Reciting these considerations for his action, the President, a few hours before the strike was to begin, issued Executive Order 10340 . . . The order directed the Secretary of Commerce to take possession of most of the steel mills and keep them running. The Secretary immediately issued his own possessory orders, calling upon the presidents of the various seized companies to serve as operating managers for the United States. They were directed to carry on their activities in accordance with regulations and directions of the Secretary. The next morning the President sent a message to Congress reporting his action. . . . Twelve days later he sent a second message. . . . Congress has taken no action.

Obeying the Secretary's orders under protest, the companies brought proceedings against him in the District Court. . . . The District Court was asked to declare the orders of the President and the Secretary invalid and to issue preliminary and permanent injunctions restraining their enforcement. Opposing the motion for preliminary injunction, the United States asserted that a strike disrupting steel production for even a brief period would so endanger the well-being and safety of the Nation that the President had "inherent power" to do what he had done—power "supported by the Constitution, by historical precedent, and by court decisions." . . . Holding against the Government on all points, the District Court on April 30 issued a preliminary injunction restraining the Secretary from "continuing the seizure and possession of the plants . . . and from acting under the purported authority of Executive Order No. 10340." . . . On the same day the Court of Appeals stayed the District Court's injunction. . . . Deeming it best that the issues raised be promptly decided by this Court, we granted certiorari on May 3 and set the cause for argument on May 12. . . .

The President's power, if any, to issue the order must stem either from an act of Congress or from the Constitution itself. There is no statute that expressly authorizes the President to take possession of property as he did here. Nor is there any act of Congress to which our attention has been directed from which such a power can fairly be implied. Indeed, we do not understand the Government to rely on statutory authorization for this seizure. There are two statutes which do authorize the President to take both personal and real property under certain conditions. However, the Government admits that these conditions were not met and that the President's order was not rooted in either of the statutes. . . .

Moreover, the use of the seizure technique to solve labor disputes in order to prevent work stoppages was not only unauthorized by any congressional enactment; prior to this controversy, Congress had refused to adopt that method of settling labor disputes. When the Taft-Hartley Act was under consideration in 1947, Congress rejected an amendment which would have authorized such governmental seizures in cases of emergency. Apparently it was thought that the technique of seizure, like that of compulsory arbitration, would interfere with the process of collective bargaining. Consequently, the plan Congress adopted in that Act did not provide for seizure under any circumstances. Instead, the plan sought to bring about settlements by use of the customary devices of mediation, conciliation, investigation by boards of inquiry, and public reports. In some instances temporary injunctions were authorized to provide cool-ing-off periods. All this failing, unions were left free to strike after a secret vote by employees as to whether they wished to accept their employers' final settlement offer.

It is clear that if the President had authority to issue the order he did, it must be found in some provisions of the Constitution. And it is not claimed that express constitutional language grants this power to the President. The contention is that presidential power should be implied from the aggregate of his powers under the Constitution. Particular reliance is placed on provisions in Article II which say that "The executive Power shall be vested in a President . . ."; that "he shall take Care that the Laws be faithfully executed"; and that he "shall be Commander in Chief of the Army and Navy of the United States."

The order cannot properly be sustained as an exercise of the President's military power as Commander in Chief of the Armed Forces. The Government attempts to do so by citing a number of cases upholding broad powers in military commanders engaged in day-to-day fighting in a theater of war. Such cases need not concern us here. Even though "theater of war" be an expanding concept, we cannot with faithfulness to our constitutional system hold that the Commander in Chief of the Armed Forces has the ultimate power as such to take possession of private property in order to keep labor disputes from stopping production. This is a job for the Nation's lawmakers, not for its military authorities.

Nor can the seizure order be sustained because of the several constitutional provisions that grant executive power to the President. In the framework of our Constitution, the President's power to see that the laws are faithfully executed refutes the idea that he is to be a lawmaker. The Constitution limits his functions in the lawmaking process to the recommending of laws he thinks wise and the vetoing of laws he thinks bad. And the Constitution is neither silent nor equivocal about who shall make laws which the President is to execute. The first section of the first article says that "All legislative Powers herein granted shall be vested in a Congress of the United States. . . ." After granting many powers to the Congress, Article I goes on to provide that Congress may "make all Laws which shall be necessary and proper for carrying into Execution the foregoing Powers and all other Powers vested by this Constitution in the Government of the United States, or in any Department or Officer thereof."

The President's order does not direct that a congressional policy be executed in a manner prescribed by Congress—it directs that a presidential policy be executed in a manner prescribed by the President. The preamble of the order itself, like that of many statutes, sets out reasons why the President believes certain policies should be adopted, proclaims these policies as rules of conduct to be followed, and again, like a statute, authorizes a government official to promulgate additional rules and regulations consistent with the policy proclaimed and needed to carry that policy into execution. The power of Congress to adopt such public policies as those proclaimed by the order is beyond question. It can authorize the taking of private property for public use. It can make laws regulating the relationships between employers and employees, prescribing rules designed to settle labor disputes, and fixing wages and working conditions in certain fields of our economy. The Constitution did not subject this lawmaking power of Congress to presidential or military supervision or control. . . .

The Founders of this Nation entrusted the law-making power to the Congress alone in both good and bad times. It would do no good to recall the historical events, the fears of power and the hopes for freedom that lay behind their choice. Such a review would but confirm our holding that this seizure order cannot stand.

THE TIDELANDS AND FEDERAL-STATE RELATIONS

245. *The federal government has "paramount rights."*

U.S. v. California, 332 U.S. 19 (1947).

BLACK, J.: . . . The point of difference is as to who owns, or has paramount rights in and power over several thousand square miles of land under the ocean off the coast of California. The difference involves the conflicting claims of federal and state officials as to which government, state or federal, has a superior right to take or authorize the taking of the vast quantities of oil and gas underneath that land, much of which has already been and more of which is about to be, taken by or under authority of the state. Such concrete conflicts as these constitute a controversy in the classic legal sense, and are the very kind of differences which can only be settled by agreement, arbitration, force, or judicial action. . . .

The crucial question on the merits is not merely who owns the bare legal title to the lands under the marginal sea. The United States here asserts rights in two capacities transcending those of a mere property owner. In one capacity it asserts the right and responsibility to exercise whatever power and dominion are necessary to protect this country against dangers to the security and tranquility of its people incident to the fact that the United States is located immediately adjacent to the ocean. The Government also appears in its capacity as a member of the family of nations. In that capacity it is responsible for conducting United States relations with other nations. It asserts that proper exercise of these constitutional responsibilities requires that it have power, unencumbered by state commitments, always to determine what agreements will be made concerning the control and use of the marginal sea and the land under it. . . . In the light of the foregoing, our question is whether the state or the Federal Government has the paramount right and power to determine in the first instance when, how, and by what agencies, foreign or domestic, the oil and other resources of the soil of the marginal sea, known or hereafter discovered, may be exploited. . . . [There follows a discussion of the accretion by the federal government of domination over the three-mile belt.]

Not only has acquisition, as it were, of the three-mile belt, been accomplished by the national Government, but protection and control of it has been and is a function of national external sovereignty. . . . The three-mile rule is but a recognition of the necessity that a government next to the sea must be able to protect itself from dangers incident to its location. It must have powers of dominion and regulation in the interest of its revenues, its health, and the security of its people from wars waged on or too near its coasts. And insofar as the nation asserts its rights under international law, whatever of value may be discovered in the seas next to its shores and within its protective belt, will most naturally be appropriated for its use. But whatever any nation does in the open sea, which detracts from its common usefulness to nations, or which another nation

may charge detracts from it, is a question for consideration among nations as such, and not their separate governmental units. What this Government does, or even what the states do, anywhere in the ocean, is a subject upon which the nation may enter into and assume treaty or similar international obligations. . . . The very oil about which the state and nation here contend might well become the subject of international dispute and settlement.

The ocean, even its three-mile belt, is thus of vital consequence to the nation in its desire to engage in commerce and to live in peace with the world; it also becomes of crucial importance should it ever again become impossible to preserve that peace. And as peace and world commerce are the paramount responsibilities of the nation, rather than an individual state, so, if wars come, they must be fought by the nation. . . . The state is not equipped in our constitutional system with the powers or the facilities for exercising the responsibilities which would be concomitant with the dominion which it seeks. Conceding that the state has been authorized to exercise local police power functions in the part of the marginal belt within its declared boundaries, these do not detract from the Federal Government's paramount rights in and power over this area. . . .

We decide for the reasons we have stated that California is not the owner of the three-mile marginal belt along its coast, and that the Federal Government rather than the state has paramount rights in and power over that belt, an incident to which is full dominion over the resources of the soil under that water area, including oil. . . .

The Cold War and Constitutional Problems

246. *Presidential Power to Commit American Forces in Foreign Areas*

Arthur Sears Henning, Editorial in *Washington Times-Herald*, July 3, 1950; *Congressional Record*, LXLVI, Pt. 16, 4901.

One of the most sensational aspects of American intervention in the Korean War is President Truman's demonstration of the use of the United Nations to bypass the United States Congress as the sole repository under the Constitution of the prerogative to declare war.

While the undertaking to defend South Korea from invasion by the Russian puppet republic of North Korea has received almost unanimous support in Congress, Mr. Truman's procedure for calling American armed power into action is being widely questioned as to its legality and also as to the implications of the precedent in the future.

There are misgivings and apprehensions that the United Nations will come in time to supersede Congress not only in the matter of declaring war but in the matter of legislation generally.

Mr. Truman in invoking the authority of the United Nations instead of the authority of Congress to make war, has shown how a dictator could operate to flout Congress and carry into effect a Socialist program, such as the welfare state or police state, or even impose on the country a completely totalitarian form of government. All he would need would be the approval of the United Nations which the United States is bound by treaty to carry out.

In the Korean venture, Mr. Truman wanted to make it a United Nations war, not a United States war, for the wider international support that might be obtained. There was ground for United Nations action, for the South Korean Republic was set up by the United Nations and justifiably could claim United Nations protection.

In addition, Mr. Truman wanted to avoid asking Congress for a declaration of war on any other authority for employing American Armed Forces in Korea. Such a request, he thought, would only provoke division and result in at least several days' delay before an enabling resolution could be adopted.

So Mr. Truman decided to ignore Congress. The news of the Reds' attack on South Korea reached Mr. Truman the night of June 24. He decided that the United States should enter the war. At 3 a.m. June 25, Mr. Truman, through an American U.N. delegate asked Secretary General Lie to convene a special meeting of the United Nations Security Council that day. That was done. By 6 p.m. Sunday June 25, the Council had adopted an American resolution declaring the Korean aggression a breach of the peace, calling for immediate cessation of hostilities and asking all member nations to render every assistance to execute this mandate.

Acting under the color of that authority, though it was not in accord with the act of Congress requiring congressional approval of the use of American forces by the United Nations, Mr. Truman ordered United States air and naval units to Korea.

The next day, June 26, the President warned those responsible for the act of aggression that the United States takes a very serious view of the invasion.

On June 27, Mr. Truman emphasized his by-passing of Congress by calling members of its Foreign Affairs and Armed Services Committees to the White House and reading to them his announcement that military forces were being sent to Korea and Formosa and military aid would be furnished to the Philippines and Indochina. He asked no advice. He merely stated an accomplished fact under the aegis, not of Congress but of the United Nations.

The theory that the authority of the United Nations under which Mr. Truman acted overrides the authority of Congress is based on the contention that in adhering to the Charter of the United Nations the United States bound itself to support United Nations acts, whether approved or disapproved by Congress. The United Nations Charter is a treaty and under our Constitution a treaty, no less than the Constitution and the laws, is the supreme law of the land.

247. *The Bricker Amendment and the Treaty-making Power*

A. 1954 VERSION

Senate Report No. 412, 82nd Congress, 2nd Session.

SECTION 1. A provision of a treaty which conflicts with this Constitution shall not be of any force or effect.

SECTION 2. A treaty shall become effective as internal law in the United States only through legislation which would be valid in the absence of a treaty.

SECTION 3. Congress shall have power to regulate all executive and other agreements with any foreign power or international organization. All such agreements shall be subject to the limitations imposed on treaties by this article.

B. 1956 VERSION

A provision of a treaty or other international agreement which conflicts with any provision of this Constitution shall not be of any force and effect.

CHAPTER XXVII

First Amendment Freedoms

THOUGH the Roosevelt Court elevated problems of civil liberties to new heights of judicial concern, it did not succeed in building a coherent constitutional theory out of its diverse and sometimes reversed rulings. Increasingly sharp splits indicated serious disagreements on proper judicial policy and promised major constitutional controversies in the postwar period. This tendency toward conflict was intensified by the constitutional crisis generated by the cold war against national and international Communism, which kept the United States in a more or less continuous state of national emergency. Perhaps the most difficult question that the Supreme Court has been called on to answer in recent years is that of rationalizing the encroachments on freedom made in the name of national security. Acutely aware of this problem and hopeful that the United States could avoid the excesses of intolerance which had characterized the postwar 1920's, President Truman established the President's Committee on Civil Rights in 1946, observing that "the preservation of civil rights guaranteed by the Constitution is essential to domestic tranquility, national security, the general welfare, and the continued existence of our free institutions." In its report, that Committee discussed not only violations of civil rights but also recommended a program of action designed to make "the Federal Government a friendly, vigilant defender of the rights and equalities of all Americans" (No. 248).

"To a marked degree," writes C. Herman Pritchett, the historian of the

Roosevelt and Vinson Courts, "civil liberty was the unfinished business of the Roosevelt Court." Despite its many rulings on religious liberty in the Jehovah Witnesses cases, it had not considered the First Amendment's more vital "establishment of religion" clause. This surprisingly difficult task therefore fell to the Vinson Court. Although there has been general agreement that the Amendment erects a wall of separation between Church and State, there has been, especially in recent years, a constant clash of views as to what the wall separates. In the Everson case (No. 249), both the majority and minority agreed that the wall should be kept high and impregnable, but divided sharply over whether the wall had been breached in New Jersey when local authorities provided tax-supported transportation for children attending parochial schools. Criticizing the majority's opinion upholding the New Jersey aid, Justice Jackson remarked that "the case which irresistibly comes to mind as the most fitting precedent is that of Julia who, according to Byron's reports, 'whispering "I will ne'er consent,"—consented.'"

A second facet of the conflict over church-state relations dealt with the use of public school facilities for religious instruction of students on a "released time" arrangement. A nearly unanimous Court reaffirmed the broad principles formulated the year before in the Everson case, agreeing that religious instruction classes conducted by denominational teachers during regular school time within a public school building violated the First Amendment as incorporated into the Fourteenth (*McCollum v. Board of Education*). This decision aroused a storm of protest, and the Court later upheld a "released time" program operated outside public school buildings (*Zorach v. Clauson* [No. 250]).

Other First Amendment freedoms gave the Vinson Court similar difficulty. In a novel decision that greatly widened state control over speech, a majority of five, speaking through Justice Frankfurter, upheld an Illinois group-libel law as a reasonable extension of the law of libelous utterances, which are not within "the area of constitutionally protected speech" (No. 251). Justice Black wrote a stinging dissent in which he observed that the majority had taken the case out of the mainstream of all previous free speech rulings on "the bland assumption that the First Amendment is wholly irrelevant."

Although the Vinson Court did not find the First Amendment wholly irrelevant in picketing cases, it did retreat from the Thornhill doctrine (Chapter XXIV) by balancing the speech element in picketing against other social values. Without dissent it ruled in *Giboney v. Empire Storage and Ice Co.* (No. 252) that a state may enjoin picketing designed to force an employer to violate the state's antitrust law. The speech communicated by the pickets' signs, said the Court, formed "an essential and inseparable part of a grave offense against an important public law"; when directed towards unlawful ends, communications on picket placards may be regulated by the state. In subsequent opinions, the Court continued to enlarge the discretionary power of the states to regulate picketing. *International Brotherhood of Teamsters v. Hanke* (1950) upheld a state injunction against picketing that was not making an unlawful demand. In this instance the union picketed a self-employed operator of a used-car business to force him to establish a union shop. The Court indicated that even though "picketing has an ingredient of communication, it cannot dogmatically be equated with the constitutionally protected freedom of speech." Though the Thornhill principle still seems to cancel blanket restraints against all picketing, later decisions grant legislatures and judges the power to strike a balance between the communication elements in picketing and the public objectives, which in their minds override the right to picket. Certainly the Court no longer views picketing as a "preferred" constitutional right protected by the free speech guarantees of the First Amendment.

In marked contrast to the Vinson Court's tendency to allow the states considerable discretion in the regulation of First Amendment freedoms was its unanimous opinion against state censorship of motion pictures in 1952 (*Burstyn v. Wilson* [No. 253]). The Warren Court, in a similar decision in 1957, reversed a conviction under a Michigan statute which banned books containing obscene, immoral, or lewd language for their potentially harmful influence upon youths. "The incidence of this enactment," Justice Frankfurter ruled, "is to reduce the adult population of Michigan to reading only what is fit for children" (*Butler v. Michigan* [No. 254]).

In the Burstyn case, Justice Clark observed "that motion pictures are a significant medium for the communication of ideas" and are therefore protected by the guarantees of the First Amendment, by way of the Fourteenth Amendment. Prior censorship of movies on the ground that they are "sacrilegious" establishes such a vague standard for censors that they are cast "adrift upon a boundless sea." In rescinding the ban on "The Miracle," the Court followed the doctrine of *Winters v. New York* (1948), which had voided, on the ground of vagueness, a New York statute that barred publication of "deeds of bloodshed, lust or crime." Thus, it did not rule out the possibility of prior censorship of movies, if specific standards, understandable to rational people, were provided. Although this seemed to leave the judgment on movie censorship somewhat unstable, the Court in 1954 cited the Miracle case as the basis for reversing New York's ban on "La Ronde," a French film barred on the ground that "it would tend to corrupt morals," and for lifting Ohio's ruling against "M," censored because it would "undermine confidence in the enforcement of law and government."

The whole question of undermining confidence in the government has loomed large on the postwar scene. The roots of this fear of freedom, however, lie in the prewar era. While the Supreme Court in the 1930's and early 1940's was expanding the concept of ordered liberty, Congress and state legislatures clamped on peacetime statutory restrictions unprecedented in American history. In 1938 the House set up a Committee on Un-American Activities which fanned the fears of Communism until Congress passed a misnamed Alien Registration Act in 1940 (the Smith Act [No. 255]), the first peacetime alien and sedition legislation since the Federalist laws of 1798 (Chapter IV).

Although the Smith Act is the basic anti-Communist measure, later legislation was added in the cold war period, creating critical conflicts between national security and individual liberty. In 1947, Congress wrote into the Taft-Hartley Act a requirement that labor union officials, in order to use the facilities of the National Labor Relations Board, sign affidavits denying not only membership in the Communist Party but also Communist beliefs. Three years later an enthusiastic Congress passed a sweeping Internal Security Act over President Truman's veto. The measure established a Subversive Activities Control Board, required registration of Communist organizations, strengthened espionage laws, provided for the detention of potential spies in national emergencies, and amended laws relating to immigration, deportation, and naturalization. By 1954 delays and appeals had prevented the registration of any groups with the Board, and Congress responded with the Communist Control Act, virtually outlawing the Communist Party as a legal political party.

The Court's first ruling on this new anti-Communist legislation came in *American Communication Association v. Douds* (No. 256), which sustained the non-Communist oath provisions of the Taft-Hartley Act. Although Chief Justice Vinson conceded that "Congress has undeniably discouraged the lawful exercise of political freedom" by demanding oaths relating to personal beliefs, he weighed this abridgment of free speech against the government's power to regulate commerce and upheld the oath as a commercial regulation rather than as a speech restriction. In balancing "the power of constitutional government to survive" against the "clear and present danger" test, the Chief Justice warned that the "Court's interpretations of the Constitution [should not] be reduced to the status of mathematical formulas." This ruling paved the way for the historic decision a year later in *Dennis v. U.S.*, which upheld the constitutionality of the Smith Act and the conviction of ten leading Communist Party officials under that law. Even though the Chief Justice retained the "clear and present danger" phrase, he labelled it a "verbalization" denoting an "indeterminate standard," and then redefined it in terms of the Gitlow "bad tendency" test (Chapter XXI). In this radical reversal, Vinson simply substituted "sufficient and probable" danger at some remote time in the future for the Holmes-Brandeis doctrine (No. 257). Justice Black rejected this return to the seventeenth-century test of criminality in advocacy cases, and expressed the hope that "in calmer times, when present pressures, passions and fears subside, this or some later Court will restore the First Amendment liberties to the high preferred place where they belong in a free society" (No. 258). For the present, however, the Chief Justice's reconciliation of the irreconcilable utilizes the Holmes-Brandeis "verbalization" but reads into it a meaning precisely the opposite of what its authors said it meant.

Jurisdictional conflicts between state and national legislation dealing with alien registration and sedition have been resolved in favor of national supremacy. In decisions separated by fifteen years, the Court ruled that the assumption of jurisdiction in these areas by the federal government supersedes similar state legislation. A Pennsylvania statute requiring aliens to register and carry identification cards was revoked in 1941 (*Hines v. Davidowitz*), and an anti-sedition law in the same state was rescinded in 1956 when the Court decided that Congress had treated "seditious conduct as a matter of vital national concern" and had "occupied the field to the exclusion of parallel state legislation" (No. 259).

In contrast with these jurisdictional clashes, there has been little dispute between federal and state governments over loyalty legislation, even though a recent rash of statutory regulations has reversed the historic policy of assuming the loyalty of government employees. For 150 years (1789-1939), the American people required only that government servants take an oath to support and defend the federal Constitution, but that policy has become a constitutional casualty of a hot and a cold war. As early as 1938, when the House of Representatives estab-lished the Un-American Activities Committee, Chairman Martin Dies and others launched a sensational hunt for Communists, radicals, Fascists, "crackpots," and "internationalists" on the federal payroll. In 1938 Congress passed Section 9A of the Hatch Act, making it unlawful for any government employee "to have mem-bership in any political party or organization which advocates the overthrow of our constitutional form of government." Since 1941 Congressional appropriation bills have included riders stipulating that funds may not be used to pay any person who advocates, or is a member of an association which advocates, forcible overthrow of the government.

Prodded by these legislative enactments, the executive department began the development of a federal loyalty program in 1942. With the approval of President Roosevelt, the Civil Service Commission issued regulations providing for dismissal of any employee if there was a "reasonable doubt" as to his loyalty to the government. It was not until the period of the cold war, however, that a comprehensive loyalty program was developed. In the Republican sweep of the 1946 Congressional elections, the charge of "Communists in government" had been an important campaign issue, and President Truman responded to this political pressure by establishing an executive program in an effort to forestall legislative action by a hostile Congress. Moreover, the Supreme Court, by refusing to review the case of a federal officer dismissed on an adverse loyalty finding by the Civil Service Commission, seemed to approve of loyalty proceedings by the executive branch. In March, 1947, less than a month after this ruling (*Friedman v. Schwellenbach*), President Truman issued Executive Order No. 9835 (No. 260). Four years later, the original standard of "reasonable grounds for belief that the person involved is disloyal" was changed to "reasonable doubts" of his loyalty, thus shifting the burden of proof from the government to the accused. No longer did the government have to prove disloyalty; instead, the employee had to prove his loyalty. In 1953 President Eisenhower broadened the basis for dismissal by substituting "security" for "loyalty." Executive Order No. 10450 repealed the Truman order and abolished the line between loyalty and security-risk cases. Al-though the order retains "subversive activities or associations" as grounds for re-moval, it also includes acts of indiscretion, or "any behavior, activities, or associa-tions which tend to show that the individual is not trustworthy." Thus, gossips, heavy drinkers, and other undesirables are barred along with subversives.

Despite severe criticisms of the loyalty and security-risk programs as viola-tions of the due process, bill of attainder, and First Amendment provisions, only procedural phases have reached the Supreme Court. In *Joint Anti-Fascist Refugee Committee v. McGrath* (1951), the majority held that the Attorney General's list of subversive organizations, compiled without prior notice and hearing, violated due process. This adverse ruling did not abolish the list or the loyalty program. Subversive organizations are still listed but hearings now precede this step. On the same day that McGrath was decided, the Court divided evenly in *Bailey v. Rich-ardson*, and thus sustained a loyalty board order barring Miss Bailey from government employment for disloyalty on the basis of accusations made by persons whose identities were never revealed to her or to the board. Although the Court did not write an opinion in the Bailey case, Justices Jackson, Black, and Douglas discussed it in their concurring opinions in McGrath. A more important decision, however, came in 1956 when the Court rejected summary procedures in dismissals from nonsensitive jobs (*Cole v. Young*). In a thoughtful and dispassionate report on the government's civilian personnel security system, a special committee of the Association of the Bar of the City of New York has suggested extensive revisions in the federal loyalty-security program (No. 261).

Paralleling the loyalty program and anti-Communist laws of the federal government are restrictive regulations imposed on state and municipal employees. The Supreme Court in a per curiam opinion unanimously upheld a Maryland statute requiring a candidate for public office to take an oath that he was not then engaged in, nor a member of an organization engaged in, an attempt to overthrow the government by force or violence (*Gerende v. Board of Supervisors*, 1951), and it sustained the Los Angeles loyalty oath by 5 to 4 (*Garner v. Board of Public Works*, 1951). The Court also approved the dismissal of public school teachers on grounds of disloyalty under New York's Feinberg law (*Adler v. Board of Education*, 1952). This statute directed the State Board of Regents to list organizations which it found to advocate the forceable overthrow of the government. Unlike the Attorney General's list, which had been criticized in the Joint Anti-Fascist decision, the state law provided for notice and hearing before listing. Membership in the banned organization was prima-facie evidence for removal. Perhaps the outstanding feature of the decision was the difference between the majority and minority over the concept of "guilt by association." In *Wieman v. Updegraff* (No. 262), however, the Court unanimously revoked a retroactive Oklahoma loyalty oath statute barring teachers for mere membership in a proscribed organization. "There can be no dispute," said the Court, "about the consequences visited upon a person excluded from public employment on disloyalty grounds. In the view of the community the stain is a deep one; indeed it has become a badge of infamy."

The Elusive Goal: To Secure These Rights

248. *"A friendly, vigilant defender of the rights and equalities of all Americans."*

To Secure These Rights: The Report of the President's Committee on Civil Rights (Washington, 1947), 4-10.

The central theme in our American heritage is the importance of the individual person. From the earliest moment of our history we have believed that every human being has an essential dignity and integrity which must be respected and safeguarded. Moreover, we believe that the welfare of the individual is the final goal of group life. Our American heritage further teaches that to be secure in the rights he wishes for himself, each man must be willing to respect the rights of other men. This is the conscious recognition of a basic moral principle: that all men are created equal as well as free. Stemming from this principle is the obligation to build social institutions that will guarantee equality of opportunity to all men. Without this equality freedom becomes an illusion. Thus the only aristocracy that is consistent with the free way of life is an aristocracy of talent and achievement. The grounds on which our society accords respect, influence or reward to each of its citizens must be limited to the quality of his personal character and his social contribution.

This concept of equality which is so vital a part of the American heritage knows no kinship with notions of human uniformity or regimentation. We abhor the totalitarian arrogance which makes one man say that he will respect another man as his equal only if he has "*my* race, *my* religion, *my* political views, *my* social position." In our land men are equal, but they are free to be different. From these very differences among our people has come the great human and national strength of America. . . .

The men who founded our Republic, as those who have built any constitutional democracy, faced the task of reconciling personal liberty and group authority, or of establishing an equilibrium between them. In a democratic state we recognize that the common interests of the people must be managed by laws and procedures established by majority rule. But a democratic majority, left unrestrained, may be as ruthless and tyrannical as were the earlier absolute monarchs. Seeing this clearly, and fearing it greatly, our forefathers built a constitutional system in which valued personal liberties, carefully enumerated in a Bill of Rights, were placed

beyond the reach of popular majorities. Thus the people permanently denied the federal government power to interfere with certain personal rights and freedoms.

Freedom, however, as we now use the term, means even more than the traditional "freedoms" listed in our Bill of Rights—important as they are. Freedom has come to mean the right of a man to manage his own affairs as he sees fit up to the point where what he does interferes with the equal rights of others in the community to manage their affairs—or up to the point where he begins to injure the welfare of the whole group. It is clear that in modern democratic society a man's freedom in this broader sense is not and cannot be absolute—nor does it exist in a vacuum—but instead is hedged about by the competing rights of others and the demands of the social welfare. In this context it is government which must referee the clashes which arise among the freedoms of citizens, and protect each citizen in the enjoyment of the maximum freedom to which he is entitled.

There is no essential conflict between freedom and government. Bills of rights restrain government from abridging individual civil liberties, while government itself by sound legislative policies protects citizens against the aggressions of others seeking to push their freedoms too far. Thus in the words of the Declaration of Independence: "Man is endowed by his Creator with certain inalienable rights. Among these are life, liberty, and the pursuit of happiness. To secure these rights, *governments are instituted among men.*"

The rights essential to the citizen in a free society can be described in different words and in varying orders. The three great rights of the Declaration of Independence have just been mentioned. Another noble statement is made in the Bill of Rights of our Constitution. A more recent formulation is found in the Four Freedoms.

Four basic rights have seemed important to this Committee and have influenced its labors. We believe that each of these rights is essential to the well-being of the individual and to the progress of society.

The Right to Safety and Security of the Person

Freedom can exist only where the citizen is assured that his person is secure against bondage, lawless violence, and arbitrary arrest and punishment. Freedom from slavery in all its forms is clearly necessary if all men are to have equal opportunity to use their talents and to lead worthwhile lives. Moreover, to be free, men must be subject to discipline by society only for commission of offenses clearly defined by law and only after trial by due process of law. Where the administration of justice is discriminatory, no man can be sure of security. . . .

The Right to Equality of Opportunity

It is not enough that full and equal membership in society entitles the individual to an equal voice in the control of his government; it must also give him the right to enjoy the benefits of society and to contribute to its progress. The opportunity of each individual to obtain useful employment, and to have access to services in the fields of education, housing, health, recreation and transportation, whether available free or at a price, must be provided with complete disregard for race, color, creed, and national origin. Without this equality of opportunity the individual is deprived of the chance to develop his potentialities and to share the fruits of society. The group also suffers through the loss of the contributions which might have been made by persons excluded from the main channels of social and economic activity.

THE HERITAGE AND THE REALITY

Our American heritage of freedom and equality has given us prestige among the nations of the world and a strong feeling of national pride at home. There is much reason for that pride. But pride is no substitute for steady and honest performance, and the record shows that at varying times in American history the gulf between ideals and practice has been wide. We have had human slavery. We have had religious persecution. We have had mob rule. We still have their ideological remnants in the unwarrantable "pride and prejudice" of some of our people and practices. . . . But we have seen nothing to shake our conviction that the civil rights of the American people—all of them—can be strengthened quickly and effectively by the normal processes of democratic, constitutional government. That strengthening, we believe, will make our daily life more and more consonant with the spirit of the American heritage of freedom. But it will require as much courage, as much imagination, as much perseverance as anything which we have ever done together. . . .

The Right to Citizenship and its Privileges

. . . Because the right to participate in the political process is customarily limited to citizens there can be no denial of access to citizenship based upon race, color, creed or national origin. . . .

To deny qualified citizens the right to vote while others exercise it is to do violence to the principle of freedom and equality. Without the right to vote, the individual loses his voice in the group effort and is subjected to rule by a body from which he has been excluded. Likewise, the right of the individual to vote is important to the group itself. Democracy assumes that the majority is more likely as a general rule to make decisions which are wise and desirable from the point of view of the interests of the whole society than is any minority. Every time a qualified person is denied a voice in public affairs, one of the components of a potential majority is lost, and the formation of a sound public policy is endangered.

To the citizen in a democracy, freedom is a precious possession. Accordingly, all able-bodied citizens must enjoy the right to serve the nation and the cause of freedom in time of war. . . . In particular, any discrimination which, while imposing an obligation, prevents members of minority groups from rendering full military service in defense of their country is for them a peculiarly humiliating badge of inferiority. The nation also suffers a loss of manpower and is unable to marshal maximum strength at a moment when such strength is most needed.

The Right to Freedom of Conscience and Expression

In a free society there is faith in the ability of the people to make sound, ra-

tional judgments. But such judgments are possible only where the people have access to all relevant facts and to all prevailing interpretations of the facts. How can such judgments be formed on a sound basis if arguments, viewpoints, or opinions are arbitrarily suppressed? How can the concept of the marketplace of thought in which truth ultimately prevails retain its validity if the thought of certain individuals is denied the right of circulation? . . .

Our forefathers fought bloody wars and suffered torture and death for the right to worship God according to the varied dictates of conscience. Complete religious liberty has been accepted as an unquestioned personal freedom since our Bill of Rights was adopted. We have insisted only that religious freedom may not be pleaded as an excuse for criminal or clearly anti-social conduct. . . .

The First Freedom

RELIGION AND PUBLIC SUPPORTED EDUCATION

249. "A Wall Between Church and State"

Everson v. Board of Education, 330 U.S. 1 (1947).

BLACK, J.: A New Jersey statute authorizes its local school districts to make rules and contracts for the transportation of children to and from schools. The appellee, a township board of education, acting pursuant to this statute, authorized reimbursement to parents of money expended by them for the bus transportation of their children on regular busses operated by the public transportation system. Part of this money was for the pay-

ment of transportation of some children in the community to Catholic parochial schools. These church schools give their students, in addition to secular education, regular religious instruction conforming to the religious tenets and modes of worship of the Catholic faith. The superintendent of these schools is a Catholic priest.

The appellant, in his capacity as a district taxpayer, filed suit in a state court challenging the right of the Board to re-imburse parents of parochial school students. . . .

The only contention here is that the state statute and the resolution, insofar as they authorized reimbursement to parents of children attending parochial schools, violate the Federal Constitution. . . .

The New Jersey statute is challenged as a "law respecting the establishment of religion." The First Amendment, as made applicable to the states by the Fourteenth, . . . commands that a state "shall make no law respecting an establishment of religion, or prohibiting the free exercise thereof. . . ." These words of the First Amendment reflected in the minds of early Americans a vivid mental picture of conditions and practices which they fervently wished to stamp out in order to preserve liberty for themselves and for their posterity. Doubtless their goal has not been entirely reached; but so far has the Nation moved toward it that the expression, "law respecting the establishment of religion," probably does not so vividly remind present-day Americans of the evils, fears, and political problems that caused that expression to be written into our Bill of Rights. Whether this New Jersey law is one respecting an "establishment of religion" requires an understanding of the meaning of that language, particularly with respect to the imposition of taxes. Once again, therefore, it is not inappropriate briefly to review the background and environment of the period in which that constitutional language was fashioned and adopted. . . .

No one locality and no one group throughout the Colonies can rightly be given entire credit for having aroused the sentiment that culminated in adoption of the Bill of Rights' provisions embracing religious liberty. But Virginia, where the established church had achieved a dominant influence in political affairs and where many excesses attracted wide public attention, provided a great stimulus and able leadership for the movement. The people there, as elsewhere, reached the conviction that individual religious liberty could be achieved best under a government which was stripped of all power to tax, to support, or otherwise to assist any or all religions, or to interfere with the beliefs of any religious individual or group.

The movement toward this end reached its dramatic climax in Virginia in 1785-86 when the Virginia legislative body was about to renew Virginia's tax levy for the support of the established church. Thomas Jefferson and James Madison led the fight against this tax. Madison wrote his great Memorial and Remonstrance against the law. In it, he eloquently argued that a true religion did not need the support of law; that no person, either believer or non-believer, should be taxed to support a religious institution of any kind; that the best interest of a society required that the minds of men always be wholly free; and that cruel persecutions were the inevitable result of government-established religions. Madison's Remonstrance received strong support throughout Virginia, and the Assembly postponed consideration of the proposed tax measure until its next session. When the proposal came up for consideration at that session, it not only died in committee, but the Assembly enacted the famous "Virginia Bill for Religious Liberty" originally written by Thomas Jefferson [see Chapter III, No. 26]. . . .

This Court has previously recognized that the provisions of the First Amendment, in the drafting and adoption of which Madison and Jefferson played such leading roles, had the same objective and were intended to provide the same protection against governmental intrusion on religious liberty as the Virginia statute. . . .

The "establishment of religion" clause of the First Amendment means at least this: Neither a state nor the Federal Government can set up a church. Neither can pass laws which aid one religion, aid all religions, or prefer one religion over another. Neither can force nor influence a person to go to or to remain away from church against his will or force him to profess a belief or disbelief in any religion. No person can be punished for entertaining or professing religious beliefs or disbeliefs, for church attendance or non-attendance. No tax in any amount, large or small, can be levied to support any religious activities or institutions, whatever they may be called, or whatever form they may adopt to teach or practice religion. Neither a state nor the Federal Government can, openly or secretly, participate in the affairs of any religious organizations or groups and vice versa. In the words of Jefferson, the clause against establishment of religion by law was intended to erect "a wall of separation between Church and State." . . .

Measured by these standards, we cannot say that the First Amendment prohibits New Jersey from spending tax-raised funds to pay the bus fares of parochial school pupils as a part of a general program under which it pays the fares of pupils attending public and other schools. It is undoubtedly true that children are helped to get to church schools. There is even a possibility that some of the children might not be sent to the church schools if the parents were compelled to pay their children's bus fares out of their own pockets when transportation to a public school would have been paid for by the State. The same possibility exists where the state requires a local transit company to provide reduced fares to school children including those attending parochial schools, or where a municipally owned transportation system undertakes to carry all school children free of charge. Moreover, state-paid policemen, detailed to protect children going to and from church schools from the very real hazards of traffic, would serve much the same purpose and accomplish much the same result as state provisions intended to guarantee free transportation of a kind

which the state deems to be best for the school children's welfare. And parents might refuse to risk their children to the serious danger of traffic accidents going to and from parochial schools, the approaches to which were not protected by policemen. Similarly, parents might be reluctant to permit their children to attend schools which the state had cut off from such general government services as ordinary police and fire protection, connections for sewage disposal, public highways and sidewalks. Of course, cutting off church schools from these services, so separate and so indisputably marked off from the religious function, would make it far more difficult for the schools to operate. But such is obviously not the purpose of the First Amendment. That Amendment requires the state to be a neutral in its relations with groups of religious believers and non-believers; it does not require the state to be their adversary. State power is no more to be used so as to handicap religions than it is to favor them.

This Court has said that parents may, in the discharge of their duty under state compulsory education laws, send their children to a religious rather than a public school if the school meets the secular educational requirements which the state has power to impose. . . . It appears that these parochial schools meet New Jersey's requirements. The State contributes no money to the schools. It does not support them. Its legislation, as applied, does no more than provide a general program to help parents get their children, regardless of their religion, safely and expeditiously to and from accredited schools.

The First Amendment has erected a wall between church and state. That wall must be kept high and impregnable. We could not approve the slightest breach. New Jersey has not breached it here.

Affirmed.

250. "Released Time" Programs of Religious Instruction

Zorach v. Clauson, 343 U.S. 306 (1952).

DOUGLAS, J.: New York City has a program which permits its public schools to release students during the school day so that they may leave the school buildings and school grounds and go to religious centers for religious instruction or devotional exercises. A student is released on written request of his parents. Those not released stay in the classrooms. The churches make weekly reports to the schools, sending a list of children who have been released from public school but who have not reported for religious instruction.

This "released time" program involves neither religious instruction in public school classrooms nor the expenditure of public funds. All costs, including the application blanks, are paid by the religious organizations. The case is therefore unlike *Illinois ex rel. McCollum v. Board of Education* . . . which involved a "released time" program from Illinois. In that case the classrooms were turned over to religious instructors. We accordingly held that the program violated the First Amendment which (by reason of the Fourteenth Amendment) prohibits the states from establishing religion or prohibiting its free exercise.

Appellants, who are taxpayers and residents of New York City and whose children attend its public schools, challenge the present law, contending it is in essence not different from the one involved in the McCollum Case. Their argument, stated elaborately in various ways, reduces itself to this: the weight and influence of the school is put behind a program for religious instruction; public school teachers police it, keeping tab on students who are released; the classroom activities come to a halt while the students who are released for religious instruction are on leave; the school is a crutch on which the

churches are leaning for support in their religious training; without the cooperation of the schools this "released time" program, like the one in the McCollum Case, would be futile and ineffective. . . .

The briefs and arguments are replete with data bearing on the merits of this type of "released time" program. . . . Those matters are of no concern here, since our problem reduces itself to whether New York by this system has either prohibited the "free exercise" of religion or has made a law "respecting an establishment of religion" within the meaning of the First Amendment.

It takes obtuse reasoning to inject any issue of the "free exercise" of religion into the present case. No one is forced to go to the religious classroom and no religious exercise or instruction is brought to the classrooms of the public schools. A student need not take religious instruction. He is left to his own desires as to the manner or time of his religious devotions, if any. . . .

Moreover, apart from that claim of coercion, we do not see how New York by this type of "released time" program has made a law respecting an establishment of religion within the meaning of the First Amendment. There is much talk of the separation of Church and State in the history of the Bill of Rights and in the decisions clustering around the First Amendment. . . . There cannot be the slightest doubt that the First Amendment reflects the philosophy that Church and State should be separated. And so far as interference with the "free exercise" of religion and an "establishment" of religion are concerned, the separation must be complete and unequivocal. The First Amendment within the scope of its coverage permits no exception; the prohibition is absolute. The First Amendment, however, does not say that in every and all respects there shall be a separation of Church and State. Rather, it studiously defines the manner, the specific ways, in which there shall be no concert or union or dependency one on the other. That is the common sense of the matter. Otherwise, the state and religion would be aliens to each other—hostile, suspicious, and even unfriendly. Churches could not be required to pay even property taxes. Municipalities would not be permitted to render police or fire protection to religious groups. Policemen who helped parishioners into their places of worship would violate the Constitution. Prayers in our legislative halls; the appeals to the Almighty in the messages of the Chief Executive; the proclamations making Thanksgiving Day a holiday; "so help me God" in our courtroom oaths —these and all other references to the Almighty that run through our laws, our public rituals, our ceremonies would be flouting the First Amendment. A fastidious atheist or agnostic could even object to the supplication with which the Court opens each session: "God save the United States and this Honorable Court."

We would have to press the concept of separation of Church and State to these extremes to condemn the present law on constitutional grounds. . . .

We are a religious people whose institutions presuppose a Supreme Being. We guarantee the freedom to worship as one chooses. We make room for as wide a variety of beliefs and creeds as the spiritual needs of man deem necessary. We sponsor an attitude on the part of government that shows no partiality to any one group and that lets each flourish according to the zeal of its adherents and the appeal of its dogma. When the state encourages religious instruction or cooperates with religious authorities by adjusting the schedule of public events to sectarian needs, it follows the best of our traditions. For it then respects the religious nature of our people and accommodates the public service to their spiritual needs. To hold that it may not would be to find in the Constitution a requirement that the government show a callous indifference to religious groups. That would be preferring those who believe in no religion over those who do believe. . . .

In the McCollum Case the classrooms were used for religious instruction and the force of the public school was used to promote that instruction. Here, as we have said, the public schools do no more than accommodate their schedules to a program of outside religious instruction. We follow the McCollum Case. But we cannot expand it to cover the present released time program unless separation of Church and State means that public institutions can make no adjustments of their schedules to accommodate the religious needs of the people. We cannot read into the Bill of Rights such a philosophy of hostility to religion.

Affirmed.

CONTROL OVER VARIOUS MEDIA OF COMMUNICATION

251. *Race Hatred and Group Libel*

Beauharnais v. Illinois, 343 U.S. 250 (1952).

FRANKFURTER, J.: . . . The testimony at the trial was substantially undisputed. From it the jury could find that Beauharnais was president of the White Circle League; that, at a meeting on January 6, 1950, he passed out bundles of the lithographs in question, together with other literature, to volunteers for distribution on downtown Chicago street corners the following day; . . . and that the leaflets

were in fact distributed . . . in accordance with his plan and instructions. The
court, together with other charges on burden of proof and the like, told the jury "if
you find . . . that the defendant, Joseph
Beauharnais, did . . . manufacture, sell,
or offer for sale, advertise or publish, present or exhibit in any public place the
lithograph . . . then you are to find the
defendant guilty. . . ." He refused to
charge the jury, as requested by the defendant, that in order to convict they
must find "that the article complained
of was likely to produce a clear and present danger of a serious substantive evil
that rises far above public inconvenience,
annoyance or unrest." Upon this evidence
and these instructions, the jury brought
in the conviction here for review.

The statute before us is not a catchall
enactment left at large by the State court
which applied it. . . . It is a law specifically directed at a defined evil, its language
drawing from history and practice in Illinois and in more than a score of other
jurisdictions a meaning confirmed by the
Supreme Court of that State in upholding
this conviction. We do not, therefore, parse
the statute as grammarians or treat it as an
abstract exercise in lexicography. We read
it in the animating context of well-defined
usage. . . .

The Illinois Supreme Court tells us
that §224a "is a form of criminal libel
law." . . . The defendant, the trial court
and the Supreme Court consistently treated
it as such. The defendant offered evidence
tending to prove the truth of parts of the
utterance, and the courts below considered
and disposed of this offer in terms of
ordinary criminal libel precedents. Section 224a does not deal with the defense
of truth, but by the Illinois Constitution,
. . . "in all trials for libel, both civil and
criminal, the truth, when published with
good motives and for justifiable ends, shall
be a sufficient defense." . . . Similarly,
the action of the trial court in deciding as
a matter of law the libelous character of

the utterance, leaving to the jury only the
question of publication, follows the settled
rule in prosecutions for libel in Illinois and
other States. Moreover, the Supreme
Court's characterization of the words prohibited by the statute as those "liable to
cause violence and disorder" paraphrases
the traditional justification for punishing
libels criminally, namely their "tendency
to cause breach of the peace." . . .

No one will gainsay that it is libelous
falsely to charge another with being a
rapist, robber, carrier of knives and guns,
user of marijuana. The precise question
before us, then, is whether the protection
of "liberty" in the Due Process Clause of
the Fourteenth Amendment prevents a
State from punishing such libels—as criminal libel has been defined, limited and
constitutionally recognized time out of
mind—directed at designated collectivities
and flagrantly disseminated. There is even
authority, however dubious, that such utterances were also crimes at common law.
It is certainly clear that some American
jurisdictions have sanctioned their punishment under ordinary criminal libel statutes. We cannot say, however, that the
question is concluded by history and practice. But if an utterance directed at an individual may be the object of criminal
sanctions, we cannot deny to a State power
to punish the same utterance directed at a
defined group, unless we can say that this
is a wilful and purposeless restriction unrelated to the peace and well-being of the
State.

Illinois did not have to look beyond
her own borders or await the tragic experience of the last three decades to conclude that wilful purveyors of falsehood
concerning racial and religious groups promote strife and tend powerfully to obstruct the manifold adjustments required
for free, ordered life in a metropolitan,
polyglot community. From the murder of
the abolitionist Lovejoy in 1837 to the
Cicero riots of 1951, Illinois has been the
scene of exacerbated tension between races,

often flaring into violence and destruction. In many of these outbreaks, utterances of the character here in question, so the Illinois legislature could conclude, played a significant part. The law was passed on June 29, 1917, at a time when the State was struggling to assimilate vast numbers of new inhabitants, as yet concentrated in discrete racial or national or religious groups—foreign-born brought to it by the crest of the great wave of immigration, and Negroes attracted by jobs in war plants and the allurements of northern cities. Nine years earlier, in the very city where the legislature sat, what is said to be the first northern race riot had cost the lives of six people, left hundreds of Negroes homeless and shocked citizens into action far beyond the borders of the State. Less than a month before the bill was enacted, East St. Louis had seen a day's rioting, prelude to an outbreak, only four days after the bill became law, so bloody that it led to Congressional investigation. A series of bombings had begun which was to culminate two years later in the awful race riot which held Chicago in its grip for seven days in the summer of 1919. Nor has tension and violence between the groups defined in the statute been limited in Illinois to clashes between whites and Negroes.

In the face of this history and its frequent obligato of extreme racial and religious propaganda, we would deny experience to say that the Illinois legislature was without reason in seeking ways to curb false or malicious defamation of racial and religious groups, made in public places and by means calculated to have a powerful emotional impact on those to whom it was presented. "There are limits to the exercise of these liberties [of speech and of the press]. The danger in these times from the coercive activities of those who in the delusion of racial or religious conceit would incite violence and breaches of the peace in order to deprive others of their equal right to the exercise of their

liberties, is emphasized by events familiar to all. These and other transgressions of those limits the States appropriately may punish." This was the conclusion, again of a unanimous Court, in 1940. *Cantwell v. Connecticut.* . . .

It may be argued, and weightily, that this legislation will not help matters; that tension and on occasion violence between racial and religious groups must be traced to causes more deeply embedded in our society than the rantings of modern Know-nothings. Only those lacking responsible humility will have a confident solution for problems as intractable as the frictions attributable to differences of race, color or religion. This being so, it would be out of bounds for the judiciary to deny the legislature a choice of policy, provided it is not unrelated to the problem and not forbidden by some explicit limitation on the State's power. That the legislative remedy might not in practice mitigate the evil, or might itself raise new problems, would only manifest once more the paradox of reform. It is the price paid for the trial-and-error inherent in legislative efforts to deal with obstinate social issues. . . . Certainly the Due Process Clause does not require the legislature to be in the vanguard of science—especially sciences as young as human ecology and cultural anthropology. . . .

Libellous utterances, not being within the area of constitutionally protected speech, it is unnecessary, either for us or for the State courts, to consider the issues behind the phrase "clear and present danger." Certainly no one would contend that obscene speech, for example, may be punished only upon a showing of such circumstances. Libel, as we have seen, is in the same class.

We find no warrant in the Constitution for denying to Illinois the power to pass the law here under attack. But it bears repeating—although it should not—that our finding that the law is not constitutionally objectionable carries no implication of approval of the wisdom of the legislation or of its efficacy. These questions may raise doubts in our minds as well as in others. It is not for us, however, to make the legislative judgment. We are not at liberty to erect those doubts into fundamental law.

Affirmed.

252. *The Retreat from the Thornhill Doctrine*

Giboney v. Empire Storage & Ice Co., 336 U.S. 490 (1949).

BLACK, J.: . . . It is contended that the injunction against picketing adjacent to Empire's place of business is an unconstitutional abridgment of free speech because the picketers were attempting peacefully to publicize truthful facts about a labor dispute. See *Thornhill v. Alabama* . . . But the record here does not permit this publicizing to be treated in isolation. For according to the pleadings, the evidence, the findings, and the argument of the appellants, the sole immediate object of the publicizing adjacent to the premises of Empire, as well as the other activities of the appellants and their allies, was to compel Empire to agree to stop selling ice to nonunion peddlers. Thus all of appellants' activities—their powerful transportation combinations, their patrolling, their formation of a picket line warning union men not to cross at peril of their union membership, their publicizing—constituted a single and integrated course of conduct, which was in violation of Missouri's valid law. In this situation, the injunction did no more than enjoin an offense against Missouri law, a felony.

It rarely has been suggested that the constitutional freedom for speech and press extends its immunity to speech or writing used as an integral part of conduct in violation of a valid criminal statute. We reject the contention now. Nothing that was said or decided in any of the cases relied on by appellants calls for a different holding.

Neither *Thornhill v. Alabama*, nor *Carlson v. California* . . . supports the contention that conduct otherwise unlawful is always immune from state regulations because an integral part of that conduct is carried on by display of placards by peaceful picketers. In both these cases this Court struck down statutes which banned all dissemination of information by people adjacent to certain premises, pointing out that the statutes were so broad that they could not only be utilized to punish conduct plainly illegal but could also be applied to ban all truthful publications of the facts of a labor controversy. But in the Thornhill opinion, . . . the Court was careful to point out that it was within the province of states "to set the limits of permissible contest open to industrial combatants." . . .

After emphasizing state power over industrial conflicts, the Court in the Thornhill opinion went on to say . . . that states may not "in dealing with the evils arising from industrial disputes . . . impair the effective exercise of the right to discuss freely industrial relations. . . ." This statement must be considered in its context. It was directed toward a sweeping state prohibition which this Court found to embrace "nearly every practicable, effective means whereby those interested —including the employees directly affected —may enlighten the public on the nature and causes of a labor dispute." That the general statement of the limitation of a state's power to impair free speech was not intended to apply to the fact situation presented here is further indicated by the cases cited with approval in note 21 of the Thornhill opinion. . . .

We think the circumstances here and the reasons advanced by the Missouri courts justify restraint of the picketing which was done in violation of Missouri's valid law for the sole immediate purpose of continuing a violation of law. In holding this, we are mindful of the essential importance to our society of a vigilant protection of freedom of speech and press. . . . States cannot consistently with our Constitution abridge those freedoms to obviate slight inconveniences or annoyances. . . . But placards used as an essential and inseparable part of a grave offense against an important public law cannot immunize that unlawful conduct from state control. . . .

It is clear that appellants were doing more than exercising a right of free speech or press. . . . They were exercising their economic power together with that of their allies to compel Empire to abide by union rather than by state regulation of trade. . . .

253. *Censorship of Motion Pictures: "The Miracle"*

Burstyn v. Wilson, 343 U.S. 495 (1952)

CLARK, J.: The issue here is the constitutionality, under the First and Fourteenth Amendments, of a New York statute which permits the banning of motion picture films on the ground that they are "sacrilegious." . . .

As we view the case, we need consider only appellant's contention that the New York statute is an unconstitutional abridgment of free speech and a free press. . . .

It cannot be doubted that motion pictures are a significant medium for the communication of ideas. They may affect public attitudes and behavior in a variety of ways, ranging from direct espousal of a political or social doctrine to the subtle shaping of thought which characterizes all artistic expression. The importance of motion pictures as an organ of public opinion is not lessened by the fact that they are designed to entertain as well as to inform. As was said in *Winters v. New York* . . . (1948):

The line between the informing and the entertaining is too elusive for the protection of that basic right [a free press]. Everyone is familiar with instances of propaganda through fiction. What is one man's amusement, teaches another's doctrine.

It is urged that motion pictures do not fall within the First Amendment's aegis because their production, distribution, and exhibition is a large-scale business conducted for private profit. We cannot agree. That books, newspapers, and magazines are published and sold for profit does not prevent them from being a form of expression whose liberty is safeguarded by the First Amendment. We fail to see why operation for profit should have any different effect in the case of motion pictures.

It is further urged that motion pictures possess a greater capacity for evil, particularly among the youth of a community, than other modes of expression. Even if one were to accept this hypothesis, it does not follow that motion pictures should be disqualified from First Amendment protection. If there be capacity for evil it may be relevant in determining the permissible scope of community control, but it does not authorize substantially unbridled censorship such as we have here.

For the foregoing reasons, we conclude that expression by means of motion pictures is included within the free speech and free press guaranty of the First and Fourteenth Amendments. To the extent that language in the opinion in *Mutual Film Corp. v. Industrial Comm'n* . . . is out of harmony with the views here set forth, we no longer adhere to it.

To hold that liberty of expression by means of motion pictures is guaranteed by the First and Fourteenth Amendments, however, is not the end of our problem.

It does not follow that the Constitution requires absolute freedom to exhibit every motion picture of every kind at all times and all places. That much is evident from the series of decisions of this Court with respect to other media of communication of ideas. Nor does it follow that motion pictures are necessarily subject to the precise rules governing any other particular method of expression. Each method tends to present its own peculiar problems. But the basic principles of freedom of speech and the press, like the First Amendment's command, do not vary. Those principles, as they have frequently been enunciated by this Court, make freedom of expression the rule. There is no justification in this case for making an exception to that rule.

The statute involved here does not seek to punish, as a past offense, speech or writing falling within the permissible scope of subsequent punishment. On the contrary, New York requires that permission to communicate ideas be obtained in advance from state officials who judge the content of the words and pictures sought to be communicated. This Court recognized many years ago that such a previous restraint is a form of infringement upon freedom of expression to be especially condemned. *Near v. Minnesota*. . . .

New York's highest court says there is "nothing mysterious" about the statutory provision applied in this case: "It is simply this: that no religion, as that word is understood by the ordinary, reasonable person, shall be treated with contempt, mockery, scorn and ridicule . . ." This is far from the kind of narrow exception to freedom of expression which a state may carve out to satisfy the adverse demands of other interests of society. In seeking to apply the broad and all-inclusive definition of "sacrilegious" given by the New York courts, the censor is set adrift upon a boundless sea amid a myriad of conflicting currents of religious views, with no charts but those provided by the most vocal and powerful orthodoxies. New York cannot vest such unlimited restraining control over motion pictures in a censor. . . . Under such a standard the most careful and tolerant censor would find it virtually impossible to avoid favoring one religion over another, and he would be subject to an inevitable tendency to ban the expression of unpopular sentiments sacred to a religious minority. Application of the "sacrilegious" test in these or other respects, might raise substantial questions under the First Amendment's guaranty of separate church and state with freedom of worship for all. However, from the standpoint of freedom of speech and the press, it is enough to point out that the state has no legitimate interest in protecting any or all religions from views distasteful to them which is sufficient to justify prior restraints upon the expression of those views. It is not the business of government in our nation to suppress real or imagined attacks upon a particular religious doctrine, whether they appear in publications, speeches, or motion pictures.

Since the term "sacrilegious" is the sole standard under attack here, it is not necessary for us to decide, for example, whether a state may censor motion pictures under a clearly-drawn statute designed and applied to prevent the showing of obscene films. That is a very different question from the one now before us. We hold only that under the First and Fourteenth Amendments a state may not ban a film on the basis of a censor's conclusion that it is sacrilegious.

Reversed.

254. *Obscene Literature and the Right to Read*

Butler v. Michigan, 77 S. Ct. 524 (1957).

FRANKFURTER, J.: . . . Appellant was charged with . . . selling to a police officer what the trial judge characterized as "a book containing obscene, immoral, lewd, lascivious language, or descriptions, tending to incite minors to violent or depraved or immoral acts, manifestly tending to corruption of the morals of youth." Appellant moved to dismiss the proceeding on the claim that application of §343 unduly restricted freedom of speech as protected by the Due Process Clause of the Fourteenth Amendment in that the statute (1) prohibited distribution of a book to the general public on the basis of the undesirable influence it may have upon youth; (2) damned a book and proscribed its sale merely because of some isolated passages that appeared objectionable when divorced from the book as a whole; and (3) failed to provide a sufficiently definite standard of guilt. After hearing the evidence, the trial judge denied the motion, and, in an oral opinion, held that ". . . the defendant is guilty because he sold a book in the City of Detroit containing this language [the passages deemed offensive], and also because the Court feels that even viewing the book as a whole, it [the objectionable language] was not necessary to the proper development of the theme of the book nor of the conflict expressed therein." Appellant was fined $100. . . .

Appellant's argument here took a wide sweep. We need not follow him. Thus, it is unnecessary to dissect the remarks of the trial judge in order to determine whether he construed §343 to ban the distribution of books merely because certain of their passages, when viewed in iso-lation, were deemed objectionable. Likewise, we are free to put aside the claim that the Michigan law falls within the doctrine whereby a New York obscenity statute was found invalid in *Winters v. . . . New York.* . . .

It is clear on the record that appellant was convicted because Michigan . . . made it an offense for him to make available for the general reading public (and he in fact sold to a police officer) a book that the trial judge found to have a potentially deleterious influence upon youth. The State insists that, by thus quarantining the general reading public against books not too rugged for grown men and women in order to shield juvenile innocence, it is exercising its power to promote the general welfare. Surely, this is to burn the house to roast the pig. Indeed, the Solicitor General of Michigan has, with characteristic candor, advised the Court that Michigan has a statute specifically designed to protect its children against obscene matter "tending to the corruption of the morals of youth." But the appellant was not convicted for violating this statute.

We have before us legislation not reasonably restricted to the evil with which it is said to deal. The incidence of this enactment is to reduce the adult population of Michigan to reading only what is fit for children. It thereby arbitrarily curtails one of those liberties of the individual, now enshrined in the Due Process Clause of the Fourteenth Amendment, that history has attested as the indispensable conditions for the maintenance and progress of a free society. We are constrained to reverse this conviction.

Liberty and Loyalty

LEGISLATIVE RESTRICTIONS ON FREEDOM OF EXPRESSION

255. *The Peacetime Alien and Sedition Act of* 1940

The Alien Registration Act (Smith Act), *U. S. Stat. at L.,* LIV, 670 (1940).

An Act to prohibit certain subversive activities; to amend certain provisions of law with respect to the admission and deportation of aliens; to require the fingerprinting and registration of aliens; and for other purposes.

TITLE I

SECTION 1. (a) It shall be unlawful for any person, with intent to interfere with, impair, or influence the loyalty, morale, or discipline of the military or naval forces of the United States—

(1) to advise, counsel, urge, or in any manner cause insubordination, disloyalty, mutiny, or refusal of duty by any member of the military or naval forces of the United States; or

(2) to distribute any written or printed matter which advises, counsels, or urges insubordination, disloyalty, mutiny, or refusal of duty by any member of the military or naval forces of the United States. . . .

SEC. 2. (a) It shall be unlawful for any person—

(1) to knowingly or willfully advocate, abet, advise, or teach the duty, necessity, desirability, or propriety of overthrowing or destroying any government in the United States by force or violence, or by the assassination of any officer of any such government;

(2) with the intent to cause the overthrow or destruction of any government in the United States, to print, publish, edit, issue, circulate, sell, distribute, or publicly display any written or printed matter advocating, advising, or teaching the duty, necessity, desirability, or propriety of overthrowing or destroying any government in the United States by force or violence;

(3) to organize or help to organize any society, group, or assembly of persons who teach, advocate, or encourage the overthrow or destruction of any government in the United States by force or violence; or to be or become a member of, or affiliate with, any such society, group, or assembly of persons, knowing the purposes thereof. . . .

256. *The Non-Communist Oath in the Taft-Hartley Law*

American Communications Association v. Douds, 339 U.S. 382 (1950).

VINSON, C.J.: These cases present for decision the constitutionality of §9(h) of the National Labor Relations Act, as amended by the Labor Management Relations Act, 1947. This section, commonly referred to as the non-Communist affidavit provision, reads as follows: "No investigation shall be made by the [National Labor

Relations] Board of any question affecting commerce concerning the representation of employees, raised by a labor organization . . . , no petition . . . shall be entertained, and no complaint shall be issued pursuant to a charge made by a labor organization . . . , unless there is on file with the Board an affidavit executed contemporaneously or within the preceding twelve-month period by each officer of such labor organization and the officers of any national or international labor organization of which it is an affiliate or constituent unit that he is not a member of the Communist Party or affiliated with such party, and that he does not believe in, and is not a member of or supports any organization that believes in or teaches, the overthrow of the United States Government by force or by any illegal or unconstitutional methods. . . ."

The constitutional justification for the National Labor Relations Act was the power of Congress to protect interstate commerce by removing obstructions to the free flow of commerce. . . .

One such obstruction, which it was the purpose of §9(h) of the Act to remove, was the so-called "political strike." Substantial amounts of evidence were presented to various committees of Congress . . . that Communist leaders of labor unions had in the past and would continue in the future to subordinate legitimate trade union objectives to obstructive strikes when dictated by Party leaders, often in support of the policies of a foreign government. . . .

There can be no doubt that Congress may, under its constitutional power to regulate commerce among the several States, attempt to prevent political strikes and other kinds of direct action designed to burden and interrupt the free flow of commerce. We think it is clear, in addition, that the remedy provided by §9(h) bears reasonable relation to the evil which the statute was designed to reach. Congress could rationally find that the Communist Party is not like other political parties in

its utilization of positions of union leadership as means by which to bring about strikes and other obstructions of commerce for purposes of political advantage, and that many persons who believe in overthrow of the Government by force and violence are also likely to resort to such tactics when, as officers, they formulate union policy.

The fact that the statute identifies persons by their political affiliations and beliefs, which are circumstances ordinarily irrelevant to permissible subjects of government action, does not lead to the conclusion that such circumstances are never relevant. . . . But the more difficult problem here arises because, in drawing lines on the basis of beliefs and political affiliations, though it may be granted that the proscriptions of the statute bear a reasonable relation to the apprehended evil, Congress has undeniably discouraged the lawful exercise of political freedoms as well. . . . By exerting pressures on unions to deny office to Communists and others identified therein, §9(h) undoubtedly lessens the threat to interstate commerce, but it has the further necessary effect of discouraging the exercise of political rights protected by the First Amendment. Men who hold union offices often have little choice but to renounce Communism or give up their offices. Unions which wish to do so are discouraged from electing Communists to office. . . .

The unions contend that once it is determined that this is a free speech case, the "clear and present danger" test must apply. . . . But they disagree as to how it should be applied. Appellant in No. 10 would require that joining the Communist Party or the expression of belief in overthrow of the Government by force be shown to be a clear and present danger of some substantive evil, since those are the doctrines affected by the statute. Petitioner in No. 13, on the other hand, would require a showing that political strikes, the substantive evil involved, are a clear and present danger to the security of the Nation or threaten widespread industrial unrest.

This confusion suggests that the attempt to apply the term, "clear and present danger," as a mechanical test in every case touching First Amendment freedoms, without regard to the context of its application, mistakes the form in which an idea was cast for the substance of the idea. . . . Although the First Amendment provides that Congress shall make no law abridging the freedom of speech, press or assembly, it has long been established that those freedoms themselves are dependent upon the power of constitutional government to survive. If it is to survive it must have power to protect itself against unlawful conduct and, under some circumstances, against incitements to commit unlawful acts. Freedom of speech thus does not comprehend the right to speak on any subject at any time. The important question that came to this Court immediately after the First World War was not whether, but how far, the First Amendment permits the suppression of speech which advocates conduct inimical to the public welfare. Some thought speech having a reasonable tendency to lead to such conduct might be punished. Justice Holmes and Brandeis took a different view. They thought that the greater danger to a democracy lies in the suppression of public discussion; that ideas and doctrines thought harmful or dangerous are best fought with words. Only, therefore, when force is very likely to follow an utterance before there is a chance for counter-argument to have effect may that utterance be punished or prevented. . . .

But the question with which we are here faced is not the same one that Justices Holmes and Brandeis found convenient to consider in terms of clear and present danger. Government's interest here is not in preventing the dissemination of Communist doctrine or the holding of particular beliefs because it is feared that unlawful action will result therefrom if free speech is practiced. Its interest is in protecting the free flow of commerce from what Congress considers to be substantial evils of conduct that are not the products of speech at all. Section 9(h), in other words, does not interfere with speech because Congress fears the consequences of speech; it regulates harmful conduct which Congress has determined is carried on by persons who may be identified by their political affiliations and beliefs. . . . [It] is designed to protect the public not against what Communists and others identified therein advocate or believe, but against what Congress has concluded they have done and are likely to do again. . . .

When particular conduct is regulated in the interest of public order, and the regulation results in an indirect, conditional, partial abridgment of speech, the duty of the courts is to determine which of these two conflicting interests demands the greater protection under the particular circumstances presented. . . .

In essence, the problem is one of weighing the probable effects of the statute upon the free exercise of the right of speech and assembly against the congressional determination that political strikes are evils of conduct which cause substantial harm to interstate commerce and that Communists and others identified by §9(h) pose continuing threats to that public interest when in positions of union leadership. . . .

The "reasons advanced in support of the regulation" are of considerable weight, as even the opponents of §9(h) agreed. . . . It should be emphasized that Congress, not the courts, is primarily charged with determination of the need for regulation of activities affecting interstate commerce. This Court must, if such regulation unduly infringes personal freedoms, declare the statute invalid under the First Amendment's command that the opportunities for free public discussion be maintained. But insofar as the problem is one of drawing inferences concerning the need for regulation of particular forms of conduct from conflicting evidence, this

Court is in no position to substitute its judgment as to the necessity or desirability of the statute for that of Congress. . . .

What of the effects of §9(h) upon the rights of speech and assembly of those proscribed by its terms? The statute does not prevent or punish by criminal sanctions the making of a speech, the affiliation with any organization, or the holding of any belief. But as we have noted, the fact that no direct restraint or punishment is imposed upon speech or assembly does not determine the free speech question. Under some circumstances, indirect "discouragements" undoubtedly have the same coercive effect upon the exercise of First Amendment rights as imprisonment, fines, injunctions or taxes. . . . The "discouragements" of §9(h) proceed, not against the groups or beliefs identified therein, but only against the combination of those affiliations or beliefs with occupancy of a position of great power over the economy of the country. Congress has concluded that substantial harm, in the form of direct, positive action, may be expected from that combination. In this legislation, Congress did not restrain the activities of the Communist Party as a political organization; nor did it attempt to stifle beliefs. . . . Section 9(h) touches only a relative handful of persons, leaving the great majority of persons of the identified affiliations and beliefs completely free from restraint. And it leaves those few who are affected free to maintain their affiliations and beliefs subject only to possible loss of positions which Congress has concluded are being abused to the injury of the public by members of the described groups. . . .

It is contended that the principle that statutes touching First Amendment freedoms must be narrowly drawn dictates that a statute aimed at political strikes should make the calling of such strikes unlawful but should not attempt to bring about the removal of union officers, with its attendant effect upon First Amendment rights. We think, however, that the legislative judgment that interstate commerce must be protected from a continuing threat of such strikes is a permissible one in this case. The fact that the injury to interstate commerce would be an accomplished fact before any sanctions could be applied, the possibility that a large number of such strikes might be called at a time of external or internal crisis, and the practical difficulties which would be encountered in detecting illegal activities of this kind are factors which are persuasive that Congress should not be powerless to remove the threat, not limited to punishing the act. . . .

Previous discussion has considered the constitutional question raised by §9(h) as they apply alike to members of the Communist Party and affiliated organizations and to persons who believe in overthrow of the Government by force. The breadth of the provision concerning belief in overthrow of the Government by force would raise additional questions, however, if it were read very literally to include all persons who might, under any conceivable circumstances, subscribe to that belief.

But we see no reason to construe the statute so broadly. . . . The congressional purpose is . . . served if we construe the clause, "that he does not believe in . . . the overthrow of the United States Government by force or by any illegal or unconstitutional methods," to apply to persons and organizations who believe in violent overthrow of the Government as it presently exists under the Constitution as an objective, not merely a prophecy. . . .

As thus construed, we think that the "belief" provision of the oath presents no different problem from that present in that part of the section having to do with membership in the Communist Party. Of course we agree that one may not be imprisoned or executed because he holds particular beliefs. But to attack the straw man of "thought control" is to ignore the fact that the sole effect of the statute upon one who believes in overthrow of the Government by force and violence—and does not deny his belief—is that he may be forced to relinquish his position as a union leader. That fact was crucial in our discussion of the statute as it related to membership in the Communist Party. . . .

SEDITION, SUBVERSION, AND SUPPRESSION: THE INTERPRETATION OF THE SMITH ACT

257. The Redefinition of the "Clear and Present Danger" Test

Dennis v. U.S., 341 U.S. 494 (1951).

VINSON, C.J.: . . . The obvious purpose of the statute [the Smith Act] is to protect existing Government, not from change by peaceable, lawful and constitutional means, but from change by violence, revolution and terrorism. That it is within the *power* of the Congress to protect the Government of the United States from armed rebellion is a proposition which requires little discussion. Whatever theoretical merit there may be to the argument that there is a "right" to rebellion against dictatorial governments is without force where the existing structure of the government provides for peaceful and orderly change. We reject any principle of governmental helplessness in the face of preparation for revolution, which principle, carried to its logical conclusion, must lead to anarchy. No one could conceive that it is not within the power of Congress to prohibit acts intended to overthrow the Government by force and violence. The question with which we are concerned here is not whether Congress has such *power*, but whether the *means* which it has employed conflict with the First and Fifth Amendments to the Constitution.

One of the bases for the contention that the means which Congress has employed are invalid takes the form of an attack on the face of the statute on the grounds that by its terms it prohibits academic discussion of the merits of Marxism-Leninism, that it stifles ideas and is contrary to all concepts of a free speech and a free press. . . .

The very language of the Smith Act negates the interpretation which petitioners would have us impose on that Act. It is directed at advocacy, not discussion. Thus, the trial judge properly charged the jury that they could not convict if they found that petitioners did "no more than pursue peaceful studies and discussions or teaching and advocacy in the realm of ideas." He further charged that it was not unlawful "to conduct in an American college and university a course explaining the philosophical theories set forth in the books which have been placed in evidence." Such a charge is in strict accord with the statutory language, and illustrates the meaning to be placed on those words. Congress did not intend to eradicate the free discussion of political theories, to destroy the traditional rights of Americans to discuss and evaluate ideas without fear of governmental sanction. Rather Congress was concerned with the very kind of activity in which the evidence showed these petitioners engaged.

But although the statute is not directed at the hypothetical cases which petitioners have conjured, its application in this case has resulted in convictions for the teaching and advocacy of the overthrow of the Government by force and violence, which, even though coupled with the intent to accomplish that overthrow, contains an element of speech. For this reason, we must pay special heed to the demands of the First Amendment marking out the boundaries of speech.

We pointed out in Douds . . . that the basis of the First Amendment is the hypothesis that speech can rebut speech, propaganda will answer propaganda, free debate of ideas will result in the wisest governmental policies. It is for this reason that this Court has recognized the inherent value of free discourse. An analysis of the leading cases in this Court which have involved direct limitations on speech, however, will demonstrate that both the majority of the Court and the dissenters in particular cases have recognized that this is not an unlimited, unqualified right, but that the societal value of speech must, on occasion, be subordinated to other values and considerations. . . .

[The Chief Justice discussed several cases decided in 1919-1920, and stressed the "clear and present danger" test enunciated in Schenck.]

The rule we deduce from these cases is that where an offense is specified by a statute in nonspeech or nonpress terms, a conviction relying upon speech or press as evidence of violation may be sustained only when the speech or publication created a "clear and present danger" of attempting or accomplishing the prohibited crime, *e.g.*, interference with enlistment. The dissents, we repeat, in emphasizing the value of speech, were addressed to the argument of the sufficiency of the evidence. . . .

[The Chief Justice then discussed dissents by Justices Holmes and Brandeis in Gitlow and Whitney, when the "clear and present danger" test was not applied.]

Although no case subsequent to Whitney and Gitlow has expressly overruled the majority opinions in those cases, there is little doubt that subsequent opinions have inclined toward the Holmes-Brandeis rationale. . . . But . . . neither Justice Holmes nor Justice Brandeis ever envisioned that a shorthand phrase should be crystallized into a rigid rule to be applied inflexibly without regard to the circumstances of each case. Speech is not an absolute, above and beyond control by the legislature when its judgment, subject to review here, is that certain kinds of speech are so undesirable as to warrant criminal sanction. Nothing is more certain in modern society than the principle that there are no absolutes, that a name, a phrase, a standard has meaning only when associated with the considerations which gave birth to the nomenclature. See *American Communications Assn. v. Douds* . . . To those who would paralyze our Government in the face of impending threat by encasing it in a semantic straitjacket we must reply that all concepts are relative.

In this case we are squarely presented with the application of the "clear and present danger" test, and must decide what that phrase imports. We first note that many of the cases in which this Court has reversed convictions by use of this or similar tests have been based on the fact that the interest which the State was attempting to protect was itself too insubstantial to warrant restriction of speech. . . . Overthrow of the Government by force and violence is certainly a substantial enough interest for the Government to limit speech. Indeed, this is the ultimate value of any society, for if a society cannot protect its very structure from armed internal attack, it must follow that no subordinate value can be protected. If, then, this interest may be protected, the literal problem which is presented is what has been meant by the use of the phrase "clear and present danger" of the utterances bringing about the evil within the power of Congress to punish.

Obviously, the words cannot mean that before the Government may act, it must wait until the *putsch* is about to be executed, the plans have been laid and the signal is awaited. If Government is aware that a group aiming at its overthrow is attempting to indoctrinate its members and to commit them to a course whereby they will strike when the leaders feel the circumstances permit, action by the Government is required. The argument that there is no need for Government to concern itself, for Government is strong, it possesses ample powers to put down a rebellion, it may defeat the revolution with ease needs no answer. For that is not the question. Certainly an attempt to overthrow the Government by force, even though doomed from the outset because of inadequate numbers or power of the revolutionists, is a sufficient evil for Congress to prevent. The damage which such attempts create both physically and politically to a nation makes it impossible to measure the validity in terms of the probability of success, or the immediacy of a successful attempt. In the instant case the trial judge charged the jury that they could not convict unless they found that petitioners intended to overthrow the Government "as speedily as circumstances would permit." This does not mean, and could not properly mean, that they would not strike until there was certainty of success. What was meant was that the revolutionists would strike when they thought the time was ripe. We must therefore reject the contention that success or probability of success is the criterion.

The situation with which Justices Holmes and Brandeis were concerned in Gitlow was a comparatively isolated event bearing little relation in their minds to any substantial threat to the safety of the community. . . . They were not confronted with any situation comparable to the instant one—the development of an apparatus designed and dedicated to the overthrow of the Government, in the context of world crisis after crisis.

Chief Judge Learned Hand, writing for the majority below, interpreted the phrase as follows: "In each case [courts] must ask whether the gravity of the 'evil,' discounted by its improbability, justifies such invasion of free speech as is necessary to avoid the danger." . . . We adopt this statement of the rule. As articulated by

Chief Judge Hand, it is as succinct and inclusive as any other we might devise at this time. It takes into consideration those factors which we deem relevant, and relates their significances. More we cannot expect from words.

Likewise, we are in accord with the court below, which affirmed the trial court's finding that the requisite danger existed. The mere fact that from the period 1945 to 1948 petitioners' activities did not result in an attempt to overthrow the Government by force and violence is of course no answer to the fact that there was a group that was ready to make the attempt. The formation by petitioners of such a highly organized conspiracy, with rigidly disciplined members subject to call when the leaders, these petitioners, felt that the time had come for action, coupled with the inflammable nature of world conditions, similar uprisings in other countries, and the touch-and-go nature of our relations with countries with whom petitioners were in the very least ideologically attuned, convince us that their convictions were justified on this score. And this analysis disposes of the contention that a conspiracy to advocate, as distinguished from the advocacy itself, cannot be constitutionally restrained, because it comprises only the preparation. It is the existence of the conspiracy which creates the danger. . . . If the ingredients of the reaction are present, we cannot bind the Government to wait until the catalyst is added. . . .

We agree that the standard as defined is not a neat, mathematical formulary. Like all verbalizations it is subject to criticism on the score of indefiniteness. But petitioners themselves contend that the verbalization, "clear and present danger," is the proper standard. We see no difference from the standpoint of vagueness, whether the standard of "clear and present danger" is one contained *in haec verba* within the statute, or whether it is the judicial measure of constitutional applicability. We have shown the indeterminate standard the phrase necessarily connotes.

We do not think we have rendered that standard any more indefinite by our attempt to sum up the factors which are included within its scope. We think it well serves to indicate to those who would advocate constitutionally prohibited conduct that there is a line beyond which they may not go—a line, which they, in full knowledge of what they intend and the circumstances in which their activity takes place, will well appreciate and understand. . . .

We hold that §§2(a) (1), 2(a) (3) and 3 of the Smith Act, do not inherently, or as construed or applied in the instant case, violate the First Amendment and other provisions of the Bill of Rights, or the First and Fifth Amendments because of indefiniteness. Petitioners intended to overthrow the Government of the United States as speedily as the circumstances would permit. Their conspiracy to organize the Communist Party and to teach and advocate the overthrow of the Government of the United States by force and violence created a "clear and present danger" of an attempt to overthrow the Government by force and violence. They were properly and constitutionally convicted for violation of the Smith Act. The judgments of conviction are affirmed.

258. *The First Amendment in a Free Society*

Dennis v. U.S., 341 U.S. 494 (1951).

BLACK, J., dissenting: Here . . . my basic disagreement with the Court is not as to how we should explain or reconcile what was said in prior decisions but springs from a fundamental difference in constitutional approach. Consequently, it would serve no useful purpose to state my position at length.

At the outset I want to emphasize what the crime involved in this case is, and what it is not. These petitioners were not charged with an attempt to overthrow the Government. They were not charged with overt acts of any kind designed to overthrow the Government. They were not even charged with saying anything or writing anything designed to overthrow the Government. The charge was that they agreed to assemble and to talk and publish certain ideas at a later date: The indictment is that they conspired to organize the Communist Party and to use speech or newspapers and other publications in the future to teach and advocate the forcible overthrow of the Government. No matter how it is worded, this is a virulent form of prior censorship of speech and press, which I believe the First Amendment forbids. I would hold §3 of the Smith Act authorizing this prior restraint unconstitutional on its face and as applied.

But let us assume, contrary to all constitutional ideas of fair criminal procedure, that petitioners although not indicted for the crime of actual advocacy, may be punished for it. Even on this radical assumption, the other opinions in this case show that the only way to affirm these convictions is to repudiate directly or indirectly the established "clear and present danger" rule. This the Court does in a way which greatly restricts the protections afforded by the First Amendment. The opinions for affirmance indicate that the chief reason for jettisoning the rule is the expressed fear that advocacy of Communist doctrine endangers the safety of the Republic. Undoubtedly, a governmental policy of unfettered communication of ideas does entail dangers. To the Founders of this Nation, however, the benefits derived from free expression were worth the risk. They embodied this philosophy in the First Amendment's command that Congress "shall make no law . . . abridging the freedom of speech, or of the press. . . ." I have always believed that the First

Amendment is the keystone of our Government, that the freedoms it guarantees provide the best insurance against destruction of all freedom. At least as to speech in the realm of public matters, I believe that the "clear and present danger" test does not "mark the furthermost constitutional boundaries of protected expression" but does "no more than recognize a minimum compulsion of the Bill of Rights." *Bridges v. California* . . . [1941].

So long as this Court exercises the power of judicial review of legislation, I cannot agree that the First Amendment permits us to sustain laws suppressing freedom of speech and press on the basis of Congress' or our own notions of mere "reasonableness." Such a doctrine waters down the First Amendment so that it amounts to little more than an admonition to Congress. The Amendment as so construed is not likely to protect any but those "safe" or orthodox views which rarely need its protection. . . .

Public opinion being what it now is, few will protest the conviction of these Communist petitioners. There is hope, however, that in calmer times, when present pressures, passions and fears subside, this or some later Court will restore the First Amendment liberties to the high preferred place where they belong in a free society.

259. *Federal Versus State Control of Sedition*

Commonwealth of Pennsylvania v. Nelson, 350 U.S. 497 (1956).

WARREN, C.J.: The respondent, Steve Nelson, an acknowledged member of the Communist party, was convicted . . . of a violation of the Pennsylvania Sedition Act and sentenced to imprisonment for twenty years and to a fine of $10,000 and to costs of prosecution in the sum of $13,000. . . . The Supreme Court of Pennsylvania, recognizing but not reaching many alleged serious trial errors and conduct of the trial court infringing upon respondent's right to due process of law, decided the case on the narrow issue of supersession of the state law by the Federal Smith Act. . . .

The precise holding of the court, and all that is before us for review, is that the Smith Act of 1940, as amended in 1948, which prohibits the knowing advocacy of the overthrow of the Government of the United States by force and violence, supersedes the enforceability of the Pennsylvania Sedition Act which proscribes the same conduct. . . .

It should be said at the outset that the decision in this case does not affect the right of states to enforce their sedition laws at times when the Federal Government has not occupied the field and is not protecting the entire country from seditious conduct. The distinction between the two situations was clearly recognized by the court below. Nor does it limit the jurisdiction of the states where the Constitution and Congress have specifically given them concurrent jurisdiction. . . . Neither does it limit the right of the state to protect itself at any time against sabotage or attempted violence of all kinds. Nor does it prevent the state from prosecuting where the same act constitutes both a Federal offense and a state offense under the police power. . . .

Where, as in the instant case, Congress has not stated specifically whether a Federal statute has occupied a field in which the states are otherwise free to legislate, different criteria have furnished touchstones for decision. . . . In this case, we think that each of several tests of supersession is met.

First, "The scheme of Federal regulation

[is] so pervasive as to make reasonable the inference that Congress left no room for the states to supplement it." . . . The Congress determined in 1940 that it was necessary for it to re-enter the field of antisubversive legislation, which had been abandoned by it in 1921. In that year it enacted the Smith Act which proscribes advocacy of the overthrow of any government—federal, state or local—by force and violence and organization of and knowing membership in a group which so advocates. Conspiracy to commit any of these acts is punishable under the general criminal conspiracy provisions in 18 U. S. C. §371. The Internal Security Act of 1950 is aimed more directly at Communist organizations. It distinguishes between "Communist-action organizations" and "Communist-front organizations," requiring such organizations to register and file annual reports with the Attorney General, giving complete details as to their officers and funds. Members of Communist-action organizations who have not been registered by their organization must register as individuals. . . . The Communist Control Act of 1954 declares "that the Communist party of the United States, although purportedly a political party is in fact an instrumentality of a conspiracy to overthrow the Government of the United States" and that "its role as the agency of a hostile foreign power renders its existence a clear, present and continuing danger to the security of the United States." . . .

We examine these Acts only to determine the Congressional plan. . . . Taken as a whole they evince a Congressional plan which makes it reasonable to determine that no room has been left for the states to supplement it. Therefore a state sedition statute is superseded regardless of whether it purports to supplement the federal law. . . .

Second, the federal statutes "touch a field in which the Federal interest is so dominant that the Federal system [must] be assumed to preclude enforcement of state laws on the same subject." . . . Congress has devised an all-embracing program for resistance to the various forms of totalitarian aggression. . . . It accordingly proscribed sedition against all government in the nation—national, state and local. . . . Congress having thus treated seditious conduct as a matter of vital national concern, it is in no sense a local enforcement problem. . . .

Third, enforcement of state sedition acts presents a serious danger of conflict with the administration of the federal program. Since 1939, in order to avoid a hampering of uniform enforcement of its program by sporadic local prosecutions, the Federal Government has urged local authorities not to intervene in such matters, but to turn over to the federal authorities immediately and unevaluated all information concerning subversive activities. The President made such a request on Sept. 6, 1939, when he placed the Federal Bureau of Investigation in charge of investigation in this field. . . .

Since we find that Congress has occupied the field to the exclusion of parallel state legislation, that the dominant interest of the Federal Government precludes state intervention and that administration of state Acts would conflict with the operation of the Federal plan, we are convinced that the decision of the Supreme Court of Pennsylvania is unassailable.

THE FEDERAL GOVERNMENT'S CONTROL OVER ITS EMPLOYEES

260. *The Federal Loyalty Program, March 21, 1947*

Executive Order 9835, *Federal Register*, XII, 1935-9 (March 25, 1947).

WHEREAS each employee of the Government of the United States is endowed with a measure of trusteeship over the democratic processes which are the heart and sinew of the United States; and

WHEREAS, it is of vital importance that persons employed in the Federal service be of complete and unswerving loyalty to the United States; and

WHEREAS, although the loyalty of by far the overwhelming majority of all Government employees is beyond question, the presence within the Government service of any disloyal or subversive person constitutes a threat to our democratic processes; and

WHEREAS maximum protection must be afforded the United States against infiltration of disloyal persons into the ranks of its employees, and equal protection from unfounded accusations of disloyalty must be afforded the loyal employees of the Government:

Now, THEREFORE . . . it is hereby, in the interest of the internal management of the Government, ordered as follows:

PART I. INVESTIGATION OF APPLICANTS

1. There shall be a loyalty investigation of every person entering the civilian employment of any department or agency of the executive branch of the Federal Government. . . .

3. An investigation shall be made of all applicants at all available pertinent sources of information and shall include reference to:

A. Federal Bureau of Investigation files.
B. Civil Service Commission files.
C. Military and Naval Intelligence files.
D. The files of any other appropriate government investigative or intelligence agency.

E. House Committee on un-American Activities files.

F. Local law-enforcement files at the place of residence and employment of the applicant, including municipal, county and State law-enforcement files.

G. Schools and colleges attended by applicant.

H. Former employers of applicant.

I. References given by applicant.

J. Any other appropriate source.

4. Whenever derogatory information with respect to loyalty of an applicant is revealed, a full field investigation shall be conducted. . . .

PART IV. SECURITY MEASURES IN INVESTIGATIONS

1. . . . An investigative agency shall make available . . . all investigative material and information collected by the investigative agency concerning any employee or prospective employee. . . .

2. . . . However, the investigative agency may refuse to disclose the names of confidential informants, provided it furnishes sufficient information about such informants on the basis of which the requesting department or agency can make an adequate evaluation of the information furnished by them, and provided it advises the requesting department or agency in writing that it is essential to the protection of the informants or to the investigation of other cases that the identity of the informants not be revealed. Investigative agencies shall not use this discretion to decline to reveal sources of information where such action is not essential. . . .

PART V. STANDARDS

1. The standard for the refusal of employment or the removal from employment in an executive department or agency on grounds relating to loyalty shall be that, on all the evidence, reasonable grounds exist for belief that the person involved is disloyal to the Government of the United States.

2. Activities and associations of an applicant or employee which may be considered in connection with the determination of disloyalty may include one or more of the following:

A. Sabotage, espionage, or attempts or preparations therefor, knowingly associating with spies or saboteurs;

B. Treason or sedition or advocacy thereof;

C. Advocacy of revolution or force or violence to alter the constitutional form of Government of the United States;

D. Intentional, unauthorized disclosure to any person, under circumstances which may indicate disloyalty to the United States, of documents or information of a confidential or non-public character obtained by the person making the disclosure as a result of his employment by the Government of the United States;

E. Performing or attempting to perform his duties, or otherwise acting, so as to serve the interests of another government in preference to the interests of the United States.

F. Membership in, affiliation with or sympathetic association with any foreign or domestic organization, association, movement, group or combination of persons, designated by the Attorney General as totalitarian, Fascist, Communist, or subversive, or as having adopted a policy of advocating or approving the commission of acts of force or violence to deny other persons their rights under the Constitution of the United States, or as seeking to alter the form of Government of the United States by unconstitutional means. . . .

261. *Proposals for a New "Federal Personnel Security System"*

Report of the Special Committee on The Federal Loyalty-Security Program of the Association of the Bar of the City of New York (New York, 1956), 137-88 *passim*. Reprinted by permission of the Association of the Bar of the City of New York Fund, Inc.

A. COORDINATION AND SUPERVISION

1. *The Director of Personnel and Information Security*

[1] The Office of Director of Personnel and Information Security should be established in the Executive Office of the President.

[2] The Director should be appointed by the President subject to confirmation by the Senate and serve at the pleasure of the President.

[3] It should be the primary responsibility of the Director to conduct a continuous review of and supervision over:

(a) The personnel security programs, in order to assure efficiency, uniformity and fairness of administration, consonant with the interests of national security.

(b) The classification of information, so that only such information shall be classified as the interest of national security actually require.

[4] In the performance of his responsibility the Director should make recommendations to the President which, when embodied in regulations prepared by the Director and approved by the President, would be binding upon the departments and agencies concerned.

B. SCOPE

2. *Scope of Personal Security*

[1] Clearance under the personnel secu-

rity programs should be required for all sensitive positions and for no others.

[2] The head of each department or agency should designate as sensitive only those positions within his department or agency the occupant of which would

   (a) have access to material classified as secret or top-secret in the interests of national security, or,

   (b) have a policy-making function which bears a substantial relation to national security.

[3] The President, on recommendation of the Director, should specify criteria in accordance with which the head of each department or agency should classify positions.

3. Classification of Information

The Director should continuously review and, after consultation with the agencies involved, make recommendations to the President concerning the standards and criteria and methods to be used in the classification of information and in its declassification when secrecy is no longer important to the interests of national security. These recommendations, when approved by the President, would be binding upon the departments and agencies concerned.

C. STANDARDS AND CRITERIA

4. Standard for Personnel Security

[1] The personnel security standard for all sensitive positions should be stated as follows:

"The personnel security standard shall be whether or not in the interest of the United States the employment or retention in employment of the individual is advisable. In applying this standard a balanced judgment shall be reached after giving due weight to all the evidence, both derogatory and favorable, to the nature of the position, and to the value of the individual to the public service." . . .

5. The Employee's Associations

A person's associations with organiza-tions or individuals may properly be considered in determining his security suita-bility. But a conclusion against his security suitability on the ground of such associations should not be reached without adequate basis for determining that he shares, is susceptible to, or is influenced by, the actions or views of such organizations or individuals.

6. The Attorney General's List

[1] The Attorney General's list of subversive organizations should be abolished, unless it can be and is modified and revised in the following respects:

   (a) The list should not include any organization which has been defunct more than ten years. (Information as to such organizations, however, would be available under the procedures set forth in paragraph [2] of this recommendation.)

   (b) The list should give information as to the period and the general nature of the subversive activity of each organization listed.

   (c) The list should be kept up to date by periodical supplements eliminating organizations which have been defunct over ten years and adding new organizations found to be subversive since the last publication.

   (d) The list should include only those organizations which have been given notice and an opportunity to be heard in conformity with the requirements of due process of law.

   (e) The list should contain a statement that mere membership in any of the organizations listed is not in itself to be construed as establishing the subversive character of a member unless membership has been made illegal by statute.

[2] The Department of Justice should upon request make available to security personnel and boards relevant information in its files concerning all organizations, whether defunct or not, the character of which may be pertinent in a pending in-

quiry. Such information may be taken into consideration in the inquiry together with all other evidence presented.

D. PERSONNEL

7. *Security Personnel*

Personnel engaged in security matters should be individuals whose qualities and standing will inspire confidence in the fair, wise and courageous administration of the programs. To this end the Director should establish training courses for security personnel. The training should include intensive and thorough instruction in

   (a) the nature of Communism and the techniques of Communist espionage and infiltration in the United States and in other countries;

   (b) the political history of the United States and of the world, especially in this century;

   (c) constitutional and legal principles; and

   (d) the relative reliability of various kinds of evidence.

E. PROCEDURE[1]

8. *Central Screening Board*

[1] A central screening board should be created in the Civil Service Commission. This board should have the responsibility, except as set forth in paragraph [3] below, of determining whether or not security charges should be filed against any person covered by a security program, whether a Federal or a private employee.

[2] The central screening board should act in panels of not less than three members. At least one member of each panel should be a lawyer, and at least one member should be a person whose only government employment is his work on the board.

[1] Such highly secret investigative agencies as the Central Intelligence Agency and the Federal Bureau of Investigation would not fall within these recommendations except as the President may determine upon the advice of the Director.

[3] Subject to further action by the Director, the Atomic Energy Commission and the Department of Defense should continue their present methods of screening to determine whether or not security charges should be filed, unless they wish to utilize the services of the central screening board. The Director should determine whether any other department or agency may establish or maintain its own screening board.

9. *Screening Procedure*

[1] Screening boards should afford the employee an opportunity for an informal conference with the board or its representatives to answer adverse security information.

[2] When a screening board determines that charges should be filed, it should prepare a specific statement of charges. If a person charged contends that charges are not specific enough to enable him to prepare his defense, the board should, in the exercise of reasonable discretion within the limits of security requirements, determine what additional information shall be furnished him. . . .

[4] Every employee against whom a security question is raised should be entitled to have an attorney advise and aid him. . . .

10. *Treatment of Charged Employees Pending Disposition of Charges*

Pending the final disposition of charges against Federal employees or employees of private employers:

[1] The pay of suspended employees should continue.

[2] Employees under charges, if not retained in the positions held when charges are filed, should be transferred without loss of pay to nonsensitive positions instead of being suspended, whenever this is practicable and consistent with the interests of national security.

11. *Hearing Boards*

[1] Every charged employee, other than a probationary employee, should be entitled to a hearing before a hearing board of three members to be appointed by the

head of the charging agency. One member but not more than one member of the hearing board should be an employee of the charging agency, at least one member should be a lawyer, and at least one member should come from outside the government service. In the alternative, a hearing board may be composed entirely of persons outside the government service but in such case also one member should be a lawyer. . . .

12. Hearing Procedure

[1] The charging agency should be entitled to have an attorney present at the hearing. . . .

[3] Every charged employee should be entitled to have an attorney present at the hearing to represent him. The attorney should have the right to offer evidence and cross-examine witnesses.

[4] Hearing boards should prepare written findings of fact and conclusions. These should be furnished to the charged employee for his use with only such deletions as are required in the interests of national security.

[5] The charged employee should be furnished a copy of the transcript of the hearing for his use in the proceedings.

[6] The security hearing should not be public.

13. Appearance of Witnesses and Confrontation

[1] Except as provided below, screening boards and hearing boards should have the power in their discretion to subpoena government witnesses and witnesses for employees and to permit the submission of evidence by depositions, interrogatories, affidavits, letters, and other written statements. . . .

[3] It should be the policy of the government to permit the employee to cross-examine adverse witnesses before a hearing board when the hearing board believes this important for the development of the facts, unless the disclosure of the identity of the witness or requiring him to submit to cross-examination would be injurious to national security. . . .

[5] As to all other witnesses, including casual informants, and with due consideration of the national security and fairness to the employee

(a) the screening board should determine whether it desires a witness to appear before it for interview, and

(b) the hearing board should determine whether the witness should be produced for cross-examination, or whether because of special circumstances he should be interrogated by the board without the employee being present, or whether his evidence should be given to the board in other ways, such as by an affidavit or a signed statement. So far as consistent with the requirements of national security, a hearing board should make available to the employee the substance of all evidence it takes into consideration which was given by any witness whom the employee has not been permitted to cross-examine.

[6] In determining the probative effect of information given by informants who are not made available for cross-examination by the charged employee, under the exceptions contained in paragraphs [4] and [5] above, screening and hearing boards as well as appeal boards and agency heads should always take into account the lack of opportunity for cross-examination. . . .

15. Final Determination

The head of the charging agency should have the power to make the final security determination. . . .

THE CONSTITUTIONALITY OF STATE LOYALTY LAWS

262. *Loyalty Oaths, Innocent Membership, and Arbitrary Power*

Wieman v. Updegraff, 344 U.S. 183 (1952).

CLARK, J.: This is an appeal from a decision of the Supreme Court of Oklahoma upholding the validity of a loyalty oath prescribed by Oklahoma statute for all state officers and employees. . . . Appellants, employed by the state as members of the faculty and staff of Oklahoma Agricultural and Mechanical College, failed within the thirty days permitted, to take the oath required by the Act. . . . The appellants . . . attacked the validity of the Act on the grounds, among others, that it was a bill of attainder; an *ex post facto* law; impaired the obligation of their contracts with the State and violated the Due Process Clause of the Fourteenth Amendment. They also sought a mandatory injunction directing the state officers to pay their salaries regardless of their failure to take the oath. Their objections centered largely on the following clauses of the oath:

. . . That I am not affiliated directly or indirectly . . . with any foreign political agency, party organization or Government, or with any agency, party, organization, association, or group whatever which has been officially determined by the United States Attorney General or other authorized agency of the United States to be a communist front or subversive organization; . . . [and] that within the five (5) years immediately preceding the taking of this oath . . . I have not been a member of . . . [such] agency. . . .

The purpose of the Act, we are told, "was to make loyalty a qualification to hold public office or be employed by the State."

. . . During periods of international stress, the extent of legislation with such objectives accentuates our traditional concern about the relation of government to the individual in a free society. The perennial problem of defining that relationship becomes acute when disloyalty is screened by ideological patterns and techniques of disguise that make it difficult to identify. Democratic government is not powerless to meet this threat, but it must do so without infringing the freedoms that are the ultimate values of all democratic living. In the adoption of such means as it believes effective, the legislature is therefore confronted with the problem of balancing its interest in national security with the often conflicting constitutional rights of the individual.

In a series of cases coming here in recent years, we have had occasion to consider legislation aimed at safeguarding the public service from disloyalty. *Garner v. Board of Public Works* . . . (1951); *Adler v. Board of Education* . . . (1952); *Gerende* . . . (1951). . . . It is in the context of these decisions that we determine the validity of the oath before us.

Garner involved a Los Angeles ordinance requiring all city employees to swear that they did not advocate the overthrow of the government by unlawful means or belong to organizations with such objectives. . . . One of the attacks made on the oath in that case was that it violated due process because its negation was not limited to organizations known by the employee to be within the prescribed class. This argument was rejected because we felt justified in assuming that *scienter* was implicit in each clause of the oath.

Adler also indicated the importance of determining whether a rule of exclusion based on association applies to innocent as well as knowing activity. New York had sought to bar from employment in the public schools persons who advocate, or belong to organizations which advocate, the overthrow of the government by unlawful means. The Feinberg Law directed the New York Board of Regents to make a listing, after notice and hearing, of organizations of the type described. . . . The Regents provided by regulation that membership in a listed organization should be prima facie evidence of disqualification for office in the New York public schools. In upholding this legislation, we expressly noted that the New York courts had construed the statute to require knowledge of organizational purposes before the regulation could apply. . . .

The oath in Gerende was required of candidates for public office who sought places on a Maryland ballot. On oral argument in that case, the Maryland Attorney General assured us that he would advise the proper state authorities to accept, as complying with the statute, an affidavit stating that the affiant was not engaged in an attempt to overthrow the government by force or violence or knowingly a member of an organization engaged in such an attempt. Because we read an earlier Maryland Court of Appeals' decision as interpreting the statute so that such an affidavit would satisfy its requirements, we affirmed on the basis of this assurance.

We assumed in Garner, that if our interpretation of the oath as containing an implicit scienter requirement was correct, Los Angeles would give the petitioners who had refused to sign the oath an opportunity to take it as interpreted and resume their employment. But here, with our decision in Garner before it, the Oklahoma Supreme Court refused to extend to appellants an opportunity to take the oath. In addition, a petition for rehear-

ing which urged that failure to permit appellants to take the oath as interpreted deprived them of due process was denied. This must be viewed as a holding that knowledge is not a factor under the Oklahoma statute. We are thus brought to the question touched on in Garner, Adler, and Gerende: whether the due process clause permits a state in attempting to bar disloyal individuals from its employ to exclude persons solely on the basis of organizational membership, regardless of their knowledge concerning the organizations to which they had belonged. For, under the statute before us, the fact of membership alone disqualifies. If the rule be expressed as a presumption of disloyalty, it is a conclusive one.

But membership may be innocent. A state servant may have joined a proscribed organization unaware of its activities and purposes. In recent years, many completely loyal persons have severed organizational ties after learning for the first time of the character of groups to which they had belonged. . . . At the time of affiliation, a group itself may be innocent, only later coming under the influence of those who would turn it toward illegitimate ends. Conversely, an organization formerly subversive and therefore designated as such may have subsequently freed itself from the influences which originally led to its listing.

There can be no dispute about the consequences visited upon a person excluded from public employment on disloyalty grounds. In the view of the community, the stain is a deep one; indeed, it has become a badge of infamy. Especially is this so in time of cold war and hot emotions when "each man begins to eye his neighbor as a possible enemy." Yet under the Oklahoma Act, the fact of association alone determines disloyalty and disqualification; it matters not whether association existed innocently or knowingly. To thus inhibit individual freedom of movement is to stifle the flow of democratic expression and controversy at one of its chief sources. We hold that the distinction observed between the case at bar and Garner, Adler, and Gerende is decisive. Indiscriminate classification of innocent with knowing activity must fall as an assertion of arbitrary power. The oath offends due process. . . .

Reversed.

CHAPTER XXVIII

Procedural Safeguards and Civil Rights

HE history of American freedom," Justice Frankfurter has rightly remarked, "is, in no small measure, the history of procedure." Certainly one of the Supreme Court's most important functions is the maintenance of fair and decent standards in criminal prosecutions conducted in both federal and state courts. Although there is no question that the standards guaranteed by the Fourth through the Eighth Amendments of the Bill of Rights apply in federal prosecutions, there has long been a controversy as to whether these requirements are applicable to state trials. *Adamson v. California* is the most important discussion since *Palko v. Connecticut* (Chapter XXIV) of the Court's selective process for determining which provisions of the federal Bill of Rights are essential to due process of law and thus binding upon the states, and which are so unessential that the states may safely ignore them (No. 263). Speaking for four dissenters, Justice Black argued that all of the procedural guarantees should be incorporated into the Fourteenth Amendment just as the substantive rights of the First Amendment had been (No. 264). The Court, by rejecting this view, has continued to decide state appeals on a case-by-case basis to determine whether fundamental standards of decency have been observed.

From this judicially established test of "fairness" have emerged several important regulations of state criminal procedure. With few exceptions coerced confessions have been invalidated fairly consistently (*Watts v. Indiana*, 1949).

Indeed, the prohibition against unreasonable searches and seizures in the Fourth Amendment has won the acceptance of the Supreme Court as an integral ingredient in its concept of "ordered liberty": "The security of one's privacy against arbitrary intrusion by the police," said the majority in *Wolf v. Colorado* (1949), ". . . is basic to a free society . . . and as such is enforceable against the states through the Due Process Clause." This resounding statement was robbed of its apparent meaning, however, for the Court refused to require state courts to exclude evidence secured by admittedly unreasonable searches and seizures.

In federal prosecutions, the Fourth Amendment requires that search warrants specifically describe the things to be seized, and forbids the seizure of any item not mentioned. But the Amendment does not categorically require a search warrant to make a search reasonable; the law has long recognized the right to search a person as an incident to a lawful arrest. In recent years, this right of search without a warrent has been extended dramatically. In 1947 a closely divided court sustained a five-hour search of a four-room apartment by federal officials made in the course of a valid arrest (*Harris v. U.S.*). Although Harris was arrested for passing fraudulent checks, the search turned up illegal draft-registration forms and Harris was convicted on this charge rather than the original. Justice Frankfurter pointed out that "the novel and startling result" of this decision was to make the scope of allowable "search without warrant broader than an authorized search." When a similar case came up the next year, Justice Douglas switched sides and the new 5 to 4 majority ruled that a search without a warrant, even though made in the course of a lawful arrest, was unreasonable if there was time to obtain a warrant in advance (*Trupiano v. U.S.*, 1948). The death of two justices of the Trupiano majority opened the way for the Rabinowitz decision (No. 265), which reinstated the Harris doctrine. Not without reason did Justice Black despair that "in no other field has the law's uncertainty been more clearly manifested."

It seems reasonably clear that these postwar developments have expanded the discretionary area for federal officers to make searches without warrants, thus leaving to the courts the job of deciding the admissibility of seized evidence. An interesting example of the Court's approval of an unusual method of securing evidence came in *On Lee v. U.S.* (1952). Using a concealed "Dick Tracy" radio transmitter, an undercover agent engaged in conversation with a Chinese laundry owner suspected of peddling opium. Outside the laundry, a Narcotics Bureau agent noted the conversation, and later testified against On Lee. Although the minority protested against the use of an ambulatory wiretap, the majority held that electronic eavesdropping did not violate the Fourth Amendment.

The guarantees of the Fourth and Fifth Amendments have always been treated by the Supreme Court as closely allied. In a leading case on the Fourth Amendment (*Boyd v. U.S.*, 1886), Justice Bradley observed that "the Fourth and Fifth Amendments run almost into each other" when a law requires the compulsory production of incriminating evidence. The Fifth Amendment, he said, forbids "any forcible and compulsory extortion of a man's own testimony or of his private papers to be used as evidence to convict him of crime or to forfeit his goods." The self-incrimination clause, however, does not create any general right to refuse to give testimony; it simply stipulates that one need not be a witness against himself in proceedings which might lead to his prosecution. Witnesses before grand juries and Congressional investigating committees have increasingly invoked the protection when questioned about Communist activities and affiliations. In the Blau case (No. 266), the Supreme Court held that admission of membership or leadership in the Communist Party created more than a "mere imaginary possibility" of prosecution under the Smith Act (Chapter XXVII); it therefore upheld the right to plead the Fifth Amendment. The privilege must be invoked at the right time, however. In *Rogers v. U.S.* (1951), the Court ruled that a witness who admitted her activity as an official of the Communist Party could not invoke the privilege of self-incrimination when asked about the disposition of party records.

Although the constitutional protection of the Fifth Amendment shields a man from criminal prosecution and from contempt charges when he refuses to answer, it has not protected him from economic reprisals, either legal or unofficial. On the whole, the invocation of the self-incrimination clause has tended to be viewed as an act of self-incrimination, and several states and municipalities have made such a plea grounds for automatic dismissal from public employment. In 1956, however, a sharply divided Court struck down as a denial of due process the New York City provision requiring immediate severance of any employee pleading the Fifth Amendment (*Slochower v. Board of Education*).

In an attempt to obtain testimony from persons claiming the protection of the self-incrimination clause, Congress in 1954 passed an act granting immunity from prosecution to witnesses called to testify on matters relating to the national security. *Ullmann v. U.S.* (1956) ruled that the statute did not violate the Fifth Amendment, observing that when "immunity displaces the danger" of prosecution, constitutional rights are preserved.

Another aspect of refusal to testify was dealt with in *Barsky v. U.S.* (1948) and in *U.S. v. Rumely* (1953). The former challenged the scope of authority of the House Un-American Activities Committee, alleging that the words "subversive" and "Un-American" were undefined and not sufficiently free from ambiguity to permit a witness to determine the pertinency of Committee questions. By refusing to grant an appeal, the Supreme Court left intact the Circuit Court's ruling (1) that the Committee's authority was not void for vagueness, and (2) that the First Amendment does not establish a right of privacy that bars inquiries into political beliefs. In *U.S. v. Rumely*, however, the Court did place restraints on the House Committee on Lobbying Activities (No. 267).

As a part of the drive for greater internal security, it was perhaps inevitable that aliens should be viewed with increasing suspicion. The Alien Registration Act of 1940 established broad grounds for deportation and the Internal Security Act of 1950 expanded these. Finally, in 1952 the Immigration and Nationality Act was passed over President Truman's stinging veto, and it imposed severer restrictions on aliens. In the latter year, the Court upheld the 1940 legislation authorizing deportation of legally resident aliens because of past membership in the Communist Party, even though the affiliation had ended prior to the enactment of the statute (*Harisiades v. Shaughnessy* [No. 268]). In an important dissent, Justice

Douglas argued that the aliens were deported "not for what they are but for what they once were."

Other cases indicated the broad powers of the federal government to deal with aliens. In *Knauff v. Shaughnessy* (1950), a four-man majority held that the Attorney General's exclusion of a warbride without a hearing was not reviewable by the Court. Public reaction forced a hearing, and the House of Representatives passed a bill permitting her to stay in the United States. Eventually, the Immigration Service reversed its decision, and after nearly three years on Ellis Island the warbride was admitted. Two other decisions ruled that alien Communists could be held indefinitely without bail while the Attorney General's office determined whether to deport them (*Carlson v. Landon*, 1952), and upheld discretionary executive imprisonment of an alien, confined without accusation of crime or trial, with no other reason than an anonymous allegation that he was a danger to the national security (*Shaughnessy v. U.S. ex rel. Mezei*, 1953). In his dissent to Mezei, Justice Jackson argued for a fair hearing with fair notice of the charges. Simple justice, he added, could hardly menace the security of the country: "No one can make me believe that we are that far gone."

If the rights of aliens were diminished in the postwar years, those of other minority groups were expanded. Perhaps the greatest advances made by the Vinson-Warren court have been in the areas of suffrage, discrimination, and segregation. Although the majority ruled in *South v. Peters* (No. 269) that a state's geographical distribution of electoral strength is a political question beyond the authority of the judiciary, Justice Douglas, in a dramatic dissent, denounced the Georgia county-unit system as a device "as deeply rooted in discrimination as the practice which keeps a man from the voting booth because of his race, creed, or color" (No. 270). Building upon the anti-white primary decision in *Smith v. Allwright* (Chapter XXIV), a nearly unanimous Court ruled that the Texas Jaybird Association, a private club of white people fronting for the Democratic Party in nominating candidates, was a part of the general election machinery and violated the Fifteenth Amendment by denying Negroes their right to vote on account of their race and color (*Terry v. Adams* [No. 271]). Justice Minton, the lone dissenter, contended that the Jaybird's maneuvers amounted to private, not state, action.

With the exception of voting, discriminatory state action against Negroes ordinarily has been invalidated under the equal protection clause of the Fourteenth Amendment. Since this provision is directed against the action of states rather than individuals, the distinction between "state action" and "private action" is as important in Fourteenth Amendment cases as in those involving the Fifteenth Amendment. This was particularly true in the restrictive covenant cases, involving private agreements in land deeds binding owners not to sell or lease their property to Negroes. In two unanimous decisions, the Court, without striking down the covenants themselves, decided that their enforcement in state courts would constitute "state action" and therefore violate the equal protection guarantees of the Fifth and Fourteenth Amendments (*Hurd v. Hodge*, 1948; *Shelley v. Kraemer* [No. 272]). This rule was strengthened in 1953 when the Court held that a racially restrictive agreement could not be enforced by a suit for damages against a white covenanter who broke the contract (*Barrows v. Jackson*).

The sharpest advances on the civil rights frontier in the postwar period were made in a series of segregation decisions which culminated in the abolition of the "separate but equal" doctrine in public schooling. In an important transportation case decided in 1950, the highest tribunal came close to reversing the Plessy rule (Chapter XIV) in favor of the proposition that separate facilities, no matter how equal, are incompatible with the Constitution. *Henderson v. U.S.* (1950) dealt with the dining-car service for Negroes between Washington and Atlanta; ten tables on the Southern Railway were reserved for white passengers and one table, separated from the others by a curtain, was reserved for Negro travelers. Without upsetting the Plessy rule, a unanimous Court stated that the carrier's allocation of seats on a segregated basis interfered with equal access of passengers to facilities in violation of the Interstate Commerce Act, which forbids interstate railroads "to subject any particular person . . . to any undue or unreasonable prejudice or disadvantage in any respect whatsoever."

In the field of education, the Court followed the precedent established in the Gaines case (see Introduction to Chapter XXIV), tightening up judicial standards of equality under segregation in such a way as to make the "separate but equal" doctrine increasingly difficult to apply in practice. A series of cases between 1948 and 1950 illustrate this trend. *Sipuel v. University of Oklahoma* (1948) held that qualified Negroes must be admitted to the state law school or be furnished an equivalent education in Oklahoma. When a Negro graduate student was admitted to the University of Oklahoma, he was segregated, sitting in a separate row for Negroes in classrooms, reading at a separate table in the library, and eating at a separate table in the cafeteria. A unanimous Court held that the equal protection clause of the Fourteenth Amendment assured the Negro student the same treatment by the state as other students (*McLaurin v. Oklahoma State Regents,* 1950).

On the same day, the Court again achieved unanimity in an even more important case, which made it evident that it would be almost impossible for a state to comply with the "separate but equal" formula in the field of higher education. Although *Sweatt v. Painter* (1950) left that doctrine intact, the Court concluded that separate Negro law schools in Texas were unequal and made it clear that this shortcoming was itself the result of segregation. Nevertheless, the Court failed to "reach petitioner's contention that *Plessy v. Ferguson* should be reexamined in the light of contemporary knowledge respecting the purposes of the Fourteenth Amendment and the effects of racial segregation," but such a near miss virtually invited cases raising that very point.

In the five public school cases brought before the Court in 1952, the constitutional issue of segregation could no longer be evaded. Few cases have been more carefully considered. Moving deliberately, the Court scheduled the cases for argument in 1952 and after deliberating six months, ordered reargument in 1953. The problems that gave the Court difficulty are indicated by the questions which both sides were asked to answer (No. 273). Briefs were presented in the fall of 1953 and on May 17, 1954, a unanimous Supreme Court, speaking through

Chief Justice Warren, declared that "in the field of public education the doctrine of 'separate but equal' has no place" (*Brown v. Board of Education of Topeka* [*No. 274*]). At the same time, the Court postponed the formulation of methods of implementing this historic decision, again scheduling additional argument. A year later, the Court ordered "a prompt and reasonable start toward full compliance" with its antisegregation ruling, and left to the federal district courts the duty of supervising desegregation. Although the Court realistically recognized that this process would take time, it stressed the necessity for "all deliberate speed" (*Brown v. Board of Education, 1955*).

In many communities, the school authorities have complied fully and integrated schools are functioning. In others, steps are being taken and will be taken toward integration. In parts of the South, however—particularly in Arkansas —there has been direct defiance of the Court's decree, and political leaders have shown as much ingenuity in devising ways of circumventing the decision as was shown earlier in their attempts to bypass the anti-white primary rulings. Indeed, Virginia and several other states have resurrected the doctrine of interposition (Chapter IV) and Georgia has threatened nullification (Chapters VIII and XI). Both moves are interesting exercises in constitutional dialectics, apparently without meaning, however, except as delaying tactics. The most considered statement of constitutional theory underlying the segregationist position was the declaration on integration made by ninety-six southern Congressmen on March 11, 1956 (No. 275).

Six months later a group of distinguished leaders of the American bar from thirty-one states and territories denounced the attacks on the Supreme Court as "reckless in their abuse, . . . heedless of the value of judicial review and . . . dangerous in fomenting disrespect for our highest law" (No. 276).

Implicit in these statements is a concern about the whole issue of segregation in all sectors of public life. For there can be no doubt that the overruling of *Plessy v. Ferguson*, a railroad case, has implications far beyond its immediate relation to public schooling. In November, 1955, the Interstate Commerce Commission cited the school decision as the basis for its order banning segregation on interstate trains and buses and in public waiting rooms serving interstate travelers, and the Court itself has ordered the ending of Jim Crow laws in intrastate commerce (*Browder et al. v. Gayle, 1956*). Without writing opinions, the Court also has extended the rule to a segregated municipal golf course, a municipal housing project, public beaches, and an amphitheater in a public park. Now that it has reversed Plessy, the Court seems to have accepted the position of the lone dissenter in that case, Justice John Marshall Harlan, who insisted that "our Constitution is color-blind, and neither knows nor tolerates classes among citizens."

The Current Status of Procedural Safeguards
of Individual Rights

GENERAL THEORY

263. Interpreting the Due Process Clause of the
Fourteenth Amendment

Adamson v. California, 332 U.S. 46 (1947).

REED, J.: We shall assume, but without any intention thereby of ruling upon the issue, that permission by law to the court, counsel and jury to comment upon and consider the failure of defendant "to explain or to deny by his testimony any evidence or facts in the case against him" would infringe defendant's privilege against self-incrimination under the Fifth Amendment if this were a trial in a court of the United States under a similar law. Such an assumption does not determine appellant's rights under the Fourteenth Amendment. It is settled law that the clause of the Fifth Amendment, protecting a person against being compelled to be a witness against himself, is not made effective by the Fourteenth Amendment as a protection against state action on the ground that freedom from testimonial compulsion is a right of national citizenship, or because it is a personal privilege or immunity secured by the Federal Constitution as one of the rights of man that are listed in the Bill of Rights.

The reasoning that leads to those conclusions starts with the unquestioned premise that the Bill of Rights, when adopted, was for the protection of the individual against the federal government and its provisions were inapplicable to similar actions done by the states. . . . With the adoption of the Fourteenth Amendment, it was suggested that the dual citizenship recognized by its first sentence, secured for citizens federal protection for their elemental privileges and immunities of state citizenship. The Slaughterhouse Cases decided . . . that these rights, as privileges and immunities of state citizenship, remained under the sole protection of the state governments. This Court . . . has approved this determination. . . . The power to free defendants in state trials from self-incrimination was specifically determined to be beyond the scope of the privileges and immunities clause of the Fourteenth Amendment in *Twining v. New Jersey.* . . . After declaring that state and national citizenship coexist in the same person, the Fourteenth Amendment forbids a state from abridging the privileges and immunities of citizens of the United States. As a matter of words, this leaves a state free to abridge, within the limits of the due process clause, the privileges and immunities flowing from state citizenship. . . . It accords with the constitutional doctrine of federalism by leaving to the states the responsibility of dealing with the privileges and immunities of their citizens except those inherent in national citizenship. . . . We reaffirm the conclusion of the Twining and Palko Cases that protection against self-incrimination is not a privilege or immunity of national citizenship.

Appellant secondly contends that if the privilege against self-incrimination is not a right protected by the privileges and immunities clause of the Fourteenth Amendment against state action, this privilege, to its full scope under the Fifth Amendment, inheres in the right to a fair trial. A right to a fair trial is a right admittedly protected by the due process clause of the Fourteenth Amendment. Therefore, appellant argues, the due process clause of the Fourteenth Amendment protects his privilege against self-incrimination. The due process clause of the Fourteenth Amendment, however, does not draw all the rights of the federal Bill of Rights under its protection. That contention was made and rejected in *Palko v. Connecticut.* . . . Nothing has been called to our attention to show that either the framers of the Fourteenth Amendment or the states that adopted it intended its due process clause to draw within its scope the earlier amendments to the Constitution. Palko held that such provisions of the Bill of Rights as were "implicit in the concept of ordered liberty," . . . became secure from state interference by the clause. But it held nothing more.

Specifically, the due process clause does not protect, by virtue of its mere existence, the accused's freedom from giving testimony by compulsion in state trials that is secured to him against federal interference by the Fifth Amendment. . . . For a state to require testimony from an accused is not necessarily a breach of a state's obligation to give a fair trial. Therefore, we must examine the effect of the California law applied in this trial to see whether the comment on failure to testify violates the protection against state action that the due process clause does grant to an accused. The due process clause forbids compulsion to testify by fear of hurt, torture or exhaustion. It forbids any other type of coercion that falls within the scope of due process. California follows Anglo-American legal tradition in excusing defendants in criminal prosecutions from compulsory testimony. . . . That is a matter of legal policy and not because of the requirements of due process under the Fourteenth Amendment. So our inquiry is directed, not at the broad question of the constitutionality of compulsory testimony from the accused under the due process clause, but to the constitutionality of the provision of the California law that permits comment upon his failure to testify. . . .

However sound may be the legislative conclusion that an accused should not be compelled in any criminal case to be a witness against himself, we see no reason why comment should not be made upon his silence. . . .

We are of the view . . . that a state may control such a situation in accordance with its own ideas of the most efficient administration of criminal justice. . . .

264. "Extend to all the complete protection of the Bill of Rights."

Adamson v. California, 332 U.S. 46 (1947).

BLACK, J., dissenting: . . . This decision reasserts a constitutional theory spelled out in *Twining v. New Jersey,* . . . that this Court is endowed by the Constitution with boundless power under "natural law" periodically to expand and contract constitutional standards to conform to the Court's conception of what at a particular time constitutes "civilized decency" and "fundamental liberty and justice." Invoking this Twining rule, the Court concludes that although comment upon testimony in a federal court would violate the Fifth Amendment, identical comment in a state court does not violate today's fashion in civilized decency and fundamentals and is therefore not prohibited by the Federal Constitution as amended. . . .

But I would not reaffirm the Twining decision. I think that decision and the "natural law" theory of the Constitution upon which it relies degrade the constitutional safeguards of the Bill of Rights and simultaneously appropriate for this Court a broad power which we are not authorized by the Constitution to exercise. . . .

The first ten amendments were proposed and adopted largely because of fear that Government might unduly interfere with prized individual liberties. The people wanted and demanded a Bill of Rights written into their Constitution. The amendments embodying the Bill of Rights were intended to curb all branches of the Federal Government in the fields touched by the amendments—Legislative, Executive, and Judicial. The Fifth, Sixth, and Eighth Amendments were pointedly aimed at confining exercise of power by courts and judges within precise boundaries, particularly in the procedure used for the trial of criminal cases. . . . For the fears of arbitrary court action sprang largely from the past use of courts in the imposition of criminal punishments to suppress speech, press, and religion. . . .

But these limitations were not expressly imposed upon state court action. In 1833, *Barron v. Baltimore*. . . . specifically held inapplicable to the states that provision of the Fifth Amendment which declares: "nor shall private property be taken for public use, without just compensation." In deciding the particular point raised, the Court there said that it could not hold that the first eight amendments applied to the states. This was the controlling constitutional rule when the Fourteenth Amendment was proposed in 1866.

My study of the historical events that culminated in the Fourteenth Amendment, and the expressions of those who sponsored and favored, as well as those who opposed, its submission and passage, persuades me that one of the chief objects that the provisions of the Amendment's first section, separately, and as a whole, were intended to accomplish was to make the Bill of Rights applicable to the states. With full knowledge of the import of the Barron decision, the framers and backers of the Fourteenth Amendment proclaimed its purpose to be to overturn the constitutional rule that case had announced. This historical purpose has never received full consideration or exposition in any opinion of this Court interpreting the Amendment. . . .

Whether this Court ever will, or whether it now should, in the light of past decisions, give full effect to what the Amendment was intended to accomplish is not necessarily essential to a decision here. However that may be, our prior decisions, including Twining, do not prevent our carrying out that purpose, at least to the extent of making applicable to the states, not a mere part, as the Court has, but the full protection of the Fifth Amendment's provision against compelling evidence from an accused to convict him of crime. And I further contend that the "natural law" formula which the Court uses to reach its conclusion in this case should be abandoned as an incongruous excrescence on our Constitution. I believe that formula to be itself a violation of our Constitution, in that it subtly conveys to courts, at the expense of legislatures, ultimate power over public policies in fields where no specific provision of the Constitution limits legislative power. . . .

For under the Twining formula, which includes non-regard for the first eight amendments, what are "fundamental rights" and in accord with "canons of decency," as the Court said in Twining, and today reaffirms, is to be independently "ascertained from time to time by judicial action . . ." "what is due process of law depends on circumstances." . . . Thus the power of legislatures became what this Court would declare it to be at a particular time independently of the specific guarantees of the Bill of Rights such as the right to freedom of speech, religion and assembly, the right to just compensation for property taken for a public purpose, the right to jury trial or the right to be secure against unreasonable searches and seizures. . . .

I cannot consider the Bill of Rights to be an outworn 18th Century "strait jacket" as the Twining opinion did. Its provisions may be thought outdated abstractions by some. And it is true that they were designed to meet ancient evils. But they are the same kind of human evils that have emerged from century to century wherever excessive power is sought by the few at the expense of the many. In my judgment the people of no nation can lose their liberty so long as a Bill of Rights like ours survives and its basic purposes are conscientiously interpreted, enforced and respected so as to afford continuous protection against old, as well as new, devices and practices which might thwart those purposes. I fear to see the consequences of the Court's practice of substituting its own concepts of decency and fundamental justice for the language of the Bill of Rights as its point of departure in interpreting and enforcing that Bill of Rights. If the choice must be between the selective process of the Palko decision applying some of the Bill of Rights to the States, or the Twining rule applying none of them, I would choose the Palko selective process. But rather than accept either of these choices, I would follow what I believe was the original purpose of the Fourteenth Amendment—to extend to all the people of the nation complete protection of the Bill of Rights. . . .

SEARCH AND SEIZURE

265. *Are the Fourth Amendment Guarantees Second-class Rights?*

U.S. v. Rabinowitz, 339 U.S. 56 (1950).

MINTON, J.: . . . The question presented here is the reasonableness of a search without a search warrant of a place of business consisting of a one-room office, incident to a valid arrest. . . . The officers . . . arrested the respondent, and over his objection searched the desk, safe, and file cabinets in the office for about an hour and a half. They found and seized 573 stamps, on which it was later determined that overprints had been forged. . . .

Were the 573 stamps, the fruits of this search, admissible in evidence? If legally obtained, these stamps were competent evidence to show intent under the first count of the indictment, and they were the very things the possession of which was the crime charged in the second count. . . .

What is a reasonable search is not to be determined by any fixed formula. The Constitution does not define what are "unreasonable" searches and, regrettably, in our discipline we have no ready litmus-paper test. The recurring questions of the reasonableness of searches must find resolution in the facts and circumstances of each case. . . . Reasonableness is in the first instance for the District Court to determine. We think the District Court's conclusion that here the search and seizure were reasonable should be sustained because: (1) the search and seizure were incident to a valid arrest; (2) the place of the search was a business room to which the public, including the officers, was invited; (3) the room was small and under the immediate and complete control of respondent; (4) the search did not extend beyond the room used for unlawful purposes; (5) the possession of the forged and altered stamps was a crime, just as it is a crime to possess burglars' tools, lottery tickets or counterfeit money.

Assuming that the officers had time to procure a search warrant, were they bound to do so? We think not, because the search was otherwise reasonable, as previously concluded. In a recent opinion, *Trupiano v. United States, . . .* this Court first enunciated the requirement that search warrants must be procured when "practicable" in a case of search incident to arrest. . . .

A rule of thumb requiring that a search warrant always be procured whenever practicable may be appealing from the vantage point of easy administration. But we cannot agree that this requirement should be crystallized into a *sine qua non* to the reasonableness of a search. It is fallacious to judge events retrospectively and thus to determine, considering the time element alone, that there was time to procure a search warrant. Whether there was time may well be dependent upon considerations other than the ticking off of minutes or hours. The judgment of the officers as to when to close the trap on a criminal committing a crime in their presence or who they have reasonable cause to believe is committing a felony is not determined solely upon whether there was time to procure a search warrant. Some flexibility will be accorded law officers engaged in daily battle with criminals for

whose restraint criminal laws are essential.

It is appropriate to note that the Constitution does not say that the right of the people to be secure in their persons should not be violated without a search warrant if it is practicable for the officers to procure one. The mandate of the Fourth Amendment is that the people shall be secure against *unreasonable* searches. It is not disputed that there may be reasonable searches, incident to an arrest, without a search warrant. Upon acceptance of this established rule that some authority to search follows from lawfully taking the person into custody, it becomes apparent that such searches turn upon the reasonableness under all the circumstances and not upon the practicability of procuring a search warrant, for the warrant is not required. To the extent that *Trupiano v. United States . . .* requires a search warrant solely upon the basis of the practicability of procuring it rather than upon the reasonableness of the search after a lawful arrest, that case is overruled. The relevant test is not whether it is reasonable to procure a search warrant, but whether the search was reasonable. That criterion in turn depends upon the facts and circumstances—the total atmosphere of the case. It is a sufficient precaution that law officers must justify their conduct before courts which have always been, and must be, jealous of the individual's right of privacy within the broad sweep of the Fourth Amendment. . . .

LEGISLATIVE INVESTIGATIONS AND PROCEDURAL RIGHTS

266. *Refusal to Testify Under the Fifth Amendment*

Blau v. U.S., 340 U.S. 159 (1950).

BLACK, J.: In response to a subpoena, petitioner appeared as a witness before the United States District Court Grand Jury at Denver, Colorado. There she was asked several questions concerning the Communist Party of Colorado and her employment by it. Petitioner refused to answer these questions on the ground that the answers might tend to incriminate her. She was then taken before the district judge where the questions were again propounded and where she again claimed her constitutional privilege against self-incrimination and refused to testify. The district judge found petitioner guilty of contempt of court and sentenced her to imprisonment for one year. . . .

At the time petitioner was called before the grand jury, the Smith Act was on the statute books making it a crime among other things to advocate knowingly the desirability of overthrow of the Government by force or violence; to organize or help to organize any society or group which teaches, advocates or encourages such overthrow of the Government; to be or become a member of such a group with knowledge of its purposes. These provisions made future prosecution of petitioner far more than "a mere imaginary possibility . . ."; she reasonably could fear that criminal charges might be brought against her if she admitted employment by the Communist Party or intimate knowledge of its workings. Whether such admissions by themselves would support a conviction under a criminal statute is immaterial. Answers to the questions asked by the grand jury would have furnished a link in the chain of evidence needed in a prosecution of petitioner for violation of . . . the Smith Act. Prior decisions of this Court have clearly established that under such circumstances, the Constitution gives a witness the privilege of remaining silent. The attempt by the courts below to compel petitioners to testify runs counter to the Fifth Amendment as it has been interpreted from the beginning. . . .

Reversed.

267. *"The investigative power of Congress in the context of the First Amendment"*

U.S. v. Rumely, 345 U.S. 1 (1953).

FRANKFURTER, J.: The respondent Rumely was Secretary of an organization known as the Committee for Constitutional Government, which, among other things, engaged in the sale of books of a particular political tendentiousness. He refused to disclose to the House Select Committee on Lobbying Activities the names of those who made bulk purchases of these books for further distribution, and was convicted under . . . 2 U. S. C. §192, which provides penalties for refusal to give testimony or to produce relevant papers "upon any matter" under congressional inquiry. The Court of Appeals reversed, one judge dissenting. It held that the committee before which Rumely refused to furnish this information had no authority to compel its production. . . . This issue—whether the committee had power to exact the information which the witness withheld—must first be settled before we may consider whether Congress had the power to confer upon the committee the authority which it claimed.

Although we are here dealing with a resolution of the House of Representatives, the problem is much the same as that which confronts the Court when called upon to construe a statute that carries the seeds of constitutional controversy. The potential constitutional questions have far-reaching import. We are asked to recognize the penetrating and pervasive scope of the investigative power of Congress. The reach that may be claimed for that power is indicated by Woodrow Wilson's characterization of it:

> It is the proper duty of a representative body to look diligently into every affair of government and to talk much about what it sees. . . . The informing function of Congress should be preferred even to its legislative function. . . .

President Wilson did not write in light of the history of events since he wrote;

more particularly he did not write of the investigative power of Congress in the context of the First Amendment. . . .

Accommodation of these contending principles—the one underlying the power of Congress to investigate, the other at the basis of the limitation imposed by the First Amendment—is not called for until after we have construed the scope of the authority which the House of Representatives gave to the Select Committee on Lobbying Activities. The pertinent portion . . . reads:

> The committee is authorized and directed to conduct a study and investigation of (1) all lobbying activities intended to influence, encourage, promote, or retard legislation; and (2) all activities of agencies of the Federal Government intended to influence, encourage, promote, or retard legislation. . . .

The resolution must speak for itself, since Congress put no gloss upon it at the time of its passage. . . . Accordingly, the phrase "lobbying activities" in the resolution must be given the meaning that may fairly be attributed to it, having special regard for the principle of constitutional adjudication which makes it decisive in the choice of fair alternatives that one construction may raise serious constitutional questions avoided by another. In a long series of decisions we have acted on this principle. . . .

Surely it cannot be denied that giving the scope to the resolution for which the Government contends, that is, deriving from it the power to inquire into all efforts of private individuals to influence public opinion through books and periodicals, however remote the radiations of influence which they may exert upon the ultimate legislative process, raises doubts of constitutionality in view of the prohibition of the First Amendment. In light of the opinion of Prettyman, J., below and of some of the views expressed here, it would not be seemly to maintain that

these doubts are fanciful or factitious. Indeed, adjudication here, if it were necessary, would affect not an evanescent policy of Congress, but its power to inform itself, which underlies its policy-making function. Whenever constitutional limits upon the investigative power of Congress have to be drawn by this Court, it ought only to be done after Congress has demonstrated its full awareness of what is at stake by unequivocally authorizing an inquiry of dubious limits. . . .

Choice is left. As a matter of English, the phrase "lobbying activities" readily lends itself to the construction placed upon it below, namely, "lobbying in its commonly accepted sense," that is, "representations made directly to the Congress, its members, or its committees," . . . and does not reach what was in Chairman Buchanan's mind, attempts "to saturate the thinking of the community." . . . Certainly it does no violence to the phrase "lobbying activities" to give it a more restricted scope. To give such meaning is not barred by intellectual honesty. So to interpret is in the candid service of avoiding a serious constitutional doubt. . . .

Only a word need be said about the debate in Congress after the committee reported that Rumely had refused to produce the information which he had a right to refuse under the restricted meaning of the phrase "lobbying activities." The view taken at that time by the committee and by the Congress that the committee was authorized to ask Rumely for the information he withheld is not legislative history defining the scope of a congressional measure. What was said in the debate on August 30, 1950, after the controversy had arisen regarding the scope of the resolution of August 12, 1949, had the usual infirmity of *post litem motam*, self-serving declarations. In any event, Rumely's duty to answer must be judged as of the time of his refusal. The scope of the resolution defining that duty is therefore to be ascertained as of that time and cannot be enlarged by subsequent action of Congress.

Grave constitutional questions are matters properly to be decided by this Court but only when they inescapably come before us for adjudication. Until then it is our duty to abstain from marking the boundaries of congressional power or delimiting the protection guaranteed by the First Amendment. Only by such self-restraint will we avoid the mischief which has followed occasional departures from the principles which we profess.

The judgment below should be affirmed.

THE CONSTITUTIONAL RIGHTS OF ALIENS

268. *Deportation, and the Denial of Alien Rights*

Harisiades v. Shaughnessy, 342 U.S. 580 (1952).

JACKSON, J.: The ultimate question in these three cases is whether the United States constitutionally may deport a legally resident alien because of membership in the Communist Party which terminated before enactment of the Alien Registration Act of 1940.

Harisiades, a Greek national, accompanied his father to the United States in 1916, when thirteen years of age, and has resided here since. He has taken a wife and sired two children, all citizens. He joined the Communist Party in 1925, when it was known as the Workers Party, and served as an organizer, Branch Executive Committeeman, secretary of its Greek Bureau, and editor of its paper "Empros." The party discontinued his membership, along with that of other aliens, in 1939, but he has continued association with members. He was familiar with the principles and philosophy of the Communist Party and says he still believes in them. He disclaims personal belief in use of force and violence and asserts that the party favored their use only in defense. A warrant for his deportation because of his membership was issued in 1930 but was not served until 1946. The delay was due to inability to locate him because of his use of a number of aliases. After hearings, he was ordered deported on the grounds that after entry he had been a member of an organization which advocates overthrow of the Government by force and violence and distributes printed matter so advocating. He sought release by habeas corpus, which was denied by the District Court. The Court of Appeals for the Second Circuit affirmed. . . .

[Justice Jackson then gave brief sketches of Mascitti and Mrs. Coleman, co-appellants.]

Validity of the hearing procedures are questioned for noncompliance with the Administrative Procedure Act, which we think is here inapplicable. Admittedly, each of these deportations is authorized and required by the letter, spirit and intention of the statute. But the Act is assailed on three grounds: (1) that it deprives the aliens of liberty without due process of law in violation of the Fifth Amendment; (2) that it abridges their freedoms of speech and assembly in contravention of the First Amendment; and, (3) that it is an *ex post facto* law which Congress is forbidden to pass. . . .

We have in each case a finding, approved by the court below, that the Communist Party during the period of the alien's membership taught and advocated overthrow of the Government of the United States by force and violence. Those findings are not questioned here.

These aliens ask us to forbid their expulsion by a departure from the long-accepted application to such cases of the Fifth Amendment provision that no person shall be deprived of life, liberty or property without due process of law. Their basic contention is that admission for permanent residence confers a "vested right" on the alien, equal to that of the citizen, to remain within the country, and that the alien is entitled to constitutional protection in that matter to the same extent as the citizen. Their second line of defense is that if any power to deport domiciled aliens exists it is so dispersed that the judiciary must concur in the grounds for its exercise to the extent of finding them reasonable. The argument goes on to the contention that the grounds prescribed by the Act of 1940 bear no reasonable relation to protection of legitimate interests of the United States and concludes that the Act should be declared invalid. Admittedly these propositions are not founded in precedents of this Court.

For over thirty years each of these aliens has enjoyed such advantages as accrue from residence here without renouncing his foreign allegiance or formally acknowledging adherence to the Constitution he now invokes. . . .

Under our law, the alien in several respects stands on an equal footing with citizens, but in others has never been conceded legal parity with the citizen. Most importantly, to protract this ambiguous status within the country is not his right but is a matter of permission and tolerance. The Government's power to terminate its hospitality has been asserted and sustained by this Court since the question first arose.

War, of course, is the most usual occasion for extensive resort to the power. . . . But it does not require war to bring the power of deportation into existence or to authorize its exercise. Congressional apprehension of foreign or internal dangers short of war may lead to its use. So long as the alien elects to continue the ambiguity of his allegiance his domicile here is held by a precarious tenure.

That aliens remain vulnerable to expulsion after long residence is a practice that bristles with severities. But it is a weapon of defense and reprisal confirmed by international law as a power inherent in every sovereign state. Such is the traditional power of the Nation over the alien and we leave the law on the subject as we find it.

This brings us to the alternative defense under the Due Process Clause—that, granting the power, it is so unreasonably and harshly exercised by this enactment that it should be held unconstitutional. . . .

We are urged, because the policy inflicts severe and undoubted hardship on affected individuals, to find a restraint in the Due Process Clause. But the Due Process Clause does not shield the citizen from conscription and the consequent calamity of being separated from family, friends, home and business while he is transported to foreign lands to stem the tide of Communism. If Communist aggression creates such hardships for loyal citizens, it is hard to find justification for holding that the Constitution requires that its hardships must be spared the Communist alien. When citizens raised the Constitution as a shield against expulsion from their homes and places of business, the Court refused to find hardship a cause for judicial intervention. . . .

We hold that the Act is not invalid under the Due Process Clause. These aliens are not entitled to judicial relief unless some other constitutional limitation has been transgressed, to which inquiry we turn.

The First Amendment is invoked as a barrier against this enactment. The claim is that in joining an organization advocating overthrow of government by force and violence the alien has merely exercised freedoms of speech, press and assembly which that Amendment guarantees to him.

The assumption is that the First Amendment allows Congress to make no distinction between advocating change in the existing order by lawful elective processes and advocating change by force and violence . . .

Our Constitution sought to leave no excuse for violent attack on the status quo by providing a legal alternative—attack by ballot. To arm all men for orderly change, the Constitution put in their hands a right to influence the electorate by press, speech and assembly. This means freedom to advocate or promote Communism by means of the ballot box, but it does not include the practice or incitement of violence. . . .

The remaining claim is that this Act conflicts with Art. 1, §9, of the Constitution forbidding *ex post facto* enactments. An impression of retroactivity results from reading as a new and isolated enactment what is actually a continuation of prior legislation.

During all the years since 1920 Congress has maintained a standing admonition to aliens, on pain of deportation, not to become members of any organization that advocates overthrow of the United States by force and violence, a category repeatedly held to include the Communist Party. These aliens violated that prohibition and incurred liability to deportation. They were not caught unawares by a change of law. . . .

In 1939, this Court decided *Kessler v. Strecker* . . . in which it was held that Congress, in the statute as it then stood, had not clearly expressed an intent that Communist Party membership remained cause for deportation after it ceased. The Court concluded that in the absence of such expression only contemporaneous membership would authorize deportation.

The reaction of the Communist Party was to drop aliens from membership, at least in form, in order to immunize them from the consequences of their party membership.

The reaction of Congress was that the Court had misunderstood its legislation. In the Act here before us it supplied unmistakable language that past violators of its prohibitions continued to be deportable in spite of resignation or expulsion from the party. . . .

However, even if the Act were found to be retroactive, to strike it down would require us to overrule the construction of the *ex post facto* provision which has been followed by this Court from earliest times. It always has been considered that that which it forbids is penal legislation which imposes or increases criminal punishment for conduct lawful previous to its enactment. Deportation, however severe its consequences, has been consistently classified as a civil rather than a criminal procedure. Both of these doctrines as original proposals might be debatable, but both have been considered closed for many years and a body of statute and decisional law has been built upon them. . . .

When the Communist Party as a matter of party strategy formally expelled alien members en masse, it destroyed any significance that discontinued membership might otherwise have as indication of change of heart by the individual. Congress may have believed that the party tactics threw upon the Government an almost impossible burden if it attempted to separate those who sincerely renounced Communist principles of force and violence from those who left the party the better to serve it. Congress, exercising the wide discretion that it alone has in these matters, declined to accept that burden.

We find none of the constitutional objections to the Act well founded. The judgments accordingly are affirmed.

Elections, Suffrage, and Segregation

POLITICS, APPORTIONMENT, AND DISCRIMINATION

269. The County-Unit System and Inequality of Representation

Per curiam opinion, *South v. Peters,* 339 U.S. 276 (1950).

The Georgia statute which appellants attack as violative of the Fourteenth and Seventeenth Amendments provides that county unit votes shall determine the outcome of a primary election. Each county is allotted a number of unit votes, ranging from six for the eight most populous counties, to two for most of the counties. The candidate who receives the highest popular vote in the county is awarded the appropriate number of unit votes. Appellants, residents of the most populous county in the state, contend that their votes and those of all other voters in that county have on the average but one-tenth the weight of those in the other counties.

Urging that this amounts to an unconstitutional discrimination against them, appellants brought this suit to restrain adherence to the statute in the forthcoming Democratic Party primary for United States Senator, Governor and other state offices.

The court below dismissed appellants' petition. . . . We affirm. Federal courts consistently refuse to exercise their equity powers in cases posing political issues arising from a state's geographical distribution of electoral strength among its political subdivisions. See *MacDougall v. Green* . . . (1948); *Colegrove v. Green* . . . (1946). . . .

270. The County-Unit System and Racial Discrimination

South v. Peters, 339 U.S. 276 (1950).

DOUGLAS, J., dissenting: I suppose that if a State reduced the vote of Negroes, Catholics, or Jews so that each got only one-tenth of a vote, we would strike the law down. The right to vote in a primary was held in *Nixon v. Herndon* . . . to be covered by the Equal Protection Clause of the Fourteenth Amendment. And where, as in Georgia, a party primary election is an integral part of the state election machinery, the right to vote in it is protected by the Fifteenth Amendment. *Smith v. Allwright.* . . . Under both Amendments discriminations based on race, creed or color fall beyond the pale.

Yet there is evidence in this case showing that Georgia's County Unit System of consolidating votes in primary elections makes an equally invidious discrimination. Under this primary law the nomination does not go to the candidate who gets the majority or plurality of votes. Votes are counted county by county. The winner in each county gets a designated number of votes—six in the most populous counties, four in the next most populous, two in each of the rest.

Plaintiffs are registered voters in Georgia's most populous county—Fulton County. They complain that their votes will be counted so as drastically to reduce their voting strength.

They show that a vote in one county will be worth over 120 times each of their votes. They show that in 45 counties a vote will be given twenty times the weight of each of theirs. They show that on a state-wide average each vote outside Fulton County will have over 11 times the weight of each vote of the plaintiffs.

Population figures show that there is a heavy Negro population in the large cities. There is testimony in the record that only in those areas have Negroes been able to vote in important numbers. Yet the County Unit System heavily disenfranchises that urban Negro population. The County Unit System has indeed been called the "last loophole" around our

decisions holding that there must be no discrimination because of race in primary as well as in general elections.

The racial angle of the case only emphasizes the bite of the decision which sustains the County Unit System of voting. The discrimination against citizens in the more populous counties of Georgia is plain. Because they are city folks their voting power is only an eleventh or a hundred and twentieth of the voting power of other citizens. I can see no way to save that classification under the Equal Protection Clause. The creation by law of favored groups of citizens and the grant to them of preferred political rights is the worst of all discriminations under a democratic system of government. . . .

SUFFRAGE AND RACIAL DISCRIMINATION

271. *The Case of the Texas Jaybirds*

Terry v. Adams, 345 U.S. 461 (1953).

BLACK, J.: . . . In *Smith v. Allwright* . . . (1944), we held that rules of the Democratic Party of Texas excluding Negroes from voting in the party's primaries violated the Fifteenth Amendment. While no state law directed such exclusion, our decision pointed out that many party activities were subject to considerable statutory control. This case raises questions concerning the constitutional power of a Texas county political organization called the Jaybird Democratic Association or Jaybird Party to exclude Negroes from its primaries on racial grounds. The Jaybirds deny that their racial exclusions violate the Fifteenth Amendment. They contend that the Amendment applies only to elections or primaries held under state regulation, that their association is not regulated by the state at all, and that it is not a political party but a self-governing voluntary club. . . .

There was evidence that:

The Jaybird Association or Party was organized in 1889. Its membership was then and always has been limited to white people; they are automatically members if their names appear on the official list of county voters. It has been run like other political parties with an executive committee named from the county's voting precincts. . . . While there is no legal compulsion on successful Jaybird candidates to enter Democratic primaries they have nearly always done so and with few exceptions since 1889 have run and won without opposition in the Democratic primaries and the general elections that followed. Thus the party has been the dominant political group in the county since organization, having endorsed every county-wide official elected since 1889.

It is apparent that Jaybird activities follow a plan purposefully designed to exclude Negroes from voting and at the same time to escape the Fifteenth Amendment's command that the right of citizens to vote shall neither be denied nor abridged on account of race. These were the admitted party purposes according to the following testimony of the Jaybird's president:

> Q. . . . One of the purposes of your organization is for the specific purpose of excluding Negroes from voting, isn't it?
> A. Yes. . . .
> Q. I will ask you, that is the reason you hold your election in May rather than in June or July, isn't it?
> A. Yes.
> Q. Because if you held it in July you would have to abide by the statutes and the law by letting them vote?
> A. They do vote in July. . . .
> Q. . . . My question is that you hold yours in May so you won't have to let them vote, don't you?
> A. Yes. . . .
> Q. That is the whole policy of your Association?
> A. Yes.
> Q. And that is its purpose?
> A. Yes.

The District Court found that the Jaybird Association was a political organization or party; that the majority of white voters generally abide by the results of its primaries and support in the Democratic primaries the persons endorsed by the Jaybird primaries; and that the chief object of the Association has always been to deny Negroes any voice or part in the election of Fort Bend County officials.

The facts and findings bring this case squarely within the reasoning and holding of the Court of Appeals for the Fourth Circuit in its two recent decisions about excluding Negroes from Democratic primaries in South Carolina. . . . South Carolina had repealed every trace of statutory or constitutional control of the Democratic primaries. It did this in the hope that

thereafter the Democratic Party or Democratic "Clubs" of South Carolina would be free to continue discriminatory practices against Negroes as voters. The contention there was that the Democratic "Clubs" were mere private groups; the contention here is that the Jaybird Association is a mere private group. The Court of Appeals in invalidating the South Carolina practices answered these formalistic arguments by holding that no election machinery could be sustained if its purpose or effect was to deny Negroes on account of their race an effective voice in the governmental affairs of their country, state, or community. In doing so the Court relied on the principle announced in *Smith v. Allwright*, . . . that the constitutional right to be free from racial discrimination in voting ". . . is not to be nullified by a state through casting its electoral process in a form which permits a private organization to practice racial discrimination in the election." . . .

It is significant that precisely the same qualifications as those prescribed by Texas entitling electors to vote at county-operated primaries are adopted as the sole qualifications entitling electors to vote at the county-wide Jaybird primaries with a single proviso—Negroes are excluded. Everyone concedes that such a proviso in the county-operated primaries would be unconstitutional. The Jaybird Party thus brings into being and holds precisely the kind of election that the Fifteenth Amendment seeks to prevent. When it produces the equivalent of the prohibited election, the damage has been done. . . .

The Jaybird primary has become an integral part, indeed the only effective part, of the elective process that determines who shall rule and govern in the county. The effect of the whole procedure, Jaybird primary plus Democratic primary plus general election, is to do precisely that which the Fifteenth Amendment forbids—strip Negroes of every vestige of influence in selecting the officials who control the local county matters that intimately touch the daily lives of citizens. . . .

We affirm the District Court's holding that the combined Jaybird-Democratic-general election machinery has deprived these petitioners of their right to vote on account of their race and color. . . .

SEGREGATION

272. *Restrictive Covenants*

Shelley v. Kraemer, 334 U.S. 1 (1948).

VINSON, C.J.: . . . These cases present for our consideration questions relating to the validity of court enforcement of private agreements, generally described as restrictive covenants, which have as their purpose the exclusion of persons of designated race or color from the ownership or occupancy of real property. Basic constitutional issues of obvious importance have been raised. . . .

Petitioners urge that they have been denied the equal protection of the laws, deprived of property without due process of law, and have been denied privileges and immunities of citizens of the United States. . . .

It is well, at the outset, to scrutinize the terms of the restrictive agreements involved in these cases. . . . The covenant declares that no part of the affected property shall be "occupied by any person not of the Caucasian race, it being intended hereby to restrict the use of said property . . . against the occupancy as owners or tenants of any portion of said property for resident or other purpose by people of the Negro or Mongolian Race." . . .

It cannot be doubted that among the civil rights intended to be protected from discriminatory state action by the Fourteenth Amendment are the rights to acquire, enjoy, own and dispose of property. Equality in the enjoyment of property rights was regarded by the framers of that Amendment as an essential pre-condition to the realization of other basic civil rights and liberties which the Amendment was intended to guarantee. . . .

It is . . . clear that restrictions on the right of occupancy of the sort sought to be created by the private agreements in these cases could not be squared with the requirements of the 14th Amendment if imposed by state statute or local ordinance. We do not understand respondents to urge the contrary. . . .

But the present cases, unlike those just discussed, do not involve action by state legislatures or city councils. Here the particular patterns of discrimination and the areas in which the restrictions are to operate, are determined, in the first instance, by the terms of agreements among private individuals. Participation of the State consists in the enforcement of the restrictions so defined. The crucial issue with which we are here confronted is whether this distinction removes these cases from the operation of the prohibitory provisions of the Fourteenth Amendment.

Since the decision of this Court in the Civil Rights Cases . . . (1883), the principle has become firmly embedded in our constitutional law that the action inhibited by the first section of the Fourteenth Amendment is only such action as may fairly be said to be that of the States. That Amendment erects no shield against merely private conduct, however discriminatory or wrongful.

We conclude, therefore, that the restrictive agreements standing alone cannot be regarded as a violation of any rights guaranteed to petitioners by the Fourteenth Amendment. So long as the purposes of those agreements are effectuated by voluntary adherence to their terms, it would appear clear that there has been no action by the State and the provisions of the Amendment have not been violated. . . .

But here there was more. These are cases in which the purposes of the agreements were secured only by judicial enforcement by state courts of the restrictive terms of the agreements. The respondents urge that judicial enforcement of private agreement does not amount to state action; or, in any event, the participation of the States is so attenuated in character as not to amount to state action within the meaning of the Fourteenth Amendment. Finally, it is suggested, even if the States in these cases may be deemed to have acted in the constitutional sense, their action did not deprive petitioners of rights guaranteed by the Fourteenth Amendment. We move to a consideration of these matters. . . .

The short of the matter is that from the time of the adoption of the Fourteenth Amendment until the present, it has been the consistent ruling of this Court that the action of the States to which the Amendment has reference includes action of state courts and state judicial officials. Although, in construing the terms of the Fourteenth Amendment, differences have from time to time been expressed as to whether particular types of state action may be said to offend the Amendment's prohibitory provisions, it has never been suggested that state court action is immunized from the operation of those provisions simply because the act is that of the judicial branch of the state government.

Against this background of judicial construction, extending over a period of some three-quarters of a century, we are called upon to consider whether enforcement by state courts of the restrictive agreements in these cases may be deemed to be the acts of those States; and, if so, whether that action has denied these petitioners the equal protection of the laws which the Amendment was intended to insure. . . .

These are not cases, as has been suggested, in which the States have merely abstained from action, leaving private individuals free to impose such discriminations as they see fit. Rather, these are cases in which the States have made available to such individuals the full coercive power of government to deny to petitioners, on the grounds of race or color, the enjoyment of property rights in premises which petitioners are willing and financially able to acquire and which the grantors are willing to sell. The difference between judicial enforcement and nonenforcement of the restrictive covenants is the difference to petitioners between being denied rights of property available to other members of the community and being accorded full enjoyment of those rights on an equal footing. . . .

We hold that in granting judicial enforcement of the restrictive agreements in these cases, the States have denied petitioners the equal protection of the laws and that, therefore, the action of the state courts cannot stand. . . .

273. Education and Segregation: The Supreme Court Requests Information

Questions by the Supreme Court to Counsel in the Segregation Cases, 345 U.S. 972 (June 8, 1953).

1. What evidence is there that the Congress which submitted and the State legislatures and conventions which ratified the Fourteenth Amendment contemplated or did not contemplate, understood or

did not understand, that it would abolish segregation in public schools?

2. If neither the Congress in submitting nor the States in ratifying the Fourteenth Amendment understood that com-

pliance with it would require the immediate abolition of segregation in public schools, was it nevertheless the understanding of the framers of the Amendment

(a) that future Congresses might, in the exercise of their power under section 5 of the Amendment, abolish such segregation, or

(b) that it would be within the judicial power, in light of future conditions, to construe the Amendment as abolishing such segregation of its own force?

3. On the assumption that the answers to questions 2(a) and (b) do not dispose of the issue, is it within the judicial power, in construing the Amendment, to abolish segregation in public schools?

4. Assuming it is decided that segregation in public schools violates the Fourteenth Amendment

(a) would a decree necessarily follow providing that, within the limits set by normal geographic school districting, Negro children should forthwith be admitted to schools of their choice, or

(b) may this Court, in the exercise of its equity powers, permit an effective gradual adjustment to be brought about from existing segregated systems to a system not based on color distinctions?

5. On the assumption on which questions 4(a) and (b) are based, and assuming further that this Court will exercise its equity powers to the end described in question 4(b),

(a) should this Court formulate detailed decrees in these cases;

(b) if so what specific issues should the decrees reach;

(c) should this Court appoint a special master to hear evidence with a view to recommending specific terms for such decrees;

(d) should this Court remand to the courts of first instance with directions to frame decrees in these cases, and if so, what general directions should the decrees of this Court include and what procedures should the courts of first instance follow in arriving at the specific terms of more detailed decrees?

274. *The Court Discards the "Separate but Equal" Doctrine*

Brown v. Board of Education of Topeka, 347 U.S. 483 (1954).

WARREN, C.J.: These cases come to us from the States of Kansas, South Carolina, Virginia, and Delaware. They are premised on different facts and different local conditions, but a common legal question justifies their consideration together in this consolidated opinion.

In each of the cases, minors of the Negro race, through their legal representatives, seek the aid of the courts in obtaining admission to the public schools of their community on a nonsegregated basis. In each instance, they had been denied admission to schools attended by white children under laws requiring or permitting segregation according to race. This segregation was alleged to deprive the plaintiffs of the equal protection of

the laws under the Fourteenth Amendment. In each of the cases other than the Delaware case, a three-judge federal district court denied relief to the plaintiffs on the so-called "separate but equal" doctrine announced by this Court in *Plessy v. Ferguson.* . . . Under that doctrine, equality of treatment is accorded when the races are provided substantially equal facilities, even though these facilities be separate. In the Delaware case, the Supreme Court of Delaware adhered to that doctrine, but ordered that the plaintiffs be admitted to the white schools because of their superiority to the Negro schools.

The plaintiffs contend that segregated public schools are not "equal" and cannot be made "equal," and that hence they are deprived of the equal protection of the laws. Because of the obvious importance of the question presented, the Court took jurisdiction. Argument was heard in the 1952 Term, and reargument was heard this Term on certain questions propounded by the Court.

Reargument was largely devoted to the circumstances surrounding the adoption of the Fourteenth Amendment in 1868. It covered exhaustively consideration of the Amendment in Congress, ratification by the states, then existing practices in racial segregation, and the views of proponents and opponents of the Amendment. This discussion and our own investigation convince us that, although these sources cast some light, it is not enough to resolve the problem with which we are faced. At best, they are inconclusive. The most avid proponents of the post-War Amendments undoubtedly intended them to remove all legal distinctions among "all persons born or naturalized in the United States." Their opponents, just as certainly, were antagonistic to both the letter and the spirit of the Amendments and wished them to have the most limited effect. What others in Congress and the state legislature had in mind cannot be determined with any degree of certainty.

An additional reason for the inconclusive nature of the Amendment's history, with respect to segregated schools, is the status of public education at that time. In the South, the movement toward free common schools, supported by general taxation, had not yet taken hold. Education of white children was largely in the hands of private groups. Education of Negroes was almost nonexistent, and practically all of the race were illiterate. In fact, any education of Negroes was forbidden by law in some states. Today, in contrast, many Negroes have achieved outstanding success in the arts and sciences as well as in the business and professional world. It is true that public education had already advanced further in the North, but the effect of the Amendment on Northern

States was generally ignored in the congressional debates. Even in the North, the conditions of public education did not approximate those existing today. The curriculum was usually rudimentary; ungraded schools were common in rural areas; the school term was but three months a year in many states; and compulsory school attendance was virtually unknown. As a consequence, it is not surprising that there should be so little in the history of the Fourteenth Amendment relating to its intended effect on public education.

In the first cases in this Court construing the Fourteenth Amendment, decided shortly after its adoption, the Court interpreted it as proscribing all state-imposed discriminations against the Negro race. The doctrine of "separate but equal" did not make its appearance in this Court until 1896 in the case of Plessy v. Ferguson . . . involving not education but transportation. American courts have since labored with the doctrine for over half a century. In this Court, there have been six cases involving the "separate but equal" doctrine in the field of public education. In Cumming v. County Board of Education . . . [1899], and Gong Lum v. Rice . . . [1927], the validity of the doctrine itself was not challenged. In more recent cases, all on the graduate school level, inequality was found in that specific benefits enjoyed by white students were denied to Negro students of the same educational qualifications. . . . [Gaines, Sipuel, Sweatt, McLaurin.] In none of these cases was it necessary to reexamine the doctrine to grant relief to the Negro plaintiff. And in Sweatt v. Painter . . . , the Court expressly reserved decision on the question whether Plessy v. Ferguson should be held inapplicable to public education.

In the instant cases, that question is directly presented. Here, unlike Sweatt v. Painter, there are findings below that the Negro and white schools involved have been equalized, or are being equalized, with respect to buildings, curricula, qualifications and salaries of teachers, and other "tangible" factors. Our decision, therefore, cannot turn on merely a comparison of these tangible factors in the Negro and white schools involved in each of the cases. We must look instead to the effect of segregation itself on public education.

In approaching this problem, we cannot turn the clock back to 1868 when the Amendment was adopted, or even to 1896 when *Plessy v. Ferguson* was written. We must consider public education in the light of its full development and its present place in American life throughout the Nation. Only in this way can it be determined if segregation in public schools deprives these plaintiffs of the equal protection of the laws.

Today, education is perhaps the most important function of state and local governments. Compulsory school attendance laws and the great expenditures for education both demonstrate our recognition of the importance of education to our democratic society. It is required in the performance of our most basic public responsibilities, even service in the armed forces. It is the very foundation of good citizenship. Today it is a principal instrument in awakening the child to cultural values, in preparing him for later professional training, and in helping him to adjust normally to his environment. In these days, it is doubtful that any child may reasonably be expected to succeed in life if he is denied the opportunity of an education. Such an opportunity, where the state has undertaken to provide it, is a right which must be made available to all on equal terms.

We come then to the question presented: Does segregation of children in public schools solely on the basis of race, even though the physical facilities and other "tangible" factors may be equal, deprive the children of the minority group of equal educational opportunities? We believe that it does.

In *Sweatt v. Painter,* . . . in finding that a segregated law school for Negroes could not provide them equal educational opportunities, this Court relied in large part on "those qualities which are incapable of objective measurement but which make for greatness in a law school." In *McLaurin v. Oklahoma State Regents,* . . . the Court, in requiring that a Negro admitted to a white graduate school be treated like all other students, again resorted to intangible considerations: ". . . his ability to study, to engage in discussions and exchange views with other students, and, in general, to learn his profession." Such considerations apply with added force to children in grade and high schools. To separate them from others of similar age and qualifications solely because of their race generates a feeling of inferiority as to their status in the community that may affect their hearts and minds in a way unlikely ever to be undone. The effect of this separation on their educational opportunities was well stated by a finding in the Kansas case by a court which nevertheless felt compelled to rule against the Negro plaintiffs:

> Segregation of white and colored children in public schools has a detrimental effect upon the colored children. The impact is greater when it has the sanction of the law; for the policy of separating the races is usually interpreted as denoting the inferiority of the Negro group. A sense of inferiority affects the motivation of a child to learn. Segregation with the sanction of law, therefore, has a tendency to retard the educational and mental development of Negro children and to deprive them of some of the benefits they would receive in a racially integrated school system.

Whatever may have been the extent of psychological knowledge at the time of *Plessy v. Ferguson,* this finding is amply supported by modern authority.

Any language in *Plessy v. Ferguson* contrary to this finding is rejected.

We conclude that in the field of public education the doctrine of "separate but equal" has no place. Separate educational facilities are inherently unequal. Therefore, we hold that the plaintiffs and others similarly situated for whom the actions have been brought are, by reason of the segregation complained of, deprived of the equal protection of the laws guaranteed by the Fourteenth Amendment. This disposition makes unnecessary any discussion whether such segregation also violates the Due Process Clause of the Fourteenth Amendment.

Because these are class actions, because of the wide applicability of this decision, and because of the great variety of local conditions, the formulation of decrees in these cases presents problems of considerable complexity. On reargument, the consideration of appropriate relief was necessarily subordinated to the primary question—the constitutionality of segregation in public education. We have now announced that such segregation is a denial of the equal protection of the laws. In order that we may have the full assistance of the parties in formulating decrees, the cases will be restored to the docket, and the parties are requested to present further argument on Questions 4 and 5 previously propounded by the Court for the reargument this Term. The Attorney General of the United States is again invited to participate. The Attorneys General of the states requiring or permitting segregation in public education will also be permitted to appear as *amici curiae* upon request to do so by September 15, 1954, and submission of briefs by October 1, 1954.

It is so ordered.

275. *Declaration on Integration by Ninety-six Southern Congressmen*

The New York Times, March 12, 1956.

We regard the decision of the Supreme Court in the school cases as clear abuse of judicial power. It climaxes a trend in the Federal judiciary undertaking to legislate, in derogation of the authority of Congress, and to encroach upon the reserved rights of the states and the people.

The original Constitution does not mention education. Neither does the Fourteenth Amendment nor any other amendment. The debates preceding the submission of the Fourteenth Amendment clearly show that there was no intent that it should affect the systems of education maintained by the states.

The very Congress which proposed the amendment subsequently provided for segregated schools in the District of Columbia.

When the amendment was adopted in 1868, there were thirty-seven states of the Union. Every one of the twenty-six states that had any substantial racial differences among its people either approved the operation of segregated schools already in existence or subsequently established such schools by action of the same law-making body which considered the Fourteenth Amendment.

As admitted by the Supreme Court in the public school case (*Brown v. Board of Education*), the doctrine of separate but equal schools "apparently originated in *Roberts v. City of Boston* (1849), upholding school segregation against attack as being violative of a state constitutional guarantee of equality." This constitutional doctrine began in the North—not in the South—and it was followed not only in Massachusetts but in Connecticut, New York, Illinois, Indiana, Michigan, Minnesota, New Jersey, Ohio, Pennsylvania and other northern states until they, exercising their rights as states through the constitutional processes of local self-government, changed their school systems.

In the case of *Plessy v. Ferguson* in 1896 the Supreme Court expressly declared that under the Fourteenth Amendment no person was denied any of his rights if the states provided separate but equal public facilities. This decision has been followed in many other cases. It is notable that the Supreme Court, speaking through Chief Justice Taft, a former President of the United States, unanimously declared in 1927 in *Lum v. Rice* that the "separate but equal" principle is ". . . within the discretion of the state in regulating its public schools and does not conflict with the Fourteenth Amendment."

This interpretation, restated time and again, became a part of the life of the people of many of the states and confirmed their habits, customs, traditions and way of life. It is founded on elemental humanity and common sense, for parents should not be deprived by Government of the right to direct the lives and education of their own children.

Though there has been no constitutional amendment or act of Congress changing this established legal principle almost a century old, the Supreme Court of the United States, with no legal basis for such action, undertook to exercise their naked judicial power and substituted their personal political and social ideas for the established law of the land.

This unwarranted exercise of power by the court, contrary to the Constitution, is creating chaos and confusion in the states principally affected. It is destroying the amicable relations between the white and Negro races that have been created through ninety years of patient effort by the good people of both races. It has planted hatred and suspicion where there has been heretofore friendship and understanding.

Without regard to the consent of the governed, outside agitators are threatening immediate and revolutionary changes in our public school systems. If done, this is certain to destroy the system of public education in some of the states.

With the gravest concern for the explosive and dangerous condition created by this decision and inflamed by outside meddlers:

We reaffirm our reliance on the Constitution as the fundamental law of the land.

We decry the Supreme Court's encroachments on rights reserved to the states and to the people, contrary to established law and to the Constitution.

We commend the motives of those states which have declared the intention to resist forced integration by any lawful means.

We appeal to the states and people who are not directly affected by these decisions to consider the constitutional principles involved against the time when they too, on issues vital to them, may be the victims of judicial encroachment.

Even though we constitute a minority in the present Congress, we have full faith that a majority of the American people believe in the dual system of government which has enabled us to achieve our greatness and will in time demand that the reserved rights of the states and of the people be made secure against judicial usurpation.

We pledge ourselves to use all lawful means to bring about a reversal of this decision which is contrary to the Constitution and to prevent the use of force in its implementation.

In this trying period, as we all seek to right this wrong, we appeal to our people not to be provoked by the agitators and troublemakers invading our states and to scrupulously refrain from disorder and lawless acts.

276. *Statement by One Hundred Leading Lawyers About Recent Attacks on the Supreme Court*

The New York Times, October 28, 1956.

As members of the bar we have been deeply disturbed by recent attacks on the Supreme Court of the United States. No institution of our Government, including the judiciary, stands beyond the reach of criticism, but these attacks have been so reckless in their abuse, so heedless of the value of judicial review and so dangerous in fomenting disrespect for our highest law that they deserve to be repudiated by the legal profession and by every thoughtful citizen.

The Constitution is our supreme law. In many of its most important provisions it speaks in general terms, as is fitting in a document intended, as John Marshall declared, "to endure for ages to come." In cases of disagreement we have established the judiciary to interpret the Constitution for us. The Supreme Court is the embodiment of judicial power, and under its evolving interpretation of the great constitutional clauses—commerce among the states, due process of law and equal protection of the laws, to name examples—we have achieved national unity, a nation-wide market for goods, and government under the guarantees of the Bill of Rights.

To accuse the court of usurping authority when it reviews legislative acts or of exercising "naked power" is to jeopardize the very institution of judicial review. To appeal for "resistance" to decisions of the court "by any lawful means" is to utter a self-contradiction, whose ambiguity can only be calculated to promote disrespect for our fundamental law. The privilege of criticizing a decision of the Supreme Court carries with it a corresponding obligation, a duty to recognize the decision as the supreme law of the land as long as it remains in force.

There are ways of bringing about changes in constitutional law, but resistance is not such a way. Changes may be wrought by seeking an overruling decision, or by constitutional amendment. It is through the amending process, and not by resistance, that the people and the states stand as the ultimate authority.

The current wave of abuse was doubtless precipitated by the school segregation decisions, though it has by no means been limited to them. Since our position does not depend on agreement with those decisions, it is not our purpose to discuss their merits. As individuals we are entitled to our own views of their soundness. Some of us are definitely in disagreement with them. . . .

Our present concern is for something more fundamental than any one decision or group of decisions; our concern is for the tradition of law observance and respect for the judiciary, a tradition indispensable to the cherished independence of our judges and orderly progress under law.

The American bar has been alert to defend the judiciary against assaults which would undermine the rule of law, and to make plain to the American public the dangers lurking in such challenges. In 1937, when the court was threatened, the bar rallied to its support as an institution, regardless of individual dissatisfaction which many felt toward important decisions of that time. We must do no less today.

The signers of this statement represent diverse political outlooks and geographic associations. We are all the more firmly united in our resolve to defend the rule of law against the present challenge.

Occasionally in our history decisions of the court have met with official resistance on the part of one or more states. No section of the country has had a monopoly on such aberrations, and in their outcome these episodes have only served to strengthen the tradition of respect for the law. In 1803 the Legislature of Pennsylvania asserted that a Federal court had illegally usurped jurisdiction and that its decree ought not to be supported or obeyed. Reviewing this action, the Supreme Court in 1809, through Chief Justice Marshall took note of a supposed right of interposition:

"The act in question does not, in terms, assert the universal right of the state to interpose in every case whatever, but assigns, as a motive for its interposition in this particular case, that the sentence, the execution of which it prohibits, was rendered in a cause over which the Federal courts have no jurisdiction."

The answer which Marshall gave is as valid and compelling today as it was almost a century and a half ago:

"If the Legislatures of the several states may, at will, annul the judgments of the courts of the United States and destroy the rights acquired under these judgments, the Constitution itself becomes a solemn mockery, and the nation is deprived of the means of enforcing its laws by the instrumentality of its own tribunals. So fatal a result must be deprecated by all, and the people of Pennsylvania, not less than the citizens of every other state, must feel a deep interest in resisting principles so destructive of the Union, and in averting consequences so fatal to themselves." (5 Cranch 115, 136—1809.)

The President at the time was James Madison, whose earlier views may have given some reason to the Governor of Pennsylvania to solicit his support. But when thus approached, Madison was firm in upholding the rule of law. He said: ". . . the Executive is not only unauthor-

ized to prevent the execution of a decree sanctioned by the Supreme Court of the United States, but is expressly enjoined, by statute, to carry into effect any such decree, where opposition may be made to it." . . .

It is unnecessary to recount additional episodes of this kind. Surmounting attacks prompted by local pressures, it was this very authority of the court that served to foster reconciliation after the Civil War, when state and Federal statutes disqualifying former supporters of the Confederacy from public and professional employment were held by the court to be repugnant to the Constitution as bills of attainder. Thus, the attacks on the power of the court proved to be as short-sighted as they were short-lived.

Concerning the school cases themselves, it should be enough to point out that they do not warrant any departure from our tradition of respect for law. It has been said that they were a usurpation because the equal protection clause of the Fourteenth Amendment does not speak of schools, and Congress had not legislated on the subject. But the equal protection clause was deliberately couched in general terms; it does not speak of jury service or transportation or any of the other specific fields in which the court has been faced with racially restrictive laws. These problems must be resolved by the Court.

Whether as individuals we agree or disagree with the school decisions, we recognize that they were the culmination of a steady line of growth in the application of the concept of equal protection of the law, and that each stage was preceded by sincere and determined opposition. In 1880 the right of Negroes to be included on juries was established by judicial decision. In 1917 racial restrictions in municipal zoning laws were held unconstitutional, and in 1948 this principle was applied to prevent the enforcement of private racial covenants for housing. In 1927 the first of a series of cases applied the principle of equal protection to higher education; through Chief Justice Hughes the Court held that a State did not satisfy its constitutional duty by offering to pay for a student's tuition at a non-segregated university in another State. The elementary-school cases themselves were presented in a series of oral arguments and written briefs that advanced every possible contention; the Court heard reargument on the merits and still another argument on the form of the decree. The cases were treated with the utmost deliberation. Recognizing the problems of adjustment in some localities, the Court left the decrees to be carried out under the supervision of the district courts. The local authorities are obligated to see that the Court's decision is complied with in good faith.

Epilogue

Liberty Under Law

Editorial on the occasion of the first meeting of the Supreme Court under Chief Justice Earl Warren, *New York Times*, October 5, 1953.

LIBERTY under the law is one of the noblest of human concepts. But how much liberty and how much law?

If nine men, or five men out of nine, had to give the final answer, we could well despair, just as we might well despair if the perpetuation of this republic depended on the election or re-election every four years of a supreme genius as President. But the nine men, however detached, however scrupulously impartial, are part of the world in which they live and move. We do not vote for them or against them, and would not want to, but all honest thought has some influence upon them. They are, at their best, America thinking, just as the President, a general, a manufacturer, a labor leader, a professional man, may be America acting. We may well feel a sense of reverence as the Court walks in—not solely for nine men brought to this place in part by chance as well as by achievement and ability, but for the function they perform. They are a substitute for force—the best yet invented.

The Court resumes. When its entrance is announced we can arise with alacrity, for here in this room, where orders are sometimes given that no other power can contravene, is a symbol of our civilization and our freedom.

INDEX

Barsky v. U.S., 540
Baumgartner v. U.S., 474
Beauharnais v. Illinois, 502, 513-6
Betts v. Brady, 449
Bill of attainder, 64, 219, 258, 450, 470-1, 535, 565
Bills of credit, 64, 174, 177
Bills of rights, 45-7, 50-1, 71, 77-8, 82-3, 264, 303, 564; applicability to states, 84-5, 447, 451-2, 464-5, 538, 544-7. *See also* Assembly, right of; "Clear and present danger" doctrine; Establishment of religion clause; Freedom of press; Freedom of speech; Religion
Bituminous Coal Act of 1935, 407, 416
Black, Hugo, 504, 538; decisions by, 465-6, 470-1, 479-80, 481-3, 492-4, 495-7, 497-8, 509-11, 516-7, 548-9, 555-7; dissents by, 527-8, 545-7
Black, Jeremiah S., 210
"Black Codes," 244, 249, 263
Blackstone, Sir William, 70, 398
Blau v. U.S., 540, 548-9
Blockade of Confederate ports, 211, 222, 226, 230
Bloudy Tenet of Persecution, 4, 11
Blount Resolutions, 79, 97
Board of commissioners, 38
Book banning, 503
Borrowing power, 63
Boston Tea Party, 23
Boswell, James, 24
Boycott, 324-5, 379, 385. *See also* Secondary boycott
Boyd v. U.S., 539
Bradley, Joseph P., 269, 377
Brandagee, Frank B., 353
Brandeis, Louis D., 406, 525; testimony before Industrial Relations Committee, 314, 328; Brandeis brief, 331, 344-6; dissents by, 369, 384-5, 392, 395-7, 402-3
Brewer, David J., 291, 295-7
Bricker Amendment, 487, 500
Bridges v. California, 447, 528
Briscoe v. Bank of Kentucky, 174, 177-8
British constitution, 24, 28, 29-30, 41
Browder et al. v. Gayle, 543
Brown, Henry B., 272-3, 302-5, 306-7, 340-1
Brown, John, 372
Brown v. Board of Education of Topeka, 543, 558-62
Brown v. Maryland, 141, 148-9, 329
Buchanan, James, 210, 213-5
Buck Stove Co. v. Gompers, 313
Buck v. Bell, 369, 389-90
Bunting v. Oregon, 331, 368
Burstyn v. Wilson, 503, 517-8
Burton, Harold H., 476-7
Business. *See* Industrialism, Labor-management relations; Regulation of economic enterprise; Sherman Act
Butchers' Benevolent Association, 262

Butchers' Union Company v. Crescent City Company, 337
Butler, Pierce, 404
Butler v. Michigan, 503, 519

Cabinet, Jackson's views on, 153
Calhoun, John C., drafts *Exposition and Protest*, 157; on state sovereignty, 158, 188, 200-1; and secession, 210
California, 188
Calvin, John, 11
Cantwell v. Connecticut, 448, 515
Cardozo, Benjamin, 406, 407, 430-2, 451-2
Carlson v. California, 516
Carlson v. Landon, 541
Carolina, "Fundamental Constitutions" for, 4
Carter v. Carter Coal Co., 407, 416-8, 437, 444
Carter v. Texas, 403
Cass, Lewis, 188, 201-2
"Cease and desist" orders, 284, 313
Censorship, 188, 197, 398, 400, 447, 448, 454, 527; postal, 197-8, 353; of motion pictures, 503-4, 517-8. *See also* Sir William Blackstone; Freedom of press; Freedom of speech
Central Screening Board, 533
Chaco War, 443
Chae Chan Ping v. U.S., 301
Chambers v. Florida, 449, 465-6
Champion v. Ames, 329, 332-3
Charles II, 28
Charles River Bridge v. Warren Bridge, 173, 175-7
Charters, 29
Chase, Salmon P., 240, 245
Child labor, 330, 335, 379, 380, 448; amendment, 368, 381. *See also* Bailey v. Drexel; Hammer v. Dagenhart
Chisholm v. Georgia, 78, 85-6
Church and State, 4, 11, 46, 59-60; separation of, 502, 509, 512-3, 518. *See also* Establishment of religion; First Amendment; Religion
Cicero riots of 1951, 514
Citizenship, 244, 262; in Dred Scott case, 204; in Civil Rights Act, 250; definition of, 253, 279; in Wong Kim Ark Case, 264-5; in Slaughterhouse Cases, 266; rights pertaining to, 274; and military service, 358; of the United States, 359; right to, 508; dual, 544. *See also* Privileges and immunities clause
Civil government, 11, 12, 16, 26
Civil liberty, 47, 78, 353, 446-71, 478. *See also* Assembly, right of; Bills of Rights; First Amendment; Freedom of press; Freedom of religion; Freedom of speech
Civil-military relations, 48, 51. *See also* Commander in chief; Standing armies
Civil rights, 266, 273, 538; of British colonists, 28; Civil Rights Act, 244, 263, 269; enumerated, 250; Justice Bradley on, 263; Jus-

A NOTE ON THE TYPE

The text of this book is set in two Linotype faces as follows: the documents in CALEDONIA, designed by W. A. Dwiggins, which belongs to the family of printing types called "modern face" by printers—a term used to mark the change in style of type-letters that occurred about 1800; Caledonia borders on the general style of Scotch Modern, but is more freely drawn than that letter. The introductions and comments of the editors are set in ELECTRA, also designed by Mr. Dwiggins, a face which cannot be classified as modern or old-style; it is not based on any historical model, nor does it echo any particular period or style; it avoids the extreme contrast between thick and thin elements that marks most modern faces, and attempts to give a feeling of fluidity, power, and speed.

The book was composed, printed, and bound by H. WOLFF, New York. Paper manufactured by P. H. Glatfelter Company, Spring Grove, Penn. Designed by Harry Ford.